OXFORD JUNIOR ENCYCLOPAEDIA

VOLUME IV
COMMUNICATIONS

OXFORD JUNIOR ENCYCLOPAEDIA

GENERAL EDITORS
LAURA E. SALT AND ROBERT SINCLAIR
ILLUSTRATIONS EDITOR: HELEN MARY PETTER

VOLUME IV

COMMUNICATIONS

OXFORD UNIVERSITY PRESS

Oxford University Press, Amen House, London E.C. 4

GLASGOW NEW YORK TORONTO MELBOURNE WELLINGTON
BOMBAY CALCUTTA MADRAS KARACHI CAPE TOWN IBADAN

FIRST PUBLISHED 1951
REPRINTED WITH CORRECTIONS 1957

PRINTED IN GREAT BRITAIN
AT THE UNIVERSITY PRESS, OXFORD
BY CHARLES BATEY, PRINTER TO THE UNIVERSITY

PREFACE

IN authorizing the preparation of this work the Delegates of the Oxford University Press had foremost in mind the need to provide a basic book of reference for school libraries. In form it was to be a genuine encyclopaedia, in treatment and vocabulary suitable for the young reader. To many children (and indeed to many adults) reading is not a natural activity: they do not turn to books for their own sake. But they can be trained to go to books for information which they want for some particular purpose—and thus, very often, to form a habit which will be of lifelong value. Their capacity to read continuously for any length of time being limited, they can absorb knowledge better if they get it in small quantities: therefore they will often read reference books when they may reject the reading of more extended matter. Again, it is probably true to say of such readers that their approach is from the particular to the general, and from the application to the principle, rather than the reverse, that their main interest is in the modern world around them, and that since they are not very good at conceiving things outside their own experience, their capacity for grasping abstract ideas is limited. On the other hand, once their interest is aroused, they will often pursue a subject to remarkable lengths, so long as its development is logical and the treatment avoids dullness.

But such generalizations can easily be overdone: many children using the books will not be of this type. Moreover, it was evident from the first that a project involving so great an amount of work, however exactly it might meet its principal mark, would be fully justified only if it could be of service to a far wider circle of readers. Even for the age-group first in mind, anything like 'writing down to children' must plainly be taboo—but clear exposition and simple language are no bad qualities in writing for any audience. Here, then, it seemed was the opportunity to provide a work of reference suitable for many readers to whom the large, standard encyclopaedias are too heavy and technical, and the popular alternatives for the most part neither sufficiently complete nor authoritative. The fact that the plan allowed for an exceptionally large proportion of illustrations to text (between one-quarter and one-third of the total space) is an advantage to any reader, since pictures may, in many instances, save whole paragraphs of involved explanation. With these secondary aims well in mind, therefore, the General

Editors have ventured to hope that the encyclopaedia may find usefulness not only among certain younger children, but also among older students in clubs, libraries, and Young People's Colleges, and even to no small extent among their parents and other adults who may wish for a simple approach to some unfamiliar or forgotten subject.

SCOPE AND EMPHASIS. Within certain limits the OXFORD JUNIOR ENCY-CLOPAEDIA purports to be reasonably comprehensive, though (in common with all general encyclopaedias) not exhaustive. Chief among these limits is that matter already easily available in school text-books is included only so far as its presence is necessary for the proper understanding of the subject under discussion. Thus, although an immense field of history is surveyed, it will be found mainly under headings dealing with its effects, or in the bio-graphies of those who lived to make it. Purely technical or scientific subjects, also, are omitted except when they have some general interest. In natural history and kindred studies the immense variety of forms necessarily led at times either to their treatment by groups or to their omission on purely arbitrary decisions as to which species would, in all probability, never be looked for, or because there was nothing particularly interesting to say of them. In point of general balance the stress is laid rather on the modern world, though due space is given to the factors which have shaped it, no less than to those which are changing it.

ARRANGEMENT. The encyclopaedia is planned to consist of twelve volumes. Each is arranged alphabetically within itself, and each deals with a particular range of related subjects. Within its terms of reference, then, each volume is virtually self-contained, and, owing to the great number of single-line cross-references, can well be used alone. This arrangement, which has several incidental advantages (as of production, in difficult times, and of prompt revision later), arose mainly from one consideration. If articles were to be kept really short—and, in fact, few approach and almost none exceeds 2,000 words—many subjects could be dealt with comprehensively only by referring the reader to other relevant articles—itself a desirable thing to do. It was clearly preferable for these to be under his hand, rather than be dis-persed through any of the twelve volumes at the caprice of the alphabet. This the present arrangement achieves to a great extent. If it has led to a small amount of overlapping, that again is not without its advantages.

The cross-references play an indispensable part in the make-up of the encyclopaedia. They are of two kinds: references in the text to further articles amplifying the particular point under review, and references at the end of an article to others taking the whole subject farther. Therefore, a reader looking up any wide subject, such as LANGUAGE, and following up its cross-references either in the text or at the end of the article, can discover under what main headwords the subject is treated. These, again, will refer him to any subsidiary articles, as also, in many cases, to those of a complementary nature. Thus he may be guided either from the general to the particular or vice versa. It is believed that the titles of the twelve volumes (see p. xii), in conjunction with their sub-titles, will usually lead the reader straight to the volume containing the information he wants. In selecting headwords, the rules generally followed have been to prefer the familiar, or even the colloquial, reserving the technical alternative for a single-line entry, and to group narrow subjects under a headword of wider scope. Thus, for GRAPHOLOGY, *see* HANDWRITING; for AERODYNAMICS, *see* FLYING; for SCHOONER or CARAVEL, *see* SAILING SHIPS; and for OREGON TRAIL, *see* AMERICAN TRAILS.

L. E. S., R. S.

OXFORD, 1951

LIST OF CONTRIBUTORS

VOLUME EDITOR
Robert Sinclair

PRINCIPAL CONTRIBUTORS

Speech and Language
Alan S. C. Ross, M.A. (Oxon.), M.A. (Birmingham), Professor of English Language, University of Birmingham.

J. A. W. Bennett, M.A., D.Phil. (Oxon.), Fellow of Magdalen College, Oxford, Lecturer in English Language and Literature.

Writing
David Diringer, M.A. (Cantab.), Lecturer in Semitic Epigraphy, Cambridge, author of *The Alphabet, A Key to the History of Mankind*.

Broadcasting
Wilfrid Goatman.

T. W. Bennington, Engineering Division, B.B.C.

Post Office
The General Post Office.

Canals and Rivers
C. A. Wilson, M.Inst.C.E., F.R.S.A.

Ships
(History.) George P. B. Naish, Assistant Director, National Maritime Museum, Greenwich, and Hon. Sec. The Society for Nautical Research.

(Modern Ships.) Lieut.-Comdr. L. M. Bates, R.N.V.R.

A. C. Hardy, B.Sc., M.I.N.A., A.M.I.Mar.E. (Chartered Marine Engineer), M.Inst. Pet., M.N.E. Coast Inst. Eng. & Shipbuilders, F.R.G.S., Constr. Cdr. R.C.N.C. (Ret.), President, World Ship Society.

(Navigation.) I. A. D. Bremner, B.A. (Cantab.), Associate Editor, *The Shipping World*.

Roads
Geoffrey Boumphrey.

Railways
Cecil J. Allen, M.Inst.T., A.I.Loco.E.

Aviation
John Stroud, Aviation Writer and Artist.

F. G. Irving, M.Eng., D.I.C., Grad.R.Ae.S.

A. V. Cleaver, A.R.Ae.S.

OTHER CONTRIBUTORS

J. Anderson.

C. Andrews, A.R.Ae.S.

H. Bellis.

J. Berry, B.A., Lecturer in West African Languages, University of London.

C. K. Ricardo Bertram, M.A., Ph.D., F.L.S.

E. L. Beverley, D.F.C.

P. H. Billington.

T. W. Birch, M.Sc., M.Ed.

Robert Birley, C.M.G., M.A. (Oxon.), Headmaster of Eton College.

P. W. Blandford.

Bodleian Library.

James Boswell, A.R.C.A., F.S.I.A.

E. A. Bowen.

E. M. Boyce, M.A. (Cantab.).

British Overseas Airways Corporation.

Constance M. Broadway, B.A.

J. BROUGH, Professor of Sanskrit, University of London.

F. M. BUSS.

CAMBRIDGE UNIVERSITY LIBRARY.

CONGRESS LIBRARY, U.S.A.

SIR WILLIAM A. CRAIGIE, D.Litt., F.B.A.

EDWARD CRESSY.

MYLES DILLON, M.A., Ph.D. (Bonn), Senior Professor, Dublin Institute for Advanced Studies.

A. C. DOUGLAS.

W. D. ELCOCK, M.A. (Oxon. and Manc.), L. ès. L., Doct. d'Univ. (Paris), Professor of Romance Philology and Medieval French Literature, University of London.

J. FRICKER.

H. V. R. GEARY, M.C.

PROFESSOR H. A. R. GIBB, M.A., F.B.A., Laudian Professor of Arabic, University of Oxford.

C. H. GIBBS-SMITH, M.A., F.R.C.A.

W. MACGOWAN GRADON, B.A. (Cantab.).

WILLIAM THOMSON HILL, F.J.I.

W. D. HOGARTH, M.A.

C. W. R. HOOKER, O.B.E., M.A. (Cantab.), B.Sc. (Lond.).

MICHAEL S. HOWARD, of Messrs. Jonathan Cape Ltd.

R. L. G. IRVING, M.A.

PHILIP JAMES, Art Director, Arts Council of Great Britain.

P. A. LANYON-ORGILL, Ph.D., F.I.Sn.

R. B. LE PAGE, B.A. (Oxon.).

S. LILLEY, M.Sc., Ph.D., sometime Fellow of St. John's College, Cambridge, Resident Tutor, Extra-Mural Dept., University of Birmingham.

LONDON LIBRARY.

N. S. D. MARTIN, B.A. (Oxon.).

M. J. MIDGLEY, B.A.

D. E. MILLS, M.A. (Cantab.), B.A. (London.), Lecturer in Japanese at the School of Oriental and African Studies, University of London.

L. MINIO-PALUELLO, M.A. (Oxon.), D.Phil. (Oxon.), Doct. Phil. (Padua), Senior Lecturer in Medieval Philosophy, University of Oxford.

J. S. MORRISON, M.A., sometime Professor of Greek, University of Durham, Fellow and Tutor of Trinity College, Cambridge.

ALEX F. MOSELEY.

P. MURRAY.

NATIONAL INSTITUTE FOR THE BLIND.

NATIONAL INSTITUTE FOR THE DEAF.

H. T. NORRIS, B.A. (Cantab.).

WALTER OAKESHOTT, M.A., F.S.A., Head-master of Winchester College.

ORTHOLOGICAL INSTITUTE.

W. H. OSMAN.

E. PAGET, M.A.

H. G. RODWAY.

H. F. SIMON, B.A., Lecturer in Chinese at the School of Oriental and African Studies, University of London.

R. A. SKELTON, Sec., Hakluyt Soc.

ALISON SMITH, M.A. (Oxon.).

S. G. SOAL, M.A., D.Sc.

HERBERT SPENCER.

H. PHILIP SPRATT, B.Sc., A.S.M.E., Deputy Keeper, Science Museum, South Kensington.

ISOBEL STIRLING, M.A. (Oxon.), diplomée (Sorbonne, Paris) Dip. Psychology, London. Educational Psychologist.

BARBARA STOREY.

ALEC BAIN TONNOCHY, M.A., F.S.A., Keeper of British and Medieval Antiquities in the British Museum.

DR. IDA CAROLINE WARD, C.B.E., Emeritus Professor West African Languages, University of London.

D. WINTON THOMAS, Regius Professor of Hebrew, University of Cambridge, and Fellow of St. Catharine's College.

A. M. WOOD.

C. L. WRENN, M.A., sometime President of the Philological Society.

Assistant Editors—W. F. JEFFREY, STELLA M. RODWAY, KATHARINE ROSS.

COLOUR PLATES

ACKNOWLEDGEMENTS

THE EDITORS wish to thank all those who have helped with the compilation of the text and illustrations. They are particularly indebted to the late Dr. Edward Lynam, Superintendent of the Map Room in the British Museum; the British Railways Executive; the Port of London Authority; the School of Oriental and African Studies in the University of London; the Imperial College of Science and Technology (South Kensington); and the Directors and Staffs of the British Museum, the Science Museum, and the National Maritime Museum.

The Editors also wish to thank all others who have lent illustrations; particularly Dr. John Johnson, C.B.E., M.A., Hon. D.Litt., for his help in the selection of material from his collection of ephemeral printing at the University Press.

PLAN OF VOLUMES

HOW TO USE THIS BOOK

THIS VOLUME is one of twelve, each on a separate subject, the whole set forming what is called an encyclopaedia, or work from which you can find out almost anything you want to know. (The word comes originally from the Greek *enkuklios*, circular or complete, and *paideia*, education.) Each of the twelve volumes is arranged alphabetically within itself, as twelve dictionaries would be.

The difference between a dictionary and an encyclopaedia is that, while the first gives you no more than the meanings and derivations of words, the second tells you a very great deal more about their subjects. For instance, from a dictionary you could find that a ROTORCRAFT is an aircraft which is kept aloft by spinning blades, and you would learn little more; but an encyclopaedia will tell you why a rotorcraft can hover in the air, how it can be steered without a rudder, and how it is used for carrying mails, spraying crops, and for the police control of crowds. Then a dictionary contains nearly every word in the language; but an encyclopaedia deals only with words and subjects about which there is something interesting to be said, beyond their bare meanings. So you should not expect to find every word in an encyclopaedia—every subject is there, but not every word.

To find any subject, you have first to decide in which of the twelve volumes it comes. Each of these has a title as well as a number, and also a list of general subjects to make the title clearer. All these are set out in the Plan of Volumes on the opposite page. Very often you will be able to tell from the title alone which volume contains the information you need; but if not, the list of sub-headings on the plan opposite will help to direct you. For example, if you want to read about people, the way they have lived at different times and places, and the things they have believed and worshipped, you would turn to Volume I. If, however, you want to find out about an animal or plant, you would look it up in Volume II, Natural History; but if you wanted to know how that animal or plant is used in something like farming, fishing, or trapping, you would find it in Volume VI. If your subject were something in nature that does not have life—such as the sun, or a particular country or river, or a kind of stone—you would find it in Volume III, with tides, earthquakes, the weather, and many other things. Business and trade are in Volume VII. Recreations are in Volume IX, which includes games and sports, entertainment, clubs, animal pets, and sporting animals. How we are governed and protected by the State, the law, and the armed forces is told in Volume X. Volume XI deals with almost everything connected with our homes, from the building and furnishing of the house to the clothes and health of those who live in it. The titles of Volumes V and XII, Great Lives and The Arts, explain themselves. A rather fuller account of the volume you are now reading, on Communications, is given on page xv opposite, but if it is the engineering side of ships, trains, roads, aircraft, printing, and broadcasting that interests you, the volume to explore is Volume VIII, Engineering.

To find your subject in the volume, think of its ordinary name, and then look it up just as though you were using a dictionary—the As on the first page and the Zs (if there are any) on the last. If you cannot find it, try a more general word. For instance, if you want to read about Blind Flying, and cannot find it under that name (as you cannot), try either FLYING INSTRUMENTS or NAVIGATION, AIR—either of which will lead you to it. As you read any article, you will probably come across the titles of other articles in some way connected with what you are reading. You will know that they are titles of other articles because they will be printed in capital letters. Either they will be followed by (q.v.) in brackets (this is short for the Latin *quod vide*, and means 'which see'), or else they themselves will be in brackets, with the word *see* in front of them. You can look up these other articles at once if you want to know more about the particular point dealt with, or you can save them up until you have finished the article you are reading. At the end of any article you may find the words 'See also', followed by one or more titles in small capital letters. If you look these titles up, they will tell you still more about the subject that interests you. These last 'cross-references' are very useful if you want to look up a particularly wide subject (such as EXPLORATION or SIGNALS), because they show you at once the titles of all the main articles dealing with it. You can then decide for yourself which to read.

WHAT YOU WILL FIND IN THIS VOLUME

THIS VOLUME IS ABOUT MAN'S EFFORTS TO COMMUNICATE WITH HIS FELLOWS BY SIGNS OR SOUNDS, AND BY TRAVEL ON LAND, ON SEA, AND IN THE AIR

COMMUNICATION OF IDEAS. Man has always needed to express his thoughts and feelings to other people. You will read here of SPEECH, of the growth and structure of LANGUAGE, and of the development of the individual tongues, whether GREEK or LATIN, CHINESE, or AMERICAN ENGLISH. You will read also of the various methods man has found of communicating with people whom he could not reach by speech. At first he used SIGNS AND SYMBOLS, many of which have lasted from the remote past into our own times, and from these developed WRITING, and the various signs for COUNTING and MEASUREMENT.

BOOKS AND PRINTING. In order to give a lasting form to his thoughts man produced BOOKS, at first writing them by hand on papyrus or parchment. The use of PAPER and the invention of PRINTING enabled them to be produced in great numbers. From early times wealthy people had made collections of books, and to-day there are LIBRARIES all over the country from which books can be borrowed.

DISTRIBUTION OF NEWS. To make ideas reach farther, people devised various means of distributing news, both privately and publicly, until there grew up the two great modern organizations of the POST OFFICE and NEWSPAPERS. Of recent years, a third and even more powerful means of communication, BROADCASTING, has made it possible for a man from one place to speak directly to millions of people.

COMMUNICATION BY TRAVEL. While he was thinking of ways of exchanging ideas, man was at the same time finding his way about the world by EXPLORATION, making MAPS and CHARTS, and working out methods of NAVIGATION. He has made ROADS, BRIDGES, and CANALS all over the world. He has written TRAVEL BOOKS AND GUIDE BOOKS to direct others, and built INNS for the shelter of travellers. He has risked HIGHWAYMEN, PIRATES, and WRECKS. He has marked out TRADE ROUTES which have been followed by merchants from century to century. To travel farther and faster with increasing loads, he has built himself SHIPS, CARRIAGES, RAILWAYS, MOTOR-CARS, and, finally, AEROPLANES.

MODERN TRANSPORT—LAND, SEA, AND AIR. Since the modern world is based on complex communications, and would break down without transport, there are many articles about modern achievements in land, sea, and air travel. You may read of MOTOR TRANSPORT and ROAD TRANSPORT ENGINES, of the MOTOR-CYCLE and BICYCLE, and of the organization of LONDON TRANSPORT. You will find articles on STEAM, DIESEL, and GAS-TURBINE LOCOMOTIVES, UNDERGROUND RAILWAYS and MOUNTAIN RAILWAYS, SIGNALLING methods, and the RAILWAY SYSTEMS of the world. You will read of STEAMSHIPS, MOTOR SHIPS, and ELECTRIC SHIPS, the rules of SAFETY AT SEA, the duties of LIGHTHOUSES AND LIGHTSHIPS, and the services of PORTS AND HARBOURS. You will read about the history and principles of FLYING, about the different types of AIRCRAFT ENGINES, the remarkable achievements of modern airmen in HIGH ALTITUDE FLIGHT and SUPERSONIC FLIGHT, and their ambitious plans for INTER-PLANETARY TRAVEL, which suggest that a journey to the Moon may be the next step in man's Communications.

The words in capitals are the headings of some of the articles

A

AEROBATICS. This is the name given to aerial acrobatics, better known in the early days of aviation as 'stunts'. These manœuvres form an important part of the basic training for all pilots. They give a pilot confidence in his machines and in himself. An aircraft may get out of control through atmospheric disturbances or careless flying, and the pilot must know instinctively what action to take to regain level flight. Only a full course of aerobatics can give him this instinct. For fighter pilots knowledge of aerobatics will often mean life or death.

All elementary flying schools are equipped with low-powered aircraft, because they are safer and easier to handle during take-off and landing. Low-powered aircraft are also best for learning aerobatics; they do not allow the learner to cover up his mistakes of judgement by using his engines. A miscalculated approach to a loop, for example, may mean that the pupil pilot has no power left to reach the top. In a high-powered machine it would have been possible to open the throttle still farther and complete the loop. The pilot of the light trainer must admit failure, and determine to correct his errors in approach.

With the advent of jet engines of great power, manœuvres hitherto undreamed of are possible. In this article a brief description of the basic aerobatics only is given.

1. THE LOOP. This is probably the oldest and most popular aerobatic, in which the pilot acquires speed by diving with the throttle open. He pulls back the control column or 'stick', so that the aircraft climbs (*see* FLYING). The stick is held in position until the machine is upside down. The throttle is then closed, allowing the machine to drop and complete a circle (Fig. 1). A variation of the loop is a rocket loop, in which a higher initial speed is required and the stick is brought back rather more quickly. When the aircraft is in a vertical climbing position, pointing straight upward, the throttle is held open and the stick pushed forward until the required height is reached. Then the aeroplane is rapidly pulled over on to its back, and the loop completed by a further backward movement of the

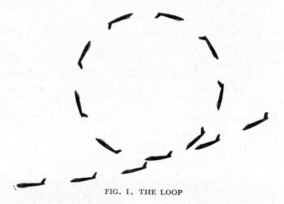

FIG. 1. THE LOOP

control column. In high-powered aircraft the rocket loop may be completed several thousand feet higher than it was begun.

2. THE BUNT. This may be most easily described as an outside loop. One may imagine an aircraft to be on top of a bunt when flying normally. The pilot pushes the stick forward, and the machine enters a dive which becomes increasingly steep. The vertical position is reached and passed; then, with the stick still held forward, the aircraft reaches a position where it is flying on its back. It then begins to climb, eventually resuming its normal attitude.

A development of the bunt, combined with a normal loop, provides an aerobatic known as 'the spectacles'. It consists of a normal loop followed immediately by a bunt, so that the machine describes a vertical figure-of-eight. The bunt is normally performed only by highly skilled pilots; the manœuvre can only be done with certain kinds of aircraft.

3. THE SPIN makes use of the liability of aircraft to stall. Stalling is the condition of an aircraft when the air ceases to flow smoothly over the upper wing-surfaces, which as a result are robbed of their lifting powers (*see* FLY-ING). There being nothing then to counteract the pull of gravity the machine will drop. The most common cause of the stall is the losing of flying speed, as in the spin and 'falling leaf'. Another cause is the rapid change of position of the aircraft, so that the smooth air-flow breaks down, as in the case of the 'flick roll'.

FIG. 2. A SPIN

It is quite possible to spin unintentionally, and for this reason special attention is paid to the pupil's ability to recover from the spin. To begin this aerobatic, the pilot will first lose flying speed until the aircraft is about to stall. At this moment he will pull the control column right back, and simultaneously push the rudder-bar hard over in the direction in which he wishes to spin, whether to left or right. The nose and one wing of the machine will then drop, and the aircraft will begin to fall in a spiral fashion. Although spinning quite rapidly, its rate of descent is, in fact, comparatively slow (Fig. 2).

In order to recover from the spin, it is necessary to bring the rudder back from its position of extreme left or right to the other extreme, while easing the control column forward. These two movements of the controls, and the subsequent centralizing of stick and rudder, will have the effect of checking the spin, from which the machine will emerge in a dive. A normal flying attitude is regained by easing the stick back.

4. THE FALLING LEAF. As with the spin, the speed of the aircraft is reduced until it reaches stalling-point, when the controls are placed in the spinning position. As soon as one wing drops, as at the start of a spin, the controls are instantly thrown to the other extreme position, and the combined effect of ailerons and rudder is to check this commenced spin and to drop the other wing. This regulated dropping of alternate wings is repeated as often as desired, and the result is rather like the action of a falling leaf. The falling leaf could well be called a spin which never really starts, in which the aircraft continually loses height by falling first to one side, then the other, while still heading in the same direction.

5. THE ROLL. There are two main types of roll, the flick roll and the slow roll. In the flick roll the machine is first flown level and at a

FIG. 3. A ROLL

fairly high speed. To begin the roll, the pilot pulls back the control column or 'stick' while at the same time working the rudder. The nose of the machine immediately rises until the effect of the rudder turns the machine on to its side, and the stalling position is reached. The aircraft then spins rapidly on its horizontal axis (Fig. 3). After one roll the machine resumes its normal course. The slow roll is a more complicated action, in which the aircraft moves through the air in a corkscrew fashion

To perform any aerobatic the controls must be moved firmly and smoothly. If the stick or

de Havilland Aircraft Co

A DE HAVILLAND 'CHIPMUNK' ROLLING

rudder must be moved rapidly, the action must not be jerky. This would throw a dangerous strain on the wings and body of the aircraft.

AERODYNAMICS, see FLYING, Section 6.

AEROPLANE. The modern aeroplane has evolved in 40 years from a lightly built apparatus made of slender wooden frames, over which fabric was stretched, and which was powered by an engine of 25 to 40 horse-power. To-day aeroplanes are sleek all-metal craft; some have an engine output of 35,000 horse-power, some can achieve speeds of well over 600 miles an hour, while others can reach heights of over 50,000 feet (10 miles) above the earth.

The term 'aeroplane' is generally used of all aircraft heavier than air, such as all types of land aeroplanes, that is, aeroplanes fitted to take off and alight on land, seaplanes and flying boats (see SEAPLANE), gliders and sailplanes (see GLIDER), and helicopters and autogyros (see ROTORCRAFT). Aircraft which are lighter than air come under the headings of BALLOON and AIRSHIPS (qq.v.).

An aeroplane consists of a number of main components. These normally are the fuselage, containing the crew and passengers or other load; the wing, which gives 'lift' (see FLYING) and enables the aircraft to remain in flight; the power unit, which makes the aeroplane move forward, this in turn enabling the wing to provide 'lift'; the tail unit, which gives stability and control; and the undercarriage, on which the aircraft is supported while on the ground.

The fuselage, which is really a sort of metal shell, is normally circular or oval in section and rather fishlike when seen from the side. It is made from a number of metal frames, placed across the structure; the frames are joined together by metal 'stringers'—long, stiffened, metal strips running fore-and-aft. The whole framework is then covered with sheet metal, known as stressed skin.

The crew compartment may be in the nose of the fuselage of a multi-engined type. In a small aeroplane the crew compartment may be just a small section in which are placed the pilot's seat, controls, and instruments, and which is covered over with a transparent hood. In large transport aeroplanes the crew compartment may fill the nose of the aeroplane, and stretch back as much as 16 or 20 feet. It houses the captain as first pilot, and first officer as second pilot (normally seated side by side, each with his own set of controls and instruments), the navigator (who has his map table and instruments), the radio officer (to work the vast array of radio receiving and transmitting equipment which keeps the aeroplane in touch with ground stations along its route), and the flight-engineer (with engine controls, as well as devices which regulate the cabin atmosphere and temperature).

Behind the crew compartment in a large aeroplane come passenger cabins, galleys, wash-rooms, and lavatories in the case of a passenger aeroplane; in a freight carrier there are large holds with very strong floors to support heavy cargo. Freight can be lashed to permanent fittings in the hold to prevent its movement in flight.

The cabins and crew compartments are normally entered by doors on the left hand or port side of the fuselage, aft of the wing. In some aeroplanes used on local routes the doors may be on the right or starboard side; this is the custom in Russia. The doors of an aircraft are some height from the ground, and to allow quicker entrance and exit, some air-liners are fitted with a flight of steps which can be lowered from the tail. Otherwise passengers cannot alight until the airport staff have brought forward a flight of steps mounted on wheels.

The wings of an aeroplane are normally built with one or two main spars, these being in effect girders running the full length of the wing. Metal ribs run from the front of the spars to the 'leading edge' or front of the wing, and also to the 'trailing edge' or rear of the wing. As with the fuselage, the whole structure is covered with metal.

The position of the wing on the sides of an aeroplane depends on the designer's intentions; speed, balance, and strength are among the many factors concerned. The wing can be mounted at the top of the fuselage; in that case it is above the windows in an air-liner, and passengers can look down more easily at the landscape. Sometimes the wing is mounted at the bottom of the fuselage; this position has many advantages for the aircraft constructor. In some cases the wing can pass right through the centre of the fuselage, although this, of course, reduces the space inside. These wing positions are known respectively as high-wing, low-wing, and mid-wing.

The wing, in addition to its main function of providing the lift, is also used to serve a number of odd purposes. In the case of the multi-engined aeroplane, the engines are either buried in the wing or else supported in front of the wing on mountings attached to it. The fuel supply (petrol for piston-engines or kerosene for gas-turbines) is stored in the wing; fuel may be contained in tanks in the wing or else allowed to flow within a section of the actual wing structure. In many aeroplanes the undercarriage is attached to the wing, and is made to fold up into it when the aircraft is flying.

The wing is one of the parts of the aeroplane most affected by ice, so it must be fitted with de-icing equipment. The most effective method of removing this ice is to heat the wing surface by a heating system inside the wing (see CLIMATE AND COMMUNICATIONS, Section 4).

In the leading edge of the wing lamps are often to be seen. These are the headlights switched on by the pilot to assist landing at night. Small lights attached to the wing tips are navigation lights, similar to those used by ships. Red is on the port (left) side and green on the starboard (right).

On the outer part of the wing (on its trailing or rear edge) are the ailerons. These are hinged parts of the wing which are moved up or down by the pilot. To turn to the left an aeroplane banks to the left. To do this the pilot turns the control wheel to the left; this action raises the left aileron and depresses the right one. The air-flow over these surfaces then forces the left wing down, and the aeroplane, with the additional aid of its rudder, turns in towards the left.

Between the ailerons and the fuselage are the flaps. These are metal panels which can be lowered to varying degrees, altering the angle of the lower surface of the wing, which action creates a drag and acts as an air brake. Flaps can also increase the wing area and enable aeroplanes to fly more slowly.

The power propelling the aeroplane may be of a number of types—the ordinary piston-engine (internal combustion) driving a propeller (air-screw), the gas-turbine driving a propeller, or the gas-turbine 'pure jet'. In single-engined aircraft having propellers, the engine is normally in the nose of the fuselage; the 'pure jet' type with single unit has its engine amidships, with its jet outlet in or under the tail. Aeroplanes can be propelled by rockets, but these are not yet widely used (see AIRCRAFT ENGINES, Section 7).

The standard type of tail unit consists of a fixed vertical fin, which helps to keep the aeroplane flying straight, and the fixed horizontal tailplane, which prevents fore-and-aft pitching. Behind the fixed vertical fin is a movable rudder to control direction; behind the fixed tailplane is a movable elevator, which controls the vertical movements of the aeroplane. When the elevator is raised, the tail of the aircraft is forced down, and the aircraft climbs. Depressing the elevator causes the aeroplane to dive. As with the wing, the surfaces of the tail are normally fitted with de-icing equipment.

While on the ground an aeroplane must have wheels on which it can move and manœuvre. The undercarriage, consisting of the wheels and their supports, is generally divided into three units. There are two main units bearing most of the weight, which are generally under the wing. A lighter unit is mounted under either the nose or tail to hold up the end of the aircraft.

The undercarriage serves no purpose in the air, and if left exposed, it would create much 'drag'; the air pressing against it when the aircraft was flying would reduce speed. Whenever possible, therefore, the wheels are drawn up out of the way. The main wheels are withdrawn or 'retracted' into the wing (or, on multi-engined aeroplanes, into the motor-housing which is built into the wing). The lighter wheel or wheels, usually under the nose, retract into the fuselage. The main wheel units are fitted with powerful brakes, so that when the aircraft is running along the ground, or taxi-ing, the pilot can gradually slow it and stop it.

Aircraft are controlled mainly by a control column held in the pilot's hands and by rudder pedals. The control column moves the ailerons and elevators, thus governing the climb, dive, and bank. The rudder pedals govern the rudder, and control the direction of flight.

The speed of an aeroplane is partly regulated by the throttles, which govern the fuel fed to the engines. A very comprehensive collection of instruments is provided. These instruments include an airspeed indicator which shows the speed of the aeroplane through the air, and an altimeter which can be set to show the height of the aeroplane above sea-level or above any desired point.

At night, or in fog or cloud, when the pilot

Port wing tip
navigation light

Metal skin

Leading edge

Mainplane

Pitot head

Aileron

Trailing edge

Landing
headlight

Wing bracing
strut

Vertical
stabilizing fin

Radial air-cooled
engine

Rudder

Metal
airscrew

Pilot's cabin

Flap

Passenger cabin

Tailplane

G-ALOW

Elevator

Steps

Passengers'
entrance door

Fuselage

Tailwheel

International
registration G= Gt. Britain

Exhaust pipe

Landing wheels

de Havilland Aircraft Co.

THE PARTS OF AN AEROPLANE
The aeroplane is a de Havilland 'Beaver'

cannot use his eyesight, an aeroplane is said to be flying under 'instrument flight' conditions. An instrument panel for 'blind flying' is the pilot's only guide. Besides his airspeed indicator and altimeter, he has a directional gyro, or gyroscopic compass (*see* GYROSCOPE, Section 2*b*, Vol. VIII), which shows him the compass-bearing on which the aeroplane is flying; an artificial horizon which shows whether the aeroplane is climbing, diving, or banking; and a climb-and-glide indicator, which shows whether the aeroplane is climbing or diving, and if so at what rate.

There are many other instruments which show such vital things as the speed of the engines, the temperature of engines and oil, and the amount of fuel available. Radio and radar equipment enable the crew to keep contact with ground stations, to find out their position, to navigate over the route, and to approach the airport in bad visibility.

See also FLYING; FLYING, HISTORY OF.

AFRICAN LANGUAGES. There are more than 700 languages in Africa, not including dialects, of which there are also very many. In most of North Africa, SEMITIC or partly Semitic languages (q.v.) are spoken. ARABIC (q.v.) is spoken in Egypt, along the Mediterranean seacoast, and in the northern Sahara—though the Berbers speak their own languages. (Berber, like Somali and ancient Egyptian is distantly related to Semitic. Some Abyssinians speak Tigre, a purely Semitic language; others Amharic, which has diverged greatly from the ancient Semitic parent language. European settlers or their descendants account for the speaking of English, French, and Portuguese in various parts of

Africa. In the Union of South Africa are spoken Afrikaans (a form of Dutch) and English; while some 250,000 settlers from India speak their own languages. This article, however, is concerned mainly with the Negro languages of Africa.

The Negro languages of Africa include the Bantu group, which stretches from an irregular line between the Cameroons and the Great Lakes near the Equator to the Cape; the Sudanic group, north of this line and stretching from the Atlantic coast to near the Nile valley; and the Nilotic and Nilo-Hamitic languages, spoken in the Nile valley and eastwards. There are also the HOTTENTOT and BUSHMAN languages (qq.v., Vol. I), of a type very different from any other African language, in the north-east of the Bantu area.

Some scholars think that there was a far-distant parent language from which the Bantu and Sudanic languages have descended; but the relationship is not fully established, nor has it been possible to discover from the two language groups what the original language was like. It is easy to see, however, that the languages which belong to the Bantu group are closely related to each other. This does not mean, however, that speakers of one can necessarily understand speakers of another, for they differ widely in much of the vocabulary and in grammar.

The chief characteristics of Bantu languages are:

(a) Nouns are grouped in classes, there being one class for the names of persons, another for the names of trees and growing things, and so on. Each class has its own particular prefix, or small addition, placed in front of the word to distinguish it, as in *Buganda* the country, *Luganda* the language, *Muganda* a Ganda person (singular), *Baganda* the Ganda people (plural). In the Swahili language we have *kisu* 'knife', *visu* 'knives', *mtu* 'person', *watu* 'persons', *mti* 'tree', *miti* 'trees', *jicho* 'eye', *macho* 'eyes'.

(b) 'Alliterative concord', that is, the prefix of each class of noun is attached in some form or other to all Bantu words agreeing with a noun of that class—as in Swahili *vikombe vyangu vikubwa* 'my big cups'. An artificial example will perhaps illustrate this more clearly. We can find no precise parallel in English, but if English had the same concord system as a Bantu language, the sentence 'little boys often climb big trees' might read something like 'ba-little ba-boys often ba-they-climb mi-big mi-trees'.

(c) Many Bantu words are tonal: that is, the tones with which a word is spoken may be the only means of distinguishing it from another word, or may be a means of showing the grammatical construction of the sentence.

(d) Bantu languages have no gender (no separate forms for masculine, feminine, and neuter). Inflexion (that is, addition to a word to show its function in the sentence) is shown mainly by prefixes.

One important Bantu language is Swahili, spoken over a wide area from Zanzibar on the east coast across central Africa into the Congo. It is a common language, often used as a means of communication between the local people and Europeans in areas where another Bantu language is the natural tongue of the inhabitants. There are so many other important Bantu languages that it is impossible to give a complete list here. The following are among the best known: Zulu and the closely related Xhosa in South Africa; Sotho and Sechuana in Basutoland and Bechuanaland; Ganda in Uganda; Kikuyu in Kenya; Kongo and Lingala in the Belgian Congo; Bemba in Northern Rhodesia; Shona in Southern Rhodesia; Nyanja in Nyasaland; Duala in the French Cameroons.

It is less easy to define the common characteristics of Sudanic and Nilotic languages, such as Twi, Ewe, and Yoruba, for example, in West Africa, or Kunama and Dinka in the East. In general these languages tend to make up their words from single syllable roots, and to make very little use of inflexion. The Nilo-Hamitic group, however, use inflexion much more, and many of them make use of a distinctive word-order in the sentence—verb, subject, object.

African languages make use of a number of sounds not met with in European languages. The Bushman and Hottentot languages include 'clicks', which have been adopted by some of the South African languages such as Zulu and Xhosa; the first sound of the name Xhosa is a click similar to that used in English to encourage a horse. In the Sudanic languages the most difficult sounds for Europeans to pronounce are those represented by 'kp' and 'gb'.

Generally, the languages of Africa have been written down by Europeans in the Latin alphabet, and unfamiliar sounds which the ordinary ALPHABET (q.v.) cannot represent have been indicated with the help of accents and other marks. In recent years, however, an 'Africa' alphabet, suggested by the International African Institute, has been adopted for many African languages. Included in it are a few new letter forms which are designed to replace as far as possible the older unsatisfactory system of letters with accent marks.

See also LANGUAGE STRUCTURE.
See also Vol. I: NEGRO AFRICANS.

AFRIKAANS LANGUAGE, *see* GERMANIC LANGUAGES.

AIRCRAFT ENGINES. An aeroplane and the engine which makes it go are extremely dependent on one another in almost every detail. This interdependence is true of communications by air in a way in which it is not true of any means of communication on land or sea. Almost every change of any kind in the design or performance of an air-engine affects the way the body of the aircraft acts on the air around it.

If a railway engine boiler is inefficient, and unsuited for modern heavy loads, the engine can still pull trains rather slowly. If a powerful motor-bus is boarded by too many passengers, it will be slowed down, but it can still complete its journey. With an aeroplane the engine, the structure, and the day-to-day use of the craft are all so interconnected that, generally speaking, none of these things can be changed without

John Stroud

AIR-COOLED PISTON ENGINE WITH CYLINDERS ARRANGED RADIALLY
The circular cowling is typical of this type of engine

changing the others. Almost every new engine designed for aircraft brings about changes in the outer shape of the craft, or in the weight it can carry, or the distance it can fly (*see* AIRCRAFT TAKE-OFF). An aircraft and its engines, therefore, must be thought of as a single structure. There are several main kinds of aircraft engine: they should not be regarded as power units which can be installed in an aircraft in the sense that any one of several kinds of railway locomotive might be coupled to a suburban train.

The power units in aircraft, which are described in technical detail in Vol. VIII (ENGINEERING), mainly belong to one of the following groups.

1. PISTON ENGINE. This is the airman's term for what the motorist calls the internal

John Stroud

LIQUID COOLED PISTON ENGINE WITH PISTONS IN LINE
The in-line engine gives a slender nose to this fighter. The cooling radiator is seen beneath the fuselage aft of the wing

combustion engine, the basic type of engine for motor-cars; it is a useful term, for no other aircraft engine uses pistons. Modern aviation was built up on the piston engine. From the first feeble flight at the beginning of the 20th century (*see* FLYING, HISTORY OF, Section 3), the piston engine was unchallenged in practical flying for 40 years. Some of the first piston engines for aircraft (particularly in the First World War) were rotary ones, in that the entire set of cylinders, arranged in the shape of a star, spun round on a fixed shaft.

The disadvantages of the piston engine are serious. One is the violent vibration imposed on the mechanical parts, and the other is the burden of weight. An engine may revolve 3,000 times a minute, which means that hundreds of pieces of metal, with perhaps a high total weight, move violently backwards and forwards 3,000 times a minute. To stand this violent shaking, metal parts must be heavy. To move these heavy parts so quickly, much power is used up, particularly at high speeds. All the moving parts need elaborate oiling systems, or they would become red-hot and stop suddenly. The advantages of the piston engine are its economical use of fuel, and its convenience for short journeys and at fairly moderate speeds, by comparison with its rival, the jet engine.

Vickers Armstrong

'VISCOUNT' AIR-LINER WITH AIRSCREW TURBINES
Note the slender cowlings which cover the engines

2. AIRSCREW TURBINE. The gas-turbine has rendered the piston engine out of date for several purposes. The turbine was experimentally devised in the years before the Second Great War by a young R.A.F. officer named Whittle (later Sir Frank Whittle) and his assistants, and also by German engineers. Britain and Germany were unaware of each others' work. The gas-turbine is based on the principle of the marine steam-turbine, but with an important simplification. The steam-turbine consists of a wheel with large numbers of curved blades set round its edge; a powerful gush of steam is forced against the blades at several points, thus making the wheel go round. The steam comes from water, which has been heated by burning coal or oil. The gas-turbine dispenses with the water and the steam. The hot gases given off by burning an oil fuel are directly forced against the blades of the turbine wheel, and push the wheel round.

The gas-turbine is widely used in aircraft to turn an ordinary propeller or airscrew. As the turbine consists essentially of one main moving part, and as that part (the wheel) spins round instead of going backwards and forwards like a piston, there is a great saving of weight, vibration, and mechanical wastage of power. The drawback of the turbine is that it consumes a good deal of fuel, which, by comparison with the piston engine, has almost to be poured into the combustion chamber. This drawback is important when the aircraft is travelling at slow speeds, or on short journeys, for the loss on fuel (and the waste of space to accommodate the extra fuel) is not made up by the speed of the journey. For long, fast journeys the airscrew-turbine is much used. Since its development for aircraft, the gas-turbine has also been tried with some forms of road, rail, and sea transport.

3. DUCTED FAN. This form of power is still in experimental form. Instead of the ordinary airscrew or propeller, a fan with many blades is used, spinning in a duct like a drain-pipe, and driven by a gas-turbine. The fan drives air forcefully backwards, and impels the aircraft forward. The ducted fan, as a development in aviation, comes somewhere between the airscrew-turbine and the turbo-jet.

4. TURBO-JET OR PURE JET. This is the logical development of Whittle's gas-turbine, and represents man's first successful means of driving an aircraft without any propeller, airscrew, or fan

de Havilland Aircraft Co.

'VAMPIRE' FIGHTER WITH TURBO-JET

The gas turbine is in the fuselage behind the pilot. The air is fed in through the opening in the front of the wing
where it joins the body, and the hot gases are released through the back of the fuselage

of any kind. Broadly, it works in the same way
as the ordinary rocket used in firework displays,
but with important differences. Just as the gas
turbine emphasized the drawbacks of the piston
engine, the turbo-jet engine has emphasized the
drawbacks of the airscrew. An airscrew is not
the best means of moving an aircraft at very high
speeds; one reason is that the blade of an airscrew has to 'grip' the air as it spins, and above
a certain speed the grip is less strong. (If one
moves one's hand too violently when swimming,
the hand slips through the water instead of
gripping it.) The other weakness of the airscrew
is that it is a moving part, and all moving parts
in machinery involve strain, wear, and the using
up of power.

The jet engine, like the rocket, is based on
what physicists call 'reaction'. The engine is
little more than an open container, with the open
end pointing backwards. Inside the engine liquid
fuel is ignited. The resulting gases expand
violently and push out in every direction. Backwards, towards the open end of the container,
the gas escapes and has little effect. But in the
forward direction the expanding gas presses hard
against the closed end of the container, pushing it forward. A continuous supply of continually igniting gas will carry a heavy aeroplane
through the sky at hundreds of miles an hour.

It is because the propeller is dispensed with, and
the aircraft is driven purely by the reactive force
of a jet of hot gas, that airmen call the turbo-jet
engine the pure jet engine. The term 'turbo'
indicates a turbine, but in this case the turbine
serves the purpose of forcing compressed air into
the ignition chamber to increase the effect of the
pressure. The turbine is itself driven by part of
the resulting hot gases.

5. THE RAMJET OR ATHODYD. This is a
further refinement of the turbo-jet or pure jet.
If an aeroplane can be made to go fast enough,
the ordinary atmosphere, which presses very
strongly against the nose of the aircraft, can be
admitted to the engine. Its pressure will be so
great at high speeds that the turbine, which
would force compressed air into the ignition
chamber, can be dispensed with. Hence the
'ramjet', in which the ordinary air is simply
rammed into the engine. Airmen call ramjet
aircraft 'flying stove-pipes', since the engine is in
effect an open tube, with air rushing in at the
front and scorching gas streaming out of the
back. In reality, the shape of the engine is not
that of a plain tube: if the front of it were completely open, the 'reaction' of the burning gas
would have nothing to press against; the entering air is admitted through a very carefully
shaped hole.

ROCKET-PROPELLED FIGHTER

The rocket outlet is at the extreme rear of the fuselage. No air intakes are required

'Flight'

The ramjet or athodyd (short for 'aero-thermo-dynamic-duct') cannot be used alone in an aircraft. From its nature, it cannot begin to work until it is moving at high speed. Then, although its fuel consumption is high, its speed and lightness are important, especially at speeds greater than 500 or 600 miles an hour, and particularly when approaching the speed of sound (*see* Supersonic Flight). Aircraft equipped with the ramjet must take off and reach a high speed with turbo-jet engine before switching on the ramjet.

One form of the ramjet was the V1, or flying bomb, used by the Germans for the bombing of London and south-east England in the closing stages of the Second World War. The V1, which flew without a human pilot, used a 'pulse-jet'—that is, a ramjet operating in intermittent bursts in order to save fuel. The V1 was fitted with a mechanism to cause the engine to stop after a flight of a certain distance; the flying bomb then fell to the ground and exploded (*see* Guided Missiles, Vol. X).

6. Rocket. A rocket is like a ramjet except that it does not need to combine air with liquid fuel to cause the ignition and expansion of hot gas. The explosive chemicals in a rocket will burn when there is no air. Rocket craft can therefore fly at great heights above the earth, where a ramjet craft would be starved of air. The farther it rises, the more a rocket aircraft gains, for the thinner the air the less the friction or 'drag' against the outside of the craft (*see*

High Altitude Flight). The solid propellant used in fireworks makes their speed difficult to control. Rockets in aviation use a liquid propellant; its supply to the combustion chamber can be controlled.

So far, rockets have been used only as auxiliaries to aircraft. Some have been used to help aircraft to leave the ground (*see* Aircraft Take-off). Others are used to increase the speed of fighter aircraft for short periods of emergency. During the Second World War the Germans dropped V2 rocket bombs on the London region. The V2, which had to rise to a height of 70 miles in order to reach London from a firing point about 250 miles away, was not an aircraft in the true sense.

Rockets have been discussed as the motive power for journeys to the moon or to other parts of space (*see* Interplanetary Travel).

Some additional power is provided for aircraft by the force of the exhaust gases, pressing against the atmosphere at the rear of the craft. Even on old-fashioned piston engines, Battle of Britain pilots were believed to gain a few extra miles an hour in speed from the exhaust of their Spitfires when flying at maximum speed.

7. Aircraft Braking. One use of air engines which is growing in importance is in slowing down aircraft after they have touched down on the runway of an airport. The increased size, weight, and landing speed of craft have made this use important. On propeller-driven machines, braking airscrews are used; the pitch or angle of the blades of the airscrews is reversed, so that the airscrew presses against the air and helps to retard the craft. On jet-propelled aircraft this is impossible and some use has been made of 'thrust-spoilers', metal plates which jut out from the aircraft to check the free flow of air. Some aircraft, on landing, have released a parachute attached to the tail in order to slow them. Brakes are also applied on the motor-car principle to the wheels of the undercarriage, but the retarding effect is small.

See also Aeroplane; Flying.

AIRCRAFT, SPECIAL USES. The most efficient aeroplane for any special type of work is one specially designed to meet the requirements of that work only. For instance, British air-lines lost much money just after the Second World War when they had to use expensive bombing aircraft which had been converted for passenger use. Many aircraft are designed to carry out special work; but the high cost of producing a new kind of aircraft means that some types have to be ready to undertake a variety of tasks.

In civil aviation one of the most specialized types of aircraft is the passenger-carrying aeroplane (see AIR-LINER).

Another aeroplane needing special designing is the primary trainer, the type on which a pilot does his initial training when learning to fly. The trainer aeroplane must be easy to fly, but at the same time it must not be found so simple to handle as to encourage carelessness in the pupil. It must respond well to its control, have a slow landing speed, show the flying characteristics of the larger modern aeroplane, and be toughly built, for it will probably have to stand up to rough landings and other harsh treatment. For this reason it must also be easily maintained and, if need be, repaired. It must also usually have 'blind flying' instruments, to teach the student how to fly in bad visibility.

Special freight aircraft are produced for the steadily increasing volume of air freight. Craft of this kind must carry as big a cargo as possible economically, so they must have strong floors to take concentrated loads. Large doors are needed at a convenient height for loading from lorries. A hoist or small crane mounted in the top of the fuselage helps in handling freight.

The transport of road vehicles requires loading either at the nose or rear of the aircraft, and a ramp up which the vehicles can be driven into the hold. Some types of freight, such as meat, require refrigerated aircraft, while others need heated compartments. If animals are to make journeys at great heights where the atmosphere becomes less dense, they must be carried in 'pressure cabins' in which the air is kept at the normal pressure for healthy breathing.

In areas where communications are still primitive, such as parts of Scandinavia and the north of Canada, aircraft must be capable of carrying out a great variety of duties. They must be able to carry passengers and freight in and out of small areas, and frequently operate on floats in the summer and skis in the winter (see SEAPLANE). It is not uncommon to find bulky objects slung on the outside of such aircraft; for instance, canoes are often strapped to the tops of floats, while passengers' skis are hung in racks on the outside of the fuselage.

Air photography and survey work for photographic map-making require aircraft in which cameras may be mounted, pointing either directly downwards or sideways at a fixed angle. Aircraft for this work must be very steady, and must be fitted with instruments enabling them to be flown on a very accurate course.

Little attention has yet been given to the design of special ambulance aircraft, mainly because it is not economical to keep aircraft idle waiting for accidents or illness, when the ordinary aeroplane can be improvised to do ambulance work. Therefore stretchers have been devised to fit in many types and sizes of transport aeroplanes.

Bristol Aeroplane Co.

LOADING A BRISTOL FREIGHTER
Large double doors in the nose of the aircraft open on the hold which has tie-down points to which the freight is lashed

The carrying of mail by special aircraft is an attractive idea, and interesting models have been planned but never built. Experiments of air-mail flights by night have been carried out with a cargo aircraft equipped as a postal sorting office. Other aircraft have been modified to pick up mail-bags hanging high up from the ground on a wire between two posts in areas in which aircraft could not land. Specially designed mail-carrying helicopters (see ROTOR-CRAFT) have been used.

Crop dusting and pest control are undertaken by small aeroplanes or helicopters modified for the purposes (see INSECTICIDES, Vol. VI). Forest fire patrol, police patrol, and coastguard work are among the duties undertaken by aircraft, sometimes of seaplane or amphibious type. For fighting forest fires seaplanes can alight on lakes in such places as North America, and put ashore fire-fighting teams and equipment. In some instances fire fighters are dropped by parachute (see FOREST FIRES, Vol. VI).

Coastguard work is closely allied with air-sea rescue. Small flying boats and amphibians can go to the rescue of ships or aircraft in distress, or equally can alight on coastal waters to investigate boats suspected of smuggling.

See also AEROPLANE.

AIRCRAFT TAKE-OFF. The greatest of all flying problems is that of taking off from the ground. Once an aircraft is launched into the air, it is comparatively easy to keep it 'floating'. The soaring seagull, the soaring kite, the soaring GLIDER (q.v.), and even the slowly falling PARA-CHUTE (q.v.) all show that once an object is high in the air, with either a wing or an umbrella-like shape to support it, it does not fall fast, but tends to glide down rather gently. It can be kept up, and prevented from gliding down, by a small amount of effort, either from a bird's muscles, or an aeroplane's engines. The real conquest of the air as a medium of communication consists in the ability to launch a heavy object off the ground into the air. (For the general principles of aviation, see FLYING.)

The difficulty of launching aeroplanes has an important effect on their practical use. An aeroplane costs a great deal of money to build and run, and this money must be earned by carrying goods or people. The weight of cargo or passengers it can carry from one place to another is called the 'payload'. (The payload, of course, excludes the weight of petrol, engines, and crew.) If an aeroplane cannot lift off the ground large enough cargoes to pay for its upkeep, larger engines could perhaps succeed in lifting it off the ground. But this would mean that the aeroplane itself would become much heavier, merely to secure a small increase in cargo. If the weight is increased, the area of the wings must be increased to bear the load. Larger wings mean more weight, and call for more powerful engines. Hence the 20,000 horse-power engines of the 130-ton BRABAZON I (q.v.). To add to the weight of the aircraft without having bigger wings would mean that the aircraft, before taking off, would have to run along the aerodrome runway at greater speed in order to get 'lift'. This would mean building longer runways at all the airports at which aircraft of this kind might call. The building of airports is expensive, and aircraft using long runways might have to pay larger fees. The result of all these difficulties is that aircraft which we see in the sky are carrying far less load than they could carry, simply because they are not able to get off the ground with a 'full' load.

Many attempts have been made to devise 'assisted take-off', or the launching of aircraft into the air by special means. Slight chemical changes introduced into the fuel at the moment of taking off have sometimes been used to produce more power than the engine would normally yield. Sometimes small rockets help an aircraft into the air. This method, known in Britain as Ratog (Rocket-Assisted Take-off Gear) and in America as Jato (Jet-Assisted Take-off) consists of a battery of small rockets attached to the aircraft and pointing towards the rear. They are fired during the take-off run, and help to thrust the aircraft forward just when it needs every ounce of power. After the rockets have been fired, the bracket to which they were attached can be dropped from the aircraft.

Rocket-assisted take-off enables laden aircraft to take off from airports where the runways would otherwise be too short, and also to take off from airports at high altitudes where the thinness of the air (see HIGH ALTITUDE FLIGHT) would need a greater taking-off speed and therefore a longer run. Rockets have also been used to enable aircraft to take off from the decks of AIRCRAFT-CARRIERS (q.v. Vol. X).

An electric catapult has been used in America to launch aircraft. The principle of the device is similar to that of the ELECTRIC MOTOR (q.v. Vol. VIII), except that the moving part of the motor, instead of spinning round, is propelled in a straight line over a length of the airport runway which has been electrically energized. A fighter aeroplane attached to this electric catapult has been launched into the air within just over four seconds of a standing start, and with a run of only 100 yards as against the normal 700 yards for this craft.

One method of increasing the payload of an aeroplane is FUELLING IN FLIGHT (q.v.), which is an indirect form of assisted take-off. An aeroplane full of heavy cargo but with almost no petrol takes off from the ground in the usual way. When it is in the air, another craft, with no cargo but filled with petrol, transfers petrol through a pipe to the first craft. During long journeys fuelling from the air can be repeated at intervals, and a heavy aircraft can be spared the difficulties of taking off from successive aerodromes.

During the late 1930's an experiment was undertaken with a British composite aircraft. This was the Short-Mayo flying-boat and sea-plane combination, used for Atlantic experimental flights. A small, heavily laden, long-range seaplane, the *Mercury*, was lifted into the air on the back of a lightly loaded but powerful flying-boat, the *Maia*—named after the Greek Goddess, Mercury's mother.

The two aircraft took off locked together, and using the power of both aircrafts' engines. After climbing to a suitable height, the aircraft separated, and the long-range aircraft set course for its destination. The 'mother' aircraft then returned to base. After a few experiments the trials were ended.

The general problems of runways and loading, as discussed in this article, do not apply in the special case of helicopters. These machines, which have the unusual quality of being able to rise straight off the ground and hover in the air, do not compete with ordinary aeroplanes in the matter of speed, distance, or load-carrying (*see* ROTORCRAFT).

See also FLYING; AIRPORT.

AIRCREW. The flying staff of a passenger airliner consists of a pilot or captain and several assistants.

Boeing Airplane Co.

ROCKET-ASSISTED TAKE-OFF
This Boeing 'Stratojet' is taking off, using the full power of its 6 gas-turbines and also the short-lived power of a battery of rockets

The Captain is a man of great flying experience. Complete responsibility for the safety of his aircraft rests on him. His rank is indicated on his cuff by a minimum of two and a half rings to a maximum of four, depending on seniority. He is compelled by law to hold current licences as pilot and navigator, and, in fact, may also possess engineer's and radio officer's licences.

He will have received his first or 'A' licence when, after 8 to 10 hours' instruction in half-hourly lessons, he has flown solo for a total of 3 hours, carried out a simple flying test, and passed a spoken examination on the rules of the air. This entitles a pilot, in theory, to fly any aeroplane anywhere, and also to carry passengers, provided he is not paid.

The professional, or 'B' licence, requires at least 100 hours' piloting experience. The candidate must know air-law, navigation, and meteorology, and must have a working knowledge of his aeroplane, its engine, and aircrew. He must also make two cross-country flights and a night flight, taking off and landing in darkness. The 'B' licence is issued with a separate endorsement for each type of aeroplane on which the pilot is qualified, and a fresh test must be taken for each type added. A medical examination has to be passed every 6 months.

The First Officer, like the captain, holds a pilot's and navigator's licence. His duties on board include those of co-pilot and navigator. He wears two rings on his cuffs as an indication of rank; both pilots wear the air-line's wings on their breast.

The Radio Officer's duties are to maintain radio contact with the ground and assist with the navigation. As well as his licence, the radio officer must hold a certificate of competence, given by the Postmaster-General. The radio officer wears zig-zag rings on his cuffs varying from one to four in number, depending on seniority, and a half-wing on the breast.

The Steward has more contact with the passengers than any other member of the crew. Apart from attending to the comfort of passengers during flight, by giving them food, drinks, and newspapers, he is trained for escape-drill duties in the event of an emergency; these involve the safe and speedy leaving of the aircraft by the passengers in case of a forced landing. Stewards, who wear a half-wing on the breast, may be men or women; a stewardess is often called an air hostess.

A Navigation Officer is carried only on long flights. Otherwise navigation is the concern of the First Officer.

A Flight Engineer can be carried by a large air-liner on a long flight. His duty is to watch many panels of instruments while the aeroplane is in flight, to ensure that the engines, pressurization equipment, propellers, and other components are working well. If he notices anything wrong on his instruments, he notifies the captain, who can then decide what to do, and, if necessary, how to land the aeroplane safely. On certain lines the engineer also handles the engine controls on behalf of the pilot.

Two and sometimes three complete crews are carried by long-distance, non-stop aircraft in order to avoid the risk of an accident being caused by fatigue.

The duties of aircrews do not end on return to their home airport. The Captain and First Officer must be available for a certain period each month to practise 'blind flying' or instrument approaches to any airfield they are likely to use (*see* FLYING INSTRUMENTS). These prac-

tices are carried out on the 'Link' trainer, a dummy cockpit on the ground in which the pilot receives radio signals in exactly the same manner as he would in a real aircraft.

The steward's ground duties involve the checking of his aircraft's stores. Customs officers insist on a strict check of dutiable articles such as tobacco and spirits.

See also AIRPORT.

AIRGRAPH. The airgraph service used during the Second World War was a specialized form of AIR MAIL (q.v.). Because of the limited space which could be used for mails on transport aircraft to the Middle East, Africa, India, and Burma, letters to members of the Forces serving in those countries were written on special forms and handed in at Post Office counters. These forms were photographed in miniature and reproduced on a strip of film, 100 feet long and 16 millimetres wide, containing 1,700 airgraph messages. The film strip when enclosed in a metal container weighed $5\frac{1}{2}$ ounces, whereas the letters, if sent by ordinary post, would have weighed 50 lb. These spools of film were sent by aeroplane to their destination. There the process was reversed, and a print was made of each original message, which was then delivered in the ordinary way.

This service could also be used for letters to England from these countries, and was of great value, for it enabled members of the forces serving many thousands of miles away to communicate speedily with their people at home. From April 1941 to July 1945, when the service closed, over 350 million messages were sent by means of the 'airgraph' service.

A similar service was also operated by the United States authorities.

See also POSTAL SERVICES.

AIR HOSTESS, *see* AIRCREW.

AIR-LINER. This is an aeroplane which is normally engaged in the commercial carrying of at least five passengers.

The first passenger transport craft were small biplanes made of wood and fabric, with one or two engines. These had been used during the First World War for bombing, and were later converted for passengers; seats and windows were fitted in the enclosed types of aeroplane, while seats and a hatch-like lid or detachable

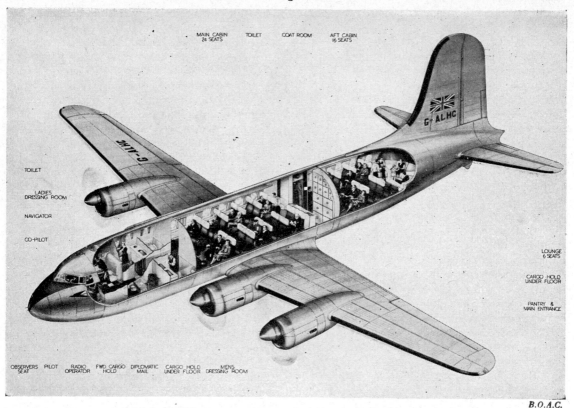

TOILET · LADIES DRESSING ROOM · NAVIGATOR · CO-PILOT

MAIN CABIN 24 SEATS · TOILET · COAT ROOM · AFT CABIN 16 SEATS

LOUNGE 6 SEATS · CARGO HOLD UNDER FLOOR · PANTRY & MAIN ENTRANCE

OBSERVERS SEAT · PILOT · RADIO OPERATOR · FWD CARGO HOLD · DIPLOMATIC MAIL · CARGO HOLD UNDER FLOOR · MENS DRESSING ROOM

B.O.A.C.

A B.O.A.C. ARGONAUT AIR-LINER CUT AWAY TO SHOW THE ACCOMMODATION
This type of aircraft is used on Far East and South American routes

roof were provided for the types with open cock-pits.

The modern air-liner carries its passengers in pressurized and air-conditioned cabins (*see* High Altitude Flight) which have been made reasonably comfortable and sound proof. Much research has gone into the designing of seats in which passengers can sit without discomfort for several hours. Sleeping-berths for night travel are generally larger than those in trains. There are lavatories and washing-rooms. Electric galleys or kitchens enable hot or cold meals to be served to passengers throughout a long flight; some aircraft have a bar, promenade deck, or lounge. For carrying goods there are pressurized and heated holds.

The crew's compartments are equipped with instruments for 'blind' flying and navigation. Radar and radio equipment is carried, and a flight engineer is frequently included to look after the engines, flying controls, and pressure pumps for high altitude flights.

In design an air-liner is normally an all-metal monoplane. It is planned for one of several special needs, such as short-range work on very crowded routes, long-range flying over water or land routes, and short-range lines on which there are few passengers. The average type used for short-range work on busy routes has two engines, which can produce 4,000 to 5,000 horse-power for short periods for the special effort of taking-off; it holds thirty to forty passengers and cruises at 250 to 350 miles an hour for 800 or 900 miles. The piston engine in this class is gradually giving way to the gas-turbine engine, still driving an airscrew, but with some increases in speed (*see* Aircraft Engines). The average weight of aircraft in this class is from 15 to 22 tons.

An average type used for long-range work has four engines, giving a take-off power of not less than 10,000 horse-power, and in many instances of 14,000 horse-power; it carries forty to seventy passengers over distances up to 3,000 miles at 300 to 400 miles an hour. In this class gas turbines both of the 'pure jet' and airscrew type are being increasingly used; speeds are rising up to about 500 to 550 miles an hour in the case of the 'pure jet'.

The following points are important in a well-designed air-liner. It must take off and land at reasonable speeds, using existing runways. It must fly under instrument-flying ('blind') conditions. Its payload (the weight it can carry in passengers and goods) must be profitable. It must have passenger comfort and ease of loading. Maintenance must be simple, and the running costs cheap. It must have a good engine 'performance', and be able to carry a worthwhile load over a required distance with ample fuel reserves in case bad weather should make a diversion necessary. The size of the aeroplane should enable it to be stowed in standard hangars without special ones having to be built. As an air-liner is expensive, and must therefore be used for some years, the design should be capable of some development to meet altering requirements.

The air-liner must comply with all national and international safety rules, which include being able to climb away from an airport should one engine fail during the take-off. It must be able to maintain height should one engine fail in flight. Four-engine types must fulfil these requirements with any two engines out of action. Although craft with two and four engines are the most common, the building of air-liners weighing over 100 tons has led to their being fitted with eight or even ten engines. Sometimes these engines are coupled in pairs, and mounted as single units.

The internal fittings of liners vary with the length and importance of the journey. 'Classes' exist on some routes, that is, different fares are charged for passages in different kinds of aircraft on the same length of journey.

Passengers see little of the organization which is necessary for their journey. At the airport of departure they show their passports to the passport control officers if they are going on a foreign trip, and their luggage is liable to be examined by Customs officers. They then walk on to the airfield and climb a short flight of steps to the door of the aeroplane, which they enter. They are shown to their seats by the steward, and are then instructed to cease smoking and to fasten their safety belts for the take-off. The safety belt is buckled round the waist of each passenger and prevents him being flung out of his seat if any mishap occurs at the take-off.

The aircraft is then taxied along a concrete runway, drawn by the action of its propellers and running along on its large rubber-tyred wheels. At the end of the runway, and at the start of the take-off path, the Captain waits for a signal from the airport control tower. On receiving this he opens the throttles of his engines, and the aircraft races along the take-off path until it rises into the air. When the aircraft is safely airborne, permission is given for passengers to unbuckle their safety belts and to smoke. During flight the radio officer and navigating officer constantly check the aircraft's exact position. A written note giving the details is passed round to passengers from time to time.

See also AEROPLANE; AIRCREW.

AIRLINES, see CIVIL AVIATION (map).

AIR MAIL. The first official air mail in the world was flown on the 18 February 1911, in India, covering a distance of 5 miles, between the Industrial and Agricultural Exhibition at Allahabad, and Naini Junction. The first air mail in the United Kingdom was flown in September 1911, between Hendon and Windsor, to celebrate the coronation of King George V and Queen Mary. Little further progress was made until immediately after the First World War, when army aeroplanes were used to carry

ENVELOPE USED ON THE FIRST OFFICIAL AIR MAIL SERVICE FROM NEW ZEALAND TO U.S.A.

mails from England to the British Forces in France and on the Rhine. This service was discontinued in August 1919.

The air mail as we know it to-day, however, may be said to have started in November 1919, with the opening of the service between London

AIR MAIL IN CENTRAL AUSTRALIA
There is a fortnightly service to many remote parts of the continent

Sunday Times

and Paris. An air fee of 2*s*. 6*d*. per ounce was charged, in addition to ordinary postage, and some 45 letters were carried daily. Services were gradually extended to other European countries, and on 30 March 1929, an air-mail service between England and India was started. This was the first stage in extending the air mail from the United Kingdom to countries outside Europe. The fee for air mail was reduced as the services expanded, until it became as low as 2*d*. per ounce to France or Belgium, and 3*d*. per ounce to Holland. To-day, 'first class mail' (letters, letter packets, and post-cards), paid for at the ordinary international rate of postage, is sent by air to those European countries (though not to Iceland or Poland) to which it will arrive more quickly than by the surface route. There is also a sixpenny 'air letter' service, serving all countries, which is specially useful when sending letters to distant places such as Canada, where an ordinary air-mail letter would cost as much as a shilling. An air letter is written on a special form supplied by the Post Office. This is made of thin paper and impressed with a sixpenny stamp.

A letter can now be sent by air to almost any country in the world, and aircraft leave London night and day with loads of mail for Australia, Canada, India, South America, South Africa, U.S.A., and other countries. A letter which, by surface mail, would take a month to reach Australia, takes only 6 days if sent by air mail. A development in inland air-mail services was the introduction in 1949, on an experimental basis, of helicopter services between Peterborough and Norwich to speed up postal services in East Anglia (*see* ROTORCRAFT).

See also POSTAL SERVICES.

AIR NAVIGATION, *see* NAVIGATION, AIR.

AIR PILOT, *see* AIRCREW.

AIRPORT. The term airport has come to mean an aerodrome or landing-ground of large size, used by regular air-passenger traffic. A great international airport may take a long time to grow. London Airport was planned to be built over a period of years, at a cost of more than £20,000,000. Even while airports grow, traffic must be handled smoothly. New York's airports cater for more than 800 aircraft movements (in or out) in a day.

The chief needs of an important airport are:

(*a*) A large area of level ground. Modern aircraft may need a run of nearly two miles along a take-off path or runway, and an airport's runways must point in more than one direction to provide for changing winds. All aircraft take off and land 'into the wind', facing the direction from which the wind is coming. This is necessary so that the wings may develop enough 'lift' (*see* FLYING).

(*b*) Firm sub-soil. Thick concrete runways are built on this. Aircraft weighing 70 tons or more may take off and alight at a speed of 100 miles an hour, and the load on the ground is severe. On the other hand, the land must be carefully drained and not allowed to become waterlogged.

(*c*) Clear weather conditions. Fog and mist caused by rivers, lakes, and reservoirs in certain conditions of temperature and humidity involve danger, expense, and delay for airport services. Mist which can hinder visibility, particularly at dusk, can be caused by the smoke from factories or from towns where many coal fires are in use.

(*d*) A site near a city with good arterial road

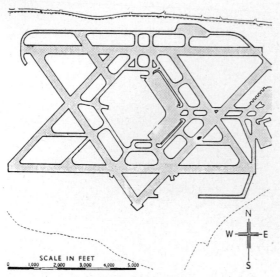

FIG. I. PLAN OF LONDON AIRPORT

Passenger buildings and the control tower occupy the central area, taxi tracks leading from them to the runways. There are hangars, workshops, and maintenance buildings to the east of the runways, and further maintenance areas to the south

and railway services. Time gained in air travel over long distances will be lost in slow ground travel unless the airport is near a capital or a group of large towns.

(e) Freedom from obstructions to flying. Neighbouring hills, blocks of flats and offices, factories and tall chimneys, power stations and electricity power lines and pylons, high railway viaducts are among obstacles to be avoided. Those very near the airport have to be lit at night or in foggy weather.

Many of those factors conflict, and in fact most of the great airports of the world are the result of compromise; none is on an ideal site.

Most airports have been shaped by the constant changes that have taken place in the design of aircraft. Every few years runways have to be made longer to accommodate faster and heavier craft (see AIRCRAFT TAKE-OFF). Airports which cannot expand, owing to the presence of a neighbouring town or river, cease to be used by the most important air-lines, which turn to new airports. These come into use before there is time to plan and build all the administrative, passenger, and storage buildings required. For that reason groups of temporary buildings are seen on many of the world's most modern airports.

The patterns of airports differ a great deal.

The pattern of each port is determined by its runways, and these in turn are influenced by the prevailing winds, the quantity, speed, and weight of the regular aircraft in use, and the area of land and financial resources available.

Many airports have three main runways, each pointing in a different direction. As each runway can serve two opposite points of the compass, an aircraft which is about to take off or alight has a choice of six directions. If the angles between the three runways are equally spaced out, no runway will ever be more than 30 degrees out of line with the direction of the wind (see Fig. 1). In some cases the three runways are laid out in a triangle. In others they cross one another in an irregular pattern. Often multi-strip runways are built to enable more air traffic to be handled at once; these are patterns in which each runway is duplicated by a parallel strip near it.

One pattern favoured by many large airports is the tangential. This consists of a central area of concrete, from the edge of which a number of runways run off at a tangent (see Fig. 2). The central area contains the ticket offices, customs sheds, and waiting-rooms. One advantage is that much taxi-ing of aircraft is avoided between the departure buildings and the chosen runway. Passengers can board aircraft near the airport buildings, and the aircraft can then

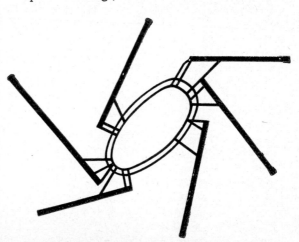

FIG. 2. FINAL PLAN FOR AMSTERDAM AIRPORT, SCHIPHOL
The taxi tracks radiate from the buildings in the centre to the tangential runways

move straight along a departure runway in the desired direction, becoming airborne at the end of the runway. A second important advantage is that arriving and departing aircraft never use the same runway. Incoming aircraft will always touch down at the far end of a runway opposite the departure runway in use; they will then taxi as far as the central buildings.

Alongside main runways, and some distance from them, auxiliary runways or taxi-ing paths are often laid down, and are connected with the main runways by cross-paths at intervals. Aircraft which have landed, and which may have a long way to taxi before reaching the airport buildings, are expected to turn off the main arrival runway on to one of these adjoining taxi-ing runways, in order to allow other craft to land.

London Airport, which is near the Bath Road, 12 to 13 miles west of central London, covers an area of 2,857 acres and was opened in 1946. There are six runways arranged in parallel pairs, the two main runways being over 9,000 feet long. The airport is designed to serve the largest kind of transport aircraft likely to be operated in the foreseeable future. The main passenger buildings and the 125-foot-high control tower occupy the centre of the airport and are reached by a road tunnel, which is half a mile long and has four traffic lanes, running under the northern runway. The main B.E.A. and B.O.A.C. maintenance bases, workshops, and hangars are to the east of the runways.

Traffic on such a scale needs an organization which compares with that of a busy harbour or of a great railway terminus. The central airport buildings have not only to provide for the comfort of passengers and to house the officials who deal directly with them. They contain staffs which deal with maps and charts; weather information; testing of aircraft engines, electrical circuits, and radio sets; control of landing aircraft; radar devices for 'blind' flying; wireless contact with foreign airports for traffic information; fuelling of aircraft from tanker lorries; control and maintenance of hundreds of powerful signal lights in various colours all over and around the airport area; provision of standby aircrews; ambulance services; fire-fighting squads; administrative and welfare work; and day and night canteens. One of the most important tasks of the staff of an airport is to see safely to the ground the landing aircraft. This becomes skilled and anxious work when bad weather reduces visibility: indeed, when an airport becomes seriously enveloped in fog, aircraft some-

B.E.A.

PASSENGERS BOARDING AN AIR-LINER AT LIVERPOOL AIRPORT
In the background is the control tower

times have to be diverted by radio to another less fog-bound port. Airports are, however, provided with various aids to landing in poor visibility. Fireworks are sometimes used for this purpose. The controller at the end of the runway on which the aircraft is to land has a selection of coloured rocket-lights which he can fire by pistol. During the aircraft's final approach he may fire several lights to mark the end of the runway. He uses another colour to tell the pilot to 'go round again' if the aircraft is still flying too high for landing. Although the controller is also in touch with the aircraft by radio-telephone, fireworks have proved useful as quick last-minute signals, especially during ground mist. Elaborate arrangements of high-powered electric lights of various colours, indicating the runway in use, can help landings at night and in poor visibility.

One aid to landing in fog, which was developed during the Second World War, was FIDO—the initial letters of Fog Investigation Dispersal Operation. Metal pipes 1,000 yards long were laid at each side of a runway. At intervals along the pipes were small holes or burners. Petrol was pumped along these pipes and set alight at all the holes. The fierce wall of flame on each side of the runway gave out so much heat that the thickest fog was cleared, up to a height of 300 feet from the ground. The device is too expensive for normal use, as 500,000 gallons of petrol an hour are needed to keep a runway fully warmed. Other disadvantages of Fido in peace-time are the bumpiness in the air caused by the rising heat, and passenger's natural dislike of making a landing between walls of flame.

See also CIVIL AVIATION; NAVIGATION, AIR.

AIR ROUTES, *see* CIVIL AVIATION.

AIR RULE OF THE ROAD, *see* RULE OF THE ROAD, Section 3.

AIRSHIPS. An airship is an engine-driven aircraft which is supported by gas that is lighter than air. The lifting gases in general use are hydrogen, which catches fire very easily, and helium, which is rare and expensive. The high cost of building airships and the large ground staffs needed for handling them make the overhead costs high. The greatest disadvantage,

A GERMAN ZEPPELIN IN 1926
This view gives some idea of the size of the airship. Its length was about seven times its width

however, is the low cruising speed—90 miles an hour is the highest practicable so far. On the other hand, landing can be made with practically no forward speed, whereas many modern aeroplanes have to touch down at over 90 miles an hour.

The popularity of the airship was highest at the beginning of the present century. Before aeroplanes had flown, and during the early years of their development, great hopes were placed on airships. Behind them lay a century of successful BALLOON ascents (q.v.); so when at the end of the 19th century the motor-car engine was available, it was felt that the two principles could be combined in the airship, or dirigible balloon, to provide a new form of transport. Within a few years the First World War had turned the aeroplane from a freak into a vital form of communication. Britain began the war with 150 aeroplanes and ended with 22,000. The airship never regained popularity.

Modern airships are classified as non-rigid, semi-rigid, and rigid.

The non-rigid type, sometimes called blimp, is simply an elongated gas-balloon with an engine-car suspended below it. It was used for patrolling the British coasts in the First World War and the American coasts in the Second World War.

The semi-rigid type, in which a long, rigid keel supports the passenger and engine-cars, has been developed mainly by the Italians. As with the non-rigid airship, the semi-rigid keeps its shape by the pressure of gas from within. If gas escapes, the vessel may become so flabby as to get out of control. Two of these airships have flown over the North Pole—the *Norge* (meaning 'Norway'), chartered by the Norwegian explorer Amundsen for an expedition across the Pole to Alaska in 1926, and the *Italia*, on an expedition organized by its designer, Umberto Nobile, two years later. After reaching the Pole, this airship was wrecked on the return.

The rigid airship, which does not depend on inflation for its shape and rigidity, has a hull made up of transverse frames of light metal alloy joined together by girders. The bay between each set of frames contains a gas-bag. The whole structure is given a stream-lined covering of fabric. Keels running through the hull add strength and provide access to various parts of the ship. Fuel tanks, water ballast tanks, and other weights are spaced out within the ship.

U.S. Navy

A NON-RIGID AIRSHIP
A G-type airship built by Goodyear, used for patrolling

the larger *Hindenburg* began operating between Europe and New York. These two craft between them had flown over a million miles when, in 1937, the *Hindenburg* burst into flames when about to moor near New York, and all its passengers and crew were killed. The craft had been unable to get supplies of the non-inflammable gas, helium.

The British rigid airships were all classified by the letter R, standing for Rigid. The best-known of these was the R34, which in 1919 made the world's first double crossing of the Atlantic. British craft, however, did not take part in a regular passenger service. The State-built R101, Britain's largest and most luxurious airship, was wrecked with great loss of life at Beauvais, in northern France, in 1930, on its first long voyage.

This disaster discouraged the building of airships in Britain. A sister ship, the R100, which had first successfully flown to Canada and back, was dismantled, and its metal parts flattened out by steam-rollers for use as scrap. A few years later came the loss of the German *Hindenburg*. These two accidents, as well as the loss of the American craft *Akron* and *Macon*, caused aircraft designers to cease building airships.

ALASKAN HIGHWAY. Alaska is a territory of the United States, but it is separated, geographically, from the United States by the western part of Canada. This part of Canada (British Columbia and the Yukon) has been so little developed, that until recently the only roads were the trails made by the early settlers or by the gold-diggers of the Klondyke Gold Rush in 1898. Alaska was more often reached by sea. During the Second World War it was realized that the Japanese might invade Alaska, and that it was so cut off from the Americans that they would not be able to defend it. So the Governments of the United States and Canada co-operated in building a highway through the wild and little known regions of north-west Canada. Most of the building was done by the United States Army; and the Canadian Government constructed a series of airfields.

The land was first surveyed by aerial photography, and then was more closely investigated by surveyors led by Indian and Canadian trappers, who were among the few people that knew the country. Bulldozers were used to clear the ground of trees and to level the track,

At the stern are fins and rudder similar to those used on aeroplanes. The control car is built into the underside in the form of a small cabin. Passenger and freight accommodation is normally within the hull. The engines, which drive propellers, are in suspended cars, called gondolas, hung beneath the hull. The gas-bags of rigid airships and the outer envelope of other airships are made of layers of cotton material proofed with rubber to prevent the gas escaping —although a slight leakage cannot be prevented. Some of the early airships had envelopes which were made of the lining of the intestines of oxen.

German rigid airships, named after their designer Count Zeppelin, were probably the most successful airships ever built. The first was constructed in 1900. Zeppelins were used to start the first air-line in the world from Berlin to Lake Constance, on the borders of Germany and Switzerland, in 1910. Airships of this type were used for bombing London in the First World War. After that war Zeppelins again took the lead in regular passenger transport by airship. From 1931 to 1937 the airship *Graf Zeppelin* flew services to a time-table between Europe and America. It made fifty Atlantic crossings and one trip round the world. In 1936

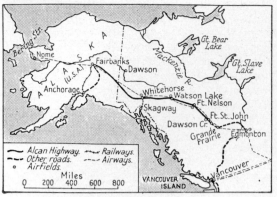

THE ALASKAN HIGHWAY

and road-building crews followed to complete the work. Settlements were built along the route, with landing-grounds for the aircraft which brought supplies. More than 10,000 soldiers and 6,000 civilian workers were employed, and they had to be provided with everything they needed: food, houses, medical supplies, doctors, and clerks. Insects in summer and intense cold in winter made the work difficult, and much of the country was mountainous or swampy. North-west of Whitehorse the road rises to a height of 4,212 feet above sea-level, and it is dry and dusty. Farther south it is wet, and lorries were often bogged. 'Muskeg', or bog of saturated peat and moss, was the worst obstacle, and crossing it needed great labour and engineering skill.

The road is 1,671 miles long. It starts at Dawson Creek in British Columbia, and goes by way of Canadian airfields at Fort St. John, Fort Nelson, Watson Lake, and Whitehorse, to Fairbanks in Alaska. It was built in 6 months, though years of work are needed to make it suitable to carry a great deal of traffic.

The road is now known as the Alaskan–Canadian Military Highway, or more briefly the 'Alcan Highway'. It did not have to be used to repel a Japanese invasion of Alaska, but it is making it possible for people to reach, settle in, and develop not only Alaska but all the rich land through which it runs.

See also Vol. III: ALASKA.
See also Vol. VIII: ROAD BUILDING.

ALDIS LAMP, *see* LIGHT SIGNALLING.

ALPHABET. The alphabet is a collection of letters, signs which represent the sounds of speech, arranged in a fixed order. The word comes from the first two letters of the Greek alphabet—*alpha* and *beta*. In the older methods of picture-writing, thousands of different symbols were required to express thoughts and objects (*see* WRITING); but in alphabetic writing only about twenty-five or so letters are needed, and by combining them in different ways any number of words can be made. An ideal alphabet would have one separate consistent letter for each sound, and only one; but no such alphabet is in general use. Actually each of the main alphabets of the world has a small number of letters, generally between twenty-two and thirty-five, which are not enough for all the sounds used in speech; our own alphabet, for instance, has only twenty-six letters to represent about forty-two different sounds. The other sounds are represented by combining different letters together, or by using the same letter to represent two different sounds. No alphabet is absolutely consistent; there are often letters such as k and c with the same sound (*see* SPELLING).

The history of the alphabet covers 3,500 years, and extends over the whole world. Most scholars think that nearly all existing alphabets are descended from one original alphabet, used some 3,000 years ago by the SEMITES (q.v. Vol. I). But they do not know for certain how this original alphabet came into being. It may have originated in Egyptian HIEROGLYPHICS (q.v.) or in another kind of picture-writing such as that used in ancient Crete (*see* MINOAN CIVILIZATION, Vol. I), or else in an already alphabetic script created by a great inventor, about whom we know nothing. Recently, ancient inscriptions have been discovered in Palestine and North Syria and on the Peninsula of Sinai, which seem to be early attempts at alphabetic writing, and some scholars believe that these may be a link in the chain between the Semitic original alphabet and the Egyptian hieroglyphic writing. One of the most valuable discoveries was that of some early inscriptions in North Syria, which are in a completely alphabetic form of script. They belong to a North Semitic language such as Phoenician, and are believed to go back about 1400 years B.C. (*see* PHOENICIAN CIVILIZATION, Vol. I). It is thought that the alphabet used in them presents certain elements similar to those of the original Semitic alphabet, and from them and many other indications it is assumed that the alphabet originated

Syria V; R. Dussaud

EARLY NORTH SEMITIC LETTERS

Part of the inscription on the coffin of Ahiram, King of Byblos, about 975 B.C. Byblos was a Phoenician town on the coast of Syria

before 1500 B.C., somewhere among the Semitic peoples of Palestine or Syria.

By about 1000 B.C. four main alphabets had arisen out of the original Semitic alphabet, and in time each of them gave rise to many others. The Canaanite branch was the ancestor of the early Hebrew alphabet, used by the ancient Israelites and other Near Eastern peoples, as well as of the Phoenician alphabet, used in Phoenicia itself and in her colonies, such as Carthage. The Aramaic branch was the ancestor not only of a great variety of scripts used throughout western and central Asia, and indirectly giving rise to many more in countries such as India, Java, Korea, and Mongolia, but also of the modern Hebrew and Arabic alphabets. The South Semitic branch was mainly confined within Arabia, where many different scripts developed from it. An offshoot spread into Africa, and became the ancestor of the Ethiopic alphabet.

The fourth, and most important branch was the Greek alphabet, which is thought to have been created somewhere between the 11th and the 9th centuries B.C. Though scholars are not agreed upon the time of its origin, there is no serious scholar to-day who doubts that the Greeks derived their alphabet from a Semitic source. The shapes of the letters are essentially the same in early Greek as in early Semitic, their sequence in the alphabet is the same, and the values of the letters are, mainly, the same. Finally, not only are the names essentially the same, but these names, meaningless in Greek, are words in Semitic languages. Hence, these alphabets must be related, and as the Semitic is without doubt the earlier, the Greek must depend upon it. The early Greek writing was not uniform; each of the many little states had its own variety, and there were perhaps about forty local alphabets. In 403 B.C. one of these, the Ionic of Miletus in Asia Minor, was officially adopted at Athens, and later became the common 'classical' Greek alphabet of twenty-four letters. The Greeks introduced various reforms. For example, the Semitic alphabet had consisted entirely of consonants, but the Greeks used some of these consonants, for which they had no use in their own language, to represent the vowels a, e, i, o, u. They discarded some Semitic letters and introduced new ones to represent the sounds ph, ps, kh, and ks. They also

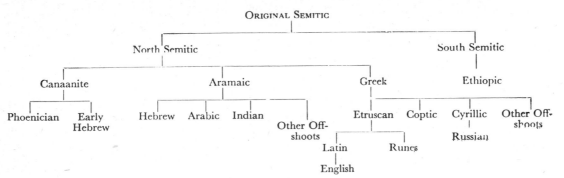

THE DEVELOPMENT OF ALPHABETS FROM THE ORIGINAL SEMITIC

simplified the form of some of the letters. The Greek alphabet has given rise to a great many alphabets, some of which, such as Coptic or Gothic or those of ancient Asia Minor, are now extinct, while others are still used; for instance, the Cyrillic in Russia, Bulgaria, Serbia, and Ukraine, and formerly also in Rumania. Most notably, however, the Greek alphabet was the ancestor of the Etruscan alphabet, the ancestor of the Latin or Roman alphabet.

The Etruscan alphabet—used in ancient Etruria, roughly corresponding to modern Tuscany in central Italy—was developed from the Greek alphabet about the 8th century B.C. It originally had twenty-six letters; but in the late 5th century B.C. classical Etruscan was developed, which had only twenty characters—sixteen consonants and four vowels. Many different alphabets arose out of the Etruscan, the most important of all being the Roman alphabet. The Romans adopted twenty-one of the original Etruscan letters. As the Etruscans had no g, the letter c was used for the Latin sounds k and g; later a new letter was invented, consisting of c with a bar added, which is our g. This replaced the Greek z, for which there was no use in Latin. In the 1st century B.C., however, z was restored for Latin words of Greek origin, and placed at the end of the alphabet. At the same time the letter y was introduced, also for Greek words which were taken into Latin, and placed before the z. By the beginning of the Christian era our alphabet of capital letters was completely developed, except for j, u, and w.

The Latin alphabet, altered in various ways, is the basis of all the alphabets of western, central, and northern Europe. It has been adapted to meet the needs of the different languages, many of which contain sounds not represented in the original alphabet. One of these adapted forms is the basis of the English alphabet.

The Runes, or 'national' script of the Teutonic peoples, are probably descended (in the 2nd or 1st century B.C.) from a North Etruscan alphabet. The Runic alphabet was generally displaced by the Latin on the conversion of its users (chiefly the Scandinavian peoples) to Christianity, but in some outlying regions of Scandinavia it lingered on into the 16th or 17th centuries.

It was also used in England between about A.D. 500 and 1000. Moreover, when the Anglo-Saxons took over the Irish style of the Roman alphabet in the 7th century A.D., they added some Runes, the *thorn*, þ, and the *wyn*, ƿ, representing the sounds of th and w. The *wyn* was dropped in the 13th century, but the *thorn* was used up till the 16th or 17th centuries, and even later. It was latterly shaped like a y. The two last lines of the inscription over Shakespeare's grave, for instance, run:

BLESTE BE YE MAN YT SPARES THES STONES,
AND CURST BE HE YT MOVES MY BONES.

Three new letters were introduced into the English alphabet in the Middle Ages: j to represent i when used as a consonant, u to represent v when used as a vowel, and w to represent vv

Arabic	Hebrew	Greek	Cyrillic (Russian)	Latin
١	א	α	а	A
ب	ב	β	б	B
س، ك	כ, ס	κ, σ	к, с	C
د	ד	δ	д	D
ى	'	ε, η	е, э	E
ف	פ	φ	ф, θ	F
ك	ג	γ	г	G
ه	ה	ʽ	г	H
ى	'	ι	и, й	I
ج	—	—	дж	J
ك	כ	κ	к	K
ل	ל	λ	л	L
م	מ	μ	м	M
ن	נ	ν	н	N
و	ו	ο, ω	о	O
ف	פ	π	п	P
ق	ק	ϙ	—	Q
ر	ר	ρ	р	R
س	שׁ, ס	σ, ς	с	S
ط، ت	ת, ט	τ	т	T
و	ו	υ	ы, ю	U
و	ו	υ	в	V
و	ו	F	—	VV
—	—	ξ	кс	X
ى	'	ι, υ	я	Y
ظ، ز	ז, צ	ζ	з	Z

COMPARATIVE TABLE OF ALPHABETS

British Museum

THE FRANKS CASKET (FRONT PANEL). MADE IN NORTHUMBRIA OF WHALEBONE, ABOUT A.D. 700
On the left is Wayland the Smith; on the right the Adoration of the Magi. The surrounding Runes read 'the fish flood (sea) lifted the whale's bones on to the mainland; the ocean became turbid where he swam aground on the shingle'

or uu. The black-letter script, incorrectly called 'Gothic', was used in England until the 16th century, when, with the development of PRINTING (q.v.), our writing was changed to its present form. The black-letter is still used in Germany.

At one time a Gaelic alphabet was used in the British Isles. This was the curious Ogham script, which consists of strokes or notches cut in the corner of a stone, varying in number, position, and direction for each letter. Most of the Ogham inscriptions which have been found are in Ireland, but there are some in Wales, and a few in the Isle of Man and in Scotland. The Oghams are not derived from the Roman alphabet, but were probably invented in the 4th century A.D. by someone familiar with Roman writing and letters.

See also SPELLING; WRITING, HISTORY OF; HIEROGLYPHICS; CUNEIFORM; HANDWRITING.

AMERICAN ENGLISH LANGUAGE. This is the variety of English spoken and written in the United States, sometimes less correctly called the American language. To a great extent educated American English does not on the whole differ from the standard English of all the countries in which it is the natural language. In all serious and cultured speech and writing there is very little by which the two can be distinguished, although there are American expressions which come as naturally to the American as Scottish expressions to the Scot.

During the period of more than three centuries, however, in which American English has been growing up, many new words, or new meanings to words, have been added which make the languages distinct from each other. The extent to which these make their appearance varies according to the subject which is being talked or written about, or to the style which is natural to the speaker or writer. They mainly belong to one of two classes: firstly, ordinary English words which have had a new meaning given to them, or are used to form new compounds or new phrases, or which are rarely used in English, but have by now become more common in America; and secondly, words which the English-speaking settlers in America have adopted from other languages with which they came in contact. Besides words from the various languages of the native Indian tribes, these include words from Dutch and German, and still more from French and Spanish, adopted from other settlers speaking these languages. The date at which any one of these words was adopted, or came into use, has a close connexion with the history of the country and of the English-speaking settlers, especially as they moved westwards across the Continent. A few examples will show the effect of both these sources of new words on the language as it now is.

Although a great many words have been adopted from other languages, comparatively few are used commonly enough to be familiar to any but Americans. The Indian languages, however, have supplied such words as 'squaw', 'wigwam', 'wampum', 'moccasin', 'tomahawk', 'pemmican', 'hickory', 'pecan' (nut), 'hominy', 'opossum', 'raccoon' (also shortened to 'coon'), and 'skunk'. Indian customs are also recorded in such phrases as 'to walk in Indian file', 'to go on the war-path', and 'to bury the hatchet'. French has contributed 'prairie', 'portage', 'chute', 'levee', 'shanty', 'cache'. From Spanish have come 'ranch', 'corral' (pen for horses or cattle), 'lariat' (rope for picketing horses), 'lasso', 'rodeo', 'canyon', 'adobe' (sun-dried brick), 'sombrero' (broad-brimmed felt hat), and others which are mainly used in connexion with the Western States, and frequently occur in short stories or novels relating to these. The most important borrowings from Dutch are 'boss', a master or employer (whence also the verb 'to boss'), 'sleigh', 'spook', and 'stoop' (a house-porch). The American use of the words 'dumb' and 'fresh' is much nearer to the German *dumm* and *frisch* than to the English use.

It is not from outside, however, but from within, that American English has made the greatest additions to its special words and their uses. This has been done in various ways. From quite early dates there are such changes in meaning as 'corn' (English: cereal plants, especially oats; American: maize), 'creek' (English: inlet on sea-coast; American: stream). Other words with a special American meaning are 'bog' for a hummock in a swamp, 'lumber' for timber, 'hemlock' for a kind of spruce, 'cedar' applied to trees which are not cedars, and 'robin' to a red-breasted thrush. So numerous are these changes of meaning that they can easily lead to misunderstandings on both sides of the Atlantic.

Another extensive source of Americanisms is the formation of a great number of new compounds, as 'back-woods', 'bee-line', 'salt-lick', 'drug-store', 'freight-train', 'log-rolling', 'camp-meeting', 'gold-hunter'. In fact, there are over thirty such compounds formed from the one word 'bear' (as 'bear-bacon', '-dance', '-grass', &c.) and no less than seventy-five from 'buffalo'. The word 'buffalo' is used in America for 'bison', whereas in English it means another species of ox, not found at all in America. This word also illustrates one way in which words acquire new

meanings—'buffalo' may be short for a 'buffalo robe'. Americans and English often use different words for the same thing, as 'baggage' for luggage, 'railroad' for railway, 'street-car' for tram, 'automobile' for motor-car, 'store' for shop, 'sidewalk' for pavement, 'gums' or 'rubbers' for overshoes. Some uses which are now American are survivals from earlier English, as 'sick' for ill; to 'guess' for to suppose; 'fall' for autumn; 'dry goods' for textile wares. These, however, are more common in the dialects.

During the past century and a half a great many colloquial and slang words have been added to American English, and some of these words have come into general use even outside the United States, such as 'blizzard', 'bogus', 'bunkum', 'crank', 'scalawag', and 'O.K.' (*see* SLANG). In some points there are also differences in spelling and pronunciation between American and English usage, such as the spelling of 'color' for colour; but these are of slight importance in comparison with the number of new words and phrases which give American English its distinctive character.

See also ENGLISH LANGUAGE.
See also Vol. I: AMERICANS.

AMERICAN INDIAN LANGUAGES. At least 2,000 different languages are spoken by the AMERICAN INDIANS (q.v. Vol. I), the original inhabitants of North and South America, of whom there are about 15,000,000 in all. These languages are very different from each other: it is possible to pick a pair which differ from each other as much as English does from Chinese, and there are no characteristics which are shared by all or even most Indian languages. Some are difficult for a European to learn, because of their difference from normal European languages, and of the great complexity of many of the words which are built up by adding suffixes (additions) to a shorter word. In Oneida, for instance, a language belonging to the Iroquois family (North America), the one word *gnaglaslizaks* means 'I am looking for a village', being made up as follows: *g*—I, *nagla*—to live, *sl*—abstract suffix like 'ness' of English 'goodness', *i*—suffix denoting that someone is taking action, *zak*—to look for, and *s*—an ending showing that the action is continuous, that is to say, that one is going on looking.

American Indian languages can be divided into 123 'families' of related languages. All the languages in one 'family' were once the same language, just as French, Spanish, and Italian were once Latin (*see* LANGUAGE, HISTORY OF); but so far no relationship has been discovered between one family of languages and another. The families vary a great deal in size—the Carib family of South America, for instance, contains fifty languages, whereas Kootenay, a language spoken in British Columbia, is the only member of one family, and is thus unrelated to any known language. Many Indian languages have died out since the coming of the Europeans to America. In South America it is probable that further separate languages will yet be discovered.

1. NORTH AMERICA. There are at least ten important families of languages each with sub-families arising out of it. Among the best-known are the Algonquin, the Iroquois, the Uto-Aztek, and the Eskimo languages. Many English and American words have been borrowed from the Algonquin group, among them 'moccasin' (*mockasin*), 'moose' (*moos*), 'mugwump' (*mug-quomp* 'big chief'), 'pow-pow' (*powwaw*), 'skunk' (*segankw*), 'squaw' (*squaws*), 'tobaggan' (*tobakun*), 'tomahawk' (*tommahick*), and 'woodchuck' (*wuchak*, with the first part corrupted to 'wood'). The Iroquois family includes many languages, among them Mohawk and Cherokee. A member of the Uto-Aztek family is Aztek, the language of the AZTECS (q.v. Vol. I), still spoken over a large part of Mexico. Eskimo is spoken along the Arctic coast, in the Aleutian Islands, in the extreme north-east of Siberia, and in Greenland. There is a considerable modern literature in Greenlandic (*see* ESKIMOES, Vol. I).

2. CENTRAL AMERICA. Maya is the most important family of languages of those which are purely Central American. Its languages are spoken over a large area in Mexico, in British Honduras, and parts of the Republics of Guatemala and Honduras. Maya is the only American Indian language with an ancient alphabet (*see* MAYA CIVILIZATION, Vol. I).

3. SOUTH AMERICA. Here again there are very many families of languages, among the largest being the Arawak, the Carib, the Chibcha, and the Tupi-Guaraní families. The numerous languages of this last family seem to have spread from the area between the Paraná and the Paraguay, up the coast of Brazil as far as the mouth of the Amazon, up the river almost to its source, and up many of its southern

Bodleian Library

PAGE FROM THE CODEX MENDOZA, 16TH-CENTURY MEXICAN PICTOGRAPHIC MANUSCRIPT

Chimalpopuca, King of Mexico (1417–1427), is seated. The years of his reign are shown by the squares on the left. On the right are two towns he conquered, Tequixquiac and Chalco. Chalco rebelled, killing five Mexicans and damaging four canoes. The explanation is given in contemporary Spanish handwriting

tributaries. In Paraguay, Guaraní is the dominant language (though Spanish is the official one), and it already has a considerable modern literature. There are many other families which cover large areas of South America, of which Quichua is of particular interest, for it was the language of the INCAS (q.v. Vol. I), and is still spoken in most of Peru and parts of the Argentine.

There are many English words derived from South American Indian words, though usually they have come to us through Spanish or Portuguese: among these are 'cocoa' (Spanish *cacao*, Aztec *caca-uatl* 'caca-tree'), 'hurricane' (Carib *huracan*), 'jaguar' (Tupi-Guaraní *yaguara*), 'tomato' Spanish and Portuguese *tomate*, Aztec *tomatl*).

See also LANGUAGE STRUCTURE.
See also Vol. I: AMERICAN INDIANS.

AMERICAN TRAILS. The word 'trail' is generally used in the United States to refer to the routes, particularly across the western part of America, that were used by traders and settlers in the early days of pioneering and development. The expression 'to blaze a trail' means to make a path through uncharted country. Usually the trails were marked out by explorers who sought the safest passages through the unknown and often difficult territory of north-west America. They were followed by traders who went out to these undeveloped regions to trade with Indian tribes, usually for furs. They established trading posts along the trails, which sometimes grew to be centres of settlement and, later, towns. The earliest trails along the Pacific Coast were particularly trade-routes established by Spaniards, and of these the Old Spanish Trail was the most important.

In the 19th century, when settlers began to cross the country from the east to seek new homes in the west, they followed the established trade-routes because they were likely to be safer and to lead to possible fording places of rivers and passages across mountain ranges or deserts. The Santa Fé Trail was one of the two main routes used by emigrants. It ran from the town of Independence, Missouri, through Texas to Santa Fé in the present State of New Mexico. It was opened in 1829 as an official trading-route, and over it passed thousands of settlers seeking land in the west. It was a dangerous route, passing through wide stretches of semi-desert country where there was uncertain water supply, and through the territory of such hostile Indian tribes as the Cheyenne, the Comanche, and the Arapaho. The use of an established route made the emigrant wagon trains more vulnerable to ambush, but insured against the greater dangers of being lost in a nearly water-less wilderness.

The Oregon Trail became in time even more important than the Santa Fé route as an emigrant passage. It ran for 2,000 miles from Independence, passing over the Rocky Mountains and near the Great Salt Lake, to the Columbia River and the Pacific coast. In 1843 a tremendous emigration began from east to west; then, following the discovery of gold in California in 1848, many thousands more went along the Oregon Trail to the Great Salt Lake and then over a new route south-westwards to the California coast and San Francisco.

The trip was at best difficult and arduous, as a covered wagon pulled by oxen travelled at a speed of about 2 miles an hour in good weather. The emigrants usually made up large parties of eighty, a hundred, or more persons for the sake of safety, and travelled armed against Indian attack. Parties were frequently accompanied by professional guides or Indian scouts, who were familiar with the dangers of the country and the hostile tribes. They usually elected one of their number as a leader, with powers like those of a general in a military organization. At night the wagon trains were formed into circles, in the centre of which the women, children, and animals could be protected; and the camps were patrolled by sentries.

In the latter part of the 19th century after the Civil War, the Chisholm Trail became of great commercial importance. This trail ran across Texas, leading from the plains to the town of Abilene, which was the railroad terminus, connected by rail with the cattle markets in Kansas City. Over the Chisholm Trail thousands of cattle were driven yearly after the round-ups, and trips along the Chisholm Trail became the subject of many cowboy songs. The phrase 'going down the Chisholm Trail' came to mean in cowboy slang, for some reason, the same thing as 'going west' or 'crossing the divide'—that is, dying.

UNITED STATES OF AMERICA, SHOWING THE CHIEF AMERICAN TRAILS

In the present day, the word 'trail' has come to be used for many modern motor roads in the United States, sometimes because the new roads follow the older routes. These include the Arrowhead Trail, running from Salt Lake City to Los Angeles, the Black and Yellow Trail, from Yellowstone Park to Chicago, the Susquehanna Trail from Buffalo, New York, to Washington D.C., and the Shenandoah and Skyline Trails, which go through the Blue Ridge and Smoky Mountains in Virginia and Tennessee, and attract many tourists because of the great beauty of the scenery.

See also TRADE ROUTES.

AMPHIBIAN AIRCRAFT, *see* SEAPLANE.

AMPHIBIOUS VEHICLES, which could be used on land or water, first came into use in the Second World War, when the British and American forces built them for the invasion of continental Europe. The amphibian resembled a boat with squared ends which had been fitted with wheels. In the water a propeller and rudder were used. A form of gear-box, known as a power transfer box, enabled the engine to be applied either to the wheels or to the propeller.

A two-purpose vehicle, not for use on land and water but on rail and road, is described in MOTOR TRANSPORT; and amphibian aircraft are described in SEAPLANE (qq.v.).

APENNINE TUNNEL. The Great Apennine railway tunnel in northern Italy, 11½ miles long, is the longest bore in the world housing a double track in a single tunnel. After the First World War, the Italian State Railways set out to build two main-line 'through' routes, known as *direttissima*, one from Rome to Naples and the other from Bologna to Florence. Both were designed to cut through all intervening obstacles, almost regardless of expense, by a series of tunnels and viaducts. The Bologna–Florence through route (which forms part of the main line from Milan to Rome) has to make its way through the main chain of the Apennine Mountains. The old route climbed on gradients as steep as 1 in 35, and with frequent bends, to a summit-level of 2,000 feet, so that express trains took 2¼ hours to cover the 82 miles from Bologna to Florence. The new through route not only smoothed out the curves, but cut the distance to 60 miles, with 1 in 85 as the steepest gradient in the open and 1 in 125 in a tunnel. As a result, the former journey of 2¼ hours could be done in 70 to 78 minutes by heavy express trains, electrically operated, while stream-lined electric expresses reduced the time to 52 minutes.

The engineering of the route involved the boring of 31 tunnels, with a total length of 22½ miles, including the 4½-mile Monte Adone tunnel, and, above all, the Great Apennine tunnel. A remarkable feature of this tunnel is the enlarged space in the centre, big enough to accommodate two sidings as well as the main line, together with a cross-over road and a signal-box, deep in the heart of the mountain. This central hall is 550 feet long, 56 feet wide, and 29½ feet high; from it two single-line tunnels, in addition to the main tunnel, have been bored to take the siding-tracks, each 1,470 feet long. This breaks up what would otherwise be a very long signalling section.

To assist in the work of boring, which was begun as usual from the two ends, two diagonal shafts were driven, and these are now used for ventilating purposes. During construction the two worst enemies were water and natural GAS (q.v. Vol. III). At certain places the latter, largely marsh gas or firedamp (methane), was abundant enough to be both poisonous and inflammable. At one point it caused an explosion and a fire which held up the work for 7 months, as the fire could be subdued only by flooding the workings. As to water, in a little less than 5 years 4,735,000 gallons were pumped from the workings. The tunnel was completed in 1934, and cost £5,100,000.

See also TUNNELS.
See also Vol. III: ITALY.

APPIAN WAY. This road, linking ancient Rome with southern Italy, was the most famous Roman highway for many centuries. Along it passed armies, envoys, missionaries, and pilgrims. St. Paul used it to travel to Rome, where he wrote some of his Epistles.

The Appian Way gained its name from a Roman official, Appius Claudius, who ordered the road to be begun in 312 B.C. It reached at first as far as Capua, 132 miles away, but was later extended to the town which is now called Brindisi, 366 miles from Rome. Remains of the old road can be seen in many places to-day, and

THE APPIAN WAY, LOOKING AWAY FROM ROME
On either side are remains of Roman tombs

show the soundness of road-building which has lasted more than 2,000 years. Here and there are fragments of old tombs: the Romans buried their dead outside cities, and often by the side of a highway; for the first few miles from ancient Rome there were tombs on both sides of this road.

A modern road of the same name runs alongside the old Appian Way.

See ROADS; ROMAN ROADS.

ARABIC LANGUAGE. Arabic is the most important living representative of the family of SEMITIC LANGUAGES (q.v.). It was spread by the conquests of the ARABS in the 7th century and the later migrations of BEDOUIN or wandering Arab tribes (qq.v. Vol. I), and is spoken to-day by the peoples of Iraq, Syria, Arabia, Egypt, most of north Africa and the northern Sudan. Although all Arabic-speaking peoples are now called Arabs, they include many millions who descend from distinct races, such as the Copts in Egypt and the Berbers in north-west Africa.

While each country and often each district has its own spoken dialect of Arabic, so that it is sometimes difficult for Arabs of different countries to understand one another, there is one common written language, which is identical in all countries from Morocco to Bagdad.

This is based on 'classical' Arabic, the written Arabic of the Middle Ages, when Arabic was the universal language of the Near and Middle East. It is the language of the Koran, the sacred book of ISLAM (q.v. Vol. I), and of the Arabic literature of the Middle Ages, which was the richest in both poetry and prose this side of China. In Europe the *Arabian Nights' Entertainments* became the most famous Arabic book.

alif (')	ا	za (z)	ز	fa (f)	ف
ba (b)	ب	sin (s)	س	qaf (q)	ق
ta (t)	ت	shin (sh)	ش	kaf (k)	ك
tha (th)	ث	ṣad (ṣ)	ص	lam (l)	ل
juin (ğ)	ج	ḍad (ḍ)	ض	mim (m)	م
ḥa (ḥ)	ح	ṭa (ṭ)	ط	nun (n)	ن
kha (kh)	خ	ẓa (ẓ)	ظ	ha (h)	ه
dal (d)	د	'ayin (')	ع	waw (w)	و
dhal (dh)	ذ	ghain (gh)	غ	ya (y)	ى
ra (r)	ر				

THE ARABIC ALPHABET

Arabic was also the chief medium of scientific and philosophical thought for some centuries, as the many traces it has left in the languages of Europe show, especially in chemical and astronomical terms such as 'alcohol', 'elixir', 'azimuth', 'nadir'. One of the main interests of the

Arabs themselves was in poetry and the study of their own language, with the result that classical Arabic never broke down into separate written languages, as the Latin of western Europe broke down into Spanish, French, and Italian (*see* ROMANCE LANGUAGES).

Written Arabic to-day is based on classical Arabic, which has been modernized in vocabulary and simplified to some extent in style. It is written in a traditional script, a very decorative cursive or running hand (*see* HANDWRITING), but the Arabic alphabet allows only consonants and long vowels to be represented. It is thus a kind of notation, like shorthand, in which *ktbw*, for example, stands for *katabū*, 'they wrote', and *kt'b* for *kitāb*, 'book'. In order to read this script correctly, the reader needs to possess a very thorough knowledge of the grammar and construction of the written language, for these often differ greatly from those of the

Bodleian Library

PAGE FROM THE 'MAQĀMAT' OF AL-ḤARĪRĪ, AN ARABIC MANU-
SCRIPT WRITTEN IN BAGDAD IN 1337

The 'Maqāmat' are scenes from the life of a witty beggar who imposes on the credulity of others

spoken dialects. The whole of Arabic grammar is, however, constructed on a regular system, each word having a 'root' of three consonants (as *ktb* 'write') which is altered by including long or short vowels, or making small additions (prefixes and suffixes) before and after the word, to show its form and function in the sentence. Learning to read, consequently, is not as difficult as it might seem.

See also LANGUAGE STRUCTURE.
See also Vol. I: ARABS.

ARAMAIC LANGUAGE, *see* HEBREW LANGUAGE.

ARK ROYAL. This galleon was built at Deptford in 1587 for Sir Walter Raleigh. She was bought into the Royal Navy the next year, and at the defeat of the Spanish Armada in 1588 she was the flagship of Lord Howard of Effingham, Lord Admiral of England. The *Ark Royal*, or *Ark Raleigh* as she was sometimes called, was 100 feet long on the keel and her beam was 37 feet. Her armament was four demi-cannon, four cannon perriers, twelve culverins, twelve demi-culverins, six sakers, two fowlers, four portpieces: fowlers and portpieces were small guns significantly known as 'murderers' (*see* NAVAL GUNS, Vol. X).

Lord Howard's fleet, which consisted of the best of the Queen's ships, reinforced by some armed merchant ships, lay in wait at Plymouth for the arrival of the 'Invincible Armada', which all Europe knew was sailing from Spain for the invasion of England. On 19 July the Spanish fleet of 120 ships was sighted. Fighting started two days later, the English ships pursuing and attacking the Armada as it continued its advance up the Channel. In the course of the action on 25 July, off the Isle of Wight, the *Ark Royal* and others of the British fleet were towed by their boats within range of the centre of the Spanish fleet, and a fierce action followed. The Spanish galleons approached, under oars, thinking the English ships lay at their mercy. But the breeze rose again, and the action became general. On the night of the 28th Howard sent eight fire-ships into the midst of the Spanish fleet anchored in Calais roads, and these threw the enemy into confusion. Next day the decisive battle of Gravelines was fought, and the Armada scattered.

The name *Ark Royal* was revived by the Admiralty in 1914 for a seaplane carrier, which

THE FIRST 'ARK ROYAL'
Engraving by Cornelis Visscher, 1629–58

National Maritime Museum

was renamed the *Pegasus* when the third *Ark Royal*, an aircraft carrier of 22,000 tons displacement was laid down by Cammell Laird & Co., the Birkenhead shipbuilders, in 1935. This is the ship which Dr. Goebbels, the Nazi Minister of Propaganda, claimed to have sunk so often. The *Ark Royal* hunted the German *Graf Spee* in 1939, and helped to trap the *Bismarck* in 1941. On 13 November 1941, when she was operating with Force H. in the Mediterranean, the *Ark Royal* was torpedoed in sight of Gibraltar and had to be abandoned. Of her ship's company of 1,541 men, only one life was lost. The Admiralty has since used the name for yet another ship.

See also SAILING SHIPS.
See also Vol. X: BATTLESHIP.

ARMOURED TRAIN, *see* TRAINS, SPECIAL USES.

ARTICULATED LOCOMOTIVES AND RAIL COACHES. The designing of locomotives to draw greater loads is limited by the 'loading gauge', that is, the measurements which set strict limits in height and width, if the locomotive is to clear tunnels, bridges, lineside structures, and adjoining tracks. The only further enlargement possible in locomotives is, therefore, in length. But in making locomotives longer, careful attention must be paid to their flexibility, or they may not be able to negotiate the curves in the track.

This difficulty has been got over by what is called articulation. The principal British articulated design is the Beyer-Garratt, of which many examples have been exported to all parts of the world. In a Garratt locomotive a boiler of large diameter is carried on a massive girder frame between two steam-driven chassis, on which it rests by means of pivots. Each chassis, like a bogie of large size (*see* LOCOMOTIVE, STEAM) is free, within limits, to rotate, so that the lengthy locomotive can adjust itself easily to the curves. Thus, an articulated locomotive, with its cylinders and driving wheels at both ends, is like two engines in one, supplied with steam from a single boiler and manned by a single crew.

A special advantage of articulation is that it enables the weight of a very powerful locomotive to be spread over a good length of track. For this reason articulated engines have found great favour in those railways of the Commonwealth on which tracks and bridges are of relatively light construction, but on which increased power is needed. Many varieties have been built, up to and including the remarkable 4–6–2+2–6–4, 4–8–2+2–8–4, and 4–6–4+4–6–4 types (*see* LOCOMOTIVES, CLASSES AND USES). In the last type mentioned the articulation is divided into six parts, as each 4–6–4 chassis has its own pivoted bogies fore and aft. The only British articulated locomotives are 33 Garratts 2–6–0+0–6–2's used on the London Midland Region and a big 2–8–0+0–8–2 built by the late L.N.E.R. for banking duty up a steep incline near Barnsley, Yorks., and has also been used at Bromsgrove, L.M.R., for similar work up the famous Lickey incline.

In the United States articulation is very popular and has led to immense locomotives. The principle generally in use is the Mallet, in which the rear chassis is a fixed part of the main frame carrying the boiler, and only the leading chassis is pivoted. The larger American loading-gauge makes it possible to mount the boiler above both chassis, instead of between them, as in the British Garratt types. The largest

U.S. MALLET ('BIG BOY' CLASS) ARTICULATED LOCOMOTIVE

Union Pacific

American Mallets are the so-called Big Boy class on the Union Pacific Railroad, which have the 4–8–0+0–8–4 wheel arrangement. With their 14-wheel tenders they weigh 534 tons apiece.

The principle of articulation has also been applied to railway coaches, by mounting the ends of two adjacent coaches on a heavy steel casting under which a single bogie is pivoted. Thus two coaches are carried on three bogies instead of four, three coaches on four bogies instead of six, and so on, with economy in both length and weight. The disadvantage is that these articulated sets cannot be broken up or marshalled in any other order, in ordinary working. In Great Britain, the Eastern Region, in whose area the idea was originated by the former Great Northern Railway, has been the most extensive user of articulated passenger stock.

ARYAN LANGUAGE, *see* INDO-EUROPEAN LANGUAGES. *See also* ARYAN, Vol. **I.**

ASTROLABE, *see* Vol. III: ASTRONOMY.

ATHODYD, *see* AIRCRAFT ENGINES, Section 5.

ATLANTIC ENGINE, *see* LOCOMOTIVES, CLASSES AND USES, Section 2.

ATLAS, *see* MAPS.

ATMOSPHERICS, *see* CLIMATE AND COMMUNICATIONS, Section 5; SHORT-WAVE WIRELESS.

AUTOGIRO, *see* ROTORCRAFT, Section 2.

AUTOMATIC SIGNALLING, RAILWAY. Where many trains follow one another closely on one line, completely automatic signalling is used, in order to prevent accidents without creating delay. The duties of the signalman, as described in SIGNALLING (RAILWAY), are taken over by self-acting apparatus.

This is the universal practice on the London tubes, where at 'rush hours' trains pass over certain routes with a frequency of forty to the hour. Automatic signalling can be either all-electric, or electro-pneumatic (a fact made apparent to any traveller in the leading coach of a tube train who hears the 'hiss' of each pneumatically operated signal returning to 'danger' as his coach passes it). The principle is an extended version of 'lock-and-block' signalling and of track circuiting worked in conjunction (*see* SIGNALLING (RAILWAY) and ELECTRIC SIGNALLING, Section 2). By suitable track circuits, each train, as it passes a stop signal, puts it to 'danger'. Then, after getting sufficiently far

C

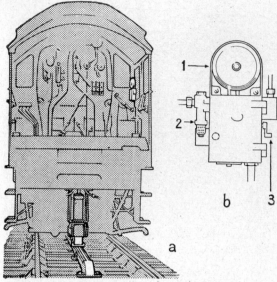

AUTOMATIC AUDIBLE SIGNAL ON WESTERN REGION MAIN LINE

a. Diagram of engine showing the electric ramp between the rails, the 'shoe' beneath the engine with which it makes contact, and the siren in driver's cab.

b. Detail of the siren in driver's cab. (1) 'All clear' bell; (2) 'Caution' siren; (3) lever to stop siren after 'caution' signal.

ahead of that signal to provide an adequate clearance for all its coaches, the train operates a second track circuit. This circuit returns to 'clear' the signal in the rear of the train.

All-electric automatic signalling is used on various surface lines round London on which electric trains run, and on other densely operated stretches of line in various parts of Britain. In many of these installations, four-aspect signalling (four coloured lights) has replaced the previous three-aspect; a red light compels a stop, a single yellow light shows that one section ahead is clear, two yellow lights that two sections ahead are clear, and green that three sections or more are clear. Drivers are able to control their speed exactly, according to the track-conditions ahead. Thus traffic is speeded up, on the principle that the first aim of signalling, beyond safe operation, is to keep the traffic moving.

On automatically signalled lines with dense traffic, the overrunning of signals by drivers must be guarded against. With electric working this is a relatively simple matter. At the side of the line, trip-levers are installed, working in conjunction with the signals. When the signal concerned is at 'clear' or 'caution', the trip-lever

falls out of action: when the signal is at 'danger', the trip-lever, in the vertical position, intercepts a corresponding lever at the side of the driving-coach of the train, cutting off the current supply to the motors and applying the brakes. This system is foolproof; the only two collisions which have ever occurred on London tube lines so equipped were the result of completely irregular action by the staff (in one case the crossing of electric connexions to a signal by a signal linesman).

The former Great Western Railway installed on all its main lines a system of audible signalling in the engine-driver's cab, which with steam trains performs in part the function of the trip-levers. Immediately in the rear of each 'distant' signal an electric ramp is fixed between the running rails, with which a 'shoe' on the under-side of the locomotive makes contact. When the 'distant' is at 'caution', the ramp is not electrically charged, and the contact of the shoe with it causes a loud horn to sound in the driver's cab, while a partial application of the brake is made. If the 'distant' is at 'clear', however, an electric current passes through the ramp; as a result, the shoe contact causes a small bell to ring in the cab instead, without any effect on the brakes. This system is particularly valuable when visibility is poor, as in fog (*see* Diagram).

In the United States considerable use is made on important main lines of an electric signalling system which gives continuous signal light indications—green, yellow, and red—on a panel immediately in front of the driver of each locomotive. This system is based on induction (*see* INDUCTION, ELECTRIC, Vol. VIII), by means of which a current running through a wire at the side of the line affects a circuit in the locomotive passing. In the event of a signal being at 'danger', the brakes are applied automatically to bring the train to a stop, unless the driver anticipates the action by applying the brakes himself. A somewhat similar system has been installed between Fenchurch Street (London) and Southend-on-Sea by British Railways.

AVIATION: (1) *History*: *see* FLYING, HISTORY of; BALLOONS; AIRSHIPS. (2) *Modern Craft*: *see* AEROPLANE; SEAPLANE; GLIDER; ROTORCRAFT; AIRCRAFT, SPECIAL USES. (3) *Navigation*: *see* NAVIGATION, AIR. (4) *Passenger Flying*: *see* CIVIL AVIATION; AIR-LINER; AIRCREW; AIRPORT.

B

BALLOON. The modern balloon dates from 1783, when two kinds of lighter-than-air methods of flight were introduced almost at once. First came the hot-air balloon, making use of the fact that hot air is lighter than cold. A balloon went aloft, filled only with hot air, which was replenished in flight from a brazier slung beneath it. A few months later the first balloon filled with hydrogen lifted a daring French airman into the air (*see* FLYING, HISTORY OF). The gas balloon has been in use ever since.

A passenger balloon consists of a thin fabric envelope with a mechanically operated valve at the top (in the 'crown'), an open neck at the base of the balloon, and a net to support the basket, which carries the crew. The envelope is filled with a gas which is so much lighter than the surrounding air that the whole balloon, its equipment, and its crew weigh less than the corresponding volume of air that they displace. It therefore rises like a cork. Ordinary air at normal pressure weighs 76 lb. a 1,000 cubic feet at sea-level; coal gas about 36 lb.; helium (which is very dear and rare) 10·5 lb.; and hydrogen (cheaper but inflammable) only 5·3 lb.

In practice the modern sporting balloon, which may be of any capacity between 10,000 and 80,000 cubic feet, has certain standard equipment which seldom varies. Ballast and valve are the most important. The ballast of sand should be adjusted just before the flight so that the balloon is almost stable and in equilibrium. Then some of the ballast is put out, and the ground crew let go. The balloon rises, and the gas inside begins to expand as the atmosphere gets thinner. The gas escapes harmlessly out of the open neck beneath, until the balloon is again in equilibrium. Then more ballast can be dropped, and the balloon will rise higher. If it is necessary to come down to a desired altitude, the valve line is pulled, the valve in the crown is opened, gas escapes through the top of the envelope, and the balloon descends. Among other important equipment is the ripping-line or rip-cord, which is painted red so that it shall not be pulled by mistake for the valve line. The rip-cord pulls open part of the envelope when the balloon is very near the ground, and so empties it in a few seconds: this prevents the basket and crew being dragged along the ground. The trail-rope, which is seldom used now, was formerly allowed to drag over the country-side, providing automatic ballast. The anchor, though not often used, is meant to be thrown out to assist in landing. An altimeter indicator to show the height above sea-level and a compass are always carried.

There is no way of steering a balloon, unless the pilot is a good meteorologist, when he may be able to choose likely heights for varying natural air-currents (*see* GLIDER). Ballooning is therefore used to-day only as a sport, and (in the United States) as a necessary preliminary

Central Press

A MODERN SPORTING BALLOON

National Geographic Society

'EXPLORER II' LANDING

In 1935 this balloon reached a height of 13·7 miles, the highest man had ever been

training for airship crews, whose craft becomes virtually a free balloon if the engines fail.

Balloons are able to rise to great heights more easily than aeroplanes. In 1862 two Englishmen, Glaisher and Coxwell, rose several miles, without oxygen for breathing and unprotected against cold, in an open basket balloon, and thus came unawares to the fringes of the stratosphere (*see* ATMOSPHERE, Vol. III). Their first hint of danger was when Glaisher fell unconscious. Coxwell, his hands numb, pulled the gas-release cord with his teeth before he, too, fainted. As the balloon fell into warmer,

breathable air, they revived in time to land safely. In 1927 another attempt was made; but the balloonist, although provided with oxygen, died from cold. Since then, stratosphere balloons have had air-tight cars, kept at ground-level pressure, painted partly black and partly white. The black portion, absorbing the sun's rays, warms the structure, while the white reflects the rays and so the car grows cooler. The crew can allow the heat or cold, at will, to alter the temperature in the car.

Successful stratosphere balloon flights were first made by the Swiss professor, Auguste Piccard, in 1931 and 1932. The car used for his second ascent is now in the Science Museum at South Kensington. In 1934 Piccard's twin brother Jean and his wife, in crossing to America by balloon, just beat his record; Madame Jean Piccard was the first to reach the stratosphere.

The world record for height is held by America. In 1934 the balloon *Explorer I* rose more than 60,500 feet (12 miles). On the way down its fabric began to split. The occupants could not jump into the rarefied air, so they went on working and speaking to the world by wireless. When they had descended to a safe height, they took to their parachutes and made a safe landing. In 1935 Captain Stevens and Captain Anderson, in the *Explorer II*, set up the still unbroken record for human beings of 72,395 feet (13·7 miles). They brought back much valuable data, including colour films of the sky-tints, infra-red photographs of the earth below, records of atmospheric electricity, and information about cosmic rays.

Crewless balloons are in constant use in meteorology for taking up instruments to high altitudes. The balloon ultimately bursts, and the instruments come down by parachute. In the Second World War the Japanese sent many crewless balloons over the Pacific, equipped with ingenious mechanisms and explosives, in the hope that they would reach the west coast of the United States. Some of them landed, but did no harm.

See also FLYING, HISTORY OF, Section 2; AIRSHIPS.

BANKING ENGINE. This is a steam locomotive used for helping a heavy train up a hill. When gradients become steep, the cost of railway working is increased. Over steeply graded main lines, the simplest solution is electrical working;

British Railways

A BEYER-GARRATT BANKING ENGINE ATTACHED TO THE REAR OF A FREIGHT TRAIN ON THE LICKEY INCLINE BETWEEN BRISTOL AND BIRMINGHAM

with high voltage alternating current (*see* ELECTRIC RAILWAYS) single locomotives up to 6,000 h.p. have been built; and on the Gotthard Railway of Switzerland, with its long stretches of 1 in 40 gradient, there are 12,000 h.p. twin locomotives in use which can handle very substantial loads even over this Alpine route. But with steam locomotives such power is not possible, and up the steepest grades, unless two engines are in use throughout the run, help has to be provided, either on the front or the rear of the train. On the Western Region, for example, all the heavier West of England trains need to be piloted between Newton Abbot and Plymouth, where there are gradients between 1 in 37 and 1 in 42 in steepness. Certain nominally non-stop expresses, like the Cornish Riviera Limited, must stop specially at Newton Abbot to attach the pilot engine in front of the main engine.

At other places the assistant engine, then called a banker, is attached to the rear of the train, as at Bromsgrove, on the Bristol–Birmingham line, for the ascent of the 1 in 38 Lickey incline; or at Beattock, on the Carlisle–Glasgow main line, for climbing the 10 miles to Beattock Summit. At such places a fleet of banking engines is kept in steam constantly; after pushing a train to the summit, the banker drops quietly off the rear—without the train stopping

for the purpose—and returns down the line to wait for the next turn of duty. In the United States, owing to the immense length of many freight trains, several 'bankers' may be used on a steep incline. One or two banking engines may be cut into different points along the length of the train, as well as attached to the rear, to distribute the power more evenly along the load.

BANTU LANGUAGES, *see* AFRICAN LANGUAGES.

BARGE. The term barge includes a great variety of vessels in use on canals, rivers, estuaries, and in coastal waters. The last include a few sailing vessels, often with an auxiliary engine. The name is sometimes given to all craft carrying goods on a canal or river; but, strictly speaking, these are either 'narrow boats' of not more than 7 feet in the beam, or barges, with a beam about twice as great.

The narrow boat, or 'monkey boat' as it is often called, after Thomas Monk (1765–1843), the inventor and first builder of the small canal cabin-boat, is possibly the commonest craft on inland waterways in England. This is because the LOCKS (q.v.) on the group of canals in the Midland counties between the four main estuaries of Mersey, Humber, Thames, and Severn can only pass a boat about 7 feet wide

BARGES AT BULL'S BRIDGE, SOUTHALL, MIDDLESEX

Topical Press

Barges from all over the country come to Bull's Bridge for repairs

and 70 feet long, with an average loaded draught of about 3 ft. 6 in. These boats generally travel in pairs—the one, a motor-boat, propelled by an 18 h.p. diesel-engine, and the other, a boat without an engine, known as a 'dumb' or 'butty' boat. The boats carry about 50 tons between them.

These narrow boats are the traditional family boats that are so often seen on the canals of the English Midlands, generally with the husband on the boat with the engine, the wife steering the butty, and the children on the cabin top or playing in the hold when the boat is travelling empty. Both boats have cabins, and although the living-space is small, everything is very compact and within reach. The cabins are painted in bright colours, with the name of the boat, the owner's name, and the registered number on the outside, for since 1887 all boats used as dwellings have to be registered. Inside the cabins, on the doors and cupboard panels, are painted the roses and castles, without which the older canal families believe that the boat is sure to be un-

lucky. The boats, which are now owned by the National Docks and Inland Waterways Executive, have 'British Waterways' on the outside of the cabins in blue and gold.

Canal-boat families keep very much to themselves and rarely marry outside their own group. They are hard-working people, and, except for their liking for gaily decorated homes, not at all like the land GYPSIES (q.v. Vol. I) with whom they are often wrongly compared. They have not been well-educated in the past; but now canal-boat children have to attend school for as long as their boats remain in one place; so that the children now growing up will at least be able to read and write. In one case an old barge has been fitted up as a school. In physical fitness and well-being, both parents and children are above the average.

In earlier years boats were pulled by horses or donkeys from the tow-paths which ran beside the canals. When the barge came to a tunnel, the animal was led outside to the other end, and the boatman and his wife would 'leg' the barge, that is, they would lie on their backs and push with their feet on the tunnel sides. It is only in fairly recent times that mechanized haulage has been introduced, but there are still a few boats under private ownership which are towed by horses or donkeys. These are now poled through tunnels with a boat shaft. Horses are used to pull barges of 14- to 16-foot beam for a short way out of ports, especially in London.

On the Leeds and Liverpool Canal 'short boats', 62 feet long and 14 ft. 3 in. wide, carrying 45 tons on a draught of 3 ft. 9 in., are operated by boat families. Barges plying inland from the sea vary in size from estuary to estuary. The River Weaver, which joins the Mersey, is used mainly by coastal vessels. From the Humber to Nottingham barges 82 feet long by 14 ft. 8 in. wide, with a draught of 5 feet, travel in trains of four, a powered barge towing three dumb barges. On the Severn single self-propelled barges, 115 feet long by 21 ft. 9 in. wide, with a draught of 8 feet, carry oil and petrol as far as Worcester. Tugs may also tow a train of narrow boats on this waterway. Barge towage by tug is common on the Thames, and barges 120 feet long by 17 feet wide can reach as far as Oxford on a draught of 3 ft. 9 in. All these barges and tugs are worked by men, for whom sleeping accommodation is provided. On the Aire and Calder Navigation a special type of compart-ment-boat is used to carry coal to the port of Goole for shipment. Each compartment is 20 feet long by 15 feet wide, with a draught of 9 feet.

A train of nineteen is towed by one tug worked by four men, and as each compartment-boat carries about 40 tons, the complete train carries over 700 tons. Single vessels, 120 feet long by 17 ft. 6 in. wide, with a draught of 7 ft. 6 in., also navigate this waterway from the Humber to Leeds, and so do trains of ordinary barges towed by tugs.

Inland navigation is on a much vaster scale on the Continent than in England. The great rivers of Germany have been linked by a net-work of canals; in Holland, Belgium, and France also, barges or tugs, fitted with a diesel-engine and towing a train of other barges, are commonly used. On some of the inland canals of France electric engines running on a metre-gauge track laid along one bank provide the traction. When two engines meet, they ex-change tow ropes and run backwards. Tractors on pneumatic tyres, with electric or internal-combustion engines, are also used. Barges on the German canals measure 213 or 262 feet long by 34 ft. 6 in. wide, with a draught of 8 feet. Those on French inland canals measure 128 feet long by 16 ft. 6 in. wide, with a draught of 6 feet. All continental towing barges have quarters for the crew, and on the larger rivers pilots are carried.

In the United States the standard 'warrior barge', which is 140 feet long by 25 feet wide, draught 8 feet, is used on the great rivers. U.S.A. barges navigate in groups, the usual arrange-ment being seven barges and a pusher barge at the rear, flanked on either side by a 'warrior

FRENCH BARGE DRAWN BY ELECTRIC ENGINE   *International Assoc. of Navigation Congresses*

barge' as a protection. The pusher or tow-boat may be either screw or stern-wheel driven, and the power may be produced by a diesel or a diesel-electric engine. Passengers are sometimes carried.

See also CANALS; CANALS, BRITISH; RIVER NAVIGATION.

BASIC ENGLISH. Basic English is designed as an INTERNATIONAL LANGUAGE (q.v.). Unlike other such systems, its words and structure are all part of a living language. It is made up of 850 normal English words; a selection undertaken with such care that anyone with a knowledge of only those words may say whatever is necessary for everyday purposes. The senses of 20,000 English words are covered by the Basic 850.

Basic was worked out in Cambridge by C. K. Ogden and a group of language experts. Their organization, formed in 1928 as the Orthological (Greek for the science of getting 'right' about words) Institute, has been responsible for its development. In their opinion international languages have made no headway because men will not take the trouble of learning one on the chance of meeting someone who has done the same. The argument for Basic is that because English is the language of North America and of the British Empire and because millions all over the earth have a little knowledge of English words, most men and women would quickly be able to make use of the 850 Basic words as a second language. Some might go on to wider English from Basic.

In Basic, unnecessary changes in the forms and endings of words are cut out. It does without 4,000 of the commonest names of acts ('verbs') by putting together the names of the twelve chief acts (such as 'put', 'take', 'give', 'get') and the twenty names of directions (such as 'in', 'out', 'over', 'through') or other words which may go with them. So 'insert' becomes 'put in', and when we 'disembark' in Basic we 'get off a ship'. In addition to the 850 words, there are fifty special words which are used in most languages, such as 'hotel' and 'sport'.

The supporters of Basic see in it a language which will be simple for learners in all countries, and which will be clear wherever wider English is used. But to some learners from the Far East, such as China, some English sounds, such as 'r', are hard to make and have to be given special attention; those who make use of picture-writing (see WRITING, HISTORY OF) will have trouble with the A B C; and in some countries where there is no love of the British and Americans, there may be a feeling against the use of English. In England Mr. Winston Churchill, when he was Prime Minister, gave his support to Basic, and in 1946 the Government made a decision to give help for the development of Basic.

Books in and about Basic have been printed in thirty countries, with learners' books in more than fifteen languages. The complete Basic Bible came out in 1949. Even the English are sometimes not conscious that they are reading Basic. This account is itself all in Basic.

See also INTERNATIONAL LANGUAGES.

BASQUE LANGUAGE, see SPANISH AND PORTUGUESE LANGUAGES.

BATH ROAD. A road between London and Bath was first made by the Romans, for Aquae Sulis, the Roman name for Bath, was a well-known health-resort noted for its baths (see ROMAN BATHS, Vol. IX). But when the Romans left Britain, the Bath Road, like most other English roads, fell into disuse. Even in the 17th century, when travelling by coach was becoming popular, the road was in very bad condition, and it was quite common for a traveller to get lost on it, as Pepys did in 1688 between Newbury and Reading.

In the 18th century, when the TURNPIKE system (q.v.) brought about an improvement in the state of the roads, the Bath Road again became active with traffic of all sorts. Bath,

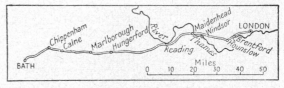

THE BATH ROAD

under the direction of the famous dandy Beau Nash, had become a fashionable holiday resort, and during the season the road was alive with gaily painted stage coaches with their six or eight horses, post-boys in their yellow coats and white beaver hats, stately private carriages of the nobility with liveried postilions and outriders, and smart lighter equipages of the young gallants with their high-stepping horses. In the summer of 1740 on three days of the week these stage coaches would leave London to run the 106 miles to Bath.

The old Bath Road is no longer the main road from London all the way to Bath. Its place has been taken at some places by the Great West Road, which follows a more direct route.

See also ROADS; STAGE COACH.

B.B.C., *see* BROADCASTING CORPORATIONS.

B.E.A., *see* CIVIL AVIATION.

BEACON, *see* SIGNALS.

BEAM WIRELESS, *see* SHORT-WAVE WIRELESS.

BEASTS OF BURDEN. 1. For many thousands of years man depended upon no other beast of burden but himself; indeed, when early man first began to domesticate animals, he did so for the purposes of food or for assistance in hunting rather than for helping him to carry things. In many parts of the world to-day, especially in south-eastern Asia, man, and especially woman, is still the chief beast of burden. The fine carriage of the people of these countries is the result of their habit of carrying burdens on their heads.

In the ancient civilizations of the Near East, and also of America, there seemed no need to make use of other animals when there were always plenty of slaves. The great buildings of ancient Egypt and Assyria, China, and India needed the transport of great quantities of stone, which was all dragged into place by gangs of slaves. But as civilization developed, it became more and more the custom to save man-power and increase efficiency by training animals to pull and to carry.

Horses and their relatives, asses and mules, have always been among the most widely used beasts of burden. These animals were first used to help in warfare. Teams of donkeys were used as early as 4000 B.C. to pull the chariots of the Kings of Sumeria, and Israelite princes used mules both for drawing chariots and for riding. Horses, from the time of the Romans till the invention of the steam-engine, were the principal means of transport in Europe (*see* HORSE TRANSPORT).

Many other animals, such as dogs, camels, llamas, elephants, reindeer, and various kinds of cattle, have been used by man. Different animals have been used in different parts of the world, according to the particular geographical and climatic conditions of the region. An animal suitable for hauling teak logs in the hot forests of Burma would be useless in the snowy pine forests of northern Europe, the rocky mountain paths of the Andes, or the stretches of waterless desert in Australia.

2. HOT DESERTS. The one-humped Arabian CAMEL or dromedary (q.v. Vol. II) has been, until the invention of the motor-car and aeroplane, the principal means of travel in the desert for thousands of years. Its broad padded feet move easily over loose, dry sand, and it has a remarkable capacity for storing fat in its hump and water in cells in its body so that it can undertake a long journey without needing

A LLAMA PACK TRAIN IN THE ANDES OF PERU

E.N.A.

Paul Popper

A HERD OF YAKS ON THE LHASA PLAIN, TIBET
Loads are fastened to the saddles. The white yak is the leader

further food and water; thus it is able to stand the conditions of DESERT TRAVEL (q.v.) as no other animal can. A loaded dromedary can cover great distances at a slow jog of 2½ to 3 miles an hour; and when ridden it can go about 10 miles an hour. As many as a thousand animals are sometimes to be seen crossing the desert in a single caravan. Arabian camels have been taken to Australia, where they are used in the desert regions of the north-east. The donkey, also, is useful in hot, dry climates, and has been the principal pack animal of the countries of the eastern Mediterranean for centuries. It can stand great heat and can work well on a poor diet.

3. COLD, HIGH DESERT. The two-humped Bactrian camel with its thick, shaggy coat is found in the cold, dry regions of central Asia, Mongolia, and parts of India. It can carry as much as 1,000 lb. or more in weight on its back and can go long distances across very rough country at a slow pace. On the Kirghiz Steppes small, shaggy camels are even yoked to draw a cart or sledge, and yokes of four are sometimes seen ploughing. The thick-coated, tough Mongolian ponies are also very important draught and riding animals of Central and East Asia.

4. MOUNTAIN COUNTRY. Although motor roads and railways have now been built in many mountain areas, most local mountain transport is still, as it always has been, by pack animal along narrow paths. Donkeys and mules are found in almost all mountain country; their ability to stand both heat and cold, their toughness and their sure-footedness make them able

to negotiate country which would be impossible to a horse. The mule has the toughness and other characteristics of its father, a jackass, and the size of its mother, a horse mare, and this makes it the ideal pack animal. A walker in mountain country may be disconcerted to meet round a corner on a narrow path what looks like a moving haystack, and what proves to be a donkey carrying home a load of hay from the field. The animal proceeds regardless of obstacles, and the walker must scramble for safety up the side of the hill. Little donkeys are often to be seen carrying their masters, whose feet almost reach the ground on each side.

In very high regions, such as large parts of Tibet, the best pack animal is the Yak (see CATTLE, Vol. II). This animal is able to work at a height in which many animals find it difficult to breathe owing to the thinness of the mountain air (see ATMOSPHERE, Vol. III). The yak is not used as a draught animal nor for ploughing, but only as a pack animal. It can carry its burden some 20 miles a day, and it is sure-footed and able to stand great cold. It has been found very useful in mountain explorations in the Himalayas. Another strong, sure-footed, and docile animal, able to stand high altitudes, is the South American LLAMA (q.v. Vol. II), which is used in the Andes regions for riding and as a pack and draught animal. The llama can carry a weight of some 100 lb. for long distances, but if it is overloaded it meets the situation by refusing to move at all.

5. NORTHERN REGIONS. In the lands of northern Europe, Asia, and America the main transport

Paul Popper

is by SLEDGE (q.v.), which is drawn in some parts by dogs and in others by reindeer. The ESKIMOES (q.v. Vol. I) of Alaska and northern Canada use long-haired, rather wolf-like dogs called huskies, which they harness in pairs or in larger teams arranged fanwise with a leader. They often cross these dogs with wolves in order to preserve the strength of the breed. The dogs can travel long distances without food and with a great capacity for endurance. The stories of Jack London, *The Call of the Wild* and *White Fang*, give a vivid picture of the lives of these animals. In the Arctic lands of northern Russia the Samoyed dogs are used for transport.

The LAPPS (q.v. Vol. I) and northern Siberian peoples use reindeer to draw their sledges, and for many other purposes; and reindeer have been successfully introduced into parts of northern America. They can keep up a pace of 10 miles an hour for long distances, and can pull a sledge loaded up to 200 lb. in weight. The driver guides them by cords attached to their antlers (*see* SNOW AND ICE TRAVEL).

6. HOT, WET LANDS. Different kinds of oxen are used in many countries as draught animals. Oxen, in fact, have been until comparatively recent times the main draught animals in Europe, and are still so in some Mediterranean countries. In India and south-eastern Asia the slow-moving bullock pulls wooden carts and is used for all farm work. In particular the Asiatic BUFFALO (q.v. Vol. II), with its long horns curved back over its shoulder and the characteristic low carriage of its head, is suitable in wet, marshy ground. The bullock has played

an important part in some of the great migratory treks of history. When the Boers left Cape Colony and trekked to Transvaal, Natal, and the Orange Free State in the 1830's, they carried their families and goods in ox-wagons; when the American pioneers set out along the Oregon Trail later in the 19th century, their covered wagons were pulled at a rate of 2 miles an hour by teams of oxen (*see* AMERICAN TRAILS).

Another important transport animal in hot, wet countries is the ELEPHANT (q.v. Vol. II), a very powerful animal, both patient and intelligent. Elephants were used in the ancient civilizations of the East for hunting and for battle. In warfare they were often taken far afield. When HANNIBAL (q.v. Vol. V) led the soldiers of Carthage over the Alps to attack Rome, he brought trained African elephants. Later, when the Romans invaded Britain in A.D. 43, they brought elephants which crossed the Thames and advanced into Essex. African elephants are now no longer domesticated; but the Indian elephant is used for agriculture and forestry in India and the countries of south-east Asia. It is invaluable in dragging the heavy logs of wood from the TEAK forests (q.v. Vol. VI) to the saw-mills. It also plays an important part in BIG GAME HUNTING (q.v. Vol. IX). It is driven by a mahout, or native driver, who sits on its head and directs it with a spiked stick. Elephants, richly draped, have always taken part in the ceremonial processions of Indian princes.

7. OTHER BEASTS OF BURDEN. Attempts at various times have been made to tame and

R. Gorbold

AN INDIAN OX-CART

train other animals. Ostriches and even giraffes have been made to pull carriages. At one time the Boers in South Africa used to catch young ZEBRAS (q.v. Vol. II), train them, and export them as draught animals to Mauritius. At the beginning of this century a pair of zebras was trained and brought back to London, where they used to be driven regularly in Hyde Park. Big dogs of various breeds have also been trained to pull carts with milk and vegetables over the cobbled streets of Holland and Belgium, or to carry packs over the mountains of Tibet.

See also HORSE TRANSPORT.

BELLS, see SIGNALS AND SIGNALLING.

BIBLIOTHÈQUE NATIONALE. The French National Library in Paris had its origin in the library of King John of France, who was captured by the Black Prince and imprisoned in London in the 14th century. His collection dwindled; but later French kings began to amass a new library, using the usual methods of the Middle Ages—plunder and gifts. In 1534 Francis I began another library at Fontaine-bleau Castle, outside Paris, and later this was brought to Paris. In the long reign of Louis XIV, when France was very prosperous, the library grew to more than 70,000 volumes, and part of the present building in the Rue Richelieu was erected. A full alphabetical catalogue was compiled. The name Bibliothèque Nationale (National Library) first came to be used during the French Revolution; the library was enriched by books belonging to noblemen who had run away or been guillotined, and others taken from convents and monasteries which had been suppressed. Later the Emperor Napoleon increased the Government grant to the Library, and added treasures taken from conquered countries. Most of these, however, had to be returned later to their rightful owners when Napoleon's armies were beaten.

Much of the present building is modern, though part of it was built in the 17th century. A large part of it is made of iron, and is fireproof. No one may enter the Students' Reading Room without a pass—visitors may only look through the glass doors, where they may see the iron pillars and wall-paintings, and the 10,000 books of reference kept there. Besides its 3,600,000 books, the Bibliothèque Nationale has many other treasures, including works by Rembrandt, Dürer, and other artists, the throne on which the Kings of France were crowned, and the chessmen which belonged to the Emperor Charlemagne, who died in 814. There are also autographs of many famous people, Mary Queen of Scots among them.

See also LIBRARIES.

BICYCLE. Machines of many shapes and sizes have led up to the bicycle that we know to-day. The first of these was the 'dandy-horse' or 'hobby-horse', introduced into England in

FIG. I. A HOBBY-HORSE

1818. Its inventor was Baron von Drais of Sauerbron on the Rhine. It had no pedals, but had to be pushed by the feet on the ground (*see* Fig. 1). John Keats, the poet, wrote of it to a friend: 'It is a wheel carriage to ride cock-horse upon, sitting astride and pushing it along with the toes, a rudder wheel in hand . . . they will go seven miles an hour.'

The first improvement on this was the invention of pedals in 1839 by Kirkpatrick Macmillan, a Scottish blacksmith. He is credited with being the first to use a lever arrangement to drive the rear wheel, so that it was not necessary to push the feet on the ground (*see* Fig. 2). By 1865 a machine was introduced in France in which pedals were attached to the front wheel, and these caused it to go round as they were pushed round themselves. The first machines to embody this principle were called velocipedes (swift feet), or boneshakers as they were called in England. They were extremely heavy,

FIG. 3. A PENNY-FARTHING

FIG. 2. KIRKPATRICK MACMILLAN'S BICYCLE

cumbersome, and uncomfortable, since they had iron tyres and poor springs or none at all. When going downhill the rider had to take his feet off the pedals, which whizzed round at a great speed.

The front wheel of the bicycle gradually grew in size until it became 50 to 60 inches in diameter; the rear wheel was only 14 to 18 inches in diameter (*see* Fig. 3). This explains the name 'penny-farthing' which was given to this bicycle, otherwise called the 'ordinary'. Since one revolution of the pedals caused one revolution of the wheel, the larger the wheel, the longer the distance covered with each push. The solid steel which had to be used for the frames, however, made them very heavy; and so experiments were made in building the frame of bamboo instead of steel. Soon, however, tubular steel frames were introduced, and these combined lightness with strength. By 1868 the

word 'bicycle' had come into general use, from the Latin *bis* 'twice', and the Greek *kuklos* 'wheel'.

The penny-farthing bicycles were used a good deal for racing and they attained some very good speeds (*see* CYCLE RACING, Vol. IX). About 1870 wheels with steel instead of wooden spokes and solid rubber tyres were introduced, and some years later springs were added. Though this made the machines more comfortable, the rider still had to be something of an athlete, for the height of the saddle made falls rather dangerous. Tricycles were safer and could be ridden by ladies, but they were very slow.

The great change came in 1885 when J. K. Starley of Coventry invented the Rover (*see* Fig. 4), the first modern or, as it was then called, 'safety' bicycle. His machine had smaller wheels of nearly the same size; the pedals were set in the bottom of the metal frame between the wheels, and drove a toothed gear-wheel which

FIG. 4. THE FIRST 'SAFETY' BICYCLE

was connected by a chain with the hub of the rear wheel.

The last improvement of fundamental importance was the introduction of pneumatic, or air-filled, tyres. In 1888 J. B. Dunlop, a Scottish veterinary surgeon practising in Belfast, made a pair of these for his son's tricycle, and they were soon in wide use, for they enormously improved both the speed and the comfort of cycling. The Dunlop Company which was started in 1889, quickly made a huge profit. It was only at this time that women began to cycle; but since the ladies' bicycle had not then been introduced, women wore 'bloomers' for bicycling—an outfit not unlike men's 'plus fours'. In the 1890's, however, the ladies' bicycle came in, and bicycling became very fashionable. In London the young people of fashionable society used to ride their bicycles in the park when their elders went out in their carriages. Until the introduction of motor-cars, bicycling was a very pleasant way of getting about.

Among later improvements was the ball-bearing, which eased the motion of the bicycle and reduced wear. The free-wheel enabled the rider to keep his feet on the pedals going downhill and so lessened the danger of falling off. Three-speed gears made going uphill easier.

THE DRESS FOR BICYCLING: 'A RATIONAL COSTUME'
From *The Girl's Own Paper*, 1895

In the last 60 years bicycling has spread all over the world, wherever there are roads with a good surface. Bicycles are most used in France, Germany, Belgium, Holland, and Great Britain, where there is much level country. In some parts of the Continent, especially in Holland, special bicycling paths are made, quite separate from the high roads. About 30 million bicycles are probably now in use in the world.

See also ROADS; ROADS, BRITISH; WHEEL.
See also Vol. IX: CYCLING; CYCLE RACING.

BLIMP, *see* AIRSHIP.

BLIND ALPHABET, *see* BRAILLE.

BLOCK SIGNALLING, *see* SIGNALLING, RAILWAY.

BLUE TRAIN. This train, named from the colour of its cars, was originally the Calais–Mediterranean express, which carried passengers to and from the sea-side towns of the French Riviera. More recently, however, the main Blue Train has worked between Paris and Mentone, a town on the coast near the frontier between France and Italy, though sleeping cars run through from Calais to Mentone without a change. These go to Paris and are worked round the city by the Ceinture ('belt' or 'circle') Railway from the Northern Region line to join the rest of the train on the South-Eastern Region line. Before the Second World War the Blue Train was made up of first and second class sleeping-cars only, but now it contains ordinary coaches as well.

See also RAILWAY COACHES, Section 4.

B.O.A.C., *see* CIVIL AVIATION.

BOAT TRAIN, *see* TRAINS, SPECIAL USES.

BODLEIAN LIBRARY. This, the library of the University of Oxford, is one of the largest libraries in England, coming after the BRITISH MUSEUM LIBRARY (q.v.). It was established by Sir Thomas Bodley (1545–1613). The first University Library had been founded in the 14th century by Bishop Cobham (d. 1327), and was housed in a room adjoining the University Church. When Humphrey, Duke of Gloucester, the youngest son of King Henry IV, gave great gifts of manuscripts and money, a new Library room was built by the University. But after about 100 years the Library was dismantled, and all the manuscripts except four disappeared, and the room was left empty for nearly 50 years. In 1598 Sir Thomas Bodley, on his retirement from Queen Elizabeth's court, undertook to start the University Library again. He furnished the empty room with bookshelves and benches, and collected about 2,000 books. In 1602 the Bodleian Library, as it came to be called, was opened.

Bodley continued to give books to the Library, and persuaded many famous people to follow his example. After his death the collections were enriched by other benefactors. Among them were Archbishop Laud, who was for a time Chancellor of the University of Oxford, and Lord Fairfax, Cromwell's commander-in-chief during the Civil War. In 1610 Bodley had arranged with the Stationers' Company that a copy of every book published by its members should be given free to the Library. This arrangement proved to be the forerunner of various 'Copyright Acts' by which the Bodleian, and certain other libraries, may each receive a free copy of every work published in Britain (*see* COPYRIGHT). To-day many thousands of copyright books are received each year, and several persons are kept continuously employed cataloguing them (*see* CATALOGUING AND INDEXING). There are now over $1\frac{1}{2}$ million books in the library, including more than 40,000 manuscript volumes.

The rapid increase in the Library's contents made it necessary for a new wing to be added during Bodley's life, and other additions were made in the years following his death, largely with money bequeathed by him for the purpose. During the following centuries the Library continued to expand and occupied space in surrounding university buildings, until a special new building had to be provided. This was designed by Sir Giles Gilbert Scott, who also designed the new CAMBRIDGE UNIVERSITY LIBRARY (q.v.), and was opened in 1946. It had to be built a short distance away from the old Bodleian; but the two are connected by an underground tunnel. Books are carried from one building to the other by means of a mechanical conveyor.

Of the other parts of the Bodleian, the best-known is the Radcliffe Camera, opened in 1749. This was built as a library quite separate from

J.R.H. Weaver

THE BODLEIAN LIBRARY, OXFORD
Part of the 15th-century room called Duke Humphrey's Library

the University's library, under the will of Dr. John Radcliffe (1650–1714), a famous London doctor who attended Queen Mary, wife of William III, and later Queen Anne. Since 1861, however, it has been used to provide extra space for the Bodleian. All the medical and scientific books are now kept in the Radcliffe Science Library near the University laboratories; books about the British Empire and the United States are in a part of Rhodes House, the Oxford headquarters of Rhodes Scholars; and, finally, books about India and Pakistan are in the Indian Institute, the centre of Indian studies in Oxford.

All members of the University are allowed to read in the library, and other people doing important research may be given special permission. Scholars come from all over the world to consult precious books and manuscripts, of some of which there is no other copy in existence. Every person who uses the library must first promise, among other things, 'not to kindle therein any fire or flame', a precaution instituted by Bodley himself.

See also LIBRARIES.
See also Vol. X: OXFORD UNIVERSITY.

BOOK. A modern book is the result of careful industrial planning, quite apart from whatever ideas may pass through the mind of the author. An idea for the subject of a new book may have occurred first to the author or to a publisher. The idea seldom comes as an author's sudden inspiration; it is often the outcome of long thinking and indecision. Few authors can afford to live solely by writing books, so an author often has to give up his spare time for thinking out a book and writing it.

Unless an author is prepared himself to pay the cost of printing, binding, and distributing a book—which will generally run into several hundred pounds—his book will not be printed unless some publisher agrees to risk that money. To do this a publisher must estimate that enough people will buy copies of the book to pay for all the costs, including a share of the cost of running the publishing business, and still leave an adequate reward for both himself and the author.

Usually a book first reaches the publisher in the form of a finished manuscript—type-written, so that a carbon copy can be taken, and also for easy reading—and he is invited to make an offer to publish it. It may have been submitted directly by the author, or have come through a literary agent, who has assessed its literary qualities, and sent it to the publisher he thinks most likely to be interested. Literary agents exist not only to find and negotiate with a publisher on the author's behalf, but also to exploit fully the author's other rights in his work, such as broadcast versions, film rights, translations, and so on—work for which some publishers have few facilities. In payment for his services the agent receives a percentage of the author's earnings.

A good publisher should know the changing demands of the book world, and the openings for new books on current affairs. That is why he himself sometimes suggests a new book to the author he considers best qualified to write it. After discussions, and often after the publisher has approved the outline of a book or read some chapters, he contracts to publish the finished book, and may perhaps pay the author an advance on his expected earnings. Such a book is said to be commissioned by the publisher. Occasionally the author commissions a publisher to handle his book, paying the manufacturing costs himself, and giving the publisher a percentage of the proceeds as a reward for the use of his organization. In this case the book is published 'on commission'.

The publisher forms his own judgement on the merits of the many manuscripts he receives; in this task he is assisted by the advice of professional experts called 'publishers' readers'. These experts often specialize in one subject; thus one 'reader' will advise on history, and another on fiction. The publisher must decide not only whether a book is good, and does not resemble some other book which would compete with it; he must also judge whether it will repay the cost of publication, yield a reward for the author, or require careful editing at the publisher's expense. As a book that costs a great deal to produce may have to be sold at such a high price that few people will buy it, the publisher may call for a detailed estimate of production and marketing costs, before he makes the author an offer.

The basis of most publishers' agreements nowadays is the payment to the author of a royalty, that is, a percentage of the published price on every copy sold. Usually provision is made for the royalty to increase after a certain number of copies have been sold; that is because, once the heavy cost of setting up type has been met, the reprinting of further copies is not in itself very expensive. Thus, if the book is very successful, the author profits accordingly; while if it is a failure, the publisher's loss is smaller than if he had paid the highest royalty on all copies. A typical arrangement in the case of a novel, which may be expected to sell quickly but for only a short period, would be a royalty of 10% on the first 3,000, 15% on the next 5,000, and 20% afterwards. If 5,000 copies were sold in all, the author would then make as much on the last 2,000 as on the first 3,000. A 10% royalty means that, for every copy sold in a bookshop, an author will receive, for instance, 1s. on a 10s. book, and 9d. on a 7s. 6d. book. At agreed intervals the publisher renders accounts and pays royalties due, although, as we have seen, the publisher may also have paid a lump sum in advance, as part of the expected royalties, so that the author might have some immediate return for his work.

The rest of the agreement mainly lays down the conditions on which the publisher may sell the author's work as a book. Although the COPYRIGHT (q.v.) remains the author's pro-

PAGE FROM THE BEDFORD BOOK OF HOURS

Written in France, 1423–1430. The illumination shows St. Mark writing his Gospel, with scenes from
his life in the margins

SIXTEEN PAGES OF TYPE LOCKED UP IN A CHASE READY FOR PRINTING

The sheet is printed on one side, then turned over and printed on the other. When cut down the centre, each half-sheet gives a complete 16-page section

perty, he normally grants the publisher an exclusive licence to publish the book; the publisher may also be granted some control over other rights (such as films and translations) which may arise from the publication of the book. Usually the publisher asks for an option on the next book or two, so that he can look forward eventually to publishing the author's entire works, and so that he may be repaid for his confidence in a new author.

Once the agreement is signed, then, providing the author has finished writing the book, the work of production can begin. The publisher must first decide what size the book is to be; he rarely departs from the standard sizes (*see* BOOK SIZES). A suitable type is then chosen; there are many different designs to choose from, wide and narrow, delicate or heavy looking. Then the length of line, number of lines to the page, arrangement of chapter openings, and headlines are decided upon. The printer then prepares specimen pages from a part of the manuscript so that appearance and legibility can be judged.

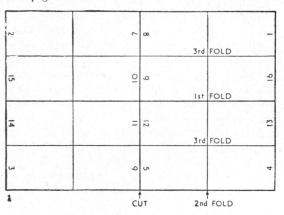

FIG. I. THE POSITION OF THE PRINTED PAGES ON THE SHEET

When one side of the sheet has been printed, the paper is turned and the other side is printed so that page 2 backs page 1, and so on. The sheet is cut in two and makes two identical sections (for two copies of the book).

FIG. 2. THE FOLDED SECTION

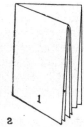

These pages are also used as a check in 'casting-off' or estimating the number of pages the book will make in the style chosen. When this is approved, the printer can begin to set up the type. Most typesetting for bookwork is now done by machines such as the monotype or linotype (*see* PRINTING, Vol. VII) from which the completed lines are taken, not in pages but in long columns of about 18 inches. A proof, called a 'galley proof', from the name of the long metal tray which holds the type, is taken, examined by the printer's readers (not to be confused with the publisher's readers who are mentioned above), and mistakes in the typesetting are corrected. Proofs may be sent out to the author in this form, or the printer may proceed at once to make up the type into pages, putting the headlines, page numbers, footnotes, and any text-illustration blocks into their proper place. The proofs then go out as page proofs.

A bound book is not an assembly of separate leaves but of folded sections which normally consist of 8, 16, or 32 pages. When, therefore, the page proofs are returned by the author, the type is first corrected and then arranged and fastened in large metal frames (chases) so that, when an impression is taken from the 'forme', as it is now called, the printed sheet can be folded into sections with the pages appearing in their correct sequence (*see* Figs. 1 and 2). A final 'imposed' proof is usually sent to the author at this stage. When the proof is returned, final corrections are made, and the forme is then ready for printing off, or 'machining'. When printed, the sheets are sent to the bindery, where they are folded, gathered into the right order (collated), sewn, glued together, and inserted into the binding case, which will already have had the title and other lettering impressed upon it with gold leaf, silver foil, or printer's ink. A jacket, intended less to protect the book than to advertise its contents, is wrapped round the case, and the book is ready for the booksellers.

While these processes are in progress the publisher is making his plans to market the finished book. He has prepared announcements and prospectuses and sent them to bookshops and libraries, and his representatives travel widely, both at home and abroad, taking advance orders. From these advance orders, called the 'subscription', the publisher gauges the demand and decides whether to bind all the sheets at once or to keep some flat for easy storage until they are needed. When sufficient bound copies are ready, he can confirm the date he had chosen for publication. Invoices are made out for the orders received, and copies ordered for bookshops are packed and dispatched to them. The remaining copies he stores in his warehouse, supplying day-by-day orders from this stock.

The publisher does not normally sell any copies direct to the public but only to booksellers, wholesalers, and public libraries, to whom he allows varying rates of discount off the published price. Nevertheless, it is he who spends the largest share of time and money in trying to interest readers in the books he publishes and to persuade them to buy copies from the bookshops. About a fortnight before publication, he sends copies to the literary editors of newspapers so that reviews can be written and published when the book appears. The publisher also prepares advertisements and inserts them in newspapers to announce publication; this item is a most expensive one. He distributes prospectuses and supplies booksellers with display material. And so, at last, the author may see his book in the shop windows. But not always: far more books are published than can be displayed at once in any bookshop.

See also ILLUSTRATION.

BOOKBINDING, *see* BOOK; BOOKS, HISTORY OF. *See also* BOOKBINDING, Vol. VII.

BOOKS, HISTORY OF. The earliest stories, stirring tales of national heroes (*see* EPIC, Vol. XII), were not written down but were sung or spoken and passed orally from generation to generation. The earliest written records, on stone, metal, clay, wax, cloth, or leaves, are described in WRITING, HISTORY OF, and WRITING INSTRUMENTS (qq.v.). The book in its proper sense can be said to begin with the handwritten roll. This was manuscript (from two Latin words meaning 'hand' and 'written'). It was in the form of a *volumen*, from which we get our word 'volume', based on the Latin word for rolling or turning, which occurs also in 'revolve'. The roll was made from papyrus, the pith of a reed which grew on the river Nile, the papyrus sheets being joined end to end (*see* PAPER). In the Egyptian city of Alexandria there was a large and famous library of these rolls (*see* LIBRARIES), collected by the Pharaohs or rulers. In the 2nd century B.C. rulers of the Ptolemy

Giraudon

A TEACHER AND SCHOLARS READING FROM ROLLS
Roman relief in Treves Museum

dynasty refused to allow the export of papyrus to the cities of Asia Minor. The people of one city, Pergamum, therefore, resorted to the skins of animals, which they split, scraped, and prepared as a writing material; it was known ever after by the name of Pergamum, of which 'parchment' is a medieval English version. The finest quality of parchment was made from the skins of lambs, kids, and calves and was known as vellum. Parchment was much stronger than papyrus and could be folded into sheets, and about the 4th century A.D. this form of writing material was used for the *Codex*, a manuscript volume which replaced the roll, and in which the sheets could be sewn together at the side to make pages, as in a modern book. In this way the BIBLE (q.v. Vol. I), the law-books of the Romans, the Greek and Roman classics, and the writings of early Christian authors which we read to-day were handed down. Lastly, the secret of making paper found its way from China through the Arabs to Europe. By the 14th century Italy was the centre of supply, and France, Germany, and Flanders were soon making their own paper.

During the Dark Ages, when the Roman Empire in the West fell to pieces through the attacks of barbarian invaders, much of the copying of manuscripts and making of books was carried on in religious communities. In monasteries books were made by MONKS (q.v. Vol. I) in a special writing-room, the *scriptorium*. This was often built in the form of a series of separate little partitions or studies. Manuscripts made for rich or noble patrons were often elaborately decorated or 'illuminated' with colours and gold-leaf. Some of the pages glowed

with initials, miniatures, and scrolls, designed by artists of great skill, which place them among the world's great works of art (see Colour Plate opposite, p. 48). Often they were finished in wonderful bindings of thick wooden boards, sometimes set with jewels or covered with stamped leather. The wood used for the boards was usually beech; the Old English word for this is related to our word 'book'. But so long as books were made of parchment and handwritten, they were rare and costly; and so long as the medieval church was the only centre of culture, there was little spur to wider reading.

Gradually, with the spread of learning and the growth of universities, more books came into use, by loan or sale. From the middle of the 14th century the universities permitted and controlled a new form of trade in books through stationers—so called because they operated in shops which were stationary or immovable, as distinct from the wandering pedlars who often sold prohibited books in secret—books which had been prohibited for either religious or political reasons. In 1403 a guild of makers and sellers of books was founded, which later, in 1557, was incorporated as the Stationers' Company, one of the ancient CITY COMPANIES (q.v. Vol. VII) which still exist in London to-day.

With the slow change from the Middle Ages to the modern world, and the growth of art, letters, and scientific thought, all was ready for the discovery of PRINTING (q.v.). Its effect on civilization was to be beyond calculation. When Johann Gutenberg, of Mainz in Germany, invented printing by movable metal type about 1445, paper was already being manufactured, as we have seen. Although few people had been taught to read, books became in great demand. By the end of the century, some 9 million printed books are believed to have been in use. Up till then, it has been recorded, 'a few score thousand manuscripts had contained the inherited wisdom and poetry of the world'. The earliest specimens of printing are fragments of a German poem, a Latin school grammar, and an astronomical calendar. The first complete printed book to have survived is the Bible in Latin, printed in Germany, which appeared not later than 1456. It was not until 1476 that William Caxton, a cloth merchant, having studied printing on the Continent, set up a press in Westminster. Books printed before 1500, when printing was still in its infancy, are known as *incunabula*, from the Latin word for an infant's cradle. They were at first made deliberately to resemble the handwriting of scribes; woodcuts which could be printed with the type were used instead of the hand-drawn coloured miniatures and initials. Indeed, collectors of fine books regarded the early printed books as inferior things. A writer of that day, describing the famous library of the Duke of Urbino, tells us: 'The collection contains no single printed book; the Duke would be ashamed to have a printed book in his library.'

Yet there was a large general demand for printed books. In England, where all paper had still to be imported, two-thirds of the printers were foreigners, and there was a big market for foreign books. In the 16th century religious works and text-books were needed for the increasing public schools and town grammar schools. After the Reformation, when England became Protestant, there was a steady demand for the Bible and other works in English. In 1526 the first New Testament in English appeared, translated by William Tyndale. Soon every church was ordered to have a copy of the English Bible; but, as books were so precious, the Bible was often chained to the desk—as, indeed, were whole libraries of books. In early Tudor England, however, with its religious disturbances and economic troubles, the progress of the book was checked; it was in Italy and France that books were so great a factor in the RENAISSANCE (q.v. Vol. I, Section 2), with its revival of learning, its pageantry, and love of the arts. Besides the ancient classics, some of whose authors were being newly discovered, there were books on medicine, astronomy, mathematics, architecture, and painting. No longer were the

Bodleian Library

PAGE FROM THE FIRST PRINTED BIBLE

This Latin Bible, known as the 42-line Bible, was printed in Mainz in 1455 by Fust and Schoeffer, partners of Gutenberg. The initials are hand-painted and the type is 'black-letter'

old manuscripts copied. The angular gothic 'black-letter' of the scribes, copied by the early printers, gave way to our present roman and italic types, which are based on the HANDWRITING (q.v.) of the 'Roman' manuscripts of antiquity. More books were made in pages of smaller size by folding each sheet of paper more often. Books are still described as folios when the sheet is only folded once (two leaves, four pages), quarto (four leaves, eight pages), octavo (eight leaves, sixteen pages), and so on (*see* BOOK SIZES). Each folded sheet is called a 'quire' or section. So that the binder might arrange the quires in the correct order when he sewed them together, the printer usually put a letter or figure at the foot of the front page of each; thus, with the quarto size, A or 1 would appear on page one, B or 2 on page nine, and so on.

From now onward, the general but gradual tendency was for books to be printed in larger numbers, at a smaller cost, and to cover an ever-widening range of subjects. Each country had its ups and downs. England, for example, enjoyed a golden age in the time of Elizabeth and Shakespeare. Poetry, plays, music, and popular ballads greatly increased in circulation. With the 17th century came the beginning of the outlook of the modern world. But in spite of the rapid development of scientific thought there were still severe restrictions on books. Printing was allowed only in London, Oxford, and Cambridge (*see* PRINTING, HISTORY OF); it was not until 1696 that anyone was free to print anywhere. Until the double disaster of the Plague and Fire of London in 1665 and 1666 scattered them, booksellers had been centred round St. Paul's Churchyard, as a few still are to-day. The Great Fire destroyed thousands of books there nearly 300 years before the Nazi bombers destroyed over a million books in one night in exactly the same spot.

In the 18th century books greatly improved in appearance. Craftsmanship was better; smoother paper allowed refinements in printing type; finer leather made for more gorgeous bindings. This was the age of great country houses, such as Holkham and Chatsworth, whose owners wanted in their newly formed libraries the same excellence as in their china, silver, furniture, and portraits.

Hitherto books had been issued in paper covers, and every buyer had to order a bookbinder to make a special cover for each book, much as men order a suit from a tailor to-day. Paper-covered boards were now brought in. The numbers of readers were increasing, and they were provided for by the increased writing of NOVELS (q.v. Vol. XII) and the setting up of circulating libraries. People began to write special books for children; in 1744 John Newbery opened a bookshop in St. Paul's Churchyard in which he stocked every sort of book for children, whether for amusement or instruction.

Changes in social habits completely changed the world of books in the 19th century. From 1800 to 1850 the population doubled itself; so did the working man's income. A different social order emerged; mechanical processes grew with startling speed. Fast communications changed daily life. The telegraph, the steam boat, and the steam printing-press came into use. The nations discovered each other, their customs and their costumes, their animal and plant life, their scenic beauties. These became the subjects of books with exquisite coloured illustrations, often by renowned artists. New means of illustration, such as aquatint and lithography, were devised. The wood engravings by Thomas Bewick in his books of birds and beasts summed up in miniature the whole of English country life and were widely read abroad. Books were made cheaper after 1825 by the use of cloth covers (instead of leather) for binding. Cheap MAGAZINES AND PERIODICALS (q.v.) multiplied; in 1848 W. H. Smith opened his bookstalls on the newly opened railways; cheap editions in yellow paper covers known as 'yellow-backs' were sold on the bookstalls. All this sacrifice to quantity and cheapness caused a decline in quality and craftsmanship. The illustration of books later suffered by the influence of photography on engravers, who lost the traditional vigour of their drawing. Such were the low standards of book production after years of mass manufacture by machinery, that at the

Bodleian Library

PAGE FROM PLINY'S 'NATURAL HISTORY'
Printed in roman type on vellum in Venice in 1476. It was illuminated by hand and bound for the Strozzi family

THE PALLISERS AT BREAKFAST

'That's what husbands always say when they're going to scold.'

'But I am not going to scold. I am only going to advise you.'

'I'd sooner be scolded. Advice is to anger just what cold anger is to hot.'

'But my dear Glencora, surely if I find it necessary to speak——'

'I don't want to stop you, Plantagenet. Pray, go on. Only it will be so nice to have it over.'

He was now more than ever averse to the task before him. Husbands, when they give their wives a talking, should do it out of hand, uttering their words hard, sharp, and quick,—and should then go. There are some works that won't bear a preface, and this work of marital fault-finding is one of them. Mr. Palliser was already beginning to find out the truth of this. 'Glencora,' he said, 'I wish you to be serious with me.'

'I am very serious,' she replied, as she settled herself in her chair with an air of mockery, while her eyes and mouth were bright and eloquent with a spirit which her husband did not love to see. Poor girl! There was seriousness enough in store for her before she would be able to leave the room.

15

PAGE FROM TROLLOPE'S NOVEL 'CAN YOU FORGIVE HER?'
Published in 1948 by the Oxford University Press (first published 1864)

end of the century a group of artist-craftsmen headed by William Morris called for a return to good workmanship and materials. Private printing-presses were set up by reformers, who published books too expensive to be of much practical value, but which had a sound artistic influence on commercial publishers. In our own time we have seen how machine production can produce books of the greatest good taste. Quality and style in book-production are combined with an ever-growing output of literature. British publishers in 1949 issued 17,000 different titles.

BOOK SIZES. Books are printed in sheets with several pages on each sheet, and their size depends on the size of the sheet of paper used and the number of times it is folded. Sheets of paper for printing are cut from the reel of paper according to one of the standard sizes, such as foolscap, crown, demy (pronounced 'demeye'), or royal, either in the single size or in one of the multiples of that size. These sheets are called 'broadsides'. After printing, these broadsides are folded down the middle of the long side to form sheets for binding. By folding once, a folio sheet of four pages is produced; by folding this sheet again in the same way, a quarto (abbreviated 4to) sheet of eight pages is produced; by folding it a third time an octavo (abbreviated 8vo) sheet of sixteen pages is produced; and so on. Each sheet can therefore be described by the size of the paper originally used and by the number of folds made, for example, a foolscap folio, a demy quarto, a crown octavo.

Here is a list of the names and dimensions, in ınches, of the principal broadsides of paper in single size, which are used in book production, with the corresponding folio, quarto, and octavo sizes, and the average dimensions of a bound volume, in which the sheets have been cut all round, that is, top, side, and bottom:

Paper size:	*Broadside*	*Folio*	*4to*	*8vo*	*Bound*
Foolscap	17 × 13½	13½ × 8½	8½ × 6¾	6¾ × 4¼	6¾ × 4⅝
Crown	20 × 15	15 × 10	10 × 7½	7½ × 5	7⅝ × 5¼
Demy	22½ × 17½	17½ × 11¼	11¼ × 8¾	8¾ × 5⅝	9 × 5¾
Royal	25 × 20	20 × 12½	12½ × 10	10 × 6¼	10 × 6½

BOUNTY, H.M.S. 'The burthen of this ship was nearly 215 tons, her length on deck 90 ft. 10 in. and breadth outside to outside of bends (thick planking near water-line) 24 ft. 3 in., a flush deck, and a pretty figurehead of a woman in a riding habit.' So wrote William Bligh, lieutenant in command of the *Bounty* when she sailed from Spithead for the South Seas on 23 December 1787. She was provisioned for 18 months and carried forty-six persons on board. The ship's company were volunteers, not pressed men. They were not told the object of the voyage until they had left Teneriffe, when Bligh had assembled the ship's company and divided them into three watches, instead of the customary watch and watch. (He promoted Mr. Fletcher Christian and put him in charge of the third watch.) But with two gardeners on board and the Great Cabin fitted up to carry 629 flower-pots, and the care with which the ship had been fitted out and provisioned, everyone on board must have realized that this was no ordinary voyage. Bligh had been for 4 years Master of the *Resolution* under Captain Cook (q.v. Vol. V). His mission now was to collect

National Maritime Museum

THE 'BOUNTY' MUTINEERS CAST ADRIFT CAPTAIN BLIGH AND EIGHTEEN OF THE SHIP'S COMPANY ON 28 APRIL 1789
Engraving by R. Dodd

bread-fruit trees from the Society Islands in the Pacific and carry them to certain West Indian islands, where it was hoped that bread-fruit could be introduced as an article of food.

On 26 October 1788 the *Bounty* anchored at Tahiti, and was well received by the islanders and their chiefs who inquired affectionately after Captain Cook. The ship remained at Tahiti for 23 weeks, and 1,015 bread-fruit plants were collected, as well as specimens of other fruits. Bligh set sail from Tahiti on 3 March 1789 and visited certain other islands. On the morning of 28 April Christian assumed command, and ordered Bligh and eighteen others to be cast adrift in the 23-foot launch, the open boat carried on deck in the *Bounty*. Twenty-three persons, including, Bligh tells us, the most able men of the ship's company, remained in the *Bounty*, some against their will. Bligh showed magnificent seamanship, and by carefully husbanding his resources, successfully navigated the launch 3,618 miles to the Dutch settlement of Timor, from where he took ship to England.

The mutineers returned in the *Bounty* to Tahiti, where they split into two parties; sixteen were disembarked, and Christian and eight other Englishmen, together with twenty-seven natives (who were always ready to sail in English ships), men, women, and children, sailed away in the *Bounty*, no one knew where. The frigate *Pandora* recovered the mutineers from Tahiti 2 years later, and ten were court-martialled, three being executed.

The cause of this famous mutiny has never been satisfactorily explained. Bligh was a good officer, not the heartless flogging tyrant he has been represented. One thing is certain: the mutiny was not long premeditated and took the ship's officers, including Bligh, entirely by surprise. Indeed, only Bligh appears to have put up any resistance. Christian, the acknowledged ringleader, had been a favourite of Bligh's.

The fate of the *Bounty* and the remaining mutineers was discovered by chance 20 years later. An American whaleship, calling at the previously uninhabited Pitcairn Island (1,200 miles from Tahiti) in 1808, found there the remains of the *Bounty* sunk in a bay, and a certain John Adams presiding in the fashion of a patriarch of old over a small community. John Adams, alias Alexander Smith, A.B., was the last survivor of Christian's party. When British men-of-war visited Pitcairn Island in 1814, he was left in peace, despite the Royal Navy's justifiable horror of mutiny. Bloody fighting had disposed of John Adams's white companions.

It is often forgotten that Bligh commanded a second and successful expedition sent to collect bread-fruit plants for transportation to the West Indies. He became Vice-Admiral of the Blue in 1814.

See also Vol. X: MUTINY.

BRABAZON I. This, the largest British transport aeroplane, was built as a model for later aircraft intended to fly non-stop from London to New York, a distance of 3,200 miles.

To achieve this range in the face of the severe head-winds of the North Atlantic, and to have enough reserve fuel to be able to fly on to some other airport in bad weather, the Brabazon had to be built to fly 5,000 miles non-stop. A total weight of nearly 130 tons was necessary to carry 100 passengers for this distance. The building of the Brabazon, as part of Britain's programme of transport aeroplane design, was recommended in 1943.

Building began in 1945 at the Bristol Aeroplane Company's works at Filton, near Bristol. Owing to the size of this aircraft it was necessary to build a very large assembly hall. For the taxi-ing and flight trials of the completed aeroplane, a concrete runway nearly 3,000 yards long and capable of heavy loads was laid down.

The aircraft, which was named after Lord Brabazon of Tara, chairman of the committee which recommended the building of this and other aircraft, made its first flight in September 1949. It is a large all-metal monoplane with a single fin and rudder. It is powered by eight normal piston-engines, each of 2,500 horse-power, housed in the wings, and coupled in pairs. Each pair drives a pair of three-bladed propellers (airscrews).

The Brabazon I was built for research and development work; future aircraft on that model were planned to have gas-turbines driving propellers. The wing span of Brabazon I is 230 feet, its length 177 feet, and its height 50 feet. The area of the wing is 5,317 square feet. The craft can cruise at 250 miles an hour at a height of 5 miles, and fly at a maximum speed of 300 miles an hour. The estimated range is 5,460 miles at cruising speed.

See also AEROPLANE.

Bristol Aeroplane Co.

THE BRISTOL 'BRABAZON' I

BRAILLE. This is a special ALPHABET (q.v.), marked by raised lumps on stiff paper, which blind persons can understand by the touch of their fingers. It was named after a blind Frenchman, Louis Braille (1809–52), who perfected it in 1834 while teaching at a school for the blind in Paris. It was not, however, much used until 20 years later.

Other systems, which had been known since the 16th century, made use of the ordinary shapes of letters. These were sometimes made of lead or wood, or cut out of cardboard, or outlined in pins stuck in cushions. One development on those lines was 'embossing'—making indentations of ordinary letters on the back of a piece of paper or card, so that the letters stood out on the other side, a method used in France in the early 19th century. But one Frenchman, Captain Charles Barbier, worked out a code of dots in place of the ordinary letters. As this method was easy to read, Braille made it the basis of his method.

Each letter in the Braille alphabet consists of one or more raised dots. There are six possible positions which a dot can occupy in any letter (*see* Fig. 1). By placing the dot or dots in various patterns, sixty-three different shapes can be devised. This number allows twenty-six shapes for the twenty-six letters of the alphabet, and thirty-seven other signs for punctuation, figures, and for the commoner words or parts of words, such as 'the', 'and', '-ing'.

The units are embossed across the page, like lines of print, and are big enough to be comfortably felt by the trained finger-tip. The thirty units given here show how the Braille alphabet is built up. The basic six positions are shown here as a guide; but in Braille books only the thick dots would appear standing up as embossed lumps.

The first-line letters, A to J, use only the first and second rows of dots. The second-line letters, K to T, are based on the corresponding first line, with one dot added; the third-liners are like the first, with two dots added. When a special sign is put in front of them, A to J stand also for the numbers 1 to 9 and 0. Even music can be written in Braille.

Blind people usually write by means of a machine on which the six dots, or any combination of dots, can be written. This is called a Braille Writer. The latest machines invented in Great Britain strike the paper from underneath, so that the lumps appear on top, and can be read as they are written.

THE BRAILLE ALPHABET

Blind people can also write by means of a hand frame, which consists of a flat board on which the paper is put, and over which is fitted a brass ruler punched with rows of six holes. A pointed instrument called a 'style' is used for pushing through the holes and making dents in the paper. As it is the lumps and not the dents that can be read, the writing is punched on the reverse side of the paper and is done from right to left. Then, when the paper is turned over, the lumps are on top, and the letter can be read in the ordinary way from left to right.

Many books and periodicals are printed in Braille, and the various societies which exist to help blind people have lending libraries of Braille books. Braille books are rather heavy and cumbersome, because of the thick, spongy paper used and because Braille letters are larger than printed ones. Long works may have to be spread over several volumes. An experienced reader can read aloud at an easy conversational pace. Nowadays gramophone records, or 'talking books', can also be bought or borrowed by blind people.

See also DEAF LANGUAGES.
See also Vol. XI: BLINDNESS.

BRAKES, AIRCRAFT, *see* AIRCRAFT ENGINES, Section 7.

BRAKES, RAILWAY. Two systems of braking are in general use on railway rolling-stock; each system allows the driver to apply the brakes throughout the entire length of a train, making a very quick stop possible. One system depends on the pressure of compressed air, and the other on the suction of a partial vacuum. In each case the train is slowed and stopped by the pressure of curved 'shoes' against all the wheels of all the coaches of the train. These shoes are controlled by a pipe, called the train-pipe, which runs the whole length of the train;

forcing a piston outwards, pushes the brake-shoes (L) against the wheel of the coach. When the driver wants to start the train again, he frees the wheel by admitting compressed air from the main reservoir into the train-pipe. This action allows the air in the brake cylinder to escape,

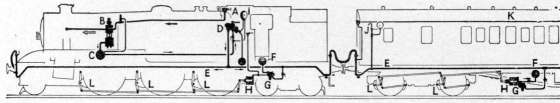

FIG. I. COMPRESSED-AIR BRAKES

A. Supply valve; B. Air pump; C. Main reservoir; D.Brake valve; E. Train pipe; F. Auxiliary reservoirs; G. Triple valves; H. Brake cylinders; I. Driver's pressure gauge; J. Guard's brake valve; K. Emergency chains in compartments; L. Brake shoes

it is carried from coach to coach by flexible piping. Normally the brakes are applied by the engine-driver, by means of the train-pipe, but each braking system is so arranged that if the train-pipe between any of the coaches is broken by the coaches parting, or if a leakage occurs in the train-pipe, the brakes will be automatically applied.

and a spring in each cylinder forces the piston back again, so drawing the shoes away from the wheels.

The same effect is achieved by vacuum braking (Fig. 2), but by a different principle. This time a larger piston in a cylinder is used to work the brake shoes. On both sides of the piston an

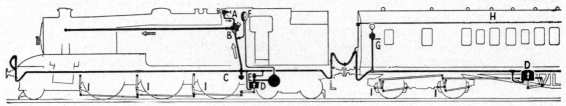

FIG. 2. VACUUM BRAKES

A. Supply valve; B. Ejector through which air is exhausted from D; C. Train pipe; D. Brake cylinder; E. One-way valve; F. Vacuum gauge; G. Guard's brake valve; H. Compartment chains; I. Brake shoe

cally applied. They can also be applied from the guard's van; while the use of the alarm chain or handle in a passenger compartment will partially apply them (see RAILWAY COACHES).

In the case of the compressed-air system (Fig. I), it is easy to distinguish a locomotive fitted with the donkey-pump or pumps (B) which compress the air, as the pumping makes a rhythmic noise, even when the train is at a standstill. The air is passed from the main reservoir (C) through a tap (D) and the train-pipe (E) to other reservoirs (F) beneath each coach. Valves (G) in the piping are designed so that if the pressure from the main reservoir is reduced by the driver opening the valve, or 'tap' of the train-pipe (D) the compressed air in each coach's auxiliary reservoir enters a cylinder (H), and by

effect of suction is produced by the state of vacuum existing in the train-pipe (C), which is induced by the exhaust of the locomotive. If the driver wishes to stop the train, he destroys this vacuum by opening the train-pipe to the ordinary atmosphere. An arrangement of valves (E) prevents this change in the train-pipe from affecting the upper part of each brake cylinder (D); therefore each piston has normal air pressure below it and a state of vacuum above it, and it moves sharply upward, forcing the brake-shoes (I) against the wheels. To release the brakes the driver causes air to be sucked from the train-pipe; the restoration of the vacuum beneath each brake piston causes the piston to drop down, and so removes the pressure from the wheels.

Compressed-air brakes, such as the Westinghouse, are in use throughout North America and in the great majority of European countries. In Great Britain, however, the use of this brake is confined mainly to electrified services, as it is much easier to compress air than to exhaust a vacuum by electrical means. British main line brakes are of the vacuum-operated type. Vacuum brakes are used also on most of the railways in India and South America. There is some tendency to change over from vacuum to compressed-air brakes; this is an outcome of increasing railway speeds, for in general 'air brakes' (as compressed-air brakes are usually called) have a more rapid retarding action than vacuum brakes.

Passenger trains in all countries are equipped with continuous brakes; but the number of countries in which braking of this type is applied universally to goods trains is limited. Among them are North America, France, and Germany. Great Britain has been backward in this respect. Certain British fast goods trains are run with vacuum brakes throughout, and are permitted, when necessary, to run at speeds up to 50 or even 60 m.p.h. Others are marshalled with half a dozen or so vacuum-braked wagons next to the engine, to give the driver additional brake-power. This allows them to travel at a slightly higher speed than the slow coal, mineral, or stopping good trains, on which the only brakes that can be worked while the train is in motion are those on the engine, tender, and guard's van. All wagons are fitted with hand-brakes, but these can be operated only when the wagons are almost or completely stationary.

See also RAILWAYS; TRAMWAYS.

BRAKES, ROAD, see MOTOR-CAR; MOTOR TRANSPORT.

BRAKING, PRINCIPLES OF, see Vol. VIII.

BREAKDOWN TRAIN. Even when every precaution has been taken, it is still not possible to avoid occasional RAILWAY ACCIDENTS (q.v.). For this reason means must be provided for clearing the line as quickly as possible after an accident has taken place. At certain strategic points on each railway (usually the principal locomotive sheds) 'breakdown trains', or, as the Americans call them, 'wrecking trains', are stationed.

The principal part of their equipment is a powerful steam-crane, so designed that, with the jib lowered, it can pass through the bridges and tunnels on the way to the scene of the accident. With the crane go a number of tool-vans, containing jacks and other appliances, as well as accommodation and means for serving meals to the breakdown crew.

At the scene of the accident, the chief pre-occupation, next to that of human safety, is to get the line cleared at all costs. To cut the clearance time to a minimum, it may be necessary, on a busy main line in particular, to deal somewhat unceremoniously with the derailed and damaged stock. Whatever can be moved on its own wheels is taken away from the site immediately; other smashed vehicles may have to be dumped at the side of the track until it is possible to dispose of them without further interruption to traffic. The use of breakdown cranes is not confined solely to accidents; they prove most useful, in particular when new bridges are being erected, or other large-scale engineering work is in progress.

BRIDGES. President Roosevelt once said in a speech, 'There can be little doubt that in many ways the story of bridge-building is the story of civilization. By it we can readily measure an important part of a people's progress.' Great rivers are themselves important means of communication for in many parts of the world they have been, and still are, the chief roads (see RIVER NAVIGATION). But they are also barriers to communication, and people have always been concerned with finding ways to cross them.

The first crossings were by FORDS (q.v.). Early man probably got the idea of a bridge from a tree fallen accidentally across a stream. From this, at a later stage, a bridge on a very simple bracket or cantilever principle was evolved. Timber beams were embedded into the banks on each side of the river with their ends extending over the water. These made simple supports for a central beam reaching across from one bracket to the other. Bridges of this type are still used a great deal in Japan, and there is an ancient Indian bridge across the river Sutlej in the Punjab which, by this method, makes a span of 200 feet.

Another early method of bridging was to roll flat-topped rocks to positions at intervals on the bed of the stream, and cover them with flat

Edgar Dale

PREHISTORIC CLAPPER BRIDGE, TARR STEPS, DEVON

stone slabs. This type of 'clapper' bridge is common in China, and is to be found in many places as a crossing over a shallow rocky stream. A simple bridge on the suspension principle was made by early man with plaited ropes, and is still used in countries such as Tibet. Two parallel ropes suspended from rocks or trees on each bank of the river or chasm, with a platform of woven mats laid across them, made a secure, even if rather swaying, crossing. Further ropes as handrails were generally added. When the Spaniards reached South America, they found that the Incas of Peru used suspension bridges made of six strong cables, four of which supported a platform and two served as rails. They were used in particular for crossing deep chasms and ravines in the Andes mountains.

All these primitive bridges made possible crossings only for narrow rivers or chasms. An early and famous bridge over a wide piece of water was built in 480 B.C. by the Persian King Xerxes over the Hellespont (the old name for the Dardanelles) to carry over his whole army during the Greek and Persian wars. This bridge is described by the Greek historian Herodotus. Two parallel lines of flat-bottomed boats were lashed together, each being securely anchored, and then a floor of brushwood and earth was laid from end to end. This type of temporary floating bridge, the pontoon-bridge, has been used ever since for military purposes; military engineers can construct a temporary bridge on this principle, able to carry all the heavy equip-

ment of a modern army, in an extremely short time. Permanent pontoon-bridges have been built in modern times—for instance, a pontoon-bridge carries the railway over the Royal Canal to the Broadstone terminus near Dublin. The longest pontoon-bridge is probably that over the River Hugli at Calcutta; this is over ¼ mile long, and is carried by fourteen pairs of iron pontoons held in place by strong chain cables.

The idea of driving wooden piles into the bed of the water in order to support a platform was put into practice as early as 2500 B.C. by the LAKE DWELLERS (q.v. Vol. I) of Switzerland and Germany, who then built wooden houses on the platforms. This is the basis of the 'trestle' or pile bridge, which makes it possible to build a wider crossing easier for the transport of animals and goods. Herodotus describes a bridge of this type built over the Euphrates at the ancient city of Babylon. Stone piles were built into the bed of the river, which possibly was diverted from its normal course during the construction, and then wooden planks were fixed to connect the piers. The Pons Sublicius (a stake or pile bridge), the famous early Roman wooden bridge across the Tiber defended by Horatius against Lars Porsena, was built on this principle (*see* Fig. 1).

The most important contribution to the evolution of bridge-making was the idea of the arch. The principle of the arch-construction is that if a number of wedge-shaped blocks are fitted together in the form of a semicircle or segment of a circle to span a gap, so long as the blocks each end are firmly anchored, the whole structure stays in position (*see* Fig. 2). It is probably that the SUMERIANS (q.v. Vol. I), the people who settled in the Euphrates–Tigris Valley as early as 4000 B.C., were the first to use the arch, which they made with sun-baked bricks; and it was known early in the history of China. But the Romans were the first to exploit it fully for the purpose of bridge-making.

Neither the Egyptians nor the Greeks were great bridge-makers; but the Romans needed bridges, as they needed roads, to enable them to administer their great empire efficiently. They built in timber, in stone, and in a combination of the two. One of the finest examples of Roman bridge-building is the huge three-tiered Pont du Gard over the Rhône near Avignon (*see* Vol. I, p. 412) which is still to be seen. This is both a viaduct and an aqueduct. The first

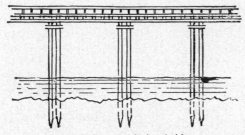

FIG. 1. Roman timber bridge

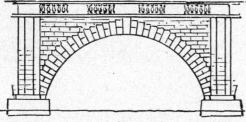

FIG. 2. Stone arch

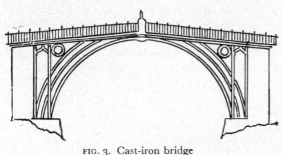

FIG. 3. Cast-iron bridge

TYPES OF BRIDGES

tier consists of six large semicircular arches which support the road and the eleven arches on the second tier, and these in turn support thirty-five arches in the third tier and the canal which is carried 190 feet above the river. The Romans established the importance of early London by building the first bridge over the Thames (*see* LONDON BRIDGE).

After the fall of the Romans in the 5th century there was little building, except in timber, for several centuries. In the 11th and 12th centuries the greatest bridge-builders were the MONKS (q.v. Vol. I), as they were the greatest roadmakers, innkeepers, makers of books, and many other things. In Italy an active order of monks called the Fratres Pontifices (the Brotherhood of Bridge-builders) laboured 'to give aid

to voyagers, to build bridges, or to establish boats for their use . . .'; and other orders of the same sort existed in France and England. The famous 12th-century Pont d'Avignon across the Rhône, renowned in the French nursery rhyme '*Sur le pont d'Avignon, on y danse tout en ronde*', was built by monks. Four out of what were originally probably twenty-eight arches are still standing. In the same century an English monk was responsible for the first London bridge in stone, the framework of which, with much repair and alteration, lasted until 1825 when the new bridge was built.

In the Middle Ages the semicircular arch of the Romans was translated into a pointed arch. An interesting specimen of a medieval pointed arch bridge is the three-way Trinity Bridge at Croyland, Lincolnshire, built by the Abbot of Croyland. Three pointed arches joined into one span the main stream and two branches, and carry roadways branching into three directions. The bridge is very steep and narrow, only suitable for foot passengers and pack animals. The steep, narrow pack-horse bridges of the Middle Ages were to be found all over Britain, for since the roads were so bad, most transport was by pack animal. Bridges of the 15th and 16th centuries often carried chapels and even houses on them. The Elizabethan London Bridge had a chapel and a whole row of houses along it, as had the famous Rialto Bridge of Venice and the Ponte Vecchio (Old Bridge) of Florence, and many others.

In the 17th and 18th centuries the French architect Jean Perronet and the Scotsman John RENNIE (q.v. Vol. V) perfected the stone arch from the point of view of beauty and efficiency. Their greater knowledge of practical mathe-

THREE-WAY BRIDGE AT CROYLAND, LINCS.

P. Hart

PONTE VECCHIO, FLORENCE
Many medieval bridges had houses built on them. This bridge dates
from the second half of the 14th century

matics and engineering enabled them to build bridges with an arch constructed on a segment of a circle less than a semicircle. Such an arch made it possible to achieve a wider span without increasing the height, but it put a greater strain on the abutments at each end. Rennie's Tweed Bridge at Kelso, built in 1803, has five arches with a 72-foot span; his Waterloo Bridge (1817) had nine arches with a 120-foot span; while the new London Bridge, begun in 1825, reaches a span of $152\frac{1}{2}$ feet. On the Continent even wider spans in stone bridges were achieved, the widest being the Plauen Bridge over the river Syra in Germany, which has an arch span of 295 feet.

With the coming of the railway in the 19th century there was a great demand for bridges, and the railways had capital for building them. The first railway bridges were built of stone or brick. In many places long lines of viaduct were built to carry railways; for instance, there are miles of brick viaducts leading railways into London, and a stone and brick viaduct over 2 miles long carries the railway by 222 arches over the marshes of the Laguna Veneta into the city of Venice.

The next important development in bridge-building was the use of iron and, later, steel. The first iron bridge, built in 1779, crossed the river Severn at Coalbrookdale in Shropshire, near the town of Ironbridge (see Fig. 3). It was of cast iron, with a single, nearly semicircular arch of 100 feet span. It is still in use, though now only for pedestrians. In 1819 John Rennie built the old Southwark Bridge over the Thames (superseded by a new bridge in 1921) of cast iron, with three arches, the central one of which has a span of 240 feet. Several important cast iron bridges were built, including the High Level Bridge over the Tyne between Newcastle and Gateshead, built by George Stephenson's son Robert, and opened by Queen Victoria in 1849. But cast iron was not a suitable material for long-span bridges, and Robert Stephenson began to experiment with wrought iron, with which material he made his famous Britannia Bridge, a tubular railway bridge over the Menai Straits, with two spans of 460 feet each, which was opened in May 1850. Another bridge of the same tubular type, the Victoria Railway Bridge, was opened in 1859 to cross the St. Lawrence at Montreal, Canada. There followed a period of great experiment in the construction of railway bridges in wrought-iron, plate-iron, and steel, as well as in reinforced concrete, on the tubular, girder, steel arch, and finally cantilever principles, which resulted in great bridges all over the world, such as the FORTH BRIDGE, the QUEBEC BRIDGE, the SYDNEY HARBOUR BRIDGE (qq.v.), and others. All this is described in the article on BRIDGES, RAILWAY.

The first great suspension bridge was the MENAI SUSPENSION BRIDGE (q.v.), built by Thomas TELFORD (q.v. Vol. V) and opened in 1823, which hung from wrought-iron chains. This was followed by Brunel's Clifton Bridge.

With the introduction of steel cables it became possible to use the suspension principle to make modern road bridges, and in this way to achieve longer spans than ever before. The GOLDEN GATE BRIDGE (q.v.), built at San Francisco in 1938, has the longest span yet made—a distance of 4,200 feet between its two great steel piers. Other famous suspension bridges are the Brooklyn Suspension Bridge, across the East River in New York, and the George Washington Bridge over the Hudson River.

The idea of a drawbridge, a bridge hinged so that it can be lifted by chains from inside to prevent passage, is an old one, and drawbridges were used over the moats of medieval CASTLES (q.v. Vol. XI). The bascule bridge, of which the TOWER BRIDGE (q.v.) London, opened in 1894, is the most obvious example, is the modern counterpart. This bridge opens its central span to allow the passage along the Thames of big ships. Another form of movable bridge is the swing-bridge. The bridge rests on a central pivot, and can be swung sideways by a system of rollers worked either by manual or steam power to clear the passage of the stream. There are swing-bridges over the river Raritan in New Jersey, U.S.A., and also at Kansas City. There are other types of 'lift' bridges, small ver-

sions of which are used a great deal on CANALS (q.v.) to allow for the passage of barges.

BRIDGES, RAILWAY. These bridges vary according to the size of opening to be bridged and the materials most readily available. Underline bridges, as their name implies, carry the railway itself; overline bridges carry main roads, other railways, footpaths, and occasionally canals or other waterways, over the railway. A lengthy underline bridge with a large number of openings is often known as a viaduct. In the building of the earlier bridges, the railway pioneers could use only stone or brick, and, later, wrought iron. A notable masonry bridge is the Royal Border Bridge on the old L.N.E.R. main line from London to Edinburgh, which crosses the River Tweed just south of Berwick, by twenty-eight arches, carrying the rails 126 feet above the water. It was designed by Robert, the son of George Stephenson, and was opened in 1850. Probably the largest single span in masonry carrying a British railway is that of Ballochmyle stone viaduct, on the old L.M.S. between Dumfries and Kilmarnock in Scotland, of which the centre arch spans 181 feet.

While masonry or brick are still used for most smaller railway bridges and viaducts, and for

British Railways

THE NORTH-BOUND 'FLYING SCOTSMAN' CROSSING THE ROYAL BORDER BRIDGE, BERWICK

Swiss Federal Railways

THE LANGWIES VIADUCT ON THE RHAETIAN RAILWAY,
SWITZERLAND

The immense span of this bridge is made possible by the
use of reinforced concrete

overline bridges in particular, the modern
counterpart for the bigger bridges is reinforced
concrete. Some very fine railway bridges have
been built with this material, one of the biggest
in the world being the Lorraine Bridge of the
Swiss Federal Railways, in the city of Berne, of
which the main span, carrying four railway
tracks, is no less than 492 feet—nearly 200 feet
wider than the span of any stone bridge. In
the United States, the Delaware, Lackawanna,
and Western Railroad Company in recent
years built the Tunkhannock viaduct in reinforced concrete with ten arches each of 180
feet span.

Before the advent of steel, some remarkable
bridges were built with wrought iron, one of
the most outstanding in Great Britain being
the Britannia Tubular Bridge, which carries the
Holyhead main railway line over the Menai
Straits from North Wales into Anglesey. Designed by Robert Stephenson, and opened in
1850, this bridge carries the two railway tracks
across the water through a pair of rectangular
box girders, set up on edge side by side, and

each nearly a quarter of a mile long. Three
supporting towers of masonry were built to carry
the tubes from one main abutment to the other,
the two widest spans being 459 feet each. Another unusual bridge, made chiefly of wrought
iron, was Brunel's Saltash Bridge, built to carry
the old G.W.R. across the river Tamar from
Devonshire into Cornwall. This waterway is
1,100 feet wide at Saltash, and 80 feet deep.
Halving the span required by sinking a foundation in the centre of the river, Brunel designed
a bridge of which the strength is mainly derived
from two arched booms of wrought iron, each
a hollow elliptical tube. Reversed arches are
used to strengthen the tubes, from which the
bridge floor is suspended by iron tie-rods.
Bridges like these would not be designed to-day,
since steel has now replaced wrought iron; but
in spite of that, these bridges, with a certain
amount of later reconditioning are now carrying
successfully the far heavier weights of modern
railway rolling-stock.

The coming of steel has both simplified the
building of the smaller bridges and made it possible to build much bigger bridges. The simplest
form of steel bridge, but suitable only for short
spans, is that in which the track is carried by
rolled steel beams, each of an 'H' section laid
on its side, one supporting each rail, and with
various types of bridge floor connecting the
beams and carrying the ballast (*see* Fig. 1).
Then we have the ordinary plate girder bridge
in which the 'H' is built up with steel plates
with cross-girders laid at intervals to carry the
bridge floor, which in its turn carries ballast
and track (*see* Fig. 2). For economy in steel, the
larger girder bridges are of the 'lattice' type.
Some of the older ones have curved upper
flanges (called 'bowstring' girders, from their
resemblance to a bent bow with its string) (*see*
Fig. 3); but more commonly they have parallel
flanges, and square or sloping ends, with massive
bracings from upper to lower flanges which, from
their resemblance to a series of capital 'N' letters,
are often called 'N' type trusses (*see* Fig. 4). A
fine example of lattice girder railway viaducts is
the Little Belt Bridge, built by the Danish State
Railways to replace a train ferry, which has
a centre span of 722 feet. The Storstrom Bridge
in Denmark, 2 miles 290 feet long, beats the
British Tay Bridge in length by 71 feet. In
America an excellent example of the lattice-
girder type of construction is the Ohio Bridge,

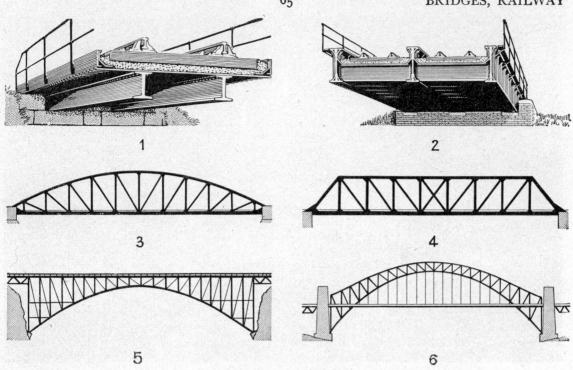

TYPES OF RAILWAY BRIDGES

1. Simple H girder span.
3. Bowstring girder truss.
5. Bridge with track above crown of arch.

2. Plate girder bridge.
4. N type girder truss.
6. Bridge with track below crown of arch.

built in 1888 to carry the Cincinnati and Covington Railroad. It carries two lines of railroad, two roadways, and two footpaths on three spans, the central one of which is 545 feet.

For bigger spans still, chiefly over waterways, the railway engineer has the choice between arch and cantilever bridges. In some of the large arches, such as the Victoria Falls Bridge in Northern Rhodesia (built in 1905), the track is laid above the crown of the arch (*see* Fig 5); this bridge has a span of 500 feet, and the railway track is 420 feet above the Zambesi River, the greatest height above water of any railway bridge. With the larger arch spans, the track is carried through the centre of the arch in such a way that whereas, at the ends of the arch, the track is built above it, at the crown the bridge floor is suspended from the arch (*see* Fig. 6). The biggest all-railway bridge of this type is Hell Gate over the East River outside New York, carrying four tracks over a span of 1,017 feet. The most notable arch bridge in the world, however, is the SYDNEY HARBOUR BRIDGE (q.v.) in New South Wales, with a clear span of 1,650

feet supporting four railway tracks, a 57-foot roadway, and two 10-foot footways.

On a larger scale still are the world's great cantilever bridges, the chief of which have all been built to carry railways. In Great Britain there is the double line FORTH BRIDGE (q.v.) with its two 1,710 feet main spans; Canada has its QUEBEC BRIDGE (q.v.), with a single span of 1,800 feet across the St. Lawrence, supporting a double main-line railway and a roadway; in India the Sukkur Bridge across the Indus spans 790 feet.

Since the building of the MENAI SUSPENSION BRIDGE (q.v.) in 1825 by Thomas Telford, many fine road suspension bridges have been built all over the world, some of the most recent American examples being of immense size. But while certain of the latter, such as Manhattan Bridge at New York or Oakland Bay Bridge at San Francisco, carry what are called 'railway' tracks, these are little more than glorified tramways. The movement of a full-size railway locomotive and train across a suspension bridge would cause such dangerous

THE BRITANNIA TUBULAR BRIDGE OVER THE MENAI STRAITS
Designed by Robert Stephenson and opened in 1850

concentrations of weight on a structure designed to carry light distributed loads that no attempt has ever been made to build a suspension bridge for ordinary railway use.

See also Vol. VIII: BRIDGE BUILDING.

BRIGHTON ROAD. The old coaching-road from London to Brighton went from Croydon through Godstone Green, East Grinstead, and Lewes, where it branched, east to Newhaven and west to the little fishing-village of Bright-helmstone. When sea-bathing and the sea air became fashionable towards the end of the 18th century, the village facing the open Channel changed its name to Brighton, and its trade from fishing and smuggling to catering for visitors (*see* SEASIDE RESORTS, Vol. IX).

The fashionable gentlemen who followed the Prince Regent in the 19th century to Brighton, instead of taking the coaching-road, took the shortest possible route through the country-side to the coast, following country lanes through Redhill, Crawley, and Cuckfield, and down the long slope of Handcross Hill to Patcham and Brighton. To-day the modern motor-road follows the same route.

It is just over 50 miles from London Bridge to Brighton. Perhaps this convenient distance decided motorists to choose the Brighton Road on which to celebrate the repeal in 1896 of the Red Flag Act (*see* MOTOR-CARS, HISTORY OF). Of the fifty-four cars that gathered for the first road-race, twenty-one refused to start, twenty broke down on the road, and only thirteen struggled into Brighton to be welcomed by the Mayor. Once a year, to commemorate this event, the 'old crocks' still splutter and struggle down the road from London to Brighton.

In 1868 a Mr. Ben Trench wagered that he would walk from London to Brighton and back in 25 hours. He did this so easily that he amused himself and the spectators by walking round and round Kennington Oval till time was up. To-day the annual Stock Exchange Walk from London to Brighton attracts some of the finest athletes in the country, who cover the 50 miles in some 7 hours.

See also ROADS.

BRITISH MUSEUM LIBRARY. This is one of the largest libraries in the world, comparable in size with the BIBLIOTHÈQUE NATIONALE and the CONGRESS LIBRARY (qq.v.). It contains over four million books, English and foreign, and, as a copy of every book, pamphlet, newspaper, and magazine published in Great Britain must be sent to the library (see COPYRIGHT), the number is continually increasing.

The library was founded in 1753, when a London physician, Sir Hans Sloane, left his valuable collection of books, manuscripts, and other treasures to start a national museum in return for £20,000 paid to his executors. A special Act of Parliament was passed to buy the collection, and money was raised by a lottery to meet the running expenses of a museum. The collection was first housed in Montague House in London; but as other libraries were bought or presented, it became too small, and in 1857 the present building in Bloomsbury was opened. To-day, the library is so large that some books which are rarely wanted are kept elsewhere, and all newspapers are stored separately at Colindale in north London.

In 1810 the library was opened to the general public, and to-day anybody can become a reader by filling up the proper form. In the Reading Room (see diagram), is the general catalogue which consists of 1,000 volumes. Readers write the number of the book they want on a slip of paper, and take it to a library official. A common book is usually brought quickly, but if a book seldom asked for is needed, two or three days' notice may have to be given. Some rare books can only be read in the North Library, which is reached from the Reading Room.

The Museum library contains a great number of very rare and valuable books, papers, and manuscripts, some of them very old. Among these are the Anglo-Saxon historical chronicles and the charters of the Saxon Kings, the romances of King Arthur, the story of Beowulf, and very early copies of Homer's *Iliad* and *Odyssey*. There are some famous illuminated manuscripts, including the Lindisfarne Gospel, the earliest English translation of the Gospels from the Latin, as well as the famous illuminated Psalter of Queen Mary. There are books of every nationality, and those in Oriental languages form a large department on their own.

See also LIBRARIES.
See also Vol. X: MUSEUMS.

BROADCASTING CORPORATIONS. 1. THE BRITISH BROADCASTING CORPORATION (B.B.C.)

was set up by Royal Charter as a public utility undertaking, and is not allowed to make any profits. It broadcasts under a licence granted by the Postmaster-General, who is the final authority for wireless in this country, whether telegraphy or the spoken word. This licence lays down certain technical regulations, and prohibits the B.B.C. from broadcasting programmes which are financially backed by anyone but itself; that is to say, the B.B.C. may not broadcast commercial or 'sponsored' programmes for advertising. The Postmaster-General has by the terms of the B.B.C. licence the right of veto over all programmes; but this is never exercised in practice. The only general restriction in force is that the B.B.C. must not broadcast any opinion of its own upon current affairs. Government departments have the right to ask for their special announcements to be broadcast, and there is provision for the Government to take over the service in time of national emergency. This right, however, has never been exercised, even in war-time.

Otherwise, the B.B.C. has complete independence in the conduct and control of its day-to-day business. The money needed to run its programmes for British listeners and viewers comes from the sale to the public of receiving licences (less a percentage retained by the issuing

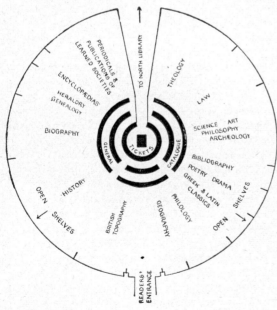

British Museum

THE READING ROOM OF THE BRITISH MUSEUM LIBRARY

B.B.C.

BROADCASTING HOUSE, PORTLAND PLACE, LONDON

The headquarters of the B.B.C. It contains offices where programmes are planned and studios from which they are broadcast

At the head of the B.B.C. is a board of seven governors appointed by the Crown on the advice of the Government. Under this governing body is a board of management, headed by the Director-General (the chief executive officer of the B.B.C.) and made up of the Directors of Technical Services, Home Broadcasting, Overseas Services, Administration, and the Spoken Word. Under this Board of Management are the many heads of departments. Altogether more than 11,000 people are employed on the staff.

The B.B.C., with regional headquarters in many parts of Britain, has established a new 'Radio City' for television broadcasts at Shepherd's Bush in London.

authority, the Post Office, to cover its administrative costs), and from the profits earned by its own publications. In 1953 there were approximately 10 million 'sound only' and 3 million television licences. Programmes directed to places outside Britain are paid for by money voted each year by Parliament.

The first British Broadcasting Company was set up in December 1922. A number of manufacturers asked the Postmaster-General for permission to broadcast (as they had to do by an old telegraphic law); but it was agreed that, instead of several companies being allowed to broadcast, the right should be given to a new joint company representing the chief manufacurers. This company ran broadcasting in Britain for 4 years. Then, on the advice of a Government committee of inquiry, the present Corporation was formed to take over the work of the company and its staff, buildings, and plant. The General Manager of the company, a Scots engineer named J. C. W. Reith (later Lord Reith), became Director-General of the Corporation.

The B.B.C.'s charter is periodically renewed by the Government (usually for a spell of 10 years) after a debate on broadcasting has been held in Parliament and approval of the Corporation's work has been given.

2. INDEPENDENT TELEVISION AUTHORITY. An important change took place in 1954. For 30 years Britain had supported the MONOPOLY system (q.v. Vol. VII); nobody but the B.B.C. could broadcast, and no advertising was allowed But when television grew popular, it was claimed that it was too costly to be paid for by viewers' licences alone, and that advertising should be allowed; it was also claimed that rivalry between the B.B.C. and a new television body would improve programmes.

After much discussion, a Parliamentary majority voted that an Independent Television Authority should be set up, run by governors and a Director-General, to broadcast 'sponsored' programmes linked with advertisers' names. The I.T.A. had to provide the organization and technical plant for regular transmissions, but was not to plan or produce the actual entertainment. This was to be arranged by various private contractors, on behalf of individual advertisers, each contractor paying for both the entertainers' fees and the transmission costs incurred by the Independent Television Authority.

Strict rules were made to limit the advertisers' influence in programmes, in contrast with the absolute freedom allowed in America.

3. AMERICAN CORPORATIONS. Broadcasting in

America is run in a different way. The money which is needed to pay for transmitting stations and broadcast programmes comes almost entirely from advertisers who use the programmes to make their goods known. During a broadcast, announcements are made at intervals about named brands of cigarettes, motor-cars, or other goods. Listeners need no licence and pay no fee. It is claimed that this system earns very large incomes for programme organizers, enabling them to engage the most expensive musicians and other entertainers.

There are over a thousand stations in the United States. They are mainly owned by local companies and operated by their own engineers. The stations do not provide their own principal programmes, however; these are supplied to them over a trunk telephone line by one of the 'networks', as the big radio corporations are called. Chief among these corporations are the National Broadcasting Company, Columbia Broadcasting Company, Mutual Broadcasting System, and the American Broadcasting Company. Each of these bodies, although itself owning only a few stations, provides main programmes for scores or even hundreds of others. Sometimes, if a very important programme is being broadcast, these 'networks' of telephone lines supplying local stations stretch right across the United States from the Atlantic to the Pacific.

A few broadcasting stations in the United States are independent of advertising and the 'hook-ups' of the 'networks'. These are a handful of stations the costs of which are paid by such bodies as universities, church organizations, and so on.

4. COMMONWEALTH CORPORATIONS. Broadcasting services in Commonwealth countries, though differing in other ways, have one thing in common with the B.B.C.; they are all publicly owned. The New Zealand Broadcasting Service, All India Radio, Ceylon Radio, and the Pakistan Broadcasting Service are departments of their Governments. The Australian Broadcasting Commission is appointed by the Federal Government; the Canadian Broadcasting Corporation and the South African Broadcasting Corporation (which was modelled on the B.B.C.) are public utility corporations, set up by the Dominion Governments.

An important difference from the B.B.C. is that none of these services is forbidden to 'sell' programme time to advertisers. In Australia and Canada independent private stations are also allowed to be run.

See also Vol. IX: BROADCASTING PROGRAMMES.

BROADCASTING, HISTORY OF. The first regular broadcasting station in the world was opened in America on 21 December 1920, at East Pittsburgh, Pennsylvania. Broadcasting came to the world suddenly, just after the First World War, when the public was little prepared for it. For nearly 20 years wireless telegraphy had been established, although still regarded as a marvel (*see* WIRELESS, HISTORY OF). During the same time the telephone had grown in use, though few homes had telephones (*see* SPEECH, TRANSMISSION OF, and TELEPHONE). The joining together of telephoned speech with the practice of wireless telegraphy was achieved towards the close of the First World War to help military aeroplanes, as well as ground troops. In 1919 demobilized airmen and radio operators brought back to civil life a knowledge of the fascination of wireless, of which the general public knew nothing. Large numbers of wireless sets and spare parts which had been used by the armed forces were sold by the Government. Many people, including countless schoolboys, took up wireless as a hobby. They designed, built, and operated their own sets, not only for receiving but for transmitting. They were granted experimenters' licences by the Post Office, and used their microphones for conversation with other people who owned transmitters. Some of them took to playing gramophone records in front of their microphones. Useful knowledge was gained which greatly helped professional experimenters working for telegraphic companies. Speech and music were transmitted from the Marconi Company's experimental station at Chelmsford, Essex, in 1919. A handful of amateurs were the 'listeners'; they heard a speaker reciting the names of the British railway systems and their London stations.

The first programmes—a nightly half-hour containing news, instrumental music, and songs—were put out by the same station between 23 February and 6 March 1920. But other users of the wireless, such as shipping and military authorities, complained that these broadcast tests interfered with their services. So broadcasting was stopped for some months.

Later two famous singers, Dame Nellie Melba

Marconi Wireless Telegraph Co.

DAME NELLIE MELBA BROADCASTING FROM THE MARCONI
STATION AT CHELMSFORD, 15 JUNE 1920
The programme was heard all over Europe

and Lauritz Melchoir, made test broadcasts. In December 1920 the Postmaster-General was asked by the Marconi Company to license a weekly half-hour of speech, music, and Morse telegraphy. He refused, fearing the broadcasts would hinder regular telegraph services. In the same month America started regular broadcasting from Pennsylvania. The station's identification letters, KDKA, became famous, for in those days every station used to announce its registration letters or numbers. Other stations began to be built throughout America, and within 3 years there were more than 500 stations in that country, and millions of listeners. A year later, after sixty-three societies of British amateur experimenters had petitioned the Postmaster-General, the Marconi Company was allowed to transmit a 15-minute programme of speech and music once a week. The first programme went out from Writtle, near Chelmsford, on 14 February 1922. These programmes were wholly an engineering enterprise, the programmes being planned and presented, and the transmitter operated—all as a spare-time task— by members of the Marconi Designs Department. Capt. P. P. Eckersley (who later became

the B.B.C.'s first Chief Engineer) led this team of pioneers, and himself took a foremost part in the programmes from Writtle; his amusing unscripted broadcasts were widely enjoyed.

Within a few months more than twenty telegraphic and other companies applied for rights to broadcast, and the Marconi Company had started speech transmission from Marconi House in the Strand in London—the first station to use the famous call sign 2LO. The Postmaster-General called a meeting of the manufacturers concerned, and it was agreed that they would be best served by a unified system of broadcasting, operated by a single Company. Their first programme, the announcement of General Election results, was broadcast on 14 November 1922.

The new Company started with three stations, London, Birmingham, and Manchester, and set up others at Newcastle, Cardiff, Glasgow, Aberdeen, Bournemouth, and Belfast. Relay stations were opened in eleven other centres. A 15-kilowatt transmitter—regarded as 'highpower' in those days—began test transmissions from Chelmsford, and was later moved to Daventry; from this system arose the later plan that gave listeners a choice between a 'National' and a 'Regional' programme.

During the first year of broadcasting the usual form of receiver was the 'crystal set', made with a fragment of a selected mineral, whose crystal structure enabled part of a wireless oscillation to pass through it, and any sound borne by that oscillation to be heard in an earpiece similar to the telephone's. Contact with the crystal was made with a thin metal thread known as a 'cat's whisker'. Sounds were very feeble, and in order to hear programmes, even in the earpiece, a high or long aerial had to be erected, well above all neighbouring houses if possible. Hundreds of thousands of tall wireless masts rose from the back gardens of Britain. But soon manufacturers devised valve sets, in which thermionic valves (*see* SPEECH, TRANSMISSION OF) not only detected the broadcast sounds, but strengthened them enough to be heard in a loudspeaker. Much smaller aerials could then be used.

For some years broadcasting was thought of as entertainment by sound only, but in 1936 the B.B.C. began a public service of TELEVISION (q.v.); this at first made little appeal, and ceased in the Second World War. Later, however, television became an important rival of 'sound', and the Independent Television Authority (*see* BROADCASTING CORPORATIONS) was set up to compete with the B.B.C.

See also BROADCASTING CORPORATIONS.
See also Vol. IX: BROADCASTING.

BROADCAST, NEWS, *see* NEWS BROAD-CASTING.

BULGARIAN LANGUAGE, *see* SLAVONIC LANGUAGES.

BUOYS. These are anchored floats. Buoys play an important part in communications, for they are used not only for the securing of ships in rivers and harbours, but also to mark channels, the edges of shoals, dangerous submerged wrecks, anchorage grounds, and so on. Their positions and descriptions are shown on charts, and so give the mariner invaluable help in the navigation of his ship.

In this country that side of the channel which is on the right hand of a ship going with the main stream of the flood tide or entering a harbour from seaward is marked by starboard (or right) hand buoys, which are all conical in shape and painted black or in black and white chequers. Port (or left) hand buoys, which mark the left-hand side under similar conditions, are can-shaped and are either red or red and white chequers. Middle grounds, which are shoals or shallow places in the middle of a navigable channel, are marked by spherical buoys.

Colour is an important factor in distinguishing one buoy from another; and many buoys carry easily recognizable topmarks in the form of crosses, spheres, cones, diamonds, &c. Wrecks or

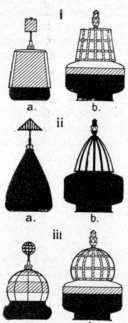

TYPES OF BUOYS
i. Port-hand buoy (*a*) unlighted, (*b*) lighted.
ii. Starboard-hand buoy (*a*) unlighted, (*b*) lighted.
iii. Spherical buoys (*a*) unlighted, (*b*) lighted.
In i (*a*) or ii (*a*) there is not always a topmark (upper shape).
The shaded part is red.

obstructions are marked by green buoys, and other special types are used to mark specific dangers.

Many buoys exhibit a light, but it is invariably an intermittent light to avoid confusion with the fixed lights in ships. Such buoys are usually lit by gas from a reservoir within the buoy. The older light buoys exhibit their light day and night; but they are gradually being superseded by buoys which automatically light up at sunset and extinguish themselves at dawn. Some buoys emit a warning noise, either from a bell or from horns and whistles. The whistles on the buoys are worked by the ingenious Courtenay device. Running down inside the buoy there is an air cylinder, the lower end of which is open to the water. When the buoy is in the trough of a wave, the water reaches a higher level within the cylinder, and the imprisoned air is forced out through the whistle or horn at the top of the buoy. As the buoy rises on the crest of a wave, air is drawn into the cylinder through two tubes which are fitted with valves so that air cannot escape through them. A post-war innovation is the introduction of buoys specially designed for use in connexion with marine radar installations (*see* RADAR, Vol. VIII).

See also NAVIGATION, MARINE.

BURMA ROAD. The Burma Road is the land-link between China and India and the West and runs from Rangoon, the capital of Burma, to Chungking in China, a distance of 2,100 miles. Until the Sino-Japanese War, and the capture by the Japanese of all China's long coast-line, only tracks, some of them very old, had crossed this formidable country. The Chinese constructed the first section of the road in 1934–5, but the most spectacular part, the 726 miles lying between Kunming and Lashio in Central Burma, was built hurriedly between December 1937 and November 1938 when the Japanese blockade was threatening to cut China off entirely from the western world.

The greater part of its course is through wild, uninhabited, and very mountainous country, though it occasionally runs through the main street of an old Chinese town which has seen little change for thousands of years. From Rangoon the road runs through hot plains and rice fields to Mandalay, on to the new town of Maymyo, then through the Goteik Gorge to Lashio, 120 miles from the Chinese border,

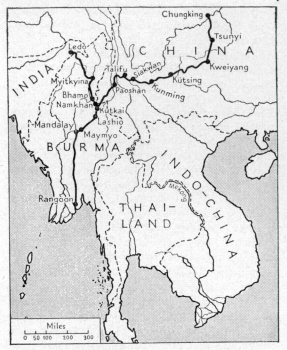

SOUTH EAST ASIA SHOWING THE BURMA AND LEDO ROADS

Rock was cut by hand; earth was removed in small baskets and often carried away on the backs of women and children; stone rollers were drawn by coolies or by water buffaloes. Over 289 bridges had to be built across ravines and rivers.

The question of repairing the road was a serious problem. The cutting and blasting had so disturbed the slope of the mountains that heavy rains caused whole hillsides to slide, so that the road might be blocked for days at a time, and coolies had to work in torrential rain to clear a way. Often lorries, piled high with supplies, sank axle deep in the loose gravel at the side of the road. After the road had been open for a little, modern road-building equipment from the west was imported to keep it in repair.

In 1943, when the Japanese had conquered Burma and made it impossible for the Burma road to be used, it became necessary to extend it into India to reopen a land-link with China. This meant that another 400 miles of road had to be built from the Upper Brahmaputra Valley in India to Namkhan, where the road joins the Burma Road, through country over which only mule tracks existed. In some ways this extension, called the Ledo Road, from its starting-point, the village of Ledo, was an even greater engineering feat than the Burma Road. Over mountains and rivers, through dense bamboo forests and jungles, and against strong Japanese resistance, the road advanced at the rate of 1 mile a day, so that by January 1945 the Ledo Road was finished and traffic moved along it to the help of the Chinese.

See also Vol. III: BURMA; CHINA.
See also Vol. VIII: ROAD BUILDING.

From Lashio it rises steeply to a height of 5,000 feet, then drops as steeply to the valley and to the town of Kutkai. After a climb to about 10,000 feet, it plunges down through some of the most magnificent scenery in the world, to the hot, steamy, fever-ridden valley of the Salween River, which it crosses by a suspension bridge 250 feet long. Then the road climbs again before it descends to the walled city of Paoshan. Another suspension bridge and many sharp-angled, hairpin bends carry the road to the Mekong Gorge, and to Siakwan, where the face of the cliff had to be blasted away for nearly a quarter of a mile. Wild country lies farther east, and the road climbs over four high passes: then the land slopes gradually to the fertile rice lands round Kunming, the capital of the Yunnan Province. Turning north-east it climbs more high mountains and eventually reaches Chungking, the war-time capital of China.

Nearly 200,000 people were employed on building the road, each village for hundreds of miles around being forced to supply its quota of labour. Some of these villages were so remote that thousands of the conscripted men did not even know that their country was at war with Japan. They worked under expert supervision, but their tools were of the most primitive kind.

BUS. The coming of the motor-bus has broken down the isolation of villages, opened up areas in which the railways could not afford to build lines, and increased the size of towns by enabling people to live a long way from their work. The design of buses takes many forms. There are the combined passenger and freight vehicles, usually consisting of a lorry chassis with special springs. Vehicles of this type are used in South Africa and other areas where development is in its early stages. Small buses were much used, particularly in Britain, before the Second World War. They are still in use in the rural parts of British Commonwealth territories. These buses seat up to twenty passengers; they are suitable for operation by one man, acting as both driver and conductor. In Britain special permission is necessary for buses with more than twenty seats to be operated by one man. The large type of single-deck bus is the most generally used throughout the world. The double-decker bus is very common in Britain and in Commonwealth cities, and a small number is to be found elsewhere; but, like the double-decker tramcar and trolley-bus, it is a type peculiarly British.

Attempts have been made from time to time to evolve international standards for the dimensions of 'public service vehicles'—the official term now in general use. Regulations vary from country to country and, in the United States, from State to State. The length of buses in Britain is limited to 30 feet for a normal single-deck vehicle, 27 feet for a four-wheel double-decker, and 30 feet for a six-wheeled bus. It is only since the Second World War that British buses and trolley-buses have been permitted an 8-foot width instead of the older limit of 7 ft. 6 in. The wider vehicles may be used only on roads which have been authorized. The many narrow streets in Britain account for these limitations; vehicles abroad are often larger. The maximum height permitted for a double-decker in Britain is 15 feet, but most are 4 or 5 inches less than this, while others, designed specially to pass beneath low bridges, have a sunken gangway on the upper deck and a correspondingly lower height. A single-seater bus, fully loaded, must be able to be tilted to an angle of 35 degrees without overturning; the angle for a double-decker is 28 degrees. The normal four-wheeled double-decker seats fifty-six passengers, and the distance between seats is governed by regulations.

Larger buses to-day are fitted almost invariably with oil-engines, as these have been developed to a stage where they are more economical to run than petrol-engines if a vehicle is kept well employed. In British buses the oil-engines developed in recent years have tended to increase in horse-power; many use 120 h.p. The engines of American buses are sometimes as large as 280 h.p. The reason for this very high power is that most of the American buses are worked by one man, owing to the high cost of labour. The bus therefore needs a high rate of acceleration to offset the time spent by the driver in collecting fares at stops.

Public service vehicles in Britain are not supposed to travel at more than 30 miles an hour, and time-tables must be worked out so that they can be kept within this speed. Oil-engines are fitted with a mechanical governing device so that very high speeds are not possible, but coaches under test in Britain for delivery to foreign countries have reached speeds of 65 miles an hour. The climbing ability of a bus can be varied by altering the ratio of the gear-box (see GEARING, Vol. VIII). Usually any coaches or buses which are intended for long-distance work are given a higher ratio, because of the amount of continuous running which they do without making stops. Where hills are particularly severe, special gears are fitted, and sometimes special brakes. The ordinary bus, however, can achieve a great deal; in South Wales there is a regular service up a hill with a gradient of 1 in $4\frac{1}{2}$.

Bus services reach almost every corner of the British Isles. The LONDON TRANSPORT Executive (q.v.) has more than 7,000 vehicles, while at the other extreme there are some 1,500 owners who each own one bus only. There were more than 60,000 public service vehicles in Britain at the beginning of 1949, compared with 58,700 in the United States. This is because many more people use private cars in America.

Both in America and on the continent of Europe it is the custom in many cities to have a standard fare payable whatever distance is travelled. If the route is a long one, it is divided into zones. On those routes in the United States where buses are operated by a single driver-conductor, the passenger pays when boarding the vehicle; he pays again when alighting if he has travelled beyond the boundary of the zone in which he boarded. One-man operation is not so common in continental Europe, but there the conductor often sits by the door and is paid by passengers as they enter. They leave the bus or tram by a separate door which is, like the entrance, pneumatically controlled by the conductor. In some cities books of tickets may be bought in advance at offices, and used to pay the fare on any bus. In Britain this practice is not followed, except for school-children's tickets issued in some areas.

The modern motor-bus is a descendant of the horse omnibus. The first omnibus was started in Paris in 1820. Nine years later a coach

THE FIRST BUS AND SHILLIBEER'S HANDBILL ADVERTISING THE SERVICE

builder named Shillibeer, who had worked in Paris, started a bus service in London, with a bus drawn by three horses. It ran between the City and a public-house near Edgware Road called The Yorkshire Stingo. Other buses were started in various parts of London, and within twenty-two years uncovered seats were built on the roofs of vehicles. These were the forerunners of our present double-decker buses.

Buses were started to get business men to their offices, and for a number of years they were not used by ordinary working people, who continued to walk to and from their work. This was not only because there were comparatively few buses, but largely because a fare of a few pence was more than they could spare from the wages then paid.

In those days there was little control of traffic in the more crowded streets; stopping places were not at fixed points, and rival buses used to compete for passengers, the conductors, who did not wear uniform, trying to persuade passers-by to board their own buses. At busy times of the day buses would race through the streets against one another, each hoping to get first to the next street crossing where would-be passengers were likely to be waiting.

By the last part of the 19th century owners of groups of buses were beginning to amalgamate and to buy up one another's concerns. At the same time TRAMWAYS (q.v.) were coming into use in south London and in some provincial cities. The London General Omnibus Company, formed in 1885, soon acquired several hundred buses. This fleet grew, in course of time, into the present fleet of London Transport buses. Early in the 20th century motor-buses came into use, and within a few years they had completely replaced horse-buses.

BUS AND COACH STATIONS. There are now so many buses and coaches that space off the public road has to be provided for them to stop; this is particularly important when they may be stationary some time or when large numbers of passengers are going to get on or off. In Britain, stations were established in London and at Canterbury and Maidstone in the early 'twenties. The largest is the coach station in London, near Victoria railway station, where, at holiday times, 1,200 coaches bringing in 40,000 passengers have been handled in 5 hours. In 1948 more than six million passengers passed through the station, using on an average 850 coaches a day.

A coach station of this size needs large offices for the control staff, which include regulators, supervisors who represent the bus and coach companies using the station, and the booking officials. These latter have to see that no more passengers are booked for a coach than it has seats, that relief vehicles are provided when they are needed and allowed (most bus and coach licences limit the number of extra journeys which may be worked on any one day), and that seats are kept for passengers who have booked places to board the coach at some point on the road.

Most stations are used by both buses and coaches. They vary in size from those in provincial cities, such as Leeds and Nottingham, to small wayside stations which exist mainly to provide food for long-distance coaches. There are many of these in the United States where distances are very long. New town-planning schemes now produced in England usually include a bus station, although the sites chosen have often been criticized for being too far from the shopping centres to and from which most passengers wish to travel.

See also BUS; MOTOR COACH.

BUSH TELEGRAPH, *see* SIGNALS.

C

CAB, *see* TAXI.

CABLE. A vital part is played by cables in telegraph and telephone communication, both on land and across the sea.

1. LAND CABLES. Long before the telephone was introduced to this country, and while telegraphy was still in its infancy, the possibility of using underground cables instead of overhead wires was being considered. The earliest cables had conductors of copper wire insulated from each other by gutta-percha, a substance rather like india-rubber, and a cable of this type was used for telegraphy as early as 1847.

With the advent of the TELEPHONE (q.v.) in 1876 the use of overhead wires increased materially, but as the transmission of speech was only satisfactory over short lengths, the use of gutta-percha-covered cable was restricted to towns; between towns, telephone and telegraph wires were still carried overhead. It was not until 1891, when the forerunner of the type of cable in use to-day was introduced, that it became practicable to use long lengths of cable for telephony. In this type of cable the copper wires, after being insulated with wrappings of paper, are twisted together in pairs and groups to form a cylindrical core of wires, which is then enclosed in a lead sheath. The first experimental long-distance telephone cable of this type was laid between London and Birmingham during 1897–9.

The thickness of wires needed for speech increases with the length of a circuit, but there are limits to the thickness of wires that can be provided in cables. The closeness of the wires to each other in cables also interferes with speech over long distances; but this has been mostly overcome by joining up inductance coils (*see* INDUCTION, Vol. VIII) in the cables at definite distances. The whole problem of telephone transmission over long distances was not satisfactorily solved until the invention of the wireless valve (*see* WIRELESS). By using valve amplifying equipment, similar in principle to the domestic wireless set, it is possible to make good the loss of power over long-distance cables. The valve acts as a repeater, so that two telephone subscribers 400 miles apart sound as if they were no more than 40 miles apart. Equipment of this kind for use on the London–Liverpool cable was first installed at Birmingham in 1916.

Telephone and telegraph cables are very expensive, and various methods of obtaining more circuits than there are wires in a cable have been in use for many years; but it was not until high-frequency methods were developed (as used in wireless communication) that great advances were made. A system for carrying twelve simultaneous conversations on each pair of wires in a cable was perfected and first introduced between Bristol and Plymouth in 1937, though multi-channel working (as this system is called) was used experimentally for transmitting telegraph messages as early as 1926.

The number of simultaneous conversations which can be sent over wires in cables is limited;

CABLE FROM TURIN TO LONDON DATED 1859

but with the coaxial cable, a new type now in use, in which one of the conductors is a hollow copper tube and the other a solid copper wire running through the centre of the tube, 600 simultaneous conversations can be carried. Although multi-channel working enables the number of conductors in a cable to be reduced, complicated electrical equipment similar to radio apparatus has to be installed at each end of the cable to work the system.

2. SEA CABLES. Cables laid on the bed of the sea have to withstand great pressures, except in shallow waters, and the conductors are usually embedded in a solid core of gutta-percha or balata, a substance similar to gutta-percha but having improved electrical properties. This, in turn, has a protective 'armour' of windings of steel or iron wire covered with a layer of tarred jute or hessian tape. In shallow waters it is possible to use cables with paper insulation, rather similar to ordinary land cables, but these cables near the shore have extra protection, as they are more likely to be damaged by ships (*see* CABLE SHIP). A submarine cable for telegraphy was laid across the Straits of Dover in 1850, and the first satisfactory telegraph cable across the Atlantic was laid in 1866. Telegraph service to India, Singapore, Hong Kong, Australia, Africa, and South America was established within a few years. Submarine cables for telephony are of similar design to those for telegraphy; but as in land cables, transmission problems restricted their use at first to comparatively short lengths. Telephone service between London and Paris was first opened in 1891, using a specially designed cable across the Channel. A cable laid between Ireland and the west coast of Scotland made it possible to introduce a London–Dublin telephone service in 1893. Many other telephone cables to the Continent and between the British Isles have since been laid, and, in 1937, multi-channel telephony over submarine cables of coaxial type was introduced between England and Holland.

The range of working of multi-channel telephony over submarine cables has been limited in the past because amplifying equipment could only be fitted at each end of the cable. Within recent years the British Post Office has designed the first submarine valve amplifying equipment in the world, which was successfully tested for 2 years in a cable in shallow water linking the Isle of Man with North Wales. The equipment consisted of several small valves inserted within the thickness of, and protected by, the normal armouring of the cable. The current which operates the repeater valves is supplied from the shore through wires within the cable. Two spare valves are embedded in the cable; if one of the valves in use becomes faulty, a spare can be switched into use in its place by electrical control from the shore. Equipment of this kind may come into use in ocean cables if means can be found of protecting the valves from the pressure of the sea at great depths.

See also TELEGRAPHY; TELEPHONE SERVICES.
See also Vol. VIII: CABLES, ELECTRICAL.

CABLE RAILWAY, *see* MOUNTAIN RAILWAYS.

CABLE SHIP. This is a ship which lays telegraph or telephone cables in the bed of the sea, and carries out repairs on them. Cable ships vary in size, but the largest tank of a large cable ship can store up to 1,000 nautical miles of deep-sea cable. Such a ship usually has four tanks, and can carry a total of some 3,000 miles of cable in all, which weighs between 5,000 and 6,000 tons.

Cable ships are equipped with a huge sheave or pulley wheel at each end of the ship, over which the cable is pulled in or paid out; in the holds are tanks in which the cable is stored. They have paying-out gear which prevents the cable being strained when the ship rises on top of a wave in stormy weather. About 200 nautical miles of deep-sea cable can be laid in a day, but perhaps only between 70 and 120 miles of heavier shallow-water cable (*see* CABLE, Section 2). Ballast tanks are used to keep the ship in trim when paying out or recovering long lengths of cable.

If it should be very stormy, and the cable ship, hampered as she is by being attached to the cable, be endangered, the cable would be cut on board, and a buoy attached to the sea end. The buoy and cable could then be recovered when the danger had passed.

Although cable-laying is now a comparatively rare duty, a cable ship is essential for repairing the breaks which sometimes occur. Much of the damage suffered by marine cables occurs in comparatively shallow water and is caused by ships' anchors or by the boards attached to the trawls of fishing-vessels. Sometimes this trouble

LAYING THE FIRST ATLANTIC CABLE IN 1857
This cable was not satisfactory and was replaced by another in 1866

can be avoided if the cable has been laid in a trench in the bed of the sea. The trench is cut by a marine plough towed by the cable ship, which automatically lays the cable in the trench. Repairs to deep-sea cables involve finding a break in a cable which may be several thousand feet down. For this, special electrical measuring instruments are used, and skilled navigation is needed to reach the exact site of the damage. When the break has been found, a grapnel attached to a strong rope made of manila and steel wire is dragged over the ocean bed, until it hooks the cable. If the water is very deep, perhaps 2 or 3 miles deep, and the cable is not broken completely into two, it may be too heavy to lift. In this case it has to be cut by a slicing device which is lowered to the bottom of the sea on a rope. One end of the cable is hauled on board, tested, then let out with a buoy attached which keeps the end afloat. Next the other end is grappled for, and hove on board, where it is spliced to a new length of cable. The ship then moves back to

the buoyed end, which is hauled on board again and jointed and spliced to the other end of the new length. Then the repaired cable is dropped back to the bed of the ocean.

A notable vessel in the early days of cable-laying was the GREAT EASTERN (q.v.). When cable-laying was begun, any type of suitable ship used to be chartered; but it was later realized that this technical work needed a special type of vessel. The most recent triumph of cable-laying resulted in PLUTO (Pipe Line Under The Ocean) (q.v. Vol. VIII). By means of hollow cables specially laid across the bed of the English Channel, petrol was pumped in 1944 and 1945 to the British, American, and French armies of liberation on the Continent.

Cable ships usually have yacht-like lines, but are stoutly built; comfortable accommodation is often provided for the crew to off-set the long spells of foreign service, and pay and conditions are among the best in the Merchant Navy.

CABLE TRAMWAYS, *see* TRAMWAYS.

CAMBRIDGE UNIVERSITY LIBRARY.
The beginnings of a University Library at Cambridge date from the 14th century, since when it has had an unbroken life. In 1415 William Loring left to the Common Library all his books of Civil Law; and soon afterwards a catalogue of the University's books (122 in number) was drawn up. By 1475 a new library over the University Schools had been built by Thomas Rotherham, Archbishop of York. During the next century the Library was neglected, until, in Queen Elizabeth's reign, Andrew Perne did much to restore and enrich it, collecting books from influential friends. By 1700, however, the Library still occupied only two rooms; but in 1715 the position was suddenly changed by the gift to the Cambridge Library by George I of Bishop Moore of Ely's library (30,000 volumes), which trebled the number of books in the Library. To find room for this new bequest it began to encroach on neighbouring rooms and departments in the block of buildings between the Senate House and Clare College until, by 1908, it occupied the whole block. Soon still more space was needed. A main factor in this growth was the Copyright Act of 1709 which included the Cambridge University Library among those entitled to a free copy of all English publications (*see* COPYRIGHT). In 1934 the Library was moved to a new building on the west side of the river, capable of holding comfortably the whole collection—about 1½ million printed books, 10,000 manuscripts, and 250,000 maps.

The Library is unusual among large libraries in two ways: most of the books are put on the open shelves where readers are free to go and select what they want; and most of the books can be borrowed from the Library for periods up to 3 months. Its greatest treasures are the *Codex Bezae* (a 5th- or 6th-century manuscript of the Gospels and Acts), given by Theodore Beza in 1581; and a copy of the first book printed with movable type, the forty-two-line Bible printed at Mainz in 1456, given by A. W. Young in 1933 (*see* PRINTING, HISTORY OF).

See also LIBRARIES; CATALOGUING AND INDEXING.
See also Vol. X: CAMBRIDGE UNIVERSITY.

CANADIAN PACIFIC RAILWAY, *see* RAILWAY SYSTEMS.

CANAL BOAT, *see* BARGE.

CANALS. Dr. Johnson defined a canal as 'any tract or course of water made by art'; in more modern terms, canals may be described as artificial channels filled with water, which may be used for navigation, irrigation, or drainage. Those designed for navigation may be either 'lateral' canals, which run alongside a river, or 'arterial' canals, which connect two stretches of water across the higher ground between them. Most canals are designed for canal boats (*see* BARGE); but there are also ship canals, which may be either lateral or arterial, and differ from barge canals only in size.

Irrigation canals were known in Egypt, India, and China long before the Christian era. The Great Canal of China, which ran from Canton to Peking, was built about the year 980 B.C.; it was 50 feet wide and 9 feet deep, and was used extensively for navigation. As there were no locks, boats were run down rapids at some changes in level, and up and down inclined planes at others. The Romans used a movable gate or sluice to retain the water at a higher level, forming chutes down which the vessel slid or floated.

The invention of the LOCK (q.v.), which enabled vessels to be transferred from one water-level to another, is claimed by the Italians, who used it in 1481 on the Brenta, near Padua; but it was not generally known in England until some 80 years later, when it was used on a short length of 3 miles of canal connecting Exeter with the sea. European countries took full advantage of the possibilities offered by the invention of locks for expanding their inland navigation. The canals and navigable rivers of Belgium, Holland, France, and Germany have had an important influence on the development of trade and commerce in these countries; goods can be carried economically and quickly both from inland towns to the sea and from one inland town to another. Canals on the Continent were made originally on a far larger scale than in England, and have been maintained and improved by State money. In France the improvement of rivers and the building of canals had been encouraged from the 15th century, Paris being the natural centre from which canals radiated to the western ports of Brest, Nantes, and Bordeaux, the Channel ports, and the canals of Belgium and the Rhine, and from these on to Switzerland and Germany. Marseilles, in the south, has connexions inland by

Paul Popper

THE DUTCH SECTION OF THE ALBERT CANAL LEADING TO MAASTRICHT

water, although the northern canals are more important means of communication. Altogether French navigable waterways cover 6,200 miles. These waterways were badly damaged in the Second World War. In rebuilding them the French are trying to standardize them more than before, so that the canals may take four classes of craft, from 300 up to 2,000 tons.

In Germany the great KIEL CANAL (q.v.), which takes ships between the North Sea and the Baltic, was completed in 1895. Much important canal construction was carried out in the years before the Second World War. The Dortmund–Ems–Weser Canal, navigable by ships and barges of 800 tons capacity, joined the Rhine and Weser and brought the Ruhr district in direct water connexion with Emden. The Berlin–Stettin Canal connected Berlin with the Oder and through the Bromberg Canal with the Vistula. There were plans to link up by canals the western and eastern waterways, to develop the upper Rhine, and make connexions with the Danube.

The large network of canals in Holland was built for drainage as well as navigation. The water from marshy country is discharged through the canals into the sea. The canals were dug through level country and made with gently sloping sides so that they are wide and deep, and the water flowing to the sea does not run so fast as to make navigation difficult. Difficulties did arise, however, as navigation requires a high water-level and drainage a low one; and, as in recent years both barges and ships have increased in size, many additional hydraulic structures and pumping-plants have had to be built to regulate the water-levels. The North Sea Canal which connects Amsterdam with Ymuiden was enlarged in 1937 and can take ships about 70 feet wide on a draft about 30 feet—nearly as large as for the MANCHESTER SHIP CANAL in England (q.v.). The Merwede Canal connects Amsterdam with the Lek and Waal Rivers and takes ships of 2,000 tons capacity; while the canal between Rotterdam, Antwerp, and other cities can be navigated by 3,500-ton ships.

An elaborate network of canals has been built up in Russia which connects Moscow with the Volga and makes it possible to travel by water from the Caspian to the Baltic (*see* RUSSIAN CANALS). British canals, except for the Manchester Ship Canal, are on a much smaller scale than the great continental canals, though in places they carry a considerable amount of traffic (*see* CANALS, BRITISH).

The great rivers and lakes of the United States and Canada are connected by waterways and canals. It is hoped that some day the waterways of the western river system will be standardized in size. A standard lock, 100 feet wide and 600 feet long, has already been decided on. The WELLAND CANAL (q.v.) is an important link in the chain of inland waterways connecting the Atlantic Ocean with the Great Lakes. It crosses the Niagara peninsula about 10 miles west of the Niagara Falls, allowing ocean-going ships to pass between Lake Erie and Lake Ontario.

The first thing to consider in building a canal is the size of the boat for which it is needed. The early English canals were built to deal with local traffic and to conform to the nature of the country, and in consequence the canals vary a good deal in size. This drawback is not found in Continental waterways, however, nor in American, for the canals were for the most part built to connect large navigable rivers and lakes for long-distance traffic. When canals were first built, before locks were used, it was necessary to keep to level ground; and so it was common to follow the contours of the ground—which is the reason why so many British canals wind about, taking a more devious route than a modern canal would. But even with modern canals, which can deal with differences of level by a lock or boat lift (see LOCKS AND WEIRS), it is desirable to use as many level stretches as possible, for passing through locks means loss of time in travelling. In some places, accordingly, the canal is on a built-up embankment, or runs along an aqueduct built of stone, brick, or concrete; in other places it runs through cuttings, or even, where cuttings would have to be too deep, through tunnels.

SECTION OF A CANAL

Canals have to be watertight. The early canal-builders used to line the bed of the canal with 'puddle clay', a clay of an even texture worked up with water until it was like putty. They plastered this in layers up to 2 or 3 feet thick both on the bed and sides of the canal. When, however, the boats began to be propelled by engines instead of animal power, stronger banks were needed to resist the force of the wash from the propellers. Modern canals, therefore, have concrete walls. The 6- or 7-foot wide towing-path along one side of the canal, essential in early days, is now no longer necessary. In a modern canal the cross-section of the waterway has nearly straight lines, the top width being four or five times the width of the barge, and the depth 2 or 3 feet below the depth of the loaded barge.

The importance of canals varies much between one country and another; and so does the way they are developed, this depending largely upon what other methods of transport are available. Industries on the banks of canals benefit from them, and so do the ports where canals enter the sea. But the canals must be adequately maintained, and often improved, so that traffic can go fast enough for modern industrial requirements.

See also BARGE; CANALS, BRITISH; DREDGERS; PANAMA CANAL; SUEZ CANAL; RUSSIAN CANALS.

CANALS, BRITISH. In England the waterways form an inland network connected by canalized rivers with the four main estuaries, Humber, Thames, Severn, and Mersey. They are on a very small scale compared with the great continental rivers and canals, although the traffic is in some places denser in proportion to the size and length of the canals. Apart from the Manchester Ship Canal, the only other large canal is the Gloucester and Berkeley Canal connecting Gloucester with the Bristol Channel. This can take ships 250 feet long, carrying 1,200 tons.

The first canals in Britain were built by the Romans. These were the Caerdike, a canal connecting the Rivers Nene and Witham, and the Foss Dike, which ran from Lincoln to the River Trent. After the Romans left Britain, there was no canal-building of any importance until in the early 18th century some canals, such as the Aire and Calder Navigation, were built. But with the building of the Bridgewater Canal about 1762, the great age of canal-building began. The growth of industry in England in the 18th century found the country unprepared to take full advantage of the increased production of goods, because of the poor state of road transport. The roads were fit for wagons for a few months of the year only, and pack-horses were uneconomical and could not carry very heavy loads.

The advantages of the canal as a means of conveyance were well known on the Continent, and had been proved in Holland and France. It was no doubt from the Continent that Francis Egerton, 3rd Duke of Bridgewater, derived the idea for a canal to take coal from his estate at Worsley to Manchester. This was followed by the Bridgewater Canal between Manchester and Liverpool, which was an outstanding commercial success, and opened the way for many others. The engineer was James Brindley (1716-72), who will always be remembered as the 'Father of British Canals'. It was mainly due to his energy, originality, and perseverance that many of these early canals were built.

Brindley realized the value of aqueducts which are a special feature of English canals, especially the earlier ones. When he proposed to carry the Bridgewater canal over the River Irwell, near Barton Bridge, some 5 miles west of Manchester, he was laughed at. But in fact the canal is carried in an aqueduct 39 feet above

John Murray

THE DUKE OF BRIDGEWATER AND HIS CANAL OVER THE RIVER
IRWELL

Engraving from *Lives of the Engineers*, by Samuel Smiles

the river and is supported by three semicircular arches. A contemporary reporter wrote of 'the new and surprising sight of vessels sailing aloft in the air, high above the vessels sailing below in the river'. Later the Barton aqueduct was replaced by a movable one in the form of a steel lattice girder swing-bridge (*see* BRIDGES), containing a steel trough filled with water.

Brindley was also responsible for the Trent and Mersey or Grand Trunk Canal, which formed a route between the River Trent, near Nottingham, and the Mersey and Bridgewater Canal at Preston Brook. It enabled the salt producers of Cheshire and the earthenware manufacturers of Staffordshire to bring raw materials—pottery clay from Devon and Cornwall and flints from the south-east ports of England—right to the factories; it gave them a safe way of sending away their pottery, without much risk of its breaking.

Next came the Stafford and Worcester Canal, which led into the Severn; the Coventry and Birmingham Canals, bringing coal and iron to the blast furnaces round Walsall and to Birmingham; the Oxford Canal making a link with the Thames; and lastly, in 1793, the Grand Junction, and Leicester and Northampton Canals, which connected the Thames and Trent. Ten years later the Kennet and Avon Canal connecting the Thames and Severn, and the Leeds and Liverpool Canal connecting the Humber and Mersey on the north route, were completed, and the estuaries of these four important rivers were now connected by water (*see* map).

The Trent and Mersey Canal is now connected with the canalized River Weaver and so with the Mersey estuary by means of the Anderton lift, an enormous lock. The Anderton boat lift, the only one in Britain, has two tanks which can each take two narrow canal-boats carrying about 50 tons of cargo. The tanks are lowered or raised by electric power (*see* LOCKS AND WEIRS).

In Scotland the Forth and Clyde Canal, which could pass small coasters and fishing-vessels, was opened in 1790; the Crinan, which provided a passage from the Clyde to the Western Islands, 10 years later; and in the 1820's the Caledonian, a Government undertaking on a larger scale, for coasting and fishing craft. The Caledonian, which runs right across Scotland joining up the lakes of the Great Glen, was carried out by the great engineer, Thomas TELFORD (q.v. Vol. V).

The success of the earlier canals and the outburst of industrial activity of the age led, at the end of the 18th century, to a canal mania, like the railway mania which followed it. Many canals were built which could not possibly be made to pay, and speculation in canal shares reached fantastic figures. After 1840, when the railways were working fully, almost no more canals were built. Many of the existing ones were taken over by the railways, and in some cases the water was drained from them, and a railway laid down on the same route. The smaller canals in some districts, such as the Shropshire Union and Birmingham Canals Navigation, were amalgamated under railway control. Other canals, such as the Aire and Calder Navigation between Leeds and the Humber, the Leeds and Liverpool, the Bridgewater, and the Grand Union, kept abreast of the times by improvements, and continued to

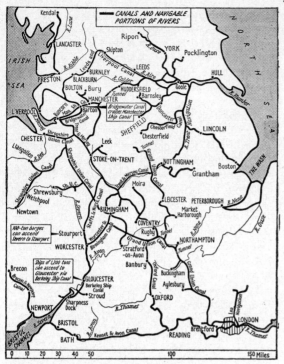

THE CHIEF CANALS IN ENGLAND AND WALES

hold their own against the railways, although they no longer made such big profits. In 1894 the very important MANCHESTER SHIP CANAL (q.v.) was opened, linking Manchester with the sea. In 1932 the Grand Union Company was formed by the merging of eleven companies, and this company, prior to nationalization, controlled 264 miles of canal between the Thames and the Midlands.

Before the Second World War there were approximately 2,100 miles of navigable canal in Great Britain, of which 600 miles were under railway control. By the Transport Act of 1947, British canals, with the exception of the Manchester Ship Canal and the Bridgewater Canal, came under national control. They are now operated by the Docks and Inland Waterways Executive, and are grouped into divisions based on the estuaries Humber, Thames, Severn, and Mersey, with the Scottish canals as a fifth division.

See also BARGE; CANALS; LOCKS AND WEIRS; MANCHESTER SHIP CANAL.

CANOE.

1. This word is derived from a Caribbean word for boat, and comes to the English language through the Spanish *canoa*.

It is a word, therefore, which takes the modern reader's mind back to the days of the Elizabethan adventurers and the buccaneers of the Spanish Main, who used to meet at sea the native Caribs in their rude boats. To-day the word canoe has a very wide meaning: indeed, it is only possible to hint at a definition, for the varieties are infinite. A canoe, then, is a small boat propelled by paddle or sail, which is primitive in design, probably long and narrow, and usually open from end to end. Craft which can be called canoes are used by peoples all over the world. Canoes are made from all sorts of materials. The simplest are constructed of reeds, such canoes being found on lakes in South America and in Africa on the upper Nile. The best-known type of river canoe is probably the birch-bark used by the AMERICAN INDIANS of the North (q.v. Vol. I). The Iroquois are expert canoe-builders. A wooden skeleton is made, and is covered with the bark of the birch tree laid on, not lengthwise but transversely, and the thin sheets are sewn together with long, pliant pine roots. The seams are rendered watertight with gum from the balsam tree (*see* Fig. 1). Birch-bark canoes are very light and are easily carried. They vary in size from the 36-foot canoe, with a crew of sixteen paddlers, besides a bowman and a steersman, to the light

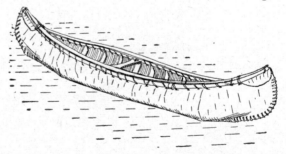

FIG. 1. IROQUOIS BIRCH BARK CANOE

hunting canoe, 12 feet long, paddled by one man. These canoes have no keel, stem, or stern-post, nor is a single nail or peg used in their construction. Long voyages are made in them through river and lake, and a sail is sometimes set when the wind is fair. But these canoes are very unstable.

2. In the far north the ESKIMOES (q.v. Vol. I) use a canoe, called a *kayak*, which has a framework of wood entirely covered with sealskin. A round hole is left for the Eskimo to sit in, and round the hole is a loose piece of sealskin which

FIG. 2. ESKIMO KAYAK

FIG. 3. WELSH CORACLE

FIG. 4. CURRAGH, GREAT BLASKET ISLAND (IRELAND)

FIG. 5. KRU CANOE, SIERRA LEONE (WEST AFRICA)

is fastened round his waist (*see* Fig. 2). The Eskimo uses a double paddle, a pole with a blade at each end. Kayaks are very swift and can face any weather: if upset at sea they can be righted, for the Eskimo, strapped into his watertight canoe, is an expert waterman. The Eskimo women use a clumsier, larger, and heavier open canoe, also skin-covered, which is called an *umiak*. This canoe can hold a complete family, and is propelled with short spoon-like single-bladed paddles.

3. Julius Caesar mentions that the boats used in Britain when the Romans came were made of wicker-work covered with hide. Of this type, the almost circular one-man coracle still survives as a fishing-boat, used principally on the Welsh rivers; but modern coracles are covered with canvas, not skins (*see* Fig. 3). On the west coast of Ireland sea-going, canvas-covered canoes, called *curraghs*, are used by the fishermen of Dingle Bay and Blasket Island off the Kerry coast, and Aran Island off Donegal. The Dingle curraghs are about 25 feet long and have four rowing thwarts and a mast thwart: the oars are worked on thole pins. A mast can be stepped forward and a sail set. Curraghs are built on a wooden framework, over which is stretched canvas which is tarred and black (*see* Fig. 4). These boats are very light and buoyant. They are carried ashore when not in use, and stowed upside down on trestles. Heavy stones are tied to the curraghs in this position so that the wind cannot blow them away. The curraghs are carried ashore bottoms upwards over the heads of the crews, and this has gained them the nickname of 'beetles'.

4. A primitive and very common type of canoe the world over is the dug-out, that is a canoe hewn or burnt from the solid tree trunk. Some dug-outs are quite crude, particularly those used on inland waters, but very many are curious works of art. The *kru* canoe, for example, used for inshore fishing off Freetown, Sierra Leone, on the west coast of Africa, is made from the cotton tree. This type has a long and tapered hull, and is carefully hollowed so as to have a very thin skin (*see* Fig. 5). Another very seaworthy little fishing canoe is the *hori* used on the other side of Africa. These little craft set a rectangular sail which is supported by two light spars, both of which can be called masts, and they come racing into the old harbour of Mombasa from the sea, the fisherman sitting back and resting himself in preparation for the strenuous work of marketing his catch ashore in the hot sun: he looks very comfortable in his minute canoe which he only occasionally has to bale vigorously. Dug-out canoes are restricted by the size of the tree, and can never be anything but narrow and unstable.

5. Some of the finest sea-going canoes are found in the Pacific. To gain stability under sail and also great carrying capacity, it was usual in the Pacific islands to form double canoes, two similar craft being lashed close together and parallel by means of beams across the gunwales. Platforms were erected over the space between across the beams, thus forming a deck (*see* Fig. 6). Some were as much as 70 feet long, and were paddled by large crews, or sailed, the mast being stepped on the platform and between the hulls. Captain Cook observed at Tahiti the great travelling canoes of this type, with thatched cabins: in such canoes the migrations had been made between the islands and New Zealand (*see* MAORIS and POLYNESIANS, Vol. I). These canoes contained hulls which were plank built. Even more impressive were the war canoes: in 1774 Cook witnessed at Tahiti a naval review of 330 canoes which he estimated carried about 8,000 men.

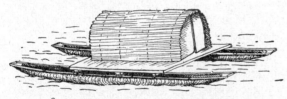

FIG. 6. DOUBLE CANOE USED ON RIVERS IN CEYLON

These big double canoes have now disappeared, except in a few places; but the outrigger canoe is common over the Pacific and Indian Oceans.

6. The most famous sailing canoe is probably the *Flying Proa* of the Ladrones or Mariana Islands in the Pacific. Drake, Dampier, and Anson were in turn astonished as these boats sailed by their stout ships at quite 20 miles an hour in the brisk trade wind. The *Flying Proa* was an outrigger canoe, and the type survives to-day. A light hull is given stability by a log shaped like a cigar, which is kept parallel with the hull and apart from it by beams lashed across the gunwale and to the log. The canoe is sailed with the outrigger always to windward, and so the ends of the canoe are the same shape,

FIG. 7. OUTRIGGER CANOE, COLOMBO, CEYLON

either end becoming the bow end according to circumstances. To balance the canoe in a breeze members of the crew can squat on the outrigger; but this canoe is tricky to sail before the wind as the outrigger may drop into a wave and cause a capsize. Single outrigger canoes (*see* Fig. 7) are to-day much commoner than the double-outrigger type, probably the older form, which has an outrigger either side of the hull. Double-outriggers are found in Indonesia and on the east coast of Africa.

7. Although mostly regarded as primitive craft, many of the types of canoes described have been developed through the centuries and are elaborately and skilfully built by conservative peoples. Nor is decoration omitted. Carvings and other ornaments are common. The Maoris of New Zealand formerly beautified their canoes with the most elaborately carved figureheads, which are now museum pieces.

8. Portable boats or canoes make handy and cheap pleasure craft, suitable for camping holidays on lakes and rivers or even round the coast. The famous Rob Roy canoe, of kayak shape but built of wood, became immensely popular in England in the 1890's. Between the two wars the 'falbot' collapsible canoe was developed in Germany, and these craft have been paddled long distances, particularly through Central Europe and down the Danube. The falbot has a wooden framework, canvas covered, and can be folded up and packed into a small suitcase.

9. Small boats, which may be classed as canoes, were extensively used during the Second World War. Aircraft were equipped with life-saving boats and rafts made of balloon fabric, which could be automatically blown up quickly by compressed air when required for use. The 'frogmen' (men equipped in rubber suits who attached explosives to the hulls of ships below the water-line) were supplied with canoes very similar to the Eskimo kayak, for use in approaching their objective preparatory to taking to the water and swimming. Commandos and other special units were similarly equipped.

See also PRIMITIVE SHIPS; SAILING.
See also Vol. IX: CANOEING.

CAPTAIN (AIRCRAFT), *see* AIRCREW; (SHIP), *see* SHIP'S COMPANY.

CAR, *see* MOTOR-CAR.

CARAVAN ROUTES, *see* DESERT TRAVEL.

CARAVEL, *see* SAILING SHIPS.

CARGO, *see* MERCHANT SHIPPING.

CARRIAGES. The word carriage has several meanings, all connected with 'carrying' something. It is taken here to mean a four-wheeled, horse-drawn vehicle (for the most part privately owned) used for carrying people. The first four-wheeled carriage we know of was perhaps the most magnificent vehicle built. When Alexander the Great died in 323 B.C., no less than 2 years were spent in building a funeral-carriage to bear his body from Babylon to Alexandria. It was 18 feet long and 12 feet wide. On a platform was set a throne with the coffin before it, and above stretched a lofty roof supported on eighteen pillars. The whole carriage was decorated with gold, jewels, silk, and bells. To draw it, sixty-four mules were yoked eight abreast. Scholars wonder whether the front wheels of this monstrous carriage were designed to pivot when turning a corner. Probably they were not. At any rate, it is almost certain that the four-wheeled wagons of the Romans, even some centuries later, were not made for turning corners. For this reason it seems likely that all their vehicles which had to travel at more than a walking-pace were two-wheeled, even their state-coaches, and the luxurious coaches of the rich.

With the fall of the Roman Empire nearly 1,000 years passed before carriages came into use again at the beginning of the 15th century. They were known as whirlicotes or chariots. They must have been very uncomfortable on the appalling roads of those days, with their complete absence of any form of springing and the lack of glass to keep out the weather. They were considered an effeminate way of travelling for anyone but ladies, but even among them the popularity of coaches had a set-back when Richard II's queen preferred to ride side-saddle rather than be bumped about in a coach —'so was riding in those Whirlicotes and Chariots forsaken except at Coronations and such like Spectacles', says an old chronicler. Also there was a general feeling of shame attached to all such travelling because criminals were taken to their execution on four-wheeled carts.

In 1550 there were still only three carriages in Paris: one was the Queen's and another was used by Royal permission by a nobleman, René de Laval, who was too fat to sit on a horse. Gradually as the wealth of Europe increased, princes and nobles could not resist the opportunity of displaying their magnificence by riding in luxurious carriages. Soon we find the Pope reproving his cardinals for such unmanly extravagance. England, which at the end of the 18th century was to lead the world in coach-building, was still rather behind the times. Both Catherine of Aragon and Anne Boleyn went to their coronations in horse-LITTERS (q.v.); Mary Tudor, however, travelled to hers in a coach drawn by six horses. Queen Elizabeth ordered the building of a state-coach in 1564 (apparently only the second to be built in England), and we can guess that this was something of an improvement on the whirlicote of the Middle Ages when we read that on a progress through Warwick she caused 'every part and side of her coach to be opened that all her subjects present might behold her, which gladly they desired'. But however much extravagance was used in carving and gilding these vehicles, and in covering their panels with pictures painted by the leading artists of Europe, their construction remained very crude. Queen Elizabeth herself complained that after a coach

POST-CHAISE   HIGH PERCH PHAETON

BROUGHAM   STATE LANDAU

BAROUCHE   PARK VICTORIA

WAGONETTE   AMERICAN BUGGY

TYPES OF ENGLISH CARRIAGES OF THE LATE 18TH AND THE 19TH CENTURIES

17TH-CENTURY CARRIAGE
Leather straps are attached to the pillars between the wheels

Bodleian Library

Springs were improved step by step. In 1665 Samuel Pepys tells in his diary how he tried several new coaches. He writes: 'And several we tried, but one did prove mighty easy, . . . and we all one after another rid in it, and it is very fine, and likely to take.' This coach was swung on two big curved springs attached to the bottom of the undercarriage, with the body of the coach held to the springs by strong leather straps. Pepys soon owned his own coach, and in 1669 he describes how he drove after dinner 'through the town with our new liveries of serge, and the horses' manes and tails tied up with red ribbons, and new green reins'.

journey in London she was unable to sit down for several days!

It was not until the 17th century that a French coach-builder first slung the body of the carriage from four straps secured at their upper ends to stout pillars set on the chassis. This construction did something to eliminate the worst jolts; but its disadvantage was that the passenger was liable to undergo a violent swinging motion which tested the strongest stomach. In 1665 steel springs were used for the first time; these did not add greatly to the passengers' comfort, but, they reduced the vibration of the body of the coach, and enabled it to be built more lightly. Also, as a lighter body could be carried on a lighter chassis, less damage was done to the road-surface. At about the same time, with the founding of the Turnpike Trusts in 1663 (*see* Turnpikes), Britain took the first effective step for centuries towards improving her roads. During the next 200 years there was a steady improvement culminating in the great coaching days of the early 19th century, when speeds of almost 20 miles an hour were scheduled over some stages, compared with 4 or 5 miles an hour (or far less in winter) at the beginning of the period. The design of private carriages showed a parallel improvement, and rich people took an even greater pride in their 'turn-outs'. The use of glass in carriage windows is first mentioned in 1650.

But gay as were these 17th-century coaches, they were still heavy, cumbersome vehicles with iron tires. The introduction of solid rubber tires in 1852 marked a great advance. Many kinds of carriages were designed and adopted in the 19th century, such as the victoria, named after the Queen, a low, light, four-wheeled carriage; the brougham, a one-horse, closed carriage called after a prime minister, Lord Brougham; the phaeton, a light, four-wheeled, open carriage drawn by two horses; and the landau of which the roof could either be closed or open. For a first-class finish, eighteen or twenty coats of paint and varnish were required. Such was the English carriage at its heyday, before the motor-car came to take its place.

See also Stage coach; Roads, British; Horse Transport.

CART AND WAGON. These are vehicles used mainly for the transport of goods. A cart is strictly a vehicle with two wheels, and a wagon one with four; but the words are used loosely. It is probable that the first cart was made by the men of the New Stone Age, who appeared in south-eastern Europe some 12,000 years ago, since it was they who were the first farmers, and crops are awkward things to transport without some vehicle to carry them. The earliest vehicle used was, no doubt, a rough Sledge (q.v.), which serves well enough over short turf on a hard soil, and can be found on some farms in Great Britain even to-day. There was a word for 'wheel' in the Aryan language, spoken 7,000 or 8,000 years ago; so we may guess that by then some enterprising farmer had fixed his sledge on a pair of WHEELS (q.v.)—and had found that it was very much easier to pull.

In Britain we know that carts or wagons were in general use in the Bronze Age, about 3,000 years ago, for carrying Cornish tin right across England to ports in Essex, Kent, and the Isle of Wight. But we do not know whether they had two wheels or four. Probably they had only two, because it seems that even the Romans some centuries later, who certainly had four-wheeled wagons, never discovered how to make the front wheels pivot when turning a corner. On the straight Roman roads with their good surface this would not matter so much; but on the unmade trackways of Britain two-wheeled carts would be much easier to handle. No doubt when the Romans occupied Britain and had given it good roads, they introduced the four-wheeled wagon, if it had not already arrived.

The first picture of a cart in Britain is dated about 1100—a two-wheeled farm-cart with wicker sides. When Thomas Beckett went to France in 1168, he travelled with eight carts, each drawn by five horses. These, too, may have been two-wheeled. But when King John lost his baggage in the Wash, we read that it was in carts and wagons; so it seems that by then at latest, four-wheeled vehicles had come into use again. The great stones used in building the cathedrals, too, were carried on wagons drawn by oxen, though they would be taken as near to the site as possible by water. Indeed, with the roads as bad as they then were, either barges or pack-animals were always preferred for the carriage of heavy or bulky goods.

During the 15th and 16th centuries the trade of the country increased very rapidly, the towns grew in size, and each year more and more goods had to be carried from place to place. Light carriers' carts had been plying in some parts from at least the beginning of this period; but by the end of it, regular services of stage-wagons had been started between most of the big towns. These were huge, clumsy vehicles, drawn by eight or ten horses and able to do no more than 10 or 12 miles a day; but they could take a very heavy load, compared with any other land transport then available.

As trade continued to increase, and with it the number and weight of vehicles using the roads, the condition of these grew rapidly worse. Little was known then of how to mend or make roads and little effort was made to gain the knowledge: it was easier to blame the new vehicles and to hamper them, in spite of the country's need for them, than to mend the roads. Wagons were condemned as public nuisances which 'galled the roads'. In 1621 an Act of Parliament forbade the use of any four-wheeled vehicle or the carriage of goods weighing more than 1 ton; in 1629 the use of more than five horses was forbidden, although animals struggling to pull a load too heavy for them actually damage a road far more than would a team of the proper size. In 1751 Parliament, thinking that if wagons were to be fitted with very broad wheels they would do less damage and might roll the roads flat again, decreed that the tires of almost all carts and wagons must be at least 9 inches wide. In 1764 it went further and offered to excuse from all tolls the drivers of wagons with 16-inch tires! But the use of such huge wheels merely made the vehicles much heavier and far harder to draw, so that still more damage was done to the roads.

17TH-CENTURY CART
From an engraving by David Loggan, 1635-1692

A COMMON STAGE WAGON

A heavy wagon with broad wheels which ran a regular service for carrying goods. Early 19th-century woodcut

Dozens of different Acts were passed in the belief that by controlling the design of vehicles in some way or other the roads could be made to mend themselves. They all failed; and in the end they failed to restrict the development of road transport, because this had by then become quite necessary to the country. At last the lesson was learned, for the time being, and it was seen that the proper course was to build roads good enough to stand up to their work. This had a double effect, because as the roads were improved, it became possible to make the vehicles using them far lighter in construction, since they no longer had to stand such jolts and strains; and in their turn the lighter vehicles did less damage to the roads. The introduction of steel springs in the second half of the 18th century also did much to reduce the wear on roads. Then, early in the 19th century came the railways, which for many years took away most of the heavy traffic from the roads and reduced them to comparative unimportance. Now motor vehicles have replaced carts and wagons for practically all road transport, except for farm work (*see* FARM WAGONS AND CARTS, Vol. VI) and a little local haulage.

See also WHEEL; CARRIAGES; ROADS; HORSE TRANSPORT.

CATALOGUING AND INDEXING. 1. In all large LIBRARIES (q.v.) there is a catalogue of the books to help readers in finding what they want. A catalogue is nothing more than a list. The reason it takes such great skill in arranging is that the list is changing every day. Some libraries receive hundreds of new books every week, and a fixed list would never be up to date.

Modern library catalogues usually consist of a cabinet of drawers, each containing a number of cards, in alphabetical order, slotted on to a movable rod which keeps the cards from getting jumbled. One card is used for each separate entry, so that a new card can easily be put in its right place, or a card of a book no longer in the library can be withdrawn.

There are two main kinds of catalogue, an 'authors' catalogue and a 'subject' catalogue. The 'authors' catalogue is easy to use, provided you know an author's name. If you want Carlyle's book about the French Revolution, you turn to Carlyle (Thomas) and you find a list of his books set out; in that list is the title *French Revolution*, and probably the number of the shelf on which you will find the book. But some reader may not know or remember Carlyle's name; he may simply want to read a book about the French Revolution. So he goes to the 'subject' catalogue, and looks up such subjects as 'France' and 'French'. He will come across French Geography, French History, French Literature, and so on, all in alphabetical order. Under French History, again in alphabetical order he will find the entry 'French Revolution'. And there he will find a list of many works on the Revolution, including, of course, *French Revolution* by Carlyle (Thomas). He will then go to the 'authors' catalogue to find the number of the shelf. But the reader in the first place may have turned up, not the word 'France', but the word 'Revolution'. Then he will find Revolution

(American), Revolution (French), Revolution (Mexican), Revolution (Russian), and so on, all in alphabetical order. Under Revolution (French), of course, he will find once more *French Revolution* by Carlyle (Thomas).

In some libraries the 'authors' catalogue and 'subject' catalogue are combined in a single set of cards from A to Z. In most libraries books on one subject are arranged together. For instance, all the travel books will be on one set of shelves, ranged according to the authors' surnames from A to Z. Many public libraries have adopted a standardized system of figures for numbering the separate subjects on their shelves.

The system which is called the Dewey decimal system is based on decimals because decimals enable extra sections to be fitted in as required. For instance, all subjects related to places and their history are allotted the numbers 900 to 999, Europe is 940 to 949, Asia 950, and so on. Each of the countries of Europe has a number somewhere between 940 and 949: England, for instance, is 942. Places within England would have this same number followed by a decimal; London, for instance, is 942·1, and a place within London would have a further number after the decimal point; thus West London is 942·13. In the same way, the Midlands are 942·5, Oxfordshire is 942·57, and Oxford 942·571, and so on. Thus with a little patience one may get quickly to the numbered shelf dealing with any subject.

2. INDEXES. A book index is an alphabetical list of the people, places, and events mentioned in a book, indicating the number of the page on which each mention is made. An index is necessary to almost all books except novels and dictionaries.

Various people who turn to an index to look up a subject may not all think of the same word. For instance, if four people were interested in stamp-collecting, one might look up 'Postage Stamp', another might look up 'Stamps', a third 'Philately', and the fourth 'Collections'. A good index would have three or four of those words, all referring to the same entry.

Sometimes an entry will have a reference beginning 'See' or 'See also', directing the reader to another part of the index. Entries of a very unimportant nature are generally omitted, to save space and the reader's time. If one person or subject is mentioned a great many times, the index will be more useful if a clue is given to the particular topic dealt with on each page, instead of just a long list of page numbers.

In making an index the first stage is to read through the book, writing down every subject, including people and places, with which it deals, and the number of the page on which each appears. In making some indexes a separate small slip of paper is used for each written entry. In other cases entries are written or typed on long sheets of paper, and after careful checking and improving, the sheets are cut with scissors into small slips. In each case the slips are then arranged in alphabetical order. With names of persons the surname comes first, as in telephone directories, except, of course, with Kings and Queens and certain other historical persons.

See also LIBRARIES; REFERENCE BOOKS.

CATAPULTED AIRCRAFT, *see* AIRCRAFT TAKE-OFF.

CATERPILLAR CLUB, *see* PARACHUTE.

CATERPILLAR TRACK, *see* TRACKED VEHICLE.

CELTIC LANGUAGES, *see* IRISH; WELSH; GAELIC.

CENTURION, H.M.S. The tale of the voyage round the world in 1740 of H.M.S. *Centurion*, manned by 507 men and carrying sixty guns, commanded by Commodore Anson, is an epic of heroic endurance. The *Centurion* was one of a powerful British squadron of six men-of-war and two victualling ships which was sent to harass Spanish trade and Pacific outposts— much as Drake had done, but on a larger scale. The *Centurion* on its return home brought about £300,000 in Spanish treasure, and so her trip was hailed as a very successful venture.

But this raiding expedition was an outstanding example of bad staff work and criminal mismanagement. The Admiralty dispatched the ships ill-provisioned and ill-manned. They even sent as marines on active service, and beyond Cape Horn, 500 Chelsea Pensioners; all of them who could walk are said to have deserted before embarkation; the remainder all perished on the voyage. But sickness did not strike down only the Chelsea Pensioners. When the *Centurion* reached the island of Juan Fernandez (off the coast of Chile) hardly more than 200 of the original ship's company were still alive, and those were weakened by scurvy. Meanwhile

National Maritime Museum

MODEL OF H.M.S. CENTURION

This model was made for Lord Anson after his voyage round the world in the *Centurion*

the *Wager*, a store-ship, had been lost by shipwreck, and two men-of-war, the *Severn* and the *Pearl*, had put back. But Anson, in the face of such adversity, still determined courageously to go on; and after meeting many difficulties and being forced to sink the two ships which still remained to him besides the *Centurion*, he intercepted and captured a Spanish treasure ship bound for Manila. The voyage lasted altogether 3 years and 9 months, and added much to men's knowledge of navigation and geography. Anson's *Voyage round the World* was an extremely popular book.

The figurehead of the *Centurion*, which was long treasured by the Pensioners in Greenwich Hospital, is now destroyed; but Lord Anson's own model of the *Centurion* is exhibited at Greenwich in the National Maritime Museum.

CHARTS. A chart is the navigator's map of the sea. MAPS (q.v.) depict the land, charts the water and the sea, lake, and river bottoms covered by water. Coast-lines are shown on both, and are especially important to the users of charts because the danger of shipwreck increases as shallow water and shore are approached. In early times charts showed little more than the coast-lines, because sailors rarely ventured far out of sight of land, and sea depths or soundings, which form so important a feature of modern charts, were rarely shown.

The Mediterranean Sea, although by no means the only sea on which men sailed, was the first to be charted. The oldest aids to navigation which have come down from the past are Greek and Roman descriptions of ports, and these may have been intended for use with charts no longer in existence. The oldest chart that survives is a Portolan Chart, which dates from 1300, and shows considerable skill. These Portolan Charts (the name comes from an Italian word referring to ports) were produced for about three centuries, largely by Italian and other Mediterranean seamen, and later by the Portuguese (*see chart*). They show chiefly the coast-lines of the Mediterranean and Black Seas, and finally extend to the Atlantic coasts of Europe and North Africa. They were drawn by hand in bright colours on parchment. They were not drawn to a very exact scale, but full use was made of the skin or parchment, whatever its size and natural shape. Nor were lines of latitude or longitude shown, for these early charts did not follow any formal MAP PROJECTION (q.v.). The most striking feature, apart from colour, consists of the sets of lines which radiate from and join up numerous points all over the charts like spiders' webs. These lines, known as 'rhumb lines', gave mariners the approximate compass direction from place to place. One central line through each of these points was always orientated to True North, but the others were not necessarily true compass bearings. They were probably as nearly true as it was possible to steer by compass in those days.

Charts were first printed towards the end of the 15th century, and engraved on copper after 1560; this is a process still largely employed in their production. It will be recalled that this was a period of great EXPLORATION (q.v.) by sea, for Columbus first crossed the Atlantic in 1492, and the first ship to sail round the world arrived back in Spain in 1522. A chart of 1529 by Diego Ribero, a Portuguese in the employment of the King of Spain, was the first to show the Pacific and Atlantic Oceans in nearly the shape known now. Until about this time English sailors, though they knew the coasts of Europe quite well, possessed no sea charts except a few drawn by foreigners. Indeed, sailors like Drake and Frobisher later carried globes on their ventures across the oceans. Henry VIII, however, having realized the disadvantages of this lack, had introduced skilled navigators and mathematicians, mainly from northern France, and had manuscript charts made of many English

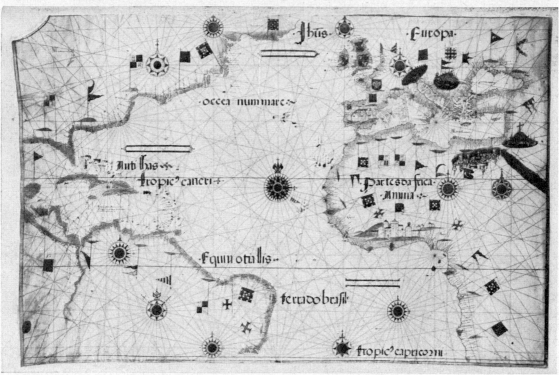

PORTOLAN CHART OF THE ATLANTIC OCEAN, OF ABOUT 1550

harbours, a few of which are still in existence. He also founded the Brethren of the Trinity to help coastal mariners with pilots, beacons, land-marks and buoys (*see* TRINITY HOUSE).

The Dutch, as enterprising sea-traders and men who saw the possibility of making money in the publishing business, produced many charts. The first volume of engraved charts was published in 1583 by the Dutchman, Lucas Waghenaer. Shoals, banks, shingle beaches, soundings, and good anchorages were marked; a silhouette, or outline view, was given of the coast as seen from a few miles out at sea, a feature which is retained on British charts. The work became so well known that English sailors long called any volume of charts a 'Waggoner'. Another Dutchman, known as Mercator, had published a chart for which he had devised a novel kind of projection, enabling ships to determine accurate compass bearings from place to place. Mercator's method has become the standard projection for all charts except those meant for special uses such as entry to ports. By the middle of the 17th century the Dutch were publishing charts under Government authority.

A little over half a century later the French established a central chart office in Paris.

In the 18th century so much material had been collected at the British Admiralty, includ-ing surveys from the voyages of Vancouver, Captain Cook, and others whose names have a permanent place on world maps, that in 1795 the British Hydrographic Department was founded. It was 'to take charge and custody of such plans and charts as then were, or should thereafter be, deposited in the Admiralty, and so select and compile such information as might appear to be requisite for the purpose of im-proving navigation'. From that date systematic surveying, carried out specially to produce charts, became increasingly important. The department was fortunate in having as hydro-graphers brilliant men such as Rear-Admiral Beaufort, who is more widely known by the Beaufort weather scale (*see* WIND, Vol. III). During the following century nearly every other civilized seafaring country founded departments whose whole business was to publish charts and carry out marine surveys; but the pre-eminent position which Britain finally gained has been retained. Most of the world's surveying has been done by the Royal Navy, and British Admiralty charts are used all over the world.

Every sea and coast important to navigation has now been charted, but only a few of the charts are up to the highest modern standards. Changes in sea bed and coasts, owing to erosion or other causes (*see* COASTS, Vol. III), the presence of wrecks, and the deeper draught of large ships make frequent revision necessary. Once it was difficult to establish longitude at all; the construction of an accurate time-keeping CHRONOMETER (q.v.) in the 18th century was a great step forward; and to-day wireless time-signals make the chronometer no longer essential. Sailing ships were more difficult to control when surveying than modern steamships are. Soundings in the deep oceans, which once took hours by wires and weights, now take only seconds by ECHO-SOUNDING (q.v. Vol. VIII). Decca, a method of locating position by means of radio (*see* NAVIGATION, AIR and MARINE), is proving of great assistance in surveying, and the Danish Navy has recently completed a survey of the coast of Greenland using portable Decca transmitting stations, which were set up on shore and moved as necessary. Aeroplanes assist by photographing coasts not already adequately mapped by land surveys.

The British Admiralty employs about half a dozen surveying ships, which are usually frigates

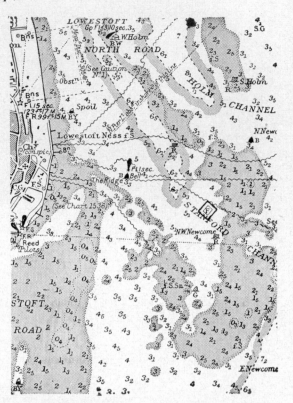

DETAIL OF A MODERN CHART OF LOWESTOFT ROADS

By courtesy of the Controller of H.M.S.O. and the Hydrographer of the Navy

or mine-sweepers converted for this work, but easily revertible in case of war. They are in the charge of the Hydrographer of the Navy, who is usually a Vice-Admiral. Thus charts are constantly revised, and the Hydrography Department of His Majesty's Navy prints over half a million copies every year, varying in scale from those covering a whole ocean to those showing the detailed approach to a single harbour.

See also NAVIGATION, HISTORY OF; NAVIGATION, AIR; NAVIGATION, MARINE; MAPS, HISTORY OF.

CHINESE LANGUAGE. Chinese belongs to a very large family of related languages, called the 'Sino-Tibetan' family. Chinese, Tibetan, Burmese, and Siamese were, in fact, once one language (just as French, Spanish, Italian, &c. were all once Latin (*see* LANGUAGE, HISTORY OF). Very many other far eastern languages, the names of which are not well-known to the general public, also belong to this Sino-Tibetan family. Tibetan, Burmese, and Siamese are each written

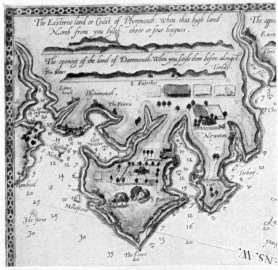

DETAIL OF A CHART OF THE ENGLISH COAST FROM PORTLAND TO PLYMOUTH

From Lucas Waghenaer's *Mariner's Mirrour*. 1588.

in their own special alphabet, but none of these three alphabets are at all like that used for Chinese. Tibetan, especially, has a large literature (mostly dealing with Buddhism) dating from the 7th century A.D. The most important of the Chinese dialects are Northern Chinese, Cantonese, Amoy (also called Hokkien), Hakka, Suchow, and Fuchow. These differ as widely from one another in their spoken form as does Spanish from French. In their written form, however, they are very similar, so that we talk of dialects rather than of languages.

There is now a standard form of Chinese, based on the Northern dialect, spoken in the capital, Peking. In the 17th century, when Manchu invaders established a new dynasty in China, this dialect became the language of their court and was spoken by all higher officials throughout the Chinese Empire. It became known as Kuanhua or official speech; and because Portuguese travellers long ago began to call Chinese officials Mandarins (a form of an old Hindu word), other Europeans took to calling this Kuanhua dialect Mandarin. After the setting up of a republic in China in 1911, in place of the old system of emperors, the new government felt that it was important to have a language that could be understood throughout the whole of China not only by officials but by every citizen; so the Northern dialect as spoken in Peking was chosen as a model. Making this national language of Kuoyü understood throughout China was part of the Government's programme for universal education. This programme, however, was interrupted by war. Nevertheless, Kuoyü is now understood and spoken by all educated Chinese—no mean achievement when one thinks of the great language barriers of Europe.

In the West we write phonetically; that is to say, we write groups of letters which represent sounds (see ALPHABET). Thus in writing and reading, as well as in speaking and listening, we depend on the sound alone to give us the meaning of the word. Not so the Chinese. Instead of representing sounds by means of an alphabet they represent each word by a drawing or 'character'. These characters have now become so shortened, through being written quickly, that it is usually quite impossible to distinguish the original drawing. But as we have examples of Chinese writing on bones and tortoise-shells that date back as far as 1000

B.C., we have been able to reconstruct many of these drawings in their earlier forms (Fig. 1). A character of a woman and a child represents

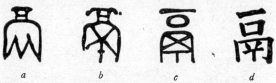

a   b   c   d

FIG. 1. EVOLUTION OF A CHINESE CHARACTER

a, Stone age pictograph of a cooking pot; *b, c*, transition forms; *d*, modern character

'love', that of a man and a child 'protect', and that of a hand over an eye 'to look', that of a woman under a roof 'peace', and that of a pig

Woman	女	child	子	love	好
man	亻	child	子	protect	仔
hand	手	eye	目	look	看
woman	女	roof	宀	peace	安
pig	豕	roof	宀	home	家

FIG. 2. EXAMPLES OF CHINESE CHARACTERS

under a roof 'home' (Fig. 2). Each character is a visual symbol of the word the writer is trying to convey and is only indirectly concerned with the sound of that word. Once a Chinese has learnt that a certain character 象 means 'elephant' he will always understand it when he sees it, even though it may be pronounced *siang* in his dialect and *jioeng* in that of the writer. Characters are usually arranged in vertical columns to be read from top to bottom, the columns being read from right to left.

In ancient Chinese, words contained only one syllable, so that all characters represent only one syllable. In modern Kuoyü, however, most words consist of combinations of two or more characters, each of which contributes to the meaning of the word. Thus *yau* 'to invite' and *ching* 'to ask' make up the modern word *yauching* 'to invite'; similarly *chu* 'to emerge' and *chü* 'to leave' make up the modern word *chuchü* 'to go out'. The single syllable words of ancient Chinese are thought to have consisted of many consonants and complicated double vowel sounds (or diphthongs). In the course of time these complications have been smoothed away, and syllables in the modern Kuoyü language consist of one initial consonant, one vowel or diphthong, and sometimes a final 'n' or 'ng'. It

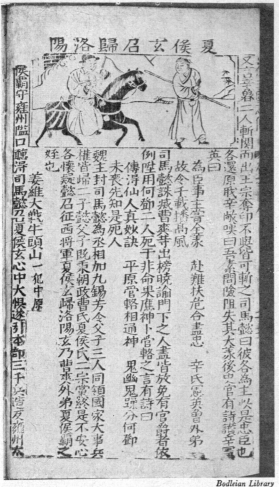

陽洛歸召玄侯夏

Bodleian Library

PAGE FROM A CHINESE HISTORICAL NOVEL, 'THE ROMANCE OF
THE THREE KINGDOMS'

Printed from wood-blocks in the 16th century

Until the beginning of the 20th century the greater part of written Chinese was in a style which imitated that of the Chinese classics, most of which were written before 200 B.C. This written style, which the Chinese call Wenyan, became more and more artificial and far removed from current speech, so that it is now almost a different language. Since, moreover, it could only be understood by scholars familiar with the classics, it appealed to only a very small proportion of the people. In 1917, however, there was a revolution in Chinese literature, and writers began to write much as they spoke; so that now, with a knowledge of some 3,000 characters and a knowledge of modern colloquial Chinese, it is possible to read with ease most of the books published to-day.

Chinese has often been described as the most difficult language in the world. It is true that it is extremely difficult to learn to speak Chinese perfectly, and the learning of characters only increases this difficulty; but since the language has no inflexions, declensions, and conjugations—that is, no special endings to show the function of the words in a sentence (*see* LANGUAGE STRUCTURE), it is one of the easiest things in the world to make oneself understood. If one does make the effort, moreover, one has the satisfaction of speaking one of the two languages which are spoken by more people than any other languages in the world—the other being English.

See also WRITING, HISTORY OF; LANGUAGE STRUCTURE.
See also Vol. I: CHINESE CIVILIZATION.

may have been as a result of the dropping out of initial consonants that there grew up a system of tones or pitches of the voice whereby each syllable may be pronounced in one of several different ways. The tone helps to distinguish several characters which would otherwise be pronounced in exactly the same way. In Kuoyü there are four of these tones; the first is pitched high and even, the second is pitched high and rises sharply, the third is pitched low and falls a little before it rises, and the fourth is pitched high and falls sharply. The syllable *tu*, for example (pronounced rather like English 'two'), means 'bald' in the first tone, 'disciple' in the second, 'earth' in the third, and 'rabbit' in the fourth.

CHRONOMETER is an accurate timepiece used for time-keeping at sea. Accurate time is needed when fixing the position of a ship by observing the stars, and before the advent of wireless time-signals, a ship might go for many weeks without being able to check its time. The chronometer was invented by John Harrison in 1735 (*see* NAVIGATION), and was later improved, and manufactured for the first time on a large scale, by two English makers, John Arnold and Thomas Earnshaw. Harrison's first chronometer was a massive affair: later models resembled more a small clock of to-day, and were mounted with a sprung suspension in a wooden box. By the end of the 18th century Earnshaw's chronometers were very similar in mechanism and appearance to those now in use. Even to-day the chronometer is still a delicate instrument, and must be looked after carefully if it is to remain accurate. Its box is kept in a special compartment as free as possible from vibration and changes of temperature.

Wireless time-signals all over the world have greatly reduced the importance of the chronometer, and nowadays, particularly in aircraft, an accurate wrist watch with a centre second-hand is often used instead. Before the invention of wireless, a ship would carry three chronometers which would be compared daily—three, because then if one were to lose or gain it would be obvious which one it was. This is still done in large ships to-day, so that accurate navigation can be maintained if the wireless breaks down.

See also COMPASS; SEXTANT.
See also Vol. VIII: CLOCKS.

CIVIL AVIATION. 1. AIR ROUTES. Many of the world's long-distance air routes follow the old tracks of sailing ships and land travel, and do not try to cut across the world in a straight line 'as the crow flies'. This is because long-established seaports and other cities, besides providing passengers for air lines, possess hotels, electric power, skilled technicians, food supplies, and facilities for oil storage, which would be difficult to organize in the middle of a desert. For that reason an air route will often go the 'long way round'. The flight from London to Australia, instead of going the shortest way across central Asia, passes through Rome, Cairo, Karachi, Calcutta, Singapore, and Batavia (Jakarta).

Britain, being a small country with well-developed land transport, is less dependent on internal air transport than large countries like U.S.A. British airports, however, form an important link between North America and the continent of Europe. The busiest airport in Europe is on the outskirts of London; at peak periods it handles an aircraft every 2 minutes on one runway alone. There are twelve major airports in Britain licensed to handle regular passenger air-liners, and another fifty on the continent.

The air lines of the world, in 1949, carried 25 million passengers. Day and night, throughout the year, aircraft took off and landed at an average of 720 craft an hour. There were 11,000 flights across the North Atlantic. Of the 70,000 passengers carried on the world's airlines on an average day, 10,000 used European airfields.

Air lines may be State-run or private corporations, but in all countries the air-line routes and the kinds of aircraft they are allowed to fly are under the general control of the government. In Britain this control is in the hands of the Ministry of Civil Aviation. The principal countries belong to the International Civil Aviation Organization (I.C.A.O.), which is linked with the UNITED NATIONS (q.v. Vol. X); by this means governments discuss and agree on international routes. Most countries agree that the aircraft of any country may fly with passengers to and from any other country. But a country will generally not allow its own local town-to-town air routes to be run by an air line of another country. The air lines themselves, through the International Air Transport Association (I.A.T.A.), arrange the issue of international tickets, and the transfer of fares due to one another.

British air lines are controlled by two Government corporations. British European Airways (B.E.A.) flies aircraft between Britain and European airports. The British Overseas Airways Corporation (B.O.A.C.) links Britain with other continents.

B.E.A. is the world's tenth largest air line. In 1949 its aircraft flew 15,145,000 miles, carrying 708,000 passengers, 3,400 tons of mail, and 4,770 tons of freight. Roughly four-fifths of its income comes from passenger fares, the rest being divided between mail and freight. A good proportion of B.E.A. passenger traffic connects London and Paris; more than 7,000 people use this route in each of the summer months.

Apart from the main air lines, many small companies supply aircraft on charter, rather like Tramp Ships (*see* SHIPPING, Vol. VII). They may be hired to carry a passenger on urgent business, but chiefly they carry out-of-season fruit, expensive flowers and other perishable goods, newsreels, medical supplies, urgently needed machinery, or valuable live-stock such as racehorses. One British freight-carrying aircraft has large doors through which a car can be driven straight into the hold; a party of motorists can be flown across the English Channel while sitting in their car.

Many aircraft carrying out flights within a continent are two-engined machines with a total horse-power of 2,200 to 4,400. The longer flights across oceans are mostly made by four-engined craft with a total horse-power ranging between 5,000 and 14,000 (*see* AIR-LINER).

2. SAFETY RULES. Every country makes safety rules, because carelessness in flying, aircraft building, or airport management could cause so many accidents. Since each aircraft which visits any country has to observe the local rules, most of the nations have agreed to certain standardized rules, besides other rules which are only observed by the countries that make them.

Safety standards concern four things: (*a*) the qualifications of the air crew; (*b*) the design, manufacture, and maintenance of aircraft; (*c*) the navigational facilities provided for aircraft, such as radar and weather news; (*d*) the actual method of piloting an aircraft.

In Britain each member of the AIRCREW (q.v.) must hold a licence for his own kind of work, whether pilot, engineer, or radio operator; the licence is given after an examination, which is repeated every year. High qualifications are needed: an Airline Transport Pilot's licence, which entitles the holder to command any transport craft, is granted only if an applicant has flown at least 1,200 hours as pilot-in-command or co-pilot.

Each British aircraft must have a certificate of airworthiness, which is given only if the maker satisfies Government-appointed examiners that special rules for manufacture were obeyed. The certificate must be renewed every year after examination of the aircraft, which must be maintained according to approved methods.

For every kind of flight various navigational aids are laid down, including radio equipment and radar instruments, depending on the facilities available at airports which the aircraft will use (*see* NAVIGATION, AIR).

Rules about the actual use of an aircraft govern its loading, the amount of space on the aerodrome within which it must be able to take off or land, the height by which it must clear obstacles on the ground, the fuel reserves to be carried, and the composition of the aircrew.

All pilots are regularly trained in the use of particular aerodromes; on a single route the pilot may have to know the exact way to land and take off at twenty aerodromes of different pattern. Less severe rules apply to private flying, in which a pilot is not allowed to carry passengers for payment. Interchange of rules is arranged by the International Civil Air Organization, to which fifty-four nations belong, and which has its headquarters in Montreal.

See also AEROPLANE; AIR-LINER; AIRPORT.

CLASSICAL SHIPS. On the banks of the Rivers Nile, Tigris, and Euphrates sprang up the first town civilizations (*see* ANCIENT CIVILIZATIONS, Vol. I). Growing cities in Egypt and Asia Minor, needing to draw imports from ever wider areas, relied on these rivers as highways of trade, government, and war. The monuments and burial treasures of ancient Egypt are rich in representations of notable fleets and in models of smaller vessels. Shipbuilding is also depicted. The Egyptian wooden ship was shallow, broad of beam, overhanging the water at bow and stern, keelless, with A-shaped mast, steered by one or more rudder-oars, and rowed by anything up to fifteen men a side. Simple, oared galleys with sharply up-turned bow and stern appear on the later monuments of Egypt and Mesopotamia. They seem to be typical of the seafaring peoples who dominated the Mediterranean after 1500 B.C. and yielded ultimately to the Greeks. With such ships, probably, people of the island of Crete established their wide maritime empire (*see* MINOANS, Vol. I), and the PHOENICIANS (q.v. Vol. I) of Tyre traded with Spain, founding Cadiz on the Spanish coast and Carthage in Africa, and even sailed as far as Britain.

The Cretans were followed by the GREEKS (q.v. Vol. I), who were a great seafaring people even as early as the 12th century B.C. We know this from the stories of the expedition to Troy, and of Jason's voyage in the ship *Argo* to the farthest limits of the Black Sea (*see* GREEK HEROES, Vol. I). Homer's poetry and a crude drawing of a galley from the late heroic age show the characteristic features of the early Greek war-galley, a high, up-curving stern, and a snout-like bow often painted to resemble the head of an animal (*see* JUNK), behind which the bow-post is stepped into the keel at right-angles (*see* Fig. 1). The method of construction of the bow suggests that the long, narrow, light Greek

Louvre, Paris

FIG. 1. SHIP ON THE 'FRANÇOIS VASE', EARLY 6TH CENTURY B.C.

The ship has been beached stern first

FIG. 2 *a*. TRIACONTER ON A GREEK VASE of about 500 B.C.
The oarsmen's heads can be seen above the gunwale

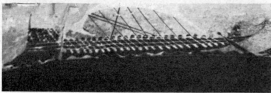

FIG. 2 *b*. PENTECONTER UNDER SAIL AND OAR
Painting on a Greek vase, 6th century B.C.

galley derives from the bark canoe, or from the intermediate type, the dug-out canoe (*see* CANOE). A single rectangular sail, which could be shortened in too strong a wind, hung from a yard-arm slung from a single mast stepped

into the keel. The steersman sat in the high stern and steered with two rudder-oars, one on each side of the ship. Oars were used where sail was unsuitable, particularly when the ship was being brought in to the beach stern first, or was being taken out. At first ships were classified by the number of oars worked, twenty usually in Homer's *Odyssey*, though fifty-oared ships are mentioned. Penteconters (twenty-five oars a side) and triaconters (fifteen oars a side) are the typical war-galleys of early Greece (*see* Fig. 2). For trade the Greeks used what they called 'round' ships (*see* Fig. 3), as opposed to the 'long' warships. These two types remained essentially unchanged throughout classical times, although between the 8th and the 5th centuries B.C. and again in the 4th century B.C. the war-galley adopted new methods of rowing.

The first developments were in the interests of efficiency, to increase oar-power without the counterbalancing increase in weight which mere lengthening of the ship would bring. By an arrangement of oars at two levels the same number of oarsmen could work a ship of half the length (see Fig. 3). The old names, penteconter and triaconter were, at first retained, but when,

FIG. 3. MERCHANT SHIP (LEFT) AND TWO-LEVEL WARSHIP (RIGHT)
Painting on a Greek cup, about 540–500 B.C.

by the invention of a projecting support for the oar, a third level could be added, a new name *trieres* (Latin: *triremis*) was introduced to indicate that the 'room' or longitudinal space allotted to each oarsman in the simple galley now accommodated three men. The classical trireme had a crew of 200 (30 officers and marines, 170 oarsmen), and was about 100 feet long and 20 feet broad. The three men in one 'room' at different levels used oars of the same length, but nevertheless the system must have required a very high degree of skill to work successfully. The citizen crews of Athens, by their mastery of a difficult weapon, won for their city, in the 5th century B.C., an empire and leadership of the civilized world.

The last development of the ancient oared galley was to meet economic needs rather than to increase efficiency. In spite of a shortage of skilled oarsmen, Athens was bent on restoring her naval power which she had lost in her struggle with Sparta. Towards the middle of the 4th century B.C. she built *tetrereis* (Latin: *quadriremes*) and *pentereis* (Latin: *quinqueremes*) by setting two or three men at larger oars probably at two levels. Later, when, after the death of Alexander the Great, the rivalry between the kingdoms of the Eastern Mediterranean was intense, the number of rowers in each 'room' went up to ten, and led to the gigantic penteconters, built in Egypt; in these the enormous oars at three levels must have been worked by sixteen or seventeen men each, half the gang pushing and half pulling, as in some French and Italian galleys of the 15th and 16th centuries A.D.

When the Romans took to the sea to defeat the powerful Phoenician colony of Carthage, they sensibly adopted the quadrireme and quinquereme, types sufficiently light and manoeuvrable, but providing a solid platform for the deck-soldiers on whom they principally relied. At the battle of Actium in 31 B.C. Augustus defeated his rival Antony, who was supported by the fleet of heavy ships of the Egyptian Queen, Cleopatra. This naval fight seemed to prove the value of lighter, more manoeuvrable craft against the heavy ships of Alexander's successors. This battle, in fact, by establishing the Roman imperial power, removed the necessity for battle fleets for three centuries. When, in the 4th century A.D., the Roman power was again disputed in a sea-battle, triremes were the heaviest vessels mustered, and all were on the losing side.

By the end of the century the three-level ships seem to have vanished; the two-level system, however, survived in the Byzantine *dromond*, which was still to be found in the eastern Mediterranean at the time of the Crusades.

See also SAILING SHIPS.

CLIMATE AND COMMUNICATIONS.
The way men travel, like their food, their clothes, and their houses, is affected by CLIMATE (q.v. Vol. III). This is particularly so in parts of the world in which the climate is extremely cold (*see* SNOW AND ICE TRAVEL) or extremely dry (*see* DESERT TRAVEL).

1. ROAD. Rain is the feature of the British climate which has caused most trouble to travellers by road in the past. Before the introduction of MACADAM ROADS (q.v.), and later of tarmac, rain covered the rough tracks with a deep layer of mud, and made travel with any wheeled cart or carriage almost impossible in winter. Even pack-horses were very much hampered. Nowadays much care has to be paid to drainage, so that roads may not remain wet, and likely to cause skids. All rubber tires now have treads of various patterns calculated to reduce the chances of skidding. There is a skid test-track at the Government Road Research Laboratory, at Harmondsworth in Middlesex, where different kinds of tire and road surface are tried out under the most difficult conditions. At the London Transport training-school for bus-drivers, pupils have to drive on a concrete track covered with mud and oil, and learn to control their skids.

Water in motor-car radiators may freeze in very cold weather, causing the radiator pipes to burst when the ice thaws. This can be avoided by adding a liquid preparation of glycerine, which has a lower freezing-point than water.

When there is snow on the ground, tires are fitted with special chains which bite into the snow and prevent slipping. In cities salt is sometimes put down; a mixture of salt and snow has a lower melting-point than ordinary snow, and as the temperature is usually above that lower point, the snow melts. If the fall is a heavy one, snow-ploughs may have to be used. These are of two kinds: a rotary plough, as used in Scotland, consists of a large spinning fan mounted on the front of a heavy lorry to cut a path through the snow; a simpler snow-plough is a vehicle on caterpillar tracks with a low, pointed

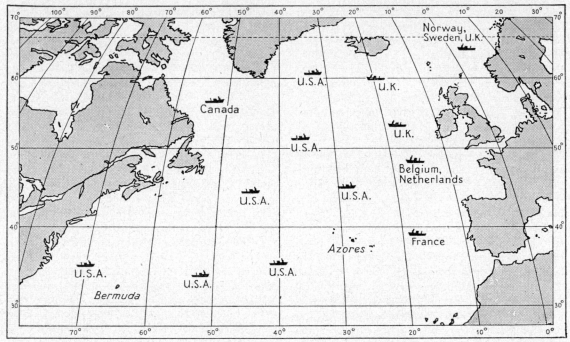

THE POSITION OF WEATHER SHIPS IN THE ATLANTIC IN 1950

front, like a bulldozer, which pushes the snow to each side. Snow-ploughs can be fitted to trams, as they are in Birmingham.

Fog (q.v. Vol. III) can do more than anything else to paralyse road traffic. Since electricity, however, is now used a great deal instead of raw coal, and smoke is reduced in cities, the dense fogs of the 19th and early 20th centuries do not occur so often.

2. RAIL. Two of the worst enemies of railways are fog and snow. Fog, by reducing visibility, deprives engine-drivers of a clear view of their signals. The dangers are considerably reduced by fog-penetrating colour-light signals in place of the old semaphores (*see* SIGNALLING, RAILWAY), and still more by the installation of automatic train-stopping apparatus (*see* AUTOMATIC SIGNALLING). Otherwise fog-signalmen armed with detonators must be stationed at every distant and home signal until the fog clears. In cold climates snow can obstruct by drifting over railway tracks, especially in cuttings, and snow protection, in the form of snow fences and snow sheds, or roofing over a line, is necessary to avoid blockage.

In mountainous areas, such as those of the Alps in Europe or the Rocky Mountains in North America, the serious danger of avalanches,

which may block lines, sweep away overhead electric equipment, and engulf trains, must be guarded against. Where railways cross recognized avalanche tracks (especially lines carried along precipitous mountain slopes, such as the Swiss Lötschberg Railway in the Lonza Valley), they must be covered by avalanche tunnels, with sharply sloping roofs which carry the avalanches harmlessly over the line. Snow-ploughs, as on roads, are used to clear falling or drifting snow on the open stretches. Exceptionally heavy rain, especially in the form of cloud-bursts, is known to wash away track and even bridges. The worst British visitation of this kind occurred in August 1948, when seven bridges on the East Coast main line between Berwick and Dunbar were carried away completely, and the track was damaged or blocked at twenty-seven different points In severe frosts the rods which operate semaphore signal arms are sometimes frozen to their joints, and the moving 'points' of the rails at junctions are frozen up. Frost on the conductor rail of electric railways can prevent the current passing to trains, and may have to be scraped off by special brushes on a pilot locomotive.

3. SEA. Although ships are no longer dependent on the wind, they may be slowed up and even endangered by gales and fog. Until quite recent times, the closing down of a sea fog in busy shipping areas was marked by the ringing of fog-bells and the rattle of anchor cables as ships were hurriedly moored; no vessel dared move until the fog lifted. The development of radar instruments for detecting objects at night or in fog, has made a change. A cargo vessel has been known to leave a Continental port in a fog too thick for even the harbour pier-heads to be seen; the ship has crossed the North Sea, and navigated through lines of fogbound shipping in the Thames to her berth at Tilbury, entirely by the use of her radar apparatus (*see* NAVIGATION, MARINE).

The danger presented by icebergs, often shrouded in fog, was brought home to people in 1912, when the British liner *Titanic*, then the largest and fastest ship in the world, struck an iceberg on her maiden voyage from Southampton to New York, and sank with the loss of more than 1,500 lives. Largely as a result of this disaster, coastguard cutters of the United States maintain by international agreement an ice patrol between March and June of each year. During this period the shipping routes of the North Atlantic are invaded by ICEBERGS (q.v. Vol. III) which break away from the ice of the Polar regions under the influence of spring thaws, and drift southward. Vessels of the ice patrol send out radio warnings of the position of icebergs and, when the bergs are not too large, sometimes destroy them by gunfire or explosive charges.

It is important for the master of a vessel to have warning of a gale, so that he can alter the ship's course and avoid the worst of the bad weather. To help aircraft and ships, weather forecasts are broadcast, based on information received from thirteen special weather-watching ships which are stationed in the Atlantic (*see* WEATHER FORECASTING, Vol. III).

4. AIR. The chief weather hazards of air travel are violent air disturbances which buffet an aircraft during storm; ground fog which impedes taking off, landing, and the recognition of landmarks; and ice forming on the aircraft.

Serious storms are avoided by a change of route, which is one reason why aircraft carry more fuel than they need for their direct journey. Ground fog, if local, can be avoided by diverting aircraft to fog-free airports. If the fog is not too thick, 'blind flying' instruments

will enable aircraft to take off and land; even with their use, a pilot is required to be able to see the ground at a distance of a few feet (*see* FLYING INSTRUMENTS). If thick fog is widespread, flying is stopped.

Ice can be a serious danger. If a thick layer of ice builds up on the leading edge of the aircraft's wing, the shape of the edge, which has been carefully designed to slip smoothly through the air (*see* FLYING), will be altered. The wing may cease to have any lifting power, and the aircraft will then 'stall', and may fall to the ground out of control. A second danger of icing is that its weight will overload the aircraft, and even upset its balance. Ice may form on the edge of the propeller, which will then cease to grip the air, and the aircraft may 'stall'. Ice in the carburettor may retard or even stop the engines. Ice on the windows will blind the pilot. Ice on the wireless aerial will interrupt communications with an airport controller. Ice in the altimeter tube will prevent the pilot knowing the height of his aircraft. Lumps of ice have been known to smash the blades of a gas-turbine engine.

It is not always easy to prevent ice forming. Ice forms where there is moisture in the air, that is, in cold cloud. There may be too much cloud in the sky for the aircraft to 'fly round it'. It may be impossible to climb above it, for the cloud may reach to 20,000 feet. Aircraft are protected from the danger of icing by devices fitted to their structure. Strips of rubber inserted in the front edges of wings and tail-fin can be made to move with a continuous rhythmic movement which breaks up thin fragments of ice before they have time to thicken and become a danger. These edges are also sometimes fitted with porous strips, through which is squeezed a liquid with a very low freezing-point to melt the ice. In some aircraft hot radiator piping is led through the wings and tail. The carburettor and other parts are also warmed. Cockpit windows are kept clear by a spray of an ice-melting fluid, by a stream of warm air, or by electrically heated wires running between the transparent layers of the window panes. Propellers are kept free from ice by an ice-melting fluid which is allowed to flow along the blades. The blades of some propellers are electrically heated.

5. TELECOMMUNICATIONS. Telegraph and telephone communications as well as broadcast programmes, whether conveyed by wire or by means of wireless, are subject to interference both by weather and by electrical disturbances from beyond the region of the earth. Overhead wires for telegraphs and telephones are sometimes broken down by snow and ice. Crackling can be heard in the earpiece of a telephone when flashes of lightning occur in the neighbourhood.

Wireless transmissions are subject to 'atmospherics' which may vary from a series of loud bangs to an almost inaudible hum, known as 'background noise'. Atmospherics are caused by electrical discharges in the atmosphere—in other words, lightning. In the vast tropical areas of the world there are thunderstorms in progress most of the time in one district or another, and these powerful discharges of electricity are 'heard' by wireless sets thousands of miles away. The continual picking-up of these distant discharges (numbering perhaps hundreds in a minute) by a wireless set is a cause of the faint background hum that is often heard. (Another cause can be a fault within the set.) As with the telephone, a storm nearby will cause loud bangs or crackling in the wireless set.

Short-wave wireless is hardly affected by atmospherics, because the natural wave-length of a flash of lightning is 'long'. A short-wave transmission, however, is likely to be affected by distortions and fading if it is received from a long distance. When transmissions from America are being heard in Britain, for example, voices may become distorted and even cease to be heard. This is more liable to occur in the day than at night, and especially during periods of intense sunspot activity (see SUN, Vol. III). An electrically charged layer above the upper atmosphere normally reflects back towards the earth all wireless transmissions, which can then be heard over a wide area (see WIRELESS, HISTORY OF). This layer sometimes becomes erratic, and parts of it cease to reflect wireless waves, which escape through the 'hole' in the layer and are lost in outer space, instead of being received in wireless sets.

See also Vol. III: FOG; ICEBERGS; WEATHER FORECASTING; WIND.

CLIPPER SHIP. The clipper was a very fast sailing ship, rigged as a full-rigged ship: that is, her three—occasionally four—masts were rigged with square sails, apart from the fore-and-aft sails on the foremast and the mizzen. Her lines were slim and yacht-like, with a lovely sheer or curve from bow to stern, which dwindled to a minimum amidships where the mainmast was stepped. Usually her masts were raked slightly aft; in the American clippers this rake was more pronounced than in the British ships, although the fine ships of the Aberdeen White Star Line, owned by George Thompson & Sons, came very close to American fashion in this respect. The tonnage of the clippers varied; on the average the British clippers did not much exceed 1,000 registered tons; but the later American clippers averaged 2,000, and some were as large as 3,000 tons. The designing of the clipper ship was the final attempt to prove the supremacy of sail over steam, and for a time the performance of the clippers brought great glory to their owners and to those who sailed and manned them. The ascendancy of the clipper ship lasted for about 30 years, from the middle of the 1840's to the middle of the 1870's.

The forerunner of the deep-sea clipper was the Baltimore clipper, built on the lower reaches of the River Potomac in the State of Maryland, U.S.A. The Baltimore ships were, however, rather small and not full rigged, for the narrowness of the river limited the size of ship that could be built in the yards on its banks. The first real ocean-going clippers were built on the same design and lines at New York and Boston. One of the earliest built was *Sea Witch*, of 907 tons, launched at New York in 1844. Her design had great influence on the form that fast deep-sea vessels were to take for many years. Shortly after, *Oriental* and *Celestial* were built at New York. *Oriental* ran the distance of over 14,000 nautical miles from New York to Hong Kong in less than 71 days, her average daily run being 200 miles; later, *Celestial* beat by 2 days *Sea Witch*'s record of 97 days for the run from New York to San Francisco. Soon afterwards these new American clippers began to appear in British waters, notably in the Thames and the Mersey, to compete against British ships for the British carrying trade. British owners became not only very concerned at this move, but also much interested in the design and performance of the ships; and shortly after 1850 Mr. Green, owner of the Blackwall Line, laid down Britain's first clipper, appropriately named *Challenger*. Mr. Green's example was soon followed by other owners; two ships were

Parker Gallery

THE RACE OF THE 'ARIEL' AND 'TAEPING' FROM CHINA TO LONDON IN 1866
Coloured lithograph showing the ships in the English Channel

ordered by Jardine, Matheson & Company, the China merchants, for the export tea trade from China; other famous British owners were Devitt & Moore, Money Wigram & Company, George Thompson & Sons of Aberdeen, Scott & Company of Greenock, and Willis of London.

The British ships put up some marvellous performances, though on the whole the Americans did better. Perhaps the most famous of the American builders was Donald McKay of East Boston. In 1851 his *Flying Cloud*, of 1,782 tons, beat the record from New York to San Francisco by a passage of 90 days, her highest run in the 24 hours being 427 nautical miles. In the following year the vessel that was perhaps his masterpiece, *Sovereign of the Seas*, of 2,421 tons, broke all records. On one occasion she logged 1,367 miles in 4 days, an average of over 14 knots. Her best day's run was 436 miles.

In those days steamers were already running regularly across the Atlantic, although they had not yet been used on the long runs round the Cape of Good Hope and Cape Horn. The American clippers did their best to beat steam across the Atlantic, and although they were eventually doomed to fail they put up some marvellous performances. *Dreadnought* ran from New York to Queenstown (Ireland) in 9 days 17 hours, at an average speed of 12 knots. *Ashburton* crossed from New York to Liverpool in 12 days, and *Gleniffer* made a passage from Quebec to Greenock in 15 days. The *Great Republic* of 3,400 tons ran from New York to Scilly in 13 days, and was only prevented from making a record passage to the Downs (off the South Foreland) by a strong easterly gale and a slow 3 days' beat up-Channel.

The opening up of California and Australia during the years that followed the gold discoveries of 1848 and 1849 gave the clipper captains a wonderful chance of showing what their ships could do. There was then no railway from the east of the United States to the far west, and miners and prospectors had to choose between 6 months of trekking across country or 3 months at sea on the long passage round the

Horn. Every day saved on the sea passage might make a great difference to those seeking their fortunes at the gold-fields; and the American clipper captains and crews were attracted to the California run by the often fantastically high rates of passage offered. Details of these Californian voyages are scanty; in any case the conditions did not make for record-breaking, as the outward voyage involved beating round the Horn against the prevailing westerly gales, and the ships had to encounter both ways a persistent belt of calms north and south of the Equator. But during the Australian gold-rush, and in the years following, when the wool trade was being developed, conditions were favourable for really fast passages, as both outward and homeward voyages were made in an easterly direction in order to use to the full the prevailing westerly winds. Racing developed between the British and American clippers, and records were established only to be immediately eclipsed. *Blackwall*, one of Green's ships, ran from Melbourne to the Downs in 1867 in 100 days. This performance was soon beaten by Money Wigram's *Sussex*, which ran from Melbourne to Plymouth in 85 days. These records were progressively beaten by the American-built clippers *Marco Polo*, which took 75 days for a run from Melbourne to Liverpool, and *Red Jacket*, on the same voyage but outward bound, in 69 days. The famous American clipper, *Lightning*, perhaps one of the most beautiful ships that ever sailed the seas, ran from Liverpool to Melbourne in 63 days, and did her return voyage in 64 days. The record on the Australian run was, however, probably achieved by the Aberdeen White Star clipper *Thermopylae*, a ship of just under 1,000 tons, which on her first voyage, from London to Melbourne, accomplished the run in 60 days exactly.

British and American clippers also competed with each other in carrying the first of the China tea crop from Shanghai to London, the race being won by the ship that could run from Shanghai to the Thames in the shortest possible time. In this race the British ships by 1870 had proved themselves altogether faster than the American. The most spectacular race was that of 1866, between *Ariel* and *Taeping*, both Scottish-built at Greenock. In that year's race *Ariel*, *Taeping*, and *Serica* left Foo-choo-foo together. At sunset on the first day out they parted company, and did not meet again until they were off the mouth of the English Channel. *Ariel* and *Taeping* ran up-Channel in company, but in coming up the Thames *Ariel* drew ahead of *Taeping* and was first to arrive off Blackwall. Unfortunately she was too late to enter the West India Docks that day, and she had to drop anchor and wait for the next tide; meanwhile *Taeping* passed her and managed to enter the locks of London Docks on that tide, and thus claimed the prize as having been the first ship to berth. In the following year there was only a difference of 5 hours between the times of *Ariel*, which was judged the winner, and of *Taeping*. Perhaps the most famous ship on the China run, and certainly the best known to most Englishmen, was CUTTY SARK (q.v.), owned by Messrs. Willis of London. She was, however, rather unlucky in the China tea races; but was more successful on the Australian run, making eight successive voyages between London and Sydney in an average of 75 days.

The opening of the Suez Canal in 1869 reduced the time taken on steamer voyages to the East, and thus allowed cargo-steamers to compete financially with the clippers so successfully that in a few more years clippers no longer sailed on the China run. For many years they sailed regularly on the Australian run, but even here they were eventually beaten by steam, and by 1890 their days were fully over.

The clippers marked a glorious stage in the history of the sea. They were lovely and graceful to look at, the tall tapering masts of the largest of them reaching a height of just under 200 feet. They were exacting ships for their crews to manage, for they were built for speed, and every change in the force of the wind meant that all hands had to turn out to make or shorten sail. For a clipper crew there was no ambling along for days on end with moderate canvas set. The clippers were handled by some of the finest shipmasters the sea has ever bred, who knew to a minute how long they dare carry on with their existing spread of sails in the face of rising wind and weather, and who never shortened sail or slacked a sheet or a brace until absolutely necessary. There is a legend of an American captain who, with all sails set as the wind began to rise to a gale, stood on the poop with a revolver in each hand and threatened to shoot the first member of his crew who should lay a hand on the braces.

See also SAILING SHIPS.

COACH, see Carriages; Stage Coach; Motor Coach; Railway Coaches.

COACH STATION, see Bus and Coach Stations.

COAST-GUARDS, see Lifeboat. *See also* Smugglers, Vol. X.

COAT OF ARMS, see Heraldry.

COCKNEY, see Slang.

CODES AND CIPHERS. Since early times men have found it necessary to write things down in such a way that they could be read only by the person for whom they were intended. From this need has developed the use of codes, ciphers, and cryptography, the terms commonly used for secret writing.

There are many examples in history of the use of cipher. Julius Caesar frequently coded his documents by the simple device of moving each letter in the message three places forward in the Roman alphabet. Cicero, the Roman statesman, used a kind of secret Shorthand (q.v.) more than 2,000 years ago. King Louis XIV of France used to issue to people of importance what we should now call identity cards. These cards carried signs and symbols which conveyed secret information about the holders, intelligible only to the King's officers.

A plot made by Anthony Babington and others to kill Queen Elizabeth in 1586, and to place on the throne the imprisoned Mary Queen of Scots, was discovered largely by the unravelling of ciphered messages which passed between the conspirators and Queen Mary; this discovery played a great part in the decision to execute her. When Samuel Pepys (q.v. Vol. V) wrote his famous secret Diary, discussing the intimate personal lives of notable people in 17th-century London, he used a kind of shorthand of which no one else had the key. More than 150 years later, a patient student named John Smith succeeded in deciphering the secret writing, and in reading the 3,000 pages of Pepys's private note-books.

In the modern world all important government telegrams are sent in some sort of code or cipher, of which the key—the secret of how to decipher the message—is carefully guarded. Also much of the cabling between business houses is done in code. This is often as much for economy as for secrecy, for certain codes use fewer letters of the alphabet than ordinary writing.

Some systems are very simple. It is said that a man once went into a shop, sniffed, and said, 'What a smell of gunpowder!' The shopkeeper was visibly upset for he was using the nine letters of the word 'Gunpowder' to mark his prices, G standing for 1, U for 2, N for 3, &c., to which he added the letter X for 0. By his remark the visitor let the shopkeeper know that his code was known.

This code is an example of the simplest and most obvious kind of cipher, a simple substitution. In such a code, which substitutes letters for figures, obviously only ten letters of the alphabet will appear, as there are only ten figures which they can represent—the figures 0 to 9. In consequence this type of code is easily recognizable.

There are also letter-for-letter substitutions which use the entire alphabet. A keyword or phrase is agreed upon—say 'Zoological Gardens'. Each letter is used only once, so this becomes 'Zolgicardens'. The letters of the alphabet which have not appeared in the keyword now follow, and under these twenty-six letters we write the alphabet in its customary order. Thus we have:

```
Z O L G I C A R D E N S B F H J K
A B C D E F G H I J K L M N O P Q

M P Q T U V W X Y
R S T U V W X Y Z
```

Any message can now be coded by reading each letter in turn from the bottom line and replacing it by the letter above. 'Meet me at the station 2 pm' in code is 'biiq bi zq qri pqzqdhf 2jb'. The man with the key phrase (Zoological Gardens) can easily read the coded message. But with patience and ordinary skill it can be read even without the key. How does one tackle it?

If we study several long passages of prose containing say, 10,000 letters each, and count the number of times each letter in the alphabet occurs, we shall find that the proportions of the various letters are very much the same for each passage. A table, called a 'frequency table', gives the order of frequency of the letters of the alphabet in ordinary English writing. Such

CIPHER LETTER FROM CHARLES I TO THE DUKE OF ORMOND

Written in a numerical cipher during the siege of Oxford, 1642. The decoding is in the handwriting of the period

tables are of immense importance in solving cryptograms. The order of frequency for English is as follows:

E T O A N I R S H D L U C M P
F Y W G B V K J X Z Q

The first step in solving a cryptogram is to make a count of the letters used. If the distribution is very uneven, some letters being common and others quite rare, we are probably dealing with a cryptogram of this kind. If the message is short, the solution may be very difficult or even impossible; if it is long, success should be certain. In English the common letter E is often followed by R or by S. Books on cryptography give all sorts of information of this sort. The final answer is obtained by trial and error, the solver being guided at every stage by the frequencies of the letters, and the fact that the letters obtained must read sensibly.

Each language has its own frequency table. In Spanish A is almost as common as E. In German Z is much more common than it is in English, and so is the letter W in Dutch. One

more point should be noted. Any 26 symbols can be used instead of letters. If odd-looking symbols are found (such as those in 'The Dancing Men', in Conan Doyle's *Return of Sherlock Holmes*), the final cryptogram may appear very mysterious, but the solution is not necessarily any more difficult. The 26 symbols are listed and counted, and the process is then just as before.

Sometimes the coded message is broken into groups of the same number of letters as the words in the original message. This is a tremendous help to the solver. He would begin by finding the letter or symbol representing E, and then make a study of the two-letter words. Common two-letter words ending in E are BE, HE, and ME. A common two-letter word ending in O is TO. More often, however, the message is divided into five-letter groups, regardless of the number of letters in the words of the message. This makes the solution more difficult.

Another type of message is that described in Jules Verne's well-known story *The Cryptogram*. The author is quite wrong in saying such a cryptogram cannot be solved. It is not even very difficult. The coding is done in this way. A key number is agreed upon. We will take as an example 1473265. Suppose we wish to code the phrase: 'Come at once; there is danger afoot'. The message is written out with a figure of the key under each letter in order, the key being continually repeated. We get:

C O M E A T O N C E T H E R E I S
1 4 7 3 2 6 5 1 4 7 3 2 6 5 1 4 7

D A N G E R A F O O T
3 2 6 5 1 4 7 3 2 6 5

Each letter is now moved on as many places in the alphabet as is decided by the figure beneath it. For instance, the first letter, C, is moved

one on to D; the second letter, O, is moved four on to S; and so on, until we have:

D S T H C Z T O G L W J K W F M Z G C
T L F V H I Q U Y

It will be noticed at once that two letters which are the same in the text need not be the same after coding. For example, the first C becomes D, but the second becomes G. So a count of the letters in the coded text will not help much.

The solution must be effected in two stages. First we must discover how many figures there are in the key. Notice that the clear text contains the sequence ER twice, once represented by KW and once by FV. But if these two ER's had happened to be above the same two figures of the key, they would clearly have given two identical pairs after coding. In the latter case, since we have a seven-figure key, it should be clear that the distance apart of these two ER's would have had to have been a multiple of seven.

So we must examine the coded text for repeated sequences. If a long sequence, say five letters, can be found repeated, it is almost certain that a sequence occurred twice in the clear text, and that the distance apart of the two occurrences is a multiple of the number of figures in the key. Once the length of the key is determined, the solution is easy to a patient and experienced person.

To return to our example, the cryptogram is written out in rows of seven letters arranged underneath each other (since there are seven figures in the key), thus:

D S T H C Z T
O G L W J K W
F M Z G C T L
F V H I Q U Y

It is now clear that the letters down any one column are obtained by the same figure of the key, as already explained. The next step is to find the key-figure for each column. For a long message this is easier to detect. Even in the very short example we have taken, the repeated letter F in the first column stands for E, which would naturally be our first guess. This means a slide forward of 1, and 1 is, in fact, the first figure of the key.

Each of the seven columns is examined in turn. When some of the key-figures have been

THE SANATORIUM,
KIMBERLEY.

Nov 18/99.

Dear Sir

Please give all offer we trorope omnipotent molars outer world since seventh Octennal

(.) Rhodes

Memnyie trustworthy Dictionary code

Bodleian Library

CODE LETTER FROM CECIL RHODES WRITTEN FROM KIMBERLEY WHEN IT WAS BESIEGED DURING THE SOUTH AFRICAN WAR
'Please give all news we have (had) no messages from the outer world since seventh November'

correctly guessed, the others follow easily, since the known letters will suggest words, and these again will suggest the missing key-figures.

One well-known cipher is the 'Playfair Cipher'. In this a diagram like a chess-board, but with only twenty-five squares, is used. A letter of the alphabet is written in each square, I and J being treated as one. The order is determined by a keyword—we will again take 'Zoological Gardens' as below:

```
Z O L G I J
C A R D E
N S B F H
K M P Q T
U V W X Y
```

To code the phrase 'At once', we divide it into pairs of letters; thus, AT-ON-CE. Find A and T in the diagram. They are at two corners of the rectangle, AETM. Replace them by EM, the two letters at the other corners of this rectangle. Similarly ON becomes ZS. C and E are on the same horizontal row. Replace C by A, the letter on its right. In order to replace E by the letter on its right, we go back to the beginning of the row and replace it by C. So 'at once' becomes, when coded, EMZSAC. In the case of a pair of letters in the same vertical column, each letter is replaced by the one immediately below it. Doubles (the same letter twice) are split up before coding by inserting a dummy letter, for instance a Q or an X, so that TT might be written TQT. Such dummy letters are easily recognizable by the decoder and are ignored by him. Thus the coded text when divided into pairs contains no doubles, and this helps to identify the Playfair Cipher. Solution without the key is difficult.

There is a large class of ciphers known as 'transposition ciphers'. Such ciphers keep the original letters of the message, but they are shuffled into some apparently haphazard order.

Most government telegrams are sent by means of specially prepared code-books consisting of words and phrases each carrying a four- or five-figure number. There is usually no relationship between the meanings and the numbers. 2016 might mean 'Liverpool', 2017 'Why did you?', 2018 a comma, and so on. There are separate volumes for coding and decoding, the former arranged alphabetically, the latter numerically. Such code-books are kept under conditions of strictest secrecy. Even so, more important messages are not sent straight from the book; but the book numbers are frequently further disguised for additional security.

COMPASS. This is an instrument which, wherever it may be, indicates the direction of a line running north and south through its position. A steady course can therefore be maintained by a ship, an aircraft, or by travellers on land. There are two main types of compass, the magnetic compass and the gyroscopic compass. The magnetic compass is based on the movement of a small magnetized steel pointer called the 'needle'. This swings freely on a central pivot on which it is balanced. We do not know who first used it. It is said that the Chinese Emperor Hwang-ti, about 2634 B.C., had an instrument on his chariot for indicating the south. It is probable that the Arabs learnt of the compass from the Chinese, and introduced it into Europe. It is mentioned in a 12th-century book about instruments, and had been in use by Europeans for over two centuries before Columbus's voyages (*see* NAVIGATION, HISTORY OF).

The compass needle points north and south because it is acted on by the MAGNETISM (q.v. Vol. III) of the earth. The earth itself acts very much as though it were a magnet with ends at the North and South Poles, and any magnet which is free to rotate will turn itself until it points north and south, if it is not affected by local magnetic conditions. Actually the magnet will not point towards the True North, but towards a point some distance away, known as the Magnetic North (*see* NAVIGATION, MARINE). This introduces an error into the compass reading which is usually described as 'variation', and for which allowance must be made in navigating. Another error is caused by the effect on the compass of the steel of the ship, aircraft, or motor-car in which it is fitted. This is known as 'deviation'. It is reduced as far as possible by fitting compensating magnets and pieces of iron in the binnacle (the compass stand); but allowance for deviation must also be made in navigation.

Once the position of the north has been indicated by the compass, a navigator, whether on land or sea or in the air, will want to measure the angle between the north and whatever course he intends to follow. That course—or in

Museum of the History of Science, Oxford

17TH-CENTURY COMPASS
The face is marked o at N. and S. and 90° at E. and W.

and quarter points are also indicated on most compass-cards.

In very small and simple kinds of compass, as used by walkers, the compass-card is fixed, and the magnetic needle swings round above it. In all aircraft and ship's compasses, however, and on the larger hand-compasses used for walking, the compass-card is laid on top of the swinging needle and attached to it, so that the whole card swings round. On larger compasses, in order to increase the magnetic effect, several strips of magnetized steel are fitted under the swinging compass-card, in place of the single needle.

A compass must be sensitive, but not affected by such motions as the rolling of a ship, and should be quick to settle down after a change in direction. In a modern ship's magnetic compass the compass-card not only rotates on a pivot, but its weight is so arranged that it nearly floats on a quantity of alcohol with which the compass bowl is filled. This liquid lessens the weight on the pivot, making the compass more sensitive, and also prevents it from swinging about too much. The casing of a compass in a ship or aeroplane swings on gimbals, an arrangement of pivots which enables a compass to remain face upward in spite of the rocking of ship or aircraft.

Walkers, mountain-climbers, and soldiers often use a prismatic compass, a hand compass with a small sighting device. The user of the compass looks through this device at some distant object, such as a church spire or mountain peak, and he then sees reflected in a prismatic mirror an engraved number on the edge of the compass-card, which tells him the exact bearing of the church or mountain peak.

The gyroscopic compass (or gyro-compass) depends for its action on the rotation of the earth. A GYROSCOPE (q.v. Vol. VIII) is a heavy wheel which is made to spin on its own axis by means of electric motors; this wheel is in a casing which is suspended on very delicate bearings and which will turn in any direction.

fact any direction which is worked out with the help of a compass—is known as a 'bearing'. Bearings nowadays are expressed in degrees in the same way that the width of an angle is expressed in degrees in ordinary geometry. There are 360 degrees to a full circle; north is o or 360 degrees; east is 90 degrees; south is 180 degrees. On the magnetic compasses usually carried in ships north and south are marked o° and east and west 90°. The degrees are printed or engraved round the edge of a circular compass-card. Also on the card are the older markings which are traditional with sailors; these show N, S, E, W, for north, south, east, and west (sometimes the 'N' is replaced by a decorative pointer); then, in between those letters come NE, SE, SW, and NW. Between these again come further subdivisions, such as NNE, ENE, and so on. There are in all thirty-two of these marks, known as 'points', on the old sea-going compass, so that a 'point' of the compass, often used in giving directions to a helmsman, equals $11\frac{1}{4}$ degrees. Half points

Any heavy wheel which is spinning fast in this way, if it is moved round some other axis as well, will try to turn itself until its axis of spin coincides with this other axis. In the case of the gyro-compass, the rotation of the earth turns the gyroscope (which is spinning fast all the time) round slowly once a day, along with the rest of the ship. If the gyroscope wheel is very carefully balanced and mounted, this movement of the earth is sufficient to make the gyroscope turn until its axis or spindle points north and south.

As the gyro-compass indicates True North, and so needs no corrections for variation and deviation, it is being increasingly used in place of the magnetic compass in ships. The actual gyroscope is installed in a special compartment low down in the ship; it controls a number of compass repeaters (compass dials driven by electric motors)

Library of Congress

MAIN READING-ROOM, LIBRARY OF CONGRESS, WASHINGTON

in the wheel-house from which the ship is steered, on the bridge, and anywhere else where one may be wanted. A ship normally carries at least two magnetic compasses, and these are retained as emergency instruments even though a gyro-compass is fitted. One is mounted in the wheel-house for the helmsman, and another, known as the standard compass, is mounted on top of the bridge as far as possible from anything which would cause deviation, and is used for taking bearings (*see* NAVIGATION, MARINE) and to check the compass in the wheel-house.

See also CHRONOMETER; SEXTANT.

CONGRESS LIBRARY, U.S.A. This is the official library of the United States President, Senate, and House of Representatives. Its vast building near the Capitol in Washington contains more than 8,300,000 books. Together with periodicals, maps, manuscripts, films, music scores, gramophone records, and photographs, its total collections number over 25,000,000 items. The library exchanges books with the national libraries of other countries.

Large staffs carry out research for the President, members of Congress, judges, military and naval departments, and also for members of the public, who are allowed to carry out private studies there.

The basis of the library was a collection of 6,500 books belonging to Thomas Jefferson, one of the early Presidents of the United States and the man who drew up the Declaration of Independence. His books were bought by Congress to form a national library after British troops occupying Washington in 1814 had burned down the Capitol building in which Congress held its meetings, and in which it had kept a small collection of books. In 1865 a law was passed requiring anyone publishing any copyright work in the United States to present a copy of it to the Library of Congress.

See also LIBRARIES.

COPYRIGHT is the exclusive right of reproducing an original work or composition, or of translating it into another language, or printing extracts from it. It applies to any piece of writing (novel, play, poem, or even a letter), to anything drawn (picture, diagram, or map), to musical compositions, and to photographs. In Great Britain the law about copyright is based on the theory that the author of a work should have first claim on any money earned by the reproduction or sale of his book. But copyright does not go on for ever. There is a time limit. Under the British Copyright Act of 1911, which is the latest law about it in Britain, copyright in published works normally lasts for 50 years after the death of the author, or in the case of photographs, after the making of the negative. When the time limit has expired, the work is said to be 'out of copyright'. While his copyright lasts, an author may sell it if he wishes to, or he may retain it while licensing a publisher to reproduce his work; and if anyone infringes, or 'pirates', his copyright, he may take him to law and get damages from him, as well as restraining him from publishing the work.

Each nation has its own copyright laws, but most European countries agreed in 1886 on a common international code known as the Berne Convention (revised 1908). The principal nations not conforming to the Berne Convention are the United States and the Soviet Union.

Under various Copyright Acts certain national libraries are entitled to a free copy of every work published in Great Britain.

CORACLE, see PRIMITIVE SHIPS; CANOE.

CORNISH RIVIERA LIMITED. This train runs between London and Penzance, with through coaches for other coastal resorts. It is the best known of all express trains on the late Great Western Railway, now Western Region. When first instituted in 1904, it held the world record for a non-stop run with its daily journey without a stop of the $245\frac{3}{4}$ miles between Paddington and Plymouth *via* Bristol. In 1906, however, with the opening of the Westbury route, the distance was shortened to $225\frac{3}{4}$ miles. This still remained for many years the longest British non-stop run, though later both L.N.E.R. and the L.M.S.R. had longer non-stop runs.

An interesting feature in the working of the 'Cornish Riviera Limited' in earlier years was that it detached at speed three slip portions in succession, at Westbury, Taunton, and Exeter, before the first stop was reached at Plymouth (*see* RAILWAY COACHES, Section 7).

COUNTING, HISTORY OF. 1. It is possible to count without having names for numbers. Early men conveyed numbers to one another by making a dumb show of counting on their fingers, and some primitive tribes still do so to-day. The ANDAMANS (q.v. Vol. I), a race of Oceanic islanders, only have names for 'one' and 'two'. But they can count up to ten by tapping their noses with their fingers, starting with the little finger of one hand, going through that hand and then starting on the other hand. At the first finger-tap they say 'one'; at the second 'two'; and for each tap after that they simply say 'and this'. By watching what finger the process stops at, the person who is receiving the information knows what number is meant.

Among peoples who have reached a more advanced stage the numbers have names, but the names are derived directly from finger counting. For 'six' a Zulu says 'taking the thumb'—meaning that you are to imagine he has counted all the fingers of one hand and has started on the thumb of the other. For 'seven' he says 'he pointed', meaning that he has reached the index finger, which is used in pointing.

Names referring to fingers have disappeared from our present number system. But we still have one important legacy from early finger counting. We count in the scale of ten, so that, for instance, 67 means 6 times *ten* added to 7. The number 'ten' is no better than any other for this purpose, but primitive people, even in our own time, think of numbers in terms of fingers, and group them in terms of the ten fingers that human beings happen to possess.

As men began to move from tribal barbarism to the first civilizations, some 5,000 to 6,000 years ago, they found a growing need to write numbers in order to keep records. Written numbers were needed by merchants for their trading accounts, by kings for regulating taxation, by priests for keeping track of temple property; and the growth of sciences such as astronomy demanded a good system for keeping records of numbers over long periods. The writing of numbers seems to have come before the writing of words—which would be expected, because numbers are more difficult to remember than names.

The earliest way of writing numbers was by repeated strokes: / for 1, // for 2, /// for 3, &c. Such a system grows very cumbersome for

THE 'VAUXHALL' OR 'NASSAU' BALLOON OVER THE MEDWAY IN 1837
Coloured engraving of the balloon which made a record flight from Vauxhall Gardens to Nassau,
Germany, in 1836. It was 157 ft. in circumference and, with car attached, 80 ft. high

numbers above 10 or 20, and so the peoples of the earliest civilizations adopted new signs for 10 and 100 and other large numbers. An example is the ancient Egyptian system shown in Fig. 1. There, the number 1,342 is written by writing the sign for 1,000 once, then the sign for 100 three times, then the sign for 10 four times, and that for unity twice. This was a great advance over writing 1,342 strokes.

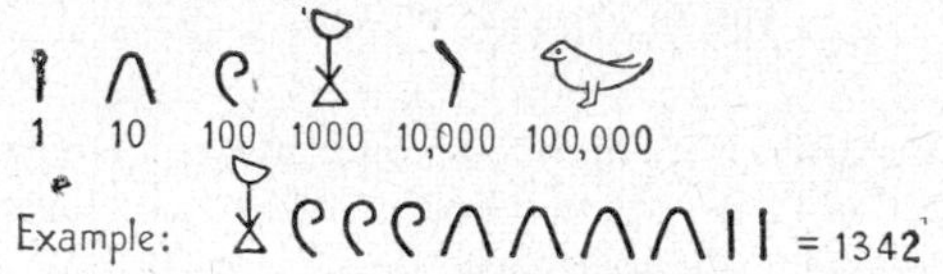

FIG. 1. EGYPTIAN NUMBERS

2. PLACE NOTATION. In the valleys of Mesopotamia, where the SUMERIANS and later the BABYLONIANS (qq.v. Vol. I) developed the other great early civilization, a similar system was used at first. But soon a more powerful one was developed (see Fig. 2). Like the Egyptians, the people of Babylon used separate signs for 'one' and 'ten', and made use of repetition to express numbers like 42 (four signs for 'ten' and two

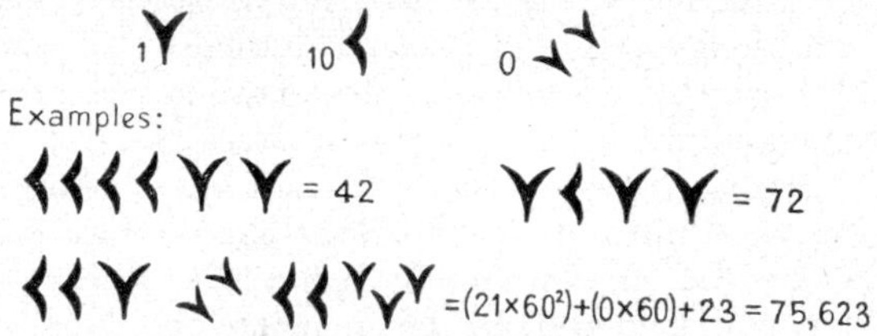

FIG. 2. BABYLONIAN NUMBERS

signs for 'one'). This method was used for numbers up to 59, but after that they used a system very like our own. We use the same sign '2' for two, twenty, two hundred, and so on, distinguishing these from one another only by the position of the figure '2' in the number. In 23, the '2' means twenty, in 264 it means two hundred, and so on. This is called a place notation or a positional notation. The Babylonians also had a place notation, but they used a scale of sixty instead of our scale of ten. Thus, to indicate 'sixty' they wrote the same sign as for 'one', and used its position to make clear that 'sixty' was meant. The picture shows how 72 was written. On the right is the sign for 'one' written twice to indicate 2; next to it comes the sign for 'ten', so that these two make 12. Then

farther to the left comes the sign for 'one' again; but as it is to the left of the other signs it means 60, so that the whole number is 60 added to 12 making 72. A system using the scale of sixty in this way is called a sexagesimal system.

3. INVENTION OF ZERO. For a long time this system was marred by the fact that the Babylonians had no sign for zero. It was as if we did not have the figure 0, and so could not be sure whether 2 3 was really 23, or 203, or 2,003. The invention of a sign for zero is often regarded as the greatest single step in mathematical history. The Babylonians invented it some time after 1000 B.C. Fig. 2 shows how it was used. The separate groups there would mean 21, 0, and 23 respectively. In view of the positional notation, the whole number means 21 times 60 times 60, added to nought times 60, added to 23. That makes 75,623.

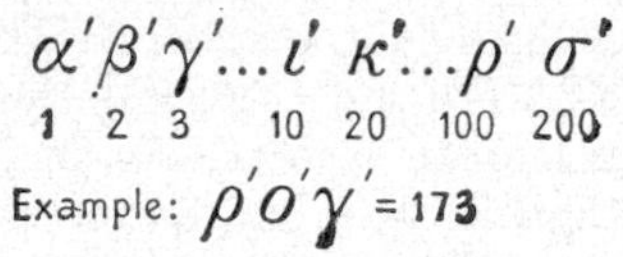

FIG. 3. GREEK NUMBERS

The Babylonians also learned to use their sexagesimal system for fractions on the same lines as our decimal fractions. A watered-down version of these fractions, having few of their advantages and most of their disadvantages, has come down to us through the Greeks as the minutes and seconds which we use to divide hours of time and degrees of angle (see NAVIGATION, HISTORY OF).

The Greeks, despite their wonderful culture which gave much to the world, took a backward step in arithmetic. At an early stage they had a system rather like that of the Egyptians. But later, under the influence of the Phoenicians, they changed to the inferior system which is illustrated in Fig. 3. They used nine different letters of the alphabet for the numbers 1 to 9; nine further different letters for 10 to 90, and so on. Such a system allows one to write numbers very neatly, but it makes calculation very difficult. In practice calculation always required the aid of an abacus, an instrument of beads strung on wire (see COUNTING INSTRUMENTS). This backward step seems to have been connected with the rise of slavery on a large scale. The earlier civilizations had used slaves, but usually only as domestic servants, whereas the Greeks used them on a large scale for all types of industry and commerce. Arithmetic came to be regarded as a task fit only for slaves and unworthy of gentlemen. For that reason the Greeks did not seek to devise a workable system of counting.

The Romans took another step backward. Their system is based, though in a different way,

I	V	X	L	C	D	M
1	5	10	50	100	500	1000

Example: MMCMLIX = 2959

FIG. 4. ROMAN NUMBERS
A lesser figure before a greater is substracted from it:
CM = 900, IX = 9

on the letters of their alphabet (*see* Fig. 4). 'M' stands for the Latin word *mille* ('thousand'), and 'C' for *centum* ('hundred'). If one tries to multiply on paper the number MMCMLIX by MDCCCXLVI ($2,959 \times 1,846$) one will find how useless the Roman system was for calculation. A Roman had to carry out the act of multiplication by repeated additions. Yet the system was used in Europe throughout the Middle Ages, and in some cases till very near modern times.

4. SCALE OF TEN. Our own system is like the Babylonian in that it uses zero, and is based on the written position of figures in their relation to one another. We happen to use the number 'ten' as the number indicated by zero, and therefore as the number which causes changes of position. Thus our system is a decimal system (from the Latin *decimus*, meaning 'tenth'). The scale of ten, as already stated, is no better than another. There is no special mathematical reason for the quantity 'ten' being chosen. It is true that ten can be divided by two and by five, which makes mental calculation easy. But twelve could be divided by two, three, and four,

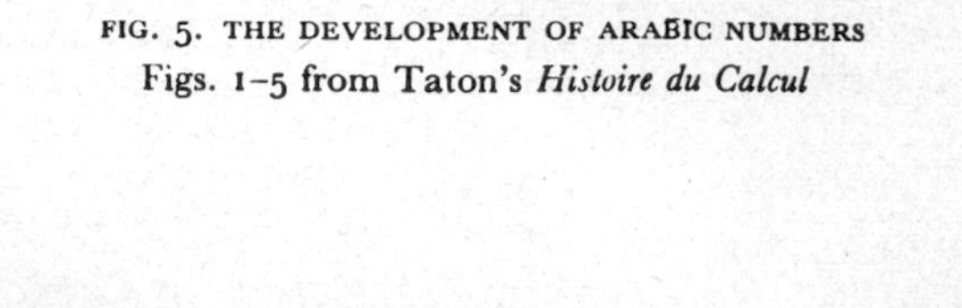

FIG. 5. THE DEVELOPMENT OF ARABIC NUMBERS
Figs. 1–5 from Taton's *Histoire du Calcul*

which would be easier still. The Babylonians, we know, used a scale of 'sixty'. Modern electronic calculating machines (*see* COUNTING INSTRUMENTS) use a scale of 'two'. The figures 101 in a scale of 'two' would have the following meaning in our scale of 'ten':

$$1 \text{ times } 2 \text{ times } 2 = 4$$
$$0 \text{ times } 2 = 0$$
$$1 = 1$$
$$\text{Value in scale of 'ten'} = \overline{5}$$

The way in which our own system originated has not yet been made clear by historical research. It probably began in India, in or before the 5th century A.D., and it may have been indirectly influenced by the Babylonian system which, like ours, used positional notation and zero. The Hindu system spread in the 8th century to the Arabs, who were then the leading commercial people, and from the Arabs it spread slowly to Europe; for this reason our written and printed figures are known as Arabic numerals. By the 15th century the new numbers were fairly generally used in Europe, although some government departments, universities, monasteries, and other institutions with settled traditions used the Roman numerals till the 18th century. They are still sometimes used for ceremonial purposes, as on monuments.

Arabic figures passed through many stages before acquiring their present shape (Fig. 5). Their use of zero made it possible later for decimal fractions to be invented by Simon Stevin, a Dutch mathematician, scientist, and engineer, in 1585. Before that time many systems of fractions had been used, for example, 'common' fractions (like $\frac{1}{257}$) and the sexagesimal fractions of the Babylonians.

The system of decimal fractions works on the assumption that the figure for unity ('1') can be divided into ten parts; the number of parts desired is then written to the right of the position of unity, with a dot between the two. Thus 1 equals one; 1·1 equals one and one-tenth, 1·2 equals one and two-tenths, 1·3 equals one and three-tenths, and so on. This process can be continued indefinitely, with each position indicating tenths of the number on its left. Thus if 1·1 equals one and one-tenth, 1·11 equals not only one and one-tenth but also a further tenth of one-tenth (the last figure, of course, equalling a hundredth). Decimal fractions are increasingly used to classify records such as books in libraries (*see* CATALOGUING AND INDEXING).

See also MATHEMATICAL NOTATION; MEASUREMENTS, HISTORY OF.

COUNTING INSTRUMENTS. Before modern methods came into use, almost all calculation had to be done by moving solid objects about by hand on a table or on the floor. Partial exception must be made in the case of the Babylonians, who made some written calculations with the help of tables of multiplication, division, and squares. From very ancient times calculations were done on various forms of the abacus (Fig. 1). An advanced type of abacus is the one still used to-day for teaching arithmetic to very young children. It consists of sets of ten beads running on each of several parallel wires. Beads on the first wire indicate units; those on the second wire indicate tens; and so on. Counting is done by moving the beads from one end of a wire to the other and then counting the number of beads that have been moved on the various wires. Simpler forms of abacus consist of boards marked out into squares, and little disks which are moved from square to square. These disks gave rise to the word 'counters' which we still use for similar disks employed in games such as draughts. The board was called a 'chequer board' or an 'exchequer', from its use in the past for counting the king's money. The title 'Chancellor of the Exchequer' is still given to the British Finance Minister.

With the coming of Arabic numbers (*see*

COUNTING, HISTORY OF, Section 4), written methods became practicable; but as few people could read and write, the abacus remained the main means of calculation in business until well into the 16th century. It is still the normal method in China, and in the hands of a good calculator, it is quicker than paper calculation, though it has the serious disadvantage that no record of the steps taken is left behind for checking.

In the 17th century there was a pressing need for improved methods of counting. Commerce was growing, government finance became more involved, and such sciences as astronomy made big demands on arithmetic. Efforts were therefore made to simplify counting. Then came a great moment in the history of mathematics and applied science—the discovery of logarithms as a means of easy reckoning. John Napier, a scholarly Scottish landowner, published in 1614 a table of figures which he had worked out to avoid the ordinary operations of multiplication and division which had slowed down all scientific calculation. Shortly afterwards Professor Henry Briggs, a Yorkshireman who had studied at Cambridge University, devised a way of relating Napier's method to the decimal system. The decimal logarithms of Briggs form the system now in use.

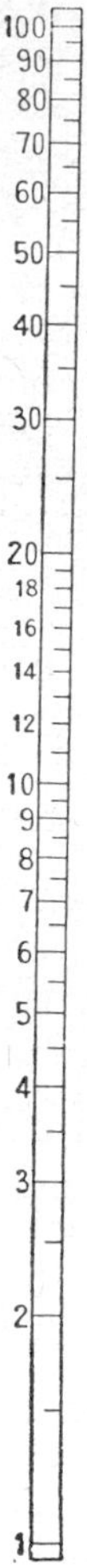

A general idea of logarithms can be gained from Fig. 2. Suppose we wish to multiply 3 by 4. On the scale shown, we measure off, with a piece of string or a strip of blank paper, the distance from 1 to 3, and again the distance from 1 to 4. We add these two distances together, and then measure from 1 the distance so obtained. The point reached will be 12—and in fact that is the product of 3 multiplied by 4. It is easy to verify that this process works with any other figures. The distances in the scale shown have been arranged in such a way that multiplying two numbers can be replaced by merely adding the corresponding distances. This principle is the basis of most slide-rule calculation.

Logarithms do not involve an actual scale of this kind, although they are based on the same clever relationship between quantities. In

FIG. 2

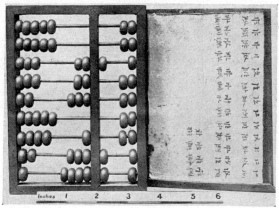

Director of the Science Museum, London

FIG. I. CHINESE ABACUS

Each bead in the left section represents one unit; each bead in the right section represents five units. To count, the beads are drawn towards the centre bar. The numbers here (reading downwards) are 0, 0, 7, 2, 3, 0, 1, 8, 9.

logarithms the scale of distances is replaced by a table of numbers; for every number the table gives another number. Long lists of logarithmic values are issued in printed books; if one wishes to multiply two large numbers, one looks up their appropriate logarithms in the book and adds them together. In the same way, division can be achieved by merely subtracting one number from another.

Later in the 17th century attempts were made to build calculating machines based on the principle of the abacus. Blaise Pascal, the French mathematician and philosopher, made an adding and subtracting machine in 1642, when he was 19 years old. Leibnitz, the German philosopher and mathematical writer, made a machine in 1694 for multiplying and dividing. These and many other machines would work when treated with great care, but broke down in everyday use. It was not until the Industrial Revolution had provided better standards of engineering that a useful calculating machine could be made. The first was that of the Frenchman, Thomas de Colmar, in 1820. Since that date there has been steady development up to the calculating machines of to-day, which are used in banks, offices, factories, and scientific laboratories. These machines carry out the elementary processes of arithmetic; that is, they add two given numbers, or multiply, or subtract, or divide them. But they have to be given separate instructions for each operation. They can do this so fast that large numbers of calculations can be made in a short time by an expert operator. But for every calculation that is done, the human operator must choose all the figures each time; so that although the actual time of doing the calculation is saved by the machine, there is no saving of the time spent by the human operator in thinking about the figures, in deciding what to make the machine do and what to do with the result. In complex calculations involving hundreds of thousands of stages (such as working out the exact shape that an aeroplane wing shall be built, in a factory) the time taken in calculating is still very great.

In calculations which involve the laborious repetition of a simple series of actions, such as computing the income-tax to be deducted from the wages of 5,000 factory workers every week, automatic machines work with great speed. The personal record of each worker is fed to a machine in the form of a card pierced with small holes, the position of each hole having a definite meaning concerning his hours of work and rates of pay (see ACCOUNTING, MACHINE, Vol. VII).

Efforts have been made for over 100 years to devise machinery which can carry out automatically very long and complex calculations, with no human assistance except for supplying certain numbers to the machine to start with. In 1833 Professor Charles Babbage of Cambridge had the idea of a machine which could do this work. His designs could not be successfully completed because they were beyond the power of engineers of his day. Every calculation would have meant large numbers of movable parts of machinery being set in motion, and the practical difficulties were too great.

To-day, after years of research arising mainly from the needs of wireless, machines are beginning to do what Babbage wanted. By using electrons (see THERMIONIC VALVES, Vol. VIII) instead of moving parts, and controlling the electrons by wireless valves, cathode-ray tubes, and similar devices, engineers have overcome the difficulties. Machines can now carry out additions, subtractions, multiplications, and divisions on 10-figure numbers at the rate of about 15,000 operations a minute. Faster machines have been experimentally designed. With their help it will be possible to solve many scientific problems which used to be impossible because the calculations would have taken a lifetime.

COUPLINGS, RAILWAY. The most primitive form of coupling between railway vehicles is the three-link coupling still fitted to almost the whole of British wagon stock (Fig. 1 a). This has no means of adjustment; wagons must be coupled and uncoupled when the buffers are touching; and it is only possible to start a heavy freight train by tautening the couplings one by one from the engine backwards, so bringing the load on to the engine gradually. This accounts

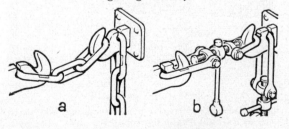

FIG. 1 a. THREE-LINK COUPLING
FIG. 1 b. TWO-LINK SCREW COUPLING

for the characteristic noise when British freight trains stop and start—the buffers hitting together one by one as the couplings slacken and the wagons bunch up towards the engine, when the train is stopping, and the couplings pulling out and straightening as the train starts.

With most passenger trains in Great Britain and in other countries (North America excepted) the method of coupling is by two links joined by a screw (Fig. 1 *b*). Unscrewing loosens the coupling, so that it can be dropped over the coupling hook, and the coupling is then tightened by the screw until it is taut, with the buffers just touching. The smooth riding of screw-coupled vehicles depends a good deal on the nicety with which this adjustment is made, neither too tight nor too loose.

Main-line corridor stock on the Eastern, North-Eastern, and Southern Regions is fitted with the 'buck-eye' type of automatic coupler, which is standard on all passenger and freight

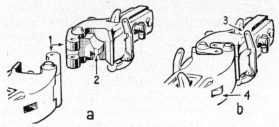

FIG. 2. BUCK-EYE COUPLING

a. Coupling up. Knuckles (1) shown open. As the coupler heads come together the part (2) is pushed in, closing the knuckles.
b. Coupled. The locked knuckle may be released by a lever (3). The knuckle protrudes at the side (4) when locked.

vehicles in the United States and Canada (Fig. 2). For this type of coupler, the coaches are built with bow ends, so that the length of the actual couplers may be shortened. The latter resemble a pair of steel hands, which clasp one another automatically as the vehicles are pushed together. This is the strongest and most satisfactory method of coupling in existence; in effect it makes a train a jointed steel frame from end to end, improves the smoothness and steadiness with which the coaches ride, and affords protection against the dreaded 'telescoping' (one coach overriding the next) in the event of a collision or derailment.

CREW, (Air) *see* AIRCREW; (SHIP) *see* SHIP'S COMPANY.

CUNEIFORM WRITING. The word 'cuneiform', from Latin *cuneus* (wedge) and *forma* (form or shape), is given to the characters used by the ancient SUMERIANS, BABYLONIANS, ASSYRIANS (qq.v. Vol. I), and other ancient peoples. These characters were formed of combinations of strokes having the shape of a wedge or cone.

Cuneiform writing was probably the earliest known system of WRITING (q.v.). It originated nearly 6,000 years ago, and was probably invented by the Sumerians, who lived in Mesopotamia for many centuries. At first, the cuneiform characters were purely pictorial; the picture-symbols were used to represent objects or abstract ideas related in meaning to these objects; for instance, the symbol 'sun' also represented the word 'day'. At a second stage, the pictures began to be simplified, and reduced to simple lines: curved lines began to disappear and to be replaced by straight lines set at angles to one another. The Sumerians lived in a country abounding in clay, which they used as a writing material. They soon found that it was possible to make the shape of a character in the wet clay much more quickly and better by stamping it than by scratching it. But curves, circles, and fine or long lines could not be stamped or impressed satisfactorily, so all these lines were substituted by short and straight strokes (which could be vertical or horizontal or oblique) and by angles. These strokes and angles were stamped in, line by line, with an instrument which the Romans later called a *stilus*. This was a small, straight piece of reed, bone, metal, or hard wood, broad at one end and pointed at the other, and used for scratching letters or signs (*see* WRITING INSTRUMENTS). In cuneiform writing the instrument was simply laid down sideways on the clay, and pressed into it. Thus the mark made in the clay was wedge-shaped.

Cuneiform writing was used by the Semitic peoples of Mesopotamia (Babylonians and Assyrians) from about 3000 B.C. almost to the beginning of the Christian era. About 1500 B.C. it became the script of the civilized peoples of the whole Near East. It was adopted by the HITTITES (q.v. Vol. I) of Asia Minor, by the ancient Elamites living to the east of the lower Tigris, by the ancient Armenians, and by various other peoples, including the ancient PERSIANS (q.v. Vol. I).

For hundreds of years the secret of reading

British Museum

BABYLONIAN WRITING ABOUT 870 B.C.
The king is worshipping the Sun god in the city of Sippar.
The inscription records the restoration of the temple

cuneiform writing was lost. In modern times scholars of many countries carried out scientific studies for years before, in the middle of the 19th century, it became possible again to read it, and in consequence to learn about the great civilizations of the Near East.

See also HIEROGLYPHICS.

CURRAGH, *see* CANOE.

CUSTOMS, *see* Vol. X: CUSTOMS AND EXCISE.

CUTTY SARK. This famous clipper ship, still afloat in the Thames in 1950, was built at Dumbarton in 1869 for Captain John Willis. She was one of the last of the clippers specially built for the tea trade with China and proved a very fast and powerful ship. Her length was 212·5 feet, and her extreme beam 36 feet, and her gross tonnage 963. She was famous for her sharp wedge-shaped bow sections, and was composite built, that is, built with wood planking laid over iron frames. Ship-rigged, with double topsails and crossing a main skysail yard, she also bent a sail to the cross-jack yard and carried studding sails on the foremast. Indeed, the *Cutty Sark* originally carried a very large spread of canvas, and in her day it was considered that no ocean-going vessel, steam or sail, merchant ship or man-of-war, could keep abreast of her in a good, strong, steady breeze of wind abeam. She is logged as averaging 15 knots for long periods and as sometimes touching 17 or even 17½ knots.

The *Cutty Sark*'s unusual name is taken from the witch in Burns's poem, *Tam o' Shanter*; and her figurehead represents a witch wearing a short skirt. Her best-remembered rival was the famous Aberdeen clipper *Thermopylae*. The great Tea Race of 1870 was won by the *Thermopylae* against the *Cutty Sark*; but the latter would probably have won if she had not carried away her rudder.

The opening of the Suez Canal in 1870 heralded the end of the famous days of the racing China tea clippers. The *Cutty Sark* stayed in the trade until 1880, when her tall spars were shortened and she was sailed to Australia and raced home with wool through stormier seas and heavier weather. As a wool clipper the *Cutty Sark* continued to make record voyages. In 1895 she was sold to the Portuguese, converted into a barquentine, and her name was changed. In 1922 she turned up in the Surrey Commercial Docks, and was greeted with great enthusiasm. Shortly afterwards she was bought back into English ownership and refitted as a clipper ship although she has never sailed again. It is hoped that it may prove possible to preserve her afloat for some years to come; for the *Cutty Sark*, with her memories of ocean racing with cargoes of tea and wool, is the sole remaining ship from a notable era in the history of the British Merchant Navy.

See CLIPPER SHIP.
See also Vol. VII: TEA TRADE.

CZECH LANGUAGE, *see* SLAVONIC LANGUAGES.

D

DAM, *see* River Navigation.
See also Vol. VIII: Dams.

DANISH LANGUAGE, *see* Scandinavian Languages.

DEAF LANGUAGES. Deaf people use various means of communication, depending partly on their kind of deafness. Some are deaf at birth, and have never heard people speak. Many others lose their hearing by illness or accident when very young, and if this occurs before the age of about 18 months or 2 years, they grow up without any recollection of having heard people speak, and so they do not know what speech is like. They are often described as 'born deaf', and although this term is not accurately applied to them, they are in just the same position as people who have been born deaf. People who lose their hearing, either wholly or in part, after they have learnt to speak have the advantage of remembering what speaking sounds like. There are also people who are both deaf and blind, and who use their own very special means of communication, which are described below.

There are some 32,000 people in Britain known as 'born deaf' (including those who became deaf in infancy) who have been educated in special schools. There they are given a means of communication and can be trained to speak by following the lip-movements of their teacher. Sometimes communication is achieved by means of the hand alphabet, known as the manual alphabet (*see* Fig. 1). In this the five fingers represent the five vowels, a, e, i, o, u, while some of the visual signs, such as those for p, s, q, and r, are based on the shape of the written letters. Communication by this alphabet is supplemented and speeded up by sign language, which was developed in 1765 by the Abbé de l'Épée, a French priest, from the natural signs used by uneducated deaf people, into a systematic and conventional language. Most of the ideas in this language are communicated by signs which have in each case grown up from an instinctive gesture to indicate some particular object or emotion. When experts use the combined systems of the manual alphabet and sign language, they almost reach the speed of speech. Indeed, at many public gatherings where the born-deaf cannot easily follow the speaker by lip-reading (that is, watching the movements of the mouth), a hearing person who can use this method of communication will interpret the speaker's words into manual alphabet and sign language for the deaf people present.

Teachers of the deaf now, however, try to give to the born-deaf the ability to understand the spoken word by sight alone, and to teach them to speak. They do this by placing the children's hands on their own chests, throats, lips, and

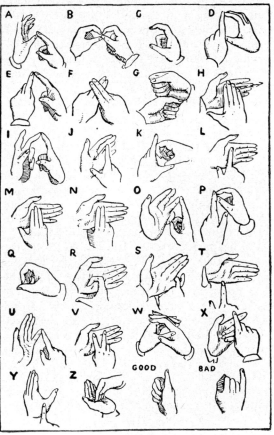

FIG. 1. MANUAL ALPHABET

noses, so that the vibration or hissing breath or other characteristic of each sound can be felt. The born-deaf then communicate either by this speaking and lip-reading or, perhaps more frequently, by skilfully combining the manual alphabet and signs. Signs are used for hundreds of common words and phrases, but unusual words and proper names are spelt letter by letter. The partially deaf or hard-of-hearing, who can communicate by ordinary speech and language like hearing people, and who can be helped by amplifying instruments, nearly all also use lip-reading in some degree.

Lip-reading is seeing speech by watching the shape and movement of the speaker's mouth, instead of listening to the sounds those movements produce. It is a difficult art to acquire completely, for not all speakers make clear correct mouth movements, and many people mumble. There are some forty sounds in English speech, each produced by a different position of the lips, teeth, and tongue (*see* VOICE, Section 2). Words are built up of two or more sounds. Each vowel sound is produced by the passage of the voice through the mouth, which is made the right shape by the position of the tongue and lips; the lips are always open. In the vowel 'ar' (as in 'far'), the tongue lies in a flat position in the mouth while the teeth are held apart, the breath escaping unimpeded. In 'ee' (as in 'tea') the tongue is pushed forward, and the corners of the lips are drawn back. Consonants, of course, produce a greater variety of mouth movements than the vowels. 'P' starts with the lips closed, blocking the breath, which bursts out as the lips open suddenly. A combination of the different positions and movements of the tongue, lips, and teeth forms a kind of picture of the sound uttered.

Although lip-reading is used by both the born-deaf and people who become deaf later in life, the two do not learn in the same way. The deafened learn by recognizing the sight of spoken words which they can remember hearing before they became deaf. The born-deaf start to learn without that advantage. It is important to remember that not every word can be lip-read, and the successful lip-reader has to watch and make use of the speaker's facial expression, gestures, and so on. Lip-reading, however skilful, cannot take the place of normal hearing.

The deaf-blind use their own alphabet, based on the manual alphabet used by the seeing deaf,

with certain important changes. When the seeing deaf use their manual alphabet, the 'speaker' uses both hands, and the 'speech' is read by the eyes of the 'listener'. With the deaf-blind, who must read by feeling, the right hand only of the 'speaker' is used, while the left hand only of the 'listener' is used as the receiving

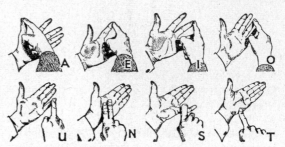

FIG. 2. SOME LETTERS OF THE DEAF-BLIND ALPHABET
The 'speaker' indicates the letters with his right hand on the left hand of the 'hearer'

medium. When the deaf-blind person becomes very skilled, he may possibly use either hand to 'receive'. When we speak of the deaf-blind, we may be speaking of a blind person who has become deaf or of a deaf person who has become blind. In the former case he may use BRAILLE (q.v.) for reading, and certain of the letter contractions evolved for Braille can be used to give his deaf-blind communication speed and fluency. Fig. 2 gives some illustrations of certain letters of the deaf-blind alphabet which can easily be identified with the illustrations of the sighted deaf alphabet. This method of communication is the only link which the deaf-blind have with other people.

There is a remarkable young man in England, called Joseph Hatton, who became totally deaf and blind when he was 4. He was taught lip-reading by touch, and somehow the idea of language was conveyed to him, although he could neither hear the words spoken by his teacher nor see the objects she referred to. Now he can follow what people say to him in four ways:

(1) By the manual alphabet as commonly used by the deaf-blind; (2) by the deaf alphabet used for sighted deaf people; Hatton reads this by holding the speaker's wrists, one in each hand, and feeling the muscles move; (3) in normal speech, which he follows by placing his thumb on the speaker's lips and his forefinger on his throat; (4) again in normal speech, which

he can also read by placing his thumb and finger on the speaker's throat alone.

Miss Helen Keller, the famous American deaf-blind woman, is the only other person who has mastered the third method. The fourth method, which Joseph Hatton alone uses, is much the most difficult, as the vibrations of the throat are the only guide; but he can use it as easily as any of the others.

See also Vol. X: SPECIAL SCHOOLS.
See also Vol. XI: EAR STRUCTURE.

DERELICTS. A derelict is a ship which, abandoned by her crew through some threatened disaster, continues to drift about the oceans, silent, unlit at night, and a deadly menace to all other vessels. Some derelicts are still afloat in the seaways, although radio and modern salvage tugs with a long range do not allow many ships to-day to become derelicts; most of them are old wooden vessels laden with timber, or some other buoyant cargo which makes them practically unsinkable.

It is the duty of any ship sighting a derelict to issue a warning to other vessels. If the abandoned ship has any value as SALVAGE (q.v.) it should be taken in tow. If, however, it is a waterlogged hulk, as it usually is, afloat near busy trade routes, a warship may be sent to sink it by gunfire or blow it up.

The most famous of all derelicts was the *Mary Celeste*. She was a small sailing-vessel which left New York in 1872 bound for Genoa, with a cargo of oils and spirits. Some time later she was discovered, completely deserted, off Gibraltar, and was taken to a Spanish port. Her sails were found set and everything on board appeared to be in perfect order. The cargo was intact, and the ship had suffered no damage; but a half-eaten meal on the table in the cabin indicated that she had been abandoned in a hurry. Many theories have been put forward to account for the disappearance of all the crew, but the mystery will probably always remain one of the unsolved puzzles of the sea.

In 1881 the American *Ellen Austin* encountered a derelict schooner whose name has not been recorded. The boarding party found all in order, but her crew were missing. A skeleton crew were put on board and for some days the ships kept company. During a gale they became separated, and when the *Ellen Austin* found the schooner again she was once more deserted. A second crew were put on board. Neither these nor the ship were ever seen again.

See also WRECKS AND WRECKERS.

DESERT TRAVEL. There are vast tracts of DESERT (q.v. Vol.. III), generally in the interior of great land masses such as Africa and Asia, the crossing of which has always presented special problems. The great stretches of desert across Asia and North Africa, from Morocco to the Gobi Desert of China, have been crossed by traders, explorers, and conquering armies for many hundreds of years. Whether the desert be high, cold, and rocky as in central Asia, a mountainous terrain as in the central Sahara or south Arabia, an expanse of sand dunes as in North Africa, or open steppe thinly carpeted with grass in spring, the general characteristics of travel are not very different, and have not changed greatly since the Israelites began to cross the desert to the Promised Land about 1700 B.C. Since the regions travelled over are at the best thinly populated and there is little cultivation, the traveller must take with him all the food he will need for himself and his beasts (or, nowadays, the petrol for his car). He must discard everything which is not a necessity. He must know, or must take a guide who knows, the routes which pass by water-holes or wells.

One problem of desert travel is the lack of ordinary landmarks, especially in sandy desert, where the very shape of the terrain changes continuously. The traveller needs, therefore, a good sense of direction. Nowadays the traveller can use a compass to guide him; in ancient days he had to depend on his knowledge of the stars by which to reckon his whereabouts. In the mountainous desert of central Asia, and again in parts of America, the traveller needs the sure-footedness of a mountaineer. In the past there were many dangers to face—the dangers of attacks by robbers or the constant possibility of becoming involved in local warfare between desert tribes; the dangers of encountering sand-storms or finding the wells dried up in a drought; or of losing the way, of running out of food, or of suffering from any of the many desert diseases. It is the conquest of such dangers that has given to journeys across the desert such a romantic appeal to adventurers and explorers.

People travelled across the desert either for purposes of trade or to make PILGRIMAGES (q.v. Vol. I). It was the duty of a strict Moslem to make a pilgrimage to Mecca at least once in his lifetime, and the same injunction rested upon the Jew to visit Jerusalem. Such journeys were generally made, for the sake of safety, in large parties or caravans. The word 'caravan', originally a Persian word, means a party of merchants with their merchandize travelling together for safety. Very long ago trade developed between the cities of the Near and Middle East, and then stretched farther east, through Persia and Afghanistan, over the Himalayas to India, and through Tibet to China. The merchants gradually established routes which took the easiest passage through difficult country (*see* TRADE ROUTES). Marco Polo (q.v. Vol. V), nearly 700 years ago, travelled along the old Silk Route on his famous visit to central Asia and beyond to China. Routes across the Sahara and Nubian Deserts in Africa also became established, and Timbuktu grew into an important caravan centre. In the 14th century the great scholar and traveller Ibn Battuta journeyed from Fez in Morocco through North Africa to Mecca and on to Persia, India, and China; and again from Fez across the Sahara to West Africa.

During the Middle Ages, as Europe became more civilized and wealthier, the demands for eastern goods, for silks and spices, precious stones and carpets, increased. The rich trade and the control of the caravan routes was in the hands of the Moslems; but during the later Middle Ages Europeans travelled more and found new routes, especially in Asia. Arab caravans from the coasts of Moslem North Africa travelled across the Sahara into Negro Africa in search of salt, ivory, and slaves. These traders not only brought precious wares with them, but also tales of strange peoples and places. The arrival of a caravan must have been a great event, for with the caravan came the news of the world.

Until the invention of the motor and aeroplane, travel was mainly by beasts of burden. The chief beast of burden on the desert has always been the camel—the tall, one-humped dromedary used in Africa and the Near East, and the sturdier, sure-footed two-humped Bactrian camel in central Asia. Donkeys are used greatly, especially for riding, and in the higher, rocky regions mules and the sure-footed, tough little Mongolian ponies carry most of the transport. Yaks in Tibet and llamas in central and South America are particularly suitable for the special conditions of those regions. Many desert people are breeders of horses, but generally speaking only the chiefs and wealthier people possess horses for riding; and the horse is not a very good pack animal in desert conditions (*see* BEASTS OF BURDEN, Sections 2 and 3).

A caravan party often consists of forty to a hundred laden beasts, though large caravans sometimes run into several thousand mules or camels. The camels are fastened head to tail by hair ropes in a long, straggling line. The leading camel is often decorated with gaily coloured trappings, tassels, and bells, and sometimes an unladen donkey leads the whole procession. The caravan party appoint a leader to take charge of the journey. Moslems consider that Friday, an hour after the noon-day prayer, is an auspicious time to start the journey. The caravan travels at the unhurried rhythm of a camel's pace, covering from 2 to $2\frac{1}{2}$ miles an hour and 23 to 26 miles a day, in two stages. They start very early in the morning and make a long pause during the midday heat. They camp at night, perhaps at one of the *caravanserai* which have grown up along the much-used routes. These are stone buildings round a central courtyard, which give shelter, but no food, to the traveller (*see* INNS). Where there are no *caravanserai* the travellers pitch tents of goat or camel hair. Caravan journeys generally take place in the spring (in high regions after the snows have melted), in early summer, or late autumn.

The business of the long-distance caravan traders has inevitably declined in the modern world. The development of sea routes in the 16th and 17th centuries, as well as political turmoil in the countries of the caravan routes, and the abolition of the slave trade, all led to its decline. Modern transport has for the most part made it a thing of the past, for modern engineers have built motor roads and even railways through the most difficult country. Pilgrims to Mecca now arrive in modern cars and aircraft. Desert journeying by beast of burden is mainly confined to the desert-dwellers themselves, pastoral nomads such as BEDOUINS, MOORS, TUAREGS, or MONGOLS (qq.v. Vol. I), who breed camels, sheep, goats, and horses; or even the primitive hunters such as the BUSHMEN of the Kalahari Desert or the AUSTRALIAN

Paul Popper

A CAMEL CARAVAN IN ERITREA, NORTH-EAST AFRICA

ABORIGINES (qq.v. Vol. I). To such, desert travel is not so much adventure or a career but life itself.

To-day the deserts are bisected by motor and air routes. The Sahara, first crossed by motor in 1922, can now be crossed in 10 days in stream-lined buses from Algiers to Zindar in French West Africa. A similar bus service runs between Syria and Bagdad. Desert patrols, aircraft, motorized armies, have disturbed districts once visited only by camels. Although caravan trade is to all intents and purposes dead, the same routes still carry the interchange of commerce, ideas, and culture. As air travel develops, the great deserts of the world become less and less the formidable barriers to communication which they were in the past.

See also TRADE ROUTES; BEASTS OF BURDEN.

DHOW. The word *dhow* is the term used by Europeans to describe any kind of Arab sailing craft. The ARABS (q.v. Vol. I) have various names for their ships: for example, the largest dhows are called *baghla*, which is Arabic for a mule. These fine great ships have long over-hanging bows and square sterns, decorated with carved ornament, originally copied from the sterns of European ships trading with India in the 17th and 18th centuries, so that one finds in them to-day poop-decks, stern windows, and quarter galleries. They have two or three short, heavy masts, raking forward and carrying tall lateen sails (*see* SAILING SHIPS). Smaller square-sterned dhows are called *sambuks*, and these are perhaps the commonest type. Some of the best-found and smartest are the *booms*, which have sharp sterns and graceful lines. They are kept very smart and gleam brightly with varnished woodwork. The merchants live on the poop-deck round which their chests are ranged. The *bedeni*, hailing from Muscat in the Persian Gulf, is a quaint type, short and wide, with one or

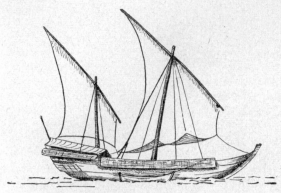

A BAGHLA, A LARGE DHOW

two upright masts and lateen sails with shorter yards and luffs. They have false stems, clipper bows, and sharp sterns with very tall false stern-posts, from which the tall rudder is slung. This rudder is operated by tackles to each quarter from a horn projecting aft from the rudder, just above the waterline. In expert hands the picturesque dhows·are excellent seaboats, and make long voyages from the Red Sea and Persian Gulf down the African coast and back again, using the north-east and south-west monsoon winds. Arabs are expert sailors, but many are happy-go-lucky; and some of the dhows sail unprepared to weather the squalls which sometimes arise. The lateen sail is not reefed, but a smaller sail is set in its place when there is a strong wind.

See also SAILING; SAILING SHIPS.

DIALECTS. When people who speak the same language live in different parts of the country or are split up by large differences in their education or work, they develop different forms of the language. When the differences become great, these forms are called dialects. Such differences last, and usually increase, as long as the speakers or writers of one group remain more or less cut off from those of another. If one dialect is influenced by conditions that do not affect the rest (for example, close contact with people speaking another language), then it may in time differ from them so much as to become a distinct language. FRENCH, SPANISH, and ITALIAN, for example, were all originally 'dialects' of LATIN (qq.v.).

But when the speakers of the various dialects of a country have a common culture as well as a common basic language, and where communication between the various parts of the country is easy and frequent, such differences are usually kept in check. This is chiefly because for political, cultural, or commercial reasons there is a strong tendency for the dialect of one class or area to gain ascendancy over the others. These last then often become confined to colloquial use, or even die out altogether.

There have been dialects in England since Old English times: for example, Old English manuscripts written in Northumbria and Kent show strongly marked differences in spelling, inflexion, and sometimes in vocabulary. By the beginning of the 11th century, when Winchester was the capital of England, the West Saxon dialect seems to have become almost a 'standard' for literary purposes. But with the Norman Conquest Wessex lost its power, and the importance of its dialect declined. For several hundred years people wrote in their local dialects, all of which were developing rapidly, and therefore differing more and more from each other. By the end of the 14th century, however, the dialect of London and the surrounding area was beginning to gain supremacy, chiefly because of the growing importance of London itself; and by Elizabeth's reign it had become the basis of the written language (*see* STANDARD ENGLISH). Yet this did not prevent Shakespeare from introducing several words and phrases from his native Warwickshire dialect into his plays ('mobled', 'muss', 'othergates'). And words and pronunciations from other dialects, such as 'fell' and 'beck' from the north of England, and the forms 'left' and 'merry' from the south-east, have at various times entered the 'standard' language. Until the late 18th century many people of the upper classes who did not live in the capital went on speaking their local dialect: Squire Western, in Fielding's *Tom Jones*, for example, says 'zee, volks, wull' for 'see, folks, will'.

Burns and other Scottish poets have given the Lowland Scots dialect the standing of a literary language. In the 19th century William Barnes attempted to do something similar for the dialect of Dorset. Edmund Blunden is an example of a modern poet who has used dialect words in his verse. Dialect has been used in dialogue by such modern writers as Thomas Hardy in his Wessex novels, and G. B. Shaw in, for example, *Major Barbara* and *Pygmalion*—'eed now bettern to spawl a pore gel's flahrz' is a specimen of his attempt to represent Cockney.

Despite the spread of education, broadcasting, and the cinema, regional dialects persist in many parts of England, as well as on the Continent, and help to keep a language from becoming monotonously uniform. In America, where the population has tended to shift more often than in Europe, differences in the spoken language are comparatively few, and there are only three main dialect areas—New England, the south, and the middle and western states. Only in a few isolated areas, such as the Appalachians and the tide-water country of Virginia, do old expressions survive to the same extent as in English dialects. 'Class' dialects scarcely exist in America and, where they do, count for very little (*see* AMERICAN ENGLISH).

See also SLANG; ENGLISH LANGUAGE.

DICTIONARY, *see* REFERENCE BOOKS.

DIESEL LOCOMOTIVE. This type of engine is increasingly taking the place of the steam locomotive in many countries, and will in time be used largely in Britain. The diesel engine is an INTERNAL COMBUSTION ENGINE (q.v. Vol. VIII), like the motor-car petrol engine, but using instead a much cheaper oil fuel. The cost of building a diesel locomotive is high. Diesels do not normally transmit their power direct to the engine wheels; a diesel is like a travelling power station; the engine works an electrical generator, the current of which is used to drive powerful electric motors, which turn the locomotive wheels. This diesel-electric form of transmission enables the many wheels of a long locomotive to be driven by electric power from the diesel plant, while two or three locomotives can be linked together and controlled by one crew in the leading locomotive. Although a diesel locomotive costs at least twice as much to build as a steam locomotive of the same power, there are great advantages. Not only is the fuel oil cheap, but the diesel uses no fuel while standing still, unlike the old steam-engine, which has to get up steam before hauling its train. A diesel locomotive will work continuously for 24 hours a day if necessary, and modern diesels are expected to be available for actual service on the road over 90 per cent. of each day, a figure which steam could not rival. In the United States diesel-electric locomotives are used without change over distances as great as from Chicago to Los Angeles and San Francisco —more than 2,200 miles, running for nearly 40 hours. Although the diesels use water for engine-cooling, refilling is seldom needed, so that the diesels do not waste time on their

J. Hardman

THE ROYAL SCOT DRAWN BY TWIN DIESEL-ELECTRIC LOCOMOTIVES
The train is climbing Shap Fell, Westmorland, on its non-stop run from Euston to Glasgow

journeys by taking water: in arid country, where water is scarce, this is an advantage. Also, the locomotive's supply of oil fuel lasts longer than the coal supply in a steam locomotive tender.

In Great Britain there has been some experimental use of diesel-electric locomotives in long-distance passenger service, on the London Midland Region, including the hauling of the Royal Scot. Their chief use, however, is in marshalling yards. The Western Region has a number of stream-lined passenger railcars which are diesel-mechanical; the wheels are driven direct, without any electrical transmission. Mechanical transmission is a fairly simple matter with engines of limited horse-power, as in these Western Region cars; but when it comes to units of 1,000 brake-horse-power and upwards the design of a direct transmission that will stand up to the work is difficult. This is why electrical generators and motors are normally interposed between the diesel engines and the axles, for this is a much more flexible and suitable method of control. The London Midland Region, however, has made experiments with a 4–8–4 diesel express passenger locomotive with direct mechanical drive.

Some of the earliest diesel locomotive experiments were made in Canada in 1925, but the greatest impetus to the use of diesel power came in 1932 with the German State Railways' 'Flying Hamburger' stream-lined train. This consisted of two articulated cars, 138 feet long and 77 tons in weight, driven by diesel electric engines of 820 brake-horse-power. The 'Flying Hamburger' was booked to run daily between Berlin and Hamburg at an average speed of 77·4 miles an hour, and maximum speeds up to 100 miles an hour became common. The use of diesel-electric stream-lined trains spread all over Germany, and runs timed from start to stop at over 80 miles an hour appeared in the German time-tables over several main routes.

It is in the United States, however, that diesel-electric traction on railways has made by far the greatest strides. It was first tried in shunting-work in 1925, and in passenger service in 1934. By the end of 1948 nearly 10,000 diesel-electric locomotives had been built for American railways. These have now been introduced for use with a great number of stream-lined trains as well as for use with a large proportion of ordinary express trains. Diesels have become popular as well in long-distance haulage

of freight, and do a great deal of shunting in marshalling yards.

The American principle is to build independent locomotive units, and to use as many of these units together as necessary, with one crew taking charge of them all by means of multiple-unit controls. For passenger work the most popular unit is one of 2,000 brake-horse-power, used either singly, or (on the heavier trains) in pairs or triplets, totalling 4,000 or 6,000 brake-horse-power. On freight work the 1,500 brake-horse-power unit is the most widely used, with a maximum of four units (6,000 brake-horse-power in all) coupled together. Shunting is mostly done by 1,000 and 660 brake-horse-power units. A 6,000 brake-horse-power combination may measure up to 200 feet in length and weigh over 400 tons.

The mechanical and electrical equipment is of a very complicated description, and helps to account for the high cost—$500,000 to $600,000 —of one 6,000 brake-horse-power locomotive.

See also LOCOMOTIVES.
See also Vol. VIII: INTERNAL COMBUSTION ENGINE.

DIESEL ROAD ENGINES, see ROAD TRANSPORT ENGINES.

DIRIGIBLE, see AIRSHIP.

DIRECTION FINDING, see NAVIGATION, AIR; NAVIGATION, MARINE.

DISCOVERY I. This ship, now owned by the Sea Scouts and moored in London, was specially designed and built for the first expedition to the Antarctic (1901–4) led by Captain R. F. SCOTT (q.v. Vol. V). The lines of her hull are normal, except that she has a long overhanging stern to protect the rudder. She is built of wood, her sides being about 26 inches in thickness to withstand ice-pressure, and her bow is tremendously strengthened internally and covered with steel plates externally, to enable her to force and batter her way through pack ice. She can be driven either by her 450 h.p. triple-expansion steam-engines, or by her sails, which are carried on three masts, the first two of which are cross-rigged.

Apart from the great strength of her hull, the other peculiar features about the *Discovery* are the special devices used for lifting both the rudder and the propeller on board, and an observatory used for the collection of magnetic data, around which no iron or steel was permitted within a distance of 30 feet.

The *Discovery* first left England in August 1901. Five months later, after calling at New Zealand, she sighted the Antarctic Continent in the Ross Sea area. She travelled south as far as Ross Island, where Scott made his shore base. She then sailed along the edge of the great Ice Barrier as far as King Edward VII Land, making surveys and collecting scientific observations. The original plan had been for her to leave Antarctica for the winter and return in the spring; but such a safe and sheltered anchorage was found in McMurdo Sound that it was decided that she should remain there. Unfortunately the next summer the ice in the Sound never broke up, so that she was held prisoner for another whole year, and was unable to move until February 1904. She then returned to England, having shown herself a most successful ship for scientific purposes in polar seas, the only serious criticism being that she carried too little sail.

After being used for carrying cargo, first by the Hudson's Bay Company and later by the Admiralty in the First World War, the *Discovery* went south again in 1923, when she became the first research ship of the Discovery Committee, which was set up to study the Antarctic whaling industry. In 1927 she was replaced by the *Discovery II*, but returned to the Antarctic for two summer expeditions in 1929 and 1930. These were her last distant cruises.

See also ICE-BREAKER; SNOW AND ICE TRAVEL.
See also Vol. III: POLAR REGIONS.

DIVERS AND DIVING APPARATUS.

Diving has a long history. We know that Alexander the Great sent down divers to remove underwater obstructions at the siege of Tyre in 332 B.C., and that he himself made a descent in a *colymba*, a machine which kept a man dry and at the same time let in light. Aristotle describes instruments used by divers for drawing air from the surface. He also writes of a cauldron lowered straight down so that the air remained inside and could be breathed by its diver.

Siebe, Gorman & Co.

A DIVER WITH HIS EQUIPMENT

Many experiments were made in the 18th century with diving equipment, and in 1830 Augustus Siebe, a Prussian engineer who fought at the Battle of Waterloo, introduced a suit which contained the principles still in use to-day.

Modern divers use a special dress as well as surface equipment. The pump supplying air to the diver is carried in a vessel anchored over the scene of the diving operations. It is usually hand operated. The diver's helmet is made of copper specially treated with tin and contains three windows of plate glass, the inlet–outlet valves, which regulate air supply and buoyancy, and telephone equipment through which he can speak to people at the surface. The helmet is screwed to a corselet, a metal covering for shoulders and chest, which is secured to a collar of vulcanized rubber on the diving dress. This dress is a suit of layers of tanned twill with pure rubber in between in which the whole body is enveloped. The sleeve cuffs are also made of vulcanized rubber and are watertight. The diver's air pipe is flexible, but will not collapse under the great pressure exerted upon it deep under water. It is fitted with couplings at each end to fix it to the helmet and air-pump. Weight is necessary to take the diver down, and this is included in his boots, which weigh 32 lb. a pair; he also carries 40 lb. weights on his chest and back. Finally, there is the life-line which can be used to haul the diver back to the surface and also as a means of communication. The life-line often contains the telephone cable as well. The greatest depth reached by divers in this kind of dress is 340 feet. They have to spend a long time after coming up in a special chamber where the pressure is gradually lowered; without this they would become seriously ill. An underwater 'decompression chamber', as it is called, has now been invented, and this reduces the time considerably.

Diving apparatus which is independent of the surface was first used about 1882; it contains oxygen and air cylinders and a watertight compartment holding caustic soda. The diver breathes in from the oxygen and air cylinders and out through the caustic soda, which purifies his breath by absorbing the carbon dioxide from his lungs; the breath then returns to the air cylinder. This system enables a diver to remain submerged up to 2 hours. This dress, when used in conjunction with the underwater decompression chamber, has enabled divers of the Royal Navy to reach a depth of 535 feet. Deep-sea diving is carried out in specially reinforced suits of cast-steel cylinders. These can withstand the enormous pressure which would crush any unprotected body; but they are not very useful, because of their lack of mobility. An underwater observation chamber is used instead. Remarkable developments in self-con-

tained diving-suits took place during the Second World War, when it was necessary to equip 'frogmen' and others for underwater attack on the enemy. These included improvements in the self-contained breathing apparatus, and the invention of detachable webbed hands and feet for underwater swimming.

Large bell-shaped vessels are used for extensive work under water. These 'diving bells', as they are called, are lowered to the bed of the sea or river, the water being kept out by compressed air. Men go down in these bells and can work in their ordinary clothes with plenty of light and air. Diving bells are also sometimes equipped with air locks. An air lock is a small chamber with two doors. When a man enters through the first the pressure inside is that of the atmosphere, but air is then pumped in until it equals the pressure inside the bell. After this has been done, the man can enter the bell through the second door.

Divers are used to inspect and report on underwater damage and to carry out small repairs themselves; they also disentangle wire ropes which have become wound round ships' propellers, and mend lock gates. Divers help in the work of salvage by placing in position the hawsers by which sunken ships are usually raised. In docks and commercial rivers visibility below surface is extremely poor owing to suspended particles of mud and other impurities; and the diver, although sometimes equipped with powerful lights, often does much of his work by touch.

See also SALVAGE.
See also Vol. III: PRESSURE.
See also Vol. X: SUBMARINE.

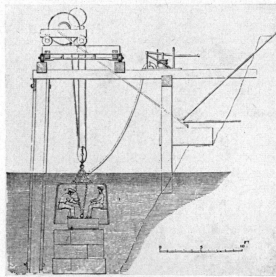

John Murray

DIVING BELL DESIGNED IN 1813 BY JOHN RENNIE FOR HARBOUR WORK AT RAMSGATE

From *Lives of the Engineers*, by Samuel Smiles

DOCKS. Docks for ship repair should not be confused with the wet docks used in Britain for the discharge of vessels, or with certain piers, such as those at New York, which are also known as docks. For ship repair, docks are designed to expose the underwater parts of a vessel's hull, so that painting or reconditioning may be carried out (*see* SHIP REPAIRS, Vol. VIII).

In Great Britain, ship repair work is usually carried out in a dry dock, often called a graving dock. It is a stone or concrete basin connected with a river or a wet dock, so that it can be readily flooded by the opening of sluices. When the dock is full of water, the vessel is floated in. The entrance is then closed with a watertight

Port of London Authority

A SHIP IN KING GEORGE V DRY DOCK, LONDON

Southampton. It is 1,200 feet long, 135 feet wide, 50½ feet deep, and can accommodate the largest vessels afloat. One of the most up-to-date dry docks is at Tilbury, on the Thames, where mechanical bilge blocks and a device called a leading-in girder avoid much of the difficulties of getting a vessel into position as the water which supports it is pumped out of the dock.

See also PORTS AND HARBOURS.

See also Vol. VIII: DOCKS AND HARBOURS.

DOVER ROAD. Long before the Romans came to Britain there was a route from London to the coast, following much the line of the modern Dover Road. The Romans greatly improved this ancient trackway. They made it part of a military road (our Watling Street) which runs right across England from Dover to Chester and thence across Wales to Caernarvon (*see* ROMAN ROADS). On the first 70-mile stretch from Dover to London the Romans built bridges across the fords, and raised a causeway to carry the road across the low-lying marshes round the Medway. Until the coming of the railways and the growth of new industrial towns in the Midlands and north, this stretch of Roman road was one of the busiest highways in the land.

The Dover Road has seen much history from the time of the Romans. Norman barons, following William the Conqueror, came from the Continent up the Dover Road to settle in the newly conquered land; bands of crusaders set off down it on their way to the Continent; Chaucer's Pilgrims and many others followed it to Canterbury; the Kentish rebels rallied along it to the call of Wat Tyler; and the first of the King's Postmen passed along it in Tudor times with news from the Continent.

In Stuart days the road surface became so bad that many travellers preferred to journey by water, at least as far as Gravesend. They thus avoided the stretch of road running across Blackheath and up Shooter's Hill, a place that already had an ugly name as the haunt of footpads and HIGHWAYMEN (q.v.). In the 19th century the Dover Road was celebrated in the writings of Charles Dickens. Among his chief characters, Mr. Micawber and Mr. Pickwick both travelled the road, and Dickens himself lived for many years at Gad's Hill Place between Dartford and Strood on the route of the road.

See also ROADS, BRITISH.

gate known as a caisson, and the water is pumped out. The vessel is supported by what are known as bilge blocks, which are enormous wedges under the bilge (the bottom part of the ship). Wooden shores or props keep the ship straight as the level of the water drops. When repairs have been completed, the dock is again flooded, the caisson is removed, and the ship floated out.

Another method of ship repair uses the floating dock. This is a floating cradle big enough to hold a ship. It has tanks which can be filled with water so that the cradle partly sinks into the sea or river. When the tanks have been filled, the ship is floated into the cradle and the tanks are pumped out. This causes the dock to rise, carrying the vessel clear of the water. Floating docks need deep berths or locations which have to be kept clear of mud by constant dredging; except for certain Government dockyards, they are now rarely used in Britain.

The largest dry dock in the world is at

DREDGER.

Ports, canals, and navigable rivers are kept clear for traffic by dredgers—special boats fitted with machinery to scoop up mud and silt from the bed of the waterway. Canals always tend to silt up, especially where the banks are unprotected by concrete piles or walls. The narrower waterways used by self-propelled craft suffer most, since the wash from the propellers is continually eating into the banks. Another cause of silting is the soil washed in from cuttings and high lands (see DENUDATION, Vol. III). Navigable rivers do not usually silt up all over, as the flow generally keeps a passage clear; but shoals form on the inside of bends, and are caused by the scouring or washing away produced by lock sluices. Silting is partly a result of river pollution. Sewage and chemical discharges and hot waste water from generating stations all tend to make a river deposit the solid particles in its water, instead of carrying them out to sea.

With the growth in the size of ships, most ports have been forced to resort to dredging to provide the deeper water required. In the Port of London, for instance, an artificial approach channel, 1,000 feet wide and 30 feet deep at ordinary low water, has been dredged from the sea into the heart of London. The tide scours

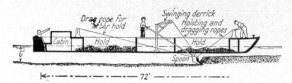

FIG. 1. SECTION OF HAND DREDGER

this channel clear of deposit, but maintenance dredging is necessary in certain areas, notably in tidal basins and the approaches to dock locks. Some 170 million tons of material have been removed from the bed of the tidal Thames by dredging.

The method of removing silt from canals is the same for most canals, but the size of the plant varies with the waterway. In the smaller canals of Great Britain the hand 'spoon dredger' is still used extensively for removing small deposits. The 'spoon' is suspended by a swivel derrick from the centre of the boat, which has compartments at each end to hold the mud. The spoon is pushed forward by the weight of the man pressing against the long handle; and when full, it is lifted by a winch at the fore-end

FIG. 2. GRAB DREDGER

and emptied into the hold. When the boat is discharging on to the tip, the process is reversed. With this machine three men can dredge about 30 tons of mud a day (see Fig. 1).

Steam-driven grab dredgers came into use about the middle of last century. In England the usual size of the vessel is 14-foot beam, and the grabs have a capacity of $\frac{1}{3}$ to $\frac{3}{4}$ cubic yards. Some dredgers have side pontoons which give stability, and can be removed to enable the dredger to pass through narrow bridges. The grab may be either free-falling and self-closing, or opened and closed under steam pressure, the pressure cylinder being attached to the top of the grab. The whole thing is suspended from the dredger crane (see Fig. 2).

The dredger is held up to the mud by ropes, and the dredged material deposited into hopper boats to be taken to the tip, and there discharged

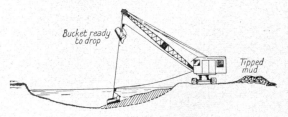

FIG. 3. DRAG-LINE CRANE

Wm. Simons & Co.

FIG. 4. CONTINUOUS BUCKET DREDGER

by a grab crane which resembles the dredger crane. Working in ordinary mud, which does not have to be carried very far, these dredgers can dredge 1,000 tons a week, or about 2 miles of narrow canal a year. Narrow canals with average protections to the banks may need re-dredging every 20 years.

When there are not many bridges and the material can be deposited direct on the banks alongside the canal, a drag-line crane on creeper track is sometimes used. This is a crane, driven by an internal-combustion engine, which moves along the bank. It has a grab shaped like an inverted bucket with teeth, which is swung out over the canal, and pulled in when it is full (see Fig. 3). This is quick and cheap to work.

In certain situations the suction dredger can be used, generally where there is a thick layer of mud or sand, and no danger of opening a soft spot in the bed of the canal. The material is sucked up through long pipes by means of pumps. Suction plant is frequently used for discharging mud from hoppers at the tip; as, however, the material is in a fluid state, there must be plenty of space and adequate banks at the tip so that the mud can settle and the water drain off. Disused gravel or clay pits made good dredging tips.

The 'ladder' or continuous bucket dredger is usually employed in rivers and estuaries (see Fig. 4). Careful preliminary work by a marine surveyor is necessary to ensure that the dredger works on the exact site of the shoal, and it is held in place by a number of strong moorings. The silt, or 'spoil' as it is called, is shot into attendant hopper barges which may be self-propelled or towed by powerful tugs. In most cases the 'spoil' is dumped at sea in deep water; Thames hoppers, for instance, carry their loads to the Black Deep in the outer Thames estuary where they are deposited without any danger of forming new shoals. The hopper barges have 'doors' in the bottoms of their holds through which the mud is dropped out.

See also RIVER NAVIGATION; PORTS AND HARBOURS.

DRY DOCK, *see* DOCKS. *See also* Vol. VIII: DOCKS AND HARBOUR CONSTRUCTION.

DUG-OUT CANOE, *see* CANOE.

DUTCH LANGUAGE, *see* GERMANIC LANGUAGES.

E

ECHO SOUNDER, *see* Vol. VIII; HYDRO-
GRAPHY.

ELECTRIC RAILWAYS. The electrification
of railway lines is gradually replacing steam
locomotives all over the world. It is costly but
is justified in dense traffic round large cities.
After each stop electric trains can speed up so
rapidly from rest that, on a route with frequent
stops, not only can the overall train times be
reduced, but trains can be packed more closely
together, so that a service both faster and more
frequent can be offered to the public. The
tremendous growth of population in the suburbs
and outer suburbs all round the south-east,
south, and south-west of London has been
largely due to the attraction of the electric train
services of the former Southern Railway, which
created the largest suburban electrified railway
system of any individual railway in the world.

A second justification for electrification is
provided by long and steep gradients, which
slow down steam working, and often make

necessary the use of two locomotives and crews
for all the heavier trains. Electric locomotives,
drawing their power from the ample resources
of the line conductors, usually avoid the need
for 'double-heading' (two locomotives), and
again make it possible to speed up the service.
An example of this in Great Britain is seen
in the electrification of the E. R. Sheffield–
Manchester main line with its 966-foot summit
level at Dunford. This station is at the eastern
end of the Woodhead tunnels, 3 miles in length,
by which the railway cuts through the main
chain of the Pennines. Very heavy freight
traffic is worked in each direction over this
route, and as the tunnel is at the summit of long
and steep inclines, and is itself on an incline,
the freight trains drawn by steam locomotives
have needed 10 to 15 minutes to clear it.
Electric working was planned to halve these
times, and so in effect will double the capacity
of the line.

In the mountainous areas of the world, where
long and steep inclines are common on almost
all railway routes, there is also the advantage of
cheap water-power, so that electric working is
doubly a profitable proposition. The rushing
streams of the high mountain valleys can be
dammed into great reservoirs, from which the
water is brought down steep pipe-lines into the
power-stations, to drive turbo-generators supplying electric power for railway use. In countries
like Switzerland, Sweden, and Italy, which have
ample water resources, but have to import all
their coal from other countries, schemes for
using HYDRO-ELECTRIC POWER (q.v. Vol. VIII)
are even more attractive. Italy has electrified
4,400 miles of her railways, Sweden 3,420 miles,

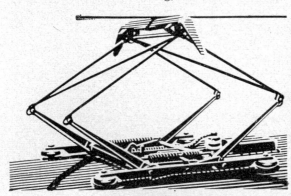

FIG. I. OVERHEAD CONDUCTOR OF CURRENT
Contact is made by the flexible 'pick-up' mounted on the
roof of the locomotive or motor-coach

FIG. 2. 'THIRD-RAIL' CONDUCTOR OF CURRENT
Contact is made by the steel shoe between the driving
wheels

Swiss Federal Railways

A SWISS ELECTRIC LOCOMOTIVE

and Switzerland all but 2,800 miles—or practically the whole of the Swiss railway system.

For suburban working, direct current (d.c.) electrification is preferred, because the locomotive equipment required is sufficiently light and compact to form part of an ordinary coach (*see* ELECTRIC MOTOR, Vol. VIII). On the latest London Tube coaches, all the control gear is packed into the limited space between the coach floor and the track, so that the entire length of the coach, apart from the small driving-cab, is available for passenger seating. On direct current lines it is customary to make up suburban trains into units, with a motor unit and a driver's cab at each outer end, and one or two ordinary trailer coaches in between; the motor units have one or both bogies (*see* LOCOMOTIVE, STEAM) which are motor-driven, and all the motors are under the control of the one motor-man at the front of the train. If more passenger accommodation is needed, as at the morning and evening rush hours, a second unit is coupled up to the first, and the motors of the second unit also come under the control of the motor-man in the original unit. This is called 'multiple-unit working', each unit self-contained with its own motive-power, as compared with the use of independent electric locomotives.

For main lines independent locomotives are customary, so that they may be able to draw trains of ordinary passenger and goods rolling stock. On main lines, also, it is customary to install alternating current (a.c.) electrification rather than direct current. As compared with the 600 to 650 volts of most direct-current railways, very high voltages are used with alternating current—such as the 11,000 volts of the Pennsylvania Railroad, U.S.A., the 15,000 volts of the Swiss Federal Railways, and the 16,000 volts of the Swedish State Railways. These high pressures cheapen the cost of feeding the current to long stretches of line; but with alternating current of high voltage it is necessary to carry a TRANSFORMER (q.v. Vol. VIII) on each locomotive, and the locomotive equipment is heavier and more bulky than in direct-current multiple-unit trains.

Alternating current is always supplied to trains by an overhead conductor, as on lengthy main routes the copper wire used for overhead conducting offers less resistance to the flow of the current than the steel conductor rails used in third rail electrification. With direct current, however, for services that are very frequent, the most reliable method of current distribution and the cheapest to maintain is the 'third rail', laid alongside the running rails, from which the current is picked up by steel shoes. On some railways, such as the Southern Region, the current is returned to the power-stations through the ordinary running rails. Greater electrical efficiency is realized by the London Transport method of laying a fourth rail, for current return, in the centre of the track.

ELECTRIC SHIP. There are many hundreds of ships in the world which are propelled by electric motors—the big brothers of those that move trams and electric trains.

The electric ship has certain advantages: the electric motor is small for the power it delivers, and can, therefore, be tucked away neatly in the stern of the ship. It does not need a long shaft connecting the propeller at the rear with the main machinery, which is often amidships. An electric motor is easy to control, and in certain cases electric ships can be operated from the navigating bridge in the way an electric train is operated from the driver's cab. This is very useful in ships like tugs and dredgers, which have to be constantly making small movements.

There are two kinds of electric ships, steam-electric and diesel-electric. In the steam-electric kind the generators which supply the electric current are driven by steam turbines. In the diesel-electric ships the generators are driven either by diesel engines or by internal-combustion engines (like those that drive motor-cars). The choice of one kind of engine or another depends upon the duties the ship is to carry out.

When the generators which supply the current that drives the screws also supply currents for other purposes, such as cooling and lighting, the generating plant is very like a central power-station.

Electric ships are not new. They were tried out by the Russians on the Volga river early in the present century. For use with internal-combustion engines, electricity was the only means known at that time of reversing the direction of rotation of the propeller shaft. The largest electric ship in the world was the 160,000 horse-power liner *Normandie*. This huge ship was burned at her pier in New York during the Second World War. She was a triumph of marine engineering; when steaming at full power at sea, at about 28 knots, her enormous generators made enough electricity to have run the whole of London's underground railways during the busiest period of the day.

In some of the earliest attempts to build an electric ship storage batteries supplied current to the electric motors. Canoes and launches were the type of craft to which this system was applied; they ran very smoothly and quickly.

For many years submarines used electric motors when they travelled submerged, as no way was known of getting rid of the poisonous exhaust gases of any oil-engine or petrol-engine. The motors took their current from enormous electric storage batteries which were placed within the hull; the batteries were charged by oil-engines, whenever it was safe for the submarine to come to the surface, especially at night. During the Second World War ways were found of using oil-engines even when a submarine was below the surface of the sea (*see* SUBMARINES, Vol. X).

Though electrical drive for ships has many advantages, it is held to be too complicated for certain uses. An electric ship must carry a greater number of highly skilled electricians than an ordinary ship. Costs are high: expensive materials such as copper are needed to make electrical machinery; the fact that there are so few electrical ships means that the mechanical parts are scarce and dear.

See also Vol. VIII: ELECTRIC MOTOR.

Nautical Photo Agency

THE 'NORMANDIE'

British Railways

DONCASTER NORTH NEW SIGNAL-BOX

ELECTRIC SIGNALLING, RAILWAY. 1.

Systems of electric signalling, which have greatly speeded up train traffic at large terminal stations and at busy junctions, are based on the general principles of safety described in SIGNAL-LING, RAILWAY (q.v.). The aim of signalling is to ensure that not more than one train at a time shall be in motion on any stretch of line (long or short, according to circumstances), and that the traffic shall be kept moving in safety with the least possible delay to trains.

The all-electric signal-box, which is gradually replacing the old manual box, has a number of miniature levers in place of the long mechanical levers. Several interconnected movements of signals and points can be made with a single lever. The working of several boxes can be concentrated in one single electric signal-frame, controlling a large area. Signalling can therefore be carried on with a much smaller staff than previously, and traffic handled more quickly.

In the electric signal-box there is generally an illuminated 'layout diagram', representing all the lines in the area; scores of electric contacts in the running lines show precisely where

every train or locomotive is moving or standing. In earlier electric signal-boxes, many of which are still in use, compressed air, electrically controlled, was used for the actual working of the signals and points; but the modern preference is for all-electric working, the power being supplied by electric motors. Many earlier installations combined mechanical locking of points with electric operation, but all-electric locking is now the general practice.

In recent years there have been even more elaborate developments aimed at simplifying and speeding up electric signal-box working. One method dispenses with levers. The controls are thumb-switches placed on the illuminated 'track diagram' in the box, exactly above both the signals and the points that they work. From this idea there developed a method in use at Doncaster. The method calls for only one action to move both junction points and their signals. The thumb-switches are located on the diagram at the signals only and not at the points. At any signal which controls the entry to two or more routes, the thumb-switch is turned to the route desired; provided the track concerned is clear, the movement of the points to the appropriate position takes place automatically, and so does the signal movement.

A still further development is the American 'NX' system, in which thumb-switches are provided round the margin of the track diagram at the entrance to and exit from every possible route controlled by the box. The signalman sets an entry switch and an exit switch; then, if the route desired is clear, the pressing of a button lines up all the points for that route, right across the diagram, and releases all the appropriate signals to 'clear'. Much time is saved by this method. Coloured lights on the diagram indicate exactly how each signal and pair of points has responded. This system was installed at Stratford (London), in the Eastern Region, for the introduction of an electric train service.

Electric signalling has to be safeguarded against current failure. Most of the larger electric signal-boxes on lines used by steam trains have petrol-driven motor-generator sets, which can be started up immediately by the signalmen if the supply from the electric mains fails. On lines worked entirely by electric trains, since the current for trains and signalling is generally derived from the same source, any general current failure would stop the train service. With some types of electric colour-light signals, twin bulbs are provided, and in the event of one failing, the other is switched automatically into position. If a driver should approach an electric colour-light signal which has failed to light up, he is required by rule to stop, and if a telephone is provided at the signal, to ask the next signal-box ahead for instructions.

2. Track-circuits. Electrical track-circuiting is an important safety device on railways. It is a means of showing, in a signal-box, whether a particular stretch of line happens to have a train on it. Many serious collisions in the past would probably have been averted if track-circuiting had been in use at signal-boxes. A stretch of track-circuited line is linked to a signal-box by electric wires; through the circuit formed by wires and rails a weak current flows; this current keeps in position part of a small electrical switching instrument known as a relay (*see* Magnets, Section 2, Vol. VIII). When a train is on that section of railway line, either moving or standing still, the steel wheels and axles of the train form a 'short circuit', by leading the current straight across from one rail to

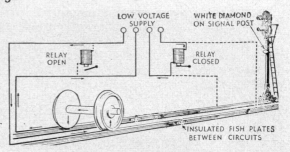

TRACK CIRCUIT

The arrows show the direction of the current, on the left when a train is on the line, and on the right when the line is clear

the other. This diversion of current causes the movable part of the relay to fall out of its normal position. By this means, an electrical indicator may be made to show, in the signal-box, a visible reminder that a train is on the line. The movement of the relay can also be made to lock a signal lever at 'danger', in order to prevent another train entering the same section of line.

Signals in a track-circuited area carry white enamelled plates of diamond shape; this is to indicate to a driver that, if he is detained at that signal for any length of time, he need not follow the old rule of sending his fireman up into the signal-box to remind the signalman, by his presence in the box, that the train is standing in the section; the track-circuit automatically does that for him.

A section of rail which is track-circuited can be detected by the pieces of copper wire which join each rail to the next one, to ensure that the current will flow along the whole section of line. Where a particular track-circuit comes to an end, insulating material can be seen underneath the fish-plates which are used for joining the rails together, and between the rail-ends. The insulation keeps each track-circuit completely self-contained.

ENCYCLOPAEDIA, *see* Reference Books.

ENDEAVOUR, H.M.S. In this barque Captain James Cook (q.v. Vol. V), Royal Navy, made his first voyage round the world in 1768–71. The *Endeavour* had been a Whitby collier. Cook himself had been brought up in the coal trade and approved the choice. The vessel's length was 97 feet along the lower deck, her beam 29 feet, her tonnage 366 tons. The purpose of the voyage was to carry out from the Pacific island of Tahiti, some astronomical observations of the planet Venus, and also to rediscover and survey the coast of New Zealand and to survey the still unexplored east coast of Australia. The result of this voyage was to establish the fact that Australia, New Zealand, and New Guinea were islands, and not part of a 'great Southern Continent', which was now shown not to exist.

Captain Cook's famous voyage in the *Endeavour* was also important for other reasons. Cook was the first to show how to conquer scurvy by the regular distribution of fresh vegetables to the ship's company and by keeping the ship clean and dry (*see* SEA TRAVEL). With the aid of the Astronomer-Royal's new Nautical Almanac Captain Cook showed that he could measure his longitude at sea correct to 1 degree by the system of measuring the lunar distances of the sun and certain selected stars; in later voyages Cook obtained greater accuracy by using the marine CHRONOMETER (q.v.) invented by John Harrison.

The voyage in the *Endeavour* lasted altogether from 25 August 1768 to 12 June 1771—nearly 3 years. The ship sailed by the Madeira Islands to Cape Horn, and then across the Pacific to Tahiti. After the astronomical observations had been made on 3 June 1769, the *Endeavour* sailed southwards round New Zealand and then northwards up the unexplored coast of eastern Australia, landing, among other places, at a bay which Cook called Botany Bay, on account of the variety of flowers they found there. They continued to sail northward, but soon ran into serious difficulties with the GREAT BARRIER REEF (q.v. Vol. III). The *Endeavour*, in the middle of the night, ran from deep water on to a coral reef and stuck fast. When she was finally floated off, she had so large a hole in her side that she was only just brought safely to shore. She took shelter in a bay now called Cook Bay, into which runs a river named after the *Endeavour*. The ship was mended at Batavia, but the men were sick with dysentery and many had died. And so they sailed westwards to the Cape of Good Hope, and then northwards until they turned safely into the English Channel and anchored at the Downs.

See also EXPLORATION; SAILING SHIPS.

ENGINE (1) *Air: see* AIRCRAFT ENGINES. (2) *Rail: see* LOCOMOTIVE, STEAM; DIESEL LOCOMOTIVE; ELECTRIC RAILWAYS; GAS TURBINE LOCOMOTIVE. (3) *Road: see* ROAD TRANSPORT ENGINES. (4) *Ship: see* SHIP.

ENGINE-DRIVER, *see* RAILWAYMEN.

ENGINE-SHEDS, RAILWAY. For maintenance purposes, all locomotives are attached to specific depots, known as engine-sheds or running-sheds. The general principle is that each steam locomotive shall spend some hours of its working day at the shed for examination, boiler washing-out, coaling, and watering, and any necessary repairs. Engines working to schedules which take them away from their home sheds for over 18 hours or so—especially express engines on long non-stop runs—receive this attention at the shed nearest the farther end of their day's run, returning to their home shed on the following day or later. The larger sheds may house up to 100 locomotives or more, and are responsible for all the locomotives in an area, which may include a number of smaller sub-sheds under the control of the main shed. Close to all modern sheds are large automatic coaling plants, and arrangements for disposing quickly of ashes—all designed to reduce to the minimum the 'idle' time spent at the shed by each locomotive.

Running-sheds in general are of two types. There are 'round' sheds, circular in design, with a central turn-table from which all the engine roads radiate; this type of shed requires the most space and is the most costly to build, but is the simplest to work, because of the ease with which engines can be got from any track on to the turn-table and out of the shed to begin a turn of duty. The more common type of shed, however, is rectangular, with a number of parallel tracks. The engine roads in the shed are all provided with deep inspection pits, to enable fitters and engine-crews to get under the engine for the inspection of the motion. Numerous hydrants are provided for the washing-out of boilers. The larger sheds are provided with well-equipped machine shops, suitable for carrying out all running repairs—as distinct from the major overhauls and reboilerings for which each locomotive must go at regular intervals to one of the main locomotive building works.

Among other equipment at the large sheds are 'wheel-drops', which make it possible by hydraulic power to release the wheels from under the locomotive, and wheel lathes for the

THE ROUND HOUSE, DERBY
The lines converge towards the turn-table in the centre

turning of worn tyres to their correct profile. Boilers are re-tubed as necessary, and much other repair work is carried out. Inspection extends to the inside of boilers, to ensure that the locomotive is not developing cracked plates or other sources of trouble.

The staff attached to an engine-shed includes engine-drivers, firemen, cleaners, boiler-washers, fire-droppers, steam-raisers, men to attend to coal, sand, and ashes—all of whom are concerned with the engine working and are under a 'running' foreman. Then there are examiners, fitters, machinists, blacksmiths, boilersmiths, and others, under the foreman mechanic. The staff is completed by storesmen, lampmen, toolmen, and 'callers-up' (whose duty it is to go the round of the houses at which the engine-crews live and to ensure that they are on time for duty). As a rule a locomotive bears somewhere on it either the name or the reference number of its home shed.

See also LOCOMOTIVES, STEAM.

ENGLISH LANGUAGE. The history of the English language begins with the conquest of England by the Angles, Saxons, and Jutes in the 5th century. These tribes probably came from the region of southern Denmark and the Frisian coast, bringing with them the language that we now call Old English, which is closely related to the dialects still spoken in Friesland,

and, less closely, to Danish, Swedish, and Norwegian (*see* GERMANIC LANGUAGES). It was an inflected language, that is to say, relations between words were expressed in Old English by endings showing case, mood, or tense (*see* LANGUAGE STRUCTURE). In modern English this is shown by the order in which they are placed, and by the use of prepositions (contrast, for example, Old English *eallum mannum* with our 'to all men'). The gradual decay of these endings is one of the chief changes that have taken place in the language since Old English times. Though the proportion of native words in the vocabulary has decreased, they remain an indispensable part of the language. The kind of changes that have taken place can be seen by comparing the form of the Lord's Prayer that we now use with an Old English version:

Faeder ure, þu þe eart on heofonum, si þin nama gehalgod. Tobecume þin rice. Gewurþe ðin willa on eorðan swa swa on heofonum. Urne gedaeghwamlican hlaf syle us to daeg. And forgyf us ure gyltas, swa swa we forgyfa ðurum gyltendum. . .

Old English was essentially a colloquial or spoken language. Most documents and manuscripts written in it were intended to be read aloud rather than studied privately, and their style often shows the awkwardness, and the sudden changes of tense or subject that are characteristic of casual speech. But by the time of Alfred, when Christianity was firmly established in England, Christian Latin writers had been translated, and something like a standard literary language was emerging; and by the late 10th century, the dialect of Wessex was coming to be recognized all over England as the official and literary language.

Christian culture brought a great extension in vocabulary. Some words were adopted from Latin, such as 'hymn', 'priest', 'school', 'cook', 'to turn'; others were translated from it. The Scandinavian invaders who settled in the Dane-law in the 9th and 10th centuries, spoke a language very like Old English, and influenced idiom—that is, phrases and turns of speech, as well as vocabulary. Many of the words they introduced—including several relating to law (itself a Scandinavian word) and settlement (-by, -thorpe, -thwaite, and -toft are Scandinavian place-name endings)—were later taken into the general language, whilst some survive only in DIALECTS (q.v.).

As a result of the Norman Conquest, French replaced English for a time as the language of literature. Writers who continued to use English wrote in their own dialect and with their own spelling. From this time the old system of in-flexions began to break down gradually, many of them weakening to -e or -es. The language acquired new pronouns ('they', 'their', 'them' were taken over from Scandinavian); nouns and pronouns ceased to have 'grammatical' gender (which had involved classifying many inanimate things as masculine or feminine, and many animate beings as neuter); and word-order grew more like that of Modern English.

For about 200 years after the Conquest, French remained the language of the new ruling classes and of the new culture; but the majority of Englishmen never learned to speak it. Soon kings and courtiers, churchmen, and adminis-trators learned to use English as well as French. After 1362 lawsuits were conducted in English; and a writer at the end of the 14th century tells us that 'in all the grammar schools of England children leave French, and construe and learn in English, and . . . know no more French than their left heel'. From the middle of the 12th century, however, English itself had steadily adopted a large part of the French vocabulary, particularly terms of art, administration, law, literature, fashion, and food. Often there was already an English word with almost the same meaning, for example: French demander, English

'ask'; and French mansion, English 'house'. In such cases the older native word sometimes disappeared except for a time in poetry; but more often it remained, so that English became particularly rich in synonyms—different words with the same or nearly the same meaning. So considerable were the French additions to the vocabulary, that it later seemed quite natural to combine French words with English affixes, or the reverse, for example 'courtship', from French court and English 'ship'; 'forbearance' from English 'forbear' and the French suffix -ance. Many French phrases were translated into English, such as 'a good time', from the French bon temps.

Certain changes in pronunciation had been going on since the 11th century, but the change was so gradual that we cannot say exactly when Old English became Middle English, the

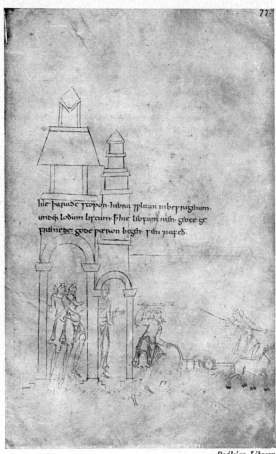

Bodleian Library

PAGE FROM 'GENESIS', A POEM OF ABOUT A.D. 1000, WRITTEN IN OLD ENGLISH AND AT ONE TIME ATTRIBUTED TO CAEDMON

PAGE FROM 'THE OWL AND THE NIGHTINGALE', A MIDDLE
ENGLISH POEM, EARLY 13TH CENTURY

A literal rendering reads:
> I was in a certain valley
> In a very hidden corner;
> I heard holding a great debate
> An owl and a nightingale.
> That debate was stiff and severe and strong,
> Sometimes soft and loud at intervals,
> And each against the other raged
> And let that evil mood all out;
> And each said of the other's character
> The very worst that she could,
> And especially of the other's song
> They held debate very strongly.

language spoken in the first 400 years after the Conquest, or when Middle English became Modern English. We know that by the 15th century most of the inflexions that had survived in one form or another in the Middle English period had been lost, and that by the 16th century many vowels had a pronunciation something like that which we now give them. On the other hand, some characteristic features of Modern English, for example, the possessive neuter pronoun 'its', the emphatic use of 'do' and 'did', and the distinction between the present and present continuous tenses (I eat, I am eating), did not exist or were rare before the 17th century.

The invention of the printing press, the spread of education, and the growth of the conception of STANDARD ENGLISH (q.v.) helped to stabilize grammar and spelling. And whilst these things were happening, the English vocabulary was being greatly enriched, not only from Latin and French sources, but also from other languages with which the English had been brought

into touch by trade contacts. Thus English now seemed fully equipped to be the language of poetry, philosophy, science, and the church; and a new-born nationalism produced many writers prepared to defend its fitness for these subjects. Some, however, ran to excess in their attempts to adopt ponderous Latin words, Latin idiom, and Latin sentence-structure; and many writers invented new words simply for the sake of novelty. Even as late as the beginning of the 18th century there were some scholars and poets who, like Pope, doubted whether their works could reach permanent fame if written in English.

In the 16th century the colloquial language, too, developed great freedom and flexibility, which is partly reflected in ELIZABETHAN DRAMA (q.v. Vol. XII) (the language of the stage usually being close to current speech). Shakespeare's plays, for example, abound in phrases illustrating how one part of speech could be given the function of almost any other part— 'But me no buts', 'Lord Angelo dukes it well', 'stranger'd with an oath', and so on.

The development of scientific thought in the late 17th century after the Restoration led to new standards of precision in the written language and to the growth of scientific vocabulary —it is at this period that words like 'chemistry', 'electricity', 'impulse', 'consciousness' came into use. The connexion of the Court with France, and the prestige of French literature are reflected in the additions now made to the vocabulary of art, literature, and social life; whilst in the 18th century, to match the modern system of trade and commerce, came words like 'banking', 'currency', 'finance', and 'capitalist'. Until well into the 20th century, however, colloquial English, even that of fashionable society, was by no means rigid in grammar or pronunciation, and used slang words and phrases (for example, 'phizz', for physiognomy). But writers such as Dryden and Swift thought such words were allowed too easy an entrance, and proposed an Academy on the French model which they hoped might 'regulate' grammar and vocabulary. The proposal, however, came to nothing. The growth of the middle classes in the 18th century stimulated afresh the desire for 'correctness'. In 1755 appeared Dr. Johnson's *Dictionary*, in which meaning is illustrated by examples from 'the best writers'; and later came dictionaries indicating correct pronunciation.

English grammar began to be thought of as a subject worth study in itself; grammars were published and ran into numerous editions. These laid down rules to be followed in writing English; but they rarely allowed alternatives, or recognized the importance of current usage as opposed to logical rule, and so they tended to widen the gap between the spoken and the written language. This gap became all the more noticeable because by the mid-18th century verse and prose were being written in carefully balanced phrases and in a Latinized style which, in the hands of its less skilled practitioners, became vague and pompous. Wordsworth's plea for simplicity in language, and the revival of old words fostered by Coleridge and Scott, helped to adjust the balance.

In the last hundred years commercial, imperial, and scientific expansion, contact with new cultures (including that of America), the growth of advertisement (which has enabled trade names, such as *kodak*, to come into the language), the influence of journalists using new and arresting words—all these have enlarged the vocabulary of the average Englishman, whilst old words such as 'broadcast' (originally applied mainly to the sowing of seeds) have taken on new meanings. Foreign words are continually being adopted; and, in turn, many European and even some Asiatic languages have borrowed English words—notably words relating to sport and politics; Russian, for example, has taken 'boycott', 'parliament', 'yacht-club'.

Since the 18th century large towns have become the centres of most of English industry, and have increased enormously in population, drawing people from many different areas. Dialects have accordingly declined, being slowly replaced by a modified form of standard English. During the 20th century English has strengthened its position as a world language; but both its written and, still more, its spoken forms vary throughout the world. An educated Indian, for example, may write a clear and grammatical English style, yet may sometimes show slight differences from that of an English writer. In Great Britain itself, the spread of education has produced a literate public; but much that this public reads in books, magazines, or newspapers is written in a style lacking either elegance or precision—for the very richness of the English vocabulary sometimes leads to careless, inexact use. The English spoken in America differs considerably from standard English; it has differences in intonation; it retains some pronunciations and usages now obsolete in England, such as 'gotten', 'mad' in the sense of 'angry', and 'fall' for 'autumn'; and has others of native growth, some peculiar to particular parts of the country; its slang—vivid, if short-lived—is spread throughout the English-speaking world by the films and books. The habits of colloquial speech seem to influence the written language more quickly in America than in England (*see* AMERICAN ENGLISH.) Differences of vocabulary are so extensive that a large dictionary has been produced in several volumes. Canadian usage is inevitably affected by American; and the other Dominions have their own speech-peculiarities, their own SLANG (q.v.), and words and meanings not found in England; but it is scarcely likely that as a whole they will diverge very much from the mother-tongue.

See also LANGUAGE, HISTORY OF; INDO-EUROPEAN.

ERSE, *see* IRISH LANGUAGE.

ESPERANTO, *see* INTERNATIONAL LANGUAGES.

EXPLORATION. From the earliest times men have travelled in search of new lands or of new routes to lands already known. They have set out from different centres; but the history of exploration describes especially the geographical discoveries by which the peoples of the Mediterranean basin and western Europe have enlarged the limits of their known world and filled in its details. While men of many races have asked the question, 'What are other lands and peoples like?' Europeans were the first to invent methods of observing and recording by which they could build their discoveries into an orderly system of geographical knowledge. The history of exploration tells of European expansion by sea and land, and the growth of the world map shows the geographical horizon widening from the Mediterranean to all parts of the earth.

Almost every human activity has created motives for exploration. The oldest and most permanent is economic necessity. When the population of a community increases or the natural resources of its homeland shrink, fresh and unexhausted territory must be sought. A nation that develops new and greater powers of production must find markets for its goods and raw materials for its industries; rivalry in trade drives merchants farther afield in search of

British Museum

A SKIRMISH BETWEEN ENGLISH SEAMEN AND ESKIMOES

From a drawing by John White. It may have been drawn on one of Frobisher's expeditions in search of a North West passage, 1576–8

these. Curiosity, the impulse to see what lies 'on the other side of the hill', has always been a spur to discovery. Captain Cook wrote of 'the pleasure which naturally results to a man from being the first discoverer, even was it nothing more than sand and shoals' and of his 'ambition not only to go farther than anyone had been before, but as far as it was possible for man to go'. To Cook and to many European travellers, a task seemed the more worth while for its difficulty and for the satisfaction of 'beating a record'. To the pursuit of personal fame may be added national ambition, the desire of a people to spread its own social organization, political ideas, and especially its religious beliefs in distant lands. Richard Hakluyt, the great Elizabethan geographer, wrote in order to 'commend our nation for their high courage and singular activity in the search and discovery of the most unknown quarters of the world'.

An explorer's reach is limited by his geographical ideas and by his equipment. In reading the stories of early travellers it is necessary to realize what stock of knowledge they carried. In the Middle Ages men thought that the equatorial zone was too hot to support life,

and this belief barred southerly exploration until the Portuguese coasted Africa in the 15th century. Only because Magellan knew the earth to be spherical and its approximate size, could he attempt to sail round it. Incorrect ideas of the earth's diameter and the lack of instruments to determine longitude hindered many early explorers from making discoveries or from placing them accurately on the map. Columbus, for instance, always believed that he had found, not a new continent, but the east coast of Asia; and the Solomon Islands, discovered by the Spaniards in 1568, were searched for in vain by later Europeans for 200 years because their longitude was wrongly plotted. In the days of sail, ignorance of prevailing winds and currents often deflected ships from their intended course; it was not until Cook in 1772–5 sailed in an easterly direction over the South Pacific, with its 'brave west winds', that the imaginary Southern Continent, supposed to lie across this ocean, could be removed from the charts.

In order to reach his destination and to return safely home, the traveller must be able to fix (and record) his position and to follow a chosen route or course. His success depends on his mobility by land, or the qualities of his ship by sea; on his instruments and methods of navigation; and on the preservation of his health. Technical improvements in these three matters mark stages in the history of exploration, especially by sea. The introduction of the magnetic COMPASS (q.v.), perhaps in the 12th century, enabled mariners to navigate out of sight of land and to draw more serviceable CHARTS (q.v.). When the 15th-century seamen crossed the Equator and lost sight of the Pole Star below the horizon, astronomers provided tables for calculating latitude from the height of the Sun at noon. The first chart of magnetic variation appeared in 1702; and soon after this a truer estimate of the earth's size and shape was made. The baffling problem of longitude, hitherto roughly found by 'dead reckoning', was solved in the middle of the 18th century, when an accurate CHRONOMETER (q.v.) was produced by John Harrison and the *Nautical Almanac* was issued for the first time. Scurvy, the sailor's greatest enemy, was gradually conquered by hygiene, diet, and good discipline; Cook, the hero of this victory, lost not a man from scurvy on his second voyage round the world lasting

3 years. In the 19th century the steamship revolutionized sea travel. The 20th century has seen the internal-combustion engine applied to travel by land and sea and in the air, and wireless used to give the navigator his position and course. These and many other inventions enable the modern explorer to penetrate farther and with better hope of return than his forerunners (*see* NAVIGATION, MARINE). Essentially, his task still calls for the same qualities of resolution, endurance, and skill as theirs.

The story of exploration begins in the eastern Mediterranean. Trade led the PHOENICIANS (q.v. Vol. I) through the Straits of Gibraltar, and about 500 B.C. Carthaginian ships explored the Atlantic coasts from Ireland almost to the Equator. Pytheas, a Greek captain of Marseilles, sailed round Britain about 300 B.C.; and the conquests of Gaul and Britain made north-west Europe known to the Romans.

In the east Alexander the Great led his Greek army to India (331–323 B.C.), and Greeks and Romans discovered the trade routes from the Red Sea to India, first coastwise and later by the open sea with the monsoons. By the time of the geographer Ptolemy (A.D. 150), Roman merchants were navigating the shores of the Indian Ocean from Zanzibar to Malaya and trading with China by both land and sea.

Except for Arabs this traffic ceased during the Dark Ages, and eastern Asia was unknown to Europeans until the great Venetian traveller, Marco Polo, reached China by land in 1271, returning in 1295 with his report of the glory and wealth of 'Cathay'. But the land ways to the East were soon blocked by the Turks, and a new sea route had to be found. In search of this, Prince Henry of Portugal (called 'the Navigator') sent expeditions south along the African coast in the 15th century. Diogo Cão reached the Congo; Bartholomew Diaz rounded the Cape of Good Hope in 1488; and in 1497–9 Vasco da Gama sailed to India.

Meanwhile, the study of Ptolemy's writings had suggested that Cathay could be reached by sailing westward from Europe. The discovery of America (A.D. 1002) by the Norseman Leif Ericsson from Greenland had long been forgotten, and Christopher Columbus, sailing west in the SANTA MARIA (q.v.) from Spain in 1492, found land (in the Bahamas), which he believed to be Cathay, or 'the Indies'. A few years later John Cabot, in a Bristol ship, reached the North American coast, and further voyages by Spaniards, English, and French showed that a great land mass, a 'new world', lay across the westward ocean route to Asia. The Spaniard Balboa was the first European to see the Pacific Ocean or 'South Sea'. Many attempts were made to find a sea passage through or round the American continent, and in 1519 Magellan led a Spanish squadron through his Strait into the Pacific; the *Victoria*, the only surviving ship, completed the first voyage round the world in 1522.

Spain and Portugal divided the newly found lands in the west and the east. Spanish conquerors, converting the Indians and winning treasure from the gold and silver mines, founded a colonial empire in south and central America, to which their galleons carried the wares of the Far East across the North Pacific. The Portuguese, sailing by the Cape of Good Hope and their fortified bases in the Indian Ocean, developed the rich spice trade of the Malay Archipelago and reached China and Japan. Cut off from the commerce of the East, English and Dutch seamen (Chancellor, Frobisher, Davis, Hudson, Barents) sought channels into the Pacific to the north of America and Asia— the North-west and North-east Passages. When they failed to make their way through these ice-bound waters, they turned to the southern sea routes. In 1577–80 Francis Drake, in the GOLDEN HIND (q.v.), defied the claims of Spain and Portugal by passing through the Magellan Strait and sailing across the Pacific to the Philippines and the 'Spice Islands' (Moluccas). This was the second voyage round the world; another Englishman, Thomas Cavendish, made the third (1586–8), and Dutchmen the next two. In 1616 the passage into the Pacific by Cape Horn was discovered.

A more serious challenge to Spanish and Portuguese control of eastern trade was made on the Cape of Good Hope route. In 1592 the East Indies were reached by an English ship, in 1596 by a Dutch squadron; and within 10 years England and Holland each had its East India Company. The Dutch drove the Portuguese from their trading stations, and by 1650 had founded a commercial empire with its capital at Batavia (Jakarta), in Java. Their pilots discovered the north coast of Australia and part of its west and south coasts, and in 1642–3 Abel Tasman made a great voyage from Batavia. By sailing round Australia he proved that it was an

H.M.S. 'RESOLUTION' IN THE ANTARCTIC IN 1773

The sailors are shooting albatrosses and collecting ice from an iceberg for drinking water. Engraving entitled 'The Ice Islands' from Cook's *Voyage towards the South Pole.*

island, although he did not see its east coast; and he discovered Tasmania and New Zealand.

To the east of New Zealand the South Pacific Ocean was unknown, and it was thought that a vast inhabited 'Southern Continent' occupied this area. Its exploration from the east was frustrated by contrary winds and by the enormous death-rate from scurvy on long voyages without fresh food. In the late 18th century the British sent expeditions to the Pacific, under Byron, Wallis, Carteret, and James Cook, all of whom sailed round the world; only Cook's last two voyages were made in an easterly direction. Captain Cook, on his three circumnavigations in H.M.S. ENDEAVOUR (q.v.) (1768–71) and H.M.S. *Resolution* (1772–5 and 1776–80), revealed a larger area of the globe than any other man has done. New Zealand was charted, and the east coast of Australia discovered; the existence of the Southern Continent was disproved, and the chief Pacific island groups were discovered or explored; the Antarctic Circle was crossed for the first time, and a latitude of 71° S. reached, in ice conditions of terrible difficulty; the north-west coast of America was explored, and the strait between Asia and

Alaska navigated as far as 70° N., within the Arctic Circle. This great achievement cost very few casualties from scurvy.

After Cook the work of exploration gathered impetus, and its character changed. There were still large blanks on the map of the world: the interior of Africa and Australia, and the Polar Regions. Most of the world's coasts were known, but few were properly charted. Within 50 years of Cook's death Australia had been settled; its coasts were surveyed by Matthew Flinders; and inland exploration had begun. Canada was crossed by land by Alexander Mackenzie (1793), and the United States by Captains Lewis and Clark (1804–6). The courses of the great African rivers were mapped; Mungo Park explored the Niger (1795–7 and 1805), Captains Speke and Grant traced the Nile (1860–3), and H. M. Stanley the Congo (1874–7). David Livingstone, the greatest of African explorers, revealed a large part of Central Africa on his missionary travels between 1849 and 1873. The Arctic channels from the Atlantic to the Pacific were again attempted and, after many failures, navigated—the Northeast Passage by the Swede A. E. Nordenskiöld

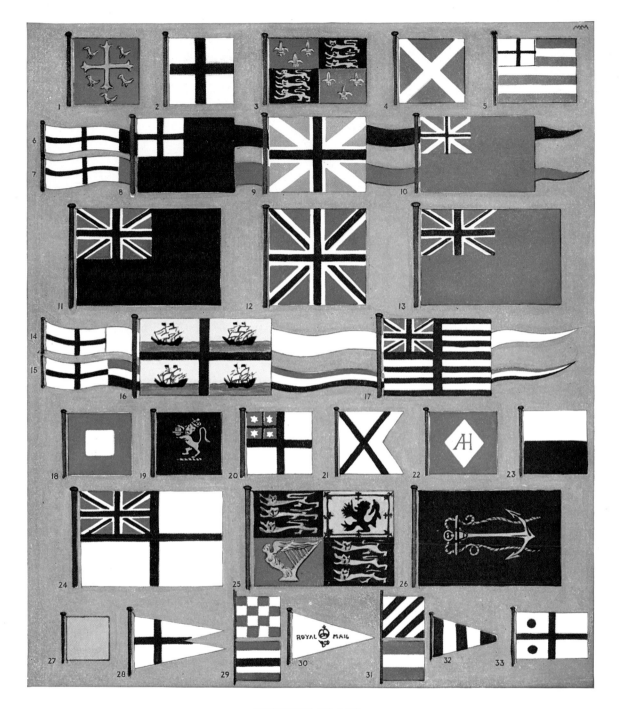

BRITISH FLAGS

1, 2, 4. Banners bearing the arms of St. Edward, St. George, and St. Andrew. 3. Tudor Royal Standard. 5. Elizabethan Ensign. 6, 7. Red and Blue Pendant (Royal Navy). 8, 11. Red Ensign, 17th century and modern. 9, 12.
Union Jack 1606 and 1801. 10, 13. Blue Ensign, 18th century (Royal Navy) and modern. 14. White or Commissioning Pendant (Royal Navy). 15. Common or Church Pendant (Royal Navy). 16. Trinity House flag or 'Jack'.
17. Ensign of Hon. East India Company. 18. 'Blue Peter'—International Code 'P'. 19, 20, 21, 22. House Flags of
Cunard White Star, Shaw Savill and Albion, British India Steam Navigation, and Blue Funnel Line. 23. Pilot Flag.
24. White Ensign, modern (Royal Navy). 25. Royal Standard, modern. 26. Admiralty Flag (Royal Navy).
27. Quarantine flag—International Code 'Q'. 28. Commodore's Broad Pendant (Royal Navy). 29. Distress
Signal—International Code 'N.C.'. 30. Royal Mail Pendant. 31. Request for fresh water—International Code
'Y.J.'. 32. Answering pendant, International Code. 33. Rear-Admiral's flag (Royal Navy).

(1879) and the North-west Passage by the Norwegian Amundsen (1903–6). The North-west Passage was first made in an easterly direction in 1942 by Inspector Larsen of the Royal Canadian Mounted Police. The exploration of the Polar lands is described in a separate article (see POLAR REGIONS, EXPLORATION, Vol. III).

For many centuries the story of exploration tells of men setting out on foot or in small ill-found sailing-ships, not knowing the dangers they would meet nor their chances of survival and return. The modern explorer is not only far better equipped; his tasks and the spirit which he brings to them have changed also. Few new discoveries remain to be made. Trade routes, precious metals, and colonies are no longer the only objectives. The passion for complete and exact knowledge is the strongest motive in modern exploration, of which Captain Cook was the true forerunner. When the pioneer has done his work, the map-maker and the specialist-explorer begin theirs. A modern geographer has said: 'The world is discovered, but I doubt whether a hundredth part of the land surface of the globe is surveyed in sufficient detail for modern requirements.' Yet the history of older and of recent exploration tell the same tale, which has no end. It is the tale of man in contact with nature.

The lives of the great explorers mentioned in this article are described in Volume V.

See also SAILING SHIPS; SEA TRAVEL; CHARTS; MAPS, HISTORY OF; MAP PROJECTIONS; TRADE ROUTES.
See also Vol. III: POLAR REGIONS.

EXPLORATION, SCHOOL.

The British (formerly Public) Schools Exploration Society was founded in 1932 by Surgeon-Commander G. Murray Levick, R.N., a member of Captain Scott's last Antarctic expedition. It takes boys of about 16 to 18 years old to uninhabited country (including such places as Lapland, and Canada) in the summer holidays, and there teaches them the technique of exploration. The boys have to carry all their equipment and fend for themselves in the wilds. They carry out scientific study of the weather, rocks, natural history, and radio conditions of their district. Above all they undertake surveys (see SURVEYING, Vol. VIII), mapping hitherto unmapped country. Records are kept of the type and quantity of food needed under varying conditions.

EXPRESS LETTER.

The Post Office in Britain offers many special services which hasten the transmission of a letter or parcel, and similar services are provided in other countries. Express services were very important in the past, though now that the telephone is so generally used, they have become less so. A special fee has to be paid, usually by the sender, which varies with each service.

A packet may be handed over the counter of a post office and taken all the way to its destination by a post office messenger. In 1950 this cost 6d. a mile, with extra fees for more than one packet. Live animals, liquids, money, or even people may be sent in this way.

Packets which go through the post in the normal way may be taken specially quickly from the delivery office either at the sender's request (shown by writing 'Express' on them) or at the request of the person to whom they are being sent. There is a service of 'Special Delivery on Sundays', which is only available between important cities, and which deals with letters only. Messages may be telephoned to an express delivery office, and delivered by special messenger.

Another quick way of sending things is the 'Railex' service. Postal packets are dispatched by rail, met at the nearest station to their destination, and specially delivered anywhere in Great Britain. A 'railway parcel' is hurried up in the same way.

A letter taken to the parcel or booking-office of most railway stations will be sent off by the next train. When it arrives at the station to which it is addressed, it will be posted in the nearest letter-box, unless it is marked 'to be called for'. It is also possible to wire for it to be delivered quickly by one of the services already described.

By the International Express service, letters can be delivered by special messenger abroad. A minimum fee is paid by the sender, and any further charge by the person to whom the packet is sent.

See also POST OFFICE.

EXPRESS TRAINS,

see BLUE TRAIN; CORNISH RIVIERA; FLYING SCOTSMAN; GOLDEN ARROW; TWENTIETH CENTURY LIMITED; RAILWAY COACHES.

F

FELUCCA. This was the name given in the 18th century to the long, low, Mediterranean galley-like craft, which could be easily rowed but were generally sailed, and because of their length were rigged with two or three masts carrying lateen sails. The larger feluccas might have square sails on the foremast. The type was common all over the Mediterranean and round the Straits of Gibraltar. Feluccas were handled by Spaniards, and were also popular with the Greek pirates amongst the islands of the Archipelago. To-day the term covers all types of small sailing-craft rigged with lateens or lug-sails, and used for fishing and other purposes which do not take them far out of sight of land.

FELUCCA, ALEXANDRIA, EGYPT

In the eastern Mediterranean Felucca describes all the smaller local sailing-craft, particularly those working out of Port Said and Alexandria in Egypt.

See also SAILING; SAILING SHIPS.

FERRY, *see* FORD AND FERRY.

FERRY, TRAIN. Where a water-way is too wide and deep to be bridged, railways on both sides can be linked by train-ferries—steamers or motor-driven vessels on whose decks railway tracks are laid. A train-load of coaches or wagons is run on to the deck at one harbour, and run ashore on reaching the other. The rise and fall of the tide must be allowed for. A hinged bridge may be used, up which the rolling stock is propelled on to the ferry at high tide, and down at low tide; or the ferry-steamer may be docked in an enclosed dock, protected by lock-gates, within which the steamer can be brought level with the land.

The larger ferry-steamers usually contain, on an enclosed middle deck, four railway tracks converging towards the bow of the vessel. The vehicles pass on to the bridge connecting the steamer with the shore tracks through a large opening in the bow. The steamers have their engine-rooms below the track level, and their funnels on one side, like an aircraft-carrier, or on both. Some of the vessels which carry passenger trains have comfortable cabin and saloon accommodation for passengers who do not wish to remain in their coaches during the crossing.

The only British passenger train-ferry is that which connects Dover with Dunkirk in France. By this means it is possible to run the 'Night Ferry' sleeping-car service between London and Paris, and passengers are carried in their sleeping-berths across the Channel without changing. For freight traffic there is the train-ferry between Harwich and Zeebrugge in Belgium. Time is saved by ferrying freight in this way; with perishable goods no time is lost in transferring them from train to steamer and from steamer back to train. Fragile goods benefit equally because they can remain in the wagons as originally packed, with much less risk of breakage.

In Europe the best-known train-ferry services are those connecting the Scandinavian countries across the Baltic and neighbouring waters. Of these, the principal ones ply between Sassnitz

DOVER–DUNKIRK TRAIN-FERRY IN DOVER DOCKS
The opening through which the trains run on to the ferry can be seen on the left

in Germany and Trelleborg in Sweden; Wärne-munde in Germany and Gjedser in Denmark; Copenhagen in Denmark and Malmö in Sweden; and across the Great Belt on the Danish route from Jutland to Copenhagen. Two other Danish ferry-crossings—the Little Belt on the Jutland–Copenhagen route, and the Störström on the Gjedser–Copenhagen line—have been replaced in recent years by very large bridges.

In the United States there are numerous wagon ferries in New York Harbour and across the great rivers such as the Mississippi; but, as elsewhere, with the development of large-scale bridge-building technique, the tendency is to replace the ferries by permanent bridges.

See also BRIDGES, RAILWAY.

FIDO, *see* AIRPORT.

FIGURES, *see* COUNTING, HISTORY OF; MEASUREMENT, HISTORY OF.

FINNISH AND ALLIED LANGUAGES. Finnish, Estonian, Hungarian, and Lappish are related as a 'family' of languages, and must have descended from one common language long ago. They are all members of the Uralian family, and languages of this family are spoken by many different peoples ranging from Hungary, Finland, and Lapp regions of northern Scandinavia

and Russia in Europe, to parts of Siberia in Soviet Asia. They differ in construction a great deal from more widely spoken languages, such as English. In English, for example, we often change the vowel in a word to express grammatical differences, such as the tense of a verb (as in 'sing', 'sang', 'sung'); whereas in Uralian, grammatical difference is often expressed by changing the consonant; thus Finnish *suku* (race), genitive *suvun*. In Finnish, the noun not only has many cases, but is also conjugated, that is, it changes according to the first, second, or third person in grammar, as our verbs do: *kirja* 'book', *kirja-ssa* 'in a book', *kirja-ssa-ni* 'in my book'. In Finnish, too, there are many verbal nouns and adjectives which, together with the different forms of the noun, lead to very complex words, such as *sanoa-kse-si* 'that thou mightest say' (the infinitive of *sanoa*—'to say', in the second person singular, in the 'translative case'). (*See also* LANGUAGE, STRUCTURE.)

The most important of the Uralian languages belong to the sub-family called the Finno-Ugrian branch, which includes Hungarian, Finnish, Estonian, and Lappish, as well as some other languages spoken in Russia. Hungarian, Finnish, and Estonian all have large literatures which date from medieval times. Hungarian, the language of about 9½ million people in Hungary, is spoken also in Transylvania and the Bukovina. Finnish and Estonian are closely related. Finnish is spoken by about 3 million people in Finland or more than three-quarters of the population. Estonian is spoken by about 1,500,000 people in Estonia and parts of Latvia. Lappish is the language of the Lapps who number nearly 32,000, and who inhabit the northernmost part of Norway, Sweden, and Finland, and the Kola peninsula in extreme north-west Russia.

Besides the Finno-Ugrian group, the Uralian family includes the Samoyede languages, which are spoken only by the 18,000 Samoyedes of north-east European Russia and north-west Siberia.

See also Language, History of.
See also Vol. I: Finns; Estonians; Hungarians; Lapps.

FLAGS. 1. History. A flag or standard is a symbol of a group. Early standards came into being to identify a tribe, a regiment, or a town. From ancient days they were treated with great respect; some were held to be of religious significance, and in war, the standard was a rallying point for the armies.

The standards of the ancient Egyptian and Assyrian armies were carved objects rather than cloth flags, though their navies displayed symbols embroidered on the sails of ships. Among the Greeks, the first standard was a piece of armour carried on a spear; later, many of the cities adopted their special emblems. The Romans used many carved standards and cloth flags; there was a standard-bearer attached to each 'century' (a unit of about 120 foot soldiers); the cavalry carried cloth flags; a legion (a unit of several thousand warriors) followed a bronze standard in the shape of the famous Roman eagle.

In later times flags came to be decorated with Christian symbols, such as the cross of St. George. By the 13th century, in the principal Christian countries of Europe, flags had become involved in the complicated customs and rules of Heraldry (q.v.).

The chief flag was then called the Standard. It is represented to-day by the rectangular Royal Standard, which is hoisted over the king's residence, and at naval and military ceremonies which he attends as head of the forces. By the 15th century the standard had grown long and tapering in shape, with its end forked. Its size depended on the importance of its owner. An upright line divided it into two parts, that nearer

the staff bearing the cross of St. George, while the owner's coat-of-arms filled up the rest. It was not intended to be carried into the thick of battle (since it might be as long as 10 yards, it was not easily carried), but elsewhere it was displayed wherever the owner happened to be—outside his tent near the battlefield or tournament ground, or over his castle when he was in residence. The old standard is not used to-day.

The Banner was the personal flag or ensign (another word for a flag) carried by a knight-banneret and persons of higher rank. (A knight-banneret, an honour which could be conferred only on the battlefield, was one degree higher in rank than an ordinary knight.) The banner, which bore the heraldic coat-of-arms of its owner, just as it appeared on his shield, was rectangular. As with the standard, its size depended on rank. The banner had begun as a flag of battle in the days when noblemen had to furnish the king with men and arms in war time. A baron's personal troop would follow his personal banner and nobody else's. Strictly speaking, the Royal Standard just mentioned is derived from the banner and not from the standard of the 15th and 16th centuries, for it bears the arms of the king without the national flag. Although it serves the purpose of the old standard, by showing the king's whereabouts, it is by nature the king's personal battle-flag.

The Pennon was a personal ensign, carried by a plain knight, who did not rank high enough for a banner. It did not compare with the banner for size, because it was designed to be borne on the end of a lance. It was either pointed, or forked like a swallow-tail, and the coat-of-arms was embroidered so that it appeared right way up when the lance was held horizontally (or 'couched') ready for action.

The Pennoncel or Pensel was a small version of the pennon. Later it came to be the distinctive ensign carried only by esquires who attended upon knights. It was mainly shown on ceremonial occasions, such as weddings and funerals.

The Guidon was a simpler form of the standard. It was generally shorter, the end was rounded rather than forked, and it did not bear the national St. George's cross. Nor did it bear the full coat-of-arms, but only the owner's heraldic crest or badge (see Heraldry). It was carried by the leader of a cavalry troop.

The Streamer was a naval flag, which might

National Maritime Museum

VISIT OF CHARLES II TO THE FLEET, 5TH JUNE 1672

Painting by William van de Velde the younger. The King was received in the *Royal Prince* (on right). She flies the Jack,
Admiralty Flag, Standard, Union, Ensign, and Streamers

be up to 60 yards long. It tapered like the standard, and the end was forked. Like the guidon, it bore only the crest or badge. To-day we call this type of flag a 'pennant' or 'pendant', and the end is often straight and not forked.

2. NATIONAL FLAGS. Every country has its national flag, and many of them have interesting histories. The cross of St. George has been an English flag since its first appearance in the middle of the 13th century. The present Union Jack is a blend of English, Scottish, and Irish flags. The English cross of St. George and the Scottish cross of St. Andrew were united to form the first Union Jack when the two kingdoms were united under James I in 1603. The cross of St. Patrick of Ireland was added soon after the union of Ireland with Great Britain in 1801. The Union Jack should be flown with the broader white diagonal line uppermost at the corner near the top of the mast.

The American flag now flown, consists of thirteen stripes (seven red and six white), with a small blue rectangle in a corner containing forty-eight white stars. The stripes refer to the original thirteen colonies which formed the first United States at the American Revolution in 1776; since 1818 this part of the flag has remained unaltered. The stars represent the number of States; as each new State has been founded or

joined to the rest, the number of stars has been increased.

3. ARMY, NAVY, AND AIR FORCE FLAGS. In the army, flags are called Colours, and each regiment generally has two: the King's colour and the regimental colour. The King's colour is the Union Jack, with various additions; the regimental colour is embroidered with badges, mottoes, and the names of battles in which the regiment has taken part. The edges are fringed with gold, and the colour has gold and silver tassels hanging from it.

The word 'colour' came into use in the 16th century. Paid soldiers under hired commanders then began to take the place of earlier fighting bands, who had consisted merely of tied agricultural tenants and personal servants of landowning knights or barons (*see* LAND WARFARE, and FEUDAL SYSTEM, Vol. X). The new professional commanders were not always men who inherited the right to show a coat-of-arms, so they began to design simple coloured flags of their own, round which each regiment could rally.

The British Navy for long had three flags which were famous in battle. It was the custom to split up the large fleets into three groups, called 'centre', 'van' (vanguard, from the French *avant-garde*, a fighting force which took the lead), and 'rear'. The centre was commanded by the admiral, the van by the vice-admiral, and the rear squadron by the rear-admiral. In order that any ship in one of the three groups could recognize its own admiral, the centre flagship flew a plain red flag, the van a plain white one, and the rear a plain blue. Each vessel in the fleet showed which of the three squadrons it belonged to by flying a red, white, or blue flag with the national flag in the top corner. These flags were called 'ensigns' (pronounced 'ensun').

In 1864 new rules were made. Ships of the Royal Navy and the Royal Yacht Squadron alone now have the right to wear the White Ensign (a white flag with the red cross of St. George, and a Union Jack in the upper quarter near the flagstaff). All other British ships may wear the Red Ensign or 'Red Duster' (a red flag with the Union Jack in the upper quarter); the right to wear the Blue Ensign (a blue flag with the Union Jack in the upper quarter) is limited to ships (other than men-of-war) in Admiralty service, merchant ships commanded by officers of the Royal Naval Reserve, and (with badge) ships belonging to various Government Offices. Each of the Dominions has its own version of the Blue and the Red, but not the White, Ensign. Foreign ships generally wear a version of their national flag as an ensign, and most countries have separate ensigns for men-of-war and merchant ships. Ensigns are worn either on a staff at the stern or at the 'peak' or yardarm. In addition to the ensign, ships may wear various other flags or pendants at their mastheads. In the Royal Navy each flag officer (rear-admiral and above) flies his own flag at the mainmast of his flagship; a commodore flies a broad pendant. Other warships fly a 'commissioning pendant' while in commission: this is a narrow strip of white bunting with a red cross of St. George near the staff.

The Royal Air Force, like the Royal Navy, has its own ensign. This is flown on the yardarm of a mast, alongside a pennon which shows the rank of the officer commanding the station or unit. Squadron-leaders and officers of higher rank are entitled to a pennon; this may be flown on an officer's motor-car, when he is on duty.

4. Miscellaneous Flags. Various plain flags have recognized symbols or meanings all over the world. A white flag is the sign of truce or surrender in war. A red flag means mutiny or revolution—although nowadays it is more usually flown as a warning signal by ships or barges carrying explosives or inflammable liquids. Formerly a black flag (the 'Jolly Roger') was the flag popularly associated with Pirates (q.v.), although in fact gangs of robbers at sea generally flew a proper national flag to avoid causing suspicion. Sometimes, in sea fights, a black flag was hoisted to indicate that no quarter was asked for or given; commanders found this a useful way of making their own men fight harder. In British prisons it was once the practice to fly a black flag as a public signal that an execution had taken place.

A flag is flown at 'half-mast' (that is to say, not flying at the top), as a sign of mourning on land or sea. 'Dipping' a flag at sea—lowering the ensign a third of the way down and hoisting it after acknowledgement—is the salute used between merchant ships or by merchant ship to man-of-war. When the King reviews his troops, the regimental colours are lowered in salute.

For many centuries, from the beginning of the 13th century, British ships insisted that foreign ships should 'strike' (haul down) their sails, later only their topsails and top-gallant sails, when they met the British flag in the 'narrow seas'. The British claimed that the narrow seas extended from Cape Finisterre in Spain to the coast of Norway. Foreigners were not expected to show their own flag at all in sight of the British one. This claim, which was called sometimes 'The Honour of the Flag' and sometimes 'The Salute in the Narrow Seas', was probably connected with the claim made by the kings of England to rule over France and Normandy. It led to bloody battles, and was one cause of the Third Dutch War (1672–4). An English admiral even fired into King Philip of Spain's ship for wearing his own royal flag in the British Seas, when he was coming over to marry Queen Mary. The claim was quietly dropped towards the end of the 18th century.

In warfare, a ship or a land fortress which is showing a flag can indicate surrender by 'striking' its flag. A ship in distress at sea may signal the fact by flying its flag upside down.

See also Flag Signalling.

FLAG SIGNALLING. This was the principal method of communication between ships at sea, before the introduction of radio. Although flags were used in very early times as a means of identification, there is no record of their having been used in England for signalling before the middle of the 14th century. An entry of that time in *The Black Book of Admiralty*, preserved in the Courts of Justice, lays down that a flag of council, hoisted 'high in the middle of the mast', is to be used by the Admiral of a fleet in calling his captains together to confer. This signal was probably used at the Battle of Sluys in 1340, during the Hundred Years War.

Elaborate systems of flag signalling, however, were apparently not developed in the British Navy until many centuries later, although they were in use by other countries. The Venetian Navy had a flag code by 1420, and the Spaniards and French were both using one by the middle of the 16th century. A French *Book of War on Land and Sea*, dated 1543, gives a list of the signals then in use, including 'a square flag between the maintop and the small square flag which is on the maintop mast', as the order to chase the enemy. When, however, the British fleet under Howard fought the Spanish Armada in 1588, they seem to have used only such signals as could be made by firing guns and dipping sails. At the time of the Commonwealth, in the mid-17th century, flag signals were again in use, however, though they seem to have been of a very simple kind. The signal 'engage the enemy' was used by the great British admiral Monk in the sea-battles against the Dutch in 1653, and later by Blake at the battle of Santa Cruz against the Spanish West Indian fleet in 1657, was given by 'shooting-off two guns and putting a red flag over the fore topmast head'. By 1688 the first books of flags had been published, giving coloured drawings of the Union Flag (a smaller version of which, when flown from the jackstaff, at the bow, was called the 'Union Jack' to distinguish it from the larger ensign or 'ancient', as it was called) and various other ensigns, flags, and pendants (*see* FLAGS). In 1714, when the first printed Signal Book was issued to the Fleet, flags were still hoisted singly, and had different meanings when hoisted in different parts of the ship. This system continued until the latter part of the century, by which time about fifty flags were in use and each could be hoisted in any one of up to seven different positions, giving altogether 330 possible meanings. Even this number was not enough to deal with the increasingly complicated signals of war at sea. Many new systems were tried,

especially while Admiral Howe was First Lord of the Admiralty from 1783 to 1788; but the only one developed was the 'numerary' or number code. Each number from 0 to 9 had its own flag; so that three flags, hoisted together one above the other, referred to the three-figure number of a word, letter, or order in the code-book. This was the method still in use in Nelson's battles of St. Vincent in 1797, Copenhagen in 1801, and Trafalgar in 1805, at the last of which he made his famous signals:

(Numeral	England	Expects	That	Every	Man
flags	253	269	863	261	471
hoisted)	Will	Do	His	D T Y
	958	220	370	4 21 19 24

followed by: 'Engage the enemy more closely.'

In 1813 Sir Home Popham enlarged the scope of the numerary code by adding twenty-three letter flags to the ten numerals; this is the basis of the system in use to-day. The flags or pendants are hoisted either singly, in pairs, in threes, or in fours on the signal halyards, and the Chief Yeoman of Signals in a warship is a master in this art of speaking from ship to ship. The same methods are used by coastguard stations and port authorities. (*See* Colour Plate opposite p. 144.)

An International Code of signals is used by all Merchant Shipping. This code consists of twenty-six letter flags, ten numeral pendants, and five substitute and answering flags and pendants. Complicated messages or unusual words are spelt out by these, but many of the letter flags have single-flag code meanings as well: P, for instance, is the well-known Blue Peter, which is a signal that the vessel hoisting it is about to put to sea; G is the Pilot flag, and Q was formerly the Quarantine flag.

See also FLAGS; SEMAPHORE; SIGNALS.
See also Vol. X: SEA WARFARE, HISTORY OF.

FLEMISH LANGUAGE, *see* GERMANIC LANGUAGES.

FLIGHT ENGINEER, *see* AIRCREW.

FLOATING DOCK, *see* DOCKS.

FLOTSAM AND JETSAM, *see* WRECKS.

FLYING. 1. LIFT. When an aeroplane is flying on a steady, level course, the wing must produce a lift force equal to the weight of the plane. When an aeroplane is climbing, for example in AIRCRAFT TAKE-OFF (q.v.), greater lift force is

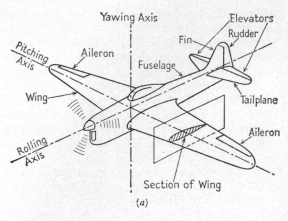

FIG. I. (*a*) DIAGRAM OF AEROPLANE
(*b*) SECTION OF WING IN AIRSTREAM

needed. The wing is generally rigidly fixed to the aeroplane, but some types of aircraft such as helicopters (*see* ROTORCRAFT) have a form of wing which spins round above the craft. If an ordinary wing were to be cut through, the shape of the cross-section would be more or less as shown in Fig. I (*b*)—the upper surface being curved differently from the lower surface. What will happen when a wing of this section is moved through the air?

Suppose two people hold each end of a model wing of this shape in their hands when a strong wind is blowing (the effect of a wind blowing past a stationary wing is the same as that of a wing passing through air at rest). These two people would feel the lift force of the wing, and if they had a suitable instrument they would notice that the speed of the air over the upper surface is greater than the wind speed, whilst the air passing the lower surface is slowed down. The result of these differences in the speed of the air is that the air pressure on the upper surface is decreased, while that on the lower surface is increased. Since the pressure on the lower surface is greater than the pressure on the upper surface, the wing will be subjected to an upward force—the lift. Because the aeroplane is being forced through the air by its propeller or jet, the air flows past the wing fast enough to give the necessary lift—the faster the speed the more the lift. This simple principle has enabled the 130-ton BRABAZON (q.v.) to rise high in the sky.

2. DRAG. When an aeroplane is moving through the air it is also subjected to a force tending to resist the motion. This force is known as the 'drag'. For an aeroplane in steady, level flight the engines must produce a forward thrust equal to the drag. The steady forward motion of the aeroplane then enables the wing to produce the necessary lift, as previously explained.

There are various forms of drag. The pressures acting on the wing which have been mentioned above, together with the pressures acting on the other parts of the aeroplane, produce a certain amount of drag, known as the 'form drag'. As the air passes over the surfaces of the aeroplane it also sets up a certain amount of friction— the drag produced in this way being termed 'skin friction drag'. The sum of the form drag and the skin friction drag is the 'profile

Aeronautics

FIG. 2. THE 'OLYMPIA' GLIDER, WHICH HAS A VERY LARGE WING-SPAN TO REDUCE
DRAG AT LOW SPEED

Compare this with the Vampire on p. 9, a fast fighter with short wing-span drag'. It is important to keep the drag of an aeroplane as low as possible, so modern high-speed aircraft have carefully designed wings, the surface being kept as smooth as possible, and projections, such as rivet-heads, eliminated. Thus the profile drag is kept low.

The remaining drag is known as 'induced drag', and is due to the disturbance of the air caused by the wing in producing lift. Now whereas the profile drag increases as the speed of the aeroplane increases, the induced drag falls. It therefore tends to be important in the case of slow-flying aircraft such as gliders; but it may be reduced by making the wing span as large as possible for a given area (*see* Fig. 2). When the aircraft is flying fast, however, the induced drag is of little significance. So in the case of a fighter the wing span can be quite short for a given wing area, which makes it easier for the aircraft to twist and turn in battle.

3. LIFT AND SPEED. The amount of lift produced by a wing of given shape and size depends

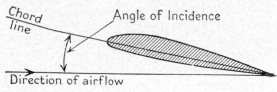

FIG. 3. SECTION OF WING SHOWING THE ANGLE OF INCIDENCE

on its speed through the air and its 'angle of incidence'. This is the angle at which the wing is inclined to the direction of the airstream, and is measured from a line called the 'chord-line' of the section (Fig. 3).

When an aeroplane is in steady flight, the lift produced by the wing must equal the weight (ignoring small amounts of lift produced by other parts of the aeroplane). In certain conditions of flight the weight may not equal the lift; thus, when the aeroplane is pulling out of a dive, the lift which is tending to push the wings upward will be considerably greater than the weight of the aeroplane.

The necessary amount of lift to support an aircraft can be produced by flying either at a low speed but with the wing inclined at a large angle of incidence, or at a higher speed and the wing inclined at a lesser angle. Sometimes a pilot wants to fly an aeroplane as slowly as possible, as when coming in to land. But if the incidence of a wing is increased beyond a certain point,

the aeroplane suddenly loses its lift, and 'stalls', or begins to fall. The speed at which stalling occurs decides the lowest speed at which the aeroplane will fly.

A wing stalls because, when the angle of incidence becomes large enough, the air will no longer flow smoothly over the upper surface

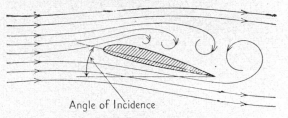

FIG. 4. AIR EDDIES ROUND WING WHEN ITS ANGLE OF INCIDENCE IS LARGE

(Fig. 4). The air breaks away and forms large eddies, and the lift is reduced. If an aeroplane is deliberately stalled, the nose suddenly drops; the aeroplane dives until the incidence is reduced below the stalling angle, and the speed is sufficient for the wing to produce lift at a smaller angle of incidence.

If a device could be fitted to the wing which would enable it to produce the required lift at a lower speed without stalling, the aeroplane would be able to fly more slowly, yet remain safe. Such a device is a 'flap' (Fig. 6). An alternative device would be one which would enable the angle to be increased beyond the ordinary stalling angle of the wing. This type of device is

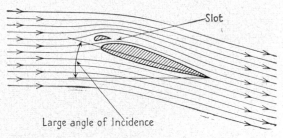

FIG. 5. SECTION OF WING WITH SLOT AT LEADING EDGE IN AIRSTREAM

termed a 'slot' (Fig. 5), and prevents the air breaking away from the upper surface; the slot guides the air round the front edge of the wing (which is called the 'leading edge' of the wing).

4. STABILITY. For an aeroplane to fly satisfactorily, it must be both stable and controllable. Imagine an aeroplane flying straight and level,

The Aeroplane

FIG. 6. PRESTWICK 'PIONEER' FLYING VERY SLOWLY
The wings are fitted with flaps at the trailing edge and
slots at the leading edge.

and then a gust causing one wing to drop a little. If the aeroplane tends to return to its original position with the wings level without the pilot having to move the controls, it is said to be stable. If the aeroplane 'pitches', its nose having moved either up or down as a result of some disturbance, a tendency to return to level flight means that the craft is longitudinally stable. If the nose is pushed to left or right by a gust (which is called 'yawing', as in a sailing ship), a tendency to right itself means that the aeroplane is directionally stable.

Lateral stability is got by inclining the wings upwards slightly from root to tip, an inclination called the 'dihedral' (see Fig. 7). The purpose of the tailplane is to provide longitudinal stability. It is a small wing, which produces a lift force in the same way as the main wing. If a disturbance makes the nose rise, the angle of incidence of the tailplane increases, and its lift also increases. This tends to raise the tail, thus restoring the aeroplane to its original level

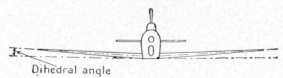

Dihedral angle

FIG. 7. CROSS-SECTION OF AEROPLANE SHOWING DIHEDRAL
ANGLE

position. The fin operates in a similar manner if the nose moves to either side.

5. CONTROL. The pilot controls an aeroplane by moving hinged flaps attached to the trailing edge of the wings, tailplane, and vertical fin, as described in the article AEROPLANE. These flaps are the ailerons, elevator, and rudder (Fig. 1 (*a*). If the pilot wishes to bank the aero-

plane to the left (that is to say, to lower the left wing and raise the right wing) he moves the control-stick in the cockpit to the left. The 'stick' is connected to the ailerons in such a way that moving the stick to the left makes the left aileron move up and the right aileron move down. The lift on the outer part of the right wing is therefore increased and the lift on the outer part of the left wing reduced, so that the aeroplane is made to bank to the left. By moving the elevator the tail can be pushed up or down. Movement of the rudder causes the tail to be pushed to one side or the other.

When a pilot is handling an aeroplane (as in a banked turn, for example), he must often use all three controls at the same time in a rather complicated way.

6. AERODYNAMICS. The forces which act on a wing, or any other body moving in air, are studied by the science of aerodynamics (*see* AERONAUTICAL ENGINEERING, Vol. VIII). A wing can be moving fast through the air, or the air can be blown at high speed past a wing which is stationary on the ground; in either case the forces are the same. For that reason, and also because it is too dangerous to make experiments with an untried aeroplane, as one can with an untried motor-car or motor-boat, all new shapes of aeroplane parts are first tried out on the ground in a WIND TUNNEL (q.v. Vol. VIII), a kind of corridor in which a model of an aeroplane (or of its wing) is suspended, and an electric fan blows a very strong current of air against it. Delicate balances show how strongly the air presses against the model. In this way a designer can tell how a full-size aeroplane would behave when flying.

See also AEROPLANE; HIGH ALTITUDE FLIGHT; SUPERSONIC FLIGHT.

FLYING-BOAT, *see* SEAPLANE.

FLYING, HISTORY OF. 1. For many centuries envy of birds and a determination to rival them caused men to try to fly. Every race created its own flying legends. The myths of ancient Greece include that of the hero Icarus, who attached birds' wings to his shoulders with wax in order to escape from danger in the island of Crete. In spite of his father's warning, he flew too near the sun; the wax melted, and Icarus crashed into the sea. A British legend tells of a mythical king called Bladud, who, long before the time of Christ, took off from the top of a temple in Britain and crashed among his people.

There were many later stories of flying men, and there is no reason to think that they were all untrue. No one, of course, can fly with false wings by the unaided power of his muscles, yet for centuries the belief persisted that this was possible. What may have happened from time to time is that some bold experimenter, jumping from a tower with artificial wings held rigid like those of a kite, may have managed to glide to earth. The legends persisted; one of the last believers was a French nobleman who tried to fly across the River Seine in Paris in 1742; he fell into a boat and broke his leg. It is now known that a vast spread of feathered wings would be needed to lift a man by bird-like flapping; these wings would require such strong muscles that human chest-bones would have to be inches thick to take the strain (see FLIGHT, Vol. II).

Some prophets, however, were able to look ahead and foretell mechanical flying. Most remarkable of the pioneers was LEONARDO DA VINCI (q.v. Vol. V), the painter, philosopher, and scientist of Florence, who studied bird flight, invented the helicopter propeller, the parachute, and possibly a balloon which was lifted by hot air.

2. LIGHTER THAN AIR FLIGHT. The lighter-than-air idea (balloons) was successful before the heavier-than-air principle (aeroplanes). An Italian designed, but did not build, a flying vessel in 1670. It was fitted with large spheres, from which the air was to be pumped out; the resulting vacuum was expected to lift the craft. It was not realized that atmospheric PRESSURE (q.v. Vol. III) would cause the thin copper spheres to collapse. In 1709 a Portuguese made and demonstrated a small model hot-air balloon in Lisbon; but no one took much notice, and it was not until 1783 that man made his first aerial voyage.

Two French brothers, named Montgolfier, who were paper-makers, built a large globe of linen and paper in a field near the River Rhône, in France. Then they lit a fire on the ground, and let the hot air float up into the globe through its open base until it began to lift it. Soon afterwards, a daring young man named de Rozier went up in a hot-air balloon lifted in this way, but still remaining tethered to the ground by a rope. Next he set off from Paris in an un-tethered balloon with a passenger, keeping up the supply of hot air with a portable brazier hung beneath the balloon. De Rozier was the world's first airman. He was followed by a French professor named Charles, who had been experimenting with filling the balloon with hydrogen gas, the lightest known substance, instead of hot air. The professor set off on the first gas-balloon voyage of history—the ancestor of all the BALLOONS and AIRSHIPS (qq.v.) that have risen since. The hot-air balloon soon went out of use, except for taking up parachute jumpers for public entertainment in the 19th century.

With the Montgolfiers, de Rozier, and Professor Charles, the air age had arrived. The idea of floating had beaten the idea of flapping wings. The first British air traveller, an Oxford grocer called Sadler, went up in 1784. The English Channel was crossed in 1785. Napoleon Bonaparte, as a young general, used balloons for military observation with the French armies in 1794. The first successful human descent in a parachute took place in 1797. With time came further conquests. Distance records were broken by a 500-mile balloon voyage in 1836. The first air-raid in history took place when the Austrian Army sent up hot-air balloons, with bombs but no pilots, to drift over Venice during the campaign of 1849. The first air photograph, a view of Paris, was taken from a balloon in 1858. A record height of 26,000 feet (5 miles) was claimed in 1875. The first Arctic exploration by air took place in 1897. (See Colour Plate opposite p. 112.)

Flying men soon thought of making their balloons long in shape, and trying to steer them, instead of having to let them drift with the wind. But for many years no one knew how to build light enough engines. Then, in 1852, a Frenchman built an airship with a steam-engine slung well below the gasbag to reduce the risk of fire. It flew for about 17 miles at 5 miles an hour; this speed was so low that the airship could be steered only on a windless day. In 1885 the French Government built an airship which was really controllable and able to return to its base: it had a 9-horse-power electric motor. A Brazilian, Santos-Dumont, made a small airship in which he flew round the Eiffel Tower in Paris in 1901. By that time the German inventor, Count Zeppelin, had launched his first craft.

3. HEAVIER THAN AIR FLIGHT. The KITE (q.v. Vol. IX) is the oldest form of aircraft in the world. Kites were used 3,000 years ago in China, where they were sometimes used for signalling in war. They have been known in Europe since the Middle Ages. British soldiers

SIR GEORGE CAYLEY'S FIRST MODEL GLIDER, 1804

flew man-lifting kites for watching their enemy in the Boer War. The significance of the kite, however, had remained undiscovered until an English baronet, Sir George Cayley, in 1804, attached a kite to a pole, and fastened fins to the other end of the pole: thus, by making the first glider, he laid the foundations of the science of flight. In the middle of the 19th century several British inventors made aircraft models, some with steam engines and propellers. The

Crown Copyright, from exhibits in the Science Museum, London
REPRODUCTION OF STRINGFELLOW'S MODEL AEROPLANE, 1848

first powered aircraft in the world to fly was a model made by John Stringfellow in 1848.

Experiments increased in Britain and France. Jet propulsion was considered but given up. One Frenchman, in 1890, at last rose from the ground in a number of hops, but this wonderful effort was not true flight—powered, sustained, and controlled.

Gliders first demonstrated the real secret of an aircraft's wing. The first person to trust himself to a glider was a German engineer, Otto Lilienthal. As a boy of 14 he had tried to fly with wings strapped to his shoulders, and he continued to experiment all his life. His first gliders were monoplanes. Then he tried using two pairs of wings, one above the other, to give the

glider more lifting surface, and from this built the first biplane. Jumping from an artificial hill, he made hundreds of glides, some as long as 750 feet, before he was killed in an accident in 1896.

Better luck came to gliding men in America, among them the brothers Wilbur and Orville Wright. The Wrights had been building gliders for several years before they made their first aeroplane. This machine was built like a glider, but was driven by an engine. Steam engines had been too heavy for flight; now the inventors of the early forms of MOTOR-CAR (q.v.) had made a light engine run by petrol, which gave enough horse-power in proportion to its weight to make flying possible. On 17 December 1903, on the lonely sands of Kitty Hawk, North Carolina, five people saw the Wrights make the first true aeroplane flight. It lasted 12 seconds. Their longest flight that day lasted 59 seconds, the machine flying half a mile, about 10 feet above the ground. Yet no one outside Kitty Hawk would believe the Wrights had flown; so they quietly went on with their work, increasing the length and height of their flights each year. At last, by 1906, the world began to take notice. Half-hearted inventors speeded up their experiments. The first aeroplane flight in Europe was made by the ingenious Brazilian, Santos-Dumont, and in 1909, amid public excitement, a Frenchman, named Blériot, flew from France to England. With this, the nations became air-minded; the British people realized that the English Channel was no longer a barrier against the rest of the world.

4. FLIGHT IN MODERN TIMES. The First World War caused an intense development in aircraft design. For the first time each leading country built up AIR FORCES (q.v. Vol. X). At the end of the war, in 1918, there were thousands of aircraft and trained pilots ready to turn to civil flying. In 1919 regular passenger services were started between many European capitals (see CIVIL AVIATION).

Much patient experiment and dangerous exploration were needed to improve aircraft and extend air routes across the world. In June 1919 the Atlantic was first flown by two young British airmen, Alcock and Brown. In the same year the brothers Ross and Keith Smith flew from England to Australia. No one had the hardihood to make this journey for another 8 years. In 1924–5 a young airman named Alan

Courtesy of the Director, Science Museum, London

THE FIRST FLIGHT BY THE WRIGHT BROTHERS, 1903

Crown Copyright, from an exhibit in the Science Museum, London

MODEL OF BLÉRIOT'S MONOPLANE 1909

Vickers-Armstrong, Ltd.

THE FIRST TRANSATLANTIC FLIGHT

The converted Vickers 'Vimy' bomber in which Alcock and Brown flew from St. John's, Newfoundland, in 1919

Cobham broke many records when he flew from England to India and back in an old machine with two friends. This route was then uncharted; so was the 16,000-mile return route to the Cape, which Cobham flew a year later. His greatest flight took him from London to Melbourne and back. He had attached floats to his trusted old machine, and after flying 28,000 miles in 320 hours, he alighted on the Thames beside the Houses of Parliament. He received a knighthood for his services to the cause of flight, for, as well as these great record flights, he made many survey flights for discovery about air-currents, storm tracks, the location of mountain ranges, and possible landing-grounds.

In 1927 the Atlantic was flown for the second time: a 25-year-old American named Lindbergh flew non-stop from the United States to Paris. In order to comply with the conditions of a prize competition, he flew solo in a small single-engined machine which carried no wireless. He was 33 hours at the controls, and won £5,000.

An Australian pilot, Kingsford Smith, made many pioneer flights, including one between America and Australia, the first mail-carrying trip from Sydney to London, and two record-breaking solo journeys between England and Australia. The first solo England–Australia flight was made by another Australian, H. Hinkler, in a tiny aircraft in appalling weather. Hinkler also made the first solo flight across the South Atlantic.

Miss Amy Johnson, of Hull, was the first woman to fly from England to Australia solo. Later she married James Mollison, a record-breaking long-distance airman, and then, flying alone, she broke her husband's own record to the Cape. As pilot to her husband, she crossed the North Atlantic in 1933. Mollison had been the first airman to cross the Atlantic in a light sports plane; he flew solo from east to west against the prevailing headwinds, all previous Atlantic flyers having flown from west to east.

But after 1930 adventure in the air had begun to give way to everyday routine. The various British air companies had united in 1924 to form Imperial Airways (predecessors of the present British Overseas Aircraft Corporation). Business men were beginning to send their letters by AIR MAIL (q.v.) and to travel in aeroplanes themselves. The Prince of Wales and other sons of King George V flew regularly. The leading statesmen saved time by flying. In 1938, when the Second World War was becoming imminent, the British Premier, Neville Chamberlain, went to Germany to try to avoid war, and no one was surprised that he should fly there. Yet it was less than 30 years since the first aeroplane had crossed the Channel. Within that time aviation had become, as it is now, as normal a part of life as trains, ships, and buses.

See also AEROPLANE; AIRCRAFT ENGINES; FLYING; CIVIL AVIATION.

FLYING INSTRUMENTS. The cockpit of a modern aircraft is fitted with a mass of instruments designed to increase the safety of flying. Instruments show: (a) the speed of the aircraft and its position in space; (b) the efficient working of the engine. Since every engine in an aircraft needs a complete set of the appropriate instruments, multi-engined aircraft are often fitted with a separate instrument panel for the flight engineer, as otherwise there would be too many dials for the pilot to watch.

All engines are fitted with tachometers, indicating the number of revolutions per minute. An engine tends to produce most power at some given speed; also, any marked variation from normal speed may suggest to the pilot that something is wrong. With piston engines, one of the most important of the other instruments is the 'boost gauge'; this shows the pressure at which petrol-laden air is being fed into the engine cylinders. For gas-turbine engines, whether 'pure jet' or driving an airscrew (see AIRCRAFT ENGINES), there is a very important instrument which records the temperature in the tail-pipe or exhaust nozzle of the turbine. This instrument works on the thermo-couple principle (see THERMOMETER, Vol. VIII), by which, if two unlike metals are joined together in an electric circuit, a current will flow, depending on the temperature at the point where they are joined.

Besides basic information of this kind, the pilot receives other indications of the state of the engine from dials which record oil pressure and temperature at many points, and pressure in the fuel-supply system.

Chief among navigating instruments are the altimeter, which records altitude, and the air-speed indicator. The standard altimeter is simply an aneroid BAROMETER (q.v. Vol. VIII); it really measures atmospheric pressure. Since this pressure falls off with height, it is possible to mark the barometer dial in terms of height, instead of air-pressure. One disadvantage is that the instrument indicates height above sea-level, which is the real 'floor' of the atmosphere, and not above such varying things as mountains, towers, or even flat land higher than sea-level. Thus a pilot lost in fog or cloud, with his altimeter showing that he was 10,000 feet up in the sky, might still fly into a mountain range 10,500 feet high. To avoid such risks, echo-sounding altimeters have been devised. Some project sound waves towards the ground, and others high-frequency wireless pulses. Both kinds of instrument measure the interval of time between projecting the waves and receiving in the aircraft the echo or reflection of the waves bouncing back from the ground or any tall obstacle below. Similar devices are used to give warning of other aircraft in the neighbourhood, a principle first developed by British military aeroplanes in the Second World War. Apart from the limitations which have already been mentioned, the barometric altimeter is a sensitive apparatus. Pressure varies with changes in weather, and in order to secure accuracy before landing, the instrument is re-set on the basis of ground barometric readings received by wireless from an airport.

The air-speed indicator is important in navigating to a definite time-and-distance plan. It is also vital when the aircraft is taking off or landing, as the pilot must then see that the air speed does not fall below 'stalling' speed (*see* FLYING); if the wing were to cease to support the aircraft when it was flying so near the ground the pilot would not have space to manœuvre, and an accident might take place. The indicator works by measuring the difference between air-pressures in two tubes. One of these tubes has a hole at its front end, which faces forward in the line of flight, and so is subject to the sum of two pressures; one is 'static' pressure (that is, the normal atmospheric pressure which is found everywhere); the other is 'dynamic' pressure, caused by the fact that air rushes into this tube owing to the speed of the aircraft. The second tube has simply a hole in its side, and so is affected only by 'static' pressure. Pipes from these two tubes are led to a pressure-gauge; this records only the difference between the two pressures, which is equal to the 'dynamic' (or 'ram') pressure alone.

This dynamic pressure varies both with the

B.E.A.

NAVIGATING AN AIR-LINER

With an 'Automatic Pilot' controlling the craft, the Captain (left) consults the first officer, who holds a computor. With this he calculates speeds, times, and wind velocity triangles and thus the course to steer. The dials show the altitude, air speed, engine revolutions, boost (power), and the course being steered

air density (governed by altitude) and with the true air speed. The actual figures on the dial of the air-speed indicator show what is called 'indicated air speed', because the instrument is unable to sort out these two effects of speed and density. To guard against stalling, it is the 'indicated' and not the 'true' air speed which the pilot needs to know. But for navigating a course from one place to another, he does need the true air speed. This can be calculated from a knowledge of his height (gained from the altimeter), which tells him the air density.

Air speed is not the same as ground speed; to estimate ground speed, that is, the actual speed the aeroplane flies over the ground, a knowledge of wind velocity is also necessary. An aeroplane flying at 350 miles an hour with a 50-mile-an-hour wind against it (headwind) is covering the ground at a speed of only 300 miles an hour. Allowances for tailwinds or crosswinds must also be made, and are only possible in flight if drift can be estimated.

The faster types of modern aircraft need an

instrument which will warn the pilot if the speed of sound is approached, either in dives or in level flight, because stability and control may be dangerously affected (*see* SUPERSONIC FLIGHT). The speed of sound varies with height and with air temperature, and these changes are allowed for by a machmeter, which measures the ratio of air speed to the speed of sound.

Other instruments make blind flying possible in cloud or fog (*see* NAVIGATION, AIR). These tell the pilot whether the aircraft is flying level, or whether it is rolling or pitching. They work on the principle of the spirit-level, or, in modern designs, with GYROSCOPES (q.v. Vol. VIII). The pilot also needs a COMPASS (q.v.). This is normally magnetic, but increasing use is made of the gyroscope and of radio (or radar) direction-finding.

See also AEROPLANE; FLYING.

FLYING SCOTSMAN. This express train runs between King's Cross station, London, and Edinburgh by the East Coast route, leaving either terminal at 10 a.m. It began making this trip in 1870, and has continued to do so through two world wars to the present date. It was operated at first by the Great Northern, North Eastern, and North British Railways, later London and North Eastern Railway. In the summer of 1928 it began a non-stop run of $392\frac{3}{4}$ miles between the two capitals, thus making a world record for a daily non-stop run. The time allowance for the run was eventually reduced to 7 hours. By using corridor tenders the engine-crews could be relieved on the way without the train being stopped. In 1949, however, the non-stop running was transferred to a new train called the 'Capitals Limited'.

FORD AND FERRY. No matter in which direction man moves, he comes sooner or later to a water obstacle, and long before the wheel or cart were used on land it became necessary to have some means of linking up trackways and land routes across water. By a ford is usually meant a place on any stream or river where the water is shallow enough to allow a crossing by man or beast by wading, and by some types of land vehicle. The word ferry can be used much more widely. It once included any system of transport or travel operating between two points, but is now more correctly confined to conveyance or passage by

boat to and fro across rivers, canals, estuaries, and straits. Recently, however, the service for flying aircraft from North America to Great Britain during the Second World War was referred to generally as the transatlantic air-ferry service. The words 'ford' and 'ferry', and also the verb to 'fare' came from the same Old English root, meaning 'go' or 'pass'.

Both types of crossing represent primitive stages in the development of communications, and are used by people who lack the engineering skill or organization to construct BRIDGES (q.v.). Both, however, survive in varied forms in all countries, no matter what their stage of development or state of communications, and both are considered of sufficient importance to be marked on the topographical maps of the British Ordnance Survey, and similar maps, where they exist, for other countries.

In parts where the height of the rivers varies widely between the wet and the dry season, it may be impossible to build bridges. In such places, where road systems are not well developed, floods may restrict travel to the dry season, and at this time rivers can be forded. In countries with modern road networks, fords are now confined almost entirely to local roads and farm tracks. Pack animals, high farm carts, carriages, or covered wagons could negotiate fairly deep water; but the modern motor-car cannot do so.

Many houses and villages were built at fords, either for farming and trading purposes, or as vantage points for guarding the crossing. Place-names ending in 'ford' usually show that these places were important road crossings, and therefore important also for the development of group settlements; most rivers show a succession of such place-names, Somerford Keynes, Duxford, Shifford, Swinford, Oxford, Sandford, Appleford, Shillingford, and Wallingford are examples along the River Thames. Often the other half of the place-name is the name of a kind of animal—for instance, Oxford is the place where oxen could cross the river; Swinford, higher up where the river was smaller, was where pigs could cross; and Shifford, higher up still, was where sheep could cross.

London grew at a point where the River Thames was fordable at low tide, for in early Roman times the main highway from Dover forded the Thames at Westminster. In pre-Roman England tracks and roads avoided

Parker Galler

DATCHET FERRY ON THE THAMES
Coloured engraving drawn by W. Havell, 1832

crossing water wherever possible, but where it was unavoidable the width and depth of the river was less important than the presence of high ground nearby and a hard bottom to the approaches. The Romans often paved the approaches to and bottoms of the fords they used. The one crossing the River Trent at Little-borough near Lincoln had a pavement 18 feet wide, of squared stones kept in place by two rows of piles.

In the 18th century, as trade and population as well as men's mathematical and engineering knowledge grew, bridges began to replace fords. These were usually built right on the site of the earlier fords, because the roads led up to that spot, and there was firm ground on which to build.

Fords have always been tactical prizes during war time. The following are two historical examples of this. Near Brentford is the place where Julius Caesar is supposed to have crossed the River Thames in 55 B.C., though his legions were impeded by stakes stuck into the river bed by the British defenders. In January 1879, while a British force was advancing into Zululand from Natal, an invaluable stand was made against the Zulus by a small garrison at a ford on the Buffalo river known as Rorke's Drift.

Unlike fords, ferries have been better adapted to modern uses. Ferries now vary in form from the floating logs, dug-out canoes, and coracles used by primitive peoples, to large steamboats capable of carrying many passengers, vehicles, and even trains. Many types are guided or drawn by rope, chain, or horses; but this is only practical where there is little other navigation and on comparatively narrow crossings.

One of the earliest references to ferrymen we find in literature is the Greek myth about Charon, the old man who conveyed the dead over the rivers of the underworld. The Romans established a number of ferries in Britain; one

FERRY-BOAT ON THE ITURI RIVER, BELGIAN CONGO

crossed the Severn and another is believed to have crossed the Wash. Ferries across the Mersey date from as early as the 13th century, when we know that King John offered freedom of toll across the river to the burgesses of Liverpool. In most countries an elaborate system of ferry rights, charges, and revenues has grown up.

The ferry that plied from Queensferry, just east of Edinburgh, across the Firth of Forth, was the chief means of communication between the capital and the Highlands. It forms the setting for the opening of Scott's novel, *The Antiquary*, and plays an important part in Stevenson's *Kidnapped*. A steam-ferry is still used by cars which wish to cross here, because the FORTH BRIDGE (q.v.) only carries a railway.

Ferries cause inevitable delays in traffic. In an undeveloped country such as the equatorial lowland of Belgian Congo where there are many ferries, it may take as much as an hour to cross a stream. But even in highly developed countries they sometimes serve a useful function, especially across rivers or estuaries, or in ports where the building of a bridge might prevent the passage of big ships, or would be an unjustifiable expense. In some places, however, tunnels for both roads and railways, such as the MERSEY TUNNEL (q.v.), are taking the place of ferries. At Le Havre on the estuary of the River Seine in France, where no tunnel exists, a ferry came into service

in 1932, connecting the port with the south bank of the estuary. In 1936 this ferry carried 300,000 passengers and 40,000 cars, but it could only work at certain hours, and only during the day because of navigational difficulties. Ferry boats plying over short distances may be pulled across by chains. Very small boats are still pulled by hand in this way across rivers; larger ones used to be worked by horses turning a wheel on the boat. Now there is usually an engine on the ferry. The chain may be dropped to the bottom to allow shipping to pass over. Wider straits are crossed by regular steamer services, such as those in the straits of Dover connecting the ferry-ports of Dunkirk, Calais, Boulogne, and Dieppe with Dover, Folkestone, and Newhaven. The only train ferry between England and France crosses between Dover and Dunkirk (*see* FERRY, TRAIN).

In time of war rivers have ceased to determine military strategy, but they are still of great tactical importance. In the advance of the Allied Armies into Germany in 1945, ferries across the Rhine and other rivers were in constant use. For the defenders, they afforded a far less conspicuous and vulnerable target from air attack than bridges, and for the assaulting armies they were essential to the rapid consolidation of bridgeheads.

FORTH BRIDGE. This bridge carries the main-line railway from Edinburgh to Aberdeen across the Firth of Forth a little to the north of Edinburgh, and is one of the largest structures of its kind in the world. The original design of Thomas Bouch, on which work began in 1879, was for a two-span suspension bridge; but after the disaster to his suspension bridge over the Tay in December of that year, Bouch's design was abandoned, and an entirely new design was prepared by John Fowler and Benjamin Baker. Despite opposition in Parliament work on the new design for a cantilever bridge began in 1883. The bridge was opened in March 1890.

It consists of three immense cantilevers, which, with their connecting girder spans, make up a total length of 5,440 feet. High-approach viaducts on both sides of the Firth, bring the total length to 8,296 feet. The site was chosen in order that the middle cantilever could be built on Inchgarvie Island; but foundations for the north and south cantilevers had to be sunk in water from 70 to 90 feet deep by the use of caissons, large, water-tight cases in which the concrete foundations are laid under water (*see* BRIDGE BUILDING, Vol. VIII). The strength of the bridge lies mainly in the 12-foot diameter tubes which form the underside of each main span, and the sides and diagonals of each cantilever. The cantilever towers which rise 361 feet above high-water mark are 120 feet wide at the base, but slope inwards to a distance of 33 feet wide at the top. The two main spans are 1,710 feet each, and the two side spans are 690 feet. The whole structure is braced from end to end by a latticework of steel girders.

As well as 54,000 tons of steel, there are 740,000 cubic feet of granite, 46,300 cubic yards of rubble masonry, and 64,300 cubic yards of

THE FORTH BRIDGE

concrete in this colossal bridge, which cost over £2,500,000. The bridge is repainted continuously to prevent rusting—a process which takes 3 years to complete, for a single coat takes no less than 54 tons of paint.

See also BRIDGES, RAILWAY.

FREEDOM OF SPEECH has always been looked upon as one of the most important liberties of people living under a democratic system of government. By freedom of speech we mean not only freedom to speak our minds to other people, either privately or at public meetings, but also freedom to put our thoughts and ideas into writing; to publish them in books, newspapers, periodicals, pamphlets, on posters and hoardings; and also to address them to the wider public that can be reached nowadays by radio broadcasting. Freedom of speech, and what is called 'the freedom of the Press' are thus closely connected, and in fact essential to each other.

Few thinkers have done more to reason out and explain the case for unrestricted freedom of speech and of publication than John Stuart MILL (q.v. Vol. V), the 19th-century philo-sopher. His argument, set forth in his famous essay *On Liberty*, was that, if any idea or opinion were sound, nothing but good could come from its being openly stated or published; while if it were unsound, and were given the fullest publicity, other people would be led to point out what might be wrong or false in it.

For 200 years before Mill, writers and printers had done a good deal, in spite of persecution, to assert the right to free speech (*see* NEWSPAPERS, HISTORY OF). In the 17th century John MILTON (q.v. Vol. V) wrote an important pamphlet, entitled *Areopagitica* (after an oration made in ancient Greece), in favour of the freedom to publish one's thoughts and ideas.

Even democratic countries, however, insist on certain limitations on complete freedom of speech and of publication—limitations which Mill himself thought reasonable, and which are still thought reasonable to-day. To start with, the right of speaking freely in public must obviously be limited to some extent, because streets and public places cannot be obstructed at the whim of anyone who wants to collect an audience around him. So laws are passed to limit and control the rights of public meeting and of public assembly. Again, some speeches may be violent, and may provoke listeners towards rioting or revolution against the established government; or the people at the meeting may be provoked to fight among themselves and to commit what the law of Britain calls 'a breach of the peace'. The law therefore forbids violent language of this kind, and also, in the interests of good order, unduly outspoken attacks on religion and morality.

In order that speech should be ideally free, speakers at public meetings ought to give others a chance of putting forward an opposite point of view. At a public debate this is, of course, the usual way of arranging things: a speaker for the motion is followed by a speaker against it; and the chairman of the meeting then puts the question to the vote, counts the voters for and against the motion, and announces the result. This, broadly, is the way in which freedom of speech is secured in PARLIAMENT (q.v. Vol. X). But not all public meetings are debates: many are meetings of persons who all hold the same views and who are not interested in hearing what their opponents have to say. Party political meetings are of this kind. Freedom of speech in political matters is assured only if every party is given the same rights of meeting, subject to the limitations mentioned above. Such meetings, however, cannot always exclude persons whose political views are different, and who may interrupt speakers with hostile questions or comments, called 'heckling'. Most political speakers expect a reasonable amount of heckling, and deal with it in good humour and often wittily; if it becomes a nuisance the audience, if they have a strong sense of justice and fair play, may check the interrupters or even hustle them from the hall. To give a speaker a fair hearing, even if what he has to say is unpalatable, is part of true freedom of speech.

With regard to private speaking, the laws of most countries forbid statements made with malice, and likely to injure the reputation of the person spoken of. One may know all sorts of unsatisfactory things about one's neighbours, but it is not part of true freedom of speech to communicate that knowledge to other persons, unless this is absolutely necessary. LIBEL (q.v. Vol. X), which is the writing or printing of things harmful to other people, is against the law of civilized countries.

See also PROPAGANDA AND ADVERTISING.
See also Vol. X: CENSORSHIP.

FREIGHT TRAIN, *see* GOODS TRAIN.

FRENCH LANGUAGE. This is one of the great languages of civilization. Its ideas and its actual words have been absorbed by other tongues in all parts of Europe. It is spoken by about 42,000,000 people in France. In the French settlements of North Africa it is widely used. In Canada it is the normal speech of 2,000,000 people in the former French province of Quebec, while in those parts of the United States which were first settled by Frenchmen there are many French place-names, such as Louisiana and New Orleans. For some centuries, until the last few years, French was an international language known to the educated people of all European nations, and used in all official letters between Governments.

The French language grew out of the changes which took place in ancient Gaul (the land which we now call France) when German tribes invaded it in the 5th and later centuries and settled there. Gaul had been one of the provinces of the Roman Empire; its various tribes, having lost their original Celtic tongues, spoke Latin, some well and some badly. When the main part of the Roman Empire, the part in western Europe, broke up in the 5th century, a Germanic tribe called the Franks settled in northern Gaul and later gained control of most of the country. The Latin spoken by the Gauls was changed by the foreign accent of the Germanic settlers, and by the many Frankish words which they brought in with them. French first appears in written form in the 9th century. Like other languages which had been based on Latin, it had developed a form of its own during the Dark Ages of tribal invasion, when reading and writing were almost at a standstill (*see* ROMANCE LANGUAGES).

Many Germanic words in early French are still in use, such as *jardin* 'garden', *haie* 'hedge', *robe* 'dress', *gant* 'glove', *farder* 'to put make-up on the face', *danser* 'to dance', *riche* 'rich', *bleu* 'blue'. Some Frankish words began with the sound of 'w'; this seems to have been hard for the Latin-speaking Gauls to pronounce, so they tended to sound the letter 'g' in front of 'w'. Later the sound of 'w' disappeared altogether, leaving only 'g' in modern French. This is shown by the many modern French words beginning with 'g', which have Germanic equivalents in English beginning with 'w', such as *guerre* 'war', *garant* 'warrant', *gage* 'wage', *guichet* 'wicket', *guise* 'wise' (as in 'likewise').

By the 12th century France had quite a large literature; works were no longer written in many local dialects, but nearly all in the dialect of the region round Paris. This dialect came to be accepted as standard French, just as the dialect of London became STANDARD ENGLISH (q.v.), for Paris was the centre of the cultural life of France. Dialects continued to be spoken, and sometimes even written; but in the poetry of the Middle Ages Parisian authors would sometimes boast of the 'purity' of their language, while provincials would apologize for local 'barbarisms' in their work.

French then must have sounded very different from the language of to-day. These differences are still reflected in French spelling which, like English spelling, has not kept pace with pronunciation. When, for example, the French scribes of the 12th century wrote *beau*, it was because they heard in the word three different vowel sounds in one group, something like a cat's cry of 'miaow'. There was a general tendency in French to split up a single Latin sound into a double sound, as in Latin *pes*, French *pied*, which may have been due to the heavy Germanic stress of the Frankish invaders. In modern spoken French the different vowels within a group have disappeared (*beau*, for instance, is pronounced 'bō').

A feature of French which began in the Middle Ages is the nasal pronunciation of certain vowels. This is found in no other living West European speeches, except Portuguese, and makes French sound very different from Spanish and Italian. The result is the French way of saying *bon* 'good' by lowering the soft palate at the back of the mouth. Old French, unlike Old Spanish or Old Italian, had adopted from Vulgar Latin two 'case' endings: nouns had different endings according to whether they were the subject or the object of a sentence. Towards the end of the 13th century, however, these different endings began to be dropped, and the word-order (first the subject, then the verb, lastly the object) became fixed, as in English.

From the 11th to the 14th centuries France became the leading country in Europe, and its influence and language spread to many other countries. After the Norman Conquest of 1066, a Norman variety of French was for nearly three centuries the language of the ruling class in England, and many French words came permanently into the English language (*see* ENGLISH LANGUAGE, HISTORY OF). During this period the Crusaders from England, France, and other countries spread the French language across Europe to the Near East. Traces of it are still to be found in the speeches of Greece, Cyprus, and Armenia. In most European countries it became customary for the upper classes to learn to speak French. Even as far afield as Norway, a land beyond the frontiers of the former Roman world, we read of a father, in the 13th century, advising his son to learn all languages, but above all Latin and French, since they were the most widely spread. From the 13th century until well into the 20th century French has been the diplomatic language, used between politicians of different countries in international negotiations. Changes in national feeling have led to the recent use of various other languages.

In the 16th century the Renaissance, the great revival of learning in Europe, spread from Italy to France, and the French language came under Italian influence, many Italian words being borrowed into the language. Many of these words have since been dropped because of a reaction towards purer French; but there are still many everyday words in French which are Italian in origin, and which date from this period, including even such familiar words as *soldat* 'soldier' and *pantalon* 'trousers'. After the Renaissance Latin was no longer considered the only language suitable for serious literary works, and French began to be adapted for this purpose, grammarians beginning to study it for the first time. In the 17th century noblemen and their wives held literary gatherings, at which the finer points of 'correct' speech were debated. In 1635 the French Academy was founded, a body which determines for French people exactly what shall be considered correct French and which new words shall be accepted into the language. In later years many new words have been added to the French vocabulary, chiefly by borrowing from English. Although modern French writers, despite the Academy, continue to experiment with the language, modern literary French remains much the same as the language of the 17th century. In the country districts of France local DIALECTS (q.v.) or 'patois' are still spoken by the peasants.

See also LANGUAGE STRUCTURE.
See also Vol. I: FRENCH.

FREQUENCY MODULATION, *see* WAVELENGTHS. *See also* Vol. VIII: WIRELESS.

FRUIT TRAIN, *see* TRAINS, SPECIAL USES.

FUELS, *see* ENGINE. *See also* Vol. VIII: FUELS.

FUELLING IN FLIGHT. The fuel tanks of an aircraft can be filled during flight by means of a pipe from another aircraft flying close by. The weight of a full load of petrol is a severe burden to an aircraft engaged on a long fast flight, particularly against head winds; a series of refuellings during the journey will enable a quicker and longer journey—and possibly a safer one—to be made. Sometimes an aeroplane can take off from the ground with a very heavy cargo provided the petrol tanks are purposely left almost empty (*see* AIRCRAFT TAKE-OFF). As soon as the craft is safely in the air the tanks are fuelled from another aeroplane.

The operation is carried out by standard

Charles E. Brown

JET FIGHTER REFUELLING IN FLIGHT
A Gloster 'Meteor' about to make contact with the hose
from the tanker

methods. The tanker aircraft (which supplies the fuel) flies to the pre-arranged meeting-place in the air; the tanker is generally a slower machine than the other aircraft (the receiver), which locates the tanker by radar.

The tanker gets into position below the receiver and a little to one side, while both craft are flying in the same direction. The receiver unwinds a light hauling line, 250 feet long, which dangles, with a hooking contrivance at the end. The tanker's crew, using a gun on the harpoon principle, fires a weight on the end of a line across the path of the receiver's dangling line, just as the receiver is overtaking the tanker. The two lines catch together, and the weight slides down the receiver's dangling line as far as the hooking contrivance, where it is gripped. The tanker hauls in the line, unhooks the projectile, and attaches instead a fuel hose to the receiver's line. The hose is hauled into the receiver, and made fast. By this time the tanker has climbed slowly until it is flying above the receiver, so that the fuel will be able to pass down through the hose by gravity. A quantity of nitrogen, which is non-inflammable, is forced through the fuel pipes as a safeguard against fire, and then the fuel is allowed to flow. It passes from one aircraft to the other at the rate of about 100 gallons a minute. When fuelling has ceased, nitrogen is again forced through the pipes. Then the hose is disconnected from the receiver's fuel system, and is attached to the receiver's hauling line, which is slowly paid out as the hose is wound in by the tanker. The hauling line includes a 'weak link', a short stretch of rope marked with a distinctive colour, and made so that it will snap under strain. At a given moment the tanker turns away, the weak link breaks, and the line and hose are hauled aboard the respective aircraft. There is some risk of fire from a slight electrical current passing along the metal hose from one aircraft to another when the petrol is pouring through, and causing a spark which might ignite the petrol fumes. The current would arise from 'static' electricity; this is the slight charge which sometimes makes a cat's fur crackle when it is stroked, or which causes a bus passenger to feel a tiny shock on touching the handrail when about to step from the ground on to the step of a bus (*see* ELECTRICITY, Vol. III). When two aircraft are to make contact for refuelling, their hauling lines (which are made of steel cable covered with hemp) are left bare at the ends; the crews of the aircraft take care that the bare steel ends touch one another when the two lines first come into contact. If one aircraft is charged with more 'static' electricity than the other, the surplus charge passes harmlessly along the steel lines until both aircraft have an equal charge; there is then no further risk of a spark passing.

Jet aircraft are refuelled more easily than propeller craft for, as there are no propellers to be fouled by hose or hauling lines, the two craft can approach more closely. A jet aircraft is refuelled through its nose by coming very near to the tail of a tanker.

FUNICULAR RAILWAYS, *see* MOUNTAIN RAILWAYS, Section 2.

G

GAELIC LANGUAGE. This is a Celtic language, and with IRISH (q.v.) and Manx, the language of the Isle of Man, makes up one group of the Celtic family. Gaelic was brought to Scotland in the 5th century by Irish settlers from Dàl Riada, a territory in what is now County Antrim. These people settled in Argyllshire (*Aireat Gaedheal* 'territory of the Gaels') and founded a kingdom of Dàl Riada in Scotland, which later became separated from the Irish Dàl Riada. They conquered the Picts and Britons and by the 10th century Gaelic was the language of all Scotland. In the 11th century Queen Margaret, a Saxon princess, brought English customs, together with the English language, to Scotland, and the tide turned against Gaelic. To-day it is spoken by perhaps 100,000 people west of a line from Kintyre through Argyllshire, West Perthshire, and on to Inverness. The HEBRIDES Islands (q.v. Vol. III) are the stronghold of Gaelic speech, but even there almost everyone can now speak English as well.

Gaelic has kept much of its ancient form, preserving sounds that appear in Old Irish; but the grammar has become much simplified. The verb has only three tenses, present-future, past, and imperfect; and is used with a personal pronoun, as in English. The nouns, which once had inflexions, or endings, varying according to the part the noun played in the sentence, now often have only one singular and one plural form, as in English, though some have distinct genitive forms.

Several English words have been borrowed from Gaelic, among them 'whisky' from Gaelic *uisge*, shortened from *uisge beatha* 'water of life'.

'Gillie' is from Gaelic *giolla* 'lad, servant', originally borrowed into Gaelic from Latin *gilda*. *Loch, bog, slogan, garron* (horse), *cairn, claymore* (sword), and *sporran* are other words which we have borrowed from Gaelic.

Manx, the language of the Isle of Man, which has recently died out completely, is closer to Gaelic than to Irish, perhaps because the island was part of the Norse Kingdom of the Hebrides in the Middle Ages, and, when the Norse were expelled in 1266, it passed into Scottish hands for a time, until the English gained control.

See also LANGUAGE STRUCTURE.
See also Vol. I: CELTIC CIVILIZATION; SCOTS.

GALLEON, *see* SAILING SHIPS.

GALLEY, *see* CLASSICAL SHIPS.

GARAGE, *see* MOTOR TRANSPORT MAINTENANCE; ROAD SERVICE STATION.

GAS TURBINE LOCOMOTIVE. The year 1949 saw the first gas-turbine-electric locomotive undergoing successful tests on the Union Pacific Railroad, U.S.A., and in February 1950 the Western Region of British Railways introduced a similar locomotive which had been built in Switzerland.

The gas turbine consists in principle of a large wheel or rotor bearing an intricate pattern of blades. The rotor is spun round at high speed

The Times

GAS TURBINE LOCOMOTIVE
Built in Switzerland for British Railways. Its power is 2,500 horsepower and it can reach a speed of 90 miles per hour.

by the pressure on the blades of a stream of hot and expanding 'gas'. This 'gas' is produced in a combustion chamber into which fuel oil and air have been forced at great pressure, and in which it is ignited. The air is forced in by a compressor which is turned by the turbine wheel, and the turning of which absorbs a great part of the power generated by the turbine. The remainder is available for moving the locomotive.

In the Swiss-built British locomotive, which is carried on twelve wheels and weighs 113 tons, the turbine develops 10,300 horse-power at full load, 7,800 of which is absorbed by the compressor, leaving 2,500 to drive the electric generator which supplies current to the traction motors. The gas-turbine-electric locomotive is designed to cost less in both fuelling and maintenance than the DIESEL LOCOMOTIVE (q.v.); and if it is eventually found practicable to fire it with pulverized coal, costs will be still lower.

See also AIRCRAFT ENGINES, Section 2; ROAD TRANSPORT ENGINES.
See also Vol. VIII: GAS TURBINES.

GAUGES, RAILWAY. The track gauge of a railway is the distance between the running edges of the rails. In Great Britain the standard gauge is 4 ft. 8½ in., and the same measurement

a. THE LIMITS IN HEIGHTS AND WIDTH OF TRAINS ON BRITISH RAILWAYS
b. A GOODS TYPE LOADING GAUGE
(P indicates platform)

is used throughout the mainland of Europe except in Russia (5 feet), and Spain and Portugal (5 ft. 6 in.). The 5 ft. 6 in. gauge is used also on most of the main lines in India and Argentina. Irish railways have a gauge of 5 ft. 3 in. Over the whole of the United States and Canada the standard 4 ft. 8½ in. gauge prevails.

It is in the Australian Continent that we find the greatest gauge problem. New South Wales and the Transcontinental Railway have the 4 ft. 8½ in. gauge; Victoria and Southern Australia 5 ft. 3 in.; and Queensland and Western Australia 3 ft. 6 in.; with break of gauge at each interstate frontier. Brisbane and Sydney are linked with 4 ft. 8¼ in. gauge lines, and Melbourne and Adelaide with 5 ft. 3 in.

In many countries the narrow gauge of 3 ft. 6 in. is standard, particularly the Dominion of South Africa and Japan; in others the closely related metre gauge is used. There are many small railways with even narrower gauges, such as 3 ft., 2 ft. 6 in., 1 ft. 11½ in. (the 'toy' railways of North Wales), and even 1 ft. 3 in. (the Ravenglass & Eskdale and Romney, Hythe, & Dymchurch Railways in Great Britain).

With each reduction in gauge, it becomes possible to lay down sharper curves, and so to adapt railway routes to the most rugged country, with less need for cuttings or embankments, tunnels, or bridges. But this is done at the expense of speed and carrying capacity. The widest gauge ever used, was the 7-foot 'broad gauge' of the Great Western Railway, which was given up in 1892 because a gauge different from other railways proved inconvenient.

Another important aspect of gauge is the

GREAT WESTERN RAILWAY.

ALTERATION OF GAUGE

OF THE

MAIN LINE

BETWEEN

EXETER & TRURO,

NOTICE IS HEREBY GIVEN,

That the lines of the Company between the above-mentioned points will be altered from the Broad to the Narrow Gauge, commencing on the night of Friday, May 20th, 1892.

During the time the alteration is being made the lines specified will be closed and all traffic upon them entirely suspended until the work is completed, which is expected to be on the night of Sunday, May 22nd.

NOTICE OF THE CHANGE OF GAUGE ON THE GREAT WESTERN RAILWAY

'loading gauge', which shows the maximum dimensions to which rolling-stock can be built if it is to have sufficient clearance through bridges and tunnels, and past platforms and other lineside structures. In this respect the British railway pioneers did not look far enough ahead, and this country has one of the most restricted loading gauges of any. In the best conditions in Britain the maximum height available above rail is 13 ft. 6 in., and the maximum width 9 ft. 6 in., though to allow for the extra room taken up by rolling-stock on curves, maximum dimensions of 13 ft. 3 in. and 9 feet respectively are seldom exceeded. In North America the height available is 15 ft. 6 in., and the width 10 ft. 9 in., which enables American railways to build locomotives up to three times the weight, size, and power of the biggest in Great Britain. The most ample railway loading-gauge in the world is that of Russia, which is able to build locomotives up to 17 feet in height above rail.

See also RAILWAYS, HISTORY OF.
See also Vol. VIII: RAILWAY ENGINEERING.

GERMANIC LANGUAGES. Many European languages, including ENGLISH and the SCANDINAVIAN LANGUAGES (qq.v.) as well as German and Dutch, are descended from the same ancient language, known as Primitive Germanic, one of the INDO-EUROPEAN LANGUAGES (q.v.). This was spoken in South Scandinavia and Denmark about 2,000 years ago. Nothing of this language survives, but some inscriptions have survived in an ancient Germanic language, which is probably very close to it. The best known of these is that on a golden horn found at Gallehus in Denmark in 1734 but now lost. It is a line of verse and reads:

ek hlewagastiz holtingaz horna tawido
'I, Hlewagastiz from Holt, the horn made.'

About 2,000 years ago the speakers of Primitive Germanic began to spread out in many directions, and their language became divided into three main sub-families, from which several of the modern languages of Europe have come. The languages descended from East Germanic have not survived to the present day; among them were those spoken by the GOTHS—we have part of the Bible in Gothic translation—and the VANDALS (qq.v. Vol. I). Gothic was spoken in the Crimea as late as the 16th century. North Germanic gave rise to the Scandinavian languages; and English, German, and Dutch are descended from the Western branch of Primitive Germanic.

German is one of the world's most important languages. It is spoken by some 90 million people in Germany, Austria, and parts of Switzerland and the Southern Tyrol. There are also important German-speaking colonies in America. German can be divided into High German, which is spoken in Austria, parts of Switzerland, and in Central Germany, and Low German, which is spoken along the coast of Northern Germany. Both have many dialects, which differ from one another far more than those of English: the speaker of a Swiss dialect, for instance, cannot understand a North German

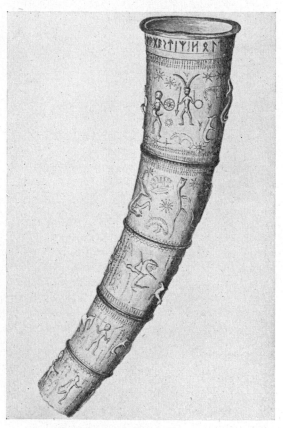

GOLDEN HORN FOUND AT GALLEHUS IN DENMARK, PROBABLY ABOUT A.D. 400

THE INSCRIPTION ROUND THE RIM OF THE HORN
It is written in runes

one. Yiddish from the German *Jüdisch* is a dialect of High German with several Hebrew words added, spoken by many Jewish people, and generally written in the Hebrew alphabet. These dialects are for the most part spoken rather than written languages. There is, however, a standard form of High German which is in use in all German-speaking countries as a written language, and as a spoken language for all official purposes. It is used in the churches, and in the law courts and parliaments, and is spoken by all educated people. It is a literary language which has been deliberately standardized—a process which began with Martin Luther's translation of the Bible in the early 16th century, and was continued by printers in the 17th and 18th centuries. Since the latter part of the 19th century congresses have met for standardizing the language. It is this standard German that we mean when we speak of German. It might be compared with STANDARD ENGLISH (q.v.), but it is probably not quite as widely spoken in Germany as Standard English is in England, for in certain districts regional dialects are used even by educated people, although they can usually speak High German as well. Although spelling is standardized, pronunciation varies a good deal, the only standard being the so-called 'German Stage pronunciation', rules for which were drawn up in 1898.

German differs from most Western European languages, such as English and French, in that it has not lost the grammatical endings of its words. It is what is called an 'inflected' language: the function of a word in a sentence is shown by changes in the word itself, as in LATIN (q.v.), instead of by means of small words, such as prepositions, as in English. The grammar of German thus seems rather complicated to English speakers. The order of words is less rigid than in English, as it can be changed according to the emphasis. For example, 'I am going to London with the car to-day' would be in German *Ich* (I) *fahre* (go) *heute* (to-day) *mit dem Auto* (with the car) *nach London* (to London). This might be written in the following different ways, each slightly different in meaning, the most important idea being placed first in the sentence:

Heute fahre ich mit dem Auto nach London 'I am going to London in the car *to-day*'. *Mit dem Auto fahre ich heute nach London* 'I am going to London *with the car* to-day'. *Nach London fahre ich heute mit dem Auto* 'I am going *to London* with the car to-day'.

The spelling and pronunciation of German are very regular; once the sounds are learnt, it is fairly easy for a foreigner to pronounce correctly words he has not seen before. Characteristic of German are the harsh 'ch' sounds pronounced in the throat, in words such as *ich* and *buch*, which are unlike any sound in English, and the 'z' sound, as in *zimmer* 'room', which is pronounced like English 'ts'. Another characteristic of German is the 'glottal stop', which in England is only found in dialects (as when a Cockney says 'wa'er' for 'water'). It often occurs in German before words or word-roots beginning with a vowel. The word *erinnern*, for instance, 'to remember', has two glottal stops, being pronounced *'er'innern*. The Gothic script, which was formerly always used in writing German and was always taught in the schools, has now been abolished in Germany.

The difference between High German and Low German arose because, in about the 9th century, a change took place in certain consonants in the south or highlands which did not reach the north. Of the two, Low German is the nearer to English: the word 'water', for instance, is spelt the same in both English and Low German, whereas it is spelt *wasser* in High German.

Dutch, the language of Holland, was also unaffected by the sound changes which took place in High German. English 'two', for instance, is *twee* in Dutch and *zwei* in High German; 'open', is *open* in Dutch and *offen* in High German. Originally Dutch was an inflected language like German, but in recent years there has been a movement for reforming both its grammar and spelling. The case endings of the nouns have been eliminated; 'the man', formerly *de man* in the nominative (that is, when subject of the sentence) and *den man* in the accusative (when object of the sentence) is now always written *de man*. Dutch pronunciation, like that of English, had drifted a long way from its spelling. *Sch*, for instance, when it appeared at the end of a word was pronounced simply like *s*, but at the beginning it represented the sound *s* followed by a sound resembling that of *ch* in Scottish 'loch'. This is a characteristic Dutch sound, unknown in German and English, and extremely difficult for a foreigner to pronounce. In 1940, when Holland was invaded and overrun by German spies, the test of the

[German handwriting of Goethe's 'Erl King' verses]

Wer reitet so spät durch Nacht und Wind?
Es ist der Vater mit seinem Kind;
Er hat den Knaben wohl in dem Arm,
Er faßt ihn sicher, er hält ihn warm.

Mein Sohn, was birgst du so bang dein Gesicht?—
Siehst, Vater, du den Erlkönig nicht?
Den Erlenkönig mit Kron' und Schweif?—
Mein Sohn, es ist ein Nebelstreif.

Who rides there so late through the night dark and drear?
The father it is, with his infant so dear;
He holdeth the boy tightly clasp'd in his arm,
He holdeth him safely, he keepeth him warm.

'My son, wherefore seek'st thou thy face thus to hide?'
'Look, father, the Erl-King is close by our side!
Dost see not the Erl-King, with crown and with train?'
'My son, 'tis the mist rising over the plain'.

claim of a suspected spy to Dutch nationality was his pronunciation of the place-name 'Scheveningen'. In the reformed spelling, *sch* at the end of a word (where it only represents the *s* sound) is changed to *s*, *Nederlandsch* becoming *Nederlands*. The effect of the reforms has been to bring Dutch nearer to English.

Dutch is spoken not only in Holland but also in North-west Belgium. This form of Dutch, often called Flemish, differs slightly in pronunciation from the Dutch of Holland, but when written, it is exactly the same. Dutch is also spoken in the former Dutch colonial possessions, such as Java; and a language based on Dutch, called Afrikaans, is spoken in South Africa by descendants of the old Boer population, who were of Dutch origin. Afrikaans is now very different from Dutch, both in grammar and vocabulary, having borrowed many words from the African native languages.

Another Germanic language is Frisian, the language spoken in the Frisian Islands off the coast of Holland, in parts of North Holland and North Germany, in islands off the German coast such as Heligoland, and in north Frisian islands such as Sylt. It is interesting because of all the languages in the world it is the one which most closely resembles English. There is an old tag which says, 'Good bread and good cheese, is good English and good Freeze'.

See also LANGUAGE, HISTORY OF; INDO-EUROPEAN LANGUAGES.

GLIDER. A glider is basically an aeroplane without an engine. It is controlled in the same way but, having no mechanical power, uses only gravity to maintain speed. Gliders, therefore, are almost silent in flight.

There are two classes of glider; the large military or commercial trailer and the sporting sailplane (*see* GLIDING, Vol. IX). The trailer is primarily a load carrier, and is capable only of gliding downward from the height at which it is released; the sailplane is designed to be able to make use of air up-currents, some of which lift the craft faster than gravity can make it sink. By this means long flights can be made. This is called soaring.

Gliders were not used for commercial or military purposes (except for the cheap training of pilots) until the Second World War. The difference between these and sporting gliders is primarily their size, and secondly, their performance. Instead of being slim and graceful, they have large bodies to carry heavy loads such as army tanks. Their wing span reaches 100 feet and over. Instead of a landing skid and single wheel, they have a fairly tall undercarriage (which can be folded if necessary) so that the fuselage will pass over small obstructions on landing in rough country. Instead of being designed to stay up in the sky, they are designed to be able to get down as rapidly as possible, relying on an aeroplane, acting as a 'tug', to take them close to their destination.

In war time, gliders are sometimes released at night at a great height and distance from their objective, and glide silently down, loaded with troops and guns, to a surprise attack. Near the ground, flaps on the wings are opened to slow down the gliders and increase the steepness of their glide; the craft can then crash-land in paddocks or spinneys without any real risk to the occupants. The greatest gliding feat of the Second World War was the towing of the airborne British soldiers who fought at Arnhem in Holland in 1944.

Glider trailers are not much used commer-

Aeronautics

'OLYMPIA' GLIDER BEING TOWED

cially as a method of increasing the payload of an aeroplane. They reduce the performance of the towing aeroplane to an uneconomical extent, and, unlike a car trailer, they require a trained crew. It has been found cheaper to use an extra aeroplane for any extra load; the aeroplane is faster, and is free to be used at once for another journey.

See also Vol. IX: GLIDING.

GOKSTAD SHIP, *see* VIKING SHIPS.

GOLDEN ARROW. This is a 'luxury' train service which runs between Victoria and Dover. The parallel French Service between Calais and Paris is called the *Flèche d'Or*. It is made up entirely of Pullman Cars, and both in France and England the cars and locomotives are painted with golden arrows, so that they may be easily recognized. The Golden Arrow provides the fastest way of covering the train part of the journey between London and Paris. Passengers have to pay extra to use it.

GOLDEN GATE BRIDGE (SAN FRANCISCO). This great suspension bridge spans the Golden Gate, the straits between two peninsulas,

through which ships enter the Bay of San Francisco from the Pacific. The city of San Francisco is situated on the tip of the southern peninsula, so that, before the building of the bridge, all traffic wishing to go northwards from the city had to travel round the long coastline of the bay or cross the bay by ferry. The great All Pacific Coast Highway, a motor road planned to run down the west coast of America from Alaska to Mexico, was faced with the problem of either a break or a long inland detour. The bridge, which took over 4 years to construct, was opened in 1937. It ran from Marin County on the north to San Francisco on the south, making a crossing of nearly 1¾ miles, and it cost some £7,000,000 to complete.

The Golden Gate Bridge is the longest single-arch suspension bridge in the world; it has a clear span of 4,200 feet between its two high steel towers. These towers, 746 feet high, that is, more than twice as high as St. Paul's Cathedral, are built on two great concrete piers, each situated a little distance from the shore. The most difficult problem was the erection of the southern pier which had to be built some 1,100 feet out from the shore. The problem was solved by building a kind of jetty from the shore to the pier site, and then sinking on to the site a cofferdam or watertight enclosure made of sheets of steel. This was pumped dry of water, and then filled with a form of concrete specially

San Francisco Chamber of Commerce

THE GOLDEN GATE BRIDGE

prepared to stand up to the action of sea water (*see* BRIDGE BUILDING, Vol. VIII).

The towers carry two main cables, each about a yard in diameter and 7,660 feet in length. From these is suspended the roadway, about 200 feet above the water, high enough to give ample clearance to the highest ship, and wide enough to allow for six lines of traffic, as well as a pavement each side.

Another suspension bridge, the Oakland Bay Bridge, has now been built to carry traffic from San Francisco across the southern branch of the bay to the city of Oakland. This bridge, which is over 4¼ miles long, is the longest bridge in the world. It is constructed with two suspensions and a cantilever, and a long causeway of 19 spans. It is double-decked, with six lanes for road traffic on the upper deck and five lines of railway on the lower deck, three for goods trains and two for passenger suburban trains.

See also BRIDGES.
See also Vol. III: SAN FRANCISCO.
See also Vol. VIII: BRIDGE BUILDING.

GOLDEN HIND. Francis DRAKE was the first Englishman to lead an expedition round the world; this he did in 1577–80, a Portuguese named Ferdinand MAGELLAN (qq.v. Vol. V) having preceded him by some 60 years. Drake's little fleet of five ships manned by 164 men sailed from Plymouth Sound on 13 December 1577. In the holds were carried the parts of four pinnaces, light craft which could be put together either for war or to explore strange coastlines and inlets. The purpose of the voyage has been variously interpreted; it seems probable that Drake had important schemes of exploration in mind, but that he shared with his mariners an overriding itch for plunder. His common failing in this respect may have disappointed some of his officers who had hoped for better things. One man, Thomas Doughty, for some reason dissatisfied, spread disaffection, and was tried for mutiny. He was executed on Drake's orders when the ships came to a very good harbour in Argentina, named by Magellan Port San Julian, where a gibbet already stood as a grim reminder of a former mutiny which had been quelled by Magellan. This deed done, Francis Drake, thoroughly master of the situation, addressed the assembled ships' companies and exhorted 'the gentleman to haul and draw with the mariner, and the mariner with the gentleman'.

National Maritime Museum
MODEL OF THE 'GOLDEN HIND'
Reconstruction from contemporary evidence

On 21 August 1578, after sending home two empty storeships, Drake with three refitted ships, the *Pelican*, the *Marigold*, and the *Elizabeth*, sailed past the Cape of the Virgins into the Straits of Magellan, between the mainland of South America and the island of Tierra del Fuego. To celebrate this happy occasion Drake changed his own ship's name from the *Pelican* to the *Golden Hind* (the hind or female deer referred to the family crest of his patron, Sir Christopher Hatton, who had paid some of the costs of the expedition). On 6 September the three ships emerged into the Pacific; then mighty storms separated the squadron, and the *Marigold* was lost, and the *Elizabeth* turned back for England. The *Golden Hind* stood on, ploughing her lonely furrow round the globe, plundering on the way the surprised Spanish ships and settlements, and visiting California, which Drake claimed for Queen Elizabeth. The ship was nearly lost through grounding heavily amongst the islands of the Celebes in the East Indies. Drake re-entered Plymouth Sound on 3 November 1580. He was summoned to sail the ship and treasure round to the Thames, and he was knighted by Queen Elizabeth when she visited the *Golden Hind* at Deptford below London Bridge. The ship was preserved for a time in a dock at Deptford; banquets were held on board, and she was an object of popular interest; but by 1662 the few surviving timbers were made into a chair which was presented to Oxford University.

Despite valiant efforts to keep this famous ship for posterity as Queen Elizabeth wished, no satisfactory picture of the *Golden Hind* remains. The Portuguese pilot, da Silva, who served Drake after being captured, thought her a stout, well-found warship, as did Drake's Spanish captives. Yet her hull was but 75 feet length overall by 19 feet beam, and she measured only 100 tons.

See also SAILING SHIPS; EXPLORATION.

GOLDEN ROAD. According to the poet J. E. Flecker (1884–1915), this route ran from the Persian Gulf to the great trading centre Samarkand in Turkestan. In fact no particular route is known to have been called 'the Golden Road', though similar names such as Old Silk Road and Lapis Lazuli Road were common (*see* ROADS).

See also TRADE ROUTES.

GONDOLA. The Gondola plies the canals of VENICE (q.v. Vol. III) and was once, before the days of motor-boats, the chief means of conveyance to and from all parts of the city. The gondolas belonging to the great families used to be extravagantly decorated, until in the 16th century it was made compulsory for all but State gondolas to be painted black. The gondola is about 30 feet long by 5 feet broad and is

A VENETIAN GONDOLA

very elegant in its appearance, having a high stem of polished steel with a standard serrated device which has been likened to the prow of a Roman galley (*see* CLASSICAL SHIPS). Amidships there is a closed cabin for passengers, comfortably fitted with windows, cushions, curtains, and a carpet. It is generally propelled by a single oar which the gondolier handles with skill from the stern-sheets. The gondola is supposed to be built with a cunning twist in its hull which assists the gondolier to handle his vessel with the one oar worked in an iron rowlock on the starboard quarter. To-day gondolas are mainly used for sight-seeing trips by visitors to Venice, and for bringing vegetables and other food for use in the city. When he comes to one of the many canal crossroads, the gondolier gives a special warning shout, just as a cyclist might ring his bell.

GOODS TRAIN. The carriage of goods and minerals, or what is generally called freight, is the backbone of railway revenue. The methods of working goods trains differ greatly in various parts of the world. In the United States and Canada high-capacity wagons alone are used, up to 50 feet long, carried on pivoting wheel-trucks (bogies), and holding 50 to 70 tons or even more of goods to a wagon. All wagons are fitted with compressed-air brakes, like passenger coaches. It is not unusual, on suitable North American routes, to marshal 100 and more wagons of this kind in a single train. The 'train crew', equivalent to a British guard and assistants, travelling in the 'caboose' at the rear, may be as much as a mile from the engine crew on the footplate. To handle these trains, very powerful 6,000 horse-power diesel-electric and steam locomotives are used on certain routes, the steam locomotives often being ARTICULATED (q.v.).

In Great Britain, with its relatively small consignments and short hauls, the number of bogie wagons in use is very limited, and reliance is placed mainly on small four-wheel wagons of 10 to 20 tons capacity. The position with British trains has been ruled largely by the layout of sidings in industrial plants, collieries, and elsewhere, with sharp curves, and by the fact that a large proportion of the wagon stock in Great Britain was not built and owned by railway companies but by various private collieries and other industrial firms. It was therefore difficult

New York Central System

U.S. FREIGHT TRAIN DRAWN BY STEAM LOCOMOTIVE
A fast train carrying perishable food in box cars (first two) and refrigerator cars (following three)

in the past to enforce general standards. In this matter, and also in the small proportion of goods wagons to be fitted with continuous brakes (*see* BRAKES, RAILWAY), British railways have been distinctly backward compared with those of other countries. Before the Second World War, all wagons in Germany and France, of considerably larger capacity than those in Britain, had been fitted with continuous brakes, and the general speed of goods trains was therefore higher on the Continent. A certain number of fast goods trains have been run in Britain with continuous brakes throughout; in the case of some other trains, which travel at higher speeds than the average slow goods and mineral train, a few continuously braked wagons are marshalled next to the engine, to give a little additional brake-power and so to allow somewhat higher speeds.

See also MARSHALLING YARDS.

GRAIN SHIP, *see* SHIP.

GRAMMAR, *see* LANGUAGE STRUCTURE.

GRAMOPHONE, *see* Vol. IX: GRAMOPHONE.

GRAPHOLOGY, *see* HANDWRITING, Section 2.

GREAT EASTERN. This ship, which has been called the wonder and failure of her age, was built by John Scott Russell & Co. at Millwall on the Thames for the Eastern Steam Navigation Company, and John Scott Russell and Isambard Brunel share the credit of her design; Launched in January 1858, the vessel was three times the size of H.M.S. *Duke of Wellington,* one of the largest line-of-battle ships of her day. Her length was 692 feet and her beam 82·5 feet. She was built of iron, and her ingenious construction was quite successful although nothing like her had been attempted before. She was double-hulled and had both traverse and longitudinal bulkheads or partitions. She was fitted with both paddle and screw propulsion, and was probably unique in having five funnels and six masts. The purpose of her great size was to enable her to reach Australia without refuelling, and her capacity for coal and cargo was 18,000 tons. The accommodation for passengers was also extraordinary—800 first class, 2,000 second class, and 1,200 third class passengers. Her crew numbered 400. The upper deck, a continuous iron-plated cellular structure, ran flush from stem to stern and was 20 feet wide each side of the hatchways.

The launch was fixed for 3 November 1857. Such a large vessel (the weight of her iron hull was 8,000 tons) had never been launched before, and, to make matters more difficult, the ship had been built broadside on to the Thames. Launching ways, laid with railway lines, were built at either end of the ship; but, although she started to move, the friction was too great, and she stuck. Finally, twenty-one powerful hydraulic rams were prepared to push her down the ways, and with these she was at last floated on 31 January 1858. The cost of these preparations, however, ruined the Company, and so the *Great Eastern* was sold and put on the transatlantic service, for which she was not designed. She was slow for this work (her average speed was 14 knots), and as her large capacity for both cargo and passengers was never made full use of, she did not pay her expenses. She was, however, most usefully employed in 1865 and 1866 laying the Atlantic cables (*see* CABLE SHIP). She was sold for breaking up in 1888 after a long period of unemployment when she had become a problem to harbour authorities.

See STEAMSHIPS, HISTORY OF.

GREAT HARRY. National or royal pride has often shown itself by the building of great ships. King Henry VIII, not less ostentatious than other monarchs of his time, ordered a great ship of 1,500 tons to be built at Woolwich. She was launched in 1514, and named the *Henry Grâce à Dieu*, 'Henry by the grace of God', an allusion to the divine right claimed by kings. Such an unhandy name was variously spelt and shortened, being seldom used in full; '*the Harry*' or '*Great Harry*' were the most popular variants. On 13 June, after her launch, there was held a great ceremony of 'hallowing' or blessing. She was a great favourite of the King's; everything was of the best, and he almost regarded her as one of his palaces, entertaining foreign ambassadors on board, even while the ship was building. The ship had four masts, as was usual, and was fitted with top-gallant sails on the fore and mainmasts. She was of carrack type (*see* SAILING SHIPS), with a lofty overhanging forecastle. Her extraordinary armament of 195 guns probably included no more than twelve heavy pieces firing through portholes low in the waist. Her ship's company numbered 907. She put to sea during the French War of 1522, but was laid up at Portsmouth until fitted out again in 1535. After that we hear no more of her.

THE 'GREAT EASTERN'
Lithograph by T. G. Dutton, 1859

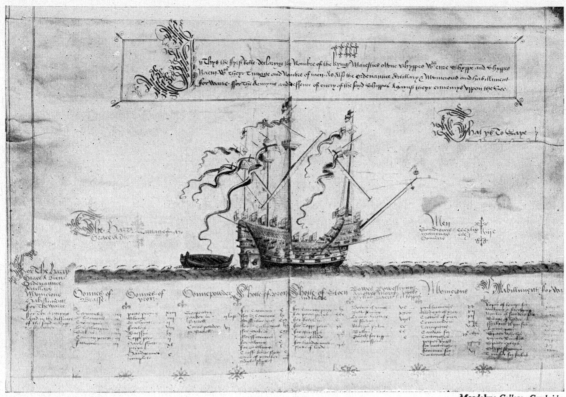

THE 'GREAT HARRY'

Magdalene College, Cambridge

Contemporary drawing which gives details of the guns, munitions, and men carried

The building of the ship had probably been suggested by the *Great Michael*, a 'very monstrous great ship' built in 1506 for King James IV of Scotland. The *Great Michael* is reputed to have been 240 feet long; she was apparently built with great bulges at the waterline, and was thought unsinkable.

In 1540 a new *Great Harry* was launched, of only 1,000 tons, 151 guns, and 800 men. She was in action with the French twice, once when Portsmouth was attacked in 1545 and the French galleys were routed. She was accidentally burnt at Woolwich in 1553.

See also Vol. X: BATTLESHIPS.

GREAT NORTH ROAD, *see* ROADS, MODERN.

GREEK LANGUAGE. This, one of the most important Indo-European languages, has been spoken and written for about 3,000 years in Greece, the Aegean Islands, Crete, and at times in parts of Western Asia, North Africa, South Italy, and Sicily. Greek was the official language of the empire of Alexander the Great (4th century B.C.) and of the kingdoms which succeeded it, and later on of the Eastern Roman Empire down to the middle of the 15th century. It was the language—and still is one of the languages—of the ORTHODOX EASTERN CHURCH (q.v., Vol. I). It was the language of culture in the Roman Empire. About 8 centuries B.C. the Homeric poems—the *Iliad* and *Odyssey*—were written in Greek; and so were, in the 5th century B.C., most of the greatest dramas that the world knew until Shakespeare. Works on medical and physical sciences, mathematics, philosophy, and history were written in Greek much earlier than in any other European language. Most of the books and letters which form the New Testament were first written in Greek. Although it has changed in the course of this long history in structure and vocabulary, the language has remained fundamentally the same.

alpha (a)	A α	*kappa* (k)	K κ	*sigma* (s)	Σ σ, ς
bēta (b)	B β	*lambda* (l)	Λ λ	*tau* (t)	T τ
gamma (g)	Γ γ	*mu* (m)	M μ	*ŭpsilon* (ŭ or ū)	
delta (d)	Δ δ	*nu* (n)	N ν		Y υ
ĕpsilon (ĕ)	E ε	*xi* (x)	Ξ ξ	*phi* (ph)	Φ φ
zēta (z)	Z ζ	*omikron* (ŏ)	O o	*chi* (kh)	X χ
ēta (ē)	H η	*pi* (p)	Π π	*psi* (ps)	Ψ ψ
thēta (th)	Θ θ	*rho* (r)	P ρ	*omega* (ō)	Ω ω
iōta (i)	I ι				

GREEK ALPHABET

Ancient Greek, as we know it, was spoken and written in a great variety of dialects, of which the more important seem to have been the Ionic, Doric, and Aeolic. Each of these became to a certain extent the standard language for some kinds of writing: Ionic for epic poetry, Doric for the choruses in the tragedies and for some mathematical and philosophical works, and Aeolic for some lyric poetry. A speech very similar to the Ionic dialect, Attic, became the standard language for most purposes in the 5th century B.C. under the powerful influence of Athenian politics and culture. It then developed, with a few changes, into the 'common' language (the *koinē*) of the people from the 3rd century B.C. down to the 15th century A.D. The fall of Constantinople to the Turks in 1453 and the disappearance of the Eastern Roman or BYZANTINE EMPIRE (q.v. Vol. I) were accompanied by the breakdown of the *koinē* as a living language; it remained in use hardly anywhere except in the Greek Church. During the following four centuries the spoken speech and dialects developed almost unchallenged, until in the 19th century, when Greece was liberated from the Turkish domination, the question of a standard language for the whole nation had to be solved. A compromise was adopted between the *koinē* and the popular Greek (*dēmotikē*). The new tongue ('pure Greek'), became the standard official language of the schools, politics, newspapers, wireless, and some literature. But the popular Greek is now gaining more and more ground, not only for conversation—where it is dominant—but also in literature.

Greek provided Latin and most European languages, especially those derived from Latin, as well as Asiatic languages, with a considerable number of words—in particular words used in the sciences, music, philosophy, and theology. The very words 'mathematics, physics, music, philosophy, theology' are borrowed from Greek. Many words which modern scientists and technicians have invented to express new ideas and discoveries are built, wholly or partly, out of Greek words or stems; such as 'telephone' (*telē* 'far', *phon-* 'sound'); 'telegraph' (*graph-* 'writing'); and 'cinema' (*kinēma* 'movement'); 'helicopter' (*helix* 'spiral', *pteron* 'wing').

Greek has always been written with an ALPHABET (q.v.) of its own, derived partly from the Phoenician model. The capitals have remained almost unaltered in shape for the last 24 centuries, while the small letters now used in print have gradually developed from the capitals.

Ancient Greek had many vowels and diphthongs which gave it a great variety of sounds. Only certain groups of consonants were used, so as to avoid the clash of unharmonious sounds. All words ended either by a vowel, a diphthong, an 'n' or an 's'—very rarely by 'k', 'l', or 'r'. Most words had one syllable pronounced with a high pitch, and the others considerably lower, giving the speech a sing-song sound. Syllables were clearly distinguished as 'short' and 'long', according to the time required to pronounce them, so that it was possible to have a variety of rhythms based on the 'quantity' or length of syllables—an opportunity which Greek poetry exploits to the full (*see* VOICE). Most Greek words (nouns, adjectives, and verbs) could be changed in many ways according to their use—at the end, at the beginning, sometimes even in the middle—while keeping the fundamental meaning and stem. For instance, the Greek verb *graphō*, 'write', had not less than 260 different forms as compared with the seven English forms of 'write' ('writest, writes, written', and so on). The adjective corresponding to 'white' (*leukos*) had about twenty forms. All these changes were bound by strict rules, resulting in a rather complicated grammar. Greek poets, especially, invented compound words freely, in order to express complicated ideas concisely (*see* LANGUAGE STRUCTURE).

Modern standard Greek has changed from ancient Greek in ways such as these. Several vowels and diphthongs have changed their sounds: in particular the long 'e' (η), the diphthong 'oy' (οι), and the sounds originally pronounced like 'ey' (ει), and the French 'u' (υ), are now all pronounced as a short 'i'. Some consonants have also changed in pronunciation: 'b', for instance, is pronounced 'v', and 'd' as 'th' (as in 'that'), and 'e' as 'y' (as in 'yes'). The

PART OF A PAGE FROM HOMER'S 'ILIAD', WRITTEN ON PAPYRUS, 1ST OR 2ND
CENTURY A.D.

British Museum

This passage is from Book XIII, 'The Battle at the Ships', lines 302 to 330, and describes a council of war between two leaders of the Greeks. Ancient writings were generally made without accents, punctuation, or spaces between words. Copies did not always agree with one another: this papyrus omits the line numbered 316 in modern texts. At some periods, and in some parts of the ancient world, the Greek letter 's' was written as above, C instead of the usual Σ. An easy line to read on this page is the third down:

ΤΟΙΟΙ ΜΗΡΙΟΝΗC ΤΕ ΚΑΙ ΙΔΟΜΕΝΕΥC ΑΓΟΙ ΑΝΔΡΩΝ
'Thus Meriones and Idomeneus, leaders of-men'

high-pitched syllable in each word, and the differences between long and short vowels,

have been lost. Verbs, nouns, and adjectives still have many more different forms than in English, but fewer than in the ancient Greek. Many words have changed their meaning, and a number of foreign words, mainly of Latin origin, have been adopted. The popular language is grammatically even simpler, but has changed the meaning, sound, and spelling of many more words, and has adopted more foreign words, including some Turkish.

Ancient Greek is still studied widely in schools and universities for its literary value, for its importance in the history of civilization, and as a model of a highly developed language. Modern Greek, on the contrary, is known to very few people outside Greece.

See also LANGUAGE, HISTORY OF; INDO-EUROPEAN LANGUAGES.
See also Vol. I: GREEK CIVILIZATION; GREEKS.
See also Vol. XII: GREEK LITERATURE.

GRID (MAPS), *see* MAP PROJECTIONS.

GUARD (RAILWAY), *see* RAILWAYMEN.

GYRO COMPASS, *see* COMPASS.

GYROSCOPE, *see* Vol. VIII: GYROSCOPE

H

HACKNEY CARRIAGE, *see* Taxi.

HANDWRITING. 1. Most forms of modern handwriting developed from Latin writing, which was first used for inscriptions in stone or other hard material for public monuments. As this was meant to last a long time, the letters, which were like our modern capital letters, were elaborately drawn and carved. These took a long time to draw and so were unsuited to business documents, literary manuscripts, or private letters. For these a new style of writing grew up, and was used side by side with that still used on monuments. Its difference from the monumental style was partly due to the different materials, for it was written in ink on papyrus, and later on parchment and Paper (q.v.) with a small brush made from a reed, later to be replaced by the pen (*see* Writing Instruments). This made the letters bolder and more rounded; and the difference was further increased by the haste and carelessness of scribes, who slurred over the forms of letters or ran them together so that it was hard to distinguish them. Sometimes part of a letter would be left off: 'H', for instance, became 'h', and 'B' became 'b'. With other letters a part might be lengthened, 'Q' becoming 'q', and 'D' becoming 'd'. Sometimes the scribes used abbreviations.

There were two fairly distinct forms of Latin handwriting, the carefully written literary or book-hand, used by trained scribes for works of literature, and the current or running hand used for everyday purposes, such as private letters. The book-hand being the more formal of the two, the letters changed more slowly. It took several different forms: there were 'square capitals', very like the writing used on monuments, only more rounded and less stiff (Fig. 1 *a*);

'rustic capitals', which were quicker and easier to write, being less elaborate and having slender strokes, and short, sloping, wavy cross-strokes (Fig. 1 *b*); and, lastly, 'uncials', in which both square capitals and small letters were used, five of the letters (a, d, e, h, m) being very rounded. The uncial style was the main book-hand from the 4th to the 8th centuries (Fig. 1 *c*).

The running hand changed much more rapidly than the book-hand; strokes were slurred, angles were curved, letters were linked together, and different individual styles began to develop. Wall-paintings and waxed tablets

a. Square capitals. 4th or 5th century A.D. MS. of Virgil in the Library of St. Gall, Switzerland

b. Rustic capitals. MS. of Virgil, written probably A.D. 494, now in the Laurenziana Library, Florence

c. Uncial script. Gospel Harmony written probably about A.D. 546, now at Fulda, Germany

d. Cursive script. Papyrus at Berlin containing portions of speeches delivered in the Senate. Ascribed to reign of Claudius, A.D. 41–54.

FIG. 1. ROMAN SCRIPTS

discovered at Pompeii in Italy show that as early as the 1st century A.D. there were many different varieties of this handwriting in Italy. From the various cursive scripts of Italy developed the particular styles of handwriting used in the different countries of western Europe, the Lombardic style used in Italy (Fig. 2 *a*), the Carolingian used in France (Fig. 2 *b*), as well as the special handwritings of Spain and Germany (Fig. 2 *c*).

The development of Latin handwriting in England was interrupted by the Saxon invasion, and Latin writing was brought to England for the second time in the 7th century, by Christian missionaries from Ireland, where writing, said to have been taken there by St. Patrick in A.D. 450, had been developed by the monks to a high degree of beauty and clearness. From this arose the Anglo-Saxon hand (Fig. 2 *d*).

After the Danish wars the Carolingian style of writing, which had spread from France to most of the countries of western Europe, was introduced into England. The idea of using large and small letters together according to a definite plan was partly due to this script. From this a most graceful style of handwriting developed in England, especially in the 12th century. In the 13th century, however, a new hand began to develop in north-west Europe, consisting of rather angular shapes. This was known as the Gothic or 'black-letter' style (*see* COLOUR PLATE opposite p. 48), and was adopted as a model for printing. It was used in England and elsewhere until the 16th century, and until recently in Germany. In the 16th century it was replaced in England and most other countries by two neat round Italian styles, which originated in Florence in the 15th century—italics, and the 'Roman' style of writing. Both are in general use now in printing, and the italic style is mainly used for handwriting. (*See* BOOKS, HISTORY OF.)

These changes in handwriting corresponded with changes in the social background against which they took place. At the time when, for instance, neither the Saxon nor the Norman noblemen could sign their own names, but employed the sign of the cross (still in use among illiterates) as the pledge of their good faith and witness to their consent, writing was a profession, and a very respected one. Handwriting at this time was regular and carefully formed.

As late as the 16th century, when it was necessary to communicate with persons at a

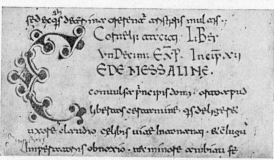

a. Lombardic script. Tacitus' *Annals* written at Monte Cassino about A.D. 1050, now in Laurenziana Library, Florence

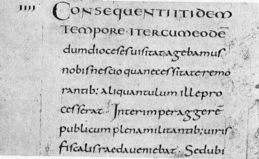

b. Carolingian script. *Life of St. Martin* written at Tours about A.D. 800, now at Quedlinburg, Germany

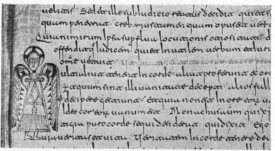

c. Spanish script. Written A.D. 945, probably in the diocese of Burgos, now in John Rylands Library, Manchester

d. Anglo-Saxon script. Lindisfarne Gospels, written in Northumbria towards the end of the 7th century, now in the British Museum

FIG. 2. EARLY MEDIEVAL SCRIPTS

FIG. 3. PAGE FROM JOHN SEDDON'S 'THE PENMAN'S PARADISE'
Writing book for the instruction of secretaries and clerks
(1695). Such books engraved on copper gave the name
'copper-plate' to clerical script

distance, a professional scribe was employed. Letter-writing did not become general till after the 16th century—even then it was restricted to the upper classes of society. In the 17th century men were the chief correspondents. One of the reasons for the scarcity of old letters is the fact that posts and messengers were not safe from inspection, and spies were freely employed. Men hesitated to set their thoughts down upon paper, and when letters were written, they were destroyed as soon as they had been read. Sometimes carelessness about letters would result in lifelong imprisonment.

However, the spread of literacy and education in the late 17th century among the leisured classes in England, and particularly among the women of the aristocracy, led to the writing of long diaries, private letters, and many everyday documents in a beautifully formed handwriting (Fig. 3). It was only in the 18th century that the art of writing became general; study grew among all classes, and the introduction of cheap postage caused an immense increase in correspondence. At this time handwriting gradually became informal, degenerating from its earlier clear, regular lettering into penmanship of every kind: each person wrote as he found it easiest. This degeneration was speeded by the introduction at the end of the 19th century of the typewriter, which quickly came into very wide use. To-day a great many well-educated people cannot write a legible handwriting.

2. GRAPHOLOGY. This is a branch of science which attempts, by careful analysis of handwriting, to indicate the personality of the writer.

In a general way handwriting can offer a record of a person's abilities, problems, and characteristics.

A specimen of handwriting is shown to the graphologist, who must know the race, age, and sex of the writer. The writing is then minutely analysed under numerous headings, of which only the most outstanding can be listed here. Each trait of the writing has its corresponding personality trait.

(*a*) *The Zones.* Writing is divided into three zones, upper, middle, and lower (Fig. 4). The upper zone consists of the upper lengths of the letters; the middle zone of everything on the writing line; the lower zone consists of the lower lengths. The upper zone corresponds to the intellect, the middle zone to the everyday behaviour; the lower zone to the subconscious.

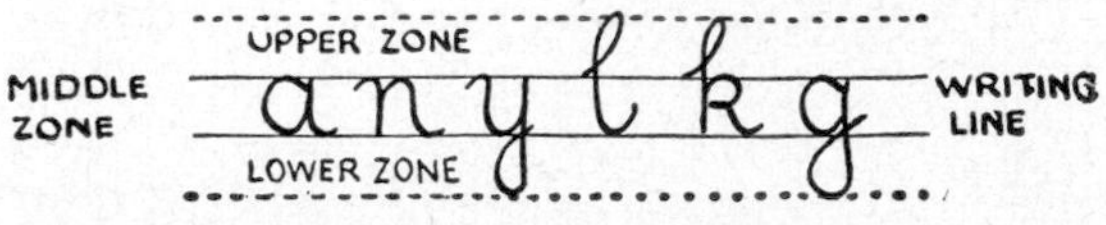

FIG. 4. THE ZONES OF WRITING

The proportion of the zones is important. The size of the writing is estimated by the middle zone of the letters, and shows the writer's opinion of himself.

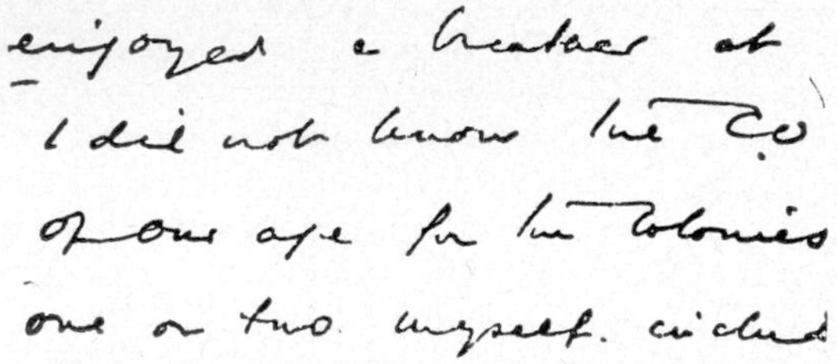

Small size, well-proportioned zones, light pressure, angle rightward, quick. Unassuming, well balanced, good mixer, energetic

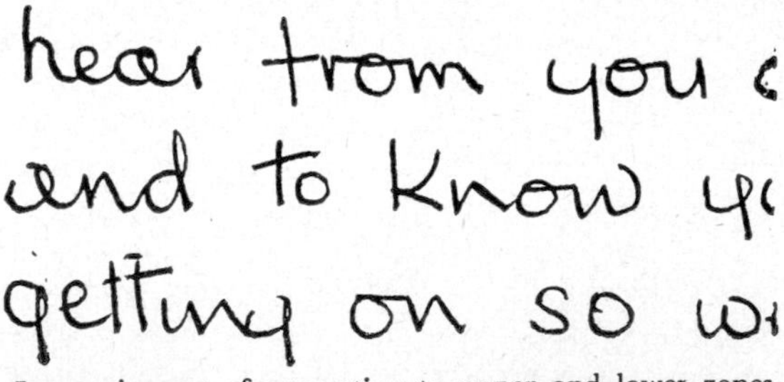

Large size out of proportion to upper and lower zones, heavy pressure, slow. Self-centred, obstinate, slow reactions

FIG. 5. THE CHARACTER OF HANDWRITING

(b) Movement. This is the way the writing runs from the left margin to the right. Here the speed is analysed—the way the letters are joined, the angle of the writing, the slope of the lines. These signs give clues to the writer's manners, temper, sociability, and speed of reaction.

(c) Spacing. The general layout of the writing on the page is studied; the width of the margins; whether the words and lines are crowded or wide apart. This relates to the writer's organization of his thoughts and emotions.

(d) Formation of Letters. Letters may be conventionally made, original, or artificial, written with strong pressure or lightly. The writer's originality, sincerity, and force of character are deduced from them.

Graphology can sometimes be of use in the selection of employees, in advising on careers, and in child-guidance clinics. Research is in progress to see whether physical and mental diseases can be detected in their early stages in handwriting. Study has been made in the United States of the writing of people suffering from rheumatoid arthritis, tuberculosis, and schizophrenia.

See also WRITING; ALPHABET.

HARBOUR, *see* PORTS AND HARBOURS.

HEBREW LANGUAGE. Hebrew is one of the group of languages known as the SEMITIC LANGUAGES (q.v.), descended from an original language spoken by the SEMITES (q.v. Vol. I) before they wandered from the direction of Arabia and spread out over much of the Near East. The Hebrews invaded Canaan in the 15th century B.C. or later, and their language mixed with that of the Canaanites to form the language known as Hebrew. This was also greatly influenced by Babylonian, which had been for a long time the international language of the Near East.

Compared with Latin and Greek, the vocabulary of ancient Hebrew was small and its grammar and sentence construction were fairly simple. The alphabet consisted of twenty-two letters, all consonants. Not until the 6th century A.D. were vowel signs added to the Hebrew text of the Old Testament, so that it could more easily be read in synagogues and schools. The Old Testament and a small number of inscriptions are the only surviving written documents in ancient Hebrew.

.1   אל אדני· יאוש ישמע

.2   יהוה את אדני· שמעת של

.3   ם· עת כים עת כים מי· עבד

.4   ך כלב כי· זכר אדני את·

.5   [ע]בדה· יבכר· יהוה את א

.6   [ˉ ˉ] י דבר· אשר לא· ידעתה

ANCIENT HEBREW SCRIPT OF THE TIME OF JEREMIAH, 597–583 B.C.

Letter written on a potsherd (a substitute for the scarce papyrus) from a soldier to his commander at Lachish, with a transliteration in square Hebrew characters. Copyright; by permission of the Trustees of the late Sir Henry S. Wellcome

Hebrew was spoken and written in Palestine for more than a thousand years. By about 500 B.C. it had come greatly under the influence of Aramaic, a Semitic language closely related to Hebrew, which was widespread in the Near East at an early date. Some of the late parts of the Old Testament, such as Esther, Ecclesiastes, and some of the Psalms, show Aramaic influence, and parts of the Books of Ezra and Daniel are written in Aramaic. By about 150 B.C. Aramaic had almost entirely replaced Hebrew as the spoken language of Palestine. When Hebrew was no longer understood by the general public of Palestine, the reading of the Hebrew text of the Old Testament in the synagogues was accompanied by the reading of an Aramaic paraphrase of the same section. Aramaic was spoken in Palestine during Christ's lifetime, and the New Testament, although written in Greek, preserves some Aramaic words. It was less straightforward than Hebrew and not so flexible as ARABIC (q.v.). Dialects of Aramaic are still spoken in some villages near Damascus, and elsewhere.

Hebrew lived on in Palestine as the language of religion and learning, and has, in fact, never ceased to be current among Jews. The vocabulary of the language has been added to throughout the centuries to meet new needs, and new types of script have been evolved. Hebrew is now re-established in Palestine as a spoken lan-

aleph (')	א	teth (t)	ט	pe (p)	פ, ף*
beth (b)	ב	yod (y)	י	ṣade (ṣ)	צ, ץ*
gimel (g)	ג	kaph (k)	כ, ך*	qof (q)	ק
daleth (d)	ד	lamed (l)	ל	resh (r)	ר
he (h)	ה	mem (m)	מ, ם*	sin (s)	שׂ
waw (w)	ו	nun (n)	נ, ן*	shin (sh)	שׁ
zayin (z)	ז	samekh (s)	ס	taw (t)	ת
ḥeth (ḥ)	ח	'ayin (')	ע		

* This form used when the letter ends a word.

HEBREW ALPHABET

guage. This modern form of Hebrew has its roots in the ancient language, but it tends to draw more and more upon the vocabularies of European languages.

See also SEMITIC LANGUAGES; LANGUAGE STRUCTURE.
See also Vol. I: HEBREW CIVILIZATION.

HELICOPTER, see ROTORCRAFT.

HELIOGRAPH, see LIGHT SIGNALLING.

HERALDRY. Heraldry is better understood if it is given its medieval name, 'armory', meaning that it is part of the arms and armour of the knight. If we picture this knight of the 12th or 13th century armed for battle or the TOURNAMENT (q.v. Vol. IX), his head completely covered by his great helm (a larger and heavier type of helmet), we shall see how heraldry, or armory, came into being. Here was a man going into battle, his features hidden, who had to be easily recognized by his followers so that they could rally about him, and by his enemies so that, it was hoped, they might be intimidated by his known powers and ferocity.

Part of the knight's armour was a shield. It had been customary in many ages for fighting-men to show on their shields some device or badge either to indicate some personal quality (such as a lion for courage or a serpent for guile), or to show that they belonged to some allegiance, such as the sprig of broom (*planta genesta*) worn by the Plantagenet kings. It was on the shield that the knight first depicted some distinguishing pattern—and the fact that it was a pattern,

rather than a symbolic emblem, marks the difference between the early development of heraldry and other systems of identification. Unlike the devices shown on Greek shields, this pattern always remained the same, and was the personal property of its owner, passed on to his descendants; a Greek hero, as far as is known, might change his shield for one with a different object or animal on it—rather as if the animal acted as a charm that would help him in the battle.

English heraldry has a special language, originally based on French words, to describe (or to 'blazon') a heraldic design. In heraldry, the colour red is called 'gules', blue 'azure', green 'vert', purple 'purpure', black 'sable', and the metal silver 'argent', and gold 'or'. The surface of the shield is called the 'field', and anything placed on the field is called a 'charge'. A very important rule in heraldry, designed so that the charges on a shield can easily be deciphered, is that colour is never placed on colour, nor metal on metal. Thus, if the field is argent (silver), the charges on it must be of colour, for instance, vert (green) or azure (blue). In describing an heraldic pattern the field must always come first: thus a very simple pattern of a blue field charged with a silver bar across it, would be described as 'Azure, a bar silver'.

The early choice of a charge was for a simple pattern by which different knights could be easily recognized—like the trade-marks by which some goods are known to-day. These simple charges, such as 'chief', 'pale', 'fesse', 'saltire', were called the 'honourable ordinaries'. The field itself could be subdivided—sometimes into two equal parts by a vertical line ('party'), or by a horizontal line ('party fessewise'), or into four parts by a combination of both ('quarterly'), or by a variety of slanting lines. The lines of these ordinaries and lines of partition could have a variety of ornamental edges (such as 'wavy', 'indented', 'engrailed', and these allowed further variety of pattern (*see* diagram).

Like good modern advertising posters, all charges on a shield were simple, easily understood, and filled the shape well—in other words, they made a good design, whether they were ordinaries, partitions of the shield, or animals, birds, or common objects chosen either to symbolize some personal quality that their owner hoped he possessed, or as a pun upon his name. This latter was a very usual reason for the choice of some object used as a charge, like the spear that appears on Shakespeare's shield. Sometimes the pun is not immediately obvious; for instance, the Arundel shield was 'silver six swallows', explained if we remember that the French for swallow is *hirondelle*.

All this shows that heraldry had a very practical purpose, which is even further emphasized when the knight, in order to make himself still more easily distinguished, fixed on his helm a crest. This carried either the same charge (or one of the charges) as on his shield (if one of the ordinaries, it would be displayed on a fan of parchment). If the charge was some suitable subject, such as an animal or bird, it would be made out of light wood, covered with tooled leather or plaster, and brightly painted. Where the crest fastened to the helm, the join was hidden by a twist of fabric, often of the chief metal and colour of the shield, called the wreath or 'torse'. A crown (not indicating any connexion with royal blood) was sometimes used instead of the torse (*see* COLOUR PLATE opposite p. 208).

When the knights were fighting in hot countries, especially on Crusades, they needed something to stop the sun's rays from beating directly on the metal of the armour, and so they wore a surcoat over it. As this, too, displayed the charge on the shield, the knight did actually carry his armory on his coat—and so came the expression a 'coat of arms'. For the same reason, there was worn a kind of curtain at the back of the helm. This, at first, was a simple piece of fabric with edges cut into scollops (a form of decoration used for the edges of most garments at this period). Later, these edges became far more deeply cut, until the curtain, called the 'mantling', had a very ragged and slashed appearance. This, it is said, represented sword cuts; but as likely as not it was done for its decorative effect, since, as the knight galloped, it would writhe and twist behind him, giving that glitter of metal and bright colour so beloved by all people of the Middle Ages.

Now we have the knight easily recognized by the charges on his shield held on his shoulder, with the helm above carrying his crest, torse, and mantling. It was an easy and more or less inevitable step for the knight to show a representation of his shield (and, later, of his shield with helm, crest, and so on above it) on his possessions as a mark of his ownership. This combination is called an 'heraldic achievement'.

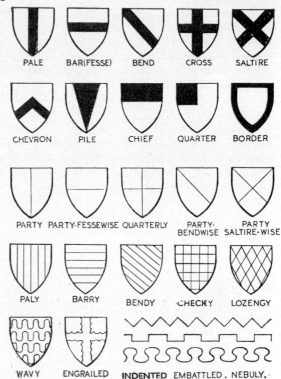

THE HONOURABLE ORDINARIES (TOP 2 ROWS), PARTITIONS OF THE FIELD (3RD AND 4TH ROWS), AND ORNAMENTAL EDGES

In the early days of heraldry only one other thing was added to it—his war cry or the saying by which he might also be known, which is called the 'motto', and is shown written on a scroll below the shield. Thus heraldry, which began by showing who a knight was, grew to signify what was his; and his heraldic achievement (a coat of arms) was displayed over his castle gate, on many of his possessions, and, most important, on his SEAL (q.v.).

Early in the 15th century two charges (often animals or birds) appeared on either side of the heraldic achievement, as if holding it up. These are called 'supporters'—the lion and the unicorn of the Royal Arms being a very well-known example. There is some uncertainty as to the reason for the appearance of supporters. It has been suggested that it was the seal-engravers who, finding they had spaces unfilled on either side of the coat of arms when they placed it in a circle (the usual shape of a seal), filled these spaces with the beast shown on the crest. This may well be one of the reasons—for such supporters for shields were actually to be seen at jousts, where it was the custom for men, often grotesquely dressed even as fabulous monsters, to hold up large shields showing the arms of the combatants—rather as the referee now proclaims the names of the boxers before a bout.

So long as the shield was used in fighting, and the crest was worn upon the helm, the pictorial representations of them remained practical. But when the shield went out of use, from the 16th century onwards, the types drawn became more and more fantastic in shape, the edges being shown as curling about in a way that would have been quite impractical on a real shield. The drawing of mantling also shows that its true nature had become forgotten—indeed, in the 17th and 18th centuries it took the form of leaves and, finally, of seaweed. Crests, when once they had merely to be drawn, and not made and worn upon the helm, also became unrealistic—until we find such strange things as landscapes with distant views, and even sunsets, drawn above the helm.

In the 18th century, when it had been forgotten that heraldry was once a practical part of the arms and armour of the fighting man, romance crept in—and writers gave to all the simple charges, such as the ordinaries, many ingenious meanings quite unknown to the medieval heralds. A charge was sometimes declared to have been granted to a man because he had some particular virtue—when he had probably chosen the charge himself because it was not carried by anyone else, or in some cases because it was a pun upon his name. In the early days of heraldry, if the same charge was chosen by different men, the matter had to be settled either by arbitration or by a joust, the loser having to make a fresh choice.

In the reign of Richard III the College of Arms was founded to put the whole business of heraldry on an organized basis; and from then onwards the granting of arms was in the hands of the Heralds of the College, or of the King. To-day the College of Arms grants all coats of arms in England; and though shields are no longer carried, nor crests worn upon helms, the arms that are designed have again much of the outlook of the medieval herald.

See also Vol. X: ARMOUR.

HIEROGLYPHICS.
The word means 'sacred carving'—the name given by the Greeks to the ancient Egyptians' pictorial symbols, carved or painted on their public stone monuments, tombs, and temples. The word is now also used of other pictorial writings, such as those of the ancient HITTITES, MAYAS, and AZTECS (qq.v. Vol. I).

Egyptian hieroglyphics began with crude pictures of natural things, such as the sun, moon, plants, parts of the human body, and animals. Later the same kind of symbols also came to express more complicated ideas—a symbol of a limb or organ of the body might represent not only the limb or organ but also its activity; a symbol of the legs would not only mean 'legs' but it would also mean 'walking'; or a symbol of the eye would mean 'seeing'. Abstract ideas could also be expressed—the eye with teardrops, for instance, indicated 'crying' or 'sadness'. As time went on the symbols became more ingenious—the arm represented 'strength', the eye 'judgement', and the hand 'authority'. All such pictorial symbols are known as 'ideographs'.

This way of writing could not express certain parts of a language, such as the words 'he', 'she', or 'it', or personal names, or the different grammatical endings of words such as 'danc-er, danc-ed, danc-ing'. So some symbols were chosen to represent sounds. They were still pictorial; for instance, the picture of a house would indicate the sounds 'p-r' in any word, because the Egyptian word for a house was 'pr' (its exact pronunciation is uncertain). Symbols of this kind, since they were given a special

| eye | giraffe | dove | flower | bread | angle |

SYMBOLS REPRESENTING THINGS SHOWN

| to dominate | to find | old age | Upper Egypt |

SYMBOLS REPRESENTING ABSTRACT IDEAS

| m-n | m-s | sh-w | n-w | ḥ-n | t-y |

SIGNS REPRESENTING TWO-CONSONANT SOUNDS

| 1 | 2 | 3 | 4 | 5 | 6 |

1. Heaven, sky, what is above. 2. Night sky with star, darkness, night. 3. Sun, sun god Ra, day, time. 4. Moon, month. 5. God or divine person. 6. Pray, worship, praise.

DETERMINATIVES

EXAMPLES OF HIEROGLYPHICS

value as sounds, or phonetic value, are called 'phonograms'. They represented only consonants: a phonogram could consist of three, two, or even one consonant. Those which were pictures of a word of one consonant came in time, of course, to be used like the single letters of our alphabet; but they were rarely used independently of the other symbols. Indeed, the ideographic and phonetic symbols were used together by the Egyptians from a very early time. As early as 3000 B.C. the hieroglyphic writing contained about twenty-four signs indicating the sound of a consonant. The script was, however, much more complicated, because, to make the meanings clearer (to indicate, for instance, whether a picture is to be read ideographically or phonetically), signs called 'determinatives' were used. These were pictures drawn after the word to be explained (or 'determined'), but they were not 'spelled'. For instance, a picture representing a man with raised hands, was the determinative of adoration, invocation, and prayer, and it was drawn after the words having the meaning of 'adoration',

British Museum

THE ROSETTA STONE WITH HIEROGLYPHIC, DEMOTIC, AND GREEK INSCRIPTIONS
It records a decree to commemorate the coronation of Ptolemy V in 196 B.C.

'invocation', or 'prayer'. A picture representing a man with a long beard was the determinative for 'gods', 'kings', or 'august persons'.

Hieroglyphics were carved on monuments, but were too difficult to use as handwriting. Therefore a simple form was devised, known as 'hieratic' or 'priests'' writing. This included, like the hieroglyphic writing, signs representing whole words, signs for two consonants, signs for single consonants, and also determinative symbols. Hieratic writing continued to grow simpler, until by the 7th century B.C. a style called 'demotic' or 'people's' writing was in common use. All resemblance to the old hieroglyphics had gone, and a whole group of hieratic signs would be joined together in a demotic sign.

Lines of the early hieroglyphic script could be written in any direction—even vertically—though normally they were written from right to left; nevertheless we always write it from left to right. The 'priests' script was first written vertically but later was written from right to left. The 'people's' script was written from right to left.

In recent times men have tried to decipher the ancient scripts. At first they failed; the writing was thought to be simpler than it really is: the pictures were taken as drawings of real things rather than symbols. Early in the 19th century scholars began to guess that some of the signs must represent sounds, and after various scholars had studied the problem, the writing was finally deciphered by the French scholar, Champollion. He examined a broken piece of black stone which had been found in Egypt, and which was covered on its one flat surface with three kinds of writing. The upper part was engraved in hieroglyphics, the next part in 'people's script', and the lowest part in Greek. With the help of the Greek text he interpreted the rest, though obviously he also made use of the previous achievements of other scholars, such as Dr. Thomas Young of Cambridge. The black stone, which is of basalt, is one of the treasures of the British Museum; it is known as the Rosetta stone from the place at which it was found. By its aid, the language and scripts of ancient Egypt have been made clear to the world, and much light thrown on history.

See also WRITING.
See also Vol. I: EGYPTIAN CIVILIZATION.

HIGH-ALTITUDE FLIGHT enables aircraft to move at high speeds for long distances with efficiency and economy. For that reason modern air-liners in peace and bombers in war are designed to fly high. Indeed, the whole history of aviation has shown a striving for height, even before men knew its usefulness.

The reason for the greater speed is that at a height of several miles the air is very thin, and offers less resistance to an aircraft. If you take a small flag on the end of a stick and whirl it round your head a few times, you will find that the quicker you whirl it the greater the resistance of the air; if you whirl it violently, something seems to be tugging at the flag to prevent you whirling it faster. This is the friction of the air, or 'drag'. Every aircraft in the sky has to face this drag all the time, and much of its engine power is used up in overcoming it. Motor-cars, trains, ships, and aeroplanes are all affected by it, but as an aeroplane moves faster than other kinds of transport, it feels the drag most. At ground-level the drag is greatest, whatever the speed of travel, because at ground-level the air is thickest, or most dense. Air, like everything else, has weight. At ground-level a cubic foot of air is heavier than a cubic foot of air 10 miles up in the sky; the reason is that at ground-level each cubic foot of space is more thickly crammed with particles of air. At a height of 7 miles above the earth, air is less than one-third as dense as at the ordinary ground-level; at a height of 10 miles, the density is only a little more than one-seventh of what it is on the ground. Therefore, if an aircraft flies at a height of several miles,

there are far fewer particles of air up there, and far less drag is felt against the sides of the cabin and the top and bottom surfaces of the wings. Speeds are increased without there being any need to increase the size of the engine or to increase the amount of fuel used.

Although speed is the chief advantage of high-altitude flight, there are other advantages. At heights greater than 20,000 feet, most of the fogs, storms, and other bad weather of the lower atmosphere are left behind. Above 35,000 feet, which is the region of the earth's upper layer of air known as the stratosphere, there is no change in temperature for a considerable distance. All the way up from ground-level to the stratosphere the temperature falls rapidly; at 35,000 feet the permanent temperature is about 100 degrees of frost. At such great heights the direction and speed of the winds are steady and can be foretold. Like the captains of sailing-ships who could rely on the Trade Winds to blow their ships in directions which never varied, so air-pilots can make use of regular winds when flying in the stratosphere on certain routes. It was thought at one time that no violent disturbances of the air took place at all at great heights—a matter of great importance to aircraft, which suffer a great increase in the stresses and strains imposed on their structure when they fly through gusts. It is known now, however, that severe gusts do sometimes occur even at high altitudes.

Far more interest has been taken in high flying since 'pure jet' gas-turbines have come into use. The propeller or airscrew, the older means of propelling an aeroplane, is somewhat at a loss at high altitudes because the spinning airscrew cannot grip the thin air so well. Besides, a piston engine driving an airscrew may weigh six times heavier than a 'pure jet' engine carrying out the same task. When flying near the ground, particularly on rather slow journeys and over short distances, the airscrew engine is much more economical. At high altitudes, for flying fast and far, the 'pure jet' is most successful (*see* AIRCRAFT ENGINES).

Navigation in the stratosphere has learnt much from military aircraft. These machines fly high because they are less likely to be found by an enemy, because they can fly faster, and because they can reconnoitre large stretches of territory by infra-red photography (*see* SURVEYING, Vol. VIII). The height also gives them plenty of room for diving, by which they

de Havilland Aircraft Co.

A DE HAVILLAND 'COMET' DESIGNED TO FLY AT A HEIGHT OF 40,000 FEET

can increase their speed for attack or defence. Civil as well as military aircraft, if flying high, have a much wider choice of a landing-place in an emergency, for the much longer time taken in descent gives time to make a choice. From a height of 10 miles a modern aeroplane can glide for over 100 miles with its engines out of action; it may take nearly half an hour to do so, and the pilot can still guide its course by using the rudder and other controls.

When an aeroplane is flying at a great height, supplies of air must be pumped to the passengers and crew to enable them to breathe normally. Oxygen, which is part of the air we breathe, is essential for life, as the proper working of every cell in the body depends on it; the brain-cells would cease to function in 1 minute without it. If one flew at the comparatively low height of 10,000 feet (2 miles up) without taking extra oxygen, one's body would begin to be affected after about an hour; among other symptoms, one's judgement would become unbalanced. At heights of 20,000 feet and over, symptoms would occur in a few minutes, and would lead to sleepiness, complete unconsciousness, and even death, unless more oxygen were breathed in.

For those reasons the cabins containing passengers and crew of high-flying aeroplanes are pressurized. Air under pressure is forced into the cabins by electric pumps, and, however high the aircraft may be flying, the air inside is kept at a density which would be natural at an altitude of 5,000 to 8,000 feet. On being drawn into the pumping system from outside, the air is first circulated through silencers, so that the hissing sound of its entry into the pumps shall not disturb passengers. Then its temperature is adjusted, and it is slightly moistened, if necessary, to make it like ordinary air at ground-level. The temperature can be raised or lowered; at certain very high speeds, in denser air, the sides of an aircraft are made so hot by the 'drag' of the air tearing past that the cockpit has to be cooled by a refrigerator; yet in the thinner air of the stratosphere, as we know, there is intense frost, and air must be heated before it can be breathed. The temperature mechanism, therefore, must be sensitive.

Each passenger needs about 1 lb. of air a minute; but if some passengers are smoking, the air will need changing more often. Therefore, 2 lb. of air a minute are usually pumped in, this being equivalent to 26 cubic feet a minute for each person. Most parts of the pressure-pump system and the devices for regulating the moisture and temperature of the air are automatic, and can be left to adjust themselves; but the flight-engineer or other officer can control them if necessary. Essential parts are duplicated in case of mechanical failure. The used air is gradually allowed to escape from the cabins while new air is taken in.

Since the lives of the passengers and crew may depend on the right pressure of air being maintained in the cabins, it is important that no air can leak out of them. All windows and doors are designed with care so that they are absolutely air-tight when closed. Even rivet holes must be sealed up. The fuselage itself is specially built to withstand the internal pressure against the walls of the aircraft.

Although the air-pumps can create an artificial pressure of air in the cabins equivalent to an altitude of 8,000 feet, no matter what the real height of the aircraft is, this pressure must be reached by slow degrees, or the passengers will feel discomfort. The human body can stand without inconvenience changes in pressure equal to a rise or fall of 300 feet a minute, and the pumps must adjust pressures accordingly, even though the aircraft may be climbing or falling five times as fast. (A quicker rate of change is not dangerous to a healthy person; a normal rate of fall with a parachute is 1,200 feet a minute.)

Flights at medium altitudes can be made without a pressurized cabin. At about 10,000 feet a passenger may inhale an occasional whiff of oxygen from a small tube held in the hand and connected to an oxygen container. Airliners on short European journeys carry oxygen for use in this way, in case they are forced up to a medium altitude to avoid storms or mountains. At greater heights a face-mask which holds a pipe of oxygen to the nose and mouth can be worn in an aircraft without cabin-pressuring plant. Above 20,000 feet the absence of normal air-pressure would cause strain to various parts of the body, and it is necessary to have a pressurized cabin or to wear a pressurized suit.

A pressurized suit is an air-tight, flexible suit, with a helmet for the head and a glass window for the eyes; it looks a little like the suit worn by DIVERS (q.v.), but is much lighter. A pressure pump forces air into the suit at the right pressure for breathing, the air being kept as warm and moist as it would be at ground-level. Pressure suits were used earlier than pressure cabins, as they are easier to make. The suits still have certain advantages in war-time, when there is a risk of pressure cabins being punctured by enemy gun-fire. A man in a pressure suit makes a smaller target, and is less likely to be hit; if there are two airmen in pressure suits in an aeroplane, one man may become a casualty from gunfire, but the other may survive.

See also SUPERSONIC FLIGHT; SPEED.
See also Vol. III: ATMOSPHERE.

HIGHWAY CODE, *see* ROAD TRAFFIC CONTROL.

HIGHWAYMEN. Throughout the centuries of slow travel, when roads were bad and travellers were in constant danger of losing their way, or of failing to reach their destination before nightfall, highway robbery was a common and profitable crime. People rarely travelled long distances unless they were on urgent business, which meant that they were worth robbing, as they were probably carrying money or goods. In the Middle Ages attacks by robbers were so common that it was almost out of the question to travel far alone. Merchants and pilgrims went in bands, armed with swords or cudgels. In 1285 laws were passed to prevent robbers from lurking in ambush at the roadside, ready to beat and rob the passers-by. By a statute of Edward I all hedges and thickets bordering the roads had to be cleared back for a distance of 200 feet. Landowners who neglected this law were liable to a fine, and were held responsible for any crimes committed on their land. The danger points were roads which joined two market towns, or which crossed parks: these last had to be cleared or enclosed by hedges, walls, or ditches.

The criminals were of many different kinds: there were labourers who had deserted the farms; outlaws liable for the death penalty perhaps for some small offence; and disbanded soldiers who could not find work. Often these took to the woods and made a living by robbing wayfarers. Robin Hood and his men, outlaws who lived in Sherwood Forest in Nottinghamshire in the 13th or 14th century, were probably highway robbers of this kind. The chief criminals were often, however, the barons, who used to send out bands of knights from their castles to waylay rich travellers, whom they robbed or held to ransom. These bands were often joined by stray vagabonds, who found it easier to work under a leader.

One notorious medieval robber was Sir

DICK TURPIN SHOOTING TOM KING
Woodcut from a series illustrating Turpin's supposed ride to York

Gosseline Denville of Northallerton, in the reign of Edward III. He led a band which plundered houses as well as robbing on the highway. He is said to have attacked the King himself. Sir Gosseline was outlawed, and was finally captured and hanged at York without a trial.

Throughout the 14th, 15th, and 16th centuries robbery and murder were common on the roads, especially after wars abroad, for many of the robbers were returned soldiers who were used to a life of pillaging, and disliked regular work even if they could find it. Chaucer, the 14th-century poet, is said to have been twice robbed in one day, while travelling between London and Eltham Palace. The robbers would frequent lonely exposed places, such as heaths and commons, and would often compel the traveller to cut across a common by blocking the roads with a fallen tree or some other obstacle. Favourite haunts in the 16th century were Salisbury Plain, Shooter's Hill at Blackheath near London, Newmarket Heath, and Gadshill near Rochester. This last was the scene of the high-

way robbery by Falstaff and his friends in Shakespeare's *Henry IV*, Part One. This, in which the gang set upon the travellers and stole their horses, was probably a faithful picture of the happenings of that time. Even inns were unsafe, for many highwaymen used them as their headquarters, and the inn servants who were often in league with them would pass on information about the guests. The highwaymen would entertain lavishly to ingratiate themselves with the travellers, even offering to act as guides.

In the 17th century travel became much more general, and private coaches and stage wagons began to be used. To this period and to the 18th century belong the famous highwaymen, many of whom worked alone and who were somewhat different in character from the footpads and vagabonds of previous ages. One man could hold up a coach, whereas it had needed a band to deal with a straggling train of travellers and pack-horses. Many of the highwaymen became the subject of ballads, broadsides, and chapbooks (little books of tales sold in the street), which, of course, exaggerated and romanticized their exploits, turning them into popular heroes. Their attacks upon the rich caused them to be presented as the champions of the poor. In actual fact the highwaymen were hardly gallant, although it is probably true that they left the very poor alone, finding them hardly worth robbing. It is also true that they rarely went as far as committing murder. Many of them tried to live up to their popular reputation by adopting eccentric tricks or clothes. Their trials and executions were often in the nature of public performances, in which the highwaymen would give a display of bravado. Many of them made speeches before they were hanged.

One of the earliest of the famous highwaymen, Gamaliel Ratsey, took to highway robbery after his return from the Irish wars in 1603. He was the hero of several ballads, which told the story of the jokes he is supposed to have played on his victims. Once, for instance, he made a Cambridge scholar deliver a learned oration before he robbed him. Ratsey was masked and apparently presented a fearsome appearance. He is mentioned by Ben Jonson in his play, *The Alchemist*. He was captured and hanged at Bedford in 1605.

The Civil War period and the years immediately following the Restoration of the Monarchy in 1660 produced many notorious highwaymen. The tradition, found in much romantic literature, that the highwayman was often a gentleman by birth, began at this time, probably because in certain cases dispossessed cavaliers took to the road in an attempt to revenge themselves on the Parliamentarians. The most famous of the Royalist highwaymen was Captain James Hind, who frequented the roads near London with a band of followers. He is said once to have attacked Cromwell. Another famous highwayman of the period, who came to England after the Restoration from fighting abroad, was John Nevison (sometimes called William and nicknamed 'Nick') who frequented the roads of York, Lincoln, Durham, and Nottingham. He was finally captured at an inn near Wakefield, and was hanged at York in 1685. It is he who is believed to have actually made the famous ride to York on a black mare, popularly attributed to the later highwayman, Dick Turpin. The story is that Nevison, wishing to prove an alibi for a robbery at Gadshill, rode to Gravesend, which he reached at 4 a.m., crossed by boat

to Essex, then rode to Cambridge and Huntingdon, and arrived at York, where he appeared at the bowling green, at 7.45 p.m., having travelled 190 miles in 15 hours. For this he became known as 'Swift Nick Nevison'. The story of a ride along the Great North Road at the end of which the horse dropped dead is, however, a local legend which has probably been attached to several different characters besides Nevison and Turpin.

Another highwayman who came to England after the Restoration, and about whom there grew up many legends, was a Frenchman named Claude Duval. He had a great reputation for gallantry to women, and is said once to have danced a coranto on the heath with a lady whose coach he had stopped, finally robbing her and her husband of only £100 of the £400 which they carried. Duval, when still in his twenties, was captured at an inn called the Hole-in-the-Wall in Chandos Street, London, and was condemned to death and hanged in 1669. He was buried behind Covent Garden churchyard, and his epitaph runs:

> Here lies Du Vall; reader if male thou art
> Look to thy purse, if female, to thy heart.

A 17th-century pamphlet, said to be a recantation of his evil life by a highwayman named John Clavel, describes some of the conditions under which the highwaymen worked. Clavel advises travellers not to go out on Sunday, as highwaymen preferred to work then, knowing that the law as it then stood would allow no redress to travellers for an assault committed on that day. For crimes committed on weekdays the traveller could claim against the town where the crime took place, if the criminal was not caught, and therefore he had no difficulty in raising a hue and cry. Clavel also advises night travel, for the highwaymen preferred to work during the day, for to be away from their lodgings all night might easily arouse suspicion. Travellers on horseback, he writes, should go in single file at intervals of 100 yards when they would be less easy to surround.

The danger of highway robbery became so serious in the 17th century that in 1642, in order to encourage the public to help in the capture of robbers, an act was passed offering rewards which included the property of the highwayman. In the early 18th century, however, highway robbery was still as serious a menace, especially during periods of general poverty and unemployment. Not only travellers but also toll-gate keepers and postmen were attacked. Highwaymen regularly frequented the heaths and commons within reach of the London slums, especially the Clare Market area, now replaced by Kingsway, where they used to go to dispose of their stolen goods. Many of them had headquarters in the taverns. *The Beggar's Opera*, written in 1728, which burlesques the idea of the romantic highwayman, shows a band of robbers who meet in a London tavern and speak in the special slang or 'thieves' cant' which was their secret language (*see* SLANG).

The most famous of all highwaymen, Dick Turpin, belongs to this period. In 1738 he took up with a certain Tom King whom he shot in what he claimed to be an accident. King, however, before he died, betrayed Turpin, who fled to York and became a horse thief under the name of John Palmer. He was hanged in the same year for stealing a black mare and foal. Turpin was a great character in contemporary ballads and also in later romantic literature, notably Harrison Ainsworth's novel *Rookwood*. Although many deeds, such as the ride to York, are probably falsely attributed to him, the stories of his coolness at his trial are probably true, and he certainly gave £3. 10s. to five men to follow his cart to the gallows as mourners. Stories of coolness and bravado at his trial are also told of Jerry Abershaw, hanged in 1795. He put on his own hat as the judge put on his black cap, and is said to have spent his time in the condemned cell drawing pictures of his exploits on the wall with cherry juice. Jack Rann, a highwayman known as 'Sixteen-string Jack' because of the eight coloured strings he wore at each knee, appeared at his trial in a pea-green costume, his hat decorated with silver string.

As travelling conditions improved, the activities of highwaymen decreased. The faster coaches on better roads were less easy to hold up. Also as the banking system and use of cheques developed, people carried less money about with them, and robbers did not make such profitable catches. Footpad robbery and general lawlessness were far from being rooted out; but by the end of the 18th century the single highwayman, the hero of the popular ballad, had almost entirely vanished.

See also ROADS, BRITISH; STAGE COACH.
See also Vol. X: OUTLAW.

HINDUSTANI LANGUAGE, *see* INDIAN LANGUAGES.

HORSE-POWER, *see* Vol. VIII: MEASUREMENTS, UNITS OF, Section 2, 1.

HORSE TRANSPORT. Prehistoric man first valued horses for their flesh and for their hides. But for at least 4,000 years man has used horses for HUNTING (*see* Vol. IX), for CAVALRY (q.v. Vol. X), for working on the land (*see* Vol. VI), for various kinds of sport and recreation (*see* Vol. IX), and for transporting himself and his possessions from one place to another. It is with this last use of the horse that we are concerned here. Of all the various animals used as BEASTS OF BURDEN (q.v.) at different times and in different places, horses are perhaps the most important, at least in Europe. The horse is an intelligent and docile animal, easy to train, and it combines strength and speed.

Horses were used for pulling things long before they were ridden. When they were first domesticated we do not know, though it was probably the wandering tribes of Central Asia who first made use of them for transport. Horses

PACK HORSES
From an engraving by David Loggan (1635–1692)

CARTS AND CARRIAGES IN THE 19TH CENTURY

were certainly used as early as 2000 B.C. by the Babylonians to pull war chariots, and they were introduced for the same purpose to Egypt about 1675 B.C. by the Hyksos, the conquering shepherd kings from Syria. Obviously an army able to move at a horse's speed had a great advantage over one confined to foot soldiers. The ancient Greeks, we know, used horses for riding, and had some mounted soldiers. The Romans used horses a great deal, both for their chariots and for riding. Travel by horse was well organized, and it was common to cover 70 miles a day by changing hired horses at certain regular INNS (q.v.). One Roman Emperor was said to have ridden 200 miles in one day on one occasion with, of course, relays of fresh horses. In Roman times, however, horses were not used for the slow moving of goods or for farming; the beasts of burden used for such purposes were oxen or slaves. The horse was needed when speed was required as well as strength.

By the 7th century stirrups were being used, adding considerably to the comfort of the rider. On long journeys a gait known as 'ambling'—something between a trot and a canter—was kept up for long periods; this gait still persists in countries, such as Peru, where long journeys on horseback are undertaken. During the Middle Ages, though oxen were still the main draught animals, the horse as a beast of burden became more and more important. Two types of horse developed: one was the heavy type capable of carrying a fully armed knight, or, towards the end of the Middle Ages, of pulling in strings of five or six the heavy, clumsy coach then coming into use; the other was the small sturdy pack-pony. Riding was for many hundreds of years the normal way of travelling. By the end of the 16th century the mails (30 lb. maximum) were carried from London to Edinburgh on horseback (see POST OFFICE, HISTORY OF). Remarkable long-distance rides were frequent—as when Sir Carbery Pryse in 1693, bearing urgent news of a lawsuit, rode from London to Gogerddan in Cardiganshire, more than 200 miles, in 48 hours.

The pack-horse, carrying its burdens bound on its back, was a vital means of transport, especially during the 16th and 17th centuries when the roads were often so bad that it was almost impossible to take any kind of wheeled traffic along them (*see* ROADS). Pack-horses and pack-mules were used for transporting nearly any type of goods, and remained quite indispensable until the end of the 18th century, when the improvement of the roads and the coming of the railway made them no longer necessary. Trains of fifty horses or more, laden with goods and led by a horse wearing a bell, whose sound they could follow, might be met with on any road in Europe. They carried trusses of hay or corn to the barns, or loads of manure to spread on the fields; they carried bales of raw wool to the ports, and sacks of grain to the mill and flour from the mill; they shifted coal from the mines, and bricks and stones from the kilns and quarries; they carried the travelling merchant's wares and baggage of the ordinary traveller. Long strings of them, tied nose to tail, wound along the packmen's routes, which, together with their inns and bridges, may still be seen in some places. They generally travelled in groups for protection against robbers on the road.

With the improvement of the roads under the TURNPIKE system (q.v.) in the late 17th and 18th centuries the CARRIAGE, and especially the STAGE COACH (qq.v.), became important ways of travelling; and so a strong, light horse, able to cover the ground at a good pace, was required. The heavy medieval horse, too slow for the new ways of travel, found a place on the farm, where, by the 18th century, horses had almost entirely replaced oxen for ploughing and other farm work (*see* HORSES, FARM, Vol. VI). The coach horse was a handsome animal, much like a modern weight-carrying hunter. High-stepping horses for pulling the light two-wheeled curricles were popular with the 19th-century gentlemen of fashion, and trotting horses for riding were also bred, principally in Norfolk. Speed records with these were set up, one horse being recorded as having trotted 17 miles in 56 minutes.

The coming of the horse-drawn omnibuses and trams in the mid-19th century provided a further use for horses. The first horse-drawn Bus (q.v.) ran in London in 1829. The horses were changed four or five times in the day, and their working life was from 5 to 7 years. By the beginning of the 20th century, just before the motor-bus began to supersede the horse-bus, there were 40,000 of these horses in London alone. The first horse-drawn trams appeared in New York in 1832, and were being introduced into England by the 1860's. They were drawn by two horses, with a third, known as a 'cock horse', added for steep hills. The horses wore bells on their head-harness to give warning of their approach. By 1880 the three London tram companies had between them 4,178 horses; but by 1915 the last horse-tram had disappeared.

The mechanization of transport has practically removed horses from the road. The carriage has almost vanished, the powerful great commercial dray-horses are replaced by lorries, the work of the pit-pony is done by a machine, the doctor does his rounds in his car instead of on his cob, the milk is more often delivered with a motor-van or electrified hand-truck than with a milk-cart and pony. In 1924 there were still 1,892,200 horses on the road; in 1948 there were only 612,000. The use of the horse is becoming almost entirely confined to sport and pleasure.

See also BEASTS OF BURDEN.
See also Vol. II: HORSE.
See also Vol. VI: HORSES, FARM.
See also Vol. IX: HORSES; HORSE RACING; RIDING.
See also Vol. X: CAVALRY.

HOSPITAL TRAIN, *see* TRAINS, SPECIAL USES.

HUNGARIAN LANGUAGE, *see* FINNISH AND ALLIED LANGUAGES.

HYDROGRAPHY, *see* CHARTS. *See also* Vol. VIII: HYDROGRAPHY.

I

ICE-BREAKER. This is a special ship for forcing a way through ice. Ice-breakers are now part of the normal equipment of ports, mainly in the Baltic Sea and Canadian waters, which habitually freeze up during the winter months. They smash the ice as it forms, and so keep the ports open to ordinary shipping for longer periods than would otherwise be possible.

All ice-breakers are designed on the same principle, and work in the same way; the front of the ship slides up on to the ice and so crushes it with its weight, and the broken ice is forced under the ice-fields on each side. By continually mounting and crushing the ice in this way, the ship gradually cuts a channel through the ice, and cargo vessels can follow into or out of the port. Ice-breakers must be very strongly built to stand the strain of the work. They are equipped with powerful engines, usually steam driven, and the propellers and rudder are specially protected against damage by the freed ice. A modern ice-breaker can crush ice-fields up to 30 feet in thickness.

See also DISCOVERY I.

ILLUSTRATION. While most pictures, so far as they represent an incident, can be said to be illustration, the true illustration, as we understand it to-day, is meant to decorate, develop, or comment on a printed text or caption. The ancestor of the modern illustrated book was the ILLUMINATED MANUSCRIPT (q.v. Vol. XII). In this the text was handwritten, and the illustrations were drawn on the pages of the book. When printed books began to displace the manuscript in the second half of the 15th century, the tradition of decorated pages and full-page illustrations was taken over, but with great simplification of method. The illustrations were engraved either on wood or copper, printed in

black, and sometimes tinted by hand. Prints from these wood-blocks, or copper plates, were often sold separately as cheap pictures, and a tradition of making separate prints, independent of text, grew up. They were often called 'broadsides', a word used by the early printers to describe a sheet printed on one side only.

A great initial stimulus was given to illustration by the Reformation. In 1511 Albrecht Dürer, the German artist, produced two classics of illustration, the *Great Passion* and the *Little Passion*, which told the story of the life of Christ in woodcuts made vividly real to the spectator by the inclusion of contemporary costume and detail. These two series of pictures were widely circulated, and filled a useful purpose among the masses of people unable to read, but able to follow in pictures a story they knew very well. These picture stories of Dürer's are the first printed ancestor of the modern comic strip. Holbein the younger and Lucas Cranach also produced illustrations and cartoons in support of the Lutheran Reformers. The work of these artists was propagandist in purposes, and much of its strength springs from the artists' urge to

British Museum

THE ADORATION OF THE SHEPHERDS
Woodcut from the *Little Passion* by Albrecht Dürer
(1471-1528)

make simple direct statement. Italian illustrators of the same period produced work of great decorative charm, but without the vigour and purpose of the Northern artists.

From these beginnings illustration keeps pace with the development of PRINTING (q.v. Vol. VII). Wood-engraving, copper-engraving, etching, lithography, and photography were to be used in turn in succeeding centuries.

Little book-illustration of high quality was produced in the 17th century; but it must be remembered that Rembrandt produced his etchings in that century, and they made ordinary woodcuts seem very crude. The influence of Rembrandt's etchings, because of their lucid realism and dramatic power, is by no means over even to-day.

Improvement in manufacturing techniques in the 18th century provided more paper and machinery; and so it became worth while for artists and printers to make better illustrations. The French school of engravers produced book-illustrations and separate prints of an elegance and polish which have rarely been equalled since. In England William Hogarth produced engravings as well as paintings which describe vividly the way people behaved in the 18th century. He was at his best with a story to tell in pictures; several series of engravings from his paintings satirize the life of his period. In Spain, at the end of the century, Goya produced *Los Caprichos*, a series of aquatints with captions which, themselves influenced by Rembrandt, had a strong influence on later illustrators.

In 1798 Alois Senefelder invented LITHO-GRAPHY (q.v. Vol. XII), a new method of printing from stone which made the modern poster a practical possibility.

By the beginning of the 19th century illustration had begun to play a part in the lives of people of all classes. Lower printing costs made possible the production of cheap children's alphabets, broadsides illustrated with crude woodcuts, and advertising handbills. Increasing skill made possible the production of richly illustrated works on natural history and on scientific and technical subjects. The political broadsides, drawn by Rowlandson, Gillray, and others, were bought from print-shops much as a magazine is bought to-day, and folios of these prints were passed from family to family to provide an evening's entertainment. Ballads and broadsheets were sold by street-hawkers, and the same

Bodleian Library

PAGE FROM WILLIAM BLAKE'S 'SONGS OF INNOCENCE', 1789
Engraved by Blake on copper by a special process

illustration often did duty for more than one sentimental song or description of a hanging.

But by the 1830's the political broadside was dead. Increasing numbers of people were able and eager to read. The first popular illustrated periodical, *The Penny Magazine*, was published in 1832, and by the end of that year was selling 200,000 copies a week. New novels were published in weekly parts and were illustrated as a matter of course.

William Blake had been, years before, the first British engraver to produce book illustrations of exceptional quality. Now George Cruikshank, who started life as an engraver of political broadsides, began to make outstanding illustrations for novels. By his mastery in both realism and fantasy, he made British book-illustration a fresh and lively art. His contemporaries, Richard Doyle, 'Phiz' (Hablôt K. Browne), and John Leech, contributed to this

ILLUSTRATION   198

LYCEUM_
DON
QUIXOTE

Victoria and Albert Museum

LYCEUM THEATRE POSTER DESIGN BY THE BEGGARSTAFF BROTHERS TO ADVERTISE SIR HENRY IRVING'S PERFORMANCE

new school of illustration. They drew for the newly founded weekly paper, *Punch*, and they illustrated the first books of Charles Dickens, which were published in monthly parts. These artists were distinguished by their imaginative understanding of picture in relation to story. When drawings began to be printed within the text, instead of appearing on a separate page, the artists were able to create a unity between the printed matter and the tone and pattern of the drawing.

The illustrated newspaper began to appear in the 1840's, and soon the artist-reporter was at work. The drawings, which these artists made on the spot (the Crimean War and the Exhibition of 1851 were the first major events to be recorded), were reproduced with astonishing skill by the wood-engravers of the period. The artists developed to a high degree the ability to produce convincing pictorial reports of events. Though they were later displaced by the camera, the tradition remained.

At first the 19th century had been remarkable for the way in which the technique of wood-engraving developed. Later, following the invention of PHOTOGRAPHY (q.v. Vol. VII), came a number of photo-engraving processes, which are the methods used for the mass production of printed illustrations to-day (*see* PROCESS REPRODUCTION, Vol. VII).

As the printing presses and processes developed, the character of illustration became more lavish. Lithographed song covers in six or seven colours were not uncommon; etchings and colour plates were bound into novels; wood-engravings of exceptional size and detail were produced for the weekly newspaper. Ingenious valentines and Christmas cards were on sale, and the artists seemed bent on cramming as much detail as they could into their illustrations. But by the end of the century a reaction took place under the leadership of William Morris and Walter Crane. Morris printed books in which the illustrations tended towards the simplicity of the early Italian book illustrations. In the 1890's, influenced by this move towards simplicity, a young artist, Aubrey Beardsley, used line and flat black masses to produce a new kind of illustration, simple yet subtle, and ideal for reproduction by the new photo-engraving methods.

At the same time large-scale production of printed posters became possible. In this field the French led the way; the early French posters, by artists such as Toulouse-Lautrec, Steinlen, Forain, and Chêret, were simple, brilliant in colour, and forceful in their message. By the turn of the century such poster-designers as James Pryde and his brother-in-law, Sir William Nicholson (who chose to be known as 'the Beggarstaff Brothers'), John Hassall, and Dudley Hardy, had made the first steps to establishing a poster tradition in England. To-day the designing of posters calls for special talents in the handling of colour and pattern (*see* POSTERS, Vol. XII). The poster was the first advertising technique to make use of gifted artists; but since then the whole field of advertisement has opened up to the illustrator. All types of work are called for, ranging from technical illustration to abstract design, from the simplest diagram to the most ambitious painting.

The modern illustrator tends to be a specialist. His work is usually very personal in style, and he usually confines himself to the perfection of his work within his chosen sphere—whether it is realistic magazine illustration, decorative illustration for books, technical drawings, newspaper cartoons and comic strips, or children's books.

See also BOOKS, HISTORY OF.
See also Vol. VII: PROCESS REPRODUCTION.

INDIAN LANGUAGES. The great majority of the inhabitants of northern India speak languages which belong to the same family as English (*see* INDO-EUROPEAN LANGUAGES). The language from which these descend was brought into India from the north-west at a very early period, probably about 1400 B.C., by one branch of the Indo-Iranian group of the Indo-European speakers. These people, who are usually referred to as the Indo-Aryans, were a vigorous and war-like people, living on their flocks of animals. Their religious hymns, which have been preserved in the great collections known as the Vedas, are among the oldest specimens of any Indo-European language which have come down to us (*see* INDIAN CIVILIZATIONS, Vol. I). Somewhere about 400 B.C., the language was fixed in its classical literary form by the composing of a grammar by a scholar named Panini, and under the name of SANSKRIT (q.v.) it has continued through the ages to be the universal language of learning in India, playing much the same part in India as Latin did in Europe. Alongside the fixed classical language, however, the common language of the people continued to develop, and just as from popular spoken Latin ('vulgar' Latin) there grew in course of time the various Romance languages such as French and Italian, so in India the popular language was gradually split up into a number of local dialects, from which the modern northern Indian languages are descended.

The oldest Indian inscriptions which have survived, the proclamations made in the 3rd century B.C. by the Emperor ASOKA (q.v. Vol. V), show a form of the language which had already changed a good deal from Sanskrit. In later inscriptions and literature we find several later languages developed from Sanskrit, which are known by the general name of Prakrit (popular) dialects. The language of the sacred books of the southern Buddhists, Pali, is really an old form of Prakrit, though the name is not usually applied to it. The latest stage of the Prakrits forms a bridge to the modern Indian languages, the most important of which are Bengali, Oriya (spoken in Orissa), Hindi, Kashmiri, Punjabi, Sindhi, Gujarati, and Marathi. Although widely

Dept. of Archaeology, Govt. of India.
DETAIL OF AN EDICT OF ASOKA CARVED ON A ROCK AT GIRNAR, INDIA, 3RD CENTURY B.C.

separated from the others geographically, Sinhalese, spoken in the southern half of Ceylon, is also Indo-Aryan.

Urdu is an important language, like Hindi in its grammar and structure, but, being spoken by the Mohammedan population, it has been built up from the Arabic and Persian spoken by the early Moslem invaders, and is written in Arabic script. Urdu means the 'language of the camp'. Literary Urdu and literary Hindi have become very much more different from each other during the past century, so that they really deserve to be ranked as distinct languages. Nevertheless, a compromise between the two, understood by speakers of either, has always been used for everyday speech, and this form of the language, known as Hindustani, has often been suggested by Indian political leaders as a common language for the whole of India. Since the formation of the two separate countries of India and Pakistan, Urdu has naturally been the official language of Pakistan, while the government of India decided in 1949 that Hindi would in the future be the official language of India.

South of the region of the Indo-Aryan languages, and occupying most of the Deccan peninsula is the Dravidian family of languages. These, spoken by some 60 million people, as against over 200 million speakers of Indo-Aryan languages, are not related to Indo-European. They have, however, borrowed large numbers of words from Sanskrit. The most important are Tamil, spoken in the extreme south-east of India and in the northern half of Ceylon; Telugu, to the north of Tamil; Malayalam in the extreme south-west; and Canarese, or Kannada, to the north of Malayalam. Brahui, spoken in Baluchistan in north-western India, is also Dravidian.

In addition to these two main families of languages, the Munda languages (Mundari, Santali, Ho, and a few others) spoken in the regions west of Calcutta, probably represent a family of languages which was formerly more widely spread. Finally, along the foothills of the Himalayas and in Assam are found a number of languages related to CHINESE (q.v.).

See also LANGUAGE, HISTORY OF.
See also Vol. I: INDIAN PEOPLES.

INDO-EUROPEAN LANGUAGES. The name 'Indo-European', which is given to the large family of languages to which English belongs, is at first sight a little misleading, since it might be supposed to include all the languages of India and Europe. In fact, several European languages, for example, Finnish and Hungarian, and several Indian languages, for example, the Dravidian languages of South India, belong to quite different families; and some Indo-European languages, such as Persian or Armenian, are at home neither in India nor in Europe. The name, however, has become established as a technical term. Other names that have been used in the past are Indo-Germanic and Aryan. The latter, however, strictly refers to the Indo-Iranian or eastern subdivision of the Indo-European family of languages only, and is now seldom used.

Scholars have discovered that some considerable time before 1500 B.C.—how long before is uncertain—there must have existed a relatively small tribe, speaking a language which we may call 'primitive Indo-European'. No records of this language have come down to us, and its existence can only be inferred from a comparison of its daughter languages.

The main subdivisions into which the primitive Indo-European language has in course of time been split up are: the Indo-Iranian or Aryan group, itself subdivided into Indo-Aryan (including SANSKRIT and a large number of more recent INDIAN LANGUAGES) and Iranian (*see* PERSIAN AND ALLIED LANGUAGES); the Hellenic group, or GREEK; the Italic group, of which the most important member is LATIN, with its daughters, FRENCH and other ROMANCE LANGUAGES; the GERMANIC LANGUAGES, to which ENGLISH belongs; the Celtic group (*see* WELSH, GAELIC, and IRISH); the Baltic languages (Lithuanian and Latvian or Lettish) and the closely related SLAVONIC LANGUAGES (qq.v.). In addition to these, Albanian forms a distinct member of the family by itself, and so does Armenian. Two important discoveries of the present century have added to the family the ancient HITTITE language (q.v. Vol. I) and Tocharian which flourished in Chinese Turkestan rather more than 1,000 years ago.

See also LANGUAGE, HISTORY OF.

INDONESIAN LANGUAGES. Over 80 million people living in the East Indies, the Malay Peninsula, Madagascar (off the east coast of Africa), Formosa (near China), and many small islands in the Indian Ocean and China Seas speak Indonesian languages. There are a great many separate languages, but not all have been recorded. These languages differ a great deal—so much so that it is not always possible for a person who usually speaks one of them to understand easily any other.

The commonest Indonesian language is Malay, which is spoken by about 40 million people, and used as an international language in much of the East Indies. It is one of the easiest languages in the world to learn a little of—enough, for instance, to go shopping with—for, like English, it has few rules of grammar. The meaning is shown by the order and grouping of the words, instead of by inflexions, that is, changes in the words themselves. As one learns more, however, one realizes that Malay is so full of close shades of meaning that no foreigner can ever speak it as a Malay does. Many of its words are borrowed from ARABIC, PERSIAN, and CHINESE (qq.v.).

Many Indonesian languages have native alphabets of their own, derived from Indian forms introduced into the islands about a thousand years or so ago, and adapted for local use. Of these the most important is Kawi, or Old Javanese, in which the earliest inscription is that at Dinaya, dated A.D. 760.

The Indonesian languages have caused many changes in the OCEANIC LANGUAGES (q.v.), and, generally therefore, the two groups are usually studied together. Many of the commonest words in Oceanic languages have been borrowed from the Indonesians, who made long voyages among the islands of the Pacific about 2,000 years ago, long before Europeans had discovered the existence of these islands. Groups settled in many of the islands and conquered the people whom they found there.

See also LANGUAGE STRUCTURE.
See also Vol. I: INDONESIANS.

INK. The word itself comes from the Latin *encaustum* (because it 'burnt in'), the name of the purple ink used by the Roman emperors. It now covers two distinct substances: writing and printing ink.

1. WRITING INKS (black and blue-black). Writing inks are liquids in which a colouring matter is present in some form. Before 2000 B.C. the Chinese and Egyptians had prepared a black ink by mixing soot, water, and gum, and forming them into a solid cake, which was probably used like a modern water-colour paint. Their invention made writing a much easier process than it had been before (*see* WRITING INSTRUMENTS). An ink similar to theirs, called Indian ink, is used to-day for drawing maps and plans. But carbon inks easily become thick and clog the pen, and by the 17th century a new writing ink was being used in Europe. It was coloured by the combination of tannic acid, got from the bark of trees, with an iron salt. Modern inks are made with these ingredients, but precautions are taken to keep them clear, and a blue dye is added to heighten the colour. Lasting clearness is, of course, essential to ink which is stored in a fountain-pen. The ink used in the modern ball-point pen (*see* WRITING INSTRUMENTS, Section 2) generally has an oil base, and is mainly composed of chemical solvents. Great care is taken to purify it after manufacture, as the most minute particle of dirt would clog the ball point.

Other kinds of writing inks are coloured inks, made by dissolving dyes in water, and indelible inks, chiefly used for marking clothing, one form of which is made by dissolving a salt of silver in water. Invisible inks, for sending secret messages, are generally made from substances which develop colour when heat or another substance known as a reagent is applied to them. Simple examples are milk and lemon juice, which respond to heat, and rice-water, which was widely used during the Indian Mutiny of 1857, and which is developed by iodine.

2. PRINTING INKS. These are thick pastes which consist of a pigment ground into a varnish, to which a dryer is added. The varnish itself hastens drying and also binds the colour to the paper. The origins of printing ink are as remote as those of writing ink, for the ancient Chinese knew how to print from wood-blocks (see CHINESE CIVILIZATION, Vol. I). When the art of printing was introduced into Europe in the middle of the 15th century the early printers used an ink consisting of lamp-black mixed with boiled linseed oil. This formula continued to be used for several hundred years, but recently new methods of manufacturing printing ink have been developed, and different kinds are made for different purposes. A wide variety of pigments is used, and inks for newspaper printing contain instant-drying varnishes made from petroleum.

See also HANDWRITING; PAPER; PRINTING, HISTORY OF.

INNS. The name 'Inn', which has the same origin as the words 'in' and 'within', means simply a place within which the traveller may find food and shelter. The word originally also meant an 'abode' or 'place of residence', being often applied to a country nobleman's town mansion. Inns of Chancery were sets of buildings in London originally used as hostels and places of study for law students.

In Biblical times and countries certain roads,

Paul Popper

A CARAVANSERAI ON THE KHYBER PASS, PAKISTAN

such as the road from Damascus to Jerusalem, were so busy that some provision had to be made for the merchants using them. Shelters were built, called *khans* if they were near towns, but *caravanserai* if they were in the open country. The shelter was square in shape, with its rooms facing on to a central courtyard, reached by a gateway under a defensive tower. Each room provided space for the traveller, his servants, and their laden camels and asses; but all travellers had to bring and prepare their own food in the courtyard. Such a *khan* at Bethlehem had no room for Mary and Joseph at the birth of Christ.

Along the Roman road inns called *tabernae* or *cauponae* were found at intervals of about a day's journey by horse. St. Paul, going as a prisoner to Rome, was met on the road from what is now called Brindisi at the Three Taverns—an important stopping place. Only poor people spent the night in these comfortless buildings, sharing with soldiers the bread and wine sold there. Innkeepers were not always respected, but the law made them responsible for the safety of their guests' slaves and belongings.

With the fall of Rome, travelling became more dangerous, and the few daring wayfarers passed the nights in monasteries or castles. In the villages the ale-house soon appeared, distinguished from other cottages by the bush or garland attached to a pole sticking out from a window, a Roman sign that wine was sold. The ale-house did not provide accommodation. The monks, upon whom the duty of charity was imposed, entertained rich or distinguished guests within the monastery; but for the humbler travellers 'God's inn' provided a guest house, sometimes on the outskirts of the monastic buildings, where food and a straw pallet in a common dormitory might be obtained. As PILGRIMAGES (q.v. Vol. I) to famous shrines became more popular, monastic hostels were placed along the pilgrim ways. Traces of some of these still survive, as in the George at Glastonbury and the hostel of God-Begot at Winchester.

The inn of the later Middle Ages, like Chaucer's Tabard Inn at Southwark, possessed its sign, hanging in the wind for all to see (see INN SIGNS). Its host cared diligently for the comfort of his guests, serving them with bread, meat, and beer. Even so, the travellers did not expect single rooms; the rush-strewn dormitory with its straw pallets was the rule. The names of

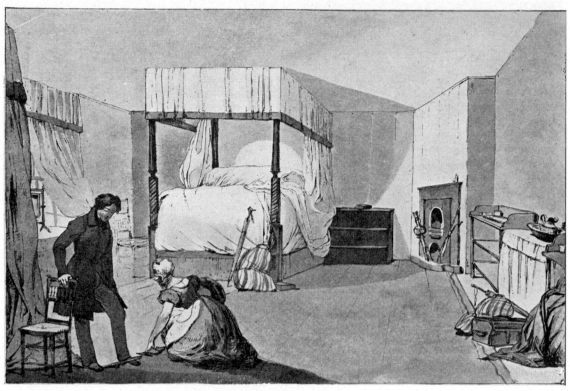

A BEDROOM AT AN INN
Coloured engraving from Eugène Lami's *Voyage en Angleterre*, 1830

inns of this period reflect the trade and travel of the time. The Woolpack and the Fleece tell of our staple trade in wool, the Packhorse reminds us that roads were too derelict to allow easy passage for the cumbersome carts. Others bear names from the crests of local families of importance, such as the Wyvern and the Chequers.

By the end of Queen Elizabeth's reign a great advance had been made. Some of the disused monastic hostels had been taken over and brought up to date. Glass windows were beginning to appear, and carpets occasionally replaced rushes on the floors. In the cobbled inn yard the traveller's horse was walked by the ostler, who would rub him down and feed him well. Whether the guest supped at the common table or in a private room, he was likely to find clean table-linen, china, and cutlery, even forks recently introduced from Italy, and a variety of foods and wines.

Some of the inns of the period had a somewhat doubtful reputation however; servants and

hosts were often in league with bands of highway robbers who learnt from them of the presence of gold in the travellers' luggage, and so prepared to attack them on their next day's journey (*see* HIGHWAYMEN).

Some inns were famous for the good company that met there. Shakespeare supped at the Mermaid in Bread Street in London, for instance, and a host of famous Elizabethans enjoyed the comfort of its panelled rooms. English inns were considered better than those of the Continent because it was said in England the host was servant to the guests and abroad he was master. Shakespeare has created the friendly atmosphere of the English inn for us, and thousands must have echoed Falstaff's words, 'Shall I not take mine ease in mine inn?'

The next great age of the English inn came with the building of the TURNPIKE roads (q.v.) and the days of coaching. The typical inn was still built around the inn yard, from which the mail and STAGE COACHES (q.v.) started their journeys or rumbled off with fresh horses, after

Henty & Constable

SIGN OF THE RICHMOND ARMS, CHICHESTER

Eldridge, Pope

SIGN OF THE CROSS KEYS, DORCHESTER

a delay long enough to enable the passengers to warm up before the log fire, and to sample the host's wine or beer. Innkeepers at first would often allow only inside passengers on the coaches to be served in the dining-room, while the outside passengers were fed with the coachmen and post-boys in the kitchen.

After some agitation by travellers in the early 19th century, innkeepers were persuaded to provide a row of jugs and basins in the hall so that the dusty passengers could wash. Upstairs massive furniture filled the rooms, and the wax candles (five shillings extra) showed up only a little of the dust in the corners. The mail coaches and stage coaches often started at dawn, and so passengers stayed at the inn the night before their journey. On busy roads from London the inns kept large numbers of horses, at Hounslow over 2,500, for the use of coaches. Some inns, such as the Red Lion at Barnet, were reserved for private posting only, and at these luxury inns the rich traveller might have to pay as much as six or seven shillings for his dinner, a sum equivalent to about £3. 10s. to-day. Such a dinner in 1820 might consist of soup, eels or freshwater fish, a roast fowl, a saddle of mutton, bread, and cheese. Wine was extra, though ale was served as a regular part of the meal.

By 1826 coaching inns had reached the peak of their prosperity, for within the next ten years the railways drew away a great deal of traffic from the roads. Old and famous inns had to close; for fifty years the rambling passages of the inns were almost empty; while in their place arose the new and often dingy Railway Hotels. Then came the age of the bicycle and motor-car, and travellers began to come back to the roads. Demand for accommodation increased. Enterprising landlords hung out signs which said at first 'stabling for motor cars'. More inns opened; guest houses and 'road houses' arose to supplement them. More and better service was given by innkeepers who still were, and are to-day, as were their medieval forerunners, bound to receive, lodge, and feed travellers as long as they have room available.

See also HORSE TRANSPORT.
See also Vol. VII: HOTEL INDUSTRY.

INN SIGNS. When most people were unable to read or write, pictures were used to draw attention to the wares of traders (*see* TRADE SIGNS, Vol. VII) and to-day inn signs are one of the

Victoria and Albert Museum

SIGN OF THE WHITE HART, WITLEY, SURREY

few remains of this practice. The early sign of an inn in England was a pole decorated with branches and leaves. This gave rise to the proverb 'Good wine needs no bush' (or advertisement). The bush sign may have been a legacy from the Roman occupation, for we know that the Romans used a bush to indicate an inn, although they also used names such as *Ad Rotam*, 'The Wheel' (which remained a popular sign for hostelries in the Middle Ages), and *Ad Gallum*, 'The Cock' (which is still popular).

There are many sources for the paintings on inn signs. The earliest is the arms of emblems of noble families who regarded the refreshment of travellers as one of their duties, and who hung their arms outside their 'inns', as their town mansions were known. Hence many inns display heraldic arms (*see* HERALDRY) of the principal landowner in the district, or of a family whom the landlord admired or to whom it was expedient to show loyalty. So there may be found the Red Lion of Lancaster, the White Hart of Richard II, the Talbot (a kind of hound) of the Earls of Shrewsbury, or the Eagle and Child

of the Stanley family. In time the word 'arms' came to be added to the name of a public house or inn even when there were no arms involved at all, as, for instance, the Cricketers' Arms. It was felt to add tone and dignity to the house.

The Church also has left its mark on inn signs, since it, too, in the Middle Ages catered for the needs of travellers. The Bell is the sign with an ecclesiastical origin which occurs most frequently, but there are many others—the Cross Keys (of St. Peter), the Mitre, or the Salutation. From the last of these have come, by an interesting transformation, the Angel and the Flower-Pot. Originally the sign showed the Virgin and the Angel Gabriel, but in the Puritan times of the 17th century the Virgin was painted out, leaving only the Angel; or the Virgin and the Angel were removed leaving only the Virgin's sheaf of lilies, to which later a flower-pot was added to complete the fancied picture.

Since members of CRAFT GUILDS (q.v. Vol. VII) often made inns their meeting-places, it is natural that many inn signs trace their origins to trades, as, for example, the Axe and Compass (of the Company of the Carpenters), the Dolphin (of the Watermen's Company). Here, again, there is an interesting corruption. The Vintner's Company marked their swans with a nick on either side of the beak, but in course of time the swan with two nicks is represented as the Swan with Two Necks.

Later on national and local figures and events, which have stirred the imagination, have been commemorated in inn signs: for instance, the sign of the Saracen's Head commemorated the Crusades, the Royal Oak, the hiding of Charles II in the oak tree, and signs with portraits commemorate great generals and admirals such as the Duke of Wellington and Lord Nelson. Inventions also have been commemorated by inn signs, such as the sign-paintings of air-balloons or railway locomotives. Trades, particularly agriculture, and typical English sports and games have all supplied subjects for signs—a fox and hounds, a plough, a harrow, a wagon and horses, a horse and jockey, a cricketer. In recent times the portrait of a particular exponent of a sport (Lord Burghley, the hurdler), or of the winner of a famous horse-race (Blenheim, the winner of the Derby of 1930) have been the subjects of inn-signs.

Not all signs can be explained by any of the origins suggested here. Some have been borrowed from older signs to which they have no real claim; some are imitations based on earlier models; the explanation of some depends on expert local knowledge; while others are plays on the original sign (15s. for the Three Crowns); and again others can only be explained as probable corruptions of earlier signs. But it is not always so easy to reconstruct the original name as it is in the case of an inn-sign in the Cotswolds, where an ill-informed correction of a local family name, Murimuth, a member of whom was the chronicler of Edward III's time, produced the Merry Mouth.

See also INNS; PLACE-NAMES.

INTERNAL-COMBUSTION ENGINE, see MOTOR-CAR, HISTORY OF. See also Vol. VIII.

INTERNATIONAL AIR CONTROL, see CIVIL AVIATION.

INTERNATIONAL BROADCASTING. In most countries broadcasting was started as a way of providing information and entertainment for the people of that country. Soon many Governments decided to broadcast as well to the peoples of foreign countries in their own languages. The chief aim of Governments was to make their national viewpoint attractive to other people. In the early years of wireless the Soviet Union set out to broadcast to as many parts of the world as it could reach. Later the German Government of Adolf Hitler broadcast regularly to groups of people of partly German ancestry who were living in countries near Germany; the broadcasts tried to persuade them to agitate against those countries in favour of Hitler. In the years just before the Second World War broadcasts directed from various lands at the peoples of other lands greatly increased. An early agreement was made by the nations that none of them would broadcast in the language of another (see WAVE-LENGTHS), but the rule was widely broken. In the end almost all nations took to making foreign broadcasts, each stating the views of its own Government and its own version of the world's news.

It is for those reasons that broadcasts to other countries are paid for by the Government of a country that sends them out. It is only for broadcasting to home audiences that wireless stations get money directly from the public, either through listeners' licence fees or through advertising (see BROADCASTING HISTORY).

Britain made its first non-English broadcasts in January 1938, when the air was already full of international arguments in many languages. The only overseas broadcasts from Britain before then had been the 'Empire service' in English to parts of the Commonwealth which, after 5 years of experiment, began in 1932.

The first foreign B.B.C. service, set up by Government request, was in Arabic; the Arab peoples had heard much propaganda from the German and Italian Governments, then hostile to British policies. Very soon the B.B.C. began broadcasting to South America in Spanish and Portuguese. After the important conference at Munich in Germany, between the British Prime Minister and the rulers of Germany and Italy in September 1938, Britain began broadcasts in French, German, and Italian. Services in various languages were greatly increased at the outbreak of war in 1939; at the height of the war the B.B.C. was speaking in forty-eight languages; every day ten overseas services, including 200 news bulletins, were issued.

The Overseas Services of the B.B.C. are now a permanent feature of broadcasting. More than forty languages are in regular use. Not all the broadcasts are in foreign languages; many programmes are for English-speaking parts of the Commonwealth.

Programmes for overseas services are, on the whole, rather shorter than home programmes. British listeners have fairly regular habits, but an overseas broadcast may be heard in remote parts of Asia by people who will not have the patience to listen for long to a programme from Britain. The speed of speech at the microphone is slower than for home broadcasts, and the transmitting station must announce itself (as 'This is London') more often.

B.B.C.

B.B.C. TRANSMITTING STATION AT DAVENTRY
Aerials with reflectors for transmitting to the Far East, Australia, and Central America

To ensure that a programme is broadcast when most listeners are free to hear it, which is often a meal-time, planners of programmes must take account of the differences in local time round the world. If Britain wants to offer listeners in Sydney a news bulletin at 6 p.m. local time, it must be broadcast from Britain at 8 a.m. Greenwich Mean Time, as the time in Sydney is 10 hours fast on Greenwich (see TIME, Vol. III). When one programme is intended for several countries, or for several time-zones in one large country, it can sometimes be recorded, and then repeated when the best listening time comes round in each time-zone. When Summer Time begins or ends in an overseas country, special care must be taken to alter the times of transmission from Britain. This may not be easy if the engineers' transmission apparatus is already fully occupied at a busy hour.

One important outcome of this nation-to-nation activity is rebroadcasting—the picking-up of a programme from elsewhere for transmission in the local programmes of the receiving country. This is only rarely done in Britain—as when, for instance, the B.B.C. home programmes rebroadcast an important concert which is being broadcast at the same time from a foreign city, such as Paris, Brussels, or The Hague. In many parts of the world programmes from the B.B.C. Overseas Services are regularly rebroadcast, particularly by stations in the Commonwealth. As most people listen to their local stations on a medium wave-length, as this is the easiest for the ordinary set to pick up, a larger audience can hear the programme. Another device for reaching a large audience is the 'outpost' station, such as the British Far Eastern Broadcasting Service at Singapore, run by the B.B.C. to supply a wide area. A B.B.C. unit in Colombo, Ceylon, supplies certain programmes for the transmitters of Radio Ceylon.

Many broadcast programmes are sent out from Britain in the shape of gramophone records, which are sent to local stations in countries all over the world, and transmitted by them at their convenience. These recordings of broadcasts in English and many other languages are known as 'transcriptions'; thousands of them are exported every week.

The needs of overseas service have led the B.B.C. to continue a 'monitoring' service, begun during the war; its duty is to listen to broadcasts from other countries and to note any statements which would help the B.B.C. editors who are preparing news for broadcasting overseas.

One form of foreign-language broadcast has

no relation to national policies; this is the use of a radio station for commercial advertising. In Britain the B.B.C. is forbidden by the terms of its charter to allow any advertising to be broadcast (*see* BROADCASTING CORPORATIONS); therefore some stations on the continent of Europe accept money to broadcast British advertisers' announcements; and to make sure that some British listeners will hear the announcements, they organize regular programmes of entertainment in English, including, if possible, well-known British entertainers.

See also BROADCASTING, HISTORY OF.

INTERNATIONAL LANGUAGES.

During the Middle Ages, Latin, which was spread through Europe by the Church, served as an international language for the western world. It was not only written but also spoken in monasteries, churches, the universities, and the law courts. It remained an international medium for learned and scientific purposes till well on into the 17th century. For instance, Milton wrote Latin prose and verse as easily as English, and even felt that he ought to put *Paradise Lost* into Latin, so that it should live! But after the Reformation Movement in the 16th century, which was a movement away from the Church of Rome, new national churches grew up in which the native language was used and learned men began to write in their own languages as well as in Latin. Soon, however, as advances were made in scientific thought, there was a need for an international language in which to express the new ideas, and philosophers such as Descartes and Leibnitz set to work to devise one. At the end of the 17th century French was replacing Latin as the language of culture: it was accepted as the diplomatic language, and was used in 'polite society' throughout Europe. In the 19th century, as British commerce and colonization spread across the globe, French slowly gave ground to English; in the 20th the rapid growth in power and population of the United States and of the British Dominions gave English an absolute superiority, which the wide distribution of American films helped to confirm. English is already the regular daily speech of more than 200,000,000 people.

But these figures, large as they are, do not mean that English is universally or broadly, and when it spreads very far among people of different changes in pronunciation are com-

struction, for it is affected by the speech-habits of peoples accustomed to other tongues and different ways of thought. The AMERICAN ENGLISH LANGUAGE (q.v.) is in many ways unlike the English spoken in England, and each Dominion has its own peculiarities of pronunciation, its own methods of expression, and its own vocabulary. In general, however, it can be said that English-speaking countries share the same grammar and roughly the same stock of words. The fact that much of the vocabulary of English is shared with the GERMANIC LANGUAGES (such as German and Dutch) or adopted from the ROMANCE LANGUAGES (such as French and Italian) (qq.v.) is helpful to foreigners familiar with these tongues who try to learn it. The fact that its grammar is simple is also an advantage, though this is perhaps counterbalanced by the fact that its spelling is not uniform or regular.

Few people now believe that it is possible or even desirable to abolish native languages and replace them by an international language—no matter whether that language be chosen from the existing tongues or artificially created. But many people feel the need of an 'auxiliary' or 'secondary' language which could be used by everyone for various forms of international communication. During the last hundred years several artificial languages, most of them based on existing languages, have been devised in the hope that they might meet this need. The best known of them are Esperanto, announced by Dr. L. L. Zamenhof in 1887, and the cumbersome Volapük, put forward by J. M. Schleyer in 1880. Esperanto builds words by adding affixes or additions to a number of one-syllable stems, which are generally derived from one or other of the European languages; it has only one auxiliary verb—the verb *to be*; all singular nouns end in -o, and all plurals in -j (as in birdoj—birds). It is perhaps not quite so cumbersome as Volapük, which claims to be based on English, and in which the opening words of the Lord's Prayer are 'O Fat obas kel binol in süls parsaladomöz nemola'! But its pronunciation is not easy, and some of its words are grotesque formations. Less eccentric than either system is Zachrissm's Anglic, which is merely English written in a partially phonetic spelling.

Critics of international language sometimes claim that even if one language were widely adopted, differences of stress and intonation

THE BLACK PRINCE AND ANOTHER KNIGHT
They are dressed in full regalia. Above is the Coat-of-Arms of the Black Prince with shield,
helm, crest, mantling, and garter. Coloured lithograph by Francis Spear

alone might eventually cause it to develop along different lines in different countries; and even the written form would probably be affected by local idioms and usages. In any case, whatever practical usefulness may be claimed for artificial languages, it must be paid for by the loss of certain qualities of flexibility, richness, and exactness that are most necessary in, for example, international negotiations.

The same criticisms can be brought against the most recent, and in many ways the most reasonable, attempt at an international language—BASIC ENGLISH (q.v.) (British American Scientific International Commercial). The advocates of Basic realize that it cannot be a substitute for STANDARD ENGLISH (q.v.). For someone beginning to learn English, Basic may prove a useful first step, but the fact that many literary works are now available in Basic (including the Bible and Shakespeare's plays) may tempt students to be content with Basic when they should pass on to normal and natural English.

See also Vol. X: INTERNATIONAL CO-OPERATION.

U.S. Navy

THE EARTH PHOTOGRAPHED FROM A ROCKET 57 MILES UP

This shows the curvature of the earth and surface haze and clouds

INTER-PLANETARY TRAVEL.

The first serious suggestion that men should find a way of leaving the Earth and of navigating in space in a rocket was made by an obscure Russian scientist named Ziolkovsky in 1895, some 30 years after Jules Verne had written his thrilling adventure story, *From the Earth to the Moon*, and 6 years before H. G. Wells published *The First Men in the Moon*. But few people then gave any thought to Ziolkovsky and his plan.

The subject was revived a generation later, after men had learnt to fly. It was realized that the desire to travel in outer space sprang from the same sense of adventure and curiosity which had impelled men to build the first sea-going ships, and later to invent aircraft. In 1927 practical study was begun with the founding in Germany of the Society for Space Travel. Some American scientists also took up the matter and, although people scoffed at first, rocket chemistry was so quickly developed by the Germans that by 1945 they were able to bombard London with rockets fired from Holland (*see* GUIDED MISSILES, Vol. X).

To-day people interested in space travel have three broad aims. First, they aim at making a careful study of the upper air, the behaviour of the COSMIC RAYS (q.v. Vol. III), and conditions in other planets. Secondly, they propose to send rockets, without crews at first, as far as the Moon; this will provide practice in aiming into space. Thirdly, they suggest that permanent 'space stations' should be established a few hundred miles above the Earth's surface.

Rockets are the only known kind of power which can propel an object through outer space in which there is no air (*see* ATMOSPHERE, Vol. III). All other forms of energy (excluding atomic energy, which is not yet fully exploited) need to consume a certain amount of air before their power can develop. The German rocket bombs on London were therefore probably the forerunners of the first space cars which will leave the Earth. Indeed, since the Second World War, British and American scientists, sometimes helped by Germans, have been working to improve rocket fuels. Liquid fuels now enable the speed of a rocket to be controlled (*see* AIRCRAFT ENGINES, Section 6).

Rockets are already being used to gather information about the upper atmosphere; but they are sent up without a crew. Recording instruments, including cameras, are carried up to great heights and set in motion. Then the instruments are often ejected and allowed to fall to the Earth gently in a container supported by a parachute, and bearing the postal address of a laboratory so that anyone who finds a container may post it on. Sometimes the rocket itself is allowed to fall back to the Earth with instruments; in that event an explosive device blows off part of the stream-lined casing of the rocket, and the remaining portion is so shaped as to be slowed down in its fall by the friction of the air, and tends to come down swaying, like a falling leaf.

The MOON (q.v. Vol. III), the first target for a rocket without men, is a dull, mountainous mass of brown volcanic rock, swinging round the Earth at a distance of some 238,000 miles. It is without air, vegetation, or life of any kind. It has a landscape of mountains as high as the Alps, many thousands of craters, and some great plains, or 'seas', as they were once thought to be and are still called. The Moon shows only one face to us. So far man has projected nothing at the Moon except radar impulses, which have reached there and bounced back again to the Earth in 2½ seconds.

A rocket aimed at the Moon (or anywhere else in space) would need a speed of 25,000 miles an hour in order to break away from the pull of the Earth's GRAVITATION (q.v. Vol. III). It would be propelled by a series of 'booster' rockets, each of which would fall off from the main projectile after it had used up its own 'boosting' charge. The rocket power would not be needed for long. When a moving body in the heavens is away from the influence of the Earth's gravity, and is not retarded by the friction of any air, it will continue to move for ever at any speed at which it happens to be travelling, unless influenced by the gravity of some other body.

It is proposed that the first rocket aimed at the Moon should carry an automatic short-wave wireless transmitter, whose signals, indicating both the direction and distance of the moving rocket, would be heard on the Earth. A large charge of white powder would also be carried, with an explosive which would blow the white powder over several acres of the Moon's surface when the rocket landed. Thus the crater caused by the rocket could be picked out from the many already there—for objects on the Moon 200 yards in breadth can be detected and photographed through large telescopes. The white patch would be an important check on the accuracy of the aim, for a rocket would have to leave the Earth at least some hours before the Moon reached the position aimed at.

A human voyage to the Moon involves much more difficult problems, such as how to sustain life outside the Earth's atmosphere. The first step would probably be to send a rocket from the Earth to make a turn round the back of the Moon and then return to Earth. When circling the Moon the rocket would follow an orbit, just like any other body in the heavens.

The most interesting plan for space-travel concerns the building and placing in position of a 'space station'. The idea is to shoot up a fairly small rocket until it reaches, say, a point 600 miles above the earth—about the distance from London to Berlin, with the intention of making it circle round the Earth steadily at that height. When the rising rocket had reached the desired height, it would be veered round by diverting some of the rocket force sideways, and a speed of 18,000 miles an hour would be set by the rocket engine. When this speed had been reached, the power could be turned off. There being no atmosphere at this height to cause friction and slow down the rocket, it would continue at this speed for ever. But instead of continuing in a straight line into space, this satellite vehicle would be affected by the force of the Earth's gravity; and because of the particular speed at which it is moving in relation to its distance from the Earth, this gravitational pull would be exactly enough to keep the rocket going round the Earth for ever, a miniature satellite.

A 'space station' without crew could first be tried, with various recording instruments automatically transmitting to the Earth. The next step might be a rocket with men aboard. If once a station could be maintained up there, it might be built up and added to, like a house, with material and crews sent up in supply rockets. A great range of scientific work, impossible on the Earth, could be carried out. Telescopes, being free of the atmosphere, would be far more efficient. Sealed cabins would be needed, filled with air for the crew to breathe. Workmen building additions to the station would need strong pressure suits to keep their bodies together in a space in which there is no PRESSURE (q.v. Vol. III). But there would be no danger of falling off this station in space. Since gravity would be cancelled out, the builders would merely need to place their tools round them, floating in space, and these would stay exactly where they were put. From space stations of this kind, it is argued, men might set out on the next stage of the conquest of space.

The British Inter-Planetary Society exists for the study of problems of this kind.

See also Vol. III: SPACE; MOTION.

IRANIAN LANGUAGES, *see* PERSIAN LANGUAGES.

IRISH LANGUAGE (ERSE). This language is one of the Celtic family of languages, and is the most important of the Irish group which includes GAELIC (q.v.) and Manx. It differs in certain distinct ways from the British group, to which belong WELSH (q.v.), Cornish, and Breton, the language of Brittany. In Welsh, for instance, the original 'q' or 'c' becomes 'p', and the original 'ū' becomes 'i'. Thus Erse *mac* (son) is Welsh *map*, and Erse *cú* (hound) is Welsh *ci*.

Erse was brought to Ireland by Celtic invaders in about 1000 B.C.; and down to the end of the 18th century it was spoken by the great majority of the people, although never so much in the cities, many of which were founded by the Norse. The native Irish were not builders of cities. In the course of the 19th century English gained ground rapidly, and there are now not more than 50,000 people who speak Erse regularly. West Kerry, Connemara, West Donegal, and a small district near Dungarvan in co. Waterford are the main areas of Irish speech. Since 1922 the Irish Government has organized the revival of Erse, and it is now taught in all the schools.

The earliest Irish documents we have are inscriptions in a peculiar script called Ogham, some of which may be as early as the 4th century, and there

British Museum

STANDING STONE FROM LLYWEL, WALES, 6TH CENTURY A.D.

Inscribed with the name MAC-CUTRENI SALICIDUNI in Latin and Ogham characters

has been a tradition of literature in Erse since the 6th century, and a great mass of material from the 9th to the 19th century. Until the 13th century Erse had a complicated grammar, especially in the forms of verbs, and was highly inflected—that is, the words had different endings according to the part they played in the sentence. In modern Erse, however, the grammar is much simpler.

Erse has not given many words to English. These, however, are some examples: 'shamrock', 'leprechaun', 'tory', 'galore', 'banshee', 'blarney', 'shillelagh', 'colleen'.

See also LANGUAGE STRUCTURE.

See also Vol. I: CELTIC CIVILIZATION; IRISH.

ITALIAN LANGUAGE. This is one of the most important of the ROMANCE LANGUAGES—those languages descended from LATIN (qq.v.). It is spoken by about 43 million people in Italy and about 7 million elsewhere, mainly in the U.S.A., Argentina, Brazil, and in parts of France, where Italian emigrants have settled in the last hundred years. It is also one of the official languages of Switzerland, one of whose confederated states or cantons, Ticino, is entirely Italian-speaking.

Modern standard Italian is based on the speech of Tuscany in Central Italy, the language in which DANTE (q.v. Vol. V), the greatest of Italian poets, wrote his works. As in Spanish, spelling in Italian is very simple, almost every sound corresponding to one letter, and every letter to one sound. There are five vowels, as in English, but Italian, unlike English, has only one sound each for 'a', 'i', and 'u', and only two each for 'e' and 'o'. Most words end in a vowel, and the nouns are either of the masculine or feminine gender—most masculine words ending in 'o' in the singular and 'i' in the plural, and most feminine words ending in 'a' in the singular and 'e' in the plural. The neuter gender, as we understand it, is not used in Romance Languages.

There are many different Italian DIALECTS (q.v.), often widely differing from each other. In one part of north-eastern Italy a dialect of the Romansh language, the language of part of eastern Switzerland, is spoken. Italian is taught in most British universities mainly for the sake of its literature, and it ranks fifth in popularity among foreign languages.

See also Vol. I: ITALIANS.

See also Vol. III: ITALY.

J

JAPANESE LANGUAGE. There is a common, though mistaken, belief that Japanese and Chinese are related languages. In fact, little is known of the origin of Japanese, and the only language with which its relationship is proved beyond doubt is that of the Ryūkyū Islands, south-west of Japan. There are several dialects of Japanese, but the differences are no greater than between the dialects of English. Nowadays, the Japanese of the capital, Tōkyō, is accepted as the standard language and understood throughout the country.

The language contains three types of words: (1) Native Japanese words, (2) Chinese words. Many were borrowed in ancient times, when Chinese was regarded in Japan as the language of learning and culture, like Latin in medieval Europe. Still more are modern words, for instance, scientific terms, often coined in Japan on the Chinese model (and sometimes re-exported to China.). (3) Some words borrowed from western languages, mostly English. The Japanese sound-system is very different from that of English. For instance, no word or syllable can end in a consonant (except 'n'), nor is there any 'l' sound. So these borrowed English words are often barely recognizable, 'spotlight', for instance, has become *supotto-raito*, and 'department-store' has been abbreviated to *depaato*.

Japanese cannot be fitted into any European system of grammar. Even adjectives can have a past tense. It has no genders (no masculine, feminine, or neuter), no article (words like 'a', 'the' in English), and no number either in nouns or verbs; thus *hito* means 'man' or 'men', and *kau* means 'I (you, he, she, we, they) buy'. Verbs and adjectives take different endings according to their function in the sentence (*kau* 'buy', *katta* 'bought', *warui* 'bad', *waruku* 'badly').

The order of words in a sentence is illustrated by the following example:

kinoo	*katta*	*mannenhitsu*
yesterday	(I) bought	fountain-pen

wa	*teeburu*	*no*	*ue*	*ni*	*arimasu.*
as for	table	's	top	on	is.

'The fountain-pen which I bought yesterday is on the table.'

The Japanese are famous for their politeness, and in their speech they use many special word-forms indicating politeness or respect for the person addressed or spoken about. This helps to make up for the vagueness caused by the fact that personal pronouns such as 'I', 'you', or 'he' are rarely used. Replace *katta* in our example by *o kai nasatta* ('honourable buying did'). Since no one would be likely to use such words about himself, the phrase must now mean 'the pen which you (or he) bought'.

The Japanese script is an adaptation of the

Bodleian Library

PAGE FROM A HISTORY OF JAPAN IN THE 19TH CENTURY, PRINTED 1875

The larger, more complicated symbols are Chinese characters. In Japanese these are used with phonetic letters called *Kana* (the smaller symbols)

Chinese system and is written in vertical columns from right to left (*see* CHINESE LANGUAGE). Because Chinese characters are pictorial the Japanese can disregard the sounds the same characters would have in Chinese and use them to write their own words. Just as in Europe the symbol 3 is used in many countries but pronounced differently in each, one character 家 means 'house' to both Japanese and Chinese alike, though the words for 'house' are different in the two languages. However, most characters in Japanese have at least two pronunciations, called *Kun* (the native Japanese words), and *On* (the borrowed Chinese sounds of the characters). The characters 人 for 'man', 力 strength', and 車 'vehicle' are given the *Kun* pronunciation when used separately for the native Japanese words *hito*, *chikara*, and *kuruma*. But the same characters used in a compound word are given their Chinese sounds (*On*), forming the word *jin-riki-sha* 'rickshaw' (a hand-drawn carriage). As the characters were borrowed well over a thousand years ago, *On* sounds are often very unlike the sounds of modern Chinese.

In Chinese words never alter in their form; *mae* means 'buy' or 'bought'. But in Japanese the difference between 'buy' and 'bought' is shown by different endings (*kau* and *katta*). So the Japanese use the Chinese character expressing the idea 'buy' and add after it phonetic letters, called *Kana*, to show the ending of the word. (In English, likewise, 3 is pronounced 'three', but 3rd is 'third'.) *Kana* are also used for the small words corresponding to English 'in', 'from', and so on, which are called prepositions in English, but are postpositions in Japanese, as they come after, not before, the noun. There are two sorts of *Kana*, both derived from Chinese characters; *hiragana* are in general use, but *katakana* are now mostly limited to official publications and to writing foreign names or words. Generally, each *Kana* represents a whole syllable (as *ka* or *so*).

Until the end of the 19th century the language in books was very different from ordinary speech, but nowadays the difference is much less marked. If you know spoken Japanese and about 3,000 characters, you can read most books, except very learned or technical works. Since the war the Japanese Government have tried to limit the number of characters in common use to 1,850, and children in primary schools are taught about

880. Attempts have been made to abolish characters altogether; but this is not satisfactory, for many words look exactly alike in Roman letters, and can only be distinguished when written with Chinese characters. The Japanese will not be able to abolish characters without making very great changes in the language itself.

See also LANGUAGE STRUCTURE.
See also Vol. I: JAPANESE.

JET PROPULSION, *see* AIRCRAFT ENGINES, Section 4.

JOURNALIST. There are many kinds of journalist; but the ordinary meaning of the word is a man (or woman) who earns his living by editing or writing for a newspaper or magazine. Thus an editor is a journalist, and so is a junior reporter. A London daily newspaper may employ a staff of a hundred trained journalists, as well as receiving part-time service from others; a small country paper may be conducted by two or three staff men, with one or more juniors. The chief difference between an important daily newspaper and a country weekly is that in the daily the work must be subdivided and specialized, while in the country weekly each senior man must be ready to turn his hand to anything. Thus the editor (who may be the proprietor) often takes a share in the reporting, and the senior reporter usually acts as deputy editor. On such papers reporters get some training in sub-editing. As reporters they have to be a good deal more than shorthand writers. Much of their work may consist in reporting speeches; but they may also have to report the local agricultural show, write a notice of a play, film, or concert, describe some outdoor event—in short, to supply an accurate and readable account of anything in which the public is interested.

Most editors claim that there is no better training for journalism than work on a good country weekly. Many distinguished journalists have begun their career in this way. Assuming an education at least of secondary type to start with and some practice in shorthand, a junior reporter on such a paper may already be doing useful work in less than a year, and in his third year he should be capable of being sent anywhere. The wide variety of events he will be called upon to cover will bring him in contact with men and women of all kinds. Such a training gives a keen young man very valuable all-round experience.

As well as serving on daily and weekly newspapers, however, journalists may be engaged on periodicals (which may contain more comment than news), on news agencies, on magazines, on the B.B.C., and on the feature and picture sides of the great dailies. The news-script read out by the B.B.C. announcer is prepared by trained journalists; and this highly skilled work is often done under pressure as great as that of producing a newspaper. Many Government departments and commercial bodies also employ trained journalists as 'public relation officers' (*see* PROPAGANDA AND ADVERTISING).

The 'free lance' is another recognized type of journalist. He does not belong to any salaried staff, but contributes to publications of many kinds. A writer who becomes widely known under his own name and writes regularly is considered to have reached the top of the tree in free-lance work.

Technical journalists are employed on the periodical publications which supply the needs of many professions, trades, and crafts, such as the law, medicine, engineering, architecture, building, the hardware industry, and the newspapers themselves. Such men are either members of their specialist callings who have turned to journalism, or else are journalists who have become specialists. Contributors have usually to be highly qualified specialists, and the editor is often a well-known member of his profession. The technical process of editing and getting a publication to press, however, has to be done by a qualified journalist.

See also NEWSPAPER.

JUNK. Junk and Sampan are the common names for Chinese ships and boats. Both terms

Parker Gallery

THE CHINESE JUNK, 'KEYING', OFF GRAVESEND, 1848
This was the first Chinese vessel to sail into Western waters

have been used by Europeans since the 17th century. There are very many types of junk, differing in size, build, and rig. Commonly junks have flat bottoms and hulls divided into watertight compartments by bulkheads. Their hulls appear box-like to Western eyes and often have high poops; but the junkman is an experienced and cunning seaman who has made up his own peculiar way of doing things, and he is in no way less cunning than the Western sailor. The most usual form of Chinese sail is the balance lug, and this has bamboo battens across the sail horizontally. The sails were formerly made of matting, but now more durable canvas is used. These sails set very flat and can be quickly reefed by tying battens together. The junkman is skilled at sculling over the stern with a big oar known as a *Yuloh*, the action of which is like that of a fish's tail. Junks have distinctive colouring; the junkmen of Foochow, particularly, attach great importance to decoration, which is always vivid yet in excellent taste. Many types of Chinese sea-going junks display a large eye painted on the bow, so that the junk can see where it is going. The largest trading junks have as many as five masts. *See also* SAILING.

KNOT, MARINE, *see* LOG, SHIP'S.

K

KAYAK, *see* CANOE, Section 2.

KIEL CANAL. This is a ship canal in North Germany, 61½ miles in length, linking the North Sea with the Baltic. It runs from the mouth of the Elbe to Holtenau, near Kiel, and very greatly reduces the sea journey from London to the Baltic ports. One of the main reasons for building the canal was to provide the German Navy with means of communication between the naval stations at Wilhelmshaven and Kiel, avoiding the long passage round north Denmark.

Construction of the canal was begun in 1887, and took 8 years. The building equipment was large for those days. There were 46 excavators, 20 dredgers, 240 steam-shovels, nearly 100 locomotives, and nearly 3,000 wagons. For part of the time 8,000 men were engaged. Although there were no unusual engineering difficulties, since most of its route is through soft ground, the canal had to cross a number of roads and railways. There are seven bridges over it and many ferries.

About two-thirds of the length was cut through dry ground. One-third crosses Lake Eider, in which the channel was excavated by DREDGERS (q.v.). Much of the mud and sand raised in this way was pumped through pipes for 2,000 feet and deposited on the sea-shore. In 1907–9 the canal was considerably enlarged; the bottom width was increased from 72 feet to 144 feet, and the depth from about 30 feet to 36 feet.

Occasionally ICE-BREAKERS (q.v.) have to be used in the winter, but the canal is never closed. Ships may pass through under their own power, or may be towed. The limits of speed allowed are 5·4 and 8·1 knots. About 56,000 ships have used the canal in a busy year, an average of more than 150 every 24 hours.

See also CANALS.

KNOTS. The word 'knot' covers in a general way all methods of joining ropes, but it is also applied to fastenings made in a single rope by twisting it or using its own strands. The word 'bend' is used for methods of joining ropes together, and a 'hitch' is used for fastening a rope to something solid, such as a pole. A 'splice' is a more permanent way of joining two ends of rope by interweaving strands. A 'sennit' or 'plait' is an interweaving of cords to form a pattern. 'Lashings' are used for roping together spars, as is done in scaffolding.

Rope has been used from prehistoric times. The peoples of ancient civilizations, such as the Egyptians, were skilled rope-makers. Therefore the knowledge of different knots for different purposes is an old one. The INCAS of Peru (q.v. Vol. I), who made elaborate suspension bridges over rivers and ravines with rope, must have been thoroughly versed in the science of knots. Of the many different knots, the majority were used by sailors in the days of SAILING SHIPS (q.v.). But knowledge of knots is important to many other people besides sailors. Mountaineers, crossing over glaciers or precipitous rocks, work in parties of three or four and are roped together in such a way that if one falls the rope will hold him (*see* MOUNTAINEERING, Vol. IX). A climber who has fallen down a crevice or cliff, and is hanging by a taut rope round his waist, can often get up again by using separate loops of rope, one for his arms and shoulders and one each for his feet, which he fastens on to the taut rope with 'prusik knots' or 'friction hitches' (*see* Fig. 1). These knots hold tight when there is strain on them, but can be slipped up the taut rope when there is no strain. So the climber, by releasing the strain on each prusik knot in turn and pulling it up, can gradually reach the top again. Knots for various purposes are used by farmers, woodmen, builders, and others; in fact, they are of such general use that training in the use of them forms an essential part in the training of BOY SCOUTS (q.v. Vol. IX). For the average person a knowledge of less than a dozen knots will suffice for all normal occasions.

A knot depends on friction to prevent its pulling undone. When a sailor has a rope about to take a heavy strain, he will throw a few turns around a post or bollard, and hold the free end in his hand. He will then be able with the aid

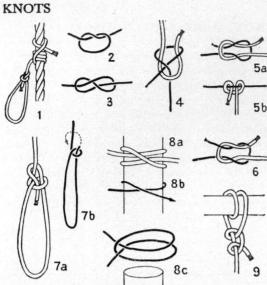

Front Front Back
11a 11b 11c 11d

KNOTS

1. Prusik knot
2. Overhand knot
3. Figure-of-eight knot
4. Sheet bend
5. Reef knot
6. Granny

7. Bowline
8. Clove hitch
9. Round turn and two half-
     hitches
10. Turk's Head
11. Eye splice

to the corner rope in a sail. Where the two ropes being joined will press against something, as the string round a parcel does, a reef knot is used (Fig. 5 a). The unskilled person ties a 'granny' (Fig. 6) by making both twists the same way. In the reef the second twist is made opposite to the first, so that each rope doubles back on itself and is held by the loop of the other. It can usually be untied by pulling the two halves of one rope into a straight line (see Fig. 5 b) and sliding the other off.

The bowline (Fig. 7 a) makes a firm loop in a rope. Allow enough for the loop, then twist a ring in the rope. Pass the end through this, around the main rope (Fig. 7 b), and back through the ring. To fasten a rope to a pole, when there is to be a load on both ends of the rope, a clove hitch is made (Fig. 8 a). This may be worked around the pole (Fig. 8 b), or if the end of the pole is free, two loops may be made (Fig. 8 c) and slipped over it. If the end of a rope is to be fastened to a pole or ring a 'round turn and two half-hitches' is a good general-purpose method (Fig. 9). The rope's end completely encircles the pole and is then made to form a clove hitch around the main part.

There are many beautiful and complicated ornamental knots. A fairly easy one is the Turk's Head, which is used to decorate a pole or as a scarf ring. It must be worked round the fingers or a pole (Fig. 10 a). Push part 1 under part 2, and take the working end over part 2 and under part 1 (Fig. 10 b). This completes a single Turk's Head, which may be doubled or trebled by following '4' around two or three times with '3' (Fig. 10 c).

The most useful splice is the eye-splice. Unlay the strands for a short distance and tuck one under a main strand (Fig. 11 a) leaving the others as shown. Use a spike to open the strands if the rope is stiff. Lift the next strand and tuck No. 1 under it, going in where No. 2 comes out (Fig. 11 b). Turn the splice over and tuck No. 3 under the only vacant strand (Fig. 11 c). Pull all the strands tight. Take each strand again 'over and under one' in turn twice more to complete the splice (Fig. 11 d).

See also Vol. VII: ROPE-MAKING.

of the friction in the turns to resist a pull of many tons. Knots for fastening rope to solid objects include one or more complete turns for this reason. Similarly, in a good knot for uniting ropes, parts are doubled back and squeezed so that a pull increases the friction within the knot. A good knot should be free from violent kinks which damage the rope; it should also be easily untied.

To stop a rope running through the hands or a hole, some form of stopper knot is used. Two simple ones are the overhand (Fig. 2) and figure-of-eight (Fig. 3). For joining ropes, whether they are the same thickness or not, a sheet bend is used (Fig. 4). The name comes from its use in joining the sheet (controlling rope)

L

LANGUAGE is the basis of human communications. It enables a man to tell other men what he is thinking. Without it there could be no exchange of ideas. It is also essential to most kinds of physical communication—the transporting of people or goods from one place to another. Most exchanges of goods between men are only a fulfilment of some agreement which has been reached by the use of words. Even the means by which a man can make his way from one village to another, or steer a ship from one continent to another, would not be known unless those who had gone before had passed on what they knew.

Although animals, birds, and insects can communicate with one another in some way, man alone can pass on complex thoughts. That, in fact, is what makes language grow. Language develops as the ideas which man wishes to express to his fellows become more complicated. It is possible, through the study of old books, to watch a particular language struggling with the problem of expressing new ideas—especially abstract ideas—and often having to borrow words for this purpose. We can see words like 'duration', 'minority', 'motive', and 'object' coming into English from Latin or French in the later Middle Ages, because Englishmen were beginning to express ideas in their own language which needed those words.

One of the great difficulties of communication is that knowledge of one's own language alone, though it enables one to talk to people who know it, also cuts one off from most of the rest of mankind. We read in the first Book of the Bible that originally 'the whole earth was of one language and of one speech', but that when men tried to build a tower which would reach to the heavens their language became split into many tongues. We know, however, that differences of speech really go back to the earliest times of man's history, and that they may have been caused by certain differences in the bodily structure of men. Thus when we find the consonants 'k', 'q', and 'f' are common in a primitive language, it seems to be because the people who use it have short upper lips, while the frequent use of 'p' denotes a people with long upper lips.

The first great change which happens to a language is that it comes to be used for writing as well as for speaking. This means that it tends to become standardized. But there is a significance in the actual regions in which one language rather than another will become standardized. In central Europe it is possible to find language frontiers for which no obvious cause exists; on one side of a line one language is spoken, and on the other quite a different one. Yet often, if we trace back the history of a region in which this occurs, we find that the people on one side of the line were converted to Christianity centuries ago by missionaries who travelled from a particular country, and that a church organization was then built up which included the converted people. With Christianity came writing; the language spoken within that church organization at that period then became fixed as the permanent tongue of those people. But other people living only a few miles away may have been converted to Christianity by missionaries coming from a different country; in that way a different language would be fixed.

The fruitfulness of language as a means of communication is shown by the development of science and the arts. No one ever makes great discoveries in science or thinks out new ideas or produces works of art entirely by himself. He depends largely on others, and needs the stimulus that is given by discussion and criticism. If we study the way in which there arise what are known as 'schools' of art or literature or music— that is, large groups of men who are producing writings or works of art of much the same kind, all at one time and in one place—we see that they usually come from the mingling of different traditions.

England in Shakespeare's day shows how the writings of French and Italian poets, along with the literature of the ancient world, influenced English traditions, offering men new possibilities in the use of language and suggesting to them new forms of literature. From Italy came the sonnet; the plays of Rome, tragedies and comedies, met the old English religious drama of the Middle Ages, and there arose the great school of play-writers, of whom Shakespeare was the greatest (*see* DRAMA, HISTORY OF, Vol. XII). Foreign writers, provided they can be understood and also that they are not too different, are particularly stimulating. To keep to the narrow native field of any country has a deadening effect on literature, art, or thought. The differences between languages have always tended to force art and thought into rather narrow divisions. Yet men have been able, time after time, to overcome the barriers of language.

There are, in fact, many people in the world who quite naturally speak more than one language, such as many of the inhabitants of Wales, who can talk and write in both Welsh and English, or many Africans, who can speak at least two or three different regional languages. It is important to realize that there is nothing strange or difficult in being able to use more than one language. It is a matter of custom. There have been several occasions in history when people living in a large area of the world have had two languages, their own and a common language used by all the various people inhabiting the area. In classical times, for instance, Greek came to be the language of the Eastern Mediterranean countries. This was due partly to the conquests of ALEXANDER (q.v. Vol. V), who invaded Asia Minor in 334 B.C. and, by the time he died 11 years later, had created an empire which stretched from the Adriatic Sea to the River Indus, and from the Black Sea to the Nile and the Indian Ocean. Partly, also, the widespread Greek speech was due to the influence of Greek traders. As a result, the people of this great area of land spoke their own various languages and also Greek. St. Paul's Epistles, written in Greek, could be understood by Christian converts equally in Rome and in Corinth (Greece) and in Ephesus (Asia Minor). Within 300 years of Alexander the eastern Mediterranean countries had become part of the Roman Empire, which extended as far as the Rhine and, later, to the Lowlands of Scotland. In the Roman Empire there must have been many people who quite naturally spoke three languages, their own native tongue as well as GREEK and LATIN (qq.v.). Educated Romans, and citizens of the Roman provinces of the West, spoke Greek as a matter of course. When Julius

Caesar was murdered, he did not make his dying exclamation to young Brutus in Latin, *Et tu, Brute*, as Shakespeare has it, but in Greek; he said, *Kai su, teknon*, which is broadly 'Even you, child!'

The Roman Empire, in fact, was made possible because the problem of communication had been solved, and the Romans were able to give Europe one civilization. They did this in two ways—by building a system of roads, which linked every part of the Empire (*see* ROMAN ROADS), and by giving to those who lived in it a common language.

It is not only through conquest, as in the times of Alexander and Caesar, that a common language comes to be adopted by different peoples. The movements of nomadic tribes have sometimes led to a single language being used over a wide area by very different peoples; it was this that caused ARABIC (q.v.) to be spoken, as it is now, from southern Arabia to the Atlantic coast of North Africa. A remarkable example of language spread by the travel of sea traders may be found in the Pacific, where the Polynesian language is spoken from Fiji to Easter Island and from Hawaii to New Zealand (*see* OCEANIC LANGUAGES). The most recent example is that of English. Trade and conquest together have made English the common language of the educated classes of India, though national feeling, an historic cause of the division of languages, is tending to the abandonment of English in India. In western Europe, the need for carrying on commerce with Britain and America is the reason for English being taught to children in many countries. Years ago the German statesman BISMARCK (q.v. Vol. V) realized the immense signification of the fact that two of the greatest states of the world spoke the same language, Great Britain and the United States. It gave them, he said, a tremendous advantage over other countries.

But although the needs of communications have sometimes caused a single language to prevail over many countries, and this in turn has strengthened later communications, some periods of history have shown an opposite tendency. The Reformation, and the loosening of the ties of a centralized Church organization, led to men abandoning Latin as a normal means of communication in speech or writing. By this Europe lost a great deal. When George I came to England as king from Hanover, he could speak no English, and most English statesmen could speak no German. Sir Robert Walpole, his Prime Minister during a large part of his reign, could communicate with his sovereign only in Latin, and neither could speak it fluently. King George had expected that the Prime Minister could at least speak French, but this he could not do.

Later the growing sense of separate nationalities—'nationalism'—affected many countries. Pride in a man's nation brought with it pride in his language. A group of Czech patriot-scholars, who lived early in the 19th century, once passed in the street two Czech girls and heard one say to the other, 'Don't speak in Czech; they will think we are kitchen-maids'. The ancient Czech language had been abandoned by the upper classes of the country after its conquest by the German-speaking Austrians. Such groups of patriots deliberately set out to make Czech once more a literary language which people could be proud to use; by doing this, they were largely responsible for the creation of the Czech nation of to-day.

In the 20th century, national feeling has become strong in many countries. As local tongues are fostered, communication by speech becomes more difficult. Modern civilization is faced with the same problem as faced the Romans—the creation of universal means of travel and a universal language. Only the first part of the problem has been solved: never before have men been able to move more easily from one part of the world to another. But the problem of different languages remains unsolved.

See also Trade Routes; Language, History of; Language Structure; Speech; International Languages.

LANGUAGE, HISTORY OF.

It is obvious that a language changes in the course of time. In English this can easily be seen by reading the Anglo-Saxon Chronicle, Chaucer, and Shakespeare, and comparing them with modern English (*see* English Language, History of). There are many different kinds of changes; some are obvious, such as changes in meaning, old words dying out, or new ones coming in. But the most important kind of linguistic change, 'sound-change'—that is change in the pronunciation of the spoken language, is not generally appreciated. The following example illustrates the nature of sound-change. The Anglo-Saxon word *stān* has changed into the Modern English word 'stone'; similarly Anglo-Saxon *bāt* has changed into Modern English 'boat'. In fact, we can state what is called a 'sound law': the Anglo-Saxon sound (or 'phoneme') *ā* normally changes into the Modern English phoneme *ou*, written in various ways, as *o* as in stone or *oa* as in boat. But sometimes there are exceptions. For instance, Anglo-Saxon *hālig* has changed into Modern English 'holy' correctly enough, but Anglo-Saxon *hālig dæg* has changed into Modern English 'holiday', not 'holy day'.

Two languages are said to be 'related' if and only if they were both once the same language. Thus Italian and Spanish are related because they were both once Latin (q.v.). From our history we know that, in Italy, the language which was once Latin is now Italian and that, in Spain, that which was once Latin is now Spanish. We may express the relationship between Latin, Italian, and Spanish by means of a diagram:

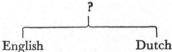

Latin / Italian / Spanish

It is not often that we are so fortunate as to have all the three members of the diagram present. For instance, we know that English and Dutch, just as much as Italian and Spanish, are related languages. Only there is no top member of the diagram:

? / English / Dutch

Virtually nothing is preserved of the language that has become, on the one hand, English, and, on the other, Dutch. But, if all our Latin had perished, we should still be able to reconstruct it to some extent, from Italian, Spanish, and the other Romance Languages (*see* French and the Romance Languages). And this is just what we have to do in the case of English and Dutch: to reconstruct partially a new language to put in the top place of the diagram. We call the family to which English and Dutch belong, the Germanic Family (q.v.) and the parent language we call 'Primitive Germanic'. It is, of course, easy to proceed from the idea of two related languages to that of a family of related languages, sub-families, sub-sub-families, and so on. Working along these lines, people interested in the scientific study of languages have been able to divide the languages of the world (some 7,000 in number) into about 200 families, and these into sub-families, and so on, with no relationship between any two of the 200 families. Some of these families are very large—INDO-EUROPEAN (q.v.) to which English and Latin belong, contains many hundreds of languages; whereas some contain just one language: JAPANESE (q.v.), for instance, is not related to any other language.

Most people think that related languages must be in some way similar, either phonetically or in grammar; but this is not true. Italian and Finnish, which are unrelated languages, sound very similar to English ears; but English and Welsh, which are related languages, are quite dissimilar in grammar. Speakers of two related languages need not have any other common characteristic, either cultural or racial. It is very important not to confuse linguistic relations with racial relations. For instance, FINNISH (q.v.) and Hungarian are certainly related languages. But, racially, the Hungarians are unlike the Finns and like the Turks, while the Finns have taken much of their culture from the Swedes. The Hungarian language, however, is not related to Turkish, nor is the Finnish language related to Swedish.

Words are related in just the same way as languages. We say, for instance, that Latin *amāre* 'to love' has become both Italian *amare* and Spanish *amar*; or, conversely, that both Italian *amare* and Spanish *amar* are derived from Latin *amāre*. Similarly, we can draw diagrams showing the descent of phonemes (or sounds) according to sound-laws; thus Anglo-Saxon *stān* 'stone' clearly corresponds to *Stein* in the related language German; and, in fact, we have:

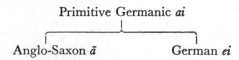

Primitive Germanic *ai*

Anglo-Saxon *ā*　　　　　German *ei*

Sound-laws do not necessarily operate only between similar sounds; often widely different sounds are concerned. Thus the word for 'warm' was *ghwermos* or *ghwormos* in Primitive Indo-European; it has become *gharmas* in Sanskrit, *thermos* in Greek, *formus* in Latin, and 'warm' in English, all with very different initial sounds. So related words do not always show any sign of similarity, and similar words are not necessarily related. Thus Danish *hoppe* 'mare' sounds like

Greek *hippos* 'horse', but the two words are not related. On the other hand, 'cow' and 'beef' are related, that is to say, that they were both once the same word in the parent language. Primitive Indo-European *gwōus* became *kwōz* in Primitive Germanic, then *cū* in Anglo-Saxon, and, finally, 'cow' in Modern English. This same Primitive Indo-European *gwōus* became *bōs* in the language of the Samnites (a dialect closely related to Latin) and passed thence into Latin; the Latin accusative *bovem* became *boef* in Old French, and, with the Normans, the word passed into Middle English as *boef*, later becoming *bēf*, and finally 'beef'.

The problem of deciding whether or not there is sufficient evidence for considering two languages as related is difficult and technical. In most words (imitative ones such as 'cuckoo' excluded) there is no direct connexion between sound and meaning: no reason is known to us why in English the word for 4 should be 'four' and that for 6 should be 'six' rather than the other way round. Let us consider some English words beginning with the sound *t*—'ten', 'tame', for example. If English and German were unrelated, there would be no reason why words of the same meaning in German should begin with one German initial sound rather than another (except in so far as one German initial is commoner than another). But, in fact, corresponding to many English words which begin with *t* we find an undue proportion of German words of the same meaning beginning with *z*—such as 'ten' *zehn*, 'tame' *zahm*. If English and German were unrelated this effect would have to be due to chance. But, if they are related (as is the case) it is due to the fact that initial English 't' and initial German 'z' were both once one and the same phoneme in their common parent language. It is, in fact, only the heaping-up of 'coincidences' like this that proves linguistic relationship.

The question whether, in fact, all languages are related, that is whether language has a common origin, cannot be answered. Man has been speaking for a very long time indeed and, during this period of time, sound-change must have removed every trace of the original state of affairs (*see* SPEECH). So-called primitive languages, such as AMERICAN INDIAN LANGUAGES (q.v.), do not represent an original state of affairs any better than 'civilized' languages. In fact, a difference between primitive and civilized does not exist in language. For instance, some civilized languages and some primitive ones have little grammar (such as English and Samoan), yet some have much (such as Greek and most North American Indian languages).

LANGUAGE STRUCTURE. Most people have held certain general ideas about the structure of language; for example, that it is composed of sentences, words (which may be grouped into parts of speech), and endings or inflexions (such as the 's' in 'dog's' or the 'er' and 'est' in 'higher' 'highest'). But philologists (those who study languages scientifically), have come to look at language in a different way, and to conclude that, although these distinctions are sometimes convenient, they do not apply always and to all languages. For example, in some languages words are built up by a number of 'suffixes' (additions) as in the English words, 'thought-ful-ness' or 'kind-li-ness'. Sometimes this results in very long words which might be regarded as phrases or sentences; for example, the Eskimo word *aulisautissarsiniarpunga*, meaning 'I wish I had something which would do for a fishing line', is built up by means of a number of suffixes from a short word meaning 'to fish'.

In ordinary grammar we learn that there is a clear distinction between a verb (a word that denotes action) and a noun (the name of something). In Hungarian, however, it seems that the verb and noun were not originally distinct: for the suffix 'unk' (denoting the first person plural 'we') may be added to either a noun or a verb: as in *ház* 'house' and *ház-unk* 'our house', or *vár* 'he waits' and *vár-unk* 'we wait'. A sentence is generally defined as being complete, a word by itself being incomplete, and there is certainly a difference of this kind between 'the man went away' and 'man'. A long argument, however (such as a mathematical proof), though it may be composed of several sentences, is not really complete until it is finished. From these and similar examples it seems that these ideas (sentence, word, part of speech, and ending), though convenient when applied to a few languages such as Latin, are not universal and cannot be defined.

There are, however, four things which apply to all languages.

1. The first is the Utterance, which may be defined as a block of intelligible speech-sound marked off by a period of silence at either end.

2. The second, and perhaps the most important, is the Phoneme, the name given to a sound which can act as the sole means of distinguishing one word from another. Thus in English the difference between the sounds 't' and 'd' is a difference between phonemes, because at least one pair of words 'tin' and 'din' is distinguished solely by it. In the name of the flower 'kingcup', however, the difference between the two 'k' sounds is not a difference between phonemes, because no two English words are distinguished solely by that difference. It is true that, in actual fact, the two 'k' sounds in 'kingcup' are different; the 'k' which is pronounced before the vowel 'i' is different from the 'k' before the vowel 'u'. Yet because the difference does not serve to distinguish two English words, it is not noticed by people who speak the language.

In Japanese, the 'h' of the word *hati* 'from' is pronounced like the 'h' of English 'house'; but another Japanese word *hito* 'one' starts with an 'h' which is pronounced like the German guttural sound 'ch'. But this is not a difference between phonemes in Japanese because no two Japanese words are distinguished solely by it. In Norwegian, however, this very same difference in sound is a difference between phonemes because it is the sole means of distinguishing two words, such as *høre* (to hear) and *kjøre* (to drive) (kj is merely a spelling for the German *ch* sound). The phoneme theory is very important in the construction of ALPHABETS (q.v.); a perfect alphabet must have only one phoneme for each letter and only one letter for each phoneme. The English alphabet is thus very imperfect ('thought' has seven letters but only three phonemes) whereas the Welsh alphabet is perfect.

3. The third is 'Class'. Instead of grouping words into nouns, verbs, adverbs, and so on, philologists group them into two classes: a 'large' class which contains words we might normally call nouns, verbs, adjectives, and adverbs, words which name things, actions, qualities, and so on, and to which words may be added at will; and a 'small' class, to which words cannot be added at will and which includes such parts of speech as pronouns, conjunctions, and prepositions. Some languages have a third, very large, class. Thus in Chukchee, a language spoken in North-east Siberia (*see* SIBERIAN PEOPLES, Vol. I), in order to say 'I'll cut your finger' you must first make a verb 'to finger-cut' and then conjugate this verb. The class to which the Chukchee 'verb' 'to finger-cut' belongs will clearly be 'very large', because it will contain a unit for every possible combination of action and object.

4. The fourth is 'Category', which includes such ideas as number (singular and plural), tense (past, present, and future), and so on. Some categories are found in many languages, some in few. The following are common categories.

(i) *Number*. In many languages singular and plural are distinguished (English, *house*: *houses*; and German *das schöne weib*, 'the beautiful woman': *die schönen weiber*, 'the beautiful women'); some languages have a dual (a special form for a pair of things) as in Greek, *hippos* a 'horse', *hippō* 'a pair of horses', *hippoi* 'horses'; and Tyattyalla, an Australian native language spoken in Victoria, has a 'trial' as well (a special form for a set of three things), for example, *gattimgattimek* 'a boomerang', *gattimgattimul* 'a pair of boomerangs, *gattimgattimurrakullik* 'a set of three boomerangs', *gattimgattimurrak* 'boomerangs'.

(ii) *Case* denotes the function of a word in a sentence: the subject of the sentence, for instance, is in the nominative case, the object in the accusative, and the possessive (a word like 'dog's') is in the genitive case. Some languages have nearly fifty cases. In Finnish we have, for instance, *kirja* 'the book', *kirja-ssa* 'in the book', *kirjaan* 'to the book', *kirja-tta* 'without a book', *kirja-lla* 'at the book'. English words formerly had more changes of endings to indicate cases than they have to-day (*see* ENGLISH LANGUAGE).

(iii) *Degree* is usually expressed by the ending of the adverb or adjective. In English there are three degrees: positive ('long'), comparative ('longer'), superlative ('longest'). Welsh has a fourth degree: *du* 'black', *dued* 'as black'. In Finnish it is possible to have the comparative in a case; for example, in the sentence *se on pohjalla laatikossa* 'it is in the box, at the bottom', the word *pohjalla* can have the form *pohjemmalla*, meaning 'more at the bottom'.

(iv) *Person*. This is generally regarded as applying only to verbs, as in Latin *amo* 'I love', *amas* 'thou lovest'; but actually it is not confined to verbs. In Finnish we have *kirja* 'book', *kirja-ni* 'my book', *kirja-si* 'thy book'; and in Welsh *at* 'to', *at-af* 'to me', *at-at* 'to thee'. In some languages there is a distinction between 'this' (near me), 'that' (near you), and 'that' (near him);

thus Spanish *este, ese, aquel*. A verb may have six or more persons. Languages often have a seventh impersonal form, such as Finnish *sanotaan*, or Welsh *dywed-ir* ('they say', or 'it is said' —in French *on dit* and German *man sagt*). The Basque personal system is very complicated and has forty forms, of which the following are examples—*eramatendet* 'I carry it', *eramatenditut* 'I carry them', *eramatendizut* 'I carry it for you', *eramatendezu* 'thou carriest it', *eramatendituzu* 'thou carriest them', *eramatendigute* 'they carry them, for us'.

(v) *Tense*. The obvious division of time into past, present, and future frequently plays a great part in language (Latin *amāvi, amo, amābo*, 'I loved, I love, I shall love'). However, many languages make no use of tense; thus Malay *bilang* means either 'spoke' 'speak', or 'shall speak', and Anglo-Saxon has no future tense.

(vi) *Voice, mood, and aspect* denote the way in which the speaker regards the action. In Latin and English we speak of the active voice 'I love' (in which the principal person or thing indicated carries out the action); the passive voice 'I am loved' (in which the action is carried out by some other person or thing); the indicative mood, 'the king lives' (which is a direct statement); the subjunctive mood, 'long live the king!' (which is a wish); the imperative mood, 'live in peace, O king!' (which is a command).

One form of 'aspect' shows the difference between something which happens instantaneously and something which takes some time in happening. Thus the verb 'kill' is 'instantaneous' in aspect because its action must take place in one instant of time, whereas the verb 'walk' is 'durative' because its action is continuous (the terms 'perfective' and 'imperfective' are common alternatives to 'instantaneous', and 'durative'). The differences of aspect expressed in some languages cannot easily be translated; in Russian both *vstretit'* and *vstrechat'* must be rendered by 'to meet' in English, but the former is instantaneous and the latter durative.

See also SPEECH; LANGUAGE, HISTORY OF.

LATIN LANGUAGE. Latin is one of the most important languages belonging to the group which experts in philology (the science of language) call INDO-EUROPEAN (q.v.). It differs from its modern descendants, and from English, in that it is a 'flexional' type of language, that is, the function of a word in a sentence is shown by changes in the word itself, instead of by means of other small words, such as prepositions, pronouns, and articles. For instance, the English sentence 'The mother gave a knife to the servant' would in Latin be: *Mater ancillae cultrum dedit*, which is literally, 'The mother' (subject), 'to the servant' (indirect object), 'a knife' (object), 'gave' (verb). This is the usual word-order in Latin. To say 'The servant gave a knife to the mother', we should simply change the position in the sentence and the endings of the words *mater* and *ancillae*, to show their new meaning: *Ancilla matri cultrum dedit*. In early times Latin was simply the local speech of the ancient province of Latium, the part of Italy in which the city of Rome stood. It was closely related to other local ways of speech or DIALECTS (q.v.) of the Italian peninsula, particularly Oscan and Umbrian, and was at first of no greater importance. The position of the city of Rome, as the centre of the rapidly expanding Roman Empire, caused its language to become the language of civilized Europe (*see* ROMAN CIVILIZATION, Vol. I). From the 1st to the 5th century A.D., most of the Western world then known was under Roman dominion. The Romans colonized far and wide as a deliberate policy, and one of their first cares was for their language. They believed that if conquered peoples learnt Latin, they would more readily accept the Roman way of life. Schools were founded in many parts of the Empire, where the Latin of Rome was taught, and any citizen of the Empire with a good command of Latin might be employed by the Roman Government.

Thus the spread of Latin was partly a matter of Roman policy; but the fact that Roman Europe was, with some important exceptions, governed from Rome made it necessary to have a language which was understood everywhere (*see* INTERNATIONAL LANGUAGES). Such a language was necessary for traders, who travelled to all parts of the Empire. Soldiers of many races, and brought up to speak various languages, were serving together in the Roman armies, and learnt to speak Latin. At the end of their service they settled in colonies and tilled the land, often in outlying parts, where again they helped to spread the Latin language. The only written code of law was Roman. Lastly, particularly in the 3rd century A.D., with the rapid growth of Christianity, Latin became the accepted language of religion.

DEDICATION INSCRIPTION OF A BUILDING ERECTED BY THE ROMAN VI LEGION AT CORSTOPITUM, A TOWN NEAR HADRIAN'S WALL, IN A.D. 192

By the 4th century A.D. the Celtic languages of western Europe (*see* WELSH, IRISH, and GAELIC LANGUAGES) had been replaced by Latin in many areas, or pushed to the outer fringes of the Roman Empire—Wales, Ireland, and Scotland —where they survive to this day. In the eastern part of the Roman Empire Latin made little headway; the Greek-speaking peoples, though less powerful politically than their Roman conquerors, had a superior civilization, and their language continued to prevail against Latin. The spread of Latin in the Roman Empire may be compared with that of English in the British Empire, for Latin, like English, became important not only as the language of the Government but also as a great literary language. Much of its literature has survived, including the work of such great Latin poets as VIRGIL, OVID, and HORACE, of orators of whom CICERO is the greatest, and of historians and prose-writers such as LIVY, JULIUS CAESAR, and TACITUS (qq.v. Vol. V).

The language actually spoken by the ordinary people of the Roman Empire, or Vulgar Latin as it is called, was very different from the refined and polished language of literature, or Classical Latin. Classical Latin, the language taught in schools, was a rather artificial language influenced partly by Greek. Vulgar Latin, however, was spoken mainly by people who could neither read nor write, and had learnt Latin by ear. They therefore adopted a style of speech which used simpler constructions than those of Classical Latin, and which included many popular words of the kind we should call 'slang'.

After the fall of the Roman Empire in the west, in the 5th century, Vulgar Latin continued to be spoken in the places once belonging to the Roman Empire, but as there was no longer a central authority and as there was less communication between different parts of the Empire, local differences in speech became more and more apparent, until, finally, completely new languages developed. These are known as the ROMANCE LANGUAGES (q.v.).

Latin, however, was still the language of the Church, which was the centre of learning, and it was therefore used as an international language amongst men of learning. This form of literary Latin, known as Low Latin, or sometimes as Church Latin, was, until about the 9th century, the only written language in general use in western Europe. Not until then did it become usual for scribes, using the letters of the Latin alphabet, to write in the speech of the ordinary people which, in the countries where it was derived from Latin, had by then become very different from Latin. Even so, literary Latin continued as the language of the Church, and became also the language of the Universities of Paris, Bologna (Italy), Oxford, and Cambridge when they were founded in the 13th and 14th centuries. Thus for a time three languages had been in use in England, English spoken by the ordinary people, Norman-French spoken by the court and noblemen and those around them, and Low Latin written (and sometimes spoken) by the churchmen who wrote all the legal and historical records. In the 16th century much serious literature was still written in Latin, and it was the international language among scholars in all countries. It remains the language of the Roman Catholic Church to-day. Only recently has it ceased to be the compulsory language for giving University formal lectures and speeches; and at many universities such as Oxford and Cambridge the granting of degrees and other ceremonies are still conducted in Latin.

English, although descended from Anglo-Saxon, the language of the tribes who invaded Britain after the Roman withdrawal, owes a great deal to Latin. Many words have been borrowed either directly from literary Latin, or from French, and now more than half the words, though for the most part the less common words, in a modern English Dictionary are Latin in origin.

It has also become a common English habit, both in speaking and in writing, to use phrases lifted directly from the Latin, sometimes quoting them in full, and sometimes in abbreviated form. Some of the best known are *vice versa*, 'the order

being reversed', *et cetera* (etc.) 'and the rest', *exempli gratia* (e.g.) 'for the sake of example', *videlicet* (viz.) 'namely', and *quod vide* (q.v.) 'which see'. The popularity of such phrases is due to their continual recurrence in the Low Latin formerly used in legal documents.

See also LANGUAGE STRUCTURE.
See also Vol. I: ROMAN CIVILIZATION.

LATITUDE, *see* MAP PROJECTIONS.

LETTER WRITING, *see* HANDWRITING. *See also* LETTERS, Vol. XII.

LIBRARIES. 1. EARLY LIBRARIES. The word 'library' means both a room in which books are kept, and also the collection of books themselves. Before the invention of printing, books were written by hand on paper or parchment (*see* PAPER) and, farther back in antiquity, on papyrus or on various surfaces such as metal, tiles, or sheets of wax (*see* WRITING INSTRUMENTS). Clay tiles formed one of the first-known libraries in Assyria about 700 B.C.—a library which was discovered about 100 years ago by archaeologists. A famous library at Alexandria in Egypt, to which scholars from many countries came to study, contained over 500,000 rolls of papyrus sheet. The greater part of this library was burnt down in 48 B.C. when Julius Caesar, at the head of the Roman force, set fire to the Egyptian fleet in Alexandria harbour. The library was partly restored by the Roman general, Mark Antony, who presented to Cleopatra, the Queen of Egypt, the contents of the royal library of the Greek city of Pergamum in Mysia, in Asia Minor. This library, which is said to have contained at that time 200,000 volumes, had previously rivalled in greatness that of Alexandria. The remains of the library of Alexandria were destroyed about A.D. 390, when the Roman Emperor Theodosius set fire to the city. After the collapse of the Roman Empire, many records of ancient pre-Christian scholarship were lost altogether or buried underground for safety, and not rediscovered until centuries later.

Meanwhile, as the Christian Church became established, a new kind of library was being gradually formed in the monasteries, where the MONKS (q.v. Vol. I) were writing and decorating books (*see* BOOKS, HISTORY OF). These monastic libraries were the forerunners of our College and

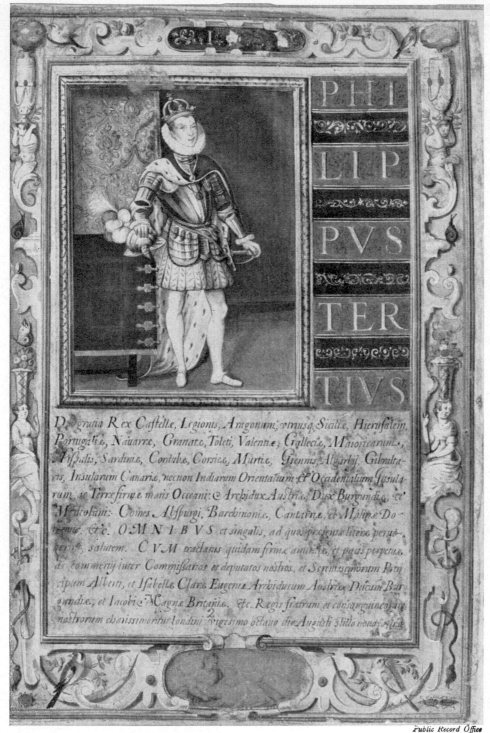

Public Record Office

ANGLO-SPANISH TREATY OF 1604 WRITTEN IN LATIN
The first page sets out the titles of the kings, starting with Philippus Tertius, Philip III of Spain
(*Exchequer, Treasury of Receipt, Diplomatic Documents (E. 30), 1705.*)

THE CHAINED LIBRARY, WIMBORNE MINSTER

University libraries. The monks made catalogues of their books and even in some cases lent books outside the monasteries. At first the books were mostly kept in the church or in chests in the cloisters; but by the 15th century the collections of books had become so large that a special room was often set apart and called the library, where the books were kept in special shelved cupboards, or presses made to take them. As the fame of a particular library spread, students from outside the monastery came to study the books; and to prevent valuable books being lost or stolen, they were chained to the shelf or table. Later libraries began to be formed in the colleges, and others were attached to the great cathedrals such as Canterbury and Durham. Rich people outside the monasteries began to form private libraries for themselves, and some of these afterwards formed the nucleus of some of the most famous libraries in the world. In the 15th century Duke Humphrey of Gloucester, son of Henry IV, gave large gifts of books to the University Library of Oxford, and many French and Italian kings and princes started collections which gradually grew into famous libraries. Very few people could read, but with the invention of PRINTING (q.v.) in the 15th century, more

people learnt to read, more books were printed, and more libraries were formed. The libraries, however, were still only for the use of a comparatively few people either at the universities or in cathedrals or other large churches. Some kings of England from earliest times had encouraged learning and had collected written records. Henry VII laid the foundations of the famous Royal Library, which was joined with the British Museum Library in 1759 by George II.

2. PUBLIC LIBRARIES. As early as the 17th century a few cities such as Norwich, Leicester, and Coventry had instituted a kind of public library supported by charitable gifts; but in later times, through lack of continued support from the townsmen, these libraries lapsed. By the 19th century the only libraries open to the ordinary people were those belonging to the mechanics' institutes, organizations founded early in the 19th century to provide workingmen with the opportunity for reading and discussion.

After 1870, when an Education Act was passed to give free education to children whose parents could not afford to pay, the demand for public libraries, paid for out of the rates, increased, and whereas in 1870 only thirty-five towns had public libraries, to-day there are over 600 library systems provided for out of the rates.

These libraries supply books to readers in their own locality, either a town or a county, and each library is managed by a committee appointed in towns by the borough council, and in counties by the county council. The first Public Libraries Act authorizing towns to maintain libraries out of the rates was passed in 1850, but it was not until 1919 that another Act was passed which allowed each authority to spend what it thought was necessary, and also allowed county councils to supply branch libraries in country districts. The library movement in Great Britain and America owes a great deal to the gifts of the American millionaire, Andrew CARNEGIE (q.v. Vol. V), who had emigrated from Scotland as a poor boy. He gave funds to present library buildings to British towns, and to help the later formation of county libraries.

In a municipal or town public library there are usually four departments—a lending library, a reference room, a children's library, and a newspaper and periodicals room. To be entitled to borrow books readers must live, work, or attend schools in the town, and if not themselves ratepayers, must obtain a written guarantee from a ratepayer. In all lending libraries to-day the reader is free to choose his own books from the shelves, where the books are arranged in a special order according to their subject (*see* CATALOGUING AND INDEXING). Each reader is given two or three tickets; only one work of fiction may be borrowed at a time, and the period of loan is usually 14 days; but after that, if no other reader needs the book, it may be kept a little longer. There are books on almost every subject, and most libraries try to keep their stock up to date. In the reference department readers may consult the books, but not take them away. There are the dictionaries, encyclopaedias, and all the other REFERENCE BOOKS (q.v.), which cannot be lent out because they are in constant use by many people. The children's library, which is usually in a separate room, includes books suitable for readers of all ages up to 15 years. Most modern children's libraries include a corner for very young children and also a reference section to help the older ones with their homework. In the news room the chief daily papers are found; technical journals and magazines may also be kept there.

Country villages, and small towns not big enough to have their own libraries, have branch libraries supplied with books from a county library, which has its headquarters in the chief town of the district. Small villages, too small for a branch library, receive boxes of books at some centre such as the village school, and these are changed at regular intervals; some counties have a travelling van which carries a stock of books, and from which the country reader may make his own selections. Students receive a special postal service direct from the headquarters library; other readers, who may want some book not at the branch, can write to the county library and order it.

All these town and county libraries are linked together by regional offices, which in turn are linked with a national central library. In this way, if a student cannot get a particular book from his own local library, he can borrow it from some other collection through the central library.

See also BIBLIOTHÈQUE NATIONALE; BODLEIAN LIBRARY; BRITISH MUSEUM LIBRARY; CAMBRIDGE UNIVERSITY LIBRARY; CONGRESS LIBRARY, U.S.A.; LONDON LIBRARY; VATICAN LIBRARY.

LIFEBOAT. For many centuries wrecks were regarded as legitimate prizes by all coast dwellers, with the result that seamen and passengers in a stranded vessel were often left to drown while local boatmen tried to plunder the ship's cargo.

Archdeacon Sharp, who lived on the Northumbrian coast in the late 18th century, had charge of certain charitable funds which he decided to use for saving life at sea. So he approached a London coachbuilder, Lionel Lukin, who was interested in the sea, and who had planned an unsinkable craft. A fishing-boat was refashioned by Lukin and was stationed at Bamburgh in Northumberland in 1786; it was the first lifeboat to be based on a shore. A second lifeboat was built and kept by a local committee at the mouth of the Tyne. During the next 14 years thirty more lifeboats were set up by local committees and charities round the coasts.

In 1823, hoping to enlarge and co-ordinate these local efforts, Sir William Hillary launched an appeal for the starting of a national lifeboat service. The Royal National Lifeboat Institution was founded, and embodied all Hillary's far-seeing plans. It is chiefly to him that the

Roy. Nat. Lifeboat Institution
THE ST. HELIER (JERSEY) LIFEBOAT

nation owes this voluntary institution, which has saved more than 76,000 lives. When the institution was founded, it was laid down that it should go to the rescue of all people, whatever their nationality, in war or peace. During the Second World War 6,376 lives were saved by its efforts.

The Institution receives great help from the coastguards, whose chief duty is now the saving of life. They man the coasts of Great Britain and Ireland and keep watch at about 180 regular stations. Roughly a third of these stations are situated at danger-points where a continuous watch is kept; at a similar number of stations a regular night watch is kept; and at the remainder watch is kept only during bad and thick weather. In addition there are nearly 180 auxiliary stations which are manned by local men, mostly members of the voluntary Coast Life-Saving Corps, about 5,000 strong, who keep watch whenever the weather is bad. The regular coastguards are nearly all recruited from naval pensioners. They are equipped with rocket apparatus and breeches-buoy gear for bringing people ashore from ships wrecked near the land, and they fire maroons to warn the lifeboat crews.

Although all coastal lifeboats in this country are maintained by the Royal National Lifeboat Institution, they are built to different designs to suit local conditions. Some are larger than others; some are very light so that they can be launched from the beaches; heavier craft are launched from slipways. All, however, are immensely strong, and virtually unsinkable by reason of their many watertight compartments. They are equipped with a number of enclosed air-chambers to make them extremely buoyant, and can automatically empty themselves of water. Many lifeboats are designed to right themselves when capsized, and some can carry up to 100 people. All are painted in the famous red, blue, and white of the R.N.L.I.

Most modern lifeboats are driven by motors housed in a watertight compartment; steam-driven lifeboats were never very efficient, and the days of rowing or sailing a lifeboat are past. The lifeboat to-day is equipped with many scientific devices to render her difficult tasks easier, such as an oil spray to smooth broken water, searchlights, radio, line-throwing apparatus, and so on. The most powerful lifeboat in the world is stationed at Dover.

Lifeboats are often launched by their own weight down a slipway. In certain areas local volunteers still run the lifeboat down the beach to the sea. On many beaches, however, launching is carried out by a specially designed tractor with engines which are protected against water.

Some of the lighter beach-launched boats can be loaded on to specially designed carriages, with caterpillar tracks; they are thus towed by a tractor to a place suitable for launching, according to the direction of wind and sea. Sailing lifeboats, in the past, were sometimes taken considerable distances by road or horse-drawn vehicles, to avoid long beats against head-on gales.

See also WRECKS AND WRECKERS.

LIFTS AND ESCALATORS. 1. LIFTS. These are cars or cages for raising goods or passengers from one level to another. They are called 'elevators' in America. Lifts became necessary when business buildings were built many stories high, or railways far underground. The sky-scraper buildings of New York make lifts vitally important.

Though hoisting machinery was used long before, the history of the lift really begins in the 17th century, when a French engineer, called Velayer, made a simple kind of lift which could be operated by hand, water, or animal power. Hydraulic lifts worked by water under pressure were introduced at the beginning of the 19th century. Another step forward was made with the invention of a lift suspended by two ropes, which used counterweights so that only the extra weight of the lift's cargo had to be pulled up. It was worked by hauling by hand on another rope.

In 1850 a crude steam lift was made in the United States, but it was not successful. In 1852, also in the United States, came the first lift to have safety devices. It was invented by Elisha Graves Otis of New York. A model was installed in London at the Crystal Palace in 1853, with a safety device which consisted of a pair of spring-loaded teeth or pawls which engaged in a vertical rack to prevent the lift from falling. About 1876 Baldwin's hydraulic lift began to take the place of earlier types.

The first electric lift was made in Germany in 1880, worked by an electric motor below the car. It was developed in America, and in 1889 Otis installed in a New York building two electric elevators, driven by individual motors.

Most passenger and goods lifts are now either hydraulic or electric, and have two sets of gates, one fixed on the landing platform, and the other attached to the travelling car itself. Both gates must be closed before the lift will work. Some lifts are operated by the passenger, who presses a button marked with the number of the floor to which he wishes to go, and then the lift will automatically stop when that floor is reached. In other cases a lift may be worked by an attendant. A small panel bearing signal lights is in the lift, and a similar panel on each landing. The lights indicate the position of the lift. A lift can also be 'called' to any floor by a press-button electric switch. In very tall buildings non-stop lifts are used, some of which reach a speed of between 1,800 and 2,000 feet per minute. The safety devices used in these lifts include electro-magnetic brakes and automatic speed governors.

London Transport uses lifts in many underground stations, the modern ones being electric and fully automatic, and running swiftly, smoothly, and silently. A gramophone record warns passengers to stand clear of the doors.

It is not possible to estimate exactly the number of passengers carried by lifts, but it has been suggested that in the U.S.A. alone some 30,000 million people are carried up and down in a year.

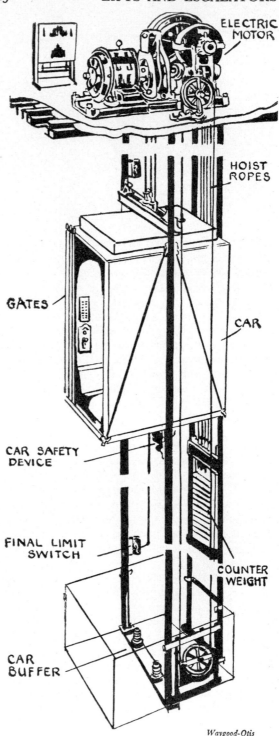

ELECTRIC MOTOR

HOIST ROPES

GATES

CAR

CAR SAFETY DEVICE

FINAL LIMIT SWITCH

COUNTER WEIGHT

CAR BUFFER

Waygood-Otis

DIAGRAM OF AN ELECTRIC LIFT

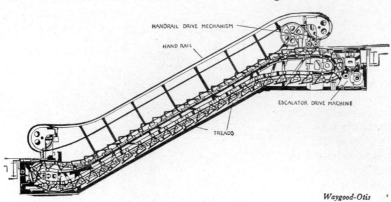

HANDRAIL DRIVE MECHANISM

HAND RAIL

ESCALATOR DRIVE MACHINE

TREADS

Waygood-Otis

DIAGRAM OF AN ESCALATOR

2. ESCALATORS are moving staircases. An escalator is made of a succession of metal and rubber treads fastened together in an endless belt, which moves round and round; the upper side, on which the passengers stand, may go either up or down. At the top and bottom the treads flatten out so that people can step on and off safely, but the rest of the way the treads are arranged like a staircase. The passenger may either stand still on one step or, if he is in a hurry, may walk up or down. The speed at which moving staircases run varies with the amount of traffic they are designed to carry.

Escalators are being used more and more in many kinds of buildings, as well as in railway stations. Modern escalator systems save time and energy, and are very popular with the public. One escalator will carry many times the number of passengers a lift can. London Transport is one of the largest users of moving staircases in the world.

See also LONDON TRANSPORT.

LIGHTHOUSES AND LIGHTSHIPS. The oldest lighthouse was the Pharos at Alexandria in Egypt which was built about 285 B.C. It was 300 feet in height, and the light is said to have been visible for about 30 miles. The oldest lighthouse on the English coast was probably the one established by the Romans at Dover.

For centuries such lighthouses as existed were merely guiding lights to particular harbours. Most of the lights were then exhibited from ordinary dwelling-houses, a small charge for the upkeep of the light being collected from shipping using the port which the light served. The inefficiencies of the lanterns or fires, as well as the false lights sometimes shown by ship-wreckers, made the night approach to our coasts extremely dangerous; and most vessels used to prefer to lay-to off the land until the dawn. Various monarchs found the sale of royal patents to establish lighthouses a useful form of raising money, the owners of the new lights recouping themselves by charges collected from the agents of passing shipping. Those early lights were often merely coal fires burning in cressets or fire-pans and kept bright by the use of bellows. Exposed to gales and rain, their brilliance was, however, very unreliable. When, later, the coal fires were enclosed in glass, the smoke nuisance and other difficulties resulted in little improvement.

Even as late as the beginning of the 19th century a great many lighthouses were in private hands; but in 1836 an Act of Parliament gave the TRINITY HOUSE Corporation (q.v.) powers to buy out private owners of lighthouses in England and Wales. To-day navigational aids are installed and maintained by three bodies: the Trinity House Corporation covering the coasts of England and Wales, and Gibraltar; the Commissioners of Northern Lighthouses, covering the Scottish coasts and the Isle of Man; the Commissioners of Irish Lights, covering the coasts of Ireland. In certain matters the Trinity House Corporation has overriding authority over the other two bodies.

With the exception of ships of the Royal Navy, fishing-boats, and certain other exempted vessels, all ships contribute to the upkeep of these navigational aids in the form of light dues. Varying according to the class of vessel and the trade on which it is engaged, these dues average only a few pence per ton per voyage.

Modern lighthouses are erected either on rocks, shoals, or in other situations exposed to the force of the sea, or on high promontories ashore. The structure of the lighthouse depends on its location; so far as lighthouses on rocks are concerned there are four different types of structure. These are masonry and concrete structures, openwork steel and iron-framed erections on pile or other foundations, cast-iron plated towers, and structures erected on caisson (watertight compartment) foundations.

Where good foundations can be found, masonry or concrete structures are generally preferred, and the tower put up by the great engineer John Smeaton on the Eddystone Rock off Plymouth in 1756 is the model upon which most later designs were based. Circular towers erected on bases with vertical sides are considered the best design, since they offer least resistance to the wind and waves, and the bases receive the full horizontal thrust of the sea. External projections from the face of the tower are usually avoided, and the tower must be high enough above sea-level for the light not to be obscured by dense spray.

Openwork steel and iron-framed erections are used where the tower has to be carried on a foundation of iron or steel piles driven or screwed to an insecure or sandy bottom. Cast-iron plated towers are used in places where the cost of stone or the scarcity of labour make other methods too expensive. Caisson foundations are used where towers have to be erected on sand-banks or shoals.

The way light is produced depends largely on the position of the lighthouse. Where it is possible to lay high-tension cables to the lighthouse or when the structure is large enough to house its own generators, electric power is used; otherwise incandescent mineral-oil burners or acetylene gas are the usual types of illuminant.

The huge glass lenses which magnify the lights are of highly scientific and complicated design and manufacture. They are housed in the lantern which, for the largest lighthouses, may be anything up to 16 feet in diameter. It is usually reached by a spiral staircase.

In order that mariners may be able to check their positions when at sea, each light shows only for a certain number of seconds at a time; this is managed either by a revolving screen with variable openings in it, or by a cylindrical screen raised and lowered around the burner. White and red are the chief colours used for lights, since these are the colours which can be seen best at a distance. The particular type of light is shown on navigation charts, for example, 'Fl. ev. 5 secs. 2 M', which means 'a white flash every 5 seconds with a visibility up to 2 miles'; or 'Gp. Fl. (5) W.R. ev. 20 secs. 188 ft. 20 M', meaning 'five white flashes every 20 seconds

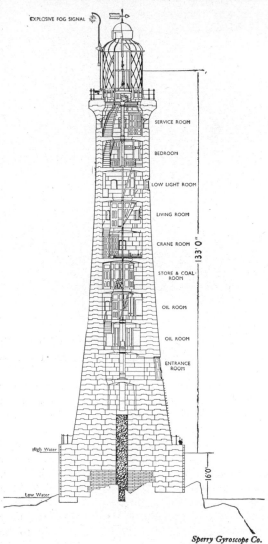

Sperry Gyroscope Co.

SECTION OF THE PRESENT EDDYSTONE LIGHTHOUSE (1882)

shown in the safety sector and five red flashes every 20 seconds in the danger sector with visibility up to 20 miles from a lighthouse 188 feet above sea-level'. The difference that can be seen between occulting and flashing lights is that the former every now and then go out, the time of darkness being always less than or equal to that of light; the latter show flashes of light at regular intervals, the time of darkness being greater than that of light.

The revolving light apparatus is sometimes rotated by clockwork mechanism actuated by weights or spring driven. Where electric current is available, electric motors are used to rotate

THE OWERS LIGHTSHIP OFF SELSEY BILL, SUSSEX

Planet News

the lights; similarly, in lighthouses with gas-lit apparatus, the gas is used to revolve·the lens table.

Fog-signals were almost unknown until the mid-19th century, but are now used in most lighthouses and lightships. Bells and gongs are the oldest forms of fog-signals; explosive sound rockets, acetylene fog-guns, whistles, horns, and sirens are now used, and also diaphones, a new type of signal invented by a Canadian in 1903, which gives a very penetrating sound from a conical horn. Whistles and reed horns are not used round the coasts of Britain, because they are thought to be wasteful and likely to be confused with steamers' whistles. Diaphones and sirens are most commonly used when space to store the equipment is available and when long-distance signals are required. These instruments are actuated by compressed air.

Shore lighthouses are looked after by two men—a third man being added when fog-signals also have to be worked. Rock lighthouses have a total crew of four, three of whom are always on duty. The men who attend isolated rock lighthouses usually spend one month out of three on shore. Rock lighthouses and lightships are relieved by tenders; and frequently when the weather is rough, men and stores have to be transferred to the lighthouse by a rope. Lighthouses and lightships in exposed places keep a

reserve of stores for the times when storms prevent the tender reaching them.

Some modern lighthouses, usually of secondary importance, such as the Rock Light at Liverpool and the light at Great Orme Head in Carnarvonshire, are unattended; but they are kept under constant observation and are generally visited once or twice a week. They are lighted by electricity or acetylene gas, and with the latter an ingenious device is used to save gas. The lamps are fitted with sun-valves which expand under the influence of daylight, and by doing so switch off the gas. This is rekindled from a pilot-jet when daylight fails.

The early lightships were Dutch galliots—strongly built cargo vessels bought for their sea-keeping qualities. Their high poops and bows and low waists made them such suitable craft that modern steel lightships are constructed on similar lines. The oldest lightship is believed to have been the Nore, established in 1732, at the mouth of the Thames. Like the lighthouses, some of the earlier lightships appear to have been privately owned. Before the Second World War the large majority of lightships were moored round the approaches to the Thames estuary, but since the war some of these have been replaced by other arrangements. The Nore light, for instance, is now shown from one of the sea forts constructed in the Thames estuary during the war to protect shipping from aerial mine-layers.

Lightships are moored to 3-ton anchors with chain cables. In open waters, where precise marking of a dangerous place is not necessary, long cables are used, which act as a steadying influence on the lightship. In more confined waters shorter cables enable the ship to mark the obstruction more exactly.

The light is supplied by incandescent acetylene or oil burners, or high-powered gas-filled electric lamps. Fog-signals are usually sirens or diaphones worked by compressed air, the compressors being driven by steam or oil engines, or in the more modern ones by semi-diesel engines. The lights of modern ships are mounted on steel lattice-work towers, and are reached by steel ladders.

Lightship crews consist of three masters, three lamplighters, three fog-signal drivers, and three seamen. Leave is so arranged that one master and eight ratings are always on board. The men are usually from the Merchant Service.

See also LIFEBOAT; SIGNALS AT SEA; WRECKS AND WRECKERS.

LIGHT SIGNALLING.

The oldest forms of signalling by means of light are beacons by night, and mirrors to reflect the sun by day. Both methods were still in use in the Second World War. The escape kits of airmen and seamen included a polished steel mirror, with a sighting device so that if they were wrecked, they could aim the signal flashes in any chosen direction. In some areas jungle troops laid out patterns of blazing oil by night, to signal to aircraft.

Mirror signalling, in the form of the heliograph, reached a high pitch of efficiency in campaigns on the north-west frontier of India and in the South African War (1899–1902). This instrument consists of a mirror mounted on a stand. The mirror is swivelled so that a signaller can aim the long and short flashes of the MORSE CODE (q.v.) towards another signaller who may be miles away. The drawback of the heliograph is that it is useless without sunshine. To-day it has been largely replaced by the portable Aldis lamp and also by the more powerful signalling lamps used in the Navy. In these an artificial light is focused by a mirror in the shape of a paraboloid, a curved surface which reflects the light in one compact beam. The Aldis lamp can be held in

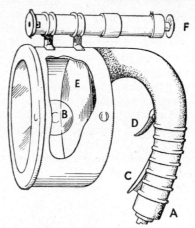

DIAGRAM OF AN ALDIS LAMP

The current is led through *A* to the bulb *B*. *C* is the light switch, *D* the trigger which moves the mirror *E*. *F* is a telescope

one hand, while the mirror is moved by a trigger (see diagram). Naval signalling lamps were first introduced in 1864. They are powerful searchlights with fixed mirrors, and are covered by metal shutters resembling the slats of a Venetian blind; the slats open and close at the movement of a lever, thus sending messages by Morse code.

Light signalling is generally used by aircraft as a special measure only. Ships use it more often to supplement radio. Ships entering or leaving harbour at night are in touch with the port authorities by light, though in daytime they would make more use of FLAG SIGNALLING (q.v.). Ships at sea during war time, rather than disclose their position to an enemy equipped with radio direction-finding, may signal with closely screened lamps, or with infra-red lights invisible except to those equipped with special glasses. Aircraft-carriers can control their pilots by showing bars of light of different shapes and colours, visible only at a certain angle from the deck.

Pyrotechnics, or fireworks, are used for identification, to summon assistance, and to make a few standard coded signals. The cartridge of the Verey pistol, after being fired into the air, throws out from itself a succession of differently coloured stars, and the various colour patterns have their special meanings in code. Rockets are used in much the same way, particularly as a distress signal, and all ships and lifeboats carry them.

See also SIGNALS; LIGHTHOUSES AND LIGHTSHIPS.

LINER. This term rightly belongs to any ship which maintains a regular service, whether for passengers and cargo, or only for cargo. The liner proper ranges from 6,000 to 80,000 gross register tonnage. Very much smaller ships, however, carry passengers in all waters of the world; they are often miniature copies of the larger ships, and the regularity of their sailings, even if only on coastal voyages, entitles them to be called liners.

No ship runs for the exclusive use of passengers; even the transatlantic giants carry mails and a certain amount of valuable cargo. In the East-bound liners cargo is very important. The Suez Canal (q.v.) limits the size of most ships going to South Africa, India and the Far East, Australia, and New Zealand, and only in the Atlantic trade can the world's largest ships be used. The East-bound liner may carry about a thousand passengers; the transatlantic ships frequently carry double that number. An immense amount of organization is necessary to look after 2,000 people for several days and nights, provide them with meals, beds, baths, service, and entertainment, when no fresh supplies can be obtained until the ship reaches the next port of call.

The liner may be driven by steam-reciprocating engines, steam-turbine, diesel, turbo-electric, or diesel-electric motors. All express passenger liners, however they are propelled, are fast ships; any that fail to maintain a cruising speed of more than 20 knots (20 sea miles per hour) soon lose their place in their fleet. In addition to the navigational aids and safety devices found in all ships, the liner is equipped with echo-sounding gear, which automatically records the depth of water beneath the vessel; radio direction-finding gear, for obtaining the liner's position when approaching land; radar, which permits the crew to avoid other ships and obstructions at night or in fog; as well as gyroscopic compasses, automatic fire-alarms, and cargo-handling machinery. Modern liners are fitted with stabilizers which prevent their rolling.

For many years there was disagreement about the interior decorations of liners; some shipowners thought that a ship should look like a ship; others thought that it should be disguised to look like an hotel, and so inspire confidence in the timid landsman. It is now clear, however, that most passengers, particularly on the eastern routes, like sea voyaging, and appreciate the change from hotel to ship.

The red plush and gaudy hangings of former years have now disappeared, but luxury and comfort have increased to a remarkable degree. The huge entrance hall with its imposing wide stairways remains. There are paintings by famous artists. Cabins and suites are very luxurious, with simple, well-designed, built-in furniture, private bathrooms, electric fires, conditioned air, telephones, and so on. There is a playroom for young children, often with an artificial beach and a paddling pool, and a trained woman in charge. The liner also has a

Cunard White Star

R.M.S. 'CARONIA' ARRIVING AT NEW YORK ON HER MAIDEN VOYAGE
She is welcomed by a firefloat

cinema, a swimming-pool, shops, gymnasium, laundry, hospital, hair-dressing saloon, and electric lifts serving all decks. The service is deft, silent, and courteous. The accommodation for the crew in these ships has also changed, and seamen now live in comfortable cabins vastly different from the forecastles, usually wet and badly ventilated, where the seamen of earlier times lived and ate. The purser is in charge of the complicated organization which provides food, linen, stores, heating, and cooking for the passengers and for the 400 or more members of the crew.

The smaller liner which specializes in cargo may not carry more than twelve passengers without a certificate from the Board of Trade. In these ships no orchestra, shops, or lifts will be found, but quarters are comfortable, and the passengers are admitted in some part into the comradeship of the sea. The passenger who books accommodation in this class of ship need not fear that he will travel in something ill-found and out of date.

It is important for the passenger or cargo liner to keep a rigid time schedule. When she leaves her home port on, say, 5 September, bound to the ends of the earth, her officers and, what is even more important, the world's shippers and merchants, know that, barring accident or unforeseen hold-up, she will be back at her berth on, say, 7 December. Factories making goods for export plan their output on these schedules, and a dock strike or some other delay to liner shipping will be felt for months afterwards in places all over the world, often far from the sea.

Outward bound from Britain, the cargo liner loads a cargo of manufactured goods such as motor-cars, railway coaches, sewing-machines, or cotton and woollen goods. On the homeward voyage, if she is a general cargo liner, she will carry chiefly raw materials and foodstuffs, such as tobacco, raw cotton, hard-woods, or sugar.

A large number of cargo liners specialize in one or more particular trades. Chief of these are Refrigerated Ships, which carry meat and fruit (*see* SHIP). Among them are special banana ships which carry no other cargo, and these graceful, fast, well-found, all-white vessels are deservedly popular with the cargo-liner passenger.

The cargo liner carries a number of derricks (a form of crane), winches, and other cargo-handling equipment. If she is one of the special-ists, her gear will include some of the intricate unloading machinery which has been devised for each particular trade. She has fewer boats than the passenger liner, and also generally less superstructure. She will carry some deck cargo, such as carboys of acid, a tram, or a railway coach. On the bridge she is probably as up to date as a passenger liner, and there is little difference on the navigational side between the two types of vessels.

The regular sailings of a liner have a great effect upon the trades and industries of the world. A liner loading at the docks causes immense activity in road, rail, and water transport. When the passengers begin their journey to the embarkation stage, hotels, passenger transport, and travel agencies are all affected. The ship's business in preparation for sailing gives rise to fresh activity in insurance offices; numerous cables and letters are sent, and hundreds of telephone calls are made. The replacement of stores and equipment calls for deliveries from paint manufacturers, furniture-makers, glass factories, electrical industries, rope-makers, cutlers, napery manufacturers, and scores of other industries. Huge quantities of fuel, either coal or oil, must be loaded; enormous freshwater tanks must be filled; and large supplies of food go into the ship's store-rooms. At the main post offices mails are sorted and dispatched to the ship, while countless clerks, dockers, and watermen work to help the ship catch the tide on sailing day.

The greatest liner port in the British Commonwealth is London, for some 700 regular sailings to more than 300 overseas ports take place from the Thames each month. Approximately 140 liners are loading or discharging at the docks of London each day. From Tilbury one can watch the great ships embarking passengers at the Tilbury Ocean Stage, and a constant stream of vessels, ranging from 28,000-ton liners in the Australian trade to little coasters, all on regular sailing schedules, pass up-stream to the docks or down-stream to the sea from 2 hours before to 2 hours after high water. 'The liner, she's a lady', as Kipling wrote, and upon her our safety and well-being largely depend.

See also SHIP; SHIP'S COMPANY; NAVIGATION, MARINE; PORTS AND HARBOURS.

See also Vol. VII: SHIPPING.

LIP READING, *see* DEAF LANGUAGES.

Bibliothèque Nationale

CHARLES V ARRIVING AT ST. DENIS IN A LITTER
15th-century miniature by Jean Fouquet

LITTER. This word comes from the Latin *lectus*, a bed. In Roman times litters were much used as means of transport by the wealthy, especially by ladies. They were shaped like a bed, without legs, but with a canopy above and curtains round the sides, which could be drawn back or across at the rider's pleasure. The litter was fixed on two long poles which rested on the shoulders of four slaves, two in front and two behind. Sometimes the litter was made like a double bed, so that two people could travel together. In medieval times, when the roads were in a very bad state, those who could not ride a horse were often carried in litters. These were usually borne by two horses, one between the poles at the front and the other at the back. Such litters were used, especially for royalty, until sprung CARRIAGES (q.v.) were introduced in the late 17th century. Queen Elizabeth, when she did not ride, often travelled in a horse litter.

A palanquin is a type of litter used especially in India for making journeys over country where there are no good roads. It is built of wood on the same pattern as the Roman litter, and has wooden shutters or slats which open on the principle of a Venetian blind. There are four rings, fixed one at each corner, through which the poles run, and the vehicle is carried by four bearers called *hammals*. The palanquins of the Indian princes are very magnificent.

LLOYD'S. Lloyd's is not, as is generally supposed, a huge insurance firm; it is an association of underwriters—that is, people who undertake insurance. Lloyd's itself issues no insurance policies; but insurances are undertaken by individual members for their own account and at their own risk. Members of Lloyd's have to be elected, and have to put down a substantial sum of money as a security against their underwriting liabilities. The purpose of Lloyd's, therefore, is an insurance of the reliability of its members. Every kind of insurance can be effected there—kinds of business which not many ordinary insurance firms can undertake. It is possible, for instance, at Lloyd's to insure the success of a fête against the disaster of bad weather; or to insure valuable personal possessions when travelling in foreign countries. Lloyd's business was at first only with shipping, and it is still used by shipowners from all over the world because of its great security. But its business now is as much non-marine as marine.

The name comes from a former coffee-house, the proprietor of which was named Lloyd, where underwriters gathered to exchange news. For their benefit, lists of shipping movements were displayed there. From this custom has grown *Lloyd's List and Shipping Gazette*, a daily newspaper, more than 200 years old, which publishes shipping news, including all recorded shipping movements. Lloyd's provides many other services for the shipping industry. It has a network of agents covering the coast-line of the globe, and from them news of shipping pours into the offices in Leadenhall Street and thence to interested shipowners and merchants. The famous Lutine Bell recovered in 1859 from the frigate, *La Lutine*, sunk off Holland in 1799, is rung to announce the arrival of news of an overdue ship; one stroke is given for bad news and two for good.

Lloyd's must not be confused with Lloyd's Register of Shipping, a separate organization with offices in Fenchurch Street. From there is published the annual volume known as *Lloyd's Register of British and Foreign Shipping*, which records the size, details of construction, propulsion, capacity, ownership, and other particulars of all vessels over 100 gross register tonnage. The system of grading ships carried out by the surveyors of Lloyd's Register has done as much to ensure a high standard of safety in both British and foreign vessels as have the regulations of governments. The highest classification of ships is '100 A 1. at Lloyd's', and the term has passed into the landsman's vocabulary as a standard of excellence.

See also Vol. VII: INSURANCE.

LOADING GAUGE, RAILWAY, *see* GAUGES, RAILWAY.

LOCKS AND WEIRS. Locks are built to control the flow of rivers and canals, so that boats may go up or down stream without danger, and so that water may not be wasted. A series of locks is like a flight of stairs. A lock is a short compartment of a canal or river, with gates at either end. It has side walls and a bottom. The reach of water or 'pound' above it is higher than the reach below it, so the lock must be deep enough to cover the distance between the bottom of the lower reach and the bank level of the upper reach. Across the top end of the lock there is a wall as high as the bed level of the upper reach. There are sluices, which open and close,

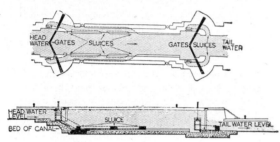

FIG. I. PLAN AND SECTION OF A LOCK

either in the lock-gates or in culverts (tunnelled passages) which pass behind the gates into the lock. The lock is filled or emptied through these. Of course, when the lock is said to be empty, it does not mean there is no water in it at all, but merely that the water in it is at the level of the lower reach (*see* Fig. 1).

Locks may be built of brick, concrete, steel sheet or concrete piling, timber, or of some combination of these. They must be large enough to take the largest vessels, fully loaded, which are likely to use the waterway; in canalized rivers, and where water is plentiful, they may be made to take several vessels at one time; if this is done, intermediate gates may be provided to shut the lock off into sections, so that the whole large lock is not used for a few small boats. Sometimes several locks of different sizes are built alongside one another, as at Teddington on the Thames where there are three locks, each of which takes a different size of vessel. When a boat descends, the lock must be full of water. The top gates are opened, the water being retained by the lower gates, and the boat enters

the lock. Then the top gates are closed, and the bottom sluices opened, so that the level of water in the lock, and the boat with it, is lowered. When the lock is 'empty', the lower gates are opened, and the boat moves into the canal at the lower level. When a boat is going up through the lock, the reverse process takes place; the lock is filled by opening the sluices at the top.

Resident lock-keepers operate all important locks, or those where river traffic is checked. At most country locks on canals in England, however, the boat crew operates the locks, and the lock-keeper may have several locks to look after. On the Thames and other rivers where there is pleasure traffic, the traditional English lock-keeper of Edwardian days, with his whitewashed or creeper-clad cottage and trim, decorative garden bright with flowers, is still to be seen by the summer visitor.

Locks vary greatly in height on different rivers and canals. In England the average rise in level for narrow canal locks is about 7 feet; the locks on the Albert Canal in Belgium have a rise of 32 feet; while in the United States rises up to 70 feet are not uncommon. The extent to which electrical and mechanical devices are used for operating the gates varies with the size of the locks.

For the smaller locks the gates are usually made of oak, and are mitred, that is, they meet at an angle across the lock, being retained in position by a sill laid in the bed and held in at the heel or lock side by anchorages; the gate chamber is recessed in the lock so as to leave no projections when the gates are open. Large gates are built of steel sections and are similar to ship lock-gates in docks.

When flood waters have to be passed through

FIG. 2. RADIAL LOCK GATE

a lock, vertical lift or radial gates are often used, as they give a quicker discharge than sluices; that is, the lock-gates, instead of opening sideways up-stream, as mitred gates do, which would be impossible against a head of water, they lift or pivot upwards, so that the water passes below them (*see* Fig. 2). As the vessels also have to pass below them, they are not so convenient for traffic unless they are built high enough not to restrict the head-room for vessels. Small gates are provided with a projecting top beam for opening and closing the gate; larger gates are worked by hand-operated gearing; while gates of the largest size are power-operated.

Where water is scarce, 'economizers' or side ponds are built alongside the lock and connected to it by sluices; the levels of these are so arranged that the top water of the lock empties into the side pond, where it is retained. When the lock is being filled again to allow a boat to go up through it, this water is used first—as the bottom layer as it were. The top layer of water has to come from the upper reach of canal as usual.

Topical Press

FIG. 3. ANDERTON BOAT LIFT, RIVER WEAVER, CHESHIRE

Lifts and inclines are an alternative to locks, and use less water. Inclined planes, where the boat is taken bodily from the water on to a carriage running on rails, are not now in use, except occasionally for boats of small size. In the inclined lift the boat is carried in a tank or trough filled with water and mounted on rails. Two counterbalanced tanks are used, one of which goes up as the other comes down. The more common arrangement, however, is the vertical lift, where the boat is again carried in a trough, gates and counterbalances being provided. There are several lifts on the Continent, but the Anderton lift, on the River Weaver in Cheshire, is the only one now in use in Great Britain. It consists of two independent movable tanks, which can each take two narrow canal boats with about 50 tons of cargo. The tanks are lowered and raised electrically through a height of about 50 feet (*see* Fig. 3).

A weir is a dam placed across a river or stream to raise the level of water above it. Often a second channel is cut for a river over a short distance, and a lock placed on one branch and a weir on the other. If a gate is placed in the weir, it is called a sluice or flood-gate; but if the gate can be raised high enough for a boat to pass under, or if it is hinged at the base and allowed to fall horizontally or to open as a lock-gate, then the arrangement is known as a 'stanch' or 'staunch'. Sometimes it is also called a 'navigation weir' and a 'flash lock'.

Staunches are the alternative to locks in a river, and are still used in isolated cases on some rivers in England to pass pleasure-craft or flats (small raft-like boats used by farmers for moving manure, hay, and so on), or maintenance boats. They are usually placed below shallow places When in position or 'set', they stop the flow, so that water accumulates, and when there is enough water above them to float the boat coming down over the shallows, the staunch gate is lowered or drawn, and the boat passes through on the flood of water into the lower level. When the boat is going up-stream, it passes through the staunch, which is then closed; the boat then has to wait until the water has risen high enough to allow it to pass over the shallow to the next reach above. Staunches waste both time and water, but they were at one time used as a means of passing navigation on certain rivers in England.

See also CANALS; RIVER NAVIGATION; BARGE.

LOCOMOTIVE, *see* LOCOMOTIVE, STEAM; DIESEL LOCOMOTIVE; ARTICULATED LOCOMO-TIVES; ELECTRIC RAILWAYS; GAS TURBINE LOCO-MOTIVE.

LOCOMOTIVE WHEEL NOTATION, *see* LOCOMOTIVES; CLASSES AND USES, Section 2.

LOCOMOTIVES: CLASSES AND USES. **1.** Steam locomotives can be classed by the kinds of work for which they are used. The nature of their work is generally made clear by their appearance. The arrangement of a locomotive's wheels is the best guide, but first all steam locomotives might be divided into two main groups, those with tenders and those without. For most journeys except very short ones, a locomotive has attached to it a separate vehicle as a tender which carries the supplies of fuel and water. For short journeys, however, and for shunting, a locomotive carries its own coal and water; the coal is kept in a small bunker at the rear, and the water is stored in tanks, either at the sides of the boiler or on top of it. A locomotive of this kind is called a 'tank'; when the tanks are on top, they are either curved (saddle tanks) or square (pannier tanks, resembling the baskets formerly carried on horses' backs). The railways of Britain, which have to make short journeys, have a greater proportion of tank engines than those of any other country.

2. WHEEL NOTATION. The principal wheels of a steam locomotive (those to which the power of the steam is applied) are known as the driving- and coupled-wheels. The steam cylinders can often be seen at the sides of an engine; the movement of the pistons in them makes the driving-wheels go round. As the coupled-wheels are linked to the driving-wheels by coupling-rods, the power from the cylinders is applied equally to all of them. Coupling the wheels together increases the locomotive's 'grip' on the rails, or, as the engineers call it, 'adhesion' and reduces the tendency of the wheels to slip when the power is applied.

On many locomotives there are other wheels besides the coupled wheels, provided to assist in distributing the weight of the locomotives over a greater length of track. These are small 'idle' wheels, which run free; no power is applied to them. All locomotives intended for fast running have four of these small wheels arranged as a swivelling truck (a 'bogie') under their leading end. At the rear end some locomotives have other small 'idle' wheels.

The arrangement of all these wheels enables engines to be classified very simply by a method known as the 'Whyte notation'. This consists of a group of three figures. The middle figure always represents the number of coupled- or driving-wheels; the first figure represents the number of 'idle' wheels at the leading or front end of the engine; the third figure refers to the 'idle' wheels at the rear. Thus an engine with four 'idle' wheels in front, then six coupled driving-wheels, then two 'idle' wheels at the rear, would be expressed by the figures 4–6–2 (Fig. 1 a). Many types, including the 'Merchant Navy' (Southern Region), have this notation.

If there happen to be no 'idle' wheels, a nought must be written in the proper place. Thus a Western Region 'King' class engine, with a four-wheel bogie in front and then six driving-wheels, is written 4–6–0. One of the many small shunting tank engines used by all railways, carried only on six coupled driving-wheels, is written 0–6–0, or sometimes 0–6–0 T to indicate that it is a tank engine (Fig. 1 b).

FIG. 1 *a*. L.M. REGION 'DUCHESS' CLASS PACIFIC LOCOMOTIVE

FIG. 1 *b*. E. & NE. REGION 'J 94' CLASS TANK ENGINE
Drawn to same scale as 1 *a*.

Various nicknames for specific wheel arrangements have now become common in all parts of the world, though they originated in the United States. The best-known are 'Pacific' for a 4–6–2 engine, 'Atlantic' for a 4–4–2, 'Mountain' for a 4–8–2, 'Consolidation' for a 2–8–0, 'Mogul' for a 2–6–0, 'Mikado' for a 2–8–2, and 'Prairie' for a 2–6–2.

3. SPECIAL PURPOSES. The size of the driving-wheels has some relation to the use of an engine. When a large driving-wheel of 18-foot circumference makes one revolution, it pulls a train 18 feet forward along the rails. When a smaller driving-wheel of 12-foot circumference makes one revolution, it pulls a train only 12 feet forward. Therefore, less effort is needed to make the smaller wheel turn once, provided the weight of the train remains the same. Most goods trains are heavier than passenger trains, so that the steam power of an average engine can haul a heavy goods train more easily if the driving-wheels are smaller than those of a passenger

FIG. 2. WESTERN REGION 'HALL' CLASS PASSENGER AND '2800' CLASS HEAVY GOODS LOCOMOTIVES

Both have the same type of boiler, and cylinders of the same dimensions. Greatest difference is the size and number of wheels, making '2800' class more powerful but with a lower speed range. (Drawn to same scale as Fig. 1)

engine (Fig. 2). The principle is similar to that of the speed-gear of a bicycle or motor-car (*see* GEARING, Vol. VIII).

Express engines have driving-wheels of 6 ft. 3 in. to 6 ft. 9 in. diameter; goods or freight engines from 4 ft. 6 in. to 5 ft. 3 in., and 'mixed traffic' engines from 5 ft. 8 in. to 6 ft. 2 in. Railways are tending to build more general-purpose engines, which can pull either passenger or goods trains, and so can be used continuously throughout the day. In this category there are the 'Green Arrow' 2–6–2 and 'Antelope' 4–6–0 classes in the Eastern Region, with 6 ft. 2 in. driving-wheels; the hundreds of Class '5' 4–6–0 engines in the Midland Region, with 6-foot wheels; and the 6-foot 'Hall' 4–6–0 engines in the Western Region.

In early days a single pair of driving-wheels, such as those of the famous 'Stirling' 8-foot single-drivers on the one-time Great Northern Railway, provided enough adhesion for express passenger work; to-day for the heaviest and fastest passenger work we need at least three pairs of wheels coupled: in the United States many eight-coupled engines are used for this purpose.

In passenger work in Great Britain the 4–6–2 and 4–6–0 types are now most usual among tender engines. Freight trains are hauled by 0–6–0, 0–8–0, and 2–8–0 locomotives. General-purpose engines are mostly of the 2–6–0, 4–6–0, and 2–6–2 types. Of tank engines, 0–6–0 and

0–8–0 tanks are used largely for shunting, and 2–6–2 and 2–6–4 tanks for suburban and other short-distance passenger trains, but there are many other varieties.

North American railways, with more space round their tracks in which to build (*see* GAUGES, RAILWAY), have developed much larger locomotives. Some require additional bogies to support their fire-boxes at the rear of the boiler, and such wheel arrangements as 4–6–4, 4–8–4, 2–8–4, 4–8–2, 2–10–2, and 2–10–4 are common. Even larger engines are built on the articulated principle, with complicated wheel notation, especially in the United States (*see* ARTICULATED LOCOMOTIVES). Tenders in America are often carried on six-wheel bogies, and on the Pennsylvania Railroad eight-wheel bogies are used.

4. POWER RATING. Steam locomotives are also classified according to their power, and this regulates the load that each class can be expected to haul over any given route. In the Midland Region this power classification is shown on the locomotive as a figure on the side of the cab above the engine number, with the letter 'P' for 'passenger' and 'F' for 'freight'. Class '7P', the highest passenger classification, comprises the Pacific engines, Class '6P' the 'Royal Scot' 4–6–0 engines, Class '8F' the standard 2–8–0 freight engines, and so on. This system is being standardized by British Railways.

The pulling power of a steam locomotive is usually calculated from an engineering formula. Horse-power is not quoted, except in cases where it has been actually measured by a dynamometer car (*see* DYNAMOMETER, Vol. VIII). With ELECTRIC RAILWAY engines and DIESEL LOCOMOTIVES (qq.v.), however, horse-power figures are used.

5. CONTINENTAL NOTATION. On the continent of Europe the notation goes by axles and not by wheels. Thus in France, a 4–6–2 engine, by the Whyte notation, becomes an engine of the 2–3–1 type. Sometimes the notation forms a part of the number; for example, engine No. 141–602 may be No. 602 of the 1–4–1 (2–8–2 in the Whyte notation) type. In other countries, letters are used instead of numbers to indicate the coupled wheels—C for 6-coupled, D for 8-coupled, and so on. In this case, the British 4–6–2 becomes an engine of the 2–C–1 type.

The notation for electric or diesel-electric locomotives follows the Continental method in indicating driving-wheels by letters. If the driving-axles are all separately motor-driven without the driving-wheels being coupled together, the driving-wheel letter has a small 'o' as a suffix. For example, the electric locomotives for the Manchester–Sheffield electrification, which are carried on four-wheel bogies of which all axles are motor-driven and uncoupled, are of the Bo-Bo type. Experimental Southern Region electric locomotives are of the Co-Co type, being carried on six-wheel bogies with all axles motor-driven.

See also LOCOMOTIVE, STEAM; ELECTRIC RAILWAYS; DIESEL LOCOMOTIVE; GAS TURBINE LOCOMOTIVE.

LOCOMOTIVE, STEAM.

The various kinds of steam-engines which are described in LOCO-MOTIVES: CLASSES AND USES (q.v.) have some features common to most British types.

1. BOILER AND CAB. The long boiler which gives its main shape to a steam locomotive is familiar to all railway passengers, although the boilers of some of the fastest passenger engines are now hidden by stream-lined casings which are intended to increase speed by reducing the friction of the air. A locomotive boiler (see Fig. 1 a) consists of three parts, the fire-box (A) at the rear end, the smoke-box (B) at the front end, and the circular barrel connecting the two. Below the smoke-box at the front are the massive cylinders and the piston-valve chests (C). At the rear the fire lies on the fire-grate (D) in the inner fire-box (E), surrounded on all four sides and on top by the water contained in the outer fire-box.

On top of the boiler barrel most locomotives have a curved steel casing called the 'dome', which houses the 'regulator' (F). This has a use similar to that of the accelerator pedal of a motor-car. It controls the admission of steam from the boiler to the main steam-pipe (G)

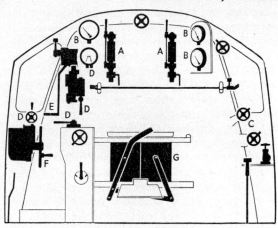

FIG. 2. FITTINGS IN A BRITISH RAILWAYS LOCOMOTIVE CAB

leading to the cylinders, and is worked by the driver's regulator handle (H) in the 'cab' in which he stands or sits. Above the fire-box are usually mounted the safety valves (I), which are spring-controlled and designed to allow steam to escape as soon as the working-pressure of the boiler is exceeded. In Western Region engines, steam is collected from the upper part of the fire-box (see Fig. 1 b J) and not in a dome; instead, the safety valves are mounted in the position of the dome (K).

Fittings in the driver's cab (see Fig. 2) include water gauges (A), to show the level of the water in the boiler; steam-pressure gauges (B); controls for the injectors (C) by which the boiler is supplied with additional water; controls for the BRAKES (D) (q.v.); in addition to the driver's regulator handle (E) and reversing gear (F). There is also the fire-hole door (G), through which the firing is done by the fireman.

2. STEAM AND CYLINDERS. The traditional principle of the railway steam-engine for more than a century has been to produce steam by heating water, and to cause the pressure of the steam in cylinders to move pistons which will turn the driving-wheels (see STEAM-ENGINE, Vol. VIII). The aim of modern locomotive design has been to make the most of the expansive properties of the steam. Boiler pressures have been raised, and the temperature of the steam has been increased by superheating to 750° F. With these improvements it is now possible for locomotives to haul very much heavier loads. In some locomotives the steam, after use in one or two high-pressure cylinders, is passed to two low-pressure cylinders for further expansion.

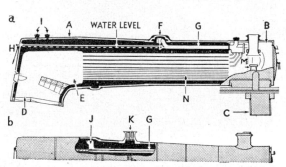

FIG. 1 a. SECTION OF BOILER
b. WESTERN REGION BOILER

This practice, which has reached its greatest development in France, is known as 'compounding'. With modern methods the pressure of the exhaust steam is relatively low, which means that a minimum of energy is being wasted up the chimney. The noisy exhaust of earlier days was often accompanied by a shower of sparks; these, however spectacular, were really particles of fuel thrown away when only partly consumed. By contrast, the modern locomotive at high speed is almost noiseless in its work.

The exhaust steam from the cylinders is used to provide the necessary draught for the fire. The steam is led to a nozzle, known as a blast-pipe (Fig. 1 M), which stands in the smoke-box under the chimney. The blast-pipe tapers inwards, so that the steam escapes from it with great force, spreading out in such a way as to fill the chimney and create strong suction. This draws air through the blazing mass of the fire, producing great heat. The heat is led through hundreds of fire tubes (N) which connect the fire-box with the smoke-box, so heating the water—though it is round the walls of the fire-box that steam is produced the most rapidly. In recent years the draught or suction has been increased by using extra blast-pipes. This is the reason for the double chimneys seen on London Midland Region 'Pacifics' and 'Royal Scot' 4–6–0's, and the large diameter chimneys on some Southern Region engines.

The cylinders, in which the pistons move, can be either outside the engine, where the passengers can see them, or inside—that is, under the boiler between the wheels. Outside cylinders are preferred nowadays; inside cylinders are less easy to get at, and also require a more complicated kind of axle. In many British locomotives, however, the use of three or four cylinders is replacing two-cylinder practice. The reason is connected with the restricted British loading gauge (see GAUGES, RAILWAY), which limits the size of engines to that of tunnels built long ago. There is insufficient room to mount two large enough cylinders either at the two sides of the engine, or inside, between the wheels. The bigger engines, therefore, have two medium-sized cylinders outside, and one or two inside. Four cylinders have been used for the 'King', 'Castle', and 'Star' class express engines of the Western Region and on some London Midland Region engines; three cylinders have been used on many Eastern and North-Eastern Region engines.

3. BOOSTERS. Many modern steam locomotives in the United States are provided with this form of auxiliary power. The booster is a small two-cylinder steam unit, usually arranged to drive a pair of small wheels at the rear of the main driving-wheels of the engine. Because of the small diameter of these wheels, the power exerted by the booster is great in relation to its size. The booster gives valuable auxiliary power when it is most needed, as when starting, or when climbing heavy inclines. As soon as the locomotive has reached a speed of 15 to 25 miles an hour, the booster is cut out of mesh (by an action somewhat similar to that of a free-wheel on a bicycle), so that at high speeds the locomotive is not hampered by frictional resistance from the auxiliary engine. Boosters have been tried in Great Britain; for various reasons they have not proved efficient, but chiefly because of the drain imposed on the steam production of the relatively small British boiler.

4. FUEL. Coal and oil are equally suitable for steam locomotives; a choice must be based on economic reasons. In Great Britain, with the best steam coal in the world, the obvious preference has been for coal; in California, with its own oil-fields and long distance from the nearest coal-fields, oil-firing is the natural choice. Some oil-firing locomotives have been used in Britain.

Anthracite coal can be burnt, but requires very large fire-boxes. Many locomotives on the Reading Railroad in the United States, which serves anthracite coal-fields, were designed with fire-boxes of such size that the driver's cab is perched on the middle of the boiler, ahead of

Reading Co., Philadelphia

'CAMEL-BACK' LOCOMOTIVE

the fire-box; the fireman has a separate shelter in the more usual position at the rear. These engines are sometimes known as 'Camel-backs'.

At times of fuel shortage, peat (in Ireland), lignite or brown coal (in central Europe), and even maize (in South America) have been used to fire locomotives, but with indifferent results. In some Eastern countries wood is used as fuel; the disadvantage is the speed with which it is used up, the constant stops needed for refilling the tenders, and the excessive throwing of sparks.

The most efficient use of oil as locomotive fuel is in the internal-combustion engine, the diesel engine in particular, and in the gas turbine. Instead of the roundabout method of turning the fuel into steam and the steam into work, as in the oil-fired steam locomotive, the burnt fuel of the internal-combustion engine provides the direct power, so that the loss of heat and energy that takes place in the process is much reduced.

See also DIESEL LOCOMOTIVE; ELECTRIC RAILWAYS; GAS TURBINE LOCOMOTIVE.

See also Vol. VIII: STEAM ENGINE.

LOG, SHIP'S. 1. This is the instrument used to measure the speed of a ship. Knowledge of the speed helps the navigating officer to calculate the position which a ship has reached (*see* NAVIGATION, MARINE). In the earlier days of sailing-ships the log was an actual piece of wood, which was tied to a very long line wound round a reel held by a sailor. The log was tossed over the side of the ship, and remained floating at the spot at which it fell. As the ship sailed on, the length of line in the sea, stretching from the ship to the log, grew longer. At intervals in the line were pieces of knotted cord; according to the number of these 'knots' which passed over the ship's side in the space of half a minute, the number of sea-miles sailed in an hour was known. Thus 5 sea-miles an hour was represented by the words '5 knots' (never 'knots an hour'). The half-minute was timed by a sand-glass (*see* CLOCKS, Vol. VIII). A sea-mile or nautical mile is 6,080 feet, or about one and a fifth ordinary or statute miles. The distance was chosen in order to make calculation easy: it equals one-sixtieth of a geographical degree.

The modern log is a precision instrument; it consists of a tiny propeller which is towed at the stern or side of a ship, or which sometimes projects through the ship's bottom. This propeller rotates a steel cable, which records the speed on dials on the ship's bridge and in the chart-room, engine-room, and other places, on the principle of a motor-car SPEEDOMETER (q.v. Vol. VIII).

2. LOG-BOOK. The word 'log' also refers to a log-book, in which the master of a ship is obliged to have a written record kept of everything of importance which concerns every journey. Changes in the speed and course of the ship, observations of wind and weather, records of other ships passed, and matters concerning the discipline of the crew must all be noted. Besides the ship's principal log-book, other log-books are kept in modern ships, including the engine-room log, which records the times of starting and stopping the various engines, and the speeds at which they are run. Such details can be important in the event of a dispute after a collision or other accident.

See also NAVIGATION, MARINE.

LONDON BRIDGE. Until the TOWER BRIDGE (q.v.) was opened in 1894, London Bridge was the last bridge across the Thames, down-stream. It connects the City of London with Bermondsey and Southwark. The Romans built a bridge near the present site of London Bridge; and so did the Saxons who succeeded them. In 1163 the whole timber structure of an existing bridge was renewed; and in 1176 a new stone bridge was begun a little farther up-stream, but was not finished until 1209. Three years later a fire swept both ends, trapping a number of people who were killed by burning or drowning. Towards the end of that century, after one of the great Thames frosts, five arches were carried away, and the bridge became 'so sore decayed for want of reparations that men were afraid to pass thereon'.

By the 14th century London Bridge had been built up again, and had shops and houses standing on it, and in the middle a chapel dedicated to St. Thomas of Canterbury. At each end stood a gate, the southern one being called the Stone Gate, and the northern one, where the heads of executed traitors were displayed, the Drawbridge Gate.

By the 16th century London Bridge had developed into a very elaborate structure. In his *Survey of London* (1603), the chronicler, John Stow describes it as 'a work very rare, having with the drawbridge twenty arches made of squared stone, of height 60 feet and in breadth 30 feet,

OLD LONDON BRIDGE FROM THE SURREY SIDE OF THE THAMES
IN 1616
From an engraving by Nicholas Visscher

distant from one another 20 feet, compact and joined together with vaults and cellars; upon both sides be houses built so that it seemeth rather a continual street than a bridge'. On the southern side the water-power of the river was put to good use, for mill-wheels were set in two of the arches.

In 1632, at a time when the river was frozen and therefore no water was available, a third of the houses were destroyed by fire. During the Great Fire of London in 1666, London Bridge

LONDON BRIDGE TO-DAY
Fox Photos.

suffered still further. Apart from these disasters, the structure was being constantly weakened by the stresses set up in the piers by ice during the hard winters. Fear for the safety of the bridge induced Parliament in 1756 to decree that all the buildings on the bridge should be pulled down. At the same time the bridge was widened to allow a 31-foot carriageway, with a 7-foot footway on either side. But by 1825 it was clear that still the bridge could not accommodate the gradually increasing traffic, and the present London Bridge, about 100 feet west of the old one, was begun. When completed in 1831 it was 53 ft. 6 in. wide; but additions made in 1902–4 increased the width to 65 feet.

See also Bridges.
See also Vol. III: London; Thames.

LONDON LIBRARY. This library was started by Thomas Carlyle (q.v. Vol. V), who found that there were no good lending-libraries in London for serious reading, and that it was not always convenient to study in the British Museum Library (q.v.), from which books could not be taken away. His aim was a library containing 'books in all departments of literature and philosophy, and in all languages, and whose subscribers should be able to have the books in their own homes, both in London and in the country'. In 1839 he began to interest some wealthy friends in his scheme, and in 1841, with their backing, the library was opened in two rooms in Pall Mall. There were about 500 members; each paid an entrance fee of £6 and a yearly subscription of £2; the library began with 3,000 books.

These books were carefully chosen, mostly by men of learning. The ordinary circulating library provided new books, especially for light reading. The London Library set out to build up stocks of books of permanent value. All the books were on open shelves, and there were no restrictions on borrowing by members, so long as books taken out were recorded.

From the beginning the London Library was used by many of the most distinguished people of the day. The first President was Lord Clarendon, the Foreign Secretary, who was succeeded by Thomas Carlyle himself. Among members have been Tennyson, Gladstone, Huxley, Darwin, Thackeray, and Macaulay, who wrote his famous history there.

The library received many valuable bequests

of books and it gradually grew in size. In 1845 it moved to its present home in St. James's Square. In 1934, after nearly a century of life, it was granted a Royal Charter. Although the library lost thousands of volumes when London was bombed in the Second World War, it contains half a million books, including much foreign literature. There are about 5,000 members; a new member must be introduced by an old member and approved by the elected committee of management.

See also LIBRARIES.

LONDON TRANSPORT. The London Transport Executive manage the largest co-ordinated road and rail system of urban passenger transport in the world. It covers a compact area of about 2,000 square miles, extending roughly 25 miles in all directions from Charing Cross, and it serves about one-fifth of the population of Britain. It carries its passengers by surface and underground trains, by buses and coaches, and by trams and trolley-buses. Its problem is to deal with nearly 13 million short journeys a day, and to deal with them with the greatest possible speed. If these journeys were spread out through the day fairly evenly, the problem would be considerably easier; but, in fact, one-half of the traffic flowing in and out of Central London is concentrated into 4 peak hours— 2 hours in the morning and 2 hours in the evening— when the mass of people are going to or from their work. As the tendency increases for those working in London to live farther and farther out in the suburbs, so do the problems of the London Transport Executive increase.

Until the beginning of the 19th century the River Thames was the only regular means of communication in London. Since then London has increased five times in size. In 1829 the first bus service was started in London with single-decker buses pulled by three horses. The buses were privately run and

competed with each other, though gradually owners of groups of buses amalgamated, and in 1885 the London General Omnibus Company was formed. In the meantime the idea of running a bus on a track had started in America, and between 1869 and 1871 the first horse-drawn trams were introduced to London. In 1863 a steam railway opened between Paddington and Farringdon Street and continued until it was electrified in 1905. The first underground railway, opened in 1890, was the City and South London Railway, an electric railway running between King William Street, in the City, and Stockwell. Before 1933, when the whole of London's transport was brought under public control, and the London Passenger Transport Board was set up, many different services ran trains, buses, and trams, all in competition with each other. When, in January 1948, the whole transport of the country was nationalized, the work of the Transport Board passed to the London Transport Executive, a body with a chairman, four full-time and three part-time members. By 1950, London's transport was carried 40% by the central buses, 30% by railways, suburban and 'tube', 21% by trams and trolley-buses, and 9% by country buses and coaches, such as the Green Line Coaches which run into London from the suburbs

London Transport Executive

LONDON'S LIFE-LINES
Poster showing how London Transport serves London and the surrounding country

as far out as Aylesbury in Buckinghamshire or Windsor in Berkshire.

The London Transport Executive have control of more than 240 miles of railway line, of which about 70 miles are 'tube'. There are six principal lines, the Metropolitan and District running mainly above ground, but including the Inner Circle which is mainly underground, and the Central, Bakerloo, Piccadilly, and Northern 'Tubes', running in 12-foot tunnels. Further 'tube' lines are being constructed. On some lines, during peak hours, as many as forty trains an hour are run. The coaches are designed to have plenty of standing space to accommodate the large numbers of standing passengers which must be carried morning and evening. Suburban lines are under the operational control of the main-line railways. Those suburban services which are still run by steam locomotives are gradually being electrified (*see* ELECTRIC RAIL-WAYS).

The road passengers of London in 1949 were carried by 7,200 buses and coaches, 1,800 trolley-buses, and 800 trams, which ran some 495 routes in all. Trams and trolley-buses are gradually being replaced by buses. For some years after the Second World War the service had to be run with a great many worn-out buses, and this put a great strain on the insufficient number of maintenance and repair garages and depots. The Chiswick Works, the main depot for major bus repairs, employs a staff of 5,000. The London Transport Executive now employ in all some 100,000 people, for whom is provided an elaborate welfare service, including some 200 canteens and good sports grounds and club rooms.

See also UNDERGROUND RAILWAY; BUS; TRAMWAY; TROLLEY-BUS; MOTOR TRANSPORT MAINTENANCE.

See also Vol. III: LONDON.

LONGITUDE, *see* MAP PROJECTIONS.

LORRY, *see* MOTOR TRANSPORT.

LOUD-SPEAKER. Electrical loud-speakers are all based on the principle of the vibrating diaphragm, which is common both to the telephone and to the wireless microphone (*see* SPEECH, TRANSMISSION OF). Differences in the size of the instrument and in the quantity of current used account for the strength of the loud-speaker's tones.

Increasing uses are being found for loud-speakers, quite apart from the part they play in the wireless receiver in the home. To make the voice of one person audible to a large audience in a hall, or to a crowd out of doors, a 'public address' system is used, made up of a microphone, amplifying apparatus, and one or more loud-speakers. Announcements and music at horse shows, gymkhanas, and sports meetings are frequently relayed by loud-speakers. In railway stations travellers are given information about trains by this means. In large hotels loud-speakers in all the public rooms will notify a particular guest if he is urgently wanted on the telephone. In factories and offices loud-speakers are sometimes used to give instructions to the staff (*see* OFFICE COMMUNICATIONS, Vol. VII).

The microphone, amplifiers, and loud-speakers can all be carried in a motor-car or van. This mobile form of public address is used by the police to control street traffic and sports crowds, and by political candidates to make announcements in the streets during elections.

Many ships are fitted with a very powerful loud-speaker known as a 'loud-hailer'; vessels can thus exchange information when within ear-shot, and in a big ship an officer can give orders to distant members of the crew. The loudest kind of loud-hailer is used for 'sky shouting'. This enables a low-flying aeroplane to address multitudes of people over an area of several square miles, whether they want to be addressed or not. During the Second World War this method was used for directing PROPAGANDA (q.v.) at enemy troops. Either someone travelling in a sky-shouting aeroplane could speak directly into the apparatus, or the aeroplane merely received on its wireless set propaganda broadcast from a distant wireless station, the programme being switched directly into the sky-shouting loud-speakers.

In some countries, particularly in time of war, loud-speakers are permanently installed in public places, so that official communications can be made to people in the streets. In the more remote parts of Asia, where the people do not possess wireless receivers in their homes, a communal loud-speaker is installed in the centre of the village, round which they may gather to hear the news.

M

MACADAM ROADS. John Loudon McAdam (1756–1836) was more than a famous road-maker: he was the inventor of the first new method of road-construction after the Roman Empire. Until his time all road-engineers had copied the Romans in laying an expensive foundation of heavy stones under their roads; McAdam proved that this was not only unnecessary, but for the traffic of those days worse than his own system. He was born at Ayr, Scotland, and when still at school showed his future bent by making a model road-section. At the age of 14 he went to the counting-house of an uncle in New York, from which he returned with a fortune only 13 years later, and settled in Ayrshire. He was made Deputy-Lieutenant of the county and road trustee, posts which encouraged him to study and experiment in road-making. In 1798 a new appointment took him to live at Falmouth, where he extended his hobby to the roads of the whole south-west of England. In 1816 he was made surveyor of the British Turnpike Trust (*see* TURNPIKE) of which he had been a trustee for some time. In less than 2 years he had put its 150 miles of roads into good repair, and by reducing the cost of upkeep, had lessened the Trust's debt by £2,000. Many other turnpike trusts now sought his advice—which he would always give free of charge—and by 1819 he had been appointed surveyor to no less than thirty-four of them. In that year he was invited to give evidence before a Parliamentary Commission which was inquiring into road administration. Despite the success of his roads and the width of his experience, his revolutionary theories met with great ridicule—though not from the other great road-builder of the time, TELFORD (q.v. Vol. V).

McAdam stated that he preferred no harder foundation for his road than the ordinary subsoil, and even had no objection to a springy one, such as a bog. A harder foundation was, he declared, undesirable because it increased the wear on the road-surface, as well as on the vehicles and the legs of the horses using it. On the subsoil he laid a single layer of from 10 to 12 inches of broken stones, both the quality and size of which were of great importance. No piece should exceed 1 inch in any direction or 6 ounces in weight; the material should be hard, but not too hard, and evenly wearing—such as hard limestone, sandstone, or certain basalts. For consolidation he relied at first on the action of the wheels themselves in grinding away a fine powder which, helped by rain, eventually formed an almost waterproof layer, cementing the surface together. Later, watering-carts and light rollers were used to give quicker results. The truth of McAdam's theories was proved not only by an examination of the roads themselves, but also by the fact that coach-horses, which were usually worn out after 3 years' service on ordinary roads, lasted much longer if their work kept them on springy macadam surfaces. In 1826 McAdam himself was made Surveyor-General of Metropolitan Turnpike Roads, an appointment which allowed him indirectly to introduce his system all over Britain. He was less successful in his efforts to institute a central road authority for the whole country (a step which was not taken until 1937—and then only partially). But the nation's gratitude to him was shown by a Parliamentary grant of £10,000. He was offered, but refused, a knighthood. Charles Dickens said of him: 'Our shops, our horses' legs, our boots, our hearts, have all been benefited by the introduction of McAdam.'

See also ROADS, BRITISH.
See also Vol. VIII: ROAD BUILDING.

MAGAZINES AND PERIODICALS. These are printed publications, issued weekly, fortnightly, monthly, or quarterly, and either sold to the public or sent to a list of subscribers or to members of some association. About 3,500 magazines and periodicals are regularly published in Britain. These do not include newspapers—that is, publications chiefly concerned with general news of passing events.

Modern magazines fall in several main groups. Among weeklies are:

Illustrated papers. Several leading magazines, originally based on American practice, publish

THINGS ONE WOULD RATHER HAVE EXPRESSED DIFFERENTLY

Fair Hostess. 'Good night, Major Jones. We're supposed to breakfast at nine; but we're not very punctual people. Indeed,
the later you appear to-morrow morning, the better pleased we shall all be!'
Drawing by George Du Maurier, from *Punch*, May 13th, 1893

topical articles accompanied by vigorous photographs taken by photographers who are among
the highest paid in the country.

'Society' papers. This is a small class of
magazines with many portraits and photographs
of people in the public eye.

News magazines. These, also inspired by
American practice, contain classified reports and
pictures of leading events of the week.

Women's papers. A large number of magazines are specially designed to appeal to women.
They are concerned with clothes and fashions,
care of the body and complexion, furnishing,
cookery, care of children, and the publication of
romantic fiction and articles about film-stars.
Some of these magazines have a very large sale.
Others reach the highest level of artistic production of any magazines in Britain.

Humorous papers. This is now a very small
class among magazines. Its most distinguished
journal is *Punch*, which has appeared weekly
since 1841. Many famous artists have drawn
in its pages, including Richard Doyle, whose

design for the front cover has been in use for
over 100 years, Sir John Tenniel, the original
illustrator of *Alice in Wonderland*, Charles Keene,
George Du Maurier, Phil May, and Sir Bernard
Partridge. Thackeray among novelists, and
Thomas Hood and Tennyson among poets, have
figured in its lists of contributors.

Literary and political papers. These include
serious journals of considerable influence, which
comment, generally every week, on politics,
finance, social problems, and on newly published books. Among these magazines are *The
Economist, The Listener, The Times Literary Supplement, The Spectator, Time and Tide*, and *The New
Statesman*. Signed articles by eminent authorities
are regularly printed by some. *The Listener*
reprints the more important B.B.C. talks, and
also publishes original articles.

Juveniles' magazines. This is a large and
popular group. It ranges from papers for growing boys and girls to 'comics' for smaller children.
At one time there was a fashion for stories about
boys and girls at imaginary public schools, and

thousands of grown-up people remember with pleasure the days when they read of such characters as 'Billy Bunter'. Many papers, including *The Scout*, have a serious and useful purpose, and convey valuable information as well as entertainment.

Film and sport papers. A large number of publications print news of film-stars and of various forms of sport and athletics.

Technical and trade papers. This is one of the largest groups. It includes trade and professional magazines which deal solely with special subjects such as building, school-teaching, road transport, engineering, film-making, shipping, the drapery trade, and similar interests.

Apart from weekly magazines, there are many monthly and quarterly journals devoted to such learned subjects as medicine, surgery, archaeology, astronomy, languages, history, geography, art, and poetry.

The early history of magazines and periodicals is closely associated with that of newspapers (*see* NEWSPAPERS, HISTORY OF). In the last quarter of the 19th century, when universal education had been established by law in England, many popular magazines were founded and reached large circulation. One of the most notable of all was the *Strand Magazine*, an illustrated monthly in which the detective stories about Sherlock Holmes, by Arthur Conan Doyle, first appeared.

In recent years magazines have met with increasing competition from films, wireless programmes, and the 'features' page of newspapers.

The largest magazine circulations in the world are achieved in America. The great size of the United States prevents any daily newspaper being distributed over the whole country, as is done in Britain. With weekly magazines, however, such as the *Saturday Evening Post, Collier's, Time*, and *Life*, there is time to arrange for distribution over the whole United States.

See also NEWSPAPERS, HISTORY OF.
See also Vol. XII: PERIODICALS.

MAIL TRAIN, *see* POST OFFICE.

MANCHESTER SHIP CANAL. At the beginning of the 18th century the Mersey was navigable for barges only as far as Warrington; and Manchester, a rapidly growing industrial city, felt the need of direct communication with the sea. In 1720 the navigation of the Rivers Irwell and Mersey was improved, so that barges could reach Manchester; and in 1761 Brindley completed the first section of the Bridgewater Canal between Worsley and Barton, and later extended it to Runcorn and on to Leigh. In the early 19th century a junction was made with the Leeds–Liverpool Canal at Leigh. But the rivers and the canal, having narrow locks, could transport only small barges, each carrying about 50 tons. The high cost of transport forced many factories to close, and so people left Manchester; soon there were more than 18,000 empty houses.

There had been several proposals from as early as 1712 to construct a canal which would bring Manchester into touch with the sea, 35 miles away. An Act of Parliament was obtained in 1885, after meeting with great opposition from the Liverpool railway shareholders and others. Construction began in 1887, the work being divided into nine sections. As Manchester stands 60 feet above sea-level, five sets of locks were made to raise the canal the necessary

Geo. Newnes, Ltd.
ORIGINAL COVER OF 'THE STRAND MAGAZINE'

MANCHESTER SHIP CANAL

height. The Eastham locks are tidal; the other four have an average rise of $13\frac{1}{4}$ feet. The outlet to the Mersey is at Eastham, where the largest entrance lock is 600 feet in length by 80 feet in width. The other locks are rather smaller. The Bridgewater Canal originally crossed the River Irwell at Barton by means of a stone aqueduct, designed and built by James Brindley for the Duke of Bridgewater in the 18th century. On the building of the Manchester Ship Canal, this fixed aqueduct was replaced by a steel swing aqueduct mounted on a pier in the middle of the ship canal. The aqueduct swings open to allow ships to navigate the Manchester Ship Canal, and when shut, it becomes once more a continuous section of the Bridgewater Canal.

The canal was opened in 1894. It cost £15,000,000, or £8,000,000 more than had been expected. It is 30 feet deep for the first 5 miles and then 28 feet deep. Large ocean-going cargo vessels regularly navigate the waterway. The total tonnage of revenue-paying traffic in the year 1918 was $3\frac{1}{2}$ millions; in 1925 nearly 6 millions, and before the Second World War it rose to just under 7 millions, with some 5,000 ships entering and clearing the canal each year.

Ellesmere Port—3 miles from Eastham—is the terminus of the Shropshire Union Canal, which runs through Chester, Shropshire, and Staffordshire to the Midlands, and there are docks, wharves, warehouses, coal-tips, and granaries at this point. $4\frac{1}{2}$ miles from Eastham, at Stanlow oil docks, there are special docks for oil-tankers, and storage tanks that will hold approximately 100,000,000 gallons of oil. The new oil dock at Eastham is for tankers of 34,000 tons. At Runcorn there are 70 acres of docks and warehouses, and at Manchester there are 6 miles of wharves, 85 miles of railway line, and scores of warehouses and cranes.

Manchester, judged by the value of its trade, is one of the principal ports in the United Kingdom. Between 1894 and 1911 all the empty houses in the city became occupied and more than 34,000 more were built. Many new industries have been established, and there is now a population of more than 14,000,000 within a radius of 75 miles.

See also CANALS, BRITISH.
See also Vol. III: MANCHESTER.

MANUSCRIPT, *see* BOOKS, HISTORY OF; WRITING. *See also* Vol. XII: ILLUMINATED MANUSCRIPTS.

MAPS, HISTORY OF. There is evidence that many ancient peoples, whether civilized or not, drew maps and plans. Both civilized and uncivilized people still do. The oldest maps in existence are on small baked clay tablets found in the ruins of Babylonian cities. Many of these are to be seen in the British Museum, and one in the Museum of Harvard University, U.S.A., is said to be 4,500 years old. The Egyptians also made maps, but since these were drawn on papyrus, a material resembling PAPER (q.v.), little of their work has survived. There is reference to a map in Chinese literature from 227 B.C. The Chinese had mapped their country long before Europeans went there.

The ancient Greeks are regarded as the pioneers of modern map-making. They were aided by their knowledge of astronomy, their belief that the earth was spherical, and their eagerness to learn all they could from travellers on land or sea. In the 3rd century before Christ, a Greek named Eratosthenes estimated the size of the earth with remarkable accuracy. In the 2nd century after Christ, another Greek named Ptolemy prepared details for the drawing of many maps, though whether he actually drew them is uncertain (*see* FIG. 1). Many scholars and sailors of much later times, including Christopher Columbus, regarded Ptolemy as an authority, and his influence was clearly seen in maps as late as A.D. 1700.

FIG. I. OUTLINE MAP FROM PTOLEMY'S 'WORLD'

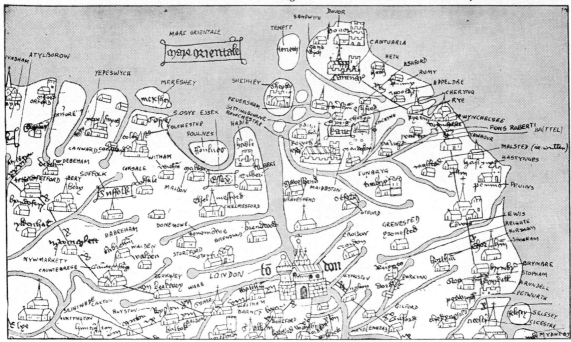

FIG. 2. DETAIL SHOWING LONDON AND PART OF KENT FROM THE GOUGH MAP OF ENGLAND, DRAWN ABOUT 1355
The map is drawn with the East at the top

No Roman maps survive, but we know that the Romans made maps; indeed, they could not have planned their fine system of roads or governed their great Empire without them; and we can obtain some idea of their maps from later maps based upon them, and from descriptions. It seems that the Empire filled nearly the whole space on their world maps, with a very small China and other countries at the outer edge, and, of course, nothing of America, South Africa, or Australia. Chinese maps of about this period show China in the centre and the rest of the world as very unimportant islands round the outside. In many ways the most remarkable map connected with the Roman Empire is one drawn in the 12th century by a monk at Colmar, a city near the river Rhine. It is believed that he copied it either from a 4th-century map, or a copy of a 4th-century map. This copy of the Roman map measures 21 feet long and 1 foot wide, and is a diagram of the road system from south-east Britain to the River Ganges in India. It was acquired by Konrad Peutinger, Keeper of the Archives at Augsburg, near Colmar, in the 16th century. It is usually known as the Peutinger Table, or Map. One difficulty in studying ancient maps is that they were copied by hand,

many of them in monasteries, and possibly no two were exactly alike.

The first notable map of England, apart from that based on Ptolemy, was produced by Matthew Paris about A.D. 1250. His information probably came from other hand-drawn maps, word accounts, and travellers. North is at the top—though Arabs and Romans usually put South at the top, while the Church favoured East. Another map a century later, known as the Gough Map (*see* FIG. 2), is accurate enough to show that all Britain had been surveyed, though nothing is known of the methods employed.

Many attempts were made in the Middle Ages to represent the world according to Scriptural references, but the resulting maps gave no help to the traveller, as they bore no more resemblance to the real world than drawings would to Heaven if based on references in the Book of Revelation. One of the best-known church maps is a large one preserved at Hereford Cathedral.

From about A.D. 1300 and onwards, for three centuries, many excellent charts were drawn, depicting especially the coast-line of the Mediterranean sea. They are called Portolan Charts (*see* CHARTS).

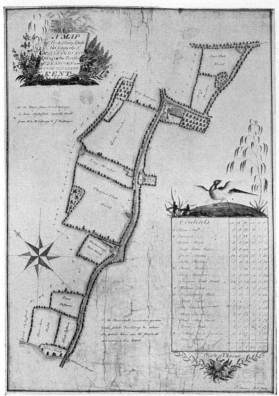

ESTATE MAP OF 1809 OF HOCKELBURY PARK IN KENT
The Ordnance Survey gradually took the place of estate
maps drawn for private landowners.

Two events occurred in the 16th century which are important to the history of maps. One was the work of a Dutchman known as Mercator. He not only worked out the MAP PROJECTION (q.v.) which bears his name, and which has helped sailors and airmen all over the world to navigate their craft from place to place, but he combined a framework of lines of latitude and longitude with the accurate type of survey work seen in Portolan Charts. The second notable event was the development of map-engraving, which enabled maps to be printed in large numbers, and all exactly alike. This gave rise to large map-publishing businesses.

At first no name existed for the numerous map collections bound in book form. Then Mercator chose to call his collection 'Atlas', perhaps because a picture of a legendary Greek giant called Atlas, who held up the heavens on his shoulders, was sometimes prefixed to such collections. So to-day all collections of maps in book form are called atlases. In 1579 a York-

shireman, Christopher Saxton, published the first national atlas of England and Wales, his maps being on fairly large scales and a blaze of brilliant hand colouring. The Dutch also published some notable atlases from about this time onward.

The 18th century saw many governments take over the task of map-making and map-publishing. At the request of King Louis XV, Caesar Cassini (1714–84), one of a very distinguished French family of mathematicians and surveyors, started to map France on a scale of about $\frac{3}{4}$ inch to the mile. Meanwhile General William Roy (1726–90), post office official, soldier, historian, antiquarian, and Surveyor-General of the Coasts, who had many years previously drawn an excellent map of Scotland with little more than a compass, started accurate surveying in South-East England with a large theodolite, the finest SURVEYING INSTRUMENT of its day (q.v. Vol. VIII), specially made for him and paid for by the king. One of the objects of the survey work done by Cassini and Roy was to determine the exact position of Paris and London relative to each other on the earth's surface. After Roy's death the surveying of England was adopted by the Board of Ordnance (the department of the army which supplied guns and ammunition), which eventually gave rise to the name Ordnance Survey. The first maps resulting from this survey were published in black and white, on a scale of 1 inch to the mile, in 1801. They were the first of a series which has remained unsurpassed in accuracy and unrivalled in completeness by the maps of any other national survey.

The Ordnance Survey has since published maps of the whole of Britain on various scales from one-millionth, where 1 inch of map shows nearly 16 miles of country, to maps where the scale is 6 inches to the mile. Maps of five-sixths of Britain have been published on a scale of 25 inches to the mile. These maps, or plans as they are called, show such details as individual fields and houses and their areas. New plans are being prepared of all towns and cities in Britain on a scale of 50 inches to the mile. On these the size of a house can be measured, and house numbers are shown. They are in black and white only, but many of the smaller-scale maps are printed in colours by methods which have been perfected since they were first introduced in the middle of last century. There is a map for every purpose: large-scale plans for engineers, surveyors, town

SOUTH OF HENLEY-ON-THAMES

Reproduced from the 6-inch Ordnance Survey Map with the sanction of the Controller of H.M. Stationery Office

planners; 6 inches to the mile plans for detailed study of small localities; 2½-inches and 1-inch maps for walkers; and ½-inch and ¼-inch maps for cyclists and motorists.

The first reference to a terrestrial globe comes from the Greeks. Crates of Mallus made a globe about 150 B.C. The oldest which has survived was made in 1492 by Martin Behaim of Nuremburg. When, a few years later, Magellan's voyage (*see* EXPLORATION) really proved the spherical shape of the earth, globes became popular. They frequently showed not only the latest discoveries, but included imaginary lands, such as Terra Australis, which were put in to give the globe a balanced look. Globes were carried as part of a ship's equipment, and used by such men as COLUMBUS, MAGELLAN, FROBISHER, and DRAKE (qq.v. Vol. V). They were also used in places of learning in Europe as early as the beginning of the 16th century. By the late 18th century they were at the height of their beauty and usefulness, and employed in the education of every young gentleman and gentlewoman. To-day maps and charts are so cheap, varied, and easily stored, that globes are largely neglected.

All highly developed areas of the world are now mapped, and work of great accuracy is not limited to Europe. Maps of the survey of India, for example, are among the most accurate in the world, and Mount Everest, the highest mountain in the world, is named after one of India's greatest surveyors, Sir George Everest. Large areas of the earth's surface, however, still remain unsurveyed and unmapped, chiefly the sparsely inhabited tropical forests, the great deserts and tundras, and the more recently discovered countries of vast extent such as the United States, Australia, South Africa, and Canada. The governments of these countries aim at mapping the whole of the usable part of their territory on a scale of about 1 inch to the mile, and at having coloured maps like those of Britain. They have large areas already mapped on this and other scales. Map-makers to-day are much helped by photographs taken from specially equipped aeroplanes.

Since 1891 a scheme has been developed to produce maps of the whole world, uniform in appearance and style, on a scale of about 16 miles to the inch. This is a great task and will take many years, but its completion will be an important landmark in the history of maps. A scheme has been evolved in the Massachusetts

Institute of Technology, U.S.A., to construct a globe on the same scale, which will be nearly 42 feet in diameter.

In recent years new kinds of maps have been developed to show such things as the distribution of rainfall, temperature, population, crops, and other things of importance and interest. These are called distribution maps, or statistical maps, to distinguish them from the topographical maps already described. At least four maps a day are made by the Air Ministry showing the weather over north-west Europe, and from a study of these, experts prepare the weather forecasts which are broadcast regularly by the B.B.C. (*see* WEATHER FORECASTING, Vol. III). Dot maps, each dot representing a certain number of, say, pigs, are used to show the distribution of crops and animals. Very few people could form as clear a picture by looking at rows of figures listing how many pigs or poultry were in the hundreds of parishes in England. Other statistical maps use colours or different kinds of shading, and still others use lines, such as the contours on topographical maps which bring out the distribution of high and low land (*see* MAP READING), or the isotherms which show the distribution of temperature.

See also MAP PROJECTIONS; MAP-READING; CHARTS; EXPLORATION.

See also Vol. VIII: SURVEYING.

MAP PROJECTIONS.

A globe is a model of the world, and if it is fairly large, all countries can be shown on it true in shape, relative size, and position, though it is impossible to see them all at the same time. If one took off the skin of the globe, as one skins an orange, and tried to lay it flat on a table, one could only succeed by slitting it, or stretching it here and shrinking it there. But if one did this the shapes and relative sizes and positions of the countries would alter; and this is what happens whenever one draws a flat map of the world.

Another way of obtaining a map of the world would be to take pencil and paper and copy the globe-skeleton—the lines of latitude and longitude—for once the skeleton is drawn it is easy to sketch in the coast-lines. The middle part of such a map would come out fairly well, but there would be uncertainty about the spacing of the meridians, or lines of longitude as they are also called, which run from pole to pole. Should they be equally spaced as on a globe, or drawn closer together towards the outsides, as they would appear on a photograph of a globe? (See p. 289.) And should all skeleton lines be straight or curved? There is no answer to these questions. The truth is that it is just as impossible to copy the skeleton, or 'net', with complete accuracy from the globe as to make a globe-skin lie flat without stretching it in places. Some plan for drawing the net has to be decided upon, and the result is called the map projection. Some projections are excellent to show Polar regions but of little use to show Equatorial lands; some maintain relative sizes of countries but distort shape; and some are valuable for navigation, but of little use for distribution or statistical maps. There is no limit to the number of projections that can be invented, though few are in constant use. An atlas contains examples of all the commonest, and the name of the particular projection used is usually printed in small letters beneath each map.

Projections are often regarded as falling into three groups called conical, zenithal, and cylindrical. The surface of a sphere cannot, as has been shown, be transferred to a flat piece of paper, but this is not so with cones and cylinders. When conical or cylindrical projections are used, the world is treated as if it were a cone or a cylinder, and maps made on these projections can be rolled up until their edges join to make a conical or cylindrical shaped world. When map-makers use zenithal projections, it is as if they were drawing the world from its zenith, that is, the point directly above some point on the earth's surface.

One of the commonest conical projections has all lines of longitude drawn as radial straight lines, like spokes of part of a wheel meeting at one point, though this point need not be shown on the map. The lines of latitude, or parallels, are all equally spaced arcs, that is, parts of circles centred on the pole. An example is seen in Fig. 1. Such a projection and many variants of it, including those which have meridians slightly curved, are much used to show countries in temperate latitudes, such as those in Europe.

Zenithal projections can be used to show Polar regions. The Pole is then at the centre of the map and the parallels are circles round it, the meridians again resembling wheel spokes, as in Fig. 2. Not all zenithal projections have the Pole at the centre.

The commonest cylindrical projection is named

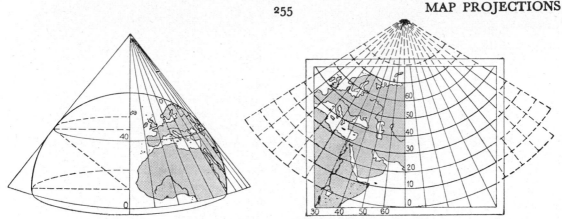

FIG. I. CONICAL PROJECTION

after a Dutchman known as Mercator, who planned it in the 16th century. Though so old, it is used by every sailor or pilot concerned with navigation. On all cylindrical projections the meridians are drawn as straight lines, all the same length from north to south, and the parallels as straight lines, all the same length from east to west. The meridians are always equally spaced, as in Fig. 3, but the parallels are not always equally spaced. Mercator said in effect 'North and south of the Equator my map has been stretched in an east-west direction so that the meridians never meet. I will balance this by stretching each part of the map equally in a north-south direction.' On Mercator's projection regions outside the tropics are therefore much larger than they should be (Iceland, for instance, appears seven times as large as it would

if it were on the Equator, and Great Britain three times as large), but because they have been stretched equally in all directions, their shape is not much distorted.

This balanced stretching has one effect of enormous importance to navigators. It maintains true compass directions between points. In Fig. 4, the position of two towns is shown, first as they appear on Mercator's projection, and secondly as on an ordinary cylindrical projection. An airman would always choose his compass direction from the Mercator map, because he knows it will get him to his destination, and that any other projection, such as an ordinary cylindrical one, would mislead him.

If a piece of string is stretched tightly on a globe between London and Australia, it will be seen to pass over Moscow and Chungking. This

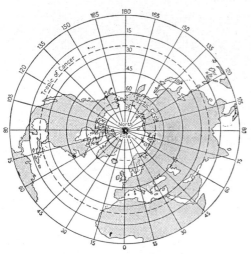

FIG. 2. ZENITHAL PROJECTION

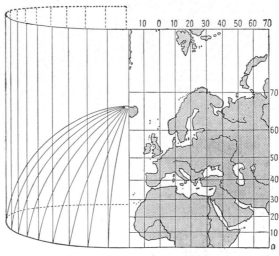

FIG. 3. MERCATOR'S PROJECTION

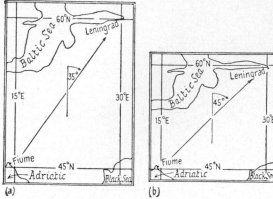

FIG. 4. COMPASS BEARING ON (a) MERCATOR'S PROJECTION, AND (b) AN ORDINARY CYLINDRICAL PROJECTION

is the shortest, or Great Circle, route, but it cannot be navigated by compass because its compass bearing is constantly changing. Thus the straight line routes on Mercator are rarely the shortest routes, but something near enough can always be plotted by transferring the route from globe to Mercator, and breaking the resulting curved lines into a series of straight legs, called loxodromes or rhumb lines, and changing compass direction wherever indicated on the chart. Thus rhumb lines London–Moscow–Chungking–Darwin–Sydney could be followed by compass and would be shorter than the line London–Sydney drawn direct on Mercator.

For practical purposes of easy reference it is often desirable to draw over a map a series of squares, called a grid (see MAP-READING), regardless of lines of latitude and longitude which may be straight or curved.

See also MAPS, HISTORY OF; MAP-READING; CHARTS; COMPASS.

MAP-READING. Just as it takes pains and skill and training to be a good map-maker, so it takes all these to be a good map-reader. The draughtsman compresses a great deal of information into a very small space by accurate scale-drawing, and using different styles of printing, colour, abbreviations, and symbols. The map-reader can get a great deal of information by careful attention to the map itself and to the key, and by coming to see not the piece of paper on which the map is printed, but the landscape as the map-maker saw it.

The Ordnance Survey, which has been responsible for producing official maps of Britain

for $1\frac{1}{2}$ centuries, prepares many kinds for different purposes. They vary in scale, the largest planned being 50 inches to 1 mile, the smallest about $\frac{1}{16}$ inch to 1 mile. The large-scale maps are published in black and white and the small-scale maps in colour. The most generally useful and interesting are on the scale of 1 inch to the mile, and $2\frac{1}{2}$ inches to the mile. They are full of detail, printed in colours, and are useful for cycling and walking.

The name of the sheet is usually taken from the name of an important town in the area, such as Dover; or a district, such as the Lake District; or a natural feature, such as a mountain or a lake, like Snowdonia or Crater Lake. Unless one is quite certain where the area lies, one should look up its exact position in an atlas. Latitude and longitude, which are always marked on the edges of the sheet, may be helpful. Next one should look at the scale of the map. This is likely to be stated in words, such as 'One inch to the mile', or by a fraction such as 1/63,360, which means that 1 inch, foot, yard, or centimetre on the map represents 63,360 inches, feet, yards, or centimetres on the ground. Scale lines are also probably drawn and divided to show miles and furlongs. The length and breadth of the land area shown on the map can then be pictured in the mind.

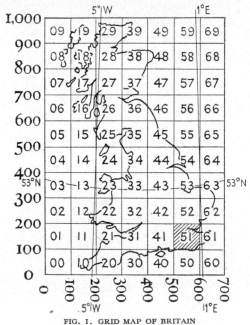

FIG. I. GRID MAP OF BRITAIN

The side of each square is 100 kilometres long

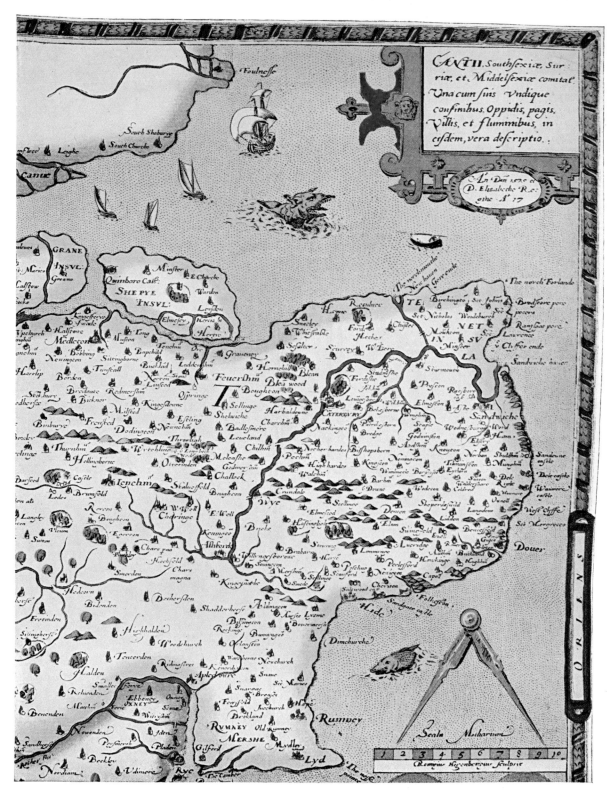

DETAIL FROM SAXTON'S MAP OF KENT, SURREY, SUSSEX, AND MIDDLESEX

Engraved on copper and coloured, 1575

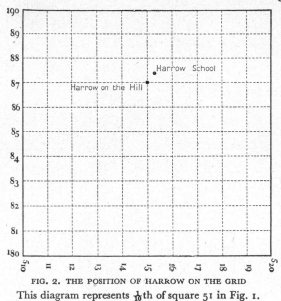

FIG. 2. THE POSITION OF HARROW ON THE GRID

This diagram represents $\frac{1}{10}$th of square 51 in Fig. 1.

The standard means of identifying a 1-inch Ordnance Survey map, or a point on it, is the grid system. This consists of a pattern of vertical and horizontal lines, forming exact squares, which is printed across every map of any part of the country (except old copies printed before the introduction of the system). Each square is a square kilometre; its side is 1,000 metres long, or 1,093 yards (about five-eighths of a mile). The bottom left-hand corner of this vast grid is at a point on the map some distance south-west of the Cornish coast (*see* Fig. 1). Once this is known, every point in Britain can be described by a group of figures. The old town of Harrow-on-the-Hill, for instance, on the north-west edge of London, is 515 kilometres east of the western edge of the grid, and 187 kilometres north of its southern edge. Therefore the figure 515187 will pick out Harrow-on-the-Hill from any other place in Britain. The reference is always derived by giving first the eastward figure, then the northward one. In practice, the figure for 'hundreds' is generally left out, since the actual region in Britain will be known. One would refer to Harrow-on-the-Hill as being at 1587 on a certain sheet of the map. One can also give a location to within 100 metres or less, since the system is based on division into tenths. The famous public school at Harrow is some 400 metres east of the '15' line. Therefore it can be located by the eastward figure 154, that is, 15

kilometres and four-tenths. Similarly, the northward figure 873 shows the school to be 87 kilometres and three-tenths northward. Thus the reference 154873 will locate Harrow School within 100 metres (*see* Fig. 2). One could go on in this way to get within 10 metres of the school tuckshop. If necessary, the figure for the 100-kilometre square can be placed in front, thus 51/154873.

The map key, which is usually printed at the bottom of the sheet, should be studied carefully. The keys which are used on Ordnance Survey maps vary with the scale, but all have much in common with that shown in Fig. 4, which is taken from the modern 1-inch map. This key is here printed in black only, and should have the following key colours to make it agree with the maps: all water should be shown blue, and glass-houses crossed with blue; woods and public parks green; National Trust areas edged in green; railway stations and Class 1 roads red; the next three road classes yellow; and contours brown.

The relief or nature of the surface of the region is shown by the contour lines. These are imaginary lines joining up points of the same height above sea-level, or depths below it. Imagine that a model of an island is put in a tank (*see* Fig. 3 A). The bottom of the tank represents sea-level; and the side of the tank is marked off in

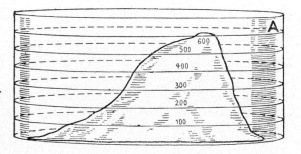

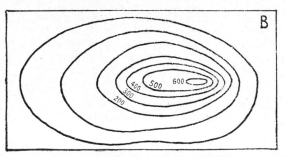

FIG. 3. DIAGRAM TO EXPLAIN CONTOURS

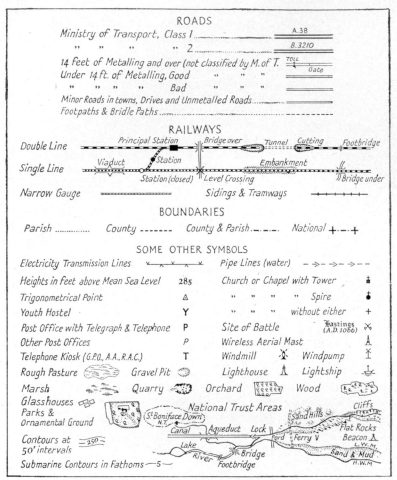

FIG. 4. SYMBOLS USED IN I-INCH ORDNANCE SURVEY MAPS
Reproduced with the sanction of the Controller of H.M. Stationery Office

are crowded, land is steep, and where they are few and far between, land is fairly flat It is possible from the contours, which are numbered to show height in feet above sea-level, to get a picture of the surface of the land. The best way to acquire this ability is to take the map to a place in the region from which a good view can be obtained, spread the map out with 'North' in the right direction, and then discover which contour forms represent the hills and valleys. A COMPASS (q.v.) helps in getting the map the right way round, because it will be seen that each map has placed on it an arrow labelled 'Magnetic North', which, when brought into line with the compass needle, means that the map is correctly arranged or orientated. As the magnetic pole is not fixed (see MAGNETISM, Vol. III), the arrow on an out-of-date map may not point exactly to the magnetic north. Sometimes

inches. Looked down on from directly above, the outline of the island would be seen as it would look on a map. If water is now poured into the tank so as to fill it up to the first inch-mark on the side, the outline of the island will be seen to have changed a little, and grown smaller. If the two outlines were drawn on a sheet of paper, they would appear as a couple of wavy shapes one inside the other, every point of the inner one being 1 inch above sea-level—that is to say, that line is a 1-inch contour line. With another inch of water in the tank, the map would show a third line, following the new water-level. That would be the 2-inch contour line, every point on it being 2 inches above sea-level. And so we could continue, until we had a complete contour map of the island, as in Fig. 3B. Where contours

an aerial photo and a map may be compared. Another excellent way to learn to read contours is to make a relief model. All but the largest scale topographical maps have contours; some have in addition layer colours, such as greens for low land and browns for high land; hachures or small lines at right angles to the contours help to give an idea of relief; shading represents shadows, as on a model; and spot heights are marked with their height above sea-level in feet printed beside them.

It will be found that many valleys contain streams, in which case V-shaped contours point up-stream. Canals mainly keep to the level, and therefore follow the contours. Sometimes streams disappear if they sink in porous rocks, such as limestone, or are artificially made to run underground, as through a town. Elsewhere numerous streams may start all at about the same level, often where a layer of clay underlies porous rocks, giving rise to a line of springs.

These maps give a good deal of information about vegetation, from rough pasture to woods and orchards. Where no distinctive vegetation is shown in the open country, the land can be assumed to be cultivated or in grass. Among the most interesting features may be those which have been made by man, such as the roads and railways which usually follow the easiest routes from place to place, or the footpaths which often take the shorter and more difficult cuts. The many signs for such things as wind-pumps and lighthouses are small drawings of the things they represent, while the symbol which is used for things such as youth hostels and post offices is the initial letter of the word. Objects which are shown fall into two groups: some, like wireless aerial masts, are easy to see in the field, and are therefore of help in locating one's position; and others, such as a post office, are things which a traveller may want to use.

See also MAPS, HISTORY OF; MAP PROJECTIONS.

MARCONI, *see* WIRELESS.

MARY CELESTE, *see* DERELICTS.

MARSHALLING YARDS form an essential part of goods train working. These yards or sidings are laid out at strategic points on the railways. Trains consisting of mixed wagons for various destinations (known as 'pick-up trains') are taken to the marshalling yards; there the wagons are sorted out and reassembled as 'through' goods trains which can be hauled for long distances. In many smaller yards the sorting is still performed by shunting engines, which pull the trains out to a shunting 'neck', and propel the wagons one by one into their appropriate sidings. Many years ago, however, it was realized that gravity could play a useful part in this operation, and the first gravity marshalling yard came into being at Edge Hill, Liverpool. In a yard of this kind, the wagons of a train to be sorted are uncoupled, and the train is pushed by a locomotive over a 'hump', a small artificial hill which is built for the purpose and over which the rails are led; on the far side of this 'hump' the track descends steeply for a short distance, so that the wagons draw away from one another;

as the switches are reached which give access to the various sidings, each wagon is switched to its proper track, either by hand or by mechanical means.

In the most modern yards, such as those at Hull, March (Cambridgeshire), and Toton (near Nottingham), the work of hump shunting has been greatly speeded up by being completely mechanized. Before each train to be sorted is taken over the hump, a list of destinations of the sequence of wagons is sent by pneumatic tube to the control tower. There, code patterns representing these destinations are punched into a card, which forms part of a long roll. This roll is fed into the machine operating the switches that give access to the groups of sidings. The effect is that each wagon automatically sets the correct switch for the wagon which follows it. By the time the wagons reach the series of electrically-worked switches leading to the individual sidings, they are well apart. The chief operator, who works in a high tower, has a wagon sequence list before him, and uses his press-button controls to turn each wagon into its appropriate siding. Immediately below the switches, rail-brakes are installed in each track; the speed of each wagon can be controlled from the tower, by the gripping

British Railways

WAGONS RUNNING OVER THE HUMP TO MARSHALLING SIDINGS
AT MARCH IN CAMBRIDGESHIRE

of the wheels as they pass through the rail-brakes, to avoid violent impacts between wagons if they run into sidings which are nearly full.

See also GOODS TRAIN.

MATHEMATICAL NOTATION.

Mathematics has to be written down in such a way that the sense is absolutely precise and cannot be misunderstood, whoever reads it. Mathematicians, therefore, have devised many signs and symbols which always have special meanings, and form a kind of international language with a special purpose. The most commonly used are those for addition (+), subtraction (−), multiplication (×) and the sign of equality (=). The division sign (÷) is used most commonly in school arithmetic books, and much less elsewhere than the others already mentioned. Instead, the figure to be divided is generally written over a horizontal line, and the divisor beneath the line $\left(12 \div 3 \text{ is written } \dfrac{12}{3}\right)$.

To most people $1+2 = 3$ means that if one is added to two the result is three. But mathematicians, as well as engineers, surveyors, accountants, and many other people who use mathematics, often want to write down things without using actual figures. They sometimes use a letter of the alphabet, in place of figures, to represent a quantity. If a bus inspector wanted to count the number of spectators who arrived by bus to see a football match, he need not count all the passengers each time. Provided that all the buses were full and that all the passengers got off, the inspector need merely count the number of bus-loads, and he could soon work out the number of passengers from that. But if there were two kinds of bus, single-deckers carrying 38 passengers and double-deckers carrying 56 passengers, he would have to be careful to distinguish between them. He could decide, to save himself trouble, to call a single-decker bus 'a' and a double-decker 'b'. Then, if he saw five single-deckers and seven double-deckers, he need simply write down $5a$ and $7b$, and later, when the rush was over, he could quietly work out five times 38 and seven times 56. To use letters in this way it is not even necessary always to know what quantity a letter represents. For instance, a foreigner, who did not know the number of passengers a full bus would hold, could just as easily write down $5a$ and $7b$, and

then make inquiries to find out the capacity of an 'a' bus and a 'b' bus.

There is no limit to what can be done by using letters as symbols of quantities in this way. The practice was acquired in the Middle Ages from learned Arabs, from whom we get its name 'algebra': the English scientist, Sir Isaac NEWTON (q.v. Vol. V) called it 'universal arithmetic'.

To every mathematician, $a+b-c = d$ means that when the quantity a is added to the quantity b and the quantity c is subtracted from this sum, the result is equal to the quantity d. So if a people get on to an empty bus at its first stop, b people get on at the second, and c people get off at the third, the number of people left on after this is d. If e people get on later without any others getting off, the number in the bus is $d+e$. If the values of a, b, c, and e were known, we should know the value of d and could tell how many people were on the bus at the time. If we do not know the exact values, we can still visualize what is happening. Mathematicians soon found that when they had written down general expressions of the form given above, they could work with the letters as if they knew what they stood for, without ever troubling to pay attention to what the letters might mean.

When this stage was reached, they found that some mathematical expressions were clumsy, and they gradually developed refinements.

When symbols are to be multiplied together, such as $a \times b$, it is customary to write this as ab. If we multiply a by a we can write it as aa. If, however, we wished to multiply six a's together and wrote the answer as $aaaaaa$, it would not be easy to see quickly how many a's there were. The trouble would be worse if the number of a's was even bigger. This clumsy way of writing is avoided by writing $a \times a \times a \times a \times a \times a$ as a^6. The ^{6} is called the index and is always written to the right of the letter. This is another example of the notation suggesting improvements, for if we multiply a^2 by a^6, we find the answer is a^8 ($aa \times aaaaaa$), and so we get the answer to the multiplication by adding the indices. This forms the basis of Logarithms (see COUNTING INSTRUMENTS).

It is often convenient to group quantities together and treat the group as one quantity. This is done by means of pairs of brackets—so $5(a+b)$ means 5 multiplied by the sum of a and b. Sometimes many brackets have to be used in a complicated expression and various shapes are employed, so that it is possible to tell exactly what is meant. The usual shapes are ( )—round brackets, [ ]—square brackets and { }—curly brackets. Another shape which serves exactly the same purpose is ————, which binds together whatever is below it.

$$\{(a+b)+2[c-(d+e)]\}$$

means that the whole quantity inside the curly bracket is made up of the sum of a and b added to twice the difference between c and the sum of d and e.

If a mathematician finds the need for a symbol that has not been wanted before (and so has not been invented), he has to invent a new one for himself and say exactly what it means. This symbol in course of time becomes understood by all without explanation. Not only are such symbols a means of international communication between mathematicians, but some of them save a great deal of writing. For instance, $<$ means 'less than', $\nless$ means 'not less than' and could (if the argument needed it) be replaced by $\geqslant$ which means 'greater than or equal to'. $5!$ is called 'factorial five', and is a recognized way of writing $5\times4\times3\times2\times1$, which equals 120. If we wrote $n!$, it would represent

$$n\times(n-1)\times(n-2)\times\ ...\ \times3\times2\times1$$

where . . . means that we are to imagine the numbers between $(n-2)$ and 3 (i.e. $n-3$ to 4) put in the expression. 2^{12} is a short way of writing $2\times2\times2\times2\times2\times2\times2\times2\times2\times2\times2\times2=4,096$.

$\sum\limits_{n=1}^{n=4} a^n$ means the sum from $n=1$ to $n=4$ of a^n, and is a short way of writing $a+a^2+a^3+a^4$.

The expression $a\sim b$ is a convenient way of saying 'Subtract b from a unless b is greater than a, in which case subtract a from b'. We usually write fractions such as $\dfrac{3}{4}$ (3 divided by 4), but for convenience in printing (to save big spaces between the lines) they are often written with an oblique stroke to separate numerator from denominator (3/4). This is a case where the development brings difficulties, because without previous knowledge we cannot know for certain that $a+b/c$ means b divided by c and the result added to a, and not the sum of b and a divided by c; if the latter, it should be printed $(a+b)/c$.

Symbols sometimes vary between countries. In decimals (*see* COUNTING, HISTORY OF), unity is divided from tenths by a point ($\cdot$) which in Britain is written a little above the line (63·5). In most European countries a comma is used instead of a point (63,5), while in the United States the point is written lower down on the line (63.5).

See also COUNTING, HISTORY OF; MEASUREMENT.
See also Vol. VIII: ARITHMETIC; ALGEBRA.

MAYFLOWER. Certain Puritan dissenters fled from religious persecution in England to Holland in 1608. They found their new life hard, and wishing to remain English, they began to look towards the empty lands newly discovered in America where they might establish an English colony. Their choice fell upon Virginia, then a colony of the English crown; they obtained a royal patent which allowed them to settle there.

Funds were difficult to raise; but a party sailed from Delftshaven to Southampton in July 1620 in the little ship *Speedwell*. At Southampton they were joined by more pilgrims with another ship, called the *Mayflower*, of 180 tons. The two ships set sail from Southampton in company; but the *Speedwell* sprang a leak, and the pilgrims had to return to England and abandon her at Plymouth. Seventy-three male and twenty-nine female colonists (some of them were children), as well as sailors, crowded into the *Mayflower* and sailed on 6 September.

The *Mayflower* was probably about 90 feet, stem to stern-posts. She was an old ship when chartered and was badly shaken in a storm on her way across the Atlantic; a main beam was bowed and cracked, and had to be raised into place by means of a great iron screw providentially brought from Holland.

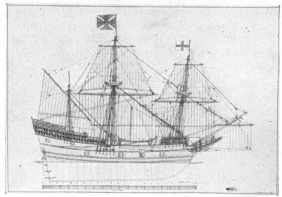

National Maritime Museum
MERCHANT SHIP OF THE SIZE AND DATE OF THE 'MAYFLOWER'
Sheer draft and rigging plan of a model

On 9 November the voyagers found themselves near Cape Cod just below Boston in Massachusetts. It was much farther north than they had intended, and in New England, not Virginia. But they were so thankful to have reached land, and the sailors so unwilling to take them farther, that they decided to settle there. They stayed in the ship until 11 December—reckoned as 21 December by the modern CALENDAR (q.v., Vol. III), and then landed and started to build their town. The place had already been named Plymouth by Captain John Smith in 1614; and Plymouth was the town in England which they had seen last. During the first winter more than half of them died from scurvy and cold.

The journal of William Bradford (1590–1657), who became the second governor of the settlement in the following year, tells the story of the voyage of the *Mayflower* and the early struggles of the Pilgrim Fathers, as they came to be called.

MEASUREMENT, HISTORY OF. Modern life depends greatly on accurate measuring and weighing. An aeroplane engine, or even a car engine of high quality, would not work well if some of its parts were a mere ten-thousandth of an inch too large or too small. Scientific research often requires even higher accuracy. In order to measure something, we must have some standard measure with which to compare it, and some method of making the comparison.

The simplest and crudest way of measuring is to compare the thing to be measured with some part of one's own body. It was therefore natural that the earlier units of length were defined in terms of parts of the body. Thus the cubit of the Egyptians and Babylonians was the length of the forearm from elbow to finger-tips (about 20 inches). Smaller things might be measured in terms of the digit, the breadth of the forefinger (about $\frac{3}{4}$ inch). Other measures of length were the hand (still used in measuring the height of

horses, and standardized at 4 inches), the span, the pace, the double pace, the fathom (length of extended arms between tips of fingers, now fixed at 6 feet as a measurement of sea depths).

In the same way units for the measurement of area at various times and places have been derived from the amount of seed necessary to sow a piece of land, or from the time taken to plough it. Measures of capacity, for things like corn, were vague units such as the basket and the boat-load. Units of weight were derived from such things as the weight of a grain of barley or wheat (a remainder of this survives in our English 'grain'—the $\frac{1}{7000}$th part of a pound). Another source of weights was the weight of gold which had the same value in money as an ox. The Babylonian talent, about 60 lb., was probably derived originally from the load a man could normally carry.

Units derived in this way have two disadvantages. First, the length of the forearm varies from one person to another; the cubit could not be an accurate unit of length unless one said whose arm was meant. Secondly, the various units (digit, hand, span, cubit, and others) would have no simple relation to one another. Very early in the history of civilization, in Egypt and Mesopotamia, these disadvantages were overcome by the process of standardization. Instead of defining the cubit as the length of a forearm, it would be defined by law as the length of a certain bar of metal, which would be kept carefully in the royal palace or the temple. The bar might be made by measuring the length of the king's forearm, just as a new standard for the English yard in the time of Henry I is said to have been fixed by measuring that monarch's arm. All measuring rods for actual use would then be made by copying as accurately as possible the standard rod. A certain piece of metal kept in safe custody would become the standard of weight.

The second disadvantage would be overcome

ONE SPAN · 7 DIGITS

ONE HAND · 4 DIGITS

20·67

Courtesy of the Director of the Science Museum, London

THE ROYAL EGYPTIAN CUBIT OF AMENOPHIS I, 1559–1539 B.C.

by agreeing that all other measurements of length should henceforth be defined as fractions or multiples of the cubit. The digit became one-twenty-eighth of a cubit in Egypt and one-thirtieth in Babylonia; the span became half a cubit; the fathom 4 cubits; and so on. Well-known units of area and capacity would be officially given a new definition in terms of units of length. Thus the Egyptian unit of area, the 'setat', was defined by a square with sides 100 cubits long.

Standardization was often difficult. Sometimes the earlier units could not be arranged neatly as multiples of one another; and so we have awkward ratios such as the rod, pole, or perch, which equals 5½ yards. Even within one country such as Egypt there were several standard cubits, differing by an inch or so from one another. There were also variations from one country to another; thus the most important cubit of ancient Egypt was the equivalent of 20·6 modern English inches; that of Babylonia equalled 19·53 modern inches, Assyria 21·8, and Asia Minor 20·37. But increasing trade helped the standards of the most powerful country to drive out the others.

The Babylonians had a unit, used chiefly for measuring bricks, which was two-thirds of a cubit, or about 13 English inches. With small variations in size, this became the 'foot' used all over Europe before the days of the metric system. In Greece the foot was 12·16 of our inches. This was taken over by the Romans, but later reduced to 11·65 inches. Another variant, nearer to the original Babylonian, was the Tungric foot of 13·1 inches, used by the barbarian tribes of nothern Europe in Roman times. Our own foot was derived from one or other of these measures, most probably the last, which seems to have been common in early medieval England. The Romans used the word *uncia* for the twelfth part of certain things. From this is derived our word 'inch' for the twelfth part of a foot. 'Ounce' is also derived from *uncia*, even though an ounce in weight (avoirdupois) is no longer a twelfth of a pound. Our yard was probably derived from the double cubit. In the same way the origin of many of our other weights and measures can be traced back to those of Babylonia, though poor copying of standards through thousands of years, besides other causes, have led to big changes in the actual size of the measures.

Crown Copyright

BURMESE BRONZE WEIGHTS, 18TH AND 19TH CENTURIES
From an exhibit in the Science Museum, London

There are traces of an early system of counting things in twelves. One is our habit of buying things by the 'dozen'. (The word comes, through Old French, from Latin words for 'a set of twelve'.) The Babylonians divided the Zodiac (their map of the skies) into twelve parts, and the day and night into twelve hours each. We have inherited this way of counting time by way of the Greeks and Romans. There are also traces of a system of reckoning by twenties in our word 'score' and in the French word for 'eighty', *quatre-vingt*, which is literally 'four-twenties'.

In Anglo-Saxon England there were official standards of weight and measure, such as the standard yard or 'gird' kept at Winchester. These standards were taken over unchanged by the Normans after the Conquest. But in practice, in a feudal society, in which there was not much trade except in the actual market place, the majority of people did not require an accurate standard of measure. So, side by side with the official standards, the people used rough definitions of measures in terms of natural objects. These definitions were even mentioned in the laws of the time along with the real standards. Thus the Statute for Measuring Land, dating from before 1284, says that 'Three grains of barley, dry and round, make an inch; twelve inches make a foot; three feet make an ulna' (yard). But then it goes on to say that the King's iron bar is the standard for the yard. So the law recognized the King's standard bar at the same time as the more natural standard of the barley grains. Our 'grain' as a measure of weight is also derived from the grain of a cereal; and an ordinance of the 13th or 14th century says that a sterling penny must weigh 32 grains of wheat,

Crown Copyright

GEORGE IV BRONZE IMPERIAL STANDARD GALLON, QUART,
AND PINT, 1824
From an exhibit in the Science Museum, London

round and dry, from the middle of the ear. An acre
was originally the amount of land that could be
ploughed in a day, and this became standardized
as 160 square rods, or 4,840 square yards.

In the time of Elizabeth, when increasing
trade once more demanded good standards of
measure, the whole system was thoroughly overhauled. The standard yard of Elizabeth differs
from the modern standard by only a little over
one-hundredth of an inch. The present system
was legally introduced in Britain in 1824, though
the standards used were ones that had been
prepared in the middle of the previous century.
In 1834 these standards were lost in the fire that
destroyed the Houses of Parliament, but they
were reconstructed from several good copies that
were in existence. The imperial yard is defined,
by the Weights and Measures Act of 1878, as the
distance, at a temperature of 62° F., between
two fine lines engraved on gold studs sunk in
a specified bronze bar known as 'No. 1 standard
bar', which was cast in 1845. The temperature is
important, as metals expand with heat. The
pound is defined as the weight of a specified
piece of metal in specified conditions.

Our present system of measures is awkward
for calculation because of the multiples 12, 16,
and even $5\frac{1}{2}$ which enter into the tables. Counting and measuring would be simpler if every
unit were 10 or 100 times the next smallest.
Business men and scientists in the 18th century
sometimes advocated a change to a system based
on multiples of 10 (*see* COUNTING, HISTORY OF).
James Watt, the inventor of the improved steam
engine, did so in 1783. But it was not till the
French Revolution that anything was done. The
revolutionary governments established the system
known as the metric system. The unit of length

became the metre (about 39·37 inches), which
was originally defined as the ten-millionth part
of the distance between the earth's Pole and the
Equator; this choice was made so that the unit
should be truly international. The centimetre
is one-hundredth of a metre and the kilometre
(which is the basis of the grid lines on British
maps) is 1,000 metres. The unit of capacity, the
litre, was defined as the capacity of a cube with
sides of 10 centimetres. The unit of weight, the
gramme, was defined to be the weight of a cubic
centimetre of pure water at a temperature of 4° C.
But one cannot measure the distance between
Equator and Pole every time one wants to make
an accurate measuring rod. So a standard bar
was constructed, based on careful calculation,
and this is taken as the standard metre. The
effective standard of weight became the kilogram
(1,000 grammes), the weight of a specified piece
of metal in specified conditions. In 1889 the
units of the metric system in France were legally
defined once more, but this time without reference to the size of the earth. The metric system
has gradually spread from one country to another. To-day it is universally used for scientific
purposes. Outside science the English-speaking
countries are the only important ones that do not
use it.

The wave-length of light of a definite colour
(*see* WAVE MOTION, Vol. III) forms an invariable
natural standard by means of which all units
of length can be defined. In 1927 the Seventh
General Congress of Weights and Measures, to
which many countries sent delegates, adopted a
further definition of the metre as 1,553,164·13
wave-lengths of red cadmium light. If the
standard metre were destroyed, this definition
could be used to reconstruct it.

In modern times two developments have taken
place which have revolutionized measurement.
One is the devising of many new standards for
measuring such things as electricity, power, the
strength of metals, and the chemical properties
of materials. The second important development concerns the great range of instruments
designed to measure, weigh, test, or classify
everything from the pitch of a violin string and
the distance of an earthquake to the flicker of
electricity in a criminal's brain.

See also COUNTING, HISTORY OF; MATHEMATICAL
NOTATION.
See also Vol. VI: AGRICULTURAL MEASUREMENTS.
See also Vol. VIII: MEASUREMENT, UNITS OF.

MENAI SUSPENSION BRIDGE
19th-century engraving

MENAI SUSPENSION BRIDGE. This link between Carnarvonshire and the Isle of Anglesey can claim to be the forefather of all modern suspension bridges. For generations men had talked about bridging the Menai Straits, since Anglesey was accessible only by ferry-boats. However, no practical steps were taken until 1801, when John Rennie presented four different schemes to the authorities. They were all turned down, chiefly because they would interfere with shipping, and for a few more years the idea was allowed to rest. Nine years later, another famous bridge-builder, Thomas Telford, prepared a plan for a cast-iron bridge of wide span, and in 1815 he was authorized to design a suspension bridge. His design was more daring than anything attempted earlier, for the site he chose required an uninterrupted span of 550 feet between the main piers.

The first stone of the chief pier was laid in August 1819, and the superstructure completed in the autumn of 1824. On 26 April 1825 the first of the great chains from which the roadway was to be hung was hauled into place. One end was attached to the pier, while a raft towed by four boats carried the other end across the Straits, to be fastened to ropes and hauled into place by capstans. When fully suspended, it hung 100 feet above the water. On 30 January 1826 the bridge, with a total length of 1,710 feet,

was formally opened, and the London to Holyhead mail-coach made the first crossing. The bridge is still in regular use by road traffic. A separate tubular bridge not far away has been built to carry the railway.

See also BRIDGES.
See also Vol. VIII: BRIDGE BUILDING.

MERCATOR PROJECTION, *see* MAP PROJECTIONS.

MERCHANT SHIPPING. The Merchant Service, or Merchant Navy, as it is now generally called, is made up of the ships of all types and sizes engaged in commerce. They range from the coasting barge using wind as a motive power (of which there are still about 100 at work, although their days are numbered) to the transatlantic passenger liner. Merchant ships are owned either singly or in fleets, sometimes by private individuals, but usually by a shipping company which offers the carrying service of its ships to the world's traders and merchants, in return for the freight money charged.

All merchant ships have distinguishing colours or marks on their funnels, and the ships of each particular line fly the Company's house flag, usually at the mainmast when entering or leaving port. The only outward sign that they have some claim to be regarded as a national service is their national ensign. In the case of British ships this is the red ensign, or red 'duster', as it is called by seamen, a red flag with a Union Jack in the upper hoist, that is, the top corner of the flag against the mast (*see* FLAGS, Section 3). If a particular merchant ship has a large enough proportion of its officers and men in the Royal Naval Reserve, it may be permitted by the Admiralty to fly the blue ensign. The crews of merchant vessels are not under the same discipline as men of the Royal Navy, but a standard of behaviour is laid down by law. Most of them do not wear uniform, and their ships are armed only in time of war so that they can defend themselves.

Crews sailing under the red ensign are British for the most part, but they probably include men of half a dozen different nationalities. A British ship, particularly a Tramp (*see* SHIP), may have Britons (of both white and coloured races), Swedes, Finns, Germans, or Danes among her deck hands, an Arab and a Negro or two in the stokehold, and a Chinese steward in the pantry.

The British Commonwealth owes much to merchant shipping. The discoveries made by explorers and adventurous travellers would have been useless without merchants and traders to develop them, and these men would not risk their investments in the new lands unless they were sure of ships to carry their merchandise. Throughout the periods of empire expansion, the British shipowner and British sailor were quick to establish sea communications with these new countries. Arduous voyages and fearful hardships were undertaken in order that manufactured goods should be taken to undeveloped parts of the world and raw materials brought back to keep Britain's valuable machinery active. Many Dominions and Colonies, and many important trades, owe their development and expansion to careful nursing by one or more British shipping lines.

See also SHIP; SHIP'S COMPANY.
See also Vol. VII: SHIPPING.

MERSEY TUNNEL. This motor traffic tunnel under the Mersey estuary is the biggest underwater tunnel in the world. Before its construction all traffic between Liverpool and Birkenhead, other than that which went by the Mersey Railway, had to use ferry boats. Although a practically continuous service was provided, delays to traffic were severe, especially in fog.

Work was started in 1928, and the tunnel was opened in 1934; in the first three months no fewer than 866,000 vehicles passed through it. The main tunnel is over 2 miles long, and in addition there are branch bores leading to the docks at both Liverpool and Birkenhead which bring the total length of the tunnel up to nearly 3 miles.

Here are some details about the tunnel's construction which show the magnitude of the work of making it: nearly $1\frac{1}{4}$ million tons of rock and other material were excavated; 82,000 tons of

Stewart Bale, Ltd.

THE MERSEY TUNNEL.

cast-iron lining and more than 1,000,000 bolts were used; the fittings and screws are all of stainless steel; 3,000 tons of steel and 270,000 tons of concrete went into its construction. Blasting operations took well over half a million pounds of explosives, and nearly $7\frac{1}{2}$ million gallons of water were pumped out of the workings during construction.

The tunnel is lighted throughout; and a special machine keeps the walls scoured and polished. The roadway is divided into four 'tracks', two in each direction. All heavy goods vehicles use the 'slow' left-hand tracks, and private cars and motor-cycles the middle 'fast' tracks. On the latter a uniform speed of 35 miles per hour is enforced by traffic police who patrol the tunnel in order to maintain a steady traffic flow. No pedal-cyclists, horse-drawn vehicles, or pedestrians are allowed to use the tunnel. The junctions leading to the docks at each side of the river are controlled by automatic traffic-light signals.

See also TUNNELS.
See also Vol. VIII: TUNNELLING.

MESSENGERS. The human courier or runner was once the quickest means of sending letters over long distances. Before there were proper organized postal services, anyone who wished to send a private letter or a parcel would probably have to find his own messenger: perhaps a friend who happened to be travelling the right way. From very early times, however, there were professional messengers, chosen for their speed, who were used to carry state documents. In China an elaborate system of couriers working in relays, some mounted and some on foot, existed as early as 1122 B.C., and was used until well into the 20th century. Marco Polo, who visited China in the 13th century, describes how the mounted couriers would change horses by leaping from saddle to saddle without dismounting. Darius, who ruled over Persia from 521 to 485 B.C., established a system of relays of couriers throughout Persia; and professional messengers were also used by the Greeks and Romans. One of the most famous journeys ever taken by a messenger was that of the Greek Pheidippides, before the battle of Marathon in 490 B.C., who ran the 150 miles between Athens and Sparta in 48 hours (*see also* MARATHON RACE, Vol. IX).

Professional messengers were widely used in Europe in the Middle Ages; they were not available for ordinary people, but carried mainly official letters. Records show that as early as the 13th century the King of England used paid messengers; and in the 14th century there were twelve on the royal staff, who earned a fixed wage while on the road, with an extra allowance for shoes. Abbots, bishops, judges, and court officials all had their staff of messengers, whom they would send on long journeys, often even abroad. Some of the medieval messengers could cover the distance from London to Scotland in as little as 6 days. They had special privileges on the roads: the 14th-century poet Langland, in *Piers Plowman*, describes how the merchant was delayed, for instance, by the keeper of the toll-gate, while the messenger had only to speak his errand and show his letters (which bore his master's seal) and he could immediately proceed. He was exempt from toll, and could order other travellers to make way for him, and the town gates to be opened for him at night. If he were a royal messenger there were severe penalties for hindering him.

Our modern POST OFFICE (q.v.) has developed from the organizing of professional messengers into a relay service. Attempts to do this were made as early as the 13th century: at this time a courier service was established in Paris for the use of the University, and private letters were also unofficially sent by it. In times of national danger, as in 1484 when Richard III feared invasion, a relay system was used in England: single horsemen were stationed at intervals of 20 miles, so that a distance of 200 miles could be covered in 2 days. The organization of royal messengers, and the appointment of a master of posts (the forerunner of our Postmaster-General) dates from the 16th century. By this time private letters were carried by the State service: by the 17th century the State had a monopoly of this (*see* POST OFFICE, HISTORY OF).

Even in modern times it is often necessary to rely upon the human messenger, especially in war time, when secret messages might be intercepted if sent by wireless. The army dispatch-rider or runner proves invaluable for messages which cannot be sent by any other method (*see* (INTELLIGENCE SERVICES, Vol. X). The ingenuity of the human messenger, and his power to adapt his route and his methods to each hazard as he meets it, make him especially useful in times of danger. During the Second World War innumerable letters and plans which it would not

KING'S MESSENGER'S BADGE

have been possible to send by telegraph passed between England and the occupied countries of Europe, handed secretly from messenger to messenger. The messages were concealed in many ingenious ways: often in the luggage of people who appeared to be ordinary travellers, going on holiday or visiting their families; on one occasion at least valuable papers were stitched inside a chicken. Even in peace time the human messenger is still used for important missions: communications between the Government and its representatives abroad are carried by members of a special corps of King's Messengers, who come under the jurisdiction of the Foreign Office. They wear a badge hanging from a garter-blue ribbon, with a silver greyhound beneath. In the past, King's messengers covered long distances on horseback; to-day they travel mainly by the passenger air routes. The 'diplomatic bag', in which they carry secret documents, is passed through the Customs unopened.

METEOROLOGICAL REPORTS, *see* CLIMATE AND COMMUNICATIONS, Section 3. *See also* Vol. III, WEATHER FORECASTING.

METRIC SYSTEM, *see* COUNTING, HISTORY OF; MEASUREMENT, HISTORY OF.

MICROPHONE, *see* SPEECH, TRANSMISSION OF.

MINIATURE RAILWAYS. The narrowest width of line on which full railway working can take place is probably the 15-inch gauge, which is in use on the Romney, Hythe & Dymchurch Railway in Kent and the Ravenglass & Eskdale Railway in Cumberland. But a scale-model steam locomotive, under test, has succeeded in pulling three full-grown adults on a gauge no wider than 2 inches. Many passenger-carrying railways have been built in pleasure grounds and private parks, worked by scale model locomotives on gauges of 15 inches (3 inches to the foot), $9\frac{1}{2}$ inches (2 inches to the foot), and $7\frac{1}{2}$ inches ($1\frac{1}{2}$ inches to the foot or one-eighth full size). Miniature lines for instructional and pleasure

purposes are in some cases on the $1\frac{3}{4}$-inch gauge, such as the well-known line of the Bekonscot model village at Beaconsfield in Buckinghamshire; amateur model railway owners concentrate mainly on Gauge 'o' ($1\frac{1}{4}$ inches) or Gauge 'oo' ($\frac{5}{8}$ inch). This smallest gauge makes it possible to assemble a model railway of great operating complexity in a very small space.

See also GAUGES, RAILWAY.
See also Vol. IX: MODEL RAILWAYS.

MORSE CODE. This international signalling code is named after its inventor Samuel MORSE (q.v. Vol. V) (1791–1872), an American who was a pioneer in the use of electric TELEGRAPHY (q.v.). It consists of an alphabet in which the letters are represented by arrangements of dots and dashes. It can be transmitted either by flags held in the hands (a short movement representing a dot, a long one a dash), by flashing lights, or by sound, the dots and dashes being represented by short and long buzzes or taps. The letters most commonly used are represented by the simplest symbols, the commonest letter of all, *e*, consisting of a single dot. The code is usually learnt by memorizing the sounds of the letter, dot being represented by 'dit', and dash by 'dah'. The code is given below:

A ·—	M ——	Y —·——
B —···	N —·	Z ——··
C —·—·	O ———	1 ·————
D —··	P ·——·	2 ··———
E ·	Q ——·—	3 ···——
F ··—·	R ·—·	4 ····—
G ——·	S ···	5 ·····
H ····	T —	6 —····
I ··	U ··—	7 ——···
J ·———	V ···—	8 ———··
K —·—	W ·——	9 ————·
L ·—··	X —··—	0 —————

There are also special combinations for punctuation marks; a full stop is AAA, inverted commas RR, brackets KK, and a query IMI.

There are various conventional short signals in use by wireless operators for conveying commonly needed phrases. Preliminary remarks between signallers are often conveyed in this way, such as 'Who are you?' RU; 'Move to your left' ML; and so on. There are several codes of these short signals, the International Q code being the most widely used. It has been universally adopted for use at sea and in commerce, and is a very convenient means of communication between operators of different nationalities. The signals consist of groups of three letters each beginning with the letter Q: among the most commonly used signals are QSA, 'Your message received', QSM, 'Repeat', and QRX, 'Please wait' or 'Come back at . . .'. There are special groups of Q signals for reporting on the clearness and readability of the signals: the QSA group, for instance, is used for reporting on the strength of the signal; QSA1 means 'unreadable', QSA2 'weak; readable now and then', QSA3 'Fairly good', and so on.

See also LIGHT SIGNALLING; FLAG SIGNALLING; CODES AND CIPHERS.

MOTOR-BOAT, *see* MOTOR-SHIP. *See also* MOTOR-BOAT, Vol. IX.

MOTOR-CAR. Although the term 'motor-car' is usually applied only to private cars (as distinct from goods-carrying vehicles or those which carry passengers for money) the general principles of the motor-car apply to almost all road vehicles which are mechanically driven.

A car has four essential parts; an engine to provide the driving-power: a transmission system to convey the power to the wheels: a body to hold the driver and passengers and their luggage; and a metal frame called the chassis to hold rigidly together the engine, transmission, and body.

1. ENGINE. The various types are described in ROAD TRANSPORT ENGINES. Technical details of each type appear in Vol. VIII under INTERNAL COMBUSTION ENGINE, GAS TURBINE, and ELECTRIC MOTORS.

2. TRANSMISSION. This is one of the most fundamental problems of motor-car design. A stationary engine, erected in a back-yard to work a circular saw, presents few difficulties. But in a car the power from a small engine has to be conveyed to bouncing wheels on the road at any speed from 1 to 60 miles an hour or more. Every time the car goes round a corner the outside wheel must go faster than the inside wheel as it has a longer way to go. In going over a bumpy road the axle of each wheel (jumping up and down on springs) may change its position

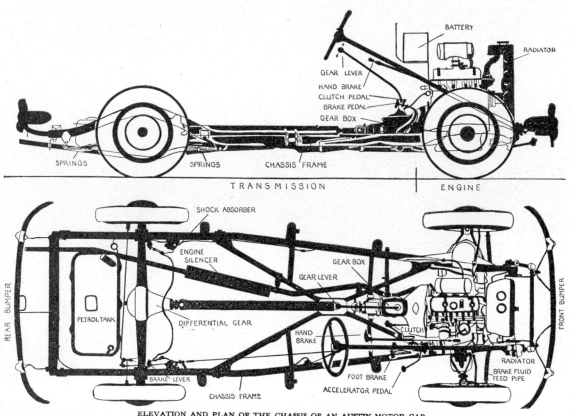

ELEVATION AND PLAN OF THE CHASSIS OF AN AUSTIN MOTOR-CAR

100 times in 60 seconds. When the car comes to a hill so steep that the engine is about to stop, the transmission (which includes the gears) is readjusted so that the engine does not stop and the car is able to go up the hill.

Since an internal-combustion engine, unlike a steam-engine, will stop completely unless it is kept spinning, every car must have some sort of gearing in order that the car can be made to travel very slowly (as when starting from rest).

The standard form of GEARS (q.v. Vol. VIII), in use since the early days of motoring, consists of a number of meshed wheels, which work on a general principle like that of the small wheels inside a watch or clock. By moving a lever—the gear-lever—a driver can decide which set of wheels shall be connected to the spinning engine. The action of the gear-lever does not decide the actual speed of the car. This speed is controlled with more exactness by the precise speed of the engine at any moment, and the engine speed is governed by the accelerator pedal, worked by the driver's foot, which admits a mixture of air and petrol to the engine. For instance, when one gear is in use, a car may travel at any speed between about 3 and 15 miles an hour, according to how far the accelerator pedal is pressed. When another gear is in use, the car may travel from about 10 to 30 miles an hour. With yet another gear, speeds from about 20 to 50 miles an hour may be achieved. The choice of gear merely determines the broad range of speeds.

Most British cars have a choice of four gears (apart from the 'reversing' gear, which enables the car to be backed). American cars, which are on the whole more powerful, generally need only three gears, besides the reversing gear. Many cars are no longer fitted with the long gear-lever which formerly rose from the floor-boards of the car; they have instead, for the driver's convenience, a short handle just under the steering wheel.

Some cars, particularly in the U.S.A., have automatic gearboxes. Their gears are independent of the driver, and change 'up' or 'down' when the mechanism registers certain relationships between the speed of the car and the effort exerted by the engine.

When it is desired to change the gear of a car, or to stop a car for a few seconds at a crossing without stopping the engine, a CLUTCH (q.v. Vol. VIII) is operated on most vehicles. This is simply a means of temporarily preventing the power of the engine from being passed on to the gears or the road-wheels. When a car is travelling normally, two round plates are pressed very hard against one another by a spring. When the plate connected with the engine goes round, it makes the plate connected with the wheels go round too. This pair of plates forms the 'clutch'. The plates can be pressed apart by the driver's foot acting on a pedal, and the engine is then 'free' of the road-wheels. Certain cars, instead, use hydraulic coupling (see Vol. VIII, p. 83).

The remainder of the transmission system of a car consists of articulated shafts, so avoiding strain when the road-wheels bounce, and a differential gear which ensures that the outside wheel goes faster than the inside wheel when cornering.

The springs, which enable each wheel to bounce, are part of the transmission too, for they have to 'hold' the wheels on to the road, however irregular the surface. The tendency to use very pliable independent springs for each wheel is increasing, as these enable the car to travel faster without rocking dangerously.

3. BODY. The body of a private car may vary from the worn seats of an old and cheap second-hand car to the luxurious fittings of a hand-built £4,000 saloon. In all bodies, however, room has to be found for the driver's controlling mechanism. The steering wheel on the steering pillar moves the two front wheels by a series of joints. Near the driver's feet are three pedals, in a standard order from left to right: Clutch, Brake, Accelerator. The brake pedal, operating through steel cables or rods, or sometimes through hydraulic pipes containing oil, affects each wheel equally, by pressing against a moving part a surface lined with gripping material, which slows it. Heavy lorries use 'servo' brakes, power-operated, as the driver's foot would be too weak. A hand-brake is provided for parking vehicles (see BRAKES AND BRAKING, Vol. VIII).

In front of the driver are many dials and switches. A speedometer dial indicates the speed at which the car is travelling and the number of miles travelled. One gauge shows the pressure of the oil. Another dial shows the condition of the electrical system which ignites the petrol in the engine, as well as providing lighting and power to work the horn and wind-screen wiper. Some cars have indicators recording the heat of the water in the radiator which cools the engine, and the actual revolutions of the engine.

At the back of the body is a large locker, known as the 'boot', which contains a spare wheel and tyres, a tool kit for repairs, and space for luggage.

The most popular type of car body in Great Britain is the four-door saloon, designed to carry four or five passengers. Ventilation is now so efficient that even small saloon cars are not stuffy, though sliding 'sunshine' roofs are not now so often fitted to saloon cars as they used to be. The drop-head coupé has a canvas roof which rolls or folds back into the rear of the body.

In Britain motorists are taxed on their car by an annual licence, and also on the petrol they buy. In 1947 the same charge was made payable on cars of all sizes, but before that the amount varied with the horse-power, which was calculated by the dimensions of the engine. These taxes led to the introduction in the 1920's of 'baby' cars of 7 and 8 horse-power, which could be run very cheaply. The horse-power tax tended to keep down the size of engines in the popular middle range of car, the engine being designed so that it should pay the least possible tax, not so that it should have the greatest engineering efficiency. In America, on the other hand, where this kind of taxation did not exist, and where distances were great and roads often bad, the car designer used a large chassis requiring a high-powered engine, so that there should be room for elaborate springs and spacious body-work. Britain has since turned to the design of larger cars with higher horse-power.

See also MOTOR-CAR, HISTORY OF; ROAD TRAFFIC CONTROL; ROAD TRANSPORT ENGINES.

See also Vol. VII: MOTOR-CAR INDUSTRY.

See also Vol. VIII: INTERNAL COMBUSTION ENGINE.

See also Vol. IX: MOTOR-CAR RACING.

MOTOR-CAR, HISTORY OF.

The first self-propelled road vehicle—which represented one of the most important steps forward in the history of transport—was designed and constructed by a Frenchman named Cugnot. He built a steam-driven carriage in Paris in 1769, which had three wheels, carried two passengers, and ran at a maximum speed of 4 miles an hour. Although much credit should be given to his achievement, this carriage was not at the time a success, for the supply of steam only lasted about 15 minutes, and the carriage had to stop to get up more steam. The next pioneers in the field were two Englishmen; William Murdock, inventor of coal-gas lighting, in 1784, and Richard Trevithick of Cornwall, the designer of steam-engines for railways, in 1801. In 1803 Trevithick's steam-driven carriage, with wheels of 10-foot diameter and a horizontal instead of a vertical engine, travelled for the first time faster than any horse-drawn carriage, and later made the journey of 90 miles from Camborne to Plymouth. Trevithick apparently developed the idea of a gear-box for varying the speed of vehicles.

At this time some people doubted whether the driving force could be transmitted to the road effectively by wheels. Sir Goldsworthy Gurney, for instance, another Cornish inventor, believed that when a vehicle was starting from rest, the wheels would spin round without biting the ground. So a few experiments were made with pushing struts or mechanical 'legs' instead of wheels. In 1825 Gurney built a steam carriage of this type which actually ascended Highgate Hill. In 1828 he accomplished the journey from London to Bath, and in 1829 made a trip through Reading, Devizes, and Melksham at such a pace that a horse-drawn 'mail-cart' had difficulty in keeping up. This vehicle carried 18 passengers. At the back were the flues, from which it was claimed that no smoke would be emitted, as charcoal and coke would be used. The steam passed from the rear, where it was generated, to the driving pistons beneath the carriage. The boiler contained forty iron pipes arranged in a horse-shoe; although this was one of the earliest applications of the tubular principle in boilers, it had actually been invented by an engineer called William Henry James some years earlier, for use in Cornish mines. Towards the end of his career Gurney met with much opposition from the farmers, who said that the machines frightened their animals, and the keepers of the TURNPIKES (q.v.), who raised their tolls on the grounds that the weight of these heavy steam-engines was tearing up the surface of the roads.

In 1831 Sir Charles Dance took over some of Gurney's steam carriages and ran them regularly four times a day between Gloucester and Cheltenham. In 4 months the carriages covered 3,500 miles and carried 3,000 passengers. The distance of 9 miles was usually covered in 45 minutes.

Meanwhile several engineers tried to produce steam carriages like Gurney's. Among the few who had some measure of success was William Henry James, the inventor of the tubular boiler, who designed a two-cylinder engine to drive his vehicle, which weighed 3 tons. It was tried out on roads in Epping Forest, and succeeded in carrying fifteen passengers at a speed of 12 to 15 miles an hour. In 1827 Walter Hancock, of London, took out a patent for a steam omnibus. His second steam carriage, named the 'Infant', ran from London to Bristol twice, and his 'Autopsy' in 1833 plied regularly from the City to Pentonville. In these machines he at first used a direct drive to the wheels from the crankshaft, but afterwards adopted a chain drive, one chain connecting two wheels with the engine. Hancock operated many other services in London and the Home Counties and was one of the most successful of these early pioneers. In 1833 Dr. Church of Birmingham started a service from there to London.

This remarkable early progress, however, met with considerable opposition. Gurney was stoned by a hostile crowd, urged on by the irate postilions of horse-drawn stage-coaches whose custom he was threatening; landowners were unhelpful. In 1832 fifty-four parliamentary bills were introduced, by which ruinous tolls on the new vehicles were authorized. The railway companies, now very powerful, won an overwhelming victory in 1865, when further progress was prevented by the introduction of the famous Locomotives Act, whereby the drivers of all power-driven vehicles were limited to a speed of 4 miles per hour, and were compelled to have a man walking in front with a red flag by day or a red lantern by night. On the continent, however, the INTERNAL-

COMBUSTION ENGINE (q.v. Vol. VIII) was developing rapidly. The first step was the perfection of the gas-engine by the German, Nikolaus Otto, in 1876. He introduced the four-stroke cycle of operation, a principle used in most petrol and diesel engines to-day. It was one of Otto's employees, however, who successfully applied this kind of engine to a road vehicle; this was Gottlieb Daimler, whose name is commemorated in the famous machines now made at Coventry. His engine, a small model produced in 1884, and made to propel a cycle in 1886, used petrol vapour.

A further step was taken by Benz, of Mannheim in Germany, who built in 1885 a three-wheeled vehicle that carried two passengers. The engine had a single cylinder which developed $\frac{3}{4}$ horse-power and was supplied with an inflammable mixture from a carburettor. Although this car was crude in comparison with later models, the ignition of the petrol mixture was caused by an electric spark from a battery and coil. Similar cars were being manufactured in France and Belgium by Panhard and Levassor, who had acquired the rights to build the Benz engine in those two countries.

The first double-cylinder engine, which had the cylinders in the form of a V, was produced by Daimler in 1889. At this time motor-cars in France were reaching such a stage that long-distance road services were being organized. In 1894 a race between Paris and Rouen was won by a steam-tractor hauling an ordinary open carriage. The next year the race run from Paris to Bordeaux was won by Levassor on a 4 horse-power Panhard, which covered the distance of 735 miles at an average speed of 15 miles an hour. A similar car won the Paris to Marseilles race (1,077 miles) in 1896 at an average speed of 16 miles an hour.

In Great Britain the progress of the motor-car at this time was much slower, and several French models were introduced into the country. An exhibition of motor-cars was held at Tunbridge Wells in 1895, but motoring really started in this country in 1896. A procession of motor-cars took place from London to Brighton, to celebrate the abolition of the 'red flag' Act and to show how reliable new vehicles were. In fact, many of the cars broke down, for although engines were reasonably dependable, the transmission system (belt or chain in most machines) gave constant trouble.

Crown Copyright

3-WHEELED MOTOR-CAR MADE BY BENZ, 1888

The cover has been removed from the engine. (From an exhibit in the Science Museum, London)

Crown Copyright

40–50 H.P. ROLLS-ROYCE MOTOR-CAR, 1908
From an exhibit in the Science Museum, London

The first order by a private customer was placed in 1897, and was for a Daimler car built at the company's works, which were established in 1896 at Coventry. This town and London became the two main centres of the motor industry, from which, during the next few years, large numbers of cars were forthcoming. Most of them were very small two-seat carts with no roofs and very poor springs, driven by an engine placed under the seat. They had wooden spoked or wire wheels, and were stopped by either a block brake acting on the outside of the wheel, or a band brake acting on a drum fitted to the transmission. Motorists had to carry large cans of fuel and several spare tires, for there were no repair or filling stations to serve them.

By 1900 the motor-car had acquired a standard shape, plan, and appearance. Multi-cylinder engines were placed under the bonnets in the front of the cars; the drive was now transmitted from the engine to the wheels by gear-boxes, with a lever for changing speed; for this, bevel gears were now used instead of a chain and sprocket. Among the important British firms which started at about this time were Humber, Riley, Lagonda, Sunbeam, Swift, Napier, and Singer. In France the Renault company was formed, and in Germany the Opel company, and 'automobile' industries were also starting in America. This rapid increase in the number of cars was partly due to their popularity with fashionable society, and especially to the great interest taken in them by King Edward VII. The name 'petrol' for the refined petroleum used in motor-car engines was introduced from the French about 1895—though the French now use the word *essence*.

In 1903 many more famous present-day manufacturers began business; these included Standard, Vauxhall, Thorneycroft, and the American Ford. Motoring remained the pastime of wealthy people until the First World War, but many manufacturers had begun to consider making light, popular cars a few years earlier. The Rover Company introduced in 1911 one of the first light cars, a 6 horse-power two-seater costing £147. Some manufacturers had earlier experimented with elaborate cycle-cars with wire wheels, chain drive, and an arm called a tiller, which steered by the single front wheel. As factory methods improved and output increased, it became possible to produce cheaper cars (*see* MOTOR-CAR INDUSTRY, Vol. VII).

A great impetus was given to the motor-car after the First World War. Wooden wheels were replaced by steel ones. A lower body line and large pneumatic tires made a great difference in appearance. In the 1920's saloon bodies began to replace the open landaulettes and tourers. Brakes became more efficient, because

Nederland Line Royal Dutch Mail

THE MOTOR-SHIP 'ORANJE'

The early internal-combustion engine for use on the road was the work of several hands (*see* MOTOR-CAR, HISTORY OF). From a marine point of view, however, the placing of internal combustion on a practical basis is usually associated with a German, Dr. Diesel. His basic patents were applied in engines fitted to the cargo liner *Selandia* in Copenhagen in 1912. Though a small oil-tanker with a motor-engine had been in service in the Dutch East Indies a few years before, the *Selandia* claims pride of place as the first ocean-going motor-ship. She was also notable in that she had no funnel; the designers of most of the early motor-ships felt that it was necessary to symbolize in this striking way a type of ship which was to revolutionize sea transport.

At the outbreak of the Second World War nearly a quarter of the total gross tonnage of ships throughout the whole world was propelled by internal-combustion engines, and merited, therefore, the title of motor-ships.

The advantage of a motor-ship is that the internal-combustion engine has the lowest rate of fuel consumption of any prime mover in the world. It burns well under $\frac{1}{2}$ lb. of oil for every horse-power it develops for every hour that it runs. The best type of oil-burning steam machinery, which is a geared turbine with water-tube boilers, used at least 0·6 lb. per horse-power per hour. An ordinary reciprocating steam-engine uses 1 lb. of oil per horse-power per hour. If the ship is coal-fired, it uses over $1\frac{1}{2}$ lb. of coal per horse-power per hour. When these differences are worked out in terms of tons of fuel which must be carried within the ship's hull to enable her to proceed at her designed speed, it will be seen that the ship which uses less fuel than any other kind is likely to be the most popular.

It was at one time claimed that as a diesel engine is rather more complicated than other engines, its upkeep cost must be greater. This is no longer true, because the increasing demand for the diesel engine has led to improvements in design and a measure of standardization which makes repair and maintenance a comparatively easy task.

There is a wide range in type and size of motor-ships. The smallest may be no more than little river tugs of 110 horse-power, while the most powerful motor-ship in the world is the 37,500 horse-power Dutch motor-liner *Oranje*, which trades between Amsterdam and the East Indies. It is among cargo-liners and coasters —ships requiring between 800 and 1,800 horse-power—that the diesel engine is most popular. Great Britain is one of the biggest owners of motor-ships in the world, being closely rivalled in this respect by the Scandinavian nations, who were among the pioneers in the use of internal-combustion engines at sea.

Motor-launches, whether used for pleasure or for carrying about harbour officials in large ports, are not regarded as motor-ships, but as being more akin to MOTOR-BOATS (q.v. Vol. IX).

See also STEAMSHIPS, HISTORY OF; ELECTRIC SHIP.
See also Vol. VIII: INTERNAL-COMBUSTION ENGINE.

MOTOR TRANSPORT. Britain and other highly developed countries have become increasingly dependent on modern organized road transport for the distribution of food and the carrying of the trade by which they live. The railways are among the largest users of road transport in Britain. They have followed a policy for many years of buying control of road haulage companies. They have closed many small railway stations to goods traffic, and have set up in their place road services worked from suitable centres. This process, which has reduced costs and quickened delivery, was hastened by the Transport Act of 1947, which brought all the principal means of transport under Government control.

Most of the 670,000 goods vehicles in Britain that year were used by some 250,000 owners for their own business. If an owner carries goods for anyone but himself, he must secure a special licence. 'A' licences, permitting general haulage for hire, covered almost 84,000 vehicles. 'A contract' licences, enabling an owner to carry goods for one firm in particular vehicles, accounted for a further 14,000 vehicles. There were over 64,000 vehicles with 'B' licences, whose owners used them mainly for themselves but could occasionally carry goods for other people. On an average, an owner of an 'A' licence owned five vehicles, an owner of an 'A contract' licence had three vehicles, and one of a 'B' licence had two vehicles. The Act of 1947 allows the national Road Haulage Executive, for the Government, to take over haulage businesses with 'A' licences for services longer than 25 miles. Lorries taken over by the Executive bear the name 'British Road Services'.

Limits are laid down in most countries to the size and shape of vehicles using the roads. In some countries the situation is complicated by the fact that restrictions vary in different parts of the country. In the U.S.A., for example, each state makes its own regulations for vehicles, and hauliers often have to transfer loads from one vehicle to another at the state border. They have for some years been trying to obtain the adoption of standard dimensions throughout the country. Lorries in other countries tend to be larger than they are in Britain, as the laws are not so strict in this respect.

In England some lorries bigger than the ordinary limits are allowed to run, under conditions. Among these are the lorries used to move locomotives from the works where they have been built to the docks for shipment, for these locomotives often cannot be carried by rail as they will not fit the loading-gauge of the British railways. These are called 'abnormal indivisible loads', and when one is going to be moved, special notice has to be given to the police in the places through which the journey will be made, and also to the road and bridge authorities. Since the Second World War special maps have been made which show the maximum weight, height, and other limits for all the important roads. During the war the military authorities made careful plans recording all the roads in the country over which a military advance was likely to be made, and the type of traffic they could handle. The necessity of this work was apparent when the Allied forces were driving the Germans out of France and Belgium in 1944. The railways had been thoroughly disorganized by air attacks, and roads had to be used to provide almost all supplies for the armies as they pressed forward. The final attack on Germany gave an even better example of what could be done with time to plan. The four American armies were kept supplied by a fleet of lorries which in April and May 1945 carried 14,000 tons a day for an average distance of 130 miles.

In Britain a lorry with more than two axles can be 30 feet long, or if it is an articulated vehicle, that is, a tractor which supports part of its trailer, it may be 3 feet longer; a two-axled vehicle may be 27 ft. 6 in. long. A separate lorry and trailer must not be longer than 60 feet together. Lorries which, unladen, weigh less than 3 tons, may travel at up to 30 miles an hour; those which weigh more are limited to 20 m.p.h. Buses may travel at the higher speed whatever their weight, and so may horse-boxes.

One of the problems of a road-haulage undertaking is to make the most of its fleet by keeping it fully used; and a method of doing this which has become steadily more popular is by the use of articulated vehicles. The mechanical horse— a small motor or electric unit, often on three wheels—was proving efficient for the local haulage work which had previously been done by horses. Then it was found that, thanks to easy coupling devices, a mechanical horse could be used to collect or deliver loads in the town, and so release the larger tractor which was necessary for moving the loaded trailer on the long-distance

Gregs Couper & Co.

SCAMMELL ARTICULATED MACHINERY CARRIER FOR 20-TON LOAD AND MOTIVE UNIT, WITH GARDNER OIL-ENGINE

journeys. For example, articulated milk tankers are to be seen making for London on many main roads. When they get there, the trailer on which the tank is mounted is detached, another trailer with an empty tank, which has been awaiting its arrival, is attached, and the tractor quickly leaves again for the country. Another method of transporting milk is by self-contained tank trailers. These are hauled by tractor to the nearest important station, where they are placed on special wagons which carry them in fast freight trains to London or other big centres. There they are hauled off and taken by another road tractor to the milk depot. After the milk has been bottled, it is then delivered to the customers, sometimes in electric vans and sometimes in small pram-like conveyances driven by a little electric or petrol motor.

There are many others tankers on the road besides those which carry milk. Most of the petrol used in Britain is distributed by road, at least on the final stages of its journey; and tar and chemicals are also carried. The tanks have to be built carefully so that they do not leak; and the material used for tanks carrying chemicals has to be carefully chosen, since some metals are eaten away by some chemicals and not by others.

Large building contractors employ lorries with special bodies for carrying liquid cement; this is

of great value when some large work, such as the construction of an aerodrome runway, is being undertaken. Instead of having a whole host of small mixers with the inevitable possibility of the quality varying from mixer to mixer, it is possible to make the whole mixture in one big plant, and to distribute it in the lorries.

Refrigerated vans have been used more since the development of 'dry ice'. This is the chemical, usually wrapped in paper, which can be seen in blocks in the bottom of the containers of ice-cream tricycles. Refrigerated lorries, with specially insulated bodies, are kept at the correct temperature in this and other ways. Many are used to carry meat from the distributing centres to smaller centres, and direct to the butchers, and also for transporting other foodstuffs. Coal is still usually carried by rail from the pit to the station nearest to the consumer; but road transport is used to shift most of the coal from opencast mining sites (see COAL MINING, Vol. VII). An organization has been built up for the movement of parcels and packages (called 'smalls' in the haulage industry) throughout the country. The parcel is first handled by a lorry in local collection work, is then transferred to a lorry on a trunk service which travels through the night, and is delivered next day by another local delivery vehicle. Containers which can be transferred by crane from one lorry to another, or from a lorry to a railway flat wagon, have so far aroused more interest on the continent of Europe than in Britain or America, but since the Second World War British firms have been considering them. There is now an International Container Bureau which works to achieve satisfactory standard types so that there can be a more easy international exchange of traffic carried in containers. The British railways were among the first to use them—in the 1920's—and they advertised them widely for household removals.

Some two-purpose vehicles are designed for use either on roads or on the railway. The London Midland and Scottish Railway experimented with a motor-coach which ran on the railway from Blisworth, Northampton, to Stratford-upon-Avon, and then travelled on the road as far as the railway hotel. This practice was abandoned, but lorries of this type are useful in remote areas for carrying gangs engaged in railway track repairs, as the men can by this means travel more directly to their work. Road-rail buses have been used in other countries, including the Netherlands and the United States.

See also MOTOR-CAR, HISTORY OF; ROADS, MODERN; ROAD TRANSPORT ENGINES.

MOTOR TRANSPORT ENGINES, *see* ROAD TRANSPORT ENGINES.

MOTOR TRANSPORT MAINTENANCE.
A bus or coach stranded by the roadside is to-day a rare sight. This is due to the efficiency of the garages from which vehicles are operated. Most bus depots look after the maintenance of their vehicles and the administration of their staff. Let the daily happenings at a London Transport garage, briefly surveyed, serve as an example.

Each weekday morning at about 4.30 a.m. and on Sundays about 6.30 a.m., the buses allocated for service are ready. During the night the garage foreman has assigned each to a route, and the buses' running numbers, obtained from a duty schedule, show the garage staff how to arrange them in order of departure. Ten minutes before each is due to leave, the engine is started; it then awaits its crew (driver and conductor).

The crew sign on for duty 10 minutes before the bus is due to leave. This allows time for the driver to look over his machine and the conductor to prepare his tickets and way-bill, which are issued to him in a fibre box with the route and duty number stencilled on the outside. Destination blinds are turned to the correct position, and the bus leaves for a day on the road, which may last for any time up to 18 hours. London Transport garages take between 20 to 200 vehicles. The departure of buses, or 'run-out', as it is called, varies with the size of the garage. It may last 3 or 4 hours, and, during its peak, buses leave the garage at 30-second intervals. An inspector usually checks the run-out, and notes each bus number, to see that none are missing and that they are leaving on time. After this, the crew follow the instructions on the time-card.

During the day, when the garage is almost bare of vehicles, plenty of people are working. Every day a certain number of buses are withheld from service, for mechanical inspection and overhaul. Some need to be sent to a central repair works for complete renovation or an overhaul. This needs careful planning to ensure that there are enough men and buses each day. The garage has to be cleaned daily, as it is generally very dirty after a hundred or more buses have been in and out within a short space of time.

Besides the clerical work that always has to be done when a large number of people are employed, arrangements must be made to provide

A LONDON TRANSPORT DOUBLE-DECK BUS BEING WASHED AT VICTORIA GARAGE AT THE END OF ITS DAY'S WORK

substitutes for drivers and conductors who are absent on holiday or sick-leave. This is done by a depot inspector. As a bus is often handled by as many as four different crews during the day, men are signing on at all times. There are early, middle, and late shifts.

At night when the bus is returning to its garage, the conductor closes all the windows, and when it arrives, one of the night depot staff drives it on to a high pressure washing-plant, where a gang of cleaners removes all the grime off its exterior in a few minutes. Then its tanks are filled with petrol or diesel fuel, and the amount put in is recorded. When the bus has finally been parked, the interior is cleaned out and the boxes for used tickets are emptied.

Meanwhile the crew have signed off, the driver reporting the condition of the bus on a mechanical report sheet, and the conductor paying in his cash and returning the tickets, punch, and equipment to the official on duty. The ticket boxes are used for 3 days without being filled up. When all the buses have returned to the garage, the night foreman checks the mechanical report sheets and notes any defects. He decides if these can be rectified immediately or whether the bus should be kept off the road the next day. The buses are allocated by the results of his examination.

See also Bus; Motor-coach; London Transport.

MOUNTAIN PASSES. These provide ways of crossing mountain barriers. The importance of a pass depends on the length of the barrier to be crossed and the extent to which the pass supplies the need for communication between the peoples living on either side of it. That is why the Alpine passes are so important, for the barrier is long, and the need for communications has been very great ever since the Roman Empire began to extend civilization beyond the Alps.

There are three great mountain barriers in Europe, the Pyrenees, the Alps, and the Caucasus (qq.v. Vol. III), all of which stretch from sea to sea. The Pyrenees are the shortest of these; but, though there are no very high peaks, the lowest passes in the central part of the chain are rarely under 6,000 feet, and as the range is only 60 miles wide, the gradients are very steep. Consequently all the traffic between France and Spain, except such as can travel by mule paths, has in the past gone round the ends close to the sea, and the Spanish side of the central Pyrenees

E.N.A.

THE STELVIO PASS, ITALY
A motor road zigzags down the side

has remained one of the most primitive regions of Europe. To cross from a popular French tourist centre, such as Gavarnie or Luchon, has been almost like passing to another continent, particularly in any season but summer. Now there are two railway lines which cross the central Pyrenees. The Caucasus is a great barrier, 700 miles long, stretching from the Black Sea to the Caspian, and the people to the south of it have been until recently very backward. There are only two passes across it suitable for heavy traffic, but it has been crossed by traders from very early times (see Trade Routes). The Alps form an immense arc over the Italian plain, with its ends reaching the Mediterranean near Nice and the Adriatic near Trieste. From very early times, ways have been found through its passes for armies, pilgrims, commerce, and pleasure seekers passing to and from Italy. Hospices kept by monks gave much needed shelter to pedestrians who braved the dangers of mountain passes in winter and spring. Hannibal's crossing of the Western Alps with all the equipment of an ancient army, including elephants, in October 219 B.C., probably by the Col de l'Argentière or the Mont Genèvre, was an extraordinary feat (*see* HANNIBAL, Vol. V).

In Asia the huge arc-like barrier of the HIMALAYAS (q.v. Vol. III), north of India, is a whole series of high mountain chains. The passes that lead through the first high range above the plains of India only lead to high, sparsely inhabited districts; but the areas separated by the Great Himalayas are so vast and so important for trade that in the season when the melting of the snow makes traffic possible, trains of packponies and yaks find their way from Tibet along routes 14,000 to 18,000 feet high.

The ROCKY MOUNTAINS and the ANDES (qq.v. Vol. III) extend the whole length of the American Continent, leaving no way round for the peoples living in the huge territories lying on either the Atlantic or Pacific side of this great barrier. Passes had to be found—first trails (*see* AMERICAN TRAILS), then roads, and, by the 19th century, railways. There are three great railway routes across the Rockies. The Transandine Railway, linking the Argentine with Valparaiso (Chile), has the highest railway pass in the world, which follows the route of the Uspallata Pass (12,800 feet) and goes through a 2-mile tunnel under the pass (*see* RAILWAY SYSTEMS).

Frontier passes may be regarded by the people on either side as gateways to be opened or locked, and in war time rather as a gap in a hedge to be closed with barbed wire. A narrowing of the valley at the foot of a pass is a favourite place for the examination of passports and the visit of the customs officers to levy tolls on certain goods, while the neighbouring heights are fortified to resist invasion. These fortifications testify to the importance of a great mountain pass in the defence of a frontier. Peace-loving nations like the Swiss feel all the more secure for holding both sides of important passes such as the Simplon and the Bernina.

The word 'pass' generally implies the crossing of a watershed; but it is also used for a defile which provides an approach to a high pass

Canadian Pacific Railway

A C.P.R. TRAIN GOING THROUGH KICKING HORSE PASS, CANADA

through a difficult bit of country; well-known examples are the Pass of Killiecrankie leading up to the main pass over the Scottish Grampians; the Dariel Pass leading up to the main pass across the Caucasus, connecting Vladikavkaz and Tiflis; the Khyber Pass, which leads from Pakistan to Afghanistan, but is far from the watershed of the Kabul River. The typical mountain pass crosses a watershed at a depression between two higher points of the chain, its nature being suggested by the word *col* (Latin *collum* a neck) in the Alps, or by the word *port* (gateway) in the Pyrenees. A valley leads up to it on either side; but owing to the erratic ways in which water works its way through the surface of the earth, the approaches to mountain passes

Swiss Federal Railways

A TÉLÉPHÉRIQUE IN SWITZERLAND

The advantage of the suspension railway is the fact that it requires no permanent way. Up a rough and irregular mountain-side, where a funicular railway would need bridges across valleys, or tunnels under projecting spurs, the *téléphérique* can swing from tower to tower, with spans of almost indefinite length if it is necessary to cross a deep valley. The disadvantage is the small carrying capacity of the cars, which must be limited in weight to reduce the strain on the supporting cables.

There are many suspension lines in the Alps, particularly in Germany, Austria, France, and Italy; a well-known railway of this kind runs up Table Mountain, in South Africa. The most striking example of a long span is at Brévent, above Chamonix, in the Alps of eastern France. This swings straight up from one height to the summit of the cliffs forming the south face of the Brévent peak—a span of 4,400 feet with no intermediate support.

See also MOUNTAIN PASSES.

buffalo-hunting Indians of the Plains, o[n the]
other hand, will invite a grandfather [or]
important man of the tribe to choose a [name]
for a new-born baby which might comm[emorate]
a brave deed of his own, such as 'St[eals-]
enemy's-horse'. Girls as well as boys [get]
these 'war' names, though they m[ay be]
called something more feminine, su[ch as]
Bird. Their names are made up [of]
everyday use, so that the literal me[aning]
even though everyone may not k[now]
behind it.

The majority of modern Am[erican Indians]
have adopted Christian names a[nd]
those of their white neighbo[urs]
combinations of Robert Yell[ow]
planter, or Mary Strikes-on-[]
old ways. Many of those [
own languages as well as [
native names as well for [
One prominent nineteen[th
of the tribe of Nez Pe[rcé
English name of Josep[h
but lacking the full d[
Thunder-coming-up-[
land.

See also PLACE NAM[ES
See also Vol. I: Am[

NAUTICAL A[
HISTORY OF; N[

NAVIGATIO[N
tional meani[
To-day the [
navigator [
can tell th[
during a [
should [
article [

The [
land, [
Ther[
losi[
cro[

n[
t[
the mor[
indication of d[
the earliest names for a[
be described by a compass b[
names given to the various winds. The [

NAMES. 1. PERSONAL NAMES. Many primitive
people believe that their names are vital parts of
themselves, and are therefore very unwilling to
let them be known. Some races, such as the
ancient Egyptians and some American Indians
to-day, customarily have two names, one for
common use, and one kept carefully concealed
for fear an enemy should use it to harm its
owner. In the German fairy story, Rumpelstilts-
kin's power was gone as soon as his name was
known.

Nowadays most people in countries with Christian traditions have two kinds of name—a surname which they get from their father, and share
with their brothers and sisters, and Christian or
personal names, which are given to them indivi-
dually. In many parts of the world, however,
particularly in the past, people have had only
one name—a personal one. Sometimes a nickname or 'the son of so-and-so' was added as an
extra way of distinguishing a person. In Anglo-
Saxon times, when one name had to do the work
of both Christian name and surname, there were
several devices for marking family connexions;
for instance, members of a family might all have
names beginning with a vowel or with the same
consonant.

Names are made up of ordinary words taken
from the language which was in use when the
names were first given. Sometimes, as in Hebrew,
several very short words are combined to make
a name which is really a sentence—the name
Michael, for instance, which is of Hebrew origin,
means 'Who is like unto the Lord?' In the
INDO-EUROPEAN family of languages (q.v.), to
which English belongs, names are usually made
up of two words. Alfred, for instance, a name of
Old English origin, consists of two words meaning 'elf' and 'counsel'.

The names brought over by the Normans in
[late] 11th century were for the most part also
of remote Germanic origin, and not unlike some
of the native English names which they largely
displaced. Many of our commonest modern
names, such as William, Robert, Geoffrey, and
Charles, were introduced at the time of the
Norman Conquest.

A few Old English names survived the Conquest. But from the 13th century onwards most
English Christian names were drawn from the
general stock of names common to Christian
Europe. These names were either taken from
the Bible (being therefore mainly Hebrew or
Greek in origin), or from the Latin names of
a large number of saints. Most names were
changed to suit English ways of speech. Thus
the German *Gottfried* (meaning 'the peace of
God') had become *Godefroi* in France, and was
turned into 'Godfrey' in England.

The Puritans in the late 16th and early 17th
centuries introduced special names of their own,
which have become more common in the U.S.A.
(where they were used by Puritan emigrants)
than in England. For a short time in England
entire religious phrases were used as names;
a famous example is 'Praise-God Barebones'.
Ancient Hebrew names were based on the same
principle. Daniel meant 'The Lord is Judge';
John meant 'Jah (God) is gracious'. In the same
way the Moslem name Abdullah means 'Servant
of God'. The English Puritans also used Old
Testament names, such as Jedidiah, Ebenezer,
Ephraim, Ezra, which have died out in England
but are still used in the U.S.A.

More recently it has been fashionable to use
surnames as Christian names, frequently out
of admiration for some great man or socially
eminent family. Cecil (the family name of the
Marquis of Salisbury), Dudley, and Percy commemorate the names of famous families, while
Gordon is in memory of General Gordon, and
Rodney of Admiral Lord Rodney. In the U.S.A.
there are many such Christian names, for
example, Calvin, Elmer (the surname of two
brothers prominent in the American Revolution, and originally from the Old English personal name Æthelmaer), Jackson, Grant, Lee,
Jefferson, Lincoln, Luther, Washington, and
Wesley.

2. SURNAMES. By the 14th century parents
tended to give most children the names of a few
popular saints, such as Thomas, John, or James.
Since many people in the same village would

These had grown from the Port Books of the Greeks. They gave courses on which to steer, and information about ports, and were the fore-runners of the modern pilotage books.

The next step was the measurement of the altitude of the Pole Star, in order to determine latitude. Sailors must have observed for centuries that as they went south the star dipped towards the horizon; and by the time of the great Portuguese explorations of the 15th century the cross-staff, the ancestor of the modern sextant, was in general use. This was a jointed stick with a sliding crosspiece, which measured the angle of the Pole Star with the horizon, thus indicating the latitude of a ship (*see* Figure; *see* NAVIGATION, MARINE).

The ability to find latitude was a great advance: longitude, however, was to defy exact calculation for several hundred years. Yet by the 16th century, when sailors were crossing great oceans and remaining for weeks out of sight of land, navigation was becoming a science, needing charts, instruments, and books of star measurements. Ships at that time used a LOG (q.v.) to measure their speed, and a 'lead', a

direction of the port of destination, and when the latitude of the port was reached, to turn and sail along the parallel of latitude until land was sighted. With the crude instruments in use at sea, the latitude could be known only roughly, and a certain amount of sailing up and down the coast was generally necessary at the other side.

Using such methods, the Portuguese and Spanish became skilled navigators and were able to voyage successfully farther than man had sailed before. One further development was necessary before they could make their greatest voyages. When they sailed south, the Pole Star gradually dipped towards the horizon and finally vanished from view as they crossed the equator, and so the latitude could not be measured. The astronomers knew that latitude could be found by measuring the height of the sun at noon—when it was at its highest point. This gave the navigator a mathematical problem to solve, for the altitude of the sun is not as directly connected with the latitude as is that of the Pole Star. Tables had to be prepared, and rules for using them written out in words that seamen could understand.

The English seaman was accustomed to making shorter voyages, and at this time used little more than the compass and lead for soundings. When Drake sailed round the world, he had to kidnap a Portuguese pilot to take him into the Pacific, then a Spaniard onward from there. But in the years that followed, the war with Spain and the growing trade with the new American colonies and other distant places forced the English to learn more of navigation. Soon they became as skilful as their teachers, and

Bibliothèque Nationale

15TH-CENTURY SHIPS WITH A MARINER USING A COMPASS
Miniature from *Livres des Merveilles*

National Maritime Museum
TERRESTRIAL GLOBE, 1588
Globes were used for navigation at this period

astronomer, complained that measurement was hindered by the inaccurate charting of the moon and stars, Charles founded the Greenwich Observatory and made Flamsteed the first Astronomer-Royal. The regular observations which Flamsteed inaugurated have been continued ever since, and form the basis of the tables in the *Nautical Almanac*, first published in 1767. These tables give the changing positions throughout each year of the sun, moon, stars, and planets. King Charles II also offered rewards to anyone who could find the longitude at sea, and in 1713 a Bill was passed by Parliament offering rewards of £10,000 to £20,000. Longitude, which is the distance west or east of the meridian at Greenwich, is equivalent to the difference in time between local time and Greenwich TIME (q.v. Vol. III). In the 18th century no clock had been produced which could keep time, despite the rolling of a ship, the dampness of the air, and the changes of temperature, so accurately that the precise longitude could be found after many weeks had been spent at sea. John Harrison, a Yorkshire clockmaker, worked on this problem for some 30 years before producing in 1735 his first CHRONOMETER (q.v.) or ship's clock. His fourth chronometer, completed in 1759, was entered for the Government award and successfully tested on a voyage to Jamaica. Harrison had to fight for his reward, and it was some years before he received it.

In 1731 John Hadley made the first SEXTANT (q.v.), though the idea had been thought of earlier. The sextant is still used to measure the altitude of sun or stars. Before Hadley's invention, measurement was made with a plumb-line, or by trying to look at the same time at the sun and at the horizon—neither method being satisfactory. The sextant, by enabling latitude to be found with great accuracy, laid the foundations of modern stellar (star) navigation. Methods of calculation have now changed, and wireless time-signals have reduced the importance of the chronometer; but the basis remains the same.

See also EXPLORATION; SEA TRAVEL.

in the next century or two were to lead the world.

England's first great contribution to navigation was the founding by Charles II in 1675 of the Royal Observatory at Greenwich. Sailors felt the need for a way of measuring longitude at sea. When John Flamsteed, a well-known

NAVIGATION, AIR. Aeroplanes are navigated first by careful planning before the flight, and then by an attempt to keep to the course planned throughout the journey. The direction and speed of the wind is the main factor to be considered. The effect of the wind on the aircraft's course

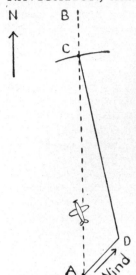

FIG. 1. WIND VELOCITY
TRIANGLE

This is a diagram to show how
an aircraft flying 150 m.p.h.
overcomes a wind to the NE.
blowing 40 m.p.h. and keeps
a straight course. The aircraft is to fly North from *A* in
the direction of *B*. Using a
scale, $\frac{1}{8}$ in. = 10 m.p.h., we
draw a line NE. from *A*, and
mark off $\frac{1}{2}$ in. (40 miles) which
fixes the point *D*. We draw a
circle centred on *D* with a
radius representing the speed
of the aircraft—$1\frac{7}{8}$ in. (150
miles). The circle cuts the
dotted line at *C*, and a line
drawn from *D* to *C* shows the
direction the pilot should steer
(NNW) to keep a straight
course N. *A* to *C* measures
the miles flown per hour if
conditions do not change.

has to be calculated. As a boat or a swimmer
crossing a river sometimes has to head not in the
direction of his objective, but into the current,
so low-flying aircraft in a cross-wind sometimes
appear to be 'flying sideways'. An aeroplane is
literally carried by the air, and as the air mass
in which it is travelling is nearly always moving,
the aircraft must tend to move with it, whatever
its course (Fig. 1).

1. PLANNING. The navigator, having arrived
at figures for the wind's speed and direction,
decides on the angle at which he must 'aim off'
his machine from the straight line between the
airports. Maps and charts of the route are
essential. An air map presents an accurate picture of the ground below, illustrating in various
colours all conspicuous geographical features
which the navigator can identify, and so tell his
position. An air chart, drawn to a much smaller
scale and without the elaborate detail of the
map, is designed simply to enable the navigator
to plot his position during the journey. The
chart is concerned not with landmarks, but with
latitude and longitude, and on it the pilot plots
all checks of position. On arrival at the destination the chart, with the navigator's notes or
'log', gives a complete story of the journey.

Before the flight the navigator, having collected his maps and charts, goes to the meteorological briefing office of the airport, where he
is informed of weather conditions. The winds
which affect him are those at a high altitude,
where there is a steady, massive movement of

air, not the gusty, changeable type of wind which
we know on the earth's surface. The navigator
then passes to the 'Flight Planning Room' where
he draws his track with protractor, ruler, and
dividers on his chart. A large patch of bad
weather may be forecast right 'on track', and if
this extends to a great height, making flying over
it impossible, he may have to make a detour,
dividing the journey into two 'legs' to take the
aircraft round the bad weather. If the aircraft,
for this or other reasons, has to make a longer
journey than was scheduled, it will have to increase the speed of travel to get to the destination
on time. This arrival time, or E.T.A. (Estimated
Time of Arrival), is important to a navigator.
He will always strive to reach home within a
minute or so of his stated E.T.A., for his passengers
may have other connexions to catch there.

2. DURING FLIGHT. Once in flight, the navigator's task is continually to 'fix' his position by
observations. He can do this in many ways—
by observing ground objects with the help of a
map, by measuring the position of sun or stars
with a SEXTANT (q.v.), or by radio and radar
navigation aids. The first two methods, of
course, depend on either the ground or the
heavens being visible, and in fact most 'position
fixing' is now done by radio or radar aids.

One radio method is just a straightforward
conversation on a radio-telephone between a
ground controller and the pilot in the sky.
Another is the sending of messages by MORSE
CODE as in TELEGRAPHY (qq.v.) A third consists in continuously transmitting a certain signal
(just as a lighthouse might flash a beam every
10 seconds), the listening pilot being guided by
the nature of the signal.

Normal telephone speech between the ground
and the aircraft is transmitted from a very high
frequency (V.H.F.) wireless set, but is limited
to a range of roughly 50 miles. Morse code is
transmitted by medium frequency (M.F.) and
high frequency (H.F.) sets, which have a range
of some 200 miles. All normal routine position
reporting, as well as weather reporting, is done
on these frequencies. At many places a direction-
finding service is available. At least three different stations take simultaneous bearings of a
signal transmitted from the aircraft. A central
station then plots these, and reports the aircraft's
position to the pilot within a few seconds.

One of the continuous signal methods is 'Consol'. Its signals, which can be picked up by an

aircraft with only an ordinary radio receiver, are transmitted from a Consol station on the ground in all directions, in a series of dots and dashes in different combinations. The proportion of the dots and dashes varies with the aircraft's bearing (north, south, east, or west of the station). The pilot counts the dots and dashes and refers them to various position lines printed on a special chart. He can get a good 'fix' by tuning in simultaneously to two Consol stations and seeing where the two position lines meet on his chart.

Another radio navigational aid is the radio compass, an appliance in an aircraft which, if tuned in to a radio beacon on the ground, automatically indicates the aircraft's bearing from the beacon. The pilot can fly direct towards the beacon, or take bearings of different beacons and plot them on his chart. If beacons are conveniently located, he may be able to make his whole flight by flying towards one beacon after another with the aid only of his radio compass. The Radio Range, a long-range navigational aid developed and much used in the U.S.A., is somewhat like a beacon, but it transmits the letters A ($\cdot$ —) and N (— $\cdot$) in Morse code simultaneously in different directions. If the pilot is flying directly on his proper course, he will be midway between the paths of the two signals, $\cdot$ — and — $\cdot$; their sounds will overlap so that he will hear only a continuous note. If he deviates to the right or left, he will hear one or other of the Morse signals, and so will know that he is off his course.

RADAR (q.v. Vol. VIII), unlike radio, is not used mainly to transmit information, but to collect it. A radar set issues wireless impulses and measures the 'echo' when this bounces back after the impulses have struck an object. Radar methods are constantly being improved in detail, and old methods discarded. Some methods of navigation employ both radar and radio at the same time.

An extremely accurate and swift method of position-fixing by radar is called 'Gee', an aid developed by the British in the Second World War to guide bombers to their targets, and now widely used in Europe. Unlike other aids, Gee is unaffected by weather, height, day and night, or atmospheric changes. The system requires a number of transmitting stations at various places on the ground, one 'master' station controlling the transmission of all the 'slave' stations. These

B.E.A.

THE WIRELESS AERIAL ON TOP OF THE CONTROL TOWER, NORTHOLT AIRPORT, LONDON

stations send out radar impulses, which are picked up on a radar set in the aeroplane and measured off by the radio officer as figures, which correspond to curved lines on special charts. The aircraft's position is the point at which the lines meet. The U.S.A. have developed an aid similar to Gee, but suitable for long-range work over the Pacific and North Atlantic Oceans, called 'Loran' (LOng RAnge Navigation), which uses longer radio waves with radar instruments.

When the navigator has obtained his 'position fixes', these either confirm or confound his earlier judgement of the wind's speed and course, and tell him whether or not he must alter his course. A pilot or navigator, however, cannot choose any course he pleases, as his is not the only aircraft in the sky; in most countries certain definite pathways or 'corridors' must be used by all aircraft to avoid accidents. In flying from one airport to another, aircraft must obey the RULE OF THE ROAD (q.v. section 3). Before the pilot

B.E.A.

IN THE MOVEMENTS CONTROL ROOMS, NORTHOLT AIRPORT, LONDON

gets to the end of his journey, he must make contact with the airport, so that he can be told how to avoid other aircraft, and when and how to land. Modern air speeds are so great that this contact is sometimes made when the aircraft is still more than 100 miles from the airport. Some of the radar and radio devices, therefore, can be used both for the main part of a flight and for the actual landing.

3. LANDING. The final approach is always made along a selected safe path to the airfield clear of buildings or hills (*see* AIRPORT). Where local obstacles, such as mountains, make landing difficult, the only safe path may be a spiral one from a point directly above the airfield itself. Before an airline starts a new service, a 'proving' flight is made, in which senior technicians make experimental approaches to each airfield to dis- cover the best landing method to be used on all flights. This method, known as the 'let-down', must be studied and practised by each pilot.

Aircraft carry a flight guide or route book, containing scale diagrams of all 'let-down' methods likely to be needed. The book gives position and frequencies of all landing aids, air traffic rules, times of weather broadcasts, and other information.

The action of landing involves steering into the wind towards the airfield, lining up the air- craft with the runway, losing height and speed at the correct rate, throttling back the engines at the right moment, and touching-down on the runway with the minimum speed and bump. The pilot is helped by many dials and meters which tell him speed, height, rate of descent, and engine revolutions (*see* FLYING INSTRUMENTS). Even in clear weather this is a task which occupies the full attention of the pilot and calls for all his skill and experience, especially if he is piloting a plane-load of passengers.

The achievement is even more difficult in bad visibility. The pilot must descend 'blind', pos- sibly through thousands of feet of cloud, until he reaches the cloud-base, which may be, per- haps, only a few feet above ground-level; and he must then level out and make his approach. When he breaks cloud, the airfield may still be obscured by mist or heavy rain. By teamwork between pilot, radio officer, and ground operators, based on intensive training, such a landing is now a safe process, carried out daily all over the world. The help of radio and radar is essential; and no aircraft is licensed to carry passengers or goods which is not equipped with efficient signalling apparatus.

An important radar and radio device is Ground Controlled Approach (G.C.A.). The only equipment required in the aircraft is a V.H.F. radio set, by which the pilot can carry on normal conversation with the ground controller. When the approaching aircraft is 30 miles away, the controller begins to watch its movements on his radar screen. At a distance of about 10 miles he begins his 'talk-you-down' instructions to the pilot. His radar set is adjusted so accurately that he can be sure of the aircraft's exact position, and can with absolute confidence direct the pilot right on to the end of the runway, even in the thickest fog. This method is the basis of more powerful equipment at very large airports. London Airport's apparatus, for instance, can 'see' a high-flying four-engined aircraft 130 miles away.

A radio device, known as Standard Beam Approach (S.B.A.), working on the same principle as Radio Range, is a method used for 'homing' an aircraft when it is near its airport. A main beacon is sited at the up-wind end of the runway in use, transmitting Morse signals. These signals are beamed along the runway and beyond it, so that the pilot has merely to follow the continuous note in order to arrive directly on the end of the runway. On the ground, below

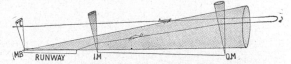

FIG. 2. S.B.A. (STANDARD BEAM APPROACH) LET-DOWN
The main beacon (M.B.) sends out a horizontal beam along which the pilot flies, and the inner and outer markers, I.M. and O.M., send vertical beams to give the lateral position. No signals are heard in the 'cone of silence' C.

the path of the beam, inner and outer radio 'markers' are situated, and transmit a high-pitched note in a very narrow vertical 'beam'. As the aircraft passes across the beam, the sudden note of the marker indicates to the pilot his distance from the end of the runway (see Fig. 2). A more elaborate version of S.B.A. is the Instrument Landing System (I.L.S.), which shows on dials the angle at which the aircraft must fly downwards. Thus the pilot can approach the runway while flying completely 'blind'.

Another 'homing' device is the Rebecca and Eureka radar system. The 'Rebecca' unit in the aircraft transmits radar impulses towards the 'Eureka' responder beacon at the destination. The Eureka responder beacon continuously reflects back these impulses to the aircraft, where

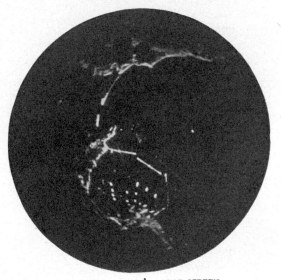

PORTLAND HARBOUR. *Left*: DETAIL OF A CHART. *Right*: THE SAME AREA SHOWN ON A SHIP'S RADAR SCREEN
The line of the coast, breakwaters, and ships show white on the screen
Reproduced by courtesy of Kelvin Hughes (Marine) Ltd. and the Controller of H.M. Stationery Office and the Hydrographer of the Navy

they appear on the screen of the radar set. To maintain an accurate course towards the Eureka beacon, the signals must be kept in the centre of the screen. A graduated scale on the screen tells the navigator his distance from the beacon.

In spite of radar and radio aids, aircraft are not allowed to attempt a landing if visibility is too bad. The pilot must be allowed at least some seconds in which he can see the runway before he attempts to touch down. If nothing at all is visible, aircraft are diverted by signal to another airfield free from fog or cloud. Aircraft always carry plenty of fuel for such an occasion.

See also RULE OF THE ROAD, Section 3; WIRELESS. See also Vol. VIII: RADAR.

NAVIGATION, MARINE.

Two basic forms of ship navigation are used to-day, coastal and deep-sea.

1. COASTAL NAVIGATION, or pilotage, is the art of directing a ship's course when within sight of land. The navigator discovers where the ship is, and so the course to steer, by direct observation of the land, by noting the position of navigational marks such as lighthouses and buoys, and by taking soundings of the depth of the sea. To interpret the information obtained from these, he uses CHARTS (q.v.), which show not only the contours of the land, and the position of all prominent objects (hills, buildings, and even conspicuous trees) and of all navigational marks, but also the depth of water and nature of the bottom.

The navigator having identified recognizable objects ashore on the chart, then, by means of the COMPASS (q.v.), notes the position of his ship relative to those objects. For example, he observes a hill bearing north-east from him and a church spire bearing north-west, and so knows that the ship must lie on lines running south-west from the hill and south-east from the spire. He draws these lines on the chart, and the point

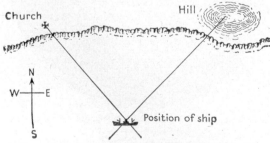

FIG. 1. OBTAINING A FIX BY CROSS-BEARINGS

at which they cross is the ship's position. This process is called 'obtaining a fix by cross-bearings' (Fig. 1).

Where suitable objects for cross-bearings are not available, methods using one object are possible. A single bearing can be taken of one object, together with a sounding; or two separate bearings of the same object can be taken, the

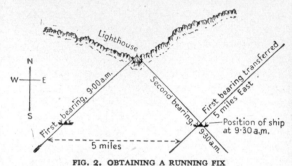

FIG. 2. OBTAINING A RUNNING FIX
The ship is travelling East at 10 knots. In ½ hour it will have travelled 5 miles

ship having moved along her course between the first and second—a method known as a 'running fix'. The first bearing is drawn on the chart and then, when the second bearing is taken, the first is transferred on the chart at a distance corresponding to the distance the ship has travelled in the interval. The bearings thus cross each other and give the ship's position at the time of the second bearing (Fig. 2). Other methods with the help of RADAR and optical RANGE-FINDERS (qq.v. Vol. VIII) are also used.

Having fixed the position of the ship, the navigator then 'rules' (draws with a ruler) the course that he wishes to follow on the chart, and notes the compass-bearing on which the ship's head must be kept. In determining the course to steer, he must take account of the tidal streams, which usually flow more rapidly close inshore than out at sea. Information about these, showing where they flow across the course, is printed on the chart.

At night, when the land cannot be seen, the coastal navigator relies mainly on the lights of LIGHTHOUSES and BUOYS (qq.v.) identifying each light by its characteristic flashes or colour. He may also have the advantage of radar to give him ranges and bearings of the land itself, and soundings will help him to keep in deep water.

When all other methods fail, as may happen in fog if radar apparatus is not fitted, the navigator must rely on 'dead reckoning', which is an estimate of his position based on the course and distance he has sailed since his last known position, with an allowance made for tidal stream and for 'leeway' if he has met strong winds.

Where navigation is particularly dangerous, or requires local knowledge, ships take on board a PILOT (q.v.) with special local knowledge to navigate through the dangerous area. Pilots are available at all the principal ports in the world, and at many ports must be employed.

2. DEEP-SEA NAVIGATION, or astro-navigation, is the art of directing the ship's course out of sight of land, when the navigator must rely on observations of celestial bodies for obtaining a 'fix'. Once he knows his position he plots it on the chart, and then decides what course to steer. Where great distances are involved the curvature of the earth must be taken into account, and a course shaped so as to follow the 'great circle'. The navigator draws an imaginary line round the earth, passing through the ship's starting-point and destination. So long as the diameters of this circle pass through the centre of the earth it will show the shortest way between the two points (*see* Fig. 3). In coastal navigation, the short distances involved make this calculation unnecessary, and the navigator can treat the earth's surface as if it were flat.

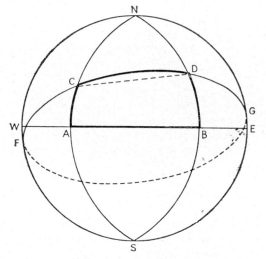

FIG. 3. GREAT CIRCLE AND PLANE SAILING

The diagram represents the earth with the Poles at N and S. Great Circle lines are NWS, NCAS, NDBS, NES (lines of longitude), WABE (the equator), and FCDG. Owing to the earth's curvature the shortest distances between AC, CD, DB, and AB lie along Great Circles and not along straight lines joining the points on a chart

The deep-sea navigator needs cross-bearings just as much as the coastal sailor, but he cannot get them by taking the bearings of objects to be seen on the coast. He has to choose two points on the surface of the earth (or sea), each of which happens to have a star directly above it at the precise moment of observation. These points, even if they are 50 or 100 or 500 miles away from him, will enable him to fix his own position.

The two stars are first located in an imaginary 'celestial sphere' (*see* diagram, p. 27, Vol. III). The sky is thought of as a vast globe surrounding the earth; on the inner surface of that globe, which is dotted with stars, are imaginary markings representing the latitude, longitude, equator, and poles, and corresponding exactly with the same markings on maps and globes of the earth. Directly above the earth's North Pole is the North Pole of the sky; on the same plane as the earth's Equator is the Equator of the sky. Thus every star in the sky has a latitude and longitude in the celestial sphere, just as any town on the earth has a latitude and longitude on maps.

When an imaginary straight line is drawn from the centre of the earth to a star, the point at which that line pierces the earth's surface at any given moment is known as the star's 'geographical position'. If that position on the earth is latitude North 64° 4′, and longitude West 13° 27′, then the position of the star in the celestial sphere at the same moment is exactly the same. By tradition, the latitude of a star is called its 'declination', and its longitude is called its 'right ascension'; mariners have to turn the degrees of longitude into clock hours in order to calculate their distance east or west of the meridian of Greenwich when using a CHRONOMETER (q.v.); therefore 'right ascension' is always expressed in hours and not degrees.

The navigator can look up the 'geographical position' of any star in the *Nautical Almanac*, a printed book issued once a year, which shows the exact position of the sun, moon, planets, and principal stars at frequent intervals on every day and night of the year. The earth, of course, is rotating, and therefore the 'geographical position' of any star is constantly moving round the earth; but rotation is related to time, and from the chronometer the navigator can find where, in its course round the earth, the 'geographical position' lies at the moment of observation.

The one important measurement which the navigator must make, and for which accuracy

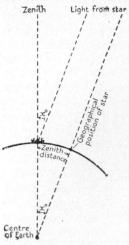

FIG. 4. FINDING THE ZENITH
DISTANCE

Because lines of light from a
star infinitely far away can
be regarded as parallel, the
angles x° are equal

is important, is that of
the altitude of each of
the two stars. This is
expressed with refer-
ence to the horizon
(any point on a level
with the eyes), and the
zenith (the point
directly overhead).
Let us suppose the
navigator is to plot
two stars, A and B,
which are nearly, but
not quite, overhead.
For this he uses a SEX-
TANT (q.v.), a simple
optical instrument
which registers the
exact angle of a star's
altitude. The naviga-
tor notes that star A
is 1 degree and star B
is 3 degrees off the zenith point overhead.
Immediately the navigator knows the distance
of his ship from the 'geographical position' of each
of those two stars on the earth's surface. The
angle measured on the ship's deck between the
zenith and the star is the same as an angle
measured at the centre of the earth between the
ship and the 'geographical position' of a star (see
Fig. 4). The navigator knows that 1 degree of the
arc at the earth's centre equals 60 sea-miles on
the surface. Therefore he is 60 miles away from the
geographical position of star A, and 180 miles
away from that of star B. (These are known as
'zenith distances'.)

The navigator then looks up in his *Nautical
Almanac* the position in the celestial sphere of
each of the two stars at the exact second at which
he made his observations. He then marks these
positions, expressed in the latitude and longitude
of 'geographical positions' on his chart, calling
them point A and point B. He then draws with
his compasses a circle of 60-mile radius round
point A and a circle of 180-mile radius round
point B. The spot at which the circular lines
cut one another on his chart represents the position of his ship (*see* Fig. 5). (If he has drawn
two complete circles, they will, of course, cut
one another at two points, but it will be clear
which point is likely to be the correct one.)

Where, as frequently happens, the zenith
distance is very large (often 2,000 miles or more),
plotting on one chart by direct measurement is
impossible. Instead, the navigator calculates the
distance from points A and B, and then draws on
the chart lines resulting from his calculations.
These lines, known as 'position lines', actually
correspond to a short section of a very large
circle, but as it is so large, the curve is ignored
and the line drawn straight. By crossing two
such lines, the ship's position is fixed.

At night, stars, planets, or the moon are used
for various observations, depending on how
cloudy the sky is. The moon is so near the earth
that the simple formula described here is not
accurate enough, and special calculations must
be made. In the day-time the sun, if it is visible,
is 'shot' with the sextant.

When the observed body is on the ship's
meridian (that is, in the plane running north
and south through the ship's position), the latitude can be found without any plotting on the
chart, and without even knowing the time (*see*
NAVIGATION, HISTORY OF). The sun is in this
position at noon (local time), and in a ship at sea
a sun 'sight' is normally taken at noon each day.
If no chronometer were available, the sight could
still be taken by observing the highest position
which the sun reaches. Knowing the latitude
accurately, the longitude may then also be found
by calculation only, without plotting. For this,
however, the Greenwich time must be known.

Astro-navigation is a big subject, and such an
account as this can include only the bare principles; there are other methods not described
here of fixing a ship's position.

3. RADIO NAVIGATION. Developments in elec-
tronics during the Second World War provided

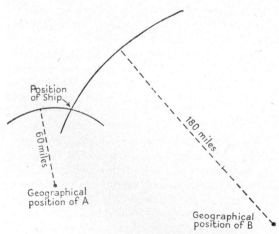

FIG. 5. PLOTTING A SHIP'S POSITION ON THE CHART

the sailor with new methods of finding his way across the ocean, which are of the greatest value when the sun or stars are hidden by cloud. Groups of transmitting-stations in various countries send out radio waves at intervals, so that ships fitted with a special receiver can calculate their position. The basic principle is that two shore stations send out waves at the same time; although these waves travel at 186,000 miles a second, which is the speed of light, the sensitive receiver can measure, in millionths of a second, how much longer the waves have taken to travel from the station which is farther off. There are several systems: 'Loran' (Long Range Navigation) is widely used for great distances in mid-ocean; nearer shore a complicated system known as 'Decca', and worked from chains of 'Decca' stations, is used in some places on the British coast.

Ships still use also the 'direction-finder' based on an older principle: this shows the direction from which any ordinary wireless message has come. Thus two ships at sea can calculate the position of an unknown ship which has sent out a wireless distress signal.

RADAR (q.v. Vol. VIII) is mainly used close to shore or in busy shipping channels, to replace the navigator's eyesight, and so avoid collision in darkness or fog. This device gives a moving diagram, on an illuminated screen, of any objects near the ship which can reflect radar waves, such as cliffs, other ships, and large buoys (see Fig. 6). It is possible to enter or leave a foggy port by radar aid, but the practice has limitations, particularly when large ships need tugs to help them to dock. More details of radio and radar navigational aids are given in the article NAVIGATION, AIR, for the principle is the same both for ships and aeroplanes.

Although the Captain of a ship is ultimately responsible for navigation, the navigating officer does most of the plotting, takes charge of the ship's charts, keeps them up to date in accordance with 'Notices to Mariners' issued weekly, and maintains such equipment as chronometers and echo-sounding equipment. Every deck officer in a ship is trained to take over navigation should the need arise.

See also NAVIGATION, HISTORY OF; MAPS.
See also Vol. VIII: RADAR.

NEWS AGENCY. This is an organization which sells news to newspapers. Small news agencies are one-man businesses, in which an energetic JOURNALIST (q.v.) collects information in a definite part of a town or county, or about a definite subject. His customers find it cheaper to buy news from him than to employ a member of their own staff to collect the information. In many countries, however, newspapers are served by one or two vast organizations which supply most of the regular news, leaving it to the papers themselves to seek for exceptional news.

In Britain this task is carried out by the Press Association, an organization which makes no profits and which is co-operatively owned by the provincial newspapers. The Association has a staff of 130 journalists, with an editor-in-chief, assistant editors, sub-editors, Parliamentary, law-court, and racing staffs, reporters, correspondents, and specialist writers, as well as some 1,500 local correspondents in all parts of the country. The Association's news is sent by teleprinter machines to more than 120 British newspapers and to the B.B.C. The news columns of a newspaper could be produced entirely with this news. In fact, all the news in some provincial evening papers, except for detailed reports of purely local events, comes from the Association.

The head offices of the Association in Fleet Street, which are never shut night or day, are shared with Reuter's Agency, an organization which deals with oversea news. Reuter's (pronounced 'Royters'), although founded by a native of Germany, has been for many years a British institution. It is owned in trust on behalf of the British and Dominions press, and works very closely with the Press Association. The sub-editors at Reuter's have to be men of wide education, well versed in foreign affairs. Reuter's employs journalists of integrity at key points all over the world. It supplies world news not only to British newspapers and the B.B.C., but to every country and every important newspaper in the world.

Most messages from abroad are received in 'cablese'—that is, the fewest possible words are used to convey the meaning, so as to save money. For instance, the following nineteen words, 'Resignation government overnight postmeeting ministry handed today einaudi exdegasperi quirinal stop president etpremier conversed two hours unregarded indication crisis', would be written out in the following fifty-two words: 'The resignation of the Government last night after a meeting of the Council of Ministers was handed today to President Einaudi by Signor de Gasperi at the Quirinal Palace. The President and the Prime Minister remained in conversation for two hours, but this is not regarded as an indication of a crisis.'

One other important agency supplies foreign news in Britain, the British United Press. This is linked with the United Press of America which, with the Associated Press of America, plays a big part in serving American newspapers.

See also NEWSPAPER; REPORTER.
See also Vol. VII: NEWSPAPER INDUSTRY.

NEWS BROADCASTING. 1. This, now one of the most important means of communication, is, unlike the printing of news, a craft of very recent origin. It was unknown before the invention of the wireless valve, which led to the start of broadcasting in the 1920's (*see* WIRELESS, HISTORY OF). News is collected for broadcasting, and assembled by editors in a central broadcasting station, in much the same way as it is for NEWSPAPERS (q.v.). Although there are important differences in the preparation of spoken and printed news, the same reporters, press conferences, and news agencies often provide news for both newspapers and broadcasting.

But printed and broadcast news reach the listener in quite a different way, and the strong emotional effect of speech compared with print calls for special safeguards in broadcasting news. When people read a newspaper, they can ponder over the printed words and analyse their meaning, if they wish to; they can read a statement twice over, and discuss its meaning with someone else, or compare it with a statement on the same subject in another newspaper. None of these methods of checking can be used for news broadcasts. A further difficulty is that the listener, because he is interrupted in some way, may hear only part of the news. He turns on the wireless in the middle of the news and hears that ten people have been killed; but he may not know whether this happened in Britain or in China, whether in a bus accident or an earthquake. Broadcast news has to be read out at a set speed which is convenient to the majority of people. But in fact some people's power of understanding works very slowly, and they may grasp only a part of what is said by the broadcaster. If they are people with little general information, they may easily misunderstand what the broadcaster has said. Scenes of panic have occurred on several occasions in America in the early days of broadcasting, when broadcast statements delivered in a rather sensational way have been only partly heard, or their meaning misunderstood—perhaps by immigrants who did not understand English well. On one occasion many people in New York left their homes on foot or by motor-car, taking their most precious possessions, and hurried into the country, in order to 'escape' from an imagined danger, the news of which they believed had been broadcast to them.

The size of the wireless audience makes it important that news should be announced with care and strict fairness. In Britain an item of broadcast news may be heard by more than ten million people at once, a fact which gives broadcasting a form of power possessed much less by a newspaper.

The emotional effect of spoken news is stronger than that of printed news. The tones of the human voice can give to a statement read out at the microphone a variety of interpretation—approval, disgust, contempt, anger, or other emotions—which the same statement, read in print, would be without. People generally listen to the news in the evening in their homes, when they are, perhaps, particularly susceptible to emotional influences, and what they hear may sway them unreasonably. Dictators have made use of this tendency; in order to win support, they have worked on the fears of their peoples by arranging for the regular broadcasting of news which would disturb them. It is well known that frightened people will often submit to any kind of leadership which promises them protection. Dictatorship Governments, who cannot count on the support of their people, generally control their broadcasting strictly, forbidding the people on pain of severe penalties, even death, to listen to unauthorized programmes. During the Second World War, for example, listeners in Germany or in countries occupied by German troops were forbidden to tune in to B.B.C. news.

2. B.B.C. NEWS. In Britain, broadcast news is the sole responsibility of the B.B.C., which is allowed to transmit its programmes by virtue of a licence granted to it by the Postmaster-General (*see* BROADCASTING CORPORATIONS). The B.B.C. is obliged, by the terms of this licence, to avoid expressing any opinions of its own. The Government may order the broadcasting of any announcement, but the B.B.C. has the right to

B.B.C.

PREPARING 'RADIO NEWSREEL'
The narrator is in the foreground

state publicly that it is doing so on the instructions of the Government, and is in no way responsible for the announcement. The B.B.C. broadcasts the news at set times from 7 a.m. until just before midnight in its main programmes every day. As well as the bulletins of general news and sports news, a radio newsreel, which is a form of broadcast news magazine, is given daily. When the occasion justifies it, extra broadcasts are made of special kinds of news, such as a cricket Test Match, or the Lord Mayor's Show. These are accompanied by the recordings of B.B.C. commentators on the spot, and sometimes by the actual sounds of the event, as at a Coronation or other great public ceremony (*see* BROADCASTING COMMENTARIES, Vol. IX).

The News bulletin is read out by one of the news-readers (the more experienced announcers), who sits at a table before a microphone, reading from a set of typewritten sheets which has been prepared in a news-room by the editors. The editors are a team of professional journalists permanently employed by the B.B.C. They receive hundreds of thousands of words a day, which arrive from their own observers or correspondents at home and abroad by tape-machine,

telephone, cable, air mail, wireless, or by messenger from the offices of one of the newspaper press agencies. The editors' task is to sift the main items of the news from this mass of material, and then to edit the selected material and condense it to not more than 2,000 words. This length, which is equal to two or three columns of space in a newspaper, will occupy nearly 15 minutes of time when spoken. The final bulletin is dictated to a typist, so that the editors may hear what the news will sound like; it is important that the sentences should be distinct, and free from tongue-twisting words, and that there should be no possibility of misunderstanding. Next, the items in the news are checked for doubtful references of fact, and for words of unusual or difficult pronunciation. Lastly, the news-reader himself reads the bulletin and gets settled any doubtful questions of phrasing, pronunciation, or emphasis before he goes to the microphone.

Occasionally news reaches listeners in the form of an international 'hook-up'; if a very important event is taking place in France, Italy, America, or some other foreign country, the B.B.C. may arrange to link up by radio-telephone with the broadcasting organization in that country. In that way an American President's voice may be heard in B.B.C. programmes while he is actually speaking. At the same time a recording of his words will be made by the B.B.C.'s recording studios in London, and may be broadcast again several times that day, during the B.B.C.'s ordinary news bulletins.

See also REPORTER.

NEWSPAPER. Most newspapers provide general news—that is, information about any subject likely to be interesting to the general reader. But a small class of newspapers, such as a daily paper devoted to finance or to sport, or a weekly paper devoted to religious news, is a specialist publication, intended only for a section of the community.

General newspapers are either national or regional. In a small country like Britain a national daily paper can easily be distributed to all parts of the country. But in countries of enormous area, such as the U.S.A., India, and the U.S.S.R., the distribution of a national daily paper to all parts would take so long that the news would be out of date before it reached the reader. There are now fewer than ten national papers in Britain, for the large wealthy papers have tended to absorb the poorer ones.

All general newspapers were roughly classified by the Royal Commission on the Press (1949) as either 'quality' or 'popular' newspapers, although several newspapers can claim to be both. Typical of 'quality' papers is *The Times*, which has been published in London every week-day since the late 18th century. In the mid-19th century, changes in taxation, education, and mechanical invention enabled newspapers to lower their prices and sell to a larger public. *The Times* decided not to compete with others, but to maintain a higher price and sell a larger and more carefully prepared selection of news to a smaller number of influential readers. This policy has been successfully carried out for 100 years, and has since been followed by a few other papers. The 'quality' papers, recognizing that the press is the public's main link with the world outside Britain, have always specialized in foreign news. Many popular papers at the beginning of this century largely ignored foreign events, but have since begun to appreciate their importance.

Most of the popular morning papers, except for two 'picture papers', follow a standardized pattern. The more important news is printed on the front page, and the sporting news on the back. In the centre of the paper is a literary or 'feature' page which may contain the leading article of editorial opinion, or a signed article by a well-known person, a cartoon, book reviews, comic strips, personal 'gossip', a humorous column, fashion news, items for children, and a selection of readers' letters to the editor. Sometimes these items appear on other pages.

Nearly every London morning paper prints some of its editions in branch printing works in Manchester, from which copies may be distributed more quickly to northern Britain. Some also print in Scotland.

A big London daily newspaper may employ as many as 3,000 men and women, who have to work as a carefully organized team. The editor, who must be a man of good organizing ability, is responsible for seeing that each editorial department is working efficiently and that the proprietor's policy is being observed in the paper's general politics and tone.

The collection of all general news is the responsibility of the news editor; foreign news, sent in from a number of foreign correspondents, is organized by the foreign editor; the sports editor arranges sporting news; a features editor sees to the features page; and so on. News is brought in by REPORTERS (q.v.), some of whom work from the head office, and others from various important points in the provinces. As well, there are contributors in hundreds of large and small towns all over the country, who are paid on results. News is also supplied by the NEWS AGENCIES (q.v.). Many reporters specialize in particular kinds of work. There are political correspondents who attend sessions in the Houses of Parliament, industrial correspondents, crime reporters, and theatre and film news correspondents, apart from the critics of the new plays and films. The news editor also receives a great deal of information from Government departments, business organizations, and from private people who are seeking publicity. Reporters have to investigate such information to sift out the small proportion which proves to be worth publishing. The 'leader' column contains an article every day which expresses the newspaper's official opinions (as distinct from news). Important papers have at least one full-time 'leader-writer', and the editor always supervises, and sometimes even writes, this article himself.

A sub-editor's task is to take all the available material relating to an item of news, and turn it into the exact form in which it will be printed, including the head-lines. Let us suppose that a murder has occurred in Wales, in a village half-way between Cardiff and Swansea. The sub-editor in charge of the account at head office may be handed as many as fifty different sheets of paper during the course of 3 or 4 hours, each containing a report or part of a report of some aspect of the murder. Reporters in Cardiff and Swansea, who have heard of the murder, will telephone reports to London, but their reports may not agree. When the sub-editor has written a summary of their information, having checked it from maps and local directories, an account may arrive from a correspondent at the actual scene of the crime, which renders the prepared summary out of date. Later the staff reporter for the South Wales region, having reached the spot by car, may telephone yet another version, ignorant of what has already been sent. Yet the sub-editor must prepare for the printer, some-times hour by hour as new editions are printed, a single, clear account from which all doubts and inconsistencies have been removed. And this is probably not the only story he is having to handle. Even more difficult to handle is a political crisis in Europe or a presidential election in the U.S.A. A London morning paper at the busiest hours, which with a morning paper are in the evening, may often have twenty sub-editors at a time. To produce some 20,000 words for an issue of a morning paper the sub-editors have had to read or glance at as much as 500,000 words. All important items are discussed and supervised by various executives such as the chief sub-editor, the chief foreign sub-editor, the night editor, various assistant editors, and per-haps the editor himself, who sometimes visits his office late at night, and is always in touch by telephone. The chief sub-editor will be told what the chief item on each page should be.

No matter how important the news or how incomplete the information, an even flow of reports from the sub-editors must reach the printing operators throughout the evening, other-wise steady production would break down (see NEWSPAPER INDUSTRY, Vol. VII). Evening papers are produced much like morning papers, except that sporting results, which may arrive as each edition is going to press, have to be handled with great speed.

In Britain national morning papers are pub-lished on week-days only, a custom due to a 19th and early 20th century prejudice against the reading of newspapers on Sunday. Manual workers, however, were thought to have little time or inclination to read papers on working days, and so special weekly newspapers, con-taining mainly news of crime and violence, were issued at week-ends for them. The publishers of morning papers then began to evade public pre-judice by printing editions on Sundays under a title different from that of their week-day editions. This practice, which became popular during the First World War, when broadcasting did not exist, has now become so widely accepted that more papers are sold on Sunday, and at higher prices, than on any week-day.

Regional newspapers range from a paper with a small circulation round a country town to a London evening paper, with an editorial staff of seventy in its head office, and a circulation of 1,500,000 copies a day in an area of several hundreds of square miles. Regional evening papers tend to be more prosperous than morning ones, because national morning papers can reach almost every city in Britain by breakfast time. But with evening papers, which often contain, especially in their sporting columns, news of events which have happened within less than an hour, the situation is different. A local evening paper, if published in a town some distance from a large city such as London or Manchester, can sell its edition before the London or Manchester evening papers can reach the district.

In a few cases regional papers have acquired a high reputation throughout Britain and the world; the *Manchester Guardian* and the Edin-burgh *Scotsman* are among them.

The simplest kind of newspaper is the 'local weekly', produced in a country town, or suburb of a great city. The weekly has no national or foreign news, and subscribes to no news agencies. It contains reports of meetings of local councils, as well as of local political meetings, lawcourts, lectures, church functions, or sports, and news of local people. Its staff may consist of an editor, who is sometimes even the proprietor, and from one to six reporters. In larger staffs, there will be a proportion of juniors in their teens, who are learning reporting before seeking work on larger papers. There are generally no sub-editors, each reporter writing head-lines on his own reports, and handing them to the printer, who will arrange the various reports in an agreed order. In some larger towns a weekly paper is owned by the same proprietor as an evening paper.

In Britain in 1950 there were fifty-six morning daily papers and eighty-eight evening ones, as well as seventeen Sunday papers. There were more than 1,300 local weekly newspapers, quite apart from the 3,500 MAGAZINES AND PERIODICALS (q.v.) All those publications, numbering more than 5,000 in all, published between them 10,000 million copies a year.

Newspapers in the more developed overseas countries, especially English-speaking ones, are broadly like those in Britain. In some countries, such as France, the press has been at times liable to corruption. While London is distinguished by a small number of very rich papers with a vast advertising revenue and immense circulations, and a tradition of independence, Paris has suffered from a large variety of papers with few readers and little money, and proprietors and journalists have sometimes yielded to the temptation of bribery, as did British journalists in the 17th and 18th centuries. Totalitarian countries, such as Germany under the Nazi Government, and the U.S.S.R. and other European countries under Communist rule, do not allow free journalism; all papers and journalistic writing must submit to State control.

See also JOURNALIST; FREEDOM OF SPEECH.
See also Vol. VII: NEWSPAPER INDUSTRY.

NEWSPAPERS, HISTORY OF. Before printing was invented, people had to rely for their news on word of mouth, and on the passing of private letters between the few people who could read and write. In ancient Rome, about the time of Julius Caesar, the practice began of writing public announcements about official matters every day on a large whitened board in the centre of the city. Important people who lived in other parts of the Roman Empire sometimes arranged for written copies of these announcements to be sent to them by messenger.

Many centuries later, long after the Roman Empire had fallen to pieces, news began to circulate again in Europe in the form of occasional written letters. News of important events, such as the battle of Agincourt, would reach the great landowners and local rulers, the abbots, bishops, and barons, in the form of private letters. These would be written by their chaplains, or other priests who formed part of their household and were probably the only members of the staff who could read and write. The letters, largely based on hearsay, would be passed from one bishop or baron to another, and so both the truth and the rumours would gradually spread.

At this time, kings and princes increasingly employed people to send them private letters with news from various parts of their own country and abroad, so that they might be aware of plotters at home and foreign enemies. Queen Elizabeth's favourite, the Earl of Essex, in order to keep abreast of court intrigue, set up a staff of clerks to provide him with news.

Although printing was invented about 1450 (see PRINTING, HISTORY OF), the first public newspapers did not appear until nearly 200 years later. During that long period, the writers of news-letters were slowly securing freedom from various kinds of control. As books had been mostly written by hand in monasteries (see BOOKS, HISTORY OF), the Church had claimed responsibility for all written things, and this continued when printing began. At the Reformation the control of the Church in England passed to the King, and for many years, therefore, the Crown claimed the right to authorize books. In those days most people thought it reasonable that men should not be free to write or print what they liked. Under Queen Elizabeth, printing was forbidden except in London, Oxford, and Cambridge, and even then the number of printers was limited by law.

Private letters containing news continued to be written after the invention of printing. Some men in London made a living by writing 'news-letters' to noblemen and rich merchants who lived in the country. But a writer would no longer send all his letters to one patron only; he would send copies to customers in different parts of the country. These writers, who used to exchange news in the busy doorway of St. Paul's Cathedral every day, were the first English journalists.

Occasional printed pamphlets or 'news-books', dealing with such events as foreign wars, began to be sold. The first to be published at regular intervals, and therefore in a sense the first newspapers, appeared in 1622, with news translated from German and other foreign news-books. They were known as 'courants' or 'corantos', to show that they were not single pamphlets but part of a running or 'current' series. Licences to print such news-books had to be obtained from

Numb 53.

A PERFECT DIVRNALL
OF THE
PASSAGES
IN
PARLIAMENT.

From Munday the 12. of June till Monday the 19. of June.

Collected by the same hand that formerly drew up the Copy for William Cooke *in* Furnivals Inne. *And now Printed by* I. Okes *and* F. Leach *and are to be sold by* Francis Coles *in the Old Baily.*

Munday the 12. of Iune 1643.

THe late treacherous conspiracy against the Parliament and City of London, doth every day more and more discover it selfe to the world, Mr. Waller the chiefe agent hath beene lately much troubled in minde at his evading some truths by his former examinations, and thereupon hath since under his own hand made a more absolute and penitent confession in discovery of some Eminent persons as maine agents in that designe, which being presented to the House of Commons this day accasioned a large and serious debate upon it, all the doores being shut, that none of their members might depart till that debate were over, and at length the matter was imparted to the Lords, the Commons then declaring that by the further confession of Master Waller concerning the plot, he had accused two members of their House to be chiefe agents in the designe, that were (he saith) privie to the whole conspiracy, and from whom

Note the is also a true re of a letter fight in westy, bet Sir willi. waller , Sir Ralpl Hoptons forcer.

HEADLINE OF THE 'EXETER POSTMAN' NEWSPAPER, 1711
One of the first provincial weekly news-sheets

one of the courts of law, known as the STAR CHAMBER (q.v. Vol. X), so called because its ceiling was painted with stars. Until this court was abolished in 1641, news-books were allowed to print only foreign news. One of the last acts of the Star Chamber was to sentence to the pillory an aggressive Puritan, William Prynne, whose ears were cut off as a punishment for publishing attacks on royalty.

The Civil War of 1642–52 gave writers a great chance to report on affairs in England. The Royalist party would start a newspaper or news-book, and the Parliament party would then start another one to attack it. Following the fashion of learned books of the time, some of these journals had Latin names. They contained news, crude woodcut pictures, leading articles, and advertisements. Their political news was violent and often dishonest. Some papers would report any abuse or untruth about their opponents; one denounced its enemies as a 'crew of brainless and brazen-faced news-scribblers'. It was at the beginning of this period that John MILTON (q.v. Vol. V) issued his famous pamphlet 'for the liberty of unlicensed printing' (see FREEDOM OF SPEECH).

After King Charles I was beheaded, the Government of Oliver Cromwell suppressed all news-books with whose opinions it did not agree. At the Restoration, the new king appointed a censor to control printed news, and the House of Commons forbade the reporting of its debates without permission. In 1665 was founded the oldest journal now living, the London Gazette, which contains official announcements.

The general setting-up of newspapers was not possible until after 1695, when Parliament ended the censorship laws. Soon there were founded many newspapers and periodicals. The first English daily paper, the Daily Courant, appeared in 1702. Papers were careful to avoid dealing with politics, because prosecutions for LIBEL (q.v. Vol. X) were freely used by the royal family, the government, and the Church authorities to punish newspaper proprietors, editors, and writers if they were too critical.

Journalism was strongly influenced by leading writers, such as Daniel DEFOE, and later STEELE, ADDISON, and SWIFT (qq.v. Vol. V). When in prison in 1704 for criticizing the Church authorities, Defoe began writing the first issues of a notable magazine, long before he started writing Robinson Crusoe.

In 1712 the Government, growing alarmed at the increasing influence of newspapers on public opinion, put a tax on them—a tax which continued under various forms for nearly 150 years. The papers survived the tax; but the violent political passions of the times often caused papers to be corrupt. If the editors and writers were paid enough money by a politician as a bribe, they would cease to criticize him.

During the 18th century newspapers reached many more parts of the country because they were carried, as were letters, by STAGE COACH (q.v.)—a service which was becoming well organized. Few people could afford books, and children were helped to learn to read by the use of newspapers. About the same time commercial firms used newspapers more and more for advertisement, and the money they paid for these encouraged editors to resist bribes and to express honest opinions. In 1761, John WILKES (q.v. Vol. V), started the *North Briton* solely to attack the Government. In his long struggle with Parliament and the lawcourts Wilkes helped to safeguard editors from the dangers of arrest by 'general warrant' at the will of the Government, and, in 1772, to establish the right to print reports of Parliamentary debates. Previously newspapers, when reporting debates in Parliament, had to use various tricks to avoid prosecution; for instance, they would pretend to be reporting the debates of an imaginary parliament in China. When Samuel JOHNSON (q.v. Vol. V) reported the debates of Lilliput in the *Gentleman's Magazine*, he was really reporting those of the House of Commons.

Until the end of the 18th century, and for some time after, the heavy taxes on newspapers kept their prices so high that people used to go to coffee-houses to read the free copies, or they used to hire copies for a small fee. This was so in the early days of *The Times*, which had been founded to help to develop a printing business. At that time papers still used to receive money, either from the Government or the opposition, as bribery for their support, and *The Times*, under its founder, John Walter, proved at first no better than the rest. But under his son, John Walter II, in the early 19th century, when the paper had a substantial circulation and received a good deal of money from advertisements, it could afford to refuse bribes. Its standard of honesty and independence became high, and its example raised the whole level of journalism. But newspapers, even though sometimes corrupt, did number among their contributors such writers as Charles LAMB, William HAZLITT, and Samuel COLERIDGE (qq.v. Vol. V).

Early in Queen Victoria's reign, *The Times*, which had the largest circulation of any newspaper, was widely read by men of the ruling classes both at their clubs and in their homes. Its editor, Thomas Barnes, was described by a Lord Chancellor as 'the most powerful man in the country'. Peers and foreign statesmen called at Barnes' houses to consult him. His successor, Delane, exercised a strong influence on the Crimean War by publishing the dispatches of W. H. Russell, the first war correspondent, who exposed British mismanagement and hastened the resignation of the Government.

By 1861 the last of the 'taxes on knowledge' had been abolished. Newspaper prices could be reduced, and new papers were founded. Mechanical improvements, following the introduction of the steam-engine, led to an increased output from printing works (*see* PRINTING, HISTORY OF), and this enabled newspapers to extend their circulation rapidly. The *Daily News* had been started in 1846, with Charles DICKENS (q.v. Vol. V) as its first editor. The *Daily Telegraph* followed in 1855, the first paper since the 17th century to be sold for a penny. Important daily papers were founded in the provinces. Until the *Manchester Guardian* was converted from a weekly into a daily in 1855, no daily paper had been published in the provinces.

A new kind of journalism was introduced by W. T. Stead, editor of the London *Pall Mall Gazette*, who began the practice of 'interviews' and 'gossip columns'. The introduction in 1876 of a simple form of compulsory education resulted in a gradual increase in the number of people able to read. In 1896 a young magazine publisher, Alfred Harmsworth (later Lord Northcliffe), founded the *Daily Mail*, which soon achieved a sale of a million copies a day, the first paper in the world to do so. Other papers of this kind were established. Inspired by the cheaper American press, they offered amusing or sensational items of news to the poorer members of the public who could spend a halfpenny on a newspaper but who had little knowledge of the world or its affairs.

In the 20th century many newspapers have grown into large industrial units (*see* NEWSPAPER INDUSTRY, Vol. VII). They have followed the tendency of other industries to merge into large groups, and a number of less successful papers have ceased to be published. Circulations of some daily papers have risen to more than 4 million copies apiece, and one Sunday paper prints more than 8 million copies. Such large circulations of newspapers are unknown elsewhere, for nowhere else in the world are so many populous cities linked so closely by rail with three such printing centres as London, Manchester, and Glasgow.

See also NEWSPAPER; MAGAZINES AND PERIODICALS; PROPAGANDA AND ADVERTISING; FREEDOM OF SPEECH.
See also Vol. VII: NEWSPAPER INDUSTRY.

NORWEGIAN LANGUAGE, *see* SCANDINAVIAN LANGUAGES.

NUMBERS, *see* COUNTING, HISTORY OF.

O

OAR AND PADDLE, *see* Vol. IX: Rowing.

OCEANIC LANGUAGES. The people who speak these are Polynesians, Melanesians, and Micronesians (qq.v. Vol. I). The first Oceanic languages probably came to the islands of the Pacific from the East Indies about 2,000 years ago. There have been at least eight other migrations since then, the last two occurring about A.D. 600–800 and A.D. 1200–1300, when the present Maori language was established in New Zealand (*see* Maoris, Vol. I). Remnants of at least two earlier tongues still survive in New Zealand.

Polynesian languages use only about ten consonants and six or seven vowels, and they have a simple flexible grammar, which does not have elaborate rules nor make changes in the endings of words; instead, little words known as particles are used to show different meanings—thus: *tika*, 'correct, proper', *tika-lu*, 'to be correct', *ta-tika-lu*, 'to cause to be correct', and so on.

The Melanesian languages, on the other hand, have elaborate grammatical rules and a large number of sounds, some of which seem rather queer to our ears. These languages vary considerably, even in the same island; it is often impossible for people living in one village to understand those living in another less than a mile away. An interesting feature of Melanesian is its 'chief's language', consisting of special words used when spoken by or to a chief. It is considered a serious offence to use a normal word when the 'chief's word' should be employed.

Polynesian and Micronesian have probably grown from Melanesian; but the origins of the Oceanic group of languages are not completely known. The main stock came from South-east Asia through the East Indies (*see* Indonesian Languages). The local languages are rapidly dying out or becoming less pure now that people from the different islands visit and mix with each other. In many places Pidgin-English (q.v.) is now spoken. English itself has borrowed a few words from Oceanic, among them *tabu* (or Taboo, q.v. Vol. I), *bamboo*, and *cockatoo*.

None of the modern languages of the Pacific were written down before the coming of missionaries at the beginning of the 19th century. Scattered records of them had been collected and preserved by the Spanish voyagers in the 16th century, and by the Dutch, English, and French navigators who followed, the best known of whom is, probably, Captain James Cook (q.v. Vol. V).

But from Easter Island, in the extreme Eastern Pacific, there have come a number of wooden tablets and other objects inscribed with pictograms, that is, a kind of writing in which pictures represent ideas. Some of these signs are clearly intended to depict men, fish, turtles, frigatebirds, and so on; others are not yet understood with any certainty. These tablets appear to be of late origin (some probably of the mid-19th century). This system of writing, unfortunately, has not yet been deciphered, so we do not know what the tablets say. It is safe to assume, however, that they have religious significance of some kind.

See also Language Structure.
See also Vol. I: Polynesians.

National Museum, Santiago

INSCRIBED WOODEN TABLET FROM EASTER ISLAND

Probably carved about A.D. 1750. It is read from the left-hand side of the bottom line, then turned round at the end of each line, so that every other line is upside down. Tablets were read out at public gatherings

ORDNANCE SURVEY, *see* Map-Reading.

OREGON TRAIL, *see* American Trails.

OMNIBUS, *see* Bus.

P

PACIFIC ENGINE, *see* LOCOMOTIVES, CLASSES AND USES, Section 2.

PACIFIC LANGUAGES, *see* OCEANIC LANGUAGES.

PACKET SHIPS, *see* STEAMSHIPS, HISTORY OF.

PADDLE STEAMER, *see* STEAMSHIPS, HISTORY OF.

PANAMA CANAL. This ship canal joins the Atlantic and Pacific Oceans, crossing the Isthmus of Panama, the narrow neck of land which connects North and South America. Before the canal was opened in 1914, ships journeying from Europe to the Pacific ports of North or South America had to make the stormy passage round Cape Horn. The Panama Canal has shortened the distance by sea between Liverpool and San Francisco by about 5,600 miles.

The idea of making a way for ships through this narrow neck of land is as old as the 16th century. Up till the early 19th century, when the Central American Colonies became independent, successive Spanish governments had made tentative plans. Then the French engineer, de Lesseps, fresh from his triumph over the SUEZ CANAL (q.v.), took up the problem. In 1879, though he was by then 74 years of age, he formed a company to raise money for the scheme. De Lesseps' engineers estimated that the canal would cost £26 million. Americans, not favouring a canal built by Europeans, refused to support the company, and most of the money was raised in France.

The canal-builders soon ran into difficulties caused both by the unhealthy, fever-infested climate, and by the magnitude of the engineering task, made worse by the behaviour of the River Chagres. This river, at some times a mere brook, during rainy seasons swelled to a raging torrent, flooding the country and sweeping everything before it. The intention was to make a sea-level canal by tunnelling through the Culebra hills which run down the middle of the isthmus. But the work of removing the enormous quantities of earth and rock was made impossible, both by the river which kept breaking through and sweeping away the machinery, and by the fever which attacked the workmen. During the 9 years that the struggle continued, as many as 16,000 men died of malaria and yellow fever. Much money was wasted in mismanagement, and after many millions had been spent, the disastrous project was abandoned; many thousands of people who had put their savings into it were ruined.

Years later, after £60 million had been spent, the U.S.A. Government became interested. During the Spanish-American War of 1898, the Americans had discovered how crippling it was to have their fleet divided between the Atlantic and the Pacific, with a journey of thousands of miles between them. Colombia, however, to whom Panama belonged, was unfriendly; but when Panama revolted and separated from Colombia, the U.S.A. Government at once bought up the canal company, the local railway, and a strip of land 10 miles wide along the line of the canal; and in 1904 work was begun.

The first step was to deal with the malaria and yellow-fever mosquito. Land was drained,

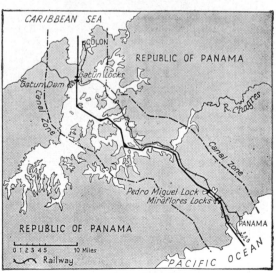

THE PANAMA CANAL

Ewing Galloway

THE PEDRO MIGUEL LOCKS ON THE PANAMA CANAL
Ships are drawn through the locks by electric cars

and all stagnant water was sprayed with petroleum to kill the mosquito larvae. All the workmen's huts were made mosquito-proof with fine copper-gauze. Arrangements were made for hospitals, schools, and amusements. In 1907 President Theodore Roosevelt put the whole work under military control in order that the workmen should come under military discipline.

It was decided to build a canal 85 feet above sea-level and to raise ships at each end by a series of locks. A great dam, the Gatun Dam, was built across the path of the River Chagres to control it and to form a huge, irregularly shaped lake at canal level. There were still many difficulties to overcome, especially in preventing landslides in the cutting through the Culebra Hills. Such landslides often meant the clearing away of millions of cubic yards of earth.

The Panama Canal has three sets of LOCKS (q.v.): Gatun, Pedro Miguel, and Miraflores. Each lock is 1,000 feet long, 110 feet wide, and from 47 to 85 feet deep. The gates are of steel, and are very thick and strong. They are hollow and filled with air so that much of their weight can be taken by floating. The inner bottom corner rests on a pivot, and the upper corner is hinged. They can be opened or closed in 2 minutes, and a lock can be emptied or filled

in 15 minutes. On the upper side of each pair of ordinary gates is an emergency gate which can be thrown across the canal in case of accident or when repairs are necessary. Ships do not pass through the locks under their own steam, but are handled by four or six electric locomotives, usually two in front and two behind. Ships take about 7 hours to pass through the whole canal, which is altogether about 50 miles long.

When the canal was opened in 1914, it had cost the United States about £75 million. In 1915, 1,072 commercial vessels passed through; by 1927 the number had increased to nearly 5,500. In consequence the income from ship dues rose steadily, and the canal, so disastrous in its early history, became a financial success as well as a tremendous contribution to communications.

See also CANALS.
See also Vol. III: PANAMA.
See also Vol. VIII: CANAL BUILDING.

PAPER. 1. In the course of history, from early civilizations until to-day, three main materials have been used for writing—papyrus, parchment or vellum, and paper. To-day paper is used for nearly all writing and printing; papyrus has long disappeared from use; and parchment is only used for special purposes, such as documents presented as testimonials to eminent people. The name 'paper' comes from papyrus; for paper was introduced into Europe when papyrus was still in general use.

2. PAPYRUS. This word was the name of a plant which grew in ancient Egypt by the River Nile, and also grew to a lesser extent in Palestine. Later the name was given also to the writing material which was made, chiefly in Egypt, from the plant. The papyrus is a straight, tall, reed-like water plant. Its leafless stem rises from 4 to 15 feet above the water, and it has an umbrella-like top of delicate green rays. A sheet of writing material was made from the plant in this way: a section of pith from the stem was cut into narrow strips which were arranged in layers, the fibres of alternate layers being at right angles. The sheets were then pressed together and dried in the sun; the natural juice of the plant made the pieces stick together. Uneven patches were smoothed away, and the surface polished (*see* p. 179).

Papyrus was cheap, and for many years it was the chief writing material of the ancient world. The Egyptians seem to have used it soon after 3000 B.C., and possibly even earlier; and the Greeks from about 500 B.C. Sheets were pasted together to form rolls, which varied in length; some of them were 30 or 40 feet long, while the 'Great Harris Papyrus', now in the British Museum, measures 150 feet. On the inner side of the roll the fibres ran across its breadth, and the writing went in the same horizontal direction. The back of the roll, the 'verso', was also used, but there the writing usually went across the fibres. Papyri have been perfectly preserved under the sands of Upper Egypt, and they have also been discovered in the ruins of synagogues and other temples in south Palestine and north Mesopotamia. Charred pieces have been found in Herculaneum (Italy). The earliest preserved papyri, which can be dated about 2750 B.C., are written in Egyptian language and are in hieratic writing (*see* HIEROGLYPHICS).

Papyrus lasted in general use down to the 9th century, and was still used occasionally in Europe until the 11th century. In Egypt it was superseded by paper, and in southern Europe by parchment or vellum.

3. PARCHMENT. The word comes from Pergamum, a city of Asia Minor, once the centre of parchment making (*see* BOOKS, HISTORY OF).

Parchment is made from the skins of sheep, goats and calves, and other animals. According to Greek writers, the Persian royal records were written on skins of sheep or goats, but skins of oxen were used for sacred writings.

The earliest documents on skins which still exist are dated about 2000 B.C. By the 2nd century, when both papyrus and parchment had been in use for some time, men found that although parchment was more expensive, its toughness enabled the sheets to be bound together like our modern books, instead of having to be pasted in a long roll. Both sides of a sheet could be written on, and writing in ink could be washed off or scraped away if the sheet was wanted again.

The finer material produced from the skins of a kid or young calf came to be known as 'vellum', but by the Middle Ages the name vellum was often applied to all parchment. In order to make parchment, the skins are first soaked in lime to remove the hair; then they are scraped, washed, stretched, and dried, and the surface is made smooth and hard by being rubbed with chalk and pumice-stone. Vellum is nearly white and has a beautiful texture (*see* Colour Plate opposite p. 48).

4. PAPER is made from a pulp of finely chopped material mixed with water and size or gum. It is spread over a wire mesh, and when the water has drained away, the solid film of material which is left is dried into a sheet of paper. Early paper was made mainly from rags; but over 400 different materials have been used at different times; the main ones are cotton rags, esparto grass, flax, and linen (from which the best quality is made), jute, hemp, rope, straw, bamboo, and wood-pulp (which is mainly used for cheaper paper). Until the 18th century, paper was made by hand: after this it began to be made by machines.

Paper was invented in China, possibly as early as 100 B.C., but it was only in the 11th century A.D. that the Arabs, who had been making it for 300 years before at their famous paper-mill at Damascus, introduced it into Europe by way of Spain, which they occupied as conquerors. From there it spread to Italy, France, and Holland. The first important paper-mill in England was built in the 15th century in Hertfordshire.

In the 14th century paper gradually became the main writing material for literary purposes, though the parchment trade naturally resisted it. By the 15th century, when printing was invented, it had become firmly established; for it was cheaper, more plentiful, and more supple than parchment. To-day paper has many uses. It is used for all books, newspapers, and writing papers; for paper money and wrapping-paper, blotting-paper, and cigarette papers. In Japan it is even used for clothes and sandals and walls of houses.

See also Books, History of; Book; Ink; Writing, History of; Writing Instruments.

PAPUAN LANGUAGES. These are spoken by the people of New Guinea. The languages vary greatly, even in a small district; in one river-valley in northern New Guinea, 30 different languages are found within a distance of 20 miles.

The languages all seem to have a comparatively small vocabulary. In order to tell a simple story it is necessary to make up for the lack of words by using many imitative sounds and by waving one's arms about. In very few cases can the people count above five or six; the method of numbering is one, two, two plus one, two plus two, after which it is impossible to go farther. The usual way of indicating any larger number is to use some word meaning 'sand on the beach' or 'leaves on the tree', implying a large, vague figure.

Since these languages vary so much, it is difficult to classify them. It has been suggested that there was an early migration across the Bay of Bengal from southern India (near the modern city of Madras) by way of the Nicobar Islands and the East Indies to New Guinea and Australia. A little later the Pacific Islanders and Indonesians (qq.v. Vol. I) started to move out from their homes in Siam and Indo-China, and so cut off the people in New Guinea and Australia from their original homeland.

See also Language Structure.
See also Vol. I: Melanesians.

PAPYRUS, see Paper.

PARACHUTE. This is a device shaped like an open umbrella, which controls the speed at which a person or object falls through the air. The resistance of the air, pressing against the large area of the parachute, slows its rate of falling according to its size.

The idea of parachutes is not new. One was designed by the Italian artist and scientist,

Leonardo da Vinci, about 1500. Soon after Balloons (q.v.) had been invented, in the late 18th century, several French pioneers made exhibition jumps from them. They used an umbrella-like structure with a stiff framework and a basket in which the parachutist stood; this structure dangled from the balloon until it was released. The word 'parachute' comes from French words for 'warding off' and 'fall'.

The first folding parachute was used in America in 1880. As the parachutist jumped, his parachute was pulled open by a cord attached to the balloon. Such parachutes were used during the First World War by observers in captive balloons; but they were not used as means of escape from damaged aeroplanes until the last stages of that war, when some German airmen made parachute escapes.

The modern parachute is of two types, the 'free', which is used for emergency escapes from aircraft at any height, and the 'static', which is used for dropping troops, weapons, and vehicles in particular areas from low-flying aircraft during war. The main difference between the two types is that with the 'static' type the folded parachute is jerked open by a cord attached to the aircraft, whereas with the 'free' type the parachutist opens the parachute.

A parachute consists of two parts, the main circular spread of silk or nylon, called the 'canopy', and the 'rigging lines' attached round the edge, which connect it to the wearer. The canopy is very carefully folded in the factory, and stowed in a pack which is strapped to harness on the wearer's body. Some packs are made to be used as a seat by an airman; others are fitted to his back, chest, or lap.

With the ordinary 'free' parachute the airman, after jumping, must take care to fall well clear of the aircraft before bringing his parachute into action, so that it may not become entangled in the machine or in bits of falling wreckage, and so that the strong 'slip-stream' of air from the propellers will not unbalance it. If he has jumped from a great height, he may decide to fall several thousand feet before opening the parachute, so that he may be exposed for the shortest possible time to the freezing temperature and shortage of oxygen at high altitudes. (Some parachute equipment carries a small bottle of oxygen which the falling airman can inhale in rarefied air.) He must, however, bring the parachute into action before coming too

Charles E. Brown

PARACHUTES OPENING
The 'pilot chute' can be seen at the head of each parachute

near the ground in order to allow adequate time for the parachute to open.

When the airman decides to open the canopy, he pulls a ring attached to a 'rip-cord' on his harness. This allows the flaps of the stowage pack to snap back under the pull of elastic cords, and releases and pulls open a small parachute, called the 'pilot chute'. The 'pilot chute', when filled with air, drags out the main canopy, which begins to inflate and to pull the folded rigging lines from the pack. The complete parachute is open and supporting the weight of the airman within a space of about one and three-fifths seconds. With the standard canopy of 24-feet diameter, the parachute then descends at about 20 feet a second. The wearer can control movement slightly as he nears the ground by tugging at some of the rigging lines and making the parachute sway. If he can, he tries to face downwind, so that he will fall forwards, and not backwards, on reaching the earth Just before touching down, he must relax all muscles to reduce the risk of broken bones.

The 'static' parachute is larger than the 'free', and enables heavily burdened soldiers to drop at the slower rate of 17 feet a second. By using several parachutes, such heavy loads as motor-cars, guns, and boats have been dropped.

Some modern air speeds are so great that an airman may be prevented by the rush of air from jumping out of the aircraft in an emergency. Very fast jet aircraft are, therefore, supplied with automatic ejector-seats. When the pilot decides to abandon the aircraft, he pulls a hood over his face to protect him from the violent impact of air; and this action fires an explosive charge, which shoots the entire seat, to which he is strapped, well clear of the aircraft. The airman then unstraps the seat, which descends on a parachute of its own, while he himself works his personal parachute. One form of parachute, designed for unconscious or wounded men, is opened by an automatic device at a safe height.

Parachutes are issued to crews of military aircraft, and to civilians engaged in special work such as test flying. Parachutes are not issued in civil air liners, because the rare accidents to craft of this kind occur near ground level, where a parachute is useless. A parachute pack, in wartime, includes an inflatable boat and some rations, in case of descent at sea. The Caterpillar Club is an organization for those who have saved their lives by parachute jumping; the name is derived from the way a caterpillar swings down on a silken thread.

See also FLYING.

PARCHMENT, *see* PAPER.

PASSPORTS, *see* Vol. X: PASSPORTS.

PEN AND PENCIL, *see* WRITING INSTRUMENTS.

PENNON, *see* FLAGS.

PERMANENT WAY, *see* Vol. VIII: RAILWAY BUILDING.

PERSIAN AND ALLIED LANGUAGES. Persian is the most important of the Iranian languages, a group within the INDO-EUROPEAN family (q.v.). The group takes its name from Irān, the national name of PERSIA (q.v. Vol III); and the languages are spoken over an area stretching from the River Euphrates to the east of the Hindu Kush Mountains. The chief languages, after Persian, are Pashto (spoken in

Bodleian Library

PAGE FROM THE POEM RUBÂ'IYÂT OF OMAR KHAYYÂM
Persian MS. written in A.D. 1460

Afghanistan), Baluchi (in Baluchistan), Ossetic (in the Caucasus), and Kurdish (on the western borders of Persia). There are also lesser languages and dialects.

The oldest records in Iranian date from the 6th century B.C. Some of the *Gathas* or psalms of the Avesta or Zoroastrian scriptures (*see* SACRED BOOKS, Vol. I) were probably composed by Zoroaster himself about 600 B.C., and are in an eastern Iranian language known as Avestan. The Persian kings of about this time made records on rocks, carved in CUNEIFORM script (q.v.) in the language called Old Persian. Avestan and Old Persian, like Sanskrit, have an elaborate grammar, the nouns, for instance, having many different grammatical endings or inflexions, and the verbs a variety of forms to indicate precise meaning. From the 3rd century onwards the only records we have of Iranian languages show that their grammar had become simpler. In Middle Persian and Parthian, for instance, two languages of this period, the nouns have no gender, and apart from a plural ending, they do not change their form according to their function in the sentence.

Modern Persian, the language spoken in Persia to-day, grew up after the Arabs had conquered Persia in the 7th century A.D. and converted most of the Persians to Islam. ARABIC (q.v.), the language of the conquerors and of the new religion, had a strong influence, and the Arabic script was used. The Persians borrowed a great number of Arabic words, which sometimes replaced Persian words, but were more often used side by side with them. These borrowings have made Modern Persian very rich and expressive, very suitable for its great literature, with its strikingly beautiful poetry. The other living Iranian languages have been deeply influenced by Modern Persian literature, but have comparatively little literature of their own.

The structure, however, of Modern Persian has not been influenced by Arabic, but has remained very much like that of Middle Persian. The constructions of everyday Persian have a good deal in common with English, as a few examples will show:

chand barādar dārid 'how-many brothers have-you?'

biyā, beravīm tā shām bekhorīm 'come, let-us-go that supper we-may-eat'.

sar-am dard mikonad 'my-head pain makes (= aches)'.

Although the Persian language can be very terse, yet in emotional or formal speech the Persians tend to enjoy the use of words, and to pile them together for effect, using several words meaning the same thing. For example, *Shāyad hikāyatī az hikāyāt -ē ān nabāshad ke az khabt o sahv o ishtebah khāli nabāshad* 'There is probably not one of its stories which is free from blunders and errors and mistakes'. They also make great use of expressive idioms and apt quotations from their poets.

See also LANGUAGE STRUCTURE.

See also Vol. I: PERSIAN ANCIENT CIVILIZATION; PERSIANS; ZOROASTRIAN.

PETROL ENGINE, *see* MOTOR-CAR, HISTORY OF.

PICTURE TRANSMISSION. The electrical transmission of photographs or other pictures over long distances is carried out either by wire or by wireless. Any means of transmission which is sensitive enough to carry speech can be used—that is, an ordinary telephone line, or a telephone trunk circuit, or any wireless telephone system which is not too distorted by electrical disturbance in the atmosphere.

Transmission first became possible because of the peculiar property of a chemical element called selenium. Changes in the amount of light which falls on a piece of selenium cause changes in the selenium itself. As the light decreases, the selenium greatly increases its resistance to any electrical current. In full light, selenium offers very little resistance to current. So when some selenium is linked up with an electrical circuit, the amount of electricity which passes through the circuit indicates how much darkness or light there is.

If an extremely small beam of light is thrown on a photograph, making a tiny point of light the size of a pin-point, that beam will either fall on a light spot or dark spot in the picture. And if a piece of selenium is held near the spot, it can effect an electric current, and so indicate to someone a long way off whether the beam of light is falling on a dark or a light spot of the photograph. Of course, a photograph does not consist of only two tones, one light and one dark. A good photograph will have many variations of tone all over the surface. But all those variations can be detected by the piece of selenium.

We have spoken only of one tiny point of light.

Cable & Wireless

TRANSMITTING A PICTURE BY WIRELESS

It takes 10 to 15 minutes to transmit a picture 10 in. × 6 in.

The mechanical problem consists in making that point of light move over every part of the photograph in a regular way, while all the time the piece of selenium is recording the amount of light or darkness in every point which it 'sees'. This is called 'scanning' the photograph. The scanning is done by wrapping the photograph round a cylinder, very much in the way a paper label is wrapped round a jam jar, except that the photograph must go all the way round the cylinder until the two ends of the photograph exactly meet on the far side. Then the cylinder begins to turn, and a beam of light is thrown on its side. The beam falls on the photograph, and as the beam is held steady while the photograph's cylinder is turning, the beam will have travelled across a thin strip, from one side of the photograph to the other, by the time the cylinder has made one complete turn. If a piece of selenium is close to the beam, the selenium will have recorded electrically all the variations in light and shade on this thin strip of the photograph, and if, at a receiving station somewhere else, another cylinder of exactly the same size is turning at exactly the same speed, with some specially treated photographic paper wrapped round it, the same variations in light and shade can be recorded on that paper by means of a varying light controlled by the varying current.

At the sending end the cylinder with the photograph wrapped round it goes on turning. But the tiny beam of light, although appearing to be held steady, is really moving extremely slowly along the side of the cylinder, so that at each turn of the cylinder the point of light avoids falling on the strip of photograph which it has first illuminated, and starts lighting up a strip next to it. The track made by the point of light round and round the cylinder is therefore spiral in shape and very like the track made by a thread which is wound on to a reel of cotton.

The high-speed commercial transmission of pictures to-day makes use of more complicated mechanism than a simple piece of selenium. Glass-bulb valves, related to those used in a broadcast receiver, now give great accuracy. Not only photographs are transmitted, generally for use in newspapers, but also black and white drawings, architects' and engineers' plans, specimens of handwriting, finger prints for police use in detecting criminals, and even ordinary printed pages. In America a 'home newspaper' has been transmitted by wireless, which reproduces a small but complete newspaper on a roll of paper in a receiver in the reader's home.

It was in 1873 that the special properties were discovered in selenium (named after a Greek word for the moon). In 1904 the first practical transmissions took place, devised by a Frenchman named Belin. Advances in scanning came from Germany. The British thermionic valve (*see* SPEECH, TRANSMISSION OF) and work by Danes and Americans were the basis of the present systems.

See also TELEVISION.

PICTURE WRITING, *see* WRITING; HIERO-GLYPHICS.

PIDGIN-ENGLISH. This is the name given to a peculiar form of English used in many parts of the world, but most commonly in the islands of the Pacific Ocean, in the East Indies, in South China, Siam, and Malaya. 'Pidgin' is said to be an attempt by some Chinese to say the English word 'business'.

Although there are many local variations, the general idea underlying the 'language' is the same—that of using simple English words but placing them in the word-order of the local language. In the native OCEANIC LANGUAGES (q.v.) there is a special distinguishing word for names of objects, verbs, descriptive words, and so on, which is placed before a word to show which class (noun, verb, or other class) it belongs to. So, in pidgin-English, the special distinguishing word is kept; for example, 'piecee' is normally used to indicate a noun, as is shown in the pidgin-English version of a well-known nursery rhyme:

Maree had little piecee lamb,
He wool all same he snow,
What time Maree all along top-side,
That lamb he all same go.

Nowadays, however, pidgin-English is often less complicated than this, as is shown in the remark once made by an islander who had become an assistant missionary in New Britain: 'You in country long way off have Good King, you have Holy Book along you long time, then you very very good people all round, yes?' The attempt to describe new conceptions sometimes results in ingenious and vivid descriptive compounds, such as 'box-you-fight-him-he-sing-out', for a piano.

Pidgin-English has changed very rapidly in the last few years and has become a little more like normal English. It is spreading quickly throughout the islands of the Pacific, and in many places is the only language now spoken, the local dialects having become extinct.

PIGEON POST. Pigeons can be used to carry messages because of their speed and remarkable power of finding their way home when set free a long distance away. They are still used in many countries, such as China, where their use has been known for centuries, and Japan, where lines of communication by land may be broken by earthquakes; many newspapers in Japan have their own pigeon services, and so have some in the United States.

The use of pigeons to carry messages probably dates back to the ancient civilizations of Assyria, Persia, and Egypt. It is certain that the ancient Greeks released pigeons at the opening of the OLYMPIC GAMES (q.v. Vol. IX) with messages that peace must be maintained during the Games. For this reason pigeons have always played a part in the revived Olympic Games. The Greeks also sent the names of the Olympic victors to their cities by pigeon post.

Julius Caesar used pigeons in his conquest of Gaul, and according to Pliny the Elder, the Roman naturalist, the general Brutus used pigeon messages at the siege of Modena (43 B.C.).

P.A.-Reuter

FASTENING A MESSAGE TO A PIGEON'S LEG
Detail from the film *This Man Reuter*

of the Rothschild family is said to have been much increased because early news of the result of the Battle of Waterloo was brought to them by pigeon post.

Until the coming of the electric telegraph, newspapers had their own pigeon service, and results of horse races and prize fights were regularly brought by this means. Even to-day some newspapers use pigeons to send results from crowded football grounds. Carrier pigeons are not now used, message carrying being done by the pedigree racing pigeon.

In the First World War pigeons were used a great deal by the Navy, Army, and Air Force. Indeed the rule was laid down that all machines reconnoitring over the sea must carry pigeons; few aircraft were then equipped with wireless telegraphy. They were not so much needed in the Second World War, since the use of radio communications had grown; but even then British fanciers gave nearly 200,000 to the Services, and aircraft carried them, so that they could be released if the wireless transmitter was damaged.

They were much used for secret messages. A number were dropped by parachute into occupied Europe, and 'partisans' or members of resistance movements in the occupied countries sent messages to the Allies by means of them. Many brought information about vital things such as the sites from which flying bombs were being launched.

See also Vol. IX: PIGEON RACING.

Since then they have been used in many sieges, among them the siege of Leyden (1574) in the Dutch War of Independence against the Spaniards. During the siege of Paris (1870–1) in the Franco-Prussian War, pigeons played a very important part; none had been sent out of the city before the siege began, so they were flown out by balloon. During the 4 months of this siege 150,000 official letters and 1,000,000 private ones were sent by pigeon post into Paris. The messages were first written, and then photographed on a thin film about 1¼ in. by 2 in. Each film could then contain 2,500 dispatches of 20 words each. The films were rolled up and pushed into a goosequill, which was fastened by a thin wire or silk thread to one of the pigeon's tail feathers. One pigeon carried as many as eighteen films in this way.

The initial success of Reuter's, the famous NEWS AGENCY (q.v.), was based on an efficient pigeon service. Many fortunes were made on the stock exchange when pigeons were first used to bring news from France; the pigeons arrived in London by mid-day, but the Paris mail did not come in until midnight. The great wealth

PILGRIMS' WAY. During the Middle Ages many people went on pilgrimages to the shrines of saints or to churches which possessed holy relics, and for this purpose they often made long journeys. They travelled in companies for safety's sake; they walked or rode according to what they could afford; or if they were ill and were seeking a cure from the holy shrine, they travelled in a cart or litter. Many people went on pilgrimages as much for a holiday as for more serious reasons (*see* PILGRIMAGES, Vol. I). The roads to well-known shrines were often called Pilgrims' Ways.

The route from Winchester to Canterbury is the best-known of English pilgrims' ways. In 1170 the archbishop Thomas Becket was murdered at Canterbury as the result of a quarrel between the Archbishop and King Henry II. Becket was canonized, and his shrine at Canterbury became a centre for pilgrimage, not only from all parts of England, but also from the Continent. Pilgrims from France landed at Southampton and came up to Winchester to start their journey from Winchester Cathedral, as did English pilgrims from the west. They followed a very old track which in prehistoric times had been used for carrying the Cornish tin to the Isle of Thanet from where it had been shipped to the Continent. The Pilgrims' Way was no defined road, for all pilgrims did not keep to the same track, some making deviations to pass monasteries or other churches or chapels containing relics. The church at Charing, for instance, on the route, possessed what was reputed to be the block on which John the Baptist was beheaded.

At the time of the Reformation Henry VIII had the Canterbury shrine destroyed, and pilgrimages ceased. Traffic along the Pilgrims' Way, therefore, declined. Later some parts of it were use by local travellers who wished to avoid paying the tolls demanded on the main roads (*see* TURNPIKE); but, as it was unpaved, travel along it was slow and rough. It is no longer possible to follow its whole 120 miles. Parts of it have become incorporated into modern roads, parts are little pathways, parts, though no longer used, can be traced over the chalky downlands, and parts have got lost altogether.

See also ROADS, BRITISH.

PILOT, AIR, *see* AIRCREW.

PILOT, SHIP'S.
All ships except very small ones are compelled to take a pilot on board before being allowed to go in or out of most harbours. One of the essential qualities in a good pilot is local knowledge; buoys, lights, bearings, leading marks, the set of local tidal currents, the vagaries of shoals (shallow water) and shifting channels, are all known to the pilot. The main channel into the harbour is as familiar to him as the High Street of his native town. The master of the vessel is responsible for its safety, the pilot being there solely as an advisor; but in actual practice he handles the vessel.

Most of the big shipping companies retain in the principal ports which they use a pilot for the exclusive pilotage of their vessels; he is known as a 'choice' pilot. In these days of easy wireless communication, however, even casual visitors to a port make advance arrangements for a pilot to meet the ship. Most harbours have a recognized boarding station, that is, the point at sea or in an estuary where the pilot cutter waits for the incoming ship, ready to put the pilot on board. In some harbours, more than one type of pilot is required. For instance, vessels entering the Thames take on a sea pilot at one of the outer pilotage stations. At Gravesend, the sea pilot leaves the ship, which is then taken up to one of the dock entrances by a river pilot. When the ship has passed through the entrance lock, it is taken to its final berth by a dock pilot.

See also NAVIGATION, MARINE; PORTS AND HARBOURS.

PIRATES.
Pirates are robbers and outlaws of the sea. But pirates at sea have played a bigger part in history than HIGHWAYMEN (q.v.) on land. This is partly because it has been harder to enforce law and order on the great no-man's land of the high seas than in most places ashore; and partly because in the past even civilized nations were often quite ready, in their rivalry with one another, to make use of the services of wild and lawless seafaring men. Indeed, it is often difficult to say at what point irregular warfare in remote seas merged into piracy. Even to-day there is no precise definition, agreed among all nations, as to what constitutes piracy; but, generally speaking, by INTERNATIONAL LAW (q.v. Vol. X), anyone who uses a ship to commit acts of violence at sea for personal profit, and not on behalf of a regular government, may be treated as a pirate. He is 'the common enemy of mankind', an OUTLAW (q.v. Vol. X) whose ship may be chased or sunk at will. In old days captured pirates might be put to death by their captors without more ado; now they must be brought to port and tried by a proper court.

There is not much piracy in the world to-day; but in the past there have been pirates at some time or other in most parts of the globe. In times when civilized peoples and their wealth were only to be found in small areas of the world, pirates from neighbouring and more backward tribes used to prey upon the trade routes along which this wealth was shipped. This happened, for instance, in the days of Greece and Rome. There were then, even in the heart of the Mediterranean, nests of pirates who lurked among the islands and inlets and lived by plunder. When the Roman Empire was falling into decline, bands of Saxon pirates from the north made

CAPTAIN BARTHOLOMEW ROBERTS WITH HIS SHIPS THE 'ROYAL FORTUNE' AND THE 'RANGER', AND ELEVEN PRIZES, LYING IN
WHYDAM ROADS, COAST OF GUINEA, 1722
Engraving from Charles Johnson's *General History of the Pirates*

bolder and more frequent descents as the Roman
defences became weaker. It was on pirate raids
that the Anglo-Saxons first found their way to
the shores of Britain; and four centuries later the
Viking pirates made widespread plundering
raids before the period when they took to extensive settlement (*see* VIKING SHIPS).

Around the coasts of western Europe in the
Middle Ages, when stable governments were
only slowly being established, there was a good
deal of small-scale piracy; and there were still
pirates along the coasts of Cornwall and Ireland
as late as the time of Queen Elizabeth and
James I. Also, before there were regular navies,
kings and princes who wanted to fight their
neighbours at sea had to charter privately owned
ships to do so; and it was not easy to ensure that
these attacked only the enemy's shipping, or
that they ceased when hostilities were over.

Edward III of England had to take special steps
to ensure that Flemish merchants (who were his
allies) could get back goods seized by English
crews who did not confine their attacks only to
the shipping of the enemy, the French king.

During the 16th century, there grew up on
the coast of north Africa whole communities of
Moslems whose chief means of livelihood was
piracy. These were the Barbary corsairs, sometimes also called Sallee Rovers or Algerines,
according to the part of the coast from which
they came. The pirates of the 'Barbary States'
were a power in the Mediterranean for some
three centuries.

At this time the goods most highly valued in
Europe—jewels, silks, and spices—came from
Eastern countries. The Barbary corsairs used to
seize or plunder vessels carrying these cargoes on
their way through the Mediterranean, or up the

west coast of Africa. For the most part corsairs were Moslems, and they used to enslave the crews of captured Christian vessels, putting them to work on building fortifications or in rowing their galleys.

The Barbary corsairs were not suppressed until the beginning of the 19th century, when the French conquest of Algiers in 1830 finally put an end to the nuisance. Probably they could have been put down much sooner if the European powers had really been united in wanting to get rid of them.

The pirates about whom we know most, however, are the ones of European origin who were to be found mostly in tropical seas and on the east coast of what is now the United States, in the late 17th and early 18th centuries. It was then that there lived some of the most notorious pirates, such as Henry Avery, William Kidd, and Bartholomew Roberts. Among them were at least two women pirates, Mary Read and Ann Bonny, who wore men's clothes and were bold and daring enough to pass for men even among their shipmates. It is from the histories of these people that most of the best-known pirate adventure stories are drawn. Daniel Defoe, the author of *Robinson Crusoe*, wrote about Henry Avery; other stories are to be found in Andrew Lang's *True Story Book*, while R. L. Stevenson's *Treasure Island* and Captain Hook in J. M. Barrie's *Peter Pan* have the same background.

This outburst of piracy was one of the results of the race among the European nations to get at the wealth of the New World. The Spaniards and Portuguese were first in the field, and the latecomers—the English, the French, and the Dutch—were only too glad to make use of private adventurers, without inquiring too closely into their activities. In some of their exploits against the Spaniards even Drake and Hawkins, for instance, were little better than pirates.

During the 17th century the prospects of looting the ill-protected Spanish settlements in the Americas attracted men of a much rougher and more lawless type—fugitives from justice, runaway servants, and the like. The English and French governments still used the services of these ruffians, or 'buccaneers' as they came to be called, because their own regular navies were too small to protect isolated colonies, and also because the buccaneers brought in Spanish gold and silver. Towards the end of the 17th century, as conditions overseas became more settled and

regular navies grew stronger, the English and French governments gradually came to disown the buccaneers.

The favourite haunts of the pirates were in the islands of the West Indies, where the buccaneers of old had had their centre. The numerous islets with hidden inlets afforded good lurking places from which attacks could be made on ships plying between the Spanish colonies, or between Europe and North America. The pirates also robbed shipping in the Pacific Ocean (then known as the South Seas), off the west coast of Africa, and in the Indian Ocean. There was a notorious pirates' base in Madagascar, whence they raided vessels belonging to rich Indian merchants and princes and sometimes also European merchantmen. Captain William Kidd was sent out from England in the year 1696 to put down these pirates in the Indian Ocean. But Kidd had been brought up in the buccaneering wars, so he himself turned pirate. He was arrested and sent for trial to England, where he was condemned and hanged in 1701.

The pirates used whatever kind of vessel they could lay hands upon—some pirate careers began with the theft of a fishing-craft by a handful of men in a rowing boat. Experienced crews liked fast light vessels, with shallow enough draught to enable them to slip into creeks and river mouths where heavier craft could not follow them. Their way of life was violent and undisciplined. They were great drinkers of rum, and it was said that a pirate who was too often sober would be suspected by his fellows of plotting to betray them. Although a pirate crew often started by agreeing to share spoils evenly and to respect their women prisoners, it seems that these agreements were seldom kept. Usually the pirates elected their own captains, and only the most ruthless could hope to keep authority over them for long. Such was Edward Teach, or 'Black-beard', who used in fights to twist lighted tapers into the ends of his hair, and to fire loaded pistols under the table at his lieutenants as an after-dinner pastime.

In early days pirates often had a good deal of support from those on shore. The inhabitants of lonely settlements were glad of their protection and of the gold pieces which the pirates spent. The Madagascar pirates were at one time fitted out by otherwise respectable merchants of the English colonies in America, who found this the cheapest way of getting valuable goods from the East. But in time the pirates became less welcome. They then grew more brutal and took to robbing all kinds of craft, until everyone on shore united to get rid of them. By the middle of the 18th century, the days of the most famous pirates were at an end.

That was not, indeed, the end of piracy. There was a serious 'epidemic' in the 1820's in the West Indies, when the Spanish American Colonies were in revolt and the American and British navies tried to stamp out the slave trade. Even to-day there are Chinese pirates who live by robbing coastal shipping in the neighbourhood of Hong Kong. A gang of pirates will board a coastal steamer disguised as passengers, and when well away from shore, seize control and hand over the ship to junks which, manned by their associates, have been lying in wait for her.

But to the world's sea-borne trade as a whole piracy is no longer, as it once was, a serious menace.

See also SEA TRAVEL.

PLACE-NAMES. The most primitive peoples give names to their villages, and the earliest written records we possess contain the names of cities. These names are generally in some way descriptive of the place: they indicate who established the first settlement, who lived there, what was its geographical situation or character, what had happened there, or some such fact. Therefore we can often learn something about a place by studying its name—though of course modern imitations often confuse the matter. We can tell, however, that if a place-name has -chester, -caster, or -cester in it, there was probably once a Roman camp (*castra*) there; if a name has a reference to an Anglo-Saxon god, such as Wednesbury, Kent (Woden), or Thundersley, Essex (Thor or Thunor), we can guess that an Anglo-Saxon settlement was made there before the Anglo-Saxons were converted to Christianity; or if it is made up with, for instance, the words *by* and *thorp* (settlement), such as Grimsby or Scunthorpe in Lincolnshire, it probably had a Viking foundation. Place-names such as Oxford or Swinford obviously indicate that at these places, before the days of bridges, the river could be forded by oxen or by swine (*see* FORD AND FERRY).

The origin of many place-names in the British Isles can be traced to the various periods in British history when the language has been affected by large settlements of people speaking another language (*see* ENGLISH LANGUAGE). We can see from the names how, after the Anglo-Saxon invasions in the 5th and 6th centuries, the British language survived mainly in the West, in Cornwall, Wales, and Cumberland. In these parts, therefore, we find the names Axe, Exe, Usk, and Esk—all derived from an ancient British word of which *isca* 'water' is an early form, and rivers named Derwent, Dart, and Darent, which come from a British word meaning 'river where oaks are common'. Some names derived from ancient British words survived in other parts of England as well as the West. Malvern comes from British words meaning 'bare hill', and the word *pen* meaning 'hill', found in a great number of Welsh names, is also found, for instance, in Yorkshire and Derbyshire. The British word *ceto* 'wood' appears in the names Chute Forest and Chetwode in Buckinghamshire. Eccles and Ecclesfield come from the British word *ecles* which, like the Welsh *eglwys* 'church', is derived through Latin from the Greek *ecclesia* 'gathering'. The English often called the British settlements which remained among them Walcot or Walton from *walh* the Anglo-Saxon word for 'foreigner', which they came to use for the Britons, and which has survived to this day in 'Wales' and 'Welsh'.

The Anglo-Saxons called the Roman roads they found in Britain *stræt*, a word which originally came from the Latin *strata*, a 'paved way'. Therefore places called Street, Streat, Stratton, Streatham, Stratford, Stratfield, Streatley are thus named because they mostly lie on Roman roads.

The Anglo-Saxons or English, as we know, named places, as they named the days of the week, after their tribal gods, especially the prehistoric earthworks, half suspected of being the work of supernatural powers. Sometimes the earthworks were given names such as Grimsbury or Grim's Ditch. *Grim*, which is related to the Old English word *grīma*, 'a mask', was a name used for Woden, the chief of the Norse gods, because of the god's habit of going about in disguise. The name 'maiden', as in Maiden Castle or Maidenbury, appears at least fifteen times in the British Isles, and is often associated with prehistoric EARTHWORKS (q.v. Vol. I); the word may indicate that these were thought never to have been captured. Curiously enough, a Byzantine fortress in Macedonia is called Avret

Hissar (Maiden's Tower), and there is an Arabic Qaṣr-el-Banāt, 'Castle of the Maidens', on the road from Aleppo to Antioch.

Early English place-names, particularly in Kent and South Hampshire, often end in -ing or -ingham, the first part generally being derived from a personal name. These indicate settlements made by a chief with a band of followers. Thus Reading and Hastings are places where 'the people of Read(a)' and 'the people of Haesta' originally made a settlement, and Sickingen in Germany means 'Siggo's people'. Names of counties often originated because of a group of people who settled there. Norfolk and Suffolk mean 'northern people' and 'southern people', and Sussex and Middlesex 'south Saxons' and 'middle Saxons'; and Amiens, Rheims, and Soissons in France are from names of Gaulish tribes.

English place-names often consist of a simple description of a place, as, for instance, Downe in Kent, which means 'hill', or Nettlebed in Oxfordshire, the meaning of which is obvious. Sometimes they consist of a word for a homestead or village, such as *ham, ton, worth, wick, stoke, borough,* or *bury,* combined either with a personal name (Padworth in Berkshire means 'Peada's enclosure'), or with a word which describes the settlement or its site, like the common Norton and Sutton, 'north' and 'south village'. In the north-east of England, where the Vikings raided and settled in the 9th and 10th centuries, they have left their mark in the characteristic place-name elements of *by* 'settlement', *thwaite* 'clearing', *holme* 'island', *fell* 'hill', and *dale* 'valley'.

Descriptive names such as Blaxton 'black stone', Radcliffe 'red cliff', and Whitchurch 'white or stone church' are common, as are those marking an occupation, as Potterton, Bickerton (bee-keeper-town), and Woodmancote; a crop, as Barley Ryton and Wheatley; or an animal, as Oxton and Shapwick (Sheep farm).

The Normans, who came in the late 11th century, bringing to Britain the early form of the French language then spoken, often gave their surnames to the places they owned. Thus *le Pugeis* has become 'Poggs' in Broughton Poggs in Oxfordshire and 'Poges' in Stoke Poges in Buckinghamshire. Stogursey in Somerset was originally Stoke Courcy, because the manor was held by William de Curci or Courcy in the time of Henry I. The place-name often shows the class of person who once held the land under the feudal system. King's Sutton or Lyme Regis, for instance, once belonged to the King; Princes Risborough and Earls Barton to a prince or earl; Compton Bishop, Kingsbury Episcopi (Latin for 'bishop'), Nuneaton, Monks Risborough, Canonsleigh, belonged to ecclesiastics, and Temple Newsam belonged to the monastic order of the Knights Templar.

Many names given by the Normans include the adjective *beau* or *bel,* 'beautiful': for example, Beaumont 'beautiful hill', Beamish 'beautiful mansion', and Belvoir 'beautiful view'. The common French place-name word, *ville* 'town', appears at a much later date, as do also the English *burg* and *ton,* and even the Greek *polis,* in the making of place-names in the U.S.A., such as Maryville, Pittsburgh, Charleston, and Minneapolis—the first part often being the name of a person.

Field-names are sometimes very old, and can be traced back to landmarks mentioned in the boundaries of estates in Anglo-Saxon charters. But the greater number are quite modern, and often consist of nicknames. Some are complimentary, such as Eden Garden, Fill Tubs, and Largess, but uncomplimentary ones, such as Beggars Bush, Hungry Hill, and Little Worth, are more common. Names such as these are often found in American place-names. In California there are Hungry Valleys, Creeks, and Hollows, and places called Humbug, where prospectors failed to find gold; and in Newfoundland there are Famish Cove, Empty Basket, Breakheart Point, and Pinchgut Point, as well as Safe Harbour, Heart's Desire, and Little Paradise.

See also NAMES.

PLANETARY TRAVEL, *see* INTER-PLANETARY TRAVEL.

PLIMSOLL MARK, *see* SAFETY AT SEA.

POLAR EXPLORATION, *see* SNOW AND ICE TRAVEL; *see also* Vol. III: POLAR REGIONS.

PORT OF LONDON AUTHORITY, *see* PORTS, HISTORY OF.

PORTS AND HARBOURS. A harbour is a place with water deep enough to float vessels, free from obstacles to navigation, and sheltered enough from storms to allow ships to lie there

THE 'BRITANNIA', 1682

The *Britannia* was the flagship of Admiral Russell (afterwards Earl of Orford) at the battle of Barfleur.
Painting by Isaac Sailmaker, 1633–1721

in safety. A port is a harbour which is regularly used by a busy community on shore for loading or unloading ships' cargoes. With the growth of sea communications during the last century, practically all harbours in densely populated countries have become ports. Most ports are found at the mouths of navigable rivers, or some way up their course, or on sheltered arms of the sea, as in the case of London on the Thames, Liverpool on the Mersey, Glasgow on the Clyde, Southampton on Southampton Water. London is the greatest port, not only in the British Isles, but in the British Commonwealth, dealing annually with ships of a registered tonnage of 45 million, and carrying 39 million tons of cargo. Some other of the biggest ports in the world are New York, Antwerp, Rotterdam, and, before the Second World War, Hamburg.

A modern port must allow ships to make a quick 'turn round' between trips, for a ship costs a good deal of money to run, yet earns it only when at sea.

All big ports are run by a governing body. Organization is complex, and differs in the ports of the world. It can be broadly divided into two sections—the one dealing with ships, the other with cargo.

Safe navigation is essential for ships (see LIGHTHOUSES AND LIGHTSHIPS, and BUOYS). Most ports have a channel kept clear by DREDGERS (q.v.). London, whose tide rises and falls about 20 feet, has a dredged channel 30 feet deep at ordinary low water and 1,000 feet wide. This allows vessels up to 35,000 tons to navigate up the Thames.

When a vessel comes near a port, it is usually boarded by a PILOT (q.v.) who advises the ship master. The Port Health Authority sends its officers aboard to see that the ship is free from infectious diseases, and, if necessary, to send infected people to hospital. All ports issue traffic rules, in which sound signals, lights, prohibited anchorages, and other details are laid down. Towage services are maintained by the port authority and private firms (see TUGS). The big ship-tugs which help large vessels in and out of docks are used not so much to pull the vessels as to help them to manœuvre.

If the ship is carrying general cargo, it will usually be moored alongside a quay or pier. It may be secured to a mooring buoy, and the cargo discharged over the side, into barges or coasting vessels. In London and Liverpool the

Mersey Docks & Harbour Board

DISCHARGING TEA AT LIVERPOOL DOCKS

big difference between the levels of high and low water has led to the building of enclosed docks, the water in which is kept at a constant level by pumps. Ships lie alongside the quays in these docks, always at the same level, whatever the height of the tide in the river outside. Vessels enter and leave through locks which, in principle, are the same as those on canals (see LOCKS AND WEIRS). Southampton has less tidal range (see TIDES, Vol. III) than the Thames, and the greater depth at low water allows large ocean liners, such as the *Queen Mary* and *Queen Elizabeth*, to lie at open quays; there is no lock between them and the sea. Small vessels and craft are not so much affected by the rise and fall of tide. Hundreds of wharves line the Thames at which barges, coasters, and even ocean-going ships, although afloat at high water, sit on the mud at low tide.

In addition to the great ship-building ports in the north of Britain, where long overhauls of vessels take place, all large ports carry out maintenance work and ship repairs, often in dry DOCKS (q.v.), which allow engineers and painters to work on the under-water parts of a vessel's hull. All ports provide ships with supplies of fresh water as well as coal, oil, and petrol. The fuel may be loaded direct from the shore or from a special ship.

A port must be easy of access to the inland population which produces goods for export and consumes the food or raw materials from overseas. Thus the port must be well served by arterial roads, rail connexions with a main line, and inland waterways. An enormous number of packages is handled in a large ship, and their movement employs a constant stream of road vehicles, rail trucks, coasters, and barges. If this distributive transport were not available, all our ports would speedily become choked with cargo and with ships waiting to unload. So the lay-out of a modern port must include railway MARSHALLING YARDS (q.v.), where goods trains can be 'broken up' and the trucks shunted alongside the ship; it must have loading bays for all forms of land transport; it must also provide tugs to tow barges to and from the steamer berths.

Much cargo is loaded and unloaded by ships' derricks, movable arms attached to the base of a mast. For very heavy objects, such as locomotives and large pieces of machinery, the bigger ports maintain a floating crane to lift weights up to 150 or even 200 tons. The lighter kinds of 'bulk cargo', such as loose grain, seeds, and nuts, are discharged by suction elevators, on the principle of a vacuum cleaner. Floating elevators alongside the ship may suck up the bulk cargo and discharge it into barges, or the ship may be taken alongside a granary or mill, where fixed elevators will suck the cargo into storage chambers.

Wide use is also made of mechanical CONVEYORS and CRANES, lifts, and hoists (qq.v. Vol. VIII). In many ports, cargo can be safely stored until needed in large WAREHOUSES (q.v. Vol. VII), specially equipped for such things as frozen meat, dairy produce, leaf tobacco, and wool.

A large reserve of labour is important in a big port. Besides pilots, dock-masters, engineers, watermen, crane drivers, tug crews, and other highly skilled men, an army of dock labourers finds employment, for a great deal of cargo can still only be dealt with by hand. Stevedores are the skilled men who load and discharge ships. Men who handle cargo at British ports are all now employed by the National Dock Labour Board.

Ports used by passengers need landing-stages, baggage halls for the Customs' examination, and railway platforms near the ship.

PORTS, HISTORY OF. The first ships were small and needed no artificial ports. They tied up to trees, posts, or mooring rings at the riverside, and were loaded by gangways up which lines of slaves could walk carrying goods. Sea-going vessels could be beached in shallow water, and were built with extra strong hulls to stand the scraping of gravel and stones. Sheltered coves and river mouths were the obvious first harbours, since calm water was necessary for beaching and unloading. When Julius Caesar came to Britain in 55 B.C. his ships were drawn up on shore, and damaged because he was unused to tidal waters.

River harbours existed at a very early date; there were two in the SUMERIAN city of Ur (q.v. Vol. I); the great Egyptian capitals of Memphis and Thebes were river ports. The port of Athens was Piræus, which is a promontory with a land-locked harbour on the west and two small harbours on the east. It was first built as a naval base with docks and 'ship-houses' (which were dry docks 150 feet long and 20 feet wide); later it was equipped with quays and warehouses for trade. The Long Walls connected the port with Athens and made the latter safe from starvation in case of siege.

The great port and city of Syracuse on the east coast of Sicily is said to have been founded by the Greeks in 734 B.C. The original settlement was in the island of Ortygia, which was joined to the mainland by a mole in the 6th century B.C.

When Alexander the Great conquered Egypt in 332 B.C., he determined to build a port which would keep open his communications with Europe and take the place of conquered Tyre in the trade of the Greek world. He sailed down the Nile from Memphis and founded his city, Alexandria, on a neck of land between the sea and Lake Mareotis. Three-quarters of a mile distant lay the island of Pharos. Alexander joined it to the mainland by a stone mole. To the east of it was the great harbour, and to the west the naval port with an inner basin. The harbours were given a trading exchange, magazines, and proper docks. Two hundred years later the Great Lighthouse was built on

DOVER HARBOUR IN 1543

Pharos Island, the first LIGHTHOUSE (q.v.) in the world.

The Phoenicians, Greeks, and Romans understood clearly the needs of sea power and chose their harbours well. They had the engineering skill and unlimited slave labour to build moles and sea walls. Their commerce was so developed as to make the erection of docks, wharves, and warehouses necessary; they levied customs duties to pay for the upkeep of the harbours. They were fortunate in living on the shores of the landlocked and almost tideless Mediterranean sea, which simplified engineering problems.

The most important harbour of Roman Britain was Richborough (Rutupiae), on the west bank of the channel which then separated the Isle of Thanet from the mainland of Kent. The original fortifications were erected by a landing party in A.D. 43 and used as a base for the Emperor Claudius's conquest of the country. A huge masonry base was erected for a lighthouse; magnificent buildings were put up, and merchants thronged the harbour; thousands of Roman coins found there testify to 400 years of business. As Roman London grew in importance, ships sailed up the Thames to Walbrook, where the first fort was built; two river gates existed at Billingsgate and Dowgate. The ports of Britain became increasingly busy as the country developed into a granary for Rome.

When the Romans left Britain, their great ports decayed. Saxon ships, like the Viking ships after them, were beached in shallow harbours or tied up in the rivers. The VIKING SHIPS (q.v.) were provided with a rope to pull up the steering oar to prevent its being damaged when the ships were dragged up the shelving beaches. As England, however, developed into a nation the five ports nearest to France—Sandwich, Dover, Hythe, Romsey, and Hastings—became important for trade and defence. They are mentioned in Edward the Confessor's time, and William the Conqueror set aside these 'Five Ports' or Cinque Ports, and the coast-line on which they lay, as a division—like a county. In the days before a regular navy was set up, these ports had to provide ships and seamen for defence. In return they had many privileges, such as exemption from taxes and the right to hold their own courts of law. At their head was the Warden of the Cinque Ports, who lived in Dover Castle. The office of warden still exists, and is conferred as an honour upon some great man of the time. The sea has now receded, and only Dover still remains an important port.

The growing trade of the Middle Ages led to important developments. It became customary for the maritime nations to have their 'streets' or head-quarters in most of the great ports of the East. By 1250 the English had their 'street', for instance, in the port of Acre. Exclusive privileges were granted to the great CHARTERED COMPANIES (q.v. Vol. VII), as well as the merchants of the HANSEATIC LEAGUE (q.v. Vol. VII), who had a depot in London. From the beginning of the 13th century certain ports were set aside to handle all the wool exported from the country to make it easier to collect the customs duties. These were called Staple towns, and the chief of them was Calais.

London, which lay at the centre of Britain's road system and also on the Thames, gradually grew into a great trading port. LONDON BRIDGE (q.v.) marked the upper limit of navigation for sea-going vessels. There were quays enough along the river for the shipping of the day, and small boats in their hundreds to help unload or to ferry passengers across the river from the 'steps' which led down to it. The masts of the Thames were to the Elizabethan a sign of his country's greatness. The new naval dockyard at Deptford founded by Henry VIII was under the control of TRINITY HOUSE (q.v.), the corporation which is still in charge of all coastwise lights and navigation signals. It was at Deptford that the GOLDEN HIND (q.v.) anchored on returning from Drake's voyage round the world.

In the west of England, Bristol was rising rapidly to pre-eminence. The harbour had been improved in the 13th century by the cutting of a new channel for the River Frome. Then its Company of MERCHANT ADVENTURERS (q.v. Vol. VII) was formed, and from its quays John and Sebastian Cabot set out in 1497 on the voyage to Newfoundland. Bristol remained the greatest of the provincial ports, engaged mainly in the slave trade, till the 19th century.

The docks at London date from the 17th century, when the increasing size of ships and volume of trade made it necessary to undertake the building of enclosed basins in which the water level could be maintained at low tide by means of gates. The first basins were built at Rotherhithe, Deptford, and Blackwall, where the East India Company berthed its ships. There were over thirty landing places by this time on the north bank of the Thames, and London was the busiest port in the world except Amsterdam. In the early 19th century the first modern walled-in docks were built for London shipping; they were at Poplar, Wapping, and Rotherhithe. Later came the large Royal Albert and Victoria Docks, to take the biggest ocean-going vessels of the day. Then a line of docks was built at Tilbury.

In 1900 a Royal Commission was set up to investigate the running of the London docks, and to make suggestions for their improvement. It reported that the river was in need of dredging, and that the port was not re-exporting as many goods as it had done earlier. In 1908 the Port of London Act set up the Port of London Authority, which now controls the port, though

Trinity House is still responsible for pilotage, lighting, and buoying from London Bridge seawards (see LONDON, Vol. III). After the First World War, the vast new King George V dock was added to the Port of London.

In the 19th century with the coming of the steamship came the rapid rise of the port of Liverpool, made efficient by the continuous dredging of the channel. The long series of docks is planned like those at Tilbury. The building of the MANCHESTER SHIP CANAL (q.v.) in 1895 made the inland city of Manchester an oceanic port. In the same way Hamburg, 75 miles from the sea, has been made a very important port by dredging the River Elbe.

Ports are always changing. The great ports of the past, such as Richborough and most of the Cinque Ports, have ceased to exist through coastal changes; some, such as King's Lynn, have been outstripped by rivals; others have been developed by the coming of the railway or have declined because the railway by-passed them. Passenger traffic keeps Southampton busy, while naval bases flourish at Portsmouth and Devonport. London and Liverpool vie for leadership in Great Britain to-day because they lie athwart great trade routes—and ports exist mainly by virtue of serving trade.

See also PORTS AND HARBOURS.

PORTUGUESE LANGUAGE, see SPANISH AND PORTUGUESE LANGUAGES.

POSTMARKS AND POSTAGE STAMPS. Post Office officials mark the outsides of letters or parcels in certain ways to facilitate their passage through the post. These postmarks may refer to dates of posting or of receipt, or to the amount of postage paid or due. They may give instructions for special treatment, as with a registered packet. The earliest British postmarks, appearing in manuscript on Tudor letters, stated that the letter so marked concerned 'His or Her Majesty's Special Affairs', and instructed the messenger to 'Haste, Post Haste for Life for Life'. In 1661 hand stamps were introduced for marking letters with a small round postmark giving the date of posting. In 1663 another hand stamp, making an oblong mark, was introduced to indicate the amount of postage due on incoming overseas letters. Until adhesive stamps came in, however, the amount of postage paid or to be collected on letters was more generally written in black or red on the front of the letter. During

Fox Photos

A PART OF THE PORT OF LONDON

The King George V Dock is in front, the Royal Albert on the right, and the Victoria at the back.

A MID-19TH-CENTURY EFFORT TO INTRODUCE A WORLD PENNY POST
Envelope decorated with propaganda and bearing a 'penny red' stamp, which succeeded the 'penny black'

the late 18th and early 19th centuries improved date-stamps were adopted with more modern designs.

In 1840, when the penny post was first introduced by Rowland Hill, the first postage stamps were issued. Stamps, as well as stamped letter sheets and envelopes, were placed on sale for public use to facilitate postal operations and in particular to bring to an end the system of collecting postage on delivery. The earliest British stamp was the 1d. black. This stamp bore the head of Queen Victoria copied from a medal designed by William Wyon of the Royal Mint, and engraved by hand.

To-day more than 7,000 million stamps are used in Britain in a year, and are printed in enormous numbers by quick modern processes. They are printed on specially watermarked paper and, apart from stamps of high value, by a process called photogravure. Reproductions of the artist's

EXPERIMENTAL DESIGN FOR
PENNY STAMP, 1839

design are transferred by a photographic process and reproduced by etching on copper-covered rollers from which the stamps are printed. Stamps of value from 2s. 6d. to £1 are still printed by a line-engraving process (see PROCESS REPRODUCTION, Vol. VII).

The stamps on letters are cancelled in sorting offices for the most part by high speed stamp cancelling machines, which overprint the stamp and also impress the date and time of posting on the letter.

See also Vol. IX: STAMP COLLECTING.

POST OFFICE, HISTORY OF. Human beings normally communicate with each other by signs and speech, but when separated by a distance greater than the range of vision or sound, they send a message. In the earliest time MESSENGERS (q.v.) delivered such messages by word of mouth; but after writing became common, they were given letters to carry. Originally the messenger carried his letters the whole distance, sometimes on foot but generally mounted: but it was soon found that his journey could be speeded up if he changed his horse for a fresh one at each stage or post along the road. Later, when letters became numerous, it was arranged for them to be passed from messenger to messenger or from post to post. This is the origin of the postal system in all countries. There are many references to such systems in the Bible and in the early histories of Persia, Greece, Rome, and China.

In this country the postal service developed from the King's Messenger service—a service which still exists under Foreign Office control, for different purposes. Messengers known as heralds, pursuivants, *nuncii*, or *cursorii* were employed by all monarchs to convey dispatches under royal warrant. They travelled the road demanding fresh horses and guides in the King's name from the authorities in the large towns on the way. London had to keep at times a stud of horses available for the use of the Royal messengers, and when not required for the use of the King's messenger service, these horses were made available for hire by the general public as hackney horses, a service which later developed into the hackney carriage and STAGE COACH services (q.v.).

About 1512 Henry VIII appointed Brian Tuke, one of Cardinal Wolsey's officials, as Master of Posts, and his duty was to organize posts along the main roads by means of which royal messengers and officers of state could travel in person, or news and instructions could be sent by letter at the speed of a horse. As time passed, such arrangements became fairly well established, and the duty of maintaining horses and men ready to meet royal requirements was transferred to innkeepers in the post-towns. These became in effect Postmasters in charge of post-houses. Gradually the public began to use this service more and more for private travel and for sending letters under private arrangements with the Postmaster-innkeepers.

During Queen Elizabeth's reign the carrying of letters became much more confined to the royal posts. Under a proclamation of 1591 the public were required to use only the royal service for travelling and for sending their letters abroad. The object of the rule was to enable a watch to be kept over the comings and goings of plotters, and over the circulation between this country and the Continent of letters dangerous to the state. The proclamation was repeated by James I, no doubt for a similar reason.

The public who used these services were required to make their own arrangements for payment with the various postmasters. In 1635, however, King Charles I issued a proclamation throwing open to the general public the royal system of posts for sending letters, but not for the hire of horses, on condition that letters were paid for at a price based on the distance covered. This postage was intended by the King to help in meeting the heavy cost of maintaining the service, then estimated at about £3,400 a year. Thomas Witherings, a courtier of experience, was made Chief Postmaster to organize the system. The Civil War of 1642–52 interfered with the development of the system; but after the war Cromwell decided to maintain and develop it as a parliamentary instead of a Crown institution. By an Act of 1657 he placed the control directly under a minister, a member of Parliament to be known as a Postmaster-General, with an office in London to be known as the General Post Office. Under Charles II, James II, and William III the service was developed still further, and the revenue from it became a valuable source of royal income. Dates of posting began to be stamped on letters from 1660, and a London Penny Post, started by William Dockwra in 1680 as a private venture, was added to the State postal service in 1682.

A continual source of difficulty at this period was the fact that postmasters could easily divert to their own pockets money which should have gone to the revenue of the Post Office. They generally did this by diverting letters from one road system to another by unofficial cross-posts, so that they avoided London, the only place where the postages on letters were assessed and checked. This difficulty was largely overcome in the 18th century when travelling surveyors were appointed to check the contents of the mails. Ralph Allen of Bath (1694–1764) set up official cross-posts joining one main-road system with another. Postmasters and others, however, continued often to abuse the 'franking' privilege —the privilege of sending letters free of postage, which had been granted to Peers, Officers of State, and members of Parliament, and later extended to Post Office officials generally. At first the sender had only to write his name or title on the letter, but in the 18th century the privilege was more closely defined, and anyone exercising his right to frank a letter had to give his full address. Even so, the privilege continued to be used too freely, frankers often sending their friends' letters under their own signature. The privilege for individuals was abolished in 1840, though it continued to be used (as it still is) for

G.P.O.

SORTING MAIL IN A TRAVELLING POST OFFICE

postal charges irrespective of distance, and this is now used all over the world. An essential feature of the reform was that all letters had to be paid for before they were sent, and special envelopes and small adhesive printed labels (now known as postage stamps) were introduced. Stamps, which were first used in Great Britain on 6 May 1840, have also been universally adopted.

Since the early 19th century, other important postal services have been developed. In 1838 it was made possible to send money by the post by the money order PAYMENT service (q.v. Vol. VII), and in 1881 the simpler method of sending small sums of money by postal order was introduced. The Travelling Post Office on railways started in 1838 (see POST OFFICE, MODERN). In 1841 the system of registering valuable letters and parcels began, and by 1878 a system of compensation for the loss of registered items in the post was working. In 1861 the Post Office Savings Bank (see NATIONAL SAVINGS, Vol. X) was opened, but the present system of savings certificates was not started until 1911. The parcel-post service both for overseas and inland delivery was working by 1883. In recent years the postal services have been further improved by the introduction of AIR MAIL and AIR-GRAPH services (qq.v.), and also by the use of helicopters to carry mail (see ROTORCRAFT).

The Universal Postal Union, through which the international postal services of all countries are now co-ordinated, was established in 1874.

In Great Britain, since 1870, the Post Office has been charged under the Postmaster-General's monopoly with the administration of all public TELECOMMUNICATION services (q.v.). At the time the only service concerned was the telegraph service, which had developed under private and railway company enterprise from the inventions of Wheatstone, Cooke, and Morse some years earlier (see TELEGRAPHY, HISTORY OF).

Soon after the Government had acquired the

government communications, such as income-tax forms.

In the 17th and 18th centuries the postal officials had great difficulties with the dishonesty and unreliability of the poorly-paid, lazy, and ill-mounted post-boys. Because of this, from 1784 onwards John Palmer's plan was adopted for sending the mails in well-guarded stage coaches, provided with good horses. This revolutionized the postal system of Great Britain, giving it a reputation, which it still holds, as a reliable and efficient service. Railways displaced the mail coach services from about 1830 onwards. In the early 19th century, mainly as a result of the Napoleonic wars, the public began to find the state postal service so costly that they would often avoid using it, and would send their letters illegally by private means, such as stage coaches or carriers, thereby depriving the State of much revenue. No solution of this problem was discovered until 1837, when Rowland HILL (q.v. Vol. V) produced his famous plan for sending letters at a uniform rate of 1d. per ½ oz., irrespective of distance. This scheme secured immediate public support; it was made official by Act of Parliament and was introduced in January 1840. Before many years had passed, most European countries had adopted the principle of uniform

telegraph service for £10,000,000, the State monopoly and revenue were threatened by a telecommunications invention known as the TELEPHONE (q.v.). Following a legal test case, however, which ruled that a telephone was a telegraph, the state monopoly was assured, and all operators of such services for public use were required to take out a licence with the Postmaster-General. These services were for the most part transferred to the State in January 1912, when the Government bought the assets of the National Telephone Company.

The British Post Office now transacts business on a vast scale. In the year 1948–9, for instance, 7,667 million letters were posted for delivery within the country and 383 million for delivery abroad. Two hundred and fourteen million parcels were delivered within Britain, and over 25½ million were handled to and from foreign countries. Over 53 million telegrams were sent, and there were altogether some 5 million telephones in use.

See also POST OFFICE, MODERN; POSTMARKS AND POSTAGE STAMPS.

POST OFFICE (MODERN). The work of the Post Office is very varied. Its primary business is the collection, conveyance, and delivery of letters, packets, and parcels, and this yields the largest annual income—nearly £85,000,000. It is also responsible for the Inland and Overseas TELEGRAPH and TELEPHONE SERVICES (qq.v.), all of which have developed during the 20th century. In January 1912 there were about 700,000 telephones; in January 1950 there were more than 5,000,000. The Post Office remits money by money order and postal order (*see* PAYMENT, Vol. VII). It also undertakes various other State services for which its vast organization affords convenient machinery. These are generally called agency services, and include the Post Office Savings Bank, the issue and repayment of NATIONAL SAVINGS Certificates, the payment of various PENSIONS (qq.v. Vol. X) and allowances on behalf of other Government departments, the issue of licences, including wireless and motor licences, and the sale of insurance and entertainment duty stamps. The Post Office is, therefore, a very large and important national service, and it has a very high reputation for efficiency.

The Postmaster-General (a political appoint-ment) is the head of the Post Office, and is responsible to Parliament for its conduct. The Director-General (a permanent appointment) is the chief adviser to the Postmaster-General. The Minister also has as advisory bodies on matters of general policy a Board of about twelve principal officials and a Post Office Advisory Council, composed of prominent men and women in public and commercial life outside the Post Office. Under the Director-General, and his two Deputies and one Assistant Director-General, are a body of heads of various departments of the Post Office and also ten Regional Directors. Post Office administration is decentralized as much as possible, Headquarters being responsible for policy, the Regional Directors for its execution, and the 56 Telephone Managers and 470 Head Postmasters for its local application. There are altogether in Great Britain and Northern Ireland some 24,000 post offices, 5,800 telephone exchanges, and a total of about 350,000 staff.

The Post Office conveys the mails by the ordinary transport facilities provided by the railways, air corporations, and, for overseas mails, shipping companies. It has the right to control the timing of certain trains essential for carrying mail, especially those on which there are Travelling Post Offices. Some trains are composed wholly or partly of coaches specially constructed as sorting offices and manned with a sorting staff. Letters with an additional fee can be posted in a special posting-box in these coaches at each station at which the Travelling Post Office stops. The staff are responsible for dropping and picking up mail-bags by means of special train and trackside apparatus while the train travels at full speed—perhaps nearly 70 miles an hour. Each of these mail-bags is enclosed in a strong leather pouch, which is suspended from a stout metal arm. The travelling train catches the trackside pouch in a strong rope net fixed to the side of the coach. It drops pouches from the train into a similar net which is fixed on the side of the railway track. In this way mail can be exchanged without stopping the train, and a very quick postal service can be provided.

In London the Post Office has used for many years a special underground 'tube' railway, which runs from the Eastern District Office to Paddington Station, linking together, over a distance of 6½ miles, a number of principal sorting offices and most of the railway termini north

G.P.O.

THE POST OFFICE UNDERGROUND RAILWAY, LONDON

of the Thames. The trains are driverless, are automatically controlled, and run at a speed of 35 miles an hour between stations. Nearly 12 million mail-bags are carried by the railway every year. Mail-bags are carried down to the railway by lifts and gravity shoots, and tipped into wheeled containers, which are then wheeled on to the trucks of the train. At their destination the containers are wheeled off and tipped into a cradle, so that the bags fall on to an elevating conveyor which carries them up to the sorting office.

The Post Office supplements the ordinary transport services, and collects and distributes mail in country districts, by a fleet of some 10,000 postal motor mail-vans; and about 17,000 bicycles are used by local postmen.

About 22 million letters, exclusive of parcels, are posted and delivered each day in Great Britain and Northern Ireland. When the postman clears a post-box, he carries the letters, either by mail-van, bicycle, or on foot, to the sorting office. Here the letters are heaped on a table and 'faced', that is, they are placed address side up with the stamp in the right-hand top corner. Small packets and newspapers are put aside to be treated separately. The faced letters are then postmarked either by hand or by being passed through an electrically operated stamp-cancelling machine at the rate of about 500 a minute. This postmark both cancels the stamp and dates the letters. Any stamps which escape the impression, as well as those on the packets and newspapers, are cancelled by hand.

The letters are then sorted into pigeon-holes, first by counties and large towns, and then subdivided into towns and districts, ready to be sent on. Letters for delivery in London are forwarded to the appropriate delivery office according to the district letters and number on the address, for example, London, S.W. 11. Packets and newspapers are sorted separately into mail-bags which are hung within iron frames called drop-bag fittings, each labelled with its place of destination. The letters, when sorted, are tied into labelled bundles and dropped into the same mail-bags. Registered letters and packets are dealt with in locked rooms, and immediately before dispatch are placed in the appropriate mail-bags. When the bags are ready, they are tied up, labelled, and sealed with specially marked sealing presses bearing the name of the sorting office. In each bag is enclosed a 'bill' which states to the receiving office what are its contents. One of the world's largest sorting offices is at Mount Pleasant in Clerkenwell, London, where all the letters for the provinces posted in the City are sorted. Letters for distribution in the centre of London or abroad go to the central sorting office in King Edward Street, where the

London Chief Office for business across the counter is situated.

The sealed mail-bags are then sent to the station either by mail-van or, if the station is close, by electric or petrol truck. The letter mails are put on to the appropriate trains by postmen, though parcel mails are generally handled by the railway staff. At the place of destination a mail-van is ready, probably drawn up on the platform, to receive the bags. At certain offices where the railway station and sorting office adjoin, the two are linked by a subway and conveyor belts.

At the delivery office the bags are 'ticked-in' and, after careful examination of the seals, opened. The bundles are then sorted for sending on or for delivery. Those for delivery are further sorted by the delivery postmen into the correct order for their delivery route or 'walk'. There are often redirection orders in the office for certain addresses, and letters for these are re-addressed and forwarded. The registered letters are handed out to each postman from the special enclosure, and for these he must bring back a signed receipt to show delivery. The postmen then proceed on their rounds, often making collections from letter-boxes on their return journeys.

Behind these operational services and departments so far described there are large departments providing all the varied equipment needed to keep the postal services running smoothly—mail-bags and uniforms, cable and telephone equipment, motor vehicles, and stationery have to be provided in large quantities. The Engineering Department has, of course, the responsibility for maintaining not only the motor vehicles, but also the plant for the TELECOMMUNICATION services (q.v.). A large research station at Dollis Hill on the outskirts of London is occupied in work in this highly specialized field.

See also POST OFFICE, HISTORY OF; POSTMARKS AND POSTAGE STAMPS; AIR MAIL; EXPRESS LETTER.

PRESSURE CABIN (AIRCRAFT), *see* HIGH ALTITUDE FLIGHT.

PRIMITIVE SHIPS. Man's first water-craft were probably used, not on the sea, but on rivers and lakes. Early settlements were formed near these, and in the days of dense forests they were easier than land to travel on (*see* RIVER NAVIGATION).

From our knowledge of primitive peoples of modern times, we suppose that man first supported himself in the water by holding on to a natural float with his hands, such as an unhusked coco-nut or drift log. The next stage depended upon the material at hand: early peoples used logs of wood, bundles of reeds, or the inflated skins of animals on which they could sit astride, or which they could build up into rafts to be stood or sat upon; in forest regions primitive man might come to use either a dug-out or bark CANOE (q.v.) or coracle, such as are still used by many primitive peoples.

The coracle was round and had a frame of wood (usually willow) covered with the skins of animals. It was very light and could be carried over land where a stretch of the river was difficult to navigate. In North America travellers by canoe regularly have to carry (or 'portage') their boats and all their goods past waterfalls. Coracles were much used in Britain; even now, covered with tarpaulin, they still survive on a few rivers; near the River Teifi in Pembrokeshire, for instance, one may easily meet a couple of men walking along the road with their coracles on their backs. The Greek historian Herodotus tells us that the Assyrians used coracles to carry wine-casks down the River Euphrates to the city of Babylon. There the willow frames were sold, and the skins carried back by donkeys to be used again. Boats of this type, and also rough rafts supported on inflated skins, are used to this day on the Tigris and Euphrates.

Another type of primitive craft still in use in India, the East Indies, and South America is the catamaran. This is formed by lashing together a group of logs, usually three; the centre one is the largest, and its fore end is slanted, as a cutwater. A sail can be carried in moderate weather if the craft is provided with an outrigger, that is, a log fixed parallel to the boat, and attached to it with timber cross-pieces. The boat cannot then turn over without submerging the log or lifting it out of the water. The MAORIS of New Zealand (q.v. Vol. I) voyaged 2,000 miles from the Cook Islands in large outrigged double canoes which ran by sail before the prevailing north-west winds. Other inhabitants of the Pacific made almost unbelievable journeys in these simple craft.

Progress in the development of the boat came chiefly through the dug-out, but it came slowly —and the first dug-out itself appears surprisingly late in man's history. A great many dug-out canoes have been discovered buried by the rivers and marshes of the British Isles. In their simplest form they have been hollowed, often with the help of fire, from a single tree trunk—mere troughs with solid blunt ends, anything from 8 feet to 35 feet in length. One ancient boat found at Brigg in Lincolnshire (Fig. 1) was made from a perfectly straight oak-tree which, allowing for the removal of bark and sapwood, must have been very large. The canoe measured 47 ft. 6 in. long, about 5 ft. wide, and 2 ft. 9 in. deep. The log had been roughly squared, and the canoe had a flat bottom and straight sides, except towards the bow end where it became semicircular. The stern end was closed by two

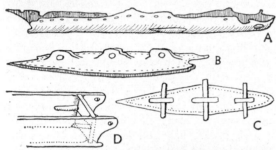

FIG. 1. BOAT FOUND AT BRIGG, LINCS.

A. The boat with tingle on bottom. B. Tingle. C. Method of attaching tingle. D. Stern board of boat

boards, slotted into the sides of the canoe and caulked with mosses. All dug-outs are liable to crack on the side and must be patched, and the Brigg boat had a remarkable patch on her side. A leaf-shaped oak board or 'tingle', 6 feet long by 6 inches in the middle, had been stitched by thongs to the outside of the canoe. Solid ridges were left across the inside of the bottom of the canoe, to strengthen the hull. This boat is valuable as a stepping-stone between the pure dug-out construction and the complex built-up plank boat which we believe evolved from the dug-out.

Two boats now in the National Maritime Museum at Greenwich were discovered at North Ferriby, on the banks of the River Humber, in 1937, and were salved in 1946. These boats show a jump from the dug-out to the built boat. The more complete of the Ferriby boats measures 43 ft. 6 in. long by 5 ft. 4 in. broad, and is built of oak. The bottom of the boat is formed of three planks—a heavier plank in the centre between two others, and at the bow end the central

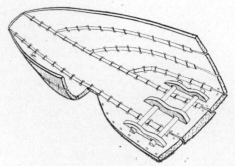

FIG. 2. SECTION OF BOAT FOUND AT NORTH FERRIBY

or keel plank turns up. The remains suggest the boat was built up with three planks each side. The seams between the planks are a remarkable example of early shipwright's work: the planks are grooved and caulked with moss; they are also stitched together with withes or twigs, and the seams are sealed with a covering strip of wood lying along the seam like a tape and held in place by the stitches. The three bottom planks are also stiffened by timbers (see Fig. 2). The blade of a paddle was found near the boats.

The boat found at Brigg and those found at Ferriby are probably earlier than the coming of the Romans to Britain; they may be as early as 500 B.C. A boat (Fig. 3) found at Hjortespring, on the island of Als, Denmark, in 1920, can be dated from about 300 B.C. and shows a definite

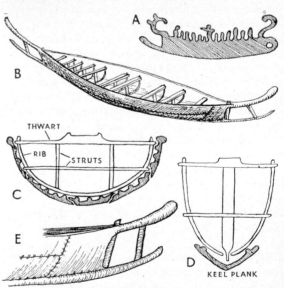

FIG. 3. BOAT FOUND AT HJORTESPRING, DENMARK

A. Scandinavian rock carving showing Stone Age boat.
B. Reconstruction of the boat. C. Midship section.
D. Section near end. E. Dug-out end of boat

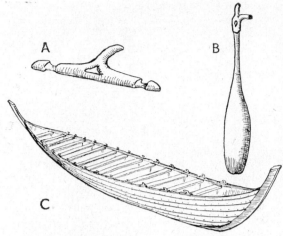

FIG. 4. SHIP FOUND AT NYDAM, SCHLESWIG, DENMARK
A. Rowlock. B. Rudder. C. Reconstruction of ship

advance in construction. It is built up of five broad oak planks, the one in the middle forming the bottom, and has a semicircular midship section. The lower edge of a plank in this boat overlaps the upper edge of the plank below, 'clinker-built' fashion, and the seams are caulked and stitched together. Beams which serve as benches or thwarts for the paddlers cross the boat, and there is a scooped seat at either side. As well as these beams which serve as thwarts, there are other struts which serve to keep the boat's shape. The ends of the Hjortespring boat show peculiar double stem and stern projections. The side planks are not carried to the ends, but are sewn to special bow and stern boards cut from the solid, like the cut-off ends of dug-out canoes. Upright struts connect the ends of the keel plank. Such ends are found to-day in canoes used in the Celebes Islands in the East Indies. The Hjortespring boat is about 40 feet long and could carry some twenty people.

A boat was found in 1863 at Nydam in Schleswig, south Denmark, which dates from about A.D. 200 and whose several new features combine to make her appear very modern when compared with the Hjortespring boat. The Nydam boat is clinker-built; both ends are alike (Fig. 4), and the side of the craft has lashed to it wooden rowlocks for fourteen oars a side. Holes in these rowlocks are for loops of rope with which to secure the oars. Benches pass across the boat for the rowers. A paddle-shaped rudder was found near the Nydam boat. There is no

trace of the use of mast or sail. Matting was laid on the bottom of the boat.

Three notable signs of progress, therefore, are apparent in the Nydam boat: rowing with oars, using rowlocks instead of paddling, must have resulted in greater endurance and speed; using iron nails instead of stitching with withes must have given boats greater strength and made them easier to build; stem and stern posts erected on the ends of the keel meant stronger construction and speed because of less resistance to the water. These boats grew into the VIKING SHIPS (q.v.). In the Mediterranean a rather different development took place. In north-west Europe boats were built with the planks overlapping, that is, they were 'clinker-built'. In the Mediterranean the skin of the boat was generally made of planks placed edge to edge to present a smooth surface outside; that is, they were 'carvel-built'.

See also CLASSICAL SHIPS; VIKING SHIPS.

PRINTING, HISTORY OF. 1. The earliest known Printing was done in Asia, perhaps as early as the 5th century, from hand-cut wood blocks. A design would be cut with a knife on a flat block of wood; it would then be inked, and paper or cloth pressed against it. That method is still used in Britain to-day by some artists to produce hand-printed woven materials (see TEXTILE PRINTING, Vol. VII). The earliest block prints still in existence are Buddhist charms, of which a million were printed in A.D. 767 by command of the Empress of Japan; several of these prints are in the British Museum. At this time Japan was strongly under Chinese influence, and it is probable that block printing was done in China earlier than the 8th century. The first printed book on record, a prayer-book known as the 'Diamond Sutra', was produced in China in 868. Wooden printing-types of Chinese origin, made in the 13th century, still exist, and movable types made of clay are known to have been cast in China in the 11th century, and probably much earlier. But there is no reason to connect Chinese work with European printing.

The first known printing with movable types in Europe occurred just before 1450. For some years earlier, a few books were being printed from wood blocks—that is, all the letters and words on a page were carved by hand, as in the ancient Asiatic way, on one flat piece of wood; a book of 100 pages would mean carving 100

A 17TH-CENTURY PRINTING SHOP

On the left are the compositors setting type from the type cases. On the right is the press, with printers inking the type ready for printing. Woodcut by Abraham von Werdt

slabs of wood, and from these many copies of a book could be printed. But the carving by hand of all the letters on each page was a slow process, requiring clever artists, and their carved work became useless once a book had been printed. The invention of movable types meant that an artist could design single letters, of which any number of copies could be made in a mould, and then assembled to make words and pages. When the printing was done, the letters could be taken apart and used again. This invention, probably one of the most important in all history, made it possible to produce many books, and helped to bring about the spread of knowledge, which led up to the developments of modern times.

The actual invention of movable type is attributed to Johann Gutenberg, at Mainz, in Germany. The great 'Forty-two Line Bible' (which had 42 lines on each page), printed in 1455 (*see* page 52), has been called the first book printed in movable type; but there were probably earlier ones which have been lost. A few years after the invention, the town of Mainz was looted during a war, and printers working or learning there were dispersed throughout Europe, carrying with them their knowledge. The first printed book in English was one relating legends of the siege of ancient Troy. It was printed at Bruges, in Flanders, in 1476, by an Englishman, William Caxton, and his partner. Caxton, after 33 years in Bruges, a city of learning, moved to London, and established the first English printing press in Westminster. In 1477 he produced a book of sayings of the philosophers, the first known book to be printed in England. In 1478 he issued the *Canterbury Tales* of Geoffrey CHAUCER (q.v. Vol. V).

Between 1500 and 1550, the 'Golden Age of Typography', the printers of Europe, and particularly of France, were scholars and authors as well as artists, who produced many beautiful books. Later, as printing passed into less skilled hands, there was a decline in workmanship.

For some centuries after Caxton's day there

was almost no change in the main methods of printing. All sheets of paper had to be printed, one at a time, by hand, much as a housewife to-day, having washed several handkerchiefs, will have to iron them by hand, one by one. The men who produced *The Times* about 1800, probably the quickest printers in the country, could hardly turn out 250 single printed sheets an hour. As for the composing of type, this continued to be done chiefly by hand (*see* PRINTING, Section 2, Vol. VII) till after 1900, although some of the wealthier newspaper printers in large cities had by then begun to use mechanical keyboards for composing.

In 1784 a former London coal merchant called John Walter bought an inventor's PATENT (q.v. Vol. VII) for speeding up printing. The idea was to keep a stock of frequently-used words or parts of words, ready-made in metal, to save printers the time needed to assemble the individual letters of each word. Although Walter started a newspaper (which later became *The Times*) to prove his theory, he was opposed by

the printers and had to go back to the old-fashioned ways.

About the same time, printing took a step forward with the development of the first iron printing-press. Until the end of the 18th century, the paper and the inked type were placed in wooden presses and squeezed by turning a large screw by hand. Thus, much time was lost in screwing and unscrewing the press for every sheet. In 1782 two Frenchmen invented a lever to apply quick pressure, instead of the slow screw; and in 1800 an English inventor, Lord Stanhope, improved on this with the first iron press, which had a more easily worked lever. Most hand-presses to-day are based on his principle.

2. MECHANICAL MACHINING. The two main operations involved in printing, the assembly of type and the actual inking and printing, or 'presswork', did not become mechanized at the same time. The presswork, now known as 'machining', became mechanized by slow stages during the 19th century, long before mechanical type-setting became common.

Common Ground Film Strip

DETAIL OF A MODERN PRINTING PRESS
The sheet of paper on the cylinder has just been printed from the type, seen lying flat

In 1814 steam printing first appeared. The early steam-engines were then being put to simple industrial uses, such as pumping water out of mines. An engine of this kind was used to print 1,000 copies an hour of *The Times*. The flat pages of type, instead of having paper squeezed against them by hand pressure, were pushed by steam power under a cylinder which pressed the paper against them. In 1848 came a rotary press: the separate columns of type were arranged round the outside of a large cylinder, and clamped to it. As the cylinder went round, it pressed the columns of type against paper sheets, of which 10,000 an hour could be printed. As only one side of a sheet was printed at a time, as in all printing in those days, the backs of the sheets had to be printed later with a second cylinder.

Modern high-speed printing became possible with the growth of stereotyping (*see* PRINTING, Section 5, Vol. VII) in the mid-19th century. This method of taking a mould of a flat page of ordinary type, and casting a duplicate page in the mould, gave rise to the idea of a curved stereotype page. In 1865 a printer in Philadelphia, U.S.A., cast molten metal in a curved mould and formed curved pages, with which he was able to print on both sides of a strip of paper at once. Instead of single sheets of paper being fed to the machine by hand, a single broad strip of great length was unwound from a spool—as with newspapers to-day. After passing through the printing rollers, the strip was automatically cut into sheets. In 1866 this method of mass production was first used in Britain by *The Times*. When in 1861 the last British tax on paper had been removed, this machine made possible the large circulations of modern newspapers (*see* NEWSPAPERS, HISTORY OF).

3. MECHANICAL TYPE-SETTING. Though invented in the 19th century, mechanical type-setting, or composition, was not widely adopted until the 20th century. Instead of the compositor having to pick up between his finger and thumb a small piece of metal for every letter he meant to print, as had been done for over 400 years, he used a keyboard like that of a typewriter. At first, machines were devised in which individual pieces of type, as used in hand-setting, were stored in separate containers, and one piece at a time was dropped from a slot as each key was pressed on the keyboard. Other machines were made to sort the type after use, each into its proper container; but it was found to be quicker in the end to melt all used type and to cast the metal again, by ordinary manufacturing methods, in groups of new letters.

The invention in America of the linotype machine in 1886 by Mergenthaler, and the monotype in 1887 by Lanston revolutionized the composition part of printing (*see* PRINTING, Section 4, Vol. VII).

See also BOOK; NEWSPAPER.
See also Vol. VII: PRINTING; PROCESS REPRODUCTION.

PRONUNCIATION, *see* LANGUAGE, HISTORY OF; VOICE.

PROPAGANDA AND ADVERTISING. One or other of these words is often used of some persuasive statement, whether written, spoken, or broadcast. More than 300 years ago the Roman Catholic church set up a missionary organization to cause its beliefs to spread or 'propagate'. The Latin term for this, *propaganda*, has come to be used for any attempt to convert people to another way of thinking, religious or otherwise.

Political propaganda is almost the only kind known to-day, and it is carried on by many methods. In countries with TOTALITARIAN systems of government (q.v. Vol. X), such as Russia and Spain, and Germany and Italy before the Second World War, propaganda is organized by the leader of the government so as to influence the minds of his people in favour of himself and of his own political party. All kinds of devices are used for this purpose. They include spectacular party congresses and meetings at which political speeches are made to large audiences, radio broadcasting, the publication of the party viewpoint through newspapers controlled and censored by the government, and the regular repeating of the government point of view in the ears of the people by an army of followers. This kind of propaganda often overflows the frontiers of the home country, and is aimed at the minds of foreigners as well. In a single-party State the government sees that there is no opposition propaganda to weaken its position, or, as it would say, mislead the people, and any form of criticism is forbidden. FREEDOM OF SPEECH (q.v.) is obviously not allowed in a single-party State. In a democratic or multi-party State, freedom of speech is not only one of the basic liberties of the people, but is, in fact, essential

The Plumb-pudding in danger: — or State Epicures taking un Petit Souper.
"*this great Globe itself, and all which it inherit*", is too small to satisfy such insatiable appetites.
295

'THE PLUMB-PUDDING IN DANGER': CARTOON BY GILLRAY, 1805
Napoleon helps himself to Europe while the British Prime Minister, Pitt, holds the sea for England

to the working of a parliamentary DEMOCRACY (q.v. Vol. X), as in Great Britain. In such a State, political propaganda can be carried out by anyone. To put before the people the attractions of their programmes and their policies, the parties make use of all available methods, which include newspapers, pamphlets, leaflets, periodicals, postal circulars, public meetings, loud-speaker vans, and radio broadcasting. In Great Britain the B.B.C. allots equal broadcasting opportunities to each of the main political parties.

The word 'advertising' originally meant bringing to people's attention a piece of information or news such as the arrival of a ship from abroad. Even to-day a newspaper may publish several columns of advertisements which aim solely at giving information: for example, the notices of births, marriages, and deaths; the various official and legal announcements; and the 'public appointments' columns, notifying vacancies on the staffs of Government or other public bodies.

But the word 'advertising' has acquired a second use; it now means not only informing people, but also persuading them—usually to buy something offered for sale.

Propaganda and advertising, therefore, are both ways of changing or influencing people's minds. In fact, just as some medicines or drugs have an effect on certain organs of the body, so propaganda, and advertising that is not merely informative, may have an undue effect on the human mind. Now that much more is known about the human mind, and the ways in which it may be influenced (*see* PSYCHOLOGY, Vol. XI), propaganda and advertising are much more efficient than they used to be, and in consequence capable of being more dangerous. Damage may be done to the peace and contentment of a home if advertisements cause unnecessary and useless goods to be bought, leaving insufficient money for important necessities. But the dangers of misused propaganda are much greater. Propaganda used for good purposes at the right time is valuable: if it urges people to be less wasteful, to save their money instead of spending it on luxuries, to grow more food in their gardens, and to avoid accidents on the roads, it is obviously useful. But in the present century many nations, previously free, have fallen victims to the propaganda of other nations, and have lost their liberties. Such political propaganda comes in time to blur people's power of seeing and judging truthfully and independently. They may in this way be led to behaviour which, were it not for the influence of the propaganda, they would shrink from. They are misled by cleverly timed exaggerations and false promises which appeal to the lower side of their nature; if such propaganda is clever, it is often very successful. But the kind that appeals to the higher instincts of men has scored some wonderful successes throughout history; this kind, like Mr. Churchill's speeches after the evacuation of Dunkirk in 1940, makes no vain promises, yet touches and rouses the hearts of men. All teaching and education, religious or other, are forms of propaganda; and civilization owes much to that type of religious propaganda that does not promise a pleasant heaven, easily reached, but asks men to do good

IT'S ALL RIGHT ... wool's *naturally* snug and warm

ADVERTISEMENTS FOR WOOL
Issued by the International Wool Secretariat

for its own sake, and not for self-love or hope of personal reward.

See also Vol. VII: ADVERTISING AND PUBLICITY; Vol. XII: POSTER.

PROPELLER, *see* Vol. VIII: PROPELLER, AIRCRAFT; PROPELLER, MARINE.

PUBLIC LIBRARY, *see* LIBRARIES, Section 2.

PUBLISHER, *see* BOOK. *See also* Vol. VII: PUBLISHING.

PULLMAN CAR, *see* RAILWAY COACHES, Section 6.

PUNCTUATION. Writing is divided into sentences and parts of sentences by a number of conventional punctuation marks or stops, which indicate pauses and help the reader to understand the meaning.

In the earliest writing the letters ran continuously without any stops. Gradually words were separated from each other, and then divided into sentences by points. Usually a single point like the full stop represented a pause; but it was normally placed high in the line of writing. Later, in some places the system was developed further: a point placed level with the top of the writing had the value of our full stop; placed in the centre, a comma; and placed near the bottom, a semicolon. These rules, however, were not always obeyed, and it was only after the invention of PRINTING (q.v.) that a standard system began to develop; the first man to encourage it was the Venetian printer, Aldus Manutius, in the 16th century. Often stops, adopted from the Greek, were altered in meaning; our semicolon, for example, was used as a question mark by the late Greeks. But fashions in punctuation have varied greatly. Generally to-day marks are used less frequently than in the 18th and 19th centuries. The main stops are these:

1. FULL STOP or PERIOD (.). This is the strongest pause and marks the end of a sentence, for example: 'Fear God. Honour the King.'

It is also used in abbreviations, as in 'Mr.' for 'Mister', 'Sept.' for 'September', 'Co.' for 'Company'.

2. COLON (:). This is an abrupt pause used particularly to connect two related sentences. The two sentences may be in contrast, as in the following:

'In peace time military discipline affects few people: in war it affects nearly everybody.'

Or the second sentence may explain or expand the first, as in:

'The choice that faced me was serious: I had to kill him or die myself.'

It may also be used to introduce a speech or quotation, for example:

'The headmaster said: "I am about to make an important announcement." '

3. SEMICOLON (;). This is less strong than the full stop or period, but stronger than the comma (*see* 4). It connects parallel or connected sentences, especially when a conjunction such as 'and' or 'but' is not used, for example, in the proverb: 'To err is human; to forgive divine.'

4. COMMA (,). It is widely used and represents the slightest pause. It separates closely connected clauses and phrases, as in:

'When I arrived in London, the day before my birthday, I met my brother.'

It separates a number of adjectives which all qualify one word, as in:

'A cold, bleak, damp room.'

5. PARENTHESES or BRACKETS (()) are put round phrases which interrupt or explain a sentence such as: 'His fortune (if you can call it that) amounted to £10.'

6. DASH (—). Dashes can be used in pairs in the same way as brackets, or one dash can be used like the colon to explain what had preceded it as in:

'These are great days—the greatest days our country has ever known.'

7. EXCLAMATION MARK (!). This is always used with certain words which in grammar are classed as exclamations, such as 'Oh!'; sometimes with the words 'what' or 'how', as in 'How I hate you!'; with wishes such as 'Heaven forbid!'; and sometimes when addressing others with emotional stress, as in 'You brave chap!' or 'Ungrateful wretches!'

It is also used to show that the words are being spoken with a particular meaning or accent; it conveys scorn, amusement, anger, horror, and so on. For example: 'So you thought it wouldn't matter!'

8. APOSTROPHE (') may show that a letter or letters have been left out of a word as in 'don't'; or it may denote possession as in 'John's book'.

9. The HYPHEN (-) looks like a shortened dash. It is used to link two or more words into a single idea, such as 'oak-apple', 'stick-in-the-mud'; or to divide words when they need to be split up at the end of a printed line.

10. QUESTION MARK (?). This is put at the end of a sentence to denote a question as in:

'Are we in time?'

11. INVERTED COMMAS ('' and " ") show speech or quotation as in:

He said to me: 'Shall we be in time?'

Some writers prefer single inverted commas; some the double ones. Whichever are chosen, the others are available for quotations within a quotation, as in the following sentence:

Edward came into the room and shouted: 'It's all very well for you to sit here, but I've got to go to the headmaster and say: "Please, can I have my dog back?" '

Although not a mark of punctuation, the device of starting a fresh paragraph when writing is an accepted way of bringing to a close one subject or one set of thoughts, and starting another. The ending of a paragraph is shown when, after a full stop, the rest of a line is blank, like this ☞

The start of a paragraph is shown when a small white space occurs at the beginning of a line of writing, typewriting, or printing, as shown below ☜

This is a short paragraph of eight words.

See also SPELLING.

Q

QUEBEC BRIDGE. This bridge, which carries a double main line of the Canadian National Railway and a main road across the River St. Lawrence west of the city of Quebec, is distinguished by having the longest single cantilever span in the world—one of 1,800 feet.

In its construction the Quebec Bridge had a tragic history. The first design was completed in 1901, and work was begun. The method of construction adopted was to work from the opposite shores at the same time towards the centre. Six years later, when the cantilever on the south side of the river had been completed, the supports of the cantilever suddenly gave way without any warning, and the entire cantilever crumpled up and fell, a tangled mass, into the river, carrying seventy-five workmen with it. At the official inquiry into the disaster it was decided that a much more substantial bridge should have been planned. A total of thirty-five new designs was prepared by bridge-builders all over the world, and the present design, which contains 66,480 tons of steel, was selected by a committee of experts.

Work on the present bridge began in 1909, and by the summer of 1916 both cantilevers were finished, and all was in readiness to receive the 640-foot centre span, which had been constructed separately some $3\frac{1}{2}$ miles down-stream on a false framework. Great steel pontoons were floated underneath the span at low tide, so that with the rising tide the 5,100 tons of the span could be lifted and towed up-stream to the site. Here elaborate hydraulic lifting engines had been prepared to hoist the span 150 feet up into position. But a second disaster took place. Early in the course of lifting, the lifting-gear at one end gave way, and the vast mass of crumpled and broken steel fell into the river, killing eleven men. By 17 September 1917, a second centre span had been built and floated to the site. This time at last, the delicate operation was successfully carried out. Three days of anxious work—lifting the span in stages of 2 feet at a time, each lift taking 15 minutes—and the great span of steelwork was into position, 150 feet above the river. A month later, on 17 October, the first train passed over the bridge, more than 16 years after work on the first bridge had been begun.

See also BRIDGES; BRIDGES, RAILWAY.
See also Vol. III: QUEBEC; ST. LAWRENCE.

QUEBEC BRIDGE

Fox Photos

THE 'QUEEN ELIZABETH'

Cunard White Star

QUEEN ELIZABETH, THE. This Cunard White Star liner is the largest vessel in the world. She was being built by John Brown & Co., Ltd., at Clydebank when the Second World War began; in March 1940, painted a drab grey, she sailed across the Atlantic to New York, where she was completed in safety from attack by the enemy. Her sailing was one of the closest secrets of the War.

The *Queen Elizabeth* is larger than her sister ship, the *Queen Mary*; her gross register tonnage is 83,673, compared with the *Queen Mary*'s 81,235. She is 987 feet long, 12 feet longer than her sister ship, and 118 feet wide. She carries 2,200 passengers in three classes—first, cabin, and tourist—and a crew of 1,250. In her twenty-seven boilers heated by oil fuel, steam is raised to a pressure of 400 lb. per square inch. This enables her sixteen steam turbines to develop 200,000 horse-power and drive the ship's four propellers. The speed of the two *Queens* is about equal, but the *Queen Mary* holds the record for the Atlantic crossing, which she achieved in August 1938 at an average speed of 31·69 knots.

The aids to navigation which the *Queen Elizabeth* carries include two direction-finders, an echo-sounding device, a gyro-compass, and two radar units of long and short ranges.

The public rooms are huge and richly furnished. In addition to the usual dining-rooms, lounges, and cocktail bars, there are two swimming-baths, shops, banks, a post office, cinema, gymnasium, a squash court, games decks, and nurseries. There is also an imitation navigation bridge to amuse the children.

The *Queen Elizabeth* was used as a troop transport during the Second World War; owing to her high speed she did not sail in convoy, and on occasions her only escort was a cruiser. The war made it impossible for her to have a trial trip, and when she was completed, she was sailed from New York to Singapore, where her career as a troopship began. During the war she carried in safety 811,324 service men and women, and steamed 492,634 miles.

Now, 'properly dressed' in the colours of the Cunard White Star line (black hull with red 'boot-topping'—a band round the water-line—white superstructure, and red funnels with black tops), the *Queen Elizabeth* is the most important vessel in the 'Atlantic ferry', and carries passengers luxuriously and safely across the ocean in 4 days.

See also SHIP; LINER.

QUINQUIREME, *see* CLASSICAL SHIPS.

R

RADIO, *see* BROADCASTING, HISTORY OF; INTERNATIONAL BROADCASTING; WIRELESS TELEGRAPHY, HISTORY OF. *See also* Vol. VIII, RADIO ENGINEERING; Vol. IX, BROADCASTING.

RADIO NAVIGATION, *see* NAVIGATION, AIR; NAVIGATION, MARINE. *See also* Vol. VIII, RADAR.

RADIO TELEPHONE, MOBILE, *see* TELEPHONE, MOBILE.

RAILWAY, *see* RAILWAYS, HISTORY OF; ELECTRIC RAILWAYS; UNDERGROUND RAILWAYS; MOUNTAIN RAILWAYS; MINIATURE RAILWAYS. *See also* Vol. VIII, RAILWAY CONSTRUCTION.

RAILWAY ACCIDENTS. Train accidents are mainly due to derailments and collisions. The chief causes of derailments are: taking curves at excessive speed; bad condition of track, which may be caused by soil subsidence, 'washing away' by rain or flood, or other natural conditions; breakage of tires, axles, the moving parts of engines, or other portions of the train. Collisions are caused chiefly by: drivers running past signals at 'danger'; errors of signalmen, especially by admitting trains to sections of line already occupied (*see* SIGNALLING, RAILWAY);

Central Press

BREAKDOWN TRAINS CLEARING THE LINE AFTER A RAILWAY ACCIDENT
The scene at Winsford (Cheshire) in 1948, when a mail train from Glasgow ran into the rear of a Glasgow–London express

the breaking away and running backwards of coaches or wagons on inclines.

The worst British example of track defect was the Tay Bridge disaster of December 1879, when part of the bridge collapsed during a wild gale and the night mail train fell into the river; 78 lives were lost. Excessive speed caused a derailment near Berkhamsted, Hertfordshire, in 1945, of an express which tried to cross from one set of lines to another without slowing; 43 people were killed. An Edinburgh–Glasgow express passed 'danger' signals in a heavy snowstorm in December 1937, and ran at full speed into a standing train at Castlecary, Stirlingshire; there were 35 deaths. The most terrible collision in British history occurred in May, 1915, in the First World War, at Gretna, near Carlisle, when a troop train collided at full speed with a shunted train, and a sleeping-car express ran into the wreckage; this accident, arising from a signal-man's oversight, cost 227 lives. It would have been prevented if track-circuiting (*see* ELECTRIC SIGNALLING) had been installed at the signal-box. The risk of vehicles out of control running backwards down an incline is largely guarded against by 'trap points' set in the rails on inclines; these points deliberately derail any such vehicle.

RAILWAY COACHES. The name 'coach', like 'guard', comes from the STAGE COACH (q.v.), for the early railway vehicles had four wheels and were built like horse-coaches.

The modern passenger coach is built on a strong steel under-frame, each end of the coach being carried on 'bogies', small pivoting trucks of four or six wheels which assist the smooth running of the train (*see* Fig. 1). The British 60-foot corridor coach of wood and steel weighs 30 to 32 tons. American coaches, formerly all-steel structures weighing 80 to 90 tons, are now being lightened by the use of light metals. France has experimented with rubber tires on express trains to increase smooth running; each coach needs a large number of wheels (sometimes as many as 32) to reduce the load on each tire to less than a ton and to retain stability if a tire bursts.

1. CORRIDOR TRAINS. Passenger coaches are divided into corridor, non-corridor, and semi-corridor types. The standard railway vehicle all over the world is the corridor coach in which passengers can move from one end of the train to the other to find seats or reach restaurant cars, and the officials can move freely to check tickets. Each coach is connected with the next by a gangway, which is protected by collapsible walls of the concertina type. For the 393-mile London–Edinburgh non-stop run, the train corridor is continued through the tender to the locomotive, so that the engine crew can be changed without stopping the train.

The traditional plan of a side corridor connecting separate compartments has given place, on many main-line British trains, to open coaches

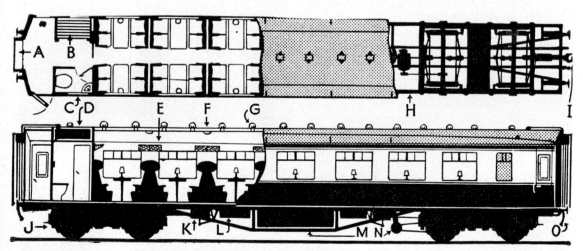

FIG. 1. PLAN AND SECTION OF A BRITISH RAILWAYS OPEN TYPE COACH

A Corridor connexion. B Heavy luggage rack. C Toilet. D Water storage tank. E Light luggage racks. F Ceiling lights. G Ventilators. H Main frame. I Buck-eye coupler. J Bogie. K Vacuum brake cylinder. L Vacuum reservoir. M Battery boxes. N Electric generator. O Brake and heating connexions.

with a central gangway and small tables between pairs of seats. Modern American long-distance trains include Pullman sleeping cars, Pullman parlour cars, in which every passenger has an armchair, and 'coaches' (equivalent to British second class). In these the seats are fitted with armrests and footrests, which can be tilted to any angle to suit the passengers' comfort. Some double-deck American express coaches have a lounge on the upper deck, with glass sides and roof, from which passengers can watch the scenery in mountain districts.

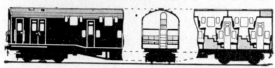

FIG. 2. SOUTHERN REGION SEMI-DOUBLE-DECK COACH
Exterior, cross-section, and longitudinal section

2. SUBURBAN TRAINS. Non-corridor compartments, which are almost unknown outside Britain, are mainly used for suburban services and minor branch lines. Modern suburban trains tend to use instead the semi-corridor 'open coach', with central gangways but no communication between coaches. Double-deck trains for suburban work are in use in America and France; the British gauge has prevented their general use in Britain, but some semi-double-deck trains were used on the Southern Region, the upper and lower compartments being dove-tailed together (Fig. 2).

3. CLASSES. Formerly passenger accommodation was divided into first, second, and third class, with different degrees of comfort. In some countries, such as Germany, there were until recent times four classes. Railways in Britain began discarding second-class accommodation in 1875, and finally abolished it in the 1920's, except for boat-trains serving the Continent. The 'third' class is now called 'second' class. The tendency in all countries now is to have only two classes. The main international expresses, however, which may run through several countries, charge additional fares, higher than first-class, for long non-stop runs in coaches of booked seats. The suburban services in parts of Britain consist of second-class coaches only.

4. SLEEPING-CARS. In 1873 sleeping-cars were introduced in Britain for first-class passengers travelling between London and Edinburgh. To-day passengers have a private room, with a box-mattress and hot and cold water. In 1928

third-class 'sleepers' came into use: these now consist of couches, or 'berths', in two layers, one above the other. Modern American 'sleepers' consist of small single-bed and double-bed compartments, as do the sleeping cars of long-distance expresses in Europe.

5. RESTAURANT CARS. The first meals were cooked and served on a train in America in 1867, and in Britain in 1879, but passengers who wanted meals had to sit in the dining-car throughout the journey. With the building of corridor trains, the dining-car can be reached by passengers from any part of the train. Coke, coal, anthracite, gas, and electricity are used for cooking. The American device of a travelling 'bar', in which drinks and light snacks are served, has been adapted to British needs.

6. PULLMAN CARS. The first luxurious 'saloon' car was devised in America in the 1860's by G. M. Pullman, the inventor of the first sleeping and restaurant cars. The use of 'Pullmans' has spread all over America and Europe. They contain comfortable armchairs, shaded lights, and tables, to which attendants bring refreshment if a passenger rings a bell. Generally the cars were built for and are owned by Pullman companies, which pay railway managements a rent for permission

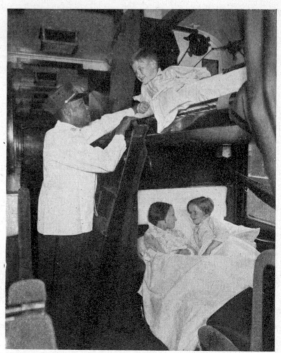

Canadian Pacific Railway
SLEEPING BERTHS ON A CANADIAN PACIFIC TRAIN

Chicago, Burlington, & Quincy Railroad

VISTA DOME CARS ON A 'ZEPHYR' TRAIN IN U.S.A.
These upper deck lounges give an uninterrupted view

to run the cars on their lines, and charge passengers a supplementary fare for their use. Sometimes an entire train will consist of Pullman cars, such as the 'Brighton Belle', the 'Devon Belle', and the GOLDEN ARROW (q.v.).

7. SLIP COACHES are less used than in former times. They are attached to the back of a train and can be disconnected at any station without the main portion of the train stopping there or even slowing down. A 'slip' may consist of one to four coaches. Passengers for a particular town are warned, before starting their journey, to take seats in the rear coaches, and as the train approaches the town, the guard disconnects the 'slip' by a special appliance. Then, while the main portion of the train continues on its way, the guard applies his handbrake and stops the 'slip' coaches at the station platform. Special coupling and braking equipment are needed, as well as a guard for each portion of the train.

8. GENERAL. Passenger coaches were formerly lit by oil lamps, and later by gas. Now they are lit by electric generators driven by the axles of the wheels; batteries maintain the lights when the train is standing. Steam trains are heated by steam led by pipes from the locomotive boiler. The coaches of most electric trains are elec-

trically heated, but on main lines on which electric locomotives pull steam-heated coaches, a special boiler vehicle has to be added to each train in winter. For the same reason, diesel-electric locomotives in America are fitted with steam boilers, fired by oil, to warm up the engine.

Modern American trains are air-conditioned. Coach windows are sealed, noise and dust being excluded, while air at a standard temperature is pumped through the coaches. In winter steam-heating warms the air, and in summer it is cooled by electric refrigerators.

In all countries, the passengers' alarm signal, worked by a lever, a chain, or a knob, is a standard feature; when operated, it applies the air or vacuum brakes slightly, thus warning the guard and engine-driver that something is wrong; a projecting device also indicates to the train staff the coach from which the signal was operated. Alarm signals were enforced by law in Britain in the late 19th century after several passengers had been robbed in trains.

RAILWAYMEN. 1. STATIONMASTER AND STAFF. The railway stationmaster has a very important task. He is not only in charge of the station staff and all the working of the trains through his

British Railways

GUARD, DRIVER, AND FIREMAN
Before the train leaves a station the guard hands the driver a paper stating the number of coaches in the train and its total weight

station, but also of the business side of the railway, making all necessary contacts with the public. On the passenger side the staff consists of porters and signalmen; at all but the smallest stations it includes also booking clerks, and at stations which have grown so much in size that booking clerks cannot cope both with the issue and collection of tickets, there are also special ticket collectors. If much goods traffic is dealt with at the station, a goods staff is necessary also, to man the goods depot.

The stationmaster is responsible for giving the guard of every passenger train that stops at his station the authority to start, though he may pass on this authority to any other responsible member of his staff, such as a foreman porter or an inspector. Inspectors are needed for the larger stations only, and at the largest, several inspectors may be on duty in relays throughout the 24 hours. In an emergency, such as a blockage of the line, the stationmaster must take control and give all necessary instructions to signalmen and drivers—though, in fact, they generally know what to do, as instructions covering most possible emergencies are given in the rules and regulations. Also, if the station lies

within a traffic control area (*see* TRAIN CONTROL), control will give all necessary general instructions for dealing with the emergency, and the stationmaster's task will be to see that these control instructions are properly carried out. In foggy weather the stationmaster must decide when the fog has thickened sufficiently to justify the calling out of the platelayers to do fogmen's duty at the various signals within his control (*see* CLIMATE AND COMMUNICATIONS, Section 2). At any large station, such as a London terminus, the stationmaster rules over a very large staff, and his job consists mainly of organizing them, while the more particular duties which would belong to the stationmaster of a smaller station are delegated to less important officials.

2. ENGINE-DRIVER. The would-be engine-driver enters the railway service while a boy as a cleaner at one of the ENGINE-SHEDS (q.v.) where locomotives are stabled. During his work of cleaning, which takes him all over the engine, both outside and inside, he becomes familiar with the various parts and the purpose that each has to serve. After a period at cleaning, if he shows aptitude, he is 'approved' to act as a fireman, first on a shunting engine, and then rising by degrees to passenger work, during which time he not only learns how to fire correctly, but also makes an intimate acquaintance with the lines over which he travels—the position of signals, gradients, and so on—which is vitally necessary when later he comes to drive. He must also gain a thorough knowledge of the rules and regulations laid down for the safe working of the traffic. After some years at firing, and after an eyesight test which includes the distinguishing of colours (vital for the observation of signals), the fireman is eventually 'passed' to assume the responsibility of driving. Once again he starts at the bottom with a shunting engine, and works his way up gradually. The most responsible and best-paid jobs at each engine-shed go to the 'top link', that is, the men with the longest and widest experience; these are paid on the basis of a fixed mileage, all excess over which is paid for by a supplementary rate, so that the longest continuous duties—such as the 299 miles without change of crew between Euston and Carlisle, London Midland Region—are the best paid.

3. GUARD. The title of guard dates back to the days of the STAGE COACH (q.v.) when the attentions of highwaymen often made the protection of the passengers on a coach no light task. To-day the railway guard is responsible, equally with the driver, for the safety of his train. His equipment consists of watch, whistle, red and green flags, hand-lamp showing red and green, and at least twelve detonators or fog-signals for use in the event of emergency. It is the responsibility of a passenger guard to see that his train is correctly formed and labelled, that the coaches are properly coupled, that the tail-lamp is in position, and that the continuous brake, which he will test before starting, is in proper working order. The driver is not permitted to start until he sees the guard's green flag or lamp waved, and hears his whistle. Before the guard gives the 'right away', he must be sure that all doors are closed, that the starting signal at the platform end is 'off', and that he has received the stationmaster's authority. Throughout the journey the guard is in charge of all luggage loaded into his van, and is responsible for seeing that the right pieces are put out at the various stops. If his train breaks down from any cause, the guard must 'protect' it; this he does by proceeding backwards along the line, with his red flag or lamp in his hand, to lay down detonators on the rails up to ¾ mile from where the train is stand-

ing, in order to warn any oncoming trains on the same line. Each guard has to keep a record of the running of his train, including all starting and stopping times, delays and the reason for them, the load, and the driver's name. The duties of goods guards are very similar to those of passenger guards.

4. SIGNALMAN. The work of a signalman is described in the article SIGNALLING, RAILWAY (q.v.). The code of bell-signalling between box and box and the rules and regulations for railwaymen cover nearly all emergencies; but in an emergency each signalman is responsible, of course, to the stationmaster in whose jurisdiction his box lies. If he is at any distance from the stationmaster's office, he is in touch with him by telephone. If the box lies in a controlled area, the signalman is subject to telephoned directions from the control office.

RAILWAYS, HISTORY OF. The first primitive railways existed long before the first steam locomotive; and the first locomotives propelled by steam ran on roads and not on rails. A reference to 'railes' appears in documents in 1597, referring to a wagonway linking coal-mines at Nottingham with the River Trent. Colliery owners found that their horses could pull more and heavier wagons of coal if the wheels ran on a straight surface of wood or iron than they could over the rough earthen roads of the period. From then onward, what were known as wagonways, plateways, tramways, or railways came into use.

Iron plates to protect the timber of the wagonways came later. (We still call 'platelayers' the men who work on modern railway tracks.) In 1767 iron angle-plates were laid for the first time on a colliery wagonway near Sheffield; the flat-tired wheels of the wagons were meant to run on the flat part of the plates, while the vertical side of the plates kept the wagon wheels from

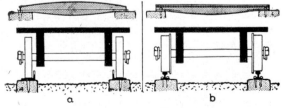

FIG. I. CROSS-SECTIONS OF 18TH-CENTURY RAILS
a. Angle plates used as rails. *b.* Flanged wheels on upright rails

Crown Copyright

THE OPENING OF THE STOCKTON AND DARLINGTON RAILWAY, 27TH SEPTEMBER 1825
Drawing in the Science Museum, London

running off the track (Fig. 1a). Wheels with flanges, which provide the models for those used to-day, were not made until about 1800 (Fig. 1b). Until the end of the 18th century all wagonways were worked by horses.

Meanwhile the first steam locomotives were being built. Nicolas Cugnot, a Frenchman, made a steam road carriage about 1770, which travelled at 3 miles an hour. William Murdock made models of steam carriages in 1786 at Redruth, in Cornwall. Richard Trevithick, a Cornish mining engineer, built in 1804 a steam locomotive to run on a horse tramway at a South Wales colliery. Other inventors were experimenting with steam engines at this time (*see* STEAM-ENGINE, Vol. VIII). When a workable engine was first evolved, therefore, the idea of well-laid rails, on which a 'train' of wagons could be drawn by a horse with little effort, was already familiar. For that reason steam railways developed very rapidly as soon as locomotives proved trustworthy.

George STEPHENSON (q.v. Vol. V), the son of a Tyneside labourer, was more responsible than anyone else for the great change that came about. He learnt engineering at a local colliery, and then became engineer to a horse-railway which was about to be laid between Stockton and Darlington. He persuaded the owners to use steam instead, and in 1825 he drove the first train with a locomotive which he had designed himself. The train went at a speed of 12 miles an hour.

The real launching of steam railways occurred in 1830, when the Liverpool and Manchester Railway line was opened. On this occasion the 'Rocket' engine, designed by Stephenson, won a competition by drawing a 20-ton train 35 miles in just under 2 hours. As a result of this triumph railways were proposed for many parts of the country; in their development George Stephenson and his son Robert played an important part. In 1837 and 1838 parts of the London and Birmingham Railway (later the London and North Western) were opened for traffic. The London and Southampton (later South-Western)

Union Pacific Railroad

THE MEETING OF THE CENTRAL PACIFIC (*left*) AND UNION PACIFIC (*right*) AT UTAH IN 1869
Two American railway companies, one serving the Atlantic and the other the Pacific, decided to join their lines. After
six years of track-laying, their workmen met in the middle of the prairie

was finished by 1840, and the Great Western from Paddington to Bristol by 1841. So in a short time railway transport, in which Britain was to lead the world for many years, was firmly established.

The 1830's and 1840's are known as the period of the 'Railway Mania', when strips of railway track were being laid in all parts of the country without any coherent plan for the future. Everyone who had any money to invest tried to buy shares in railway companies, and in consequence thousands of people lost their money in unsuccessful companies. George Hudson, known as the 'Railway King', a financier who set up many new railway companies, was courted by the richest and noblest families in England during the 'Railway Mania'.

As the railway lines had to run over people's private land, an Act of Parliament had to be passed before any line could be begun. In 1846 Parliament passed 246 Acts for the laying of new railways. Manufacturers and traders, who wanted the new form of quick and reliable trans-

port, pressed for the passing of each Act. Opposition came from influential landowners, whose demands for payment forced up considerably the costs of railway building, and from the canal companies, who were afraid of losing business to the railways.

Many towns objected to railways as being noisy, smoky, and generally unwelcome, and succeeded in preventing lines being laid near them. One company was prevented from running through Northampton, and establishing a locomotive works there; as a result, Northampton to-day stands on a loop line instead of on the London–Carlisle–Glasgow main line. The Great Northern Railway was prevented from running through the important stage-coach posting town of Stamford; the line was therefore laid through Peterborough, which has now acquired the importance as a manufacturing and communications centre which Stamford might have had.

By the 1840's Parliament had laid down the basic passenger fare of a penny a mile, which was to last until well into the 20th century. In

1842 Queen Victoria, then 23 years old, decided to sample railway travel for herself, and made her first railway journey from Windsor to Paddington. Court officials did not like this novelty; the Queen's coachman insisted on travelling on a pilot engine ahead of the royal train, but his scarlet coat and powdered wig were smothered with soot. The Queen, however, enjoyed her railway journey, and soon made a trip to Scotland in a train.

Early passenger accommodation was very simple: passengers with the cheapest tickets had to stand in trucks, like modern coal trucks, with no roofs and no seats. Gradually, however, as travelling by train became more popular, and especially after a young man called Thomas Cook had the idea of arranging cheap excursions (see Travel Agency), the accommodation was made more comfortable. Until the 1860's engines had to stop several times on a long journey to take up water for the boiler. Then a device was invented for taking up water without stopping. Long water-troughs were laid between the rails at certain places, and a metal scoop, like a large shovel, was fitted beneath locomotive tenders. When the scoop was lowered, the speed of the train caused the water to be scooped up into the tender. As railway companies became more prosperous, they began to buy up the various canal companies to prevent them competing in the transport of goods.

The railway played a big part in the growing industrial power of Britain in the 19th century. Coal-mines, iron and steel works, and a vast railway system gave Britain the lead of the whole world until the end of the century, when Germany and the U.S.A. began to draw level. In 1850 Britain had 6,600 miles of railways, and in 1920 she had 23,000 miles; after that date the railways ceased to grow, and road transport began to expand.

Other countries showed great interest in the early experiments of British railway engineers: locomotives were built in France in 1828 and in U.S.A. in 1829. Public railways were opened in Belgium and Germany in 1835, and all over the world in the next twenty years. In 1863 two American railway companies, the Union Pacific and the Central Pacific, set out to build a railway across the American continent, one company starting eastward from the Pacific coast, and the other westward from the Missouri River. After an exciting race to see which could lay the longest

line, workmen of the two companies met in Utah six years later, completing a 1,848-mile stretch of line. The Canadian Pacific line, 2,906 miles long, was completed in 1891, and the Trans-Siberian Railway, the longest in the world, 4,073 miles, was finished in 1904.

After the mid-19th century, railways all over the world gradually merged into larger and fewer companies, following the general trend of industrial unification. In almost every country except U.S.A. railway systems have been taken over by the State during the present century. After the First World War there were 120 separate railway companies in Britain, but it became clear that the smaller and less wealthy lines could not pay their way in the new conditions of wages and prices brought about by that war. From 1923, therefore, with few exceptions, all the railways were grouped by Act of Parliament into four main systems, which were, in order of size, the London Midland and Scottish, London and North Eastern, Great Western, and Southern Railways. During the Second World War, as in the earlier war, all railways in Britain were taken over and run by the Government. Soon after the Second World War Parliament passed an Act to nationalize all the railways; from 1 January 1948 they became the property of the State and are now organized in six Regions: the Southern, the Western, the London Midland, the Eastern, the North Eastern, and the Scottish.

See also Railway Systems; Locomotives; Railway Coaches; Signalling, Railway.

RAILWAY SPEED RECORDS. The highest speeds that have been reached on rails by different forms of motive power, with coaching stock of conventional design, are very similar, showing that the chief limiting factor is that of air resistance.

With steam, the highest authenticated record was that of the L.N.E.R. streamlined Pacific engine *Mallard*, on 3 July 1938, when a test train of eight coaches reached 126 miles an hour for a short distance on the downhill stretch of line from Stoke Summit towards Peterborough. A German streamlined 4-6-4 has travelled at $124\frac{1}{2}$ miles an hour, and another of the same class reached 118 miles an hour on the level with a four-coach train. The semi-streamlined 4-6-4 engines of the Chicago, Milwaukee, St. Paul, and Pacific Railroad have recorded 120

Canadian Pacific Railway

THE FIRST TRAIN INTO CALGARY ON THE CANADIAN PACIFIC RAILWAY, 1884

The Times

STEAM LOCOMOTIVE NO. 6256, 'SIR WILLIAM STANIER, F.R.S.'
Built in 1948 for north-western express services

Chicago, Burlington, & Quincy Railroad

THE DENVER 'ZEPHYR' WITH TWIN DIESEL-ELECTRIC LOCOMOTIVES WHICH RAN FROM CHICAGO TO DENVER (1,017·2 MILES) IN 12 HOURS 12½ MINUTES IN 1936

miles an hour on the 'Hiawatha' streamline-train.

Runs over long distances with steam engines include the L.N.E.R. Pacific *Silver Link*, which, with the 'Silver Jubilee' streamline train, ran 25 miles at an average speed of 107·5 miles an hour for the whole distance on 27 September 1935. The top speed on this run was 112½ miles an hour. On the L.M.S. the highest maximum ever reached was in 1937, when the Pacific loco-motive *Coronation* touched 114 miles an hour with the 'Coronation Scot' train, made up to eight coaches. On the return journey the *Coronation* averaged 89·0 miles an hour over the 72·3 miles from Welton to Kilburn. This compares with *Silver Link*'s 91·8 miles an hour over the 70 miles from Wood Green to Fletton Junction in 1935. In 1932 the G.W.R. 4–6–0 *Tregenna Castle*, with a seven-coach train, ran the 77·3 miles from Swindon to Paddington at a mean speed of 81·7 miles an hour from start to stop—the only start-to-stop run at over 80 miles an hour yet recorded in Britain.

Over a greater distance still, the L.M.S. Pacific *Princess Elizabeth* achieved a notable record in 1936 by running an eight-coach special train non-stop over the 401·4 miles from Glasgow to Euston in 5 hrs. 44¼ min., at an average speed of precisely 70 miles an hour for the whole distance, including the steep Beattock and Shap summits.

With diesel-electric power, speeds up to 100 miles an hour were run regularly by German streamline trains in the years up to the Second World War; and over certain suitable routes in the United States 100 miles an hour—even with steam—have now become commonplace. One of the most notable journeys ever made with diesel power was in 1936, when a twin-unit diesel-electric locomotive of 3,000 brake-horse-power, with eight cars, ran without a stop over the 1,017·2 miles from Chicago to Denver in 12 hrs. 12½ min., at an average of 83·3 miles an hour throughout; 26½ miles were covered at 105 miles an hour, 444¾ miles at 91·6 miles an hour, and 750 miles at 90 miles an hour. The highest maximum speed yet recorded in the United States with diesel-electric power is 122 miles an hour.

In 1939 a diesel-driven unit of three streamline cars (with a hydraulic transmission) attained a speed of 133½ miles an hour in Germany, be-tween Berlin and Hamburg. Over the same route in 1931 a curious car of very light construc-tion, which, though carried on only four wheels, was 95 feet in length, reached 143 miles an hour, the highest speed ever recorded on rails. This Krückenberg car had a petrol engine, and was propelled by an airscrew; but the vehicle was experimental, and nothing more was heard of it.

In Italy, in 1939, a three-car streamlined elec-tric unit ran the 195·8 miles from Florence to

CLEAR ROAD AHEAD

A 4–6–0 'Castle' class locomotive hauling a Western Region passenger express. Poster by Cuneo

Milan in 115¼ minutes, at an average speed of 102 miles an hour throughout—the fastest run between two stops yet recorded. The maximum speed reached was 126 miles an hour. Thus the highest speeds reached as yet by trains of rolling-stock of normal design have corresponded closely, whatever the motive power—126 miles an hour with steam or electric propulsion, and 133½ miles an hour with diesel-hydraulic drive.

See also RAILWAYS, HISTORY OF.

RAILWAY SYSTEMS. In most countries the pattern of railway lines is determined by the geography (mountains, rivers, and coastal shape), and also reveals the country's industrial and political history. Railways in Britain are strongly centred on London, which was the hub of finance and industrial enterprise when most of the main lines were projected in the 1830's and 1840's. The routes link up seaports, coalfields, and big industrial cities.

French railways radiate from Paris like the spokes of a wheel, but their biggest network of lines is in the industrial north and east. Belgium, on a railway map, looks like a mere continuation of France, for there are no geographical or political barriers between the two countries, and the French lines seem to run straight through Belgium. Many lines from both Paris and Berlin run straight to the frontier between France and Germany; ever since the war of 1870 govern-

ments of both countries have encouraged these strategic railways, to carry troops in the event of war. One of the queerest railway patterns in Europe is formed by the two main lines that run along the banks of the River Rhine, sometimes within sight of one another, for a distance of more than 100 miles. This deep and wide river, carrying much small shipping, has few bridges. The big cities of Germany are spread so widely over the country that its railway system is based on several regional capitals. The main lines of Czechoslovakia and Western Poland still show the railway pattern that was laid down when they were part of the German and Austrian Empires up till 1918. They are, therefore, centred on Berlin and Vienna.

The main lines of north Italy, joining industrial cities and receiving hydro-electric power from the Alps (see ELECTRIC RAILWAYS), are well developed. Few railways cross the mountain backbone of central Italy, and southern Italy has few industries.

Swiss railways are notable for the bold engineering which has run main-line express routes through long mountain TUNNELS (q.v.), and for the ingenious methods devised for steep climbing by MOUNTAIN RAILWAYS (q.v.). The record railway height in Europe is reached by the Jungfrau railway, one station being 11,465 feet above sea-level. This line has a gauge of 1 metre (3 ft. 3 in.), and climbs continuous gradients of 1 in 4 or

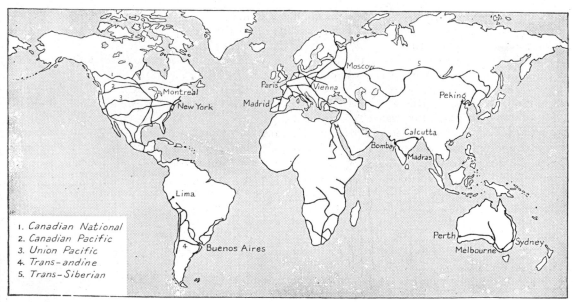

1. Canadian National
2. Canadian Pacific
3. Union Pacific
4. Trans-andine
5. Trans-Siberian

MAP SHOWING THE PRINCIPAL RAILWAY LINKS OF THE WORLD

Peruvian Corporation

DOUBLE SWITCHBACK ON THE CENTRAL RAILWAY, PERU
When the train reaches the end of one stretch it reverses up the next

1 in 5 by the rack-and-pinion method. The highest through-route in Switzerland is the metre-gauge Bernina line, which rises to 7,400 feet; it climbs a gradient of 1 in 14 by the grip of ordinary wheels on plain rails.

Of the total route mileage of the railways of the world, nearly one-third—227,244 miles—is in the U.S.A. The American lines are all privately owned by separate companies. In the Eastern States the largest railways are the New York Central (11,000 miles) and the Pennsylvania Railroad (10,000 miles). Both connect New York with Chicago, the chief railway centre of the U.S.A. Following the race between two companies in the 1860's to link the Atlantic and Pacific coasts by rail (*see* RAILWAYS, HISTORY OF), several lines were laid across the Rocky Mountains. One railway, the Atchison, Topeka, and Santa Fé, running between Chicago and Los Angeles, climbs over the 7,600-foot Raton Pass across the Rockies. Another line rises to 9,000 feet to run through the Moffat tunnel. Although the less mountainous central and eastern States have a thick network of lines, thousands of square miles of the Western States are far from a railway.

Canada has one of the biggest individual railways in the world, the Canadian National Rail-

ways, with 23,500 miles of line. The other main Canadian organization, the Canadian Pacific, not only runs 20,900 miles of line but also a fleet of ocean-going steamers with regular trading routes encircling the world. Both railways run across the whole width of the North American continent, one main line being 3,770 miles long and the other 3,360 miles. At Kicking Horse Pass in the Rocky Mountains, one line rises to 5,300 feet above sea-level.

All the greatest heights that have been reached by railways are in South America, in the Andes mountains. The mineral wealth of the mountains has encouraged the building of many railways from the Pacific coast, up to the highlands of Peru, Chile, and Bolivia. The most notable line is the Central of Peru, which runs from Callao, the port of Lima. In one stretch of over 100 miles this railway zigzags up steep valleys on a continuous gradient of 1 in 25 and using twenty-one reversing stations; these are points at which a train, having no room to turn at the end of one climb, backs towards the next stage of its climb (*see* picture). This railway rises to a height of 15,806 feet above sea-level, having passed through a tunnel at 15,694 feet. Oxygen is carried for passengers who suffer from 'mountain sickness', or faintness caused by the thin air at a high altitude. Another railway in Peru takes passengers 12,500 feet up to Lake Titicaca. One railway, starting from Antofagasta in Chile, rises to 12,000 feet and does not drop below that level for 500 miles. A branch of this line attains at Montt the world's record railway altitude of 15,817 feet—all but level with the summit of Mont Blanc. These railways, except for the Central of Peru, are all of 1-metre gauge. The Transandine Railway, linking Argentine with Chile, has to use rack-and-pinion climbing methods on steep gradients of 1 in 12½.

One of the most remarkable railway systems in the world is the Trans-Siberian Railway, which runs right across the U.S.S.R. in Asia. It is physically possible to travel by railway from Britain to China, with very few changes of train on the way, by taking the railway FERRY (q.v.) from England to France and a Trans-Siberian train for the longest stage. Even if there were no political hindrances to free travel, a change of train would still have to be made at the western frontier of Russia, for the Russian track GAUGE (q.v.) is 3½ inches wider than the European standard of 4 ft. 8½ in. From Moscow to the end of the railway, Vladivostok on the Pacific, is a

Soviet Weekly

THE TRANS-SIBERIAN RAILWAY RUNNING ALONG THE SHORE
OF LAKE BAIKAL

journey of nearly 6,000 miles, taking 9 days in normal conditions, and forming the longest journey in the world that can be made without a change of train. From one point on the line a train runs through MANCHURIA (q.v. Vol. III), connecting with a Chinese railway to Peking and other cities in the heart of China. Where the Trans-Siberian Railway reaches Lake Baikal in the mountains of central Asia, the engineers who built the line could not take it across the lake, which is 30 miles wide at its narrowest. For some years the trains were carried across the lake in ferries during the summer months; in winter the ice on the lake was thick enough to bear the weight of trains running on a railway track laid over it. Later, however, the two ends of the line were linked up by a permanent track laid round the shore of the lake.

Australia's greatest railway problem is that of GAUGES (q.v.), as various States have gauges of 5 ft. 3 in., 4 ft. 8½ in. and 3 ft. 6 in. Australia has the longest stretch of perfectly straight line in the world—328 miles across the Nullarbor Plain, an uninhabited wilderness without a single tree. Yet within a few hours' journey the passenger finds himself in Flinders Street Station in Melbourne, which claims to be the busiest in the world, handling over 300,000 passengers daily. The biggest steel arch railway bridge in the world is SYDNEY HARBOUR BRIDGE (q.v.).

The thirteen main-line railways of India and Pakistan are owned by their governments. Roughly half their mileage is the broad 5 ft. 6 in. gauge, while other railways are 1 metre, 2 ft. 6 in., and 2 foot. Famous mountain lines are the rack-and-pinion metre-gauge railway which reaches a height of 7,275 feet in the Nilgiri Hills, and the 2-foot gauge Darjeeling–Himalaya Railway, rising to 7,407 feet at Ghoom.

See also RAILWAYS, HISTORY OF; MOUNTAIN RAILWAYS.

RAILWAY TRACK, *see* Vol. VIII: RAILWAY CONSTRUCTION.

REDIFFUSION. Many of the homes in certain towns have no wireless set in the ordinary sense: they are connected by wires to a local 'wireless exchange'—just as a telephone subscriber is connected to the local post office telephone exchange. The wireless exchange or rediffusion centre receives the main B.B.C. programmes on a large and carefully tuned receiver; the programmes are transferred to a series of wires which link the wireless exchange to various subscribers in the town; each subscriber, by turning a switch, can select the programme he wants to hear. The subscriber is obliged by law to have a wireless licence.

Rediffusion services are specially useful in parts of Britain in which good reception on householders' sets is difficult to obtain; or in industrial and business areas in which tall steel-frame buildings prevent good reception on the householders' aerial, or passenger lifts and trolley-bus junctions cause clicking noises in the ordinary household wireless set. In large blocks of flats rediffusion can be economically installed in all the flats at once. Rediffusion is, of course, confined to towns in which an exchange and a wiring system have been set up. In Britain, a wireless exchange or rediffusion centre is not allowed to provide programmes of its own on the subscribers' wires.

The first British exchange was started by a Hythe engineer in 1925, and others soon followed his example. The Post Office decided to put such systems on an official basis to prevent people receiving programmes without paying for a licence. In 1926 permission was given for the relaying of programmes in this way, so long as each subscriber took out a receiving licence. By 1930 there were sixty such exchanges, serving about 14,000 subscribers, and by 1935 there were 340 exchanges with 200,000 subscribers. By the end of the Second World War the subscribers had reached 650,000. In 1935 a Government committee recommended that the exchanges should be run by the Post Office, but nothing was done.

Rediffusion has long been popular abroad, notably in Holland and Germany. It is much used in British colonies, where it is not always easy to organize a complete broadcasting service locally.

Rediffusion experts are seeking ways of expanding the services—of increasing the number of programmes available to the subscriber, developing the application of the system to larger blocks of flats and to hotels, and supplying a television service in areas where television stations have been set up. They are exploring, too, the use of the electricity mains and the telephone network as a means of carrying programmes into private homes.

See WIRELESS, HISTORY OF.

REFERENCE BOOKS. The purpose of a reference book is to give information in a brief, easily available form, so that a reader with no special knowledge of a subject can find out the facts he wants quickly. In nearly all reference books the information is arranged in alphabetical order, or the reader is directed to what he wants by means of an alphabetical index (*see* CATALOGUING AND INDEXING).

1. DICTIONARIES. A dictionary is generally a book which gives an alphabetical list of the words of a language, with an explanation of the meaning, use, and origin of each, and sometimes a key to its pronunciation. The Greek word for a dictionary was *lexicon*, from which we get our word 'lexicographer', meaning someone who compiles a dictionary. The earliest 'dictionaries' made by the Greeks and Romans only explained difficult or obscure words, and were more like what we should call glossaries or vocabularies. Dictionaries that aim at giving a complete list of words in a language, the everyday words as well as the difficult words, are comparatively modern.

The first English dictionary that became famous, and has remained so, was compiled by Dr. Samuel JOHNSON (q.v. Vol. V) and appeared in 1755. In it the 'Great Lexicographer' (as he has been called) set out to fix a standard of good English, and therefore he attempted to be comprehensive only so far as to include all of what he considered the 'best' words. He illustrated the meanings of words with quotations from different authors, a practice which has been followed in later dictionaries. Sometimes his entries make an amusing record of his personal views—such as the entry for 'Oats': 'A grain, which in England is generally given to horses, but in Scotland supports the people.' This dictionary is a great feat of scholarship, and was the basis of most English dictionaries for over a century.

The most comprehensive dictionary of any language is the *New English Dictionary* (or the *Oxford Dictionary*): the first part was published in 1884. This aims to be a record of every word in modern English (it does not include Anglo-Saxon), the changes in meanings illustrated by quotation from contemporary writings. It runs to twelve large volumes and a supplement. Smaller dictionaries, such as the *Shorter Oxford English Dictionary* and the *Concise Oxford Dictionary*, have been derived from it. The *New English Dictionary* is the accepted standard for

THE OXFORD ALMANACK OF 1674; THE FIRST OF THE ALMANACKS PUBLISHED ANNUALLY FOR THE UNIVERSITY

The illustration is symbolic of the might of Britain—the Island Fortress rising from the sea. The calendar is placed round the top of the tower, in the centre is a list of the kings of England and below are listed the chief ports with tide tables, and rates of interest at 6 per cent. on money invested

English spelling and pronunciation. The standard dictionary of America is Noah Webster's Dictionary published in 1825, and later revised and enlarged. So famous has this dictionary become in America that the word 'Webster' is now often used as meaning a dictionary. Many dictionaries, of course, explain the meaning of the words of one language in another language —such as Greek–English or English–French dictionaries. There are also special dictionaries dealing with words or terms of a particular kind, such as slang, technical terms, proverbs, and place-names.

2. ENCYCLOPAEDIAS. The word 'encyclopaedia' comes from the Greek *enkuklios,* 'circular' or 'complete', and *paedeia,* 'education'. A dictionary is normally, as we have seen, a book which explains the meaning of words, and often phrases. An encyclopaedia, such as you have in your hand, explains things and ideas. Some aim at giving information on every possible subject; others deal with some special branch of knowledge.

Books of the encyclopaedia kind were compiled even in Roman times. Pliny (A.D. 23–79) compiled a great work called *Naturalis Historia,* which dealt with the physical Universe, geography, ethnology, and anthropology (*see* page 53). One of the earliest modern encyclopaedias in English was the *Cyclopaedia, or Universal Dictionary of Arts and Sciences,* by Ephraim Chambers, published in 1728, in which a system of cross-references was used. The *Encyclopaedia Britannica* was first published at Edinburgh between 1768 and 1771. Since 1929 the *Encyclopaedia Britannica* has been published in America by the Encyclopaedia Britannica Co. Amongst other important modern encyclopaedias is *Chambers's Encyclopaedia,* published first in Edinburgh by W. and R. Chambers, between 1860 and 1868.

3. ALMANACS. An almanac is a yearly calendar of months and days, giving information, usually astronomical, about such matters as the times of sunrise and sunset, or the phases of the moon. Almanacs of the modern kind, dealing with a single year, date from about the 16th century. The most important British astronomical almanac is the *Nautical Almanac* (*see* NAVIGATION, MARINE). *Whitaker's Almanack,* first published in 1868, is much more than an almanac—it is a collection of current information of all kinds. It describes itself on the title-page as a work 'Con-

taining an account of the astronomical and other phenomena, and a vast amount of information respecting the Government, Finances, Population, Commerce, and General Statistics of the various nations of the world, with an Index containing 35,000 references'. The index is an essential key to the entries, which are not in alphabetical order.

4. MISCELLANEOUS. There is a great variety of other reference books such as gazetteers (geographical dictionaries of places) and atlases, as well as directories, such as the *Post Office Guide*— a key to all the places in Great Britain. The *Annual Register,* started by Robert Dodsley in 1758 and kept up ever since, consists of a volume for every year, in which are recorded the main events of that year. *Who's Who* is a dictionary of prominent living people, and is revised every year. *The Dictionary of National Biography,* first published between 1885 and 1900, contains in alphabetical order the lives of all notable Britons who died before 1901, over 30,000 of them. It has been regularly brought up to date by supplements every 10 years since then.

There are a great many books of reference covering a single subject; some of them, such as Black's *Medical Dictionary,* Grove's *Dictionary of Music and Musicians,* or Brewer's *Dictionary of Phrase and Fable,* are standard reference books to be found in any well-equipped library. Many others, covering subjects such as gardening, engineering, art, or natural history, are planned either for the general reader or the student.

See also LIBRARIES.

REFRIGERATED SHIP, *see* SHIP.

REPORTER. Everything that is printed in the news columns of a newspaper or broadcast in a B.B.C. news bulletin is based on the work of a reporter, and is often phrased in his own words. Only men and women of ability can carry out the responsible work of experienced reporters. A reporter may be permanently engaged on one subject which demands special knowledge, such as parliamentary, art, or sports reporting; or he may be a general reporter, which requires great versatility and enterprise. He may become a foreign correspondent, working abroad, or a B.B.C. radio reporter, frequently speaking his news into a recording machine for transmission 'on the air'.

P.A.-Reuter

REPORTERS AND PRESS PHOTOGRAPHERS IN DOWNING STREET
They are waiting to meet statesmen as they leave No. 10

The rank-and-file reporters on a morning or evening paper in a big city have to do a good deal of routine work, reporting the meetings of the town council and its committees, the regular sittings of the magistrates' courts, county courts, and occasionally the assize courts, speeches at public lunches and political meetings, interviews with notable visitors to the town, football matches, or the rapid collection of accurate information at the scene of a railway or road accident or at a serious fire, when many eye-witnesses are both confused and careless about what they say, and have to be questioned with care.

The reporter of a large newspaper must be ready for every kind of adventure. He may be called out of bed by telephone to drive to an airport, where an aeroplane privately chartered by his newspaper may be waiting to take him out to sea in search of a sunken submarine or a burning passenger liner. He may have to fly to a far part of Europe if a notable fugitive from justice is arrested, or he may have to hurry to the Old Bailey criminal court to describe the death sentence being pronounced upon a murderer. He may be posted for days at a dock or coal-mine, during a long industrial dispute, in which both parties will distrust reporters and refuse to talk to them. He may suddenly be called on to report on subjects about which he knows very little. Sometimes his jobs are exciting; often they are slow and tedious.

The foreign correspondent is one of the most responsible members of a newspaper's staff. He must have the judgement to know, from day to day, what British people at home want to read, and what policy his editor would adopt over any item of foreign news. He must be able to win the confidence of his informants—often difficult for a foreigner. He must plan his own work week by week, with only occasional instructions from headquarters, and he must make his own arrangements for telephoning or telegraphing his news to Britain, always allowing for telegraphic and censorship delays, and for differences in local time.

A radio correspondent does much of his work like other reporters. But sometimes his reports depend on listeners hearing either the radio reporter's voice, or voices and sounds as heard by him at the scene of some public event. Much use is made of recording cars. These are powerful private cars containing gramophone turntables, electrical recording apparatus, a stock of recording disks, and a long rubber cable with a small hand-microphone at the end. A recording engineer in the car starts the mechanism, and the radio reporter holds the microphone to his own mouth and speaks into it; he may then hold it to the mouth of someone whom he is interviewing, or he may turn it towards the scene he is reporting in order to pick up sounds, such as cantering horses or cheering people. Selections from these disks are then incorporated into the news programme. During the Second World War the B.B.C. devised for its war correspondents a midget recorder, about the size of a portable gramophone. Stanley Maxted took such an instrument with him when he was dropped from the air with paratroops at Arnhem, in Holland, in September 1944. While crouched in a slit trench, cut off by German armies in the middle of a very bitter battle, Maxted made his news recording. During the war radio reporters, among other dangerous tasks, were sometimes carried over enemy cities in bombers.

A skilled form of reporting is carried out by Press Photographers. A reporter who is writing a description of an event can do his work after the event has happened, or can collect informa-

THE LAST FIGHT OF THE 'REVENGE', 1591

The *Revenge* is in the centre with the foremast shot away. Tapestry lent to the National Maritime Museum, Greenwich, by M. Hypolite Worms

tion by telephone; but the photographer must be on the spot before the event occurs.

See also JOURNALIST; NEWSPAPER; NEWS BROADCASTING.

RESTAURANT CAR, *see* RAILWAY COACHES, Section 5.

REVENGE, H.M.S. The first *Revenge* was a man-of-war, of the new galleon type (*see* SAILING SHIPS), built for Queen Elizabeth at Deptford and launched in 1577. She was named, it is thought, by Elizabeth's choice, to show her wish to avenge the French religious massacre of St. Bartholomew's Day (1572) or the Spanish one at Antwerp (1576). Sir John Hawkins' sailors considered the name unlucky, revenge being the right of God alone: certainly, the *Revenge* was four times nearly lost by shipwreck before being taken by the Spaniards.

The *Revenge* was commonly rated as 500 tons and was smaller than the ARK ROYAL (q.v.) of 700 tons; she carried proportionately fewer guns, but was more serviceable for foreign service. She had four masts, and the fore and main masts were square-rigged. Her upper-works were painted green, a favourite Tudor colour. She was the flagship of Sir Francis Drake throughout the Armada campaign, capturing the flagship of Pedro de Valdes and leading the attack in the fight off Gravelines, after the Spanish fleet had been put to flight by the threat of the fire-ships.

In 1591 a considerable English squadron was sent to the Azores (Portuguese islands in the Atlantic) commanded by Lord Thomas Howard, with Sir Richard Grenville in the *Revenge* as second-in-command. This force was surprised by an overpowering Spanish fleet commanded by Alonso de Bazan. Howard got under way and led his squadron to a safe position to windward of the Spaniards; but for some reason Sir Richard Grenville hung back in the *Revenge*, and then took on the fifty-three Spanish ships single-handed and fought them for 15 hours. Two Spaniards were sunk and two so disabled that they had to be abandoned, before Grenville was persuaded to surrender, himself mortally wounded. He gave up the *Revenge* a wreck, and a hurricane shortly took the ship and the prize-crew to the bottom. The story of this engagement has been made well known by Tennyson's ballad *The Revenge*.

There have been eight ships called *Revenge* in the Royal Navy; the eighth fought at Jutland and was a unit of the Eastern Fleet during the Second World War.

See also Vol. X, SEA WARFARE.

RICKSHAW (Jinricksha). This light, two-wheeled vehicle is drawn by a man. The body of the vehicle is mounted on springs and large wire-spoked wheels, with two shafts for the man to grasp, and a movable hood to cover the passenger. It is believed to have been invented by a missionary to Japan about 1870, and its name is made up from the Japanese words for 'man' *jin*, 'power' *riki*, and 'vehicle' *sha*. It quickly became popular in Japan and China as the successor to the Oriental form of SEDAN CHAIR (q.v.), and was later introduced into Africa and India. It is used in Indian hill-stations such as Simla, where horse-drawn vehicles are not practical. In South Africa rickshaws are drawn by Zulus, who are sometimes dressed in ostrich feathers, paint, and beads. Jinricksha men have been known to run 20 miles with their carriages at a speed of 6 miles an hour.

The hand-drawn rickshaw is now little used in the big cities of China and Japan, where it has been mainly replaced by the ordinary motor-

Paul Popper

A JAPANESE RICKSHAW

taxi. In some towns rickshaw tricycles are seen, propelled by pedals.

RIGHT OF WAY.

This means the right of the public to a free passage along a road, bridle-way, or footpath. The route must be one along which the public would have a reasonable purpose for going—that is, it must lead from one public place to another, from a road to a village or another road, or a short route from one village to another; or to some special point of public interest, such as a view-point, a waterfall, or the sea-shore. A route from a road to a private house, for instance, could not be considered a reasonable right of way.

The legal establishing of a right of way depends, as does so much of English law, on continuous custom. A public right of way may be created by an Act of Parliament, but in the great majority of cases it comes into existence by a 'dedication', that is, by the owner of the land giving the public the right to use it. Dedication is not always easy to establish, and in the past so many disputes arose that the Commons, Open Spaces, and Footpaths Preservation Society made representations to Parliament, which resulted in the Rights of Way Act of 1932. This Act provided that where 20 years of continuous and undisputed use of a path by the public can be shown, then 'dedication' by the owner can be assumed. If an owner wishes to prevent a path through his land from becoming a right of way, he must do something to show that he does not intend to dedicate a public right of way; for example, he must close the path occasionally by locking gates, or he must display 'Private' notices, or take some other steps to turn back members of the public. If, however, a right of way has been established, the owner may not legally put up any obstruction to a free passage.

See also Vol. IX: Walking.

RIVER NAVIGATION.

In ancient times, when land communications were difficult because of forest and swamp and the absence of roads or wheeled vehicles, rivers were often the only means of transporting any but the lightest goods, and, indeed, often the only means of travel at all. In some little developed parts of the world, such as parts of equatorial Africa and America, where the country is largely dense forest or swamp, the great rivers, such as the Congo and Amazon (qq.v. Vol. III), are still the principal highways. It is not surprising, therefore, that early man evolved a boat (see Primitive Ships) before he evolved a cart (see Carts and Wagons).

The great cities of Ancient Civilizations (q.v. Vol. I) were almost always built on river banks. The cities of Egypt grew up along the Nile (q.v. Vol. III), and communicated with each other by boat along the river, and down the river to the Mediterranean. The cities of Mesopotamia grew up along the Tigris and Euphrates, and those of ancient India on the Ganges and Indus (qq.v. Vol. III). The fertile land in these river valleys brought wealth to the early settlers, and the different settlements began to exchange the goods they had for those they wanted by carrying them by boat. The populations in the river valleys tended to increase rapidly, and the communications made possible by the rivers in course of time resulted in the separate groups uniting into nations.

River travel in ancient days, however, was sometimes made difficult by frequent and violent floodings, by the fact that rivers changed their course, and by the silting up of the channel. The problem of controlling rivers is a very ancient one. Many great rivers extend far inland at an easy slope and could, therefore, be navigated by small craft with little more improvement of their condition than the removal, where possible, of sand-banks and fallen trees. If the river was cut up by rapids or waterfalls, the cargo from the boats, and also the boats themselves, would be carried past the rapid or up the rise in level by men and pack-horses. Some rivers, such as the Rhine, have a natural even flow of water both winter and summer. Other rivers, however, such as the great Yellow River in north China, are subject to periodic floodings, or their course is broken by rapids and sandbanks. Some rivers, especially tidal rivers, silt up with sand and mud more than others.

Most rivers have to be 'canalized', and their flow of water regulated. The aim of canalization is to provide a channel of reasonable width and depth, to protect the sides of the river so that earth will not be washed away and block the channel with mud, and to make it possible for water after rain to escape without flowing over neighbouring land. Sometimes storage reservoirs for flood water have to be built at high levels to provide for regular supplies of water

E.N.A.

BOATS ON THE YANGTZE RIVER AT HANYANG, HUPEH PROVINCE, CHINA

during dry weather. Improvement of river navigation began by increasing the length of channels which boats could use in the estuaries. Modern DREDGERS (q.v.) now serve to keep clear from silt a navigable channel for vessels.

The difficulty of raising boats from one level of water to another, without carrying the boat overland, was at first met by a method of inclined planes with rollers for raising the boat. Then changes of level were produced by the building up of rough weirs to dam up the water for a short time, so that boats could float by. Later, openings were made in these crude weirs, and these were fitted with gates or planks which could be opened or removed to allow boats to pass. Later still, a new channel with a lock was built round the shallow places, navigation depth being kept by the weir built across the river lower down (see LOCKS AND WEIRS).

These improvements in river navigation came slowly, and developed according to the nature of a river and the needs of the country or peoples it served. Sometimes a river was also used for generating power to work water-mills, as were many English rivers, or for IRRIGATION (q.v. Vol. VI) of farm land in hot, dry lands, as were

and still are the Nile in Egypt, the Ganges in India, and many great rivers in China and America. These other uses for the river have to be kept in mind when making improvements for the purposes of navigation.

In England there were many early Acts of Parliament relating to rivers and their conservancy. Navigation improvements were often prevented and traffic held up by the owners of water-mills, who were joined by landowners fearful of losing their fishing and water rights—for in the days of few waterworks and public water-mains, a stream of water running through one's land might be of great value. In spite of some improvement, rivers still contained many 'shoals' or shallow places; in times of drought there was a lack of water; in times of rain, floods destroyed the banks built to preserve navigation; few navigable rivers had towing-paths for horses, and where these existed they were frequently blocked by high stiles and fences. Action for making the river navigable was often prevented; in 1759, for instance, a clause was inserted in the Stroudwater Navigation Act prohibiting the use of locks. The first lock on the Thames at Teddington was not opened until 1811. Some

E.N.A.

DUISBURG HARBOUR ON THE RIVER RHINE

early forms of weirs called staunches are still used on the Thames above Oxford, and there were staunches on the Severn until 1842. It is not, therefore, surprising that by the middle of the 18th century the principal centres of trade were the coastal towns, since inland trade was hampered by the lack of a reasonably economical means of transport.

As good navigable rivers provide a cheap form of transport, especially for heavy goods, the great rivers of the continent of Europe have had an important influence on the commerce in the countries they serve. Large continental rivers, now mainly controlled by the State or even by an international commission, have been improved and canalized from early times, and vast sums have been expended in keeping them up to date. The RHINE (q.v. Vol. III), nearly 800 miles long, is the most important river in western Europe, serving as it does Holland, France, Germany, and Switzerland, with connexions to Belgium. It is a very busy route, with many inland ports of some size, such as Duisburg and Cologne. Mannheim and Strasbourg have large inland docks, and the Ruhr area, through which the river passes, has been the heart of industrial Germany. The Rhine BARGES (q.v.) are an economical form of transport for the heavy raw materials and goods of this manu-

facturing region. Since 1815 the Rhine has been under the control of a permanent international commission, whose duty it is to watch over the interests of the countries concerned in the navigation.

The DANUBE (q.v. Vol. III) is another river controlled by an international commission—the European Commission of the Danube, which was set up in 1856 after the Crimean War. This great river, which is navigable from the Black Sea right into Germany, links the capital cities of Belgrade, Budapest, and Vienna, as well as great river ports such as Bratislava and Turnu Severin. It is connected by canals both to the Rhine and the Elbe. The VOLGA (q.v. Vol. III), the longest European river, has been an important trade route for many centuries. It connects great industrial cities such as Stalingrad, Saratov, and Gorki, and is linked by canal to Moscow, to the River Don, and to the Baltic and White Sea (*see* RUSSIAN CANALS). In France the River Seine is navigable for vessels of 10-foot draft throughout the length from Rouen to Paris, a distance of 226 miles, over which the river is canalized.

China has three great navigable rivers, the YELLOW RIVER, the YANGTZE, and the SI-KIANG (qq.v. Vol. III), and over 25,000 miles of river are navigable by steamers and junks. The

IRRAWADDY (q.v. Vol. III) is a vital waterway navigable for some 900 miles through Burma.

The United States of America is also a country of great rivers, of which the MISSISSIPPI river system (q.v. Vol. III) is perhaps the most important. The Mississippi, with its tributaries Missouri and Ohio, has over 6,000 miles of authorized navigable waterway, as well as many hundreds of miles on the other large tributaries, such as the Arkansas. During the present century much has been done to improve the natural rivers of the United States and Canada by canalization and to connect by canals the great natural waterways, especially the Great Lakes (*see* WELLAND CANAL) and the Ohio and Hudson Rivers.

See also PRIMITIVE SHIPS; CANALS.
See also Vol. III: RIVERS.

ROAD BUILDING, *see* Vol. VIII: ROAD BUILDING.

ROADS (HISTORY OF). The modern meaning of the word 'road' dates only from about the time of Shakespeare; the earlier terms used were either 'way' or, if a properly made surface were intended, 'street'. The last comes from a Latin word meaning 'to strew or pave', and can be found to-day in the names of many English places (such as Streatham, Stratford, Streatley, Stretton) on or near one of the old ROMAN ROADS (q.v.), which were usually paved or metalled.

The earliest road-users did not have wheeled vehicles, and so the earliest roads were little more than tracks, having no artificially strengthened surface from the remains of which we might be able to trace their routes: we can only sketch some of them roughly from the finds of buried merchandise made along their courses. In this way we know that as early as 3000 B.C. a road ran from Afghanistan through Persia and Arabia to Egypt, and that along this was brought 'lapis lazuli', a valuable blue stone. About 1,000 years later there began a steady trade in amber from Denmark and the Baltic along a road running right across Europe to north Italy (*see* TRADE ROUTES). The most that was done to make and keep these ancient roads fit for traffic was perhaps the removal of large boulders or the filling of soft places with gravel, stones, or brushwood, and not even this was done if a way round could be found. In thick bush country, as in Africa, the earliest roads followed the game-trails

trampled out by heavy animals, because the tools of early man were not capable of felling trees or even hacking through bushes without great labour. In America it was the bison, a very heavy animal needing firm ground and easy gradients, which blazed the trails later followed by Indians and then by the white men (*see* AMERICAN TRAILS). So the expresses of the Canadian Pacific Railway thunder across the Rocky Mountains to-day through passes first discovered by the bison, and many modern American main roads owe their routes to the same animal.

The oldest paved road known was made by Cheops, the Egyptian king who built the Great Pyramid before 2700 B.C. Its purpose was to allow the huge granite facing-blocks to be dragged and rolled to the site. In China there is a saying that a road is good for 7 years and then bad for 4,000. The date of the first emperor, Fu Hi, is given as 2800 B.C.; and certainly, to administer his vast empire, he must have needed roads, though probably these were paved only in the towns. A later emperor, Shi Hwang Ti, who came to the throne in 246 B.C., is famous for the roads he made. The imperial

E.N.A

A ROAD OF STEPS AT PING SHA, KWANTUNG PROVINCE, CHINA

Keystone

A GERMAN HIGH-SPEED MOTOR ROAD: THE BERLIN–MUNICH AUTOBAHN

roads of China, about 2,000 miles in length, were at their best, broad, and paved with great slabs of stone. They were connected by a network of lesser roads. Rivers were bridged or crossed by ferries; mountains were tunnelled or climbed by broad easy steps suitable for pack animals. Chinese roads were deliberately made crooked to discourage evil spirits, who were believed to travel only in straight lines.

Just when trade between China and the western world began is not known; but by the 6th century B.C. Persia had already been importing raw silk for many years. The Chinese merchants are said to have linked up at Kandahar, in Afghanistan, with the travellers from the west, who no doubt used the old lapis lazuli road. In the 1st century B.C. a large trade grew up between China and Rome, silk being bartered for such things as coral, amber, ivory, and tortoise-shell. The Romans were by far the greatest road-builders of the ancient world, though they may have learned useful lessons from Carthage, the city on the north coast of Africa which, with a

population at one time of over a million and an empire stretching right along the south shore of the Mediterranean and across into Spain, must have needed a good system of roads. At its height the Roman Empire contained more than 50,000 miles of excellent roads radiating from the capital to the farthest corners of the dominions (*see* ROMAN ROADS).

For many centuries after the fall of Rome in the 5th century A.D., hardly any new roads were built in Europe, and only in France was anything done to keep the old Roman roads in repair. It was in France, too—but not until 1764—that Pierre Trésaguet made the first really successful roads since those of the Romans, whose methods he probably copied. Trésaguet, however, made the foundations of his roads, composed of stone blocks set on edge, with a camber parallel to that of the road surface. A few years later Napoleon put the whole road system of France into thorough repair to help the moving of his armies. He also built the first roads for wheeled traffic through the Western Alps to Italy (the passes through the Eastern Alps were far easier and had long carried roads). The modern *autobahnen* and *autostrade* of Germany and Italy, the most advanced examples of modern road-making in Europe, were also constructed for military reasons. With these exceptions the history of roads in Europe from Roman times onwards can be judged from ROADS, BRITISH (q.v.). In America, except in the large towns, the art of good road-making, as we know it, is little older than our own century.

See also ROADS, BRITISH; MACADAM ROADS; ROADS, MODERN; ALASKAN HIGHWAY; BURMA ROAD.

ROADS, BRITISH (HISTORY OF). Men of the Old Stone Age, who knew nothing of farming and lived by hunting the herds of bison, reindeer, and little wild horses that roamed Britain perhaps some 8,000 or 9,000 years ago, appear to have developed an extensive system of trackways and to have guided travellers along them by a series of marks so placed that the next ahead was always in sight. Thus a great stone might be reared on its end or an earthen or gravel mound (tumulus) thrown up. On sky-lines a notch might be cut; on lower ground a circular moat or pond might be dug. These marks can still be found to-day, running in dead straight lines or 'leys', and the reason we date them so far back as the Old Stone Age is that only at that particular time, when the climate was so dry and cold that hardly any trees could grow and Britain was mostly grass-covered open country, could many of them have been seen. With the warmer moister weather which followed the Great Ice Age, dense forests and thickets sprang up, which must have made them largely useless (*see* PREHISTORIC MAN, Vol. I).

Then came a new sort of man who had learned how to farm and was altogether more civilized. But because the wetter climate had turned much of the low-lying ground into vast marshes, and because the clearing of heavy or tree-covered land was too much for his crude tools, New Stone Age man lived mainly on high ground and especially on top of the chalk downs of southern England. He developed a new system of tracks, which followed the crests of the hills and are therefore called 'ridgeways'. The centre of this system was Salisbury Plain with its two great temples at STONEHENGE and AVEBURY (qq.v. Vol. I). Every few miles along these roads he made enclosures, surrounded by ramparts and ditches, into which he could drive his cattle at night. Later, some of these 'camps' were developed into immense fortresses, such as Maiden Castle in Dorset (*see* EARTHWORKS AND HILL-FORTS, Vol. I). It was in such places that the Ancient Britons put up some of their toughest fights against the Roman legions between A.D. 43 and 47. But at least 2,000 years before that Britain had begun to export tin abroad for the making of bronze. It was mined in Cornwall, and we know that long before the Romans came, it used to be sent in wagons across southern England to the Isle of Wight, Kent, or even Essex, where it was put on board ship. This could hardly have been done without reasonably good roads (*see also* CART AND WAGON).

When the Romans conquered Britain, they made their work secure by building a complete system of roads (*see* ROMAN ROADS). The great value of these was not only that their splendid construction allowed them to stand centuries of neglect, but that in choosing London as the centre of the system the Romans made a choice which has not been disputed since.

G. M. Boumphrey

THE RIDGEWAY CROSSING THE BERKSHIRE DOWNS

All through medieval times it was generally thought that if a road got bad, all it needed was a rest and it would mend itself without the need for any work. So traffic would make wider and wider detours round bad places, until some roads were in places over 100 yards wide, and equally bad from one side to the other. No one was responsible for keeping the roads in repair; and although people did not mind doing a little to mend the short lengths they themselves used, they did not see why they should keep up roads to be used by travellers from a distance. There was a vague obligation on the Lord of the Manor to have such work done, but his duty was generally neglected. On the whole it was the great abbeys and monasteries which did most for the roads; and the dissolution of these by Henry VIII led to even greater neglect just at a time when the growing trade of the country called for better transport.

Until then, trade had been so local that long-distance roads were hardly needed, except by armies on the march. In 1555 the Highway Act was passed making each parish responsible for its roads and obliging each inhabitant to do 6 days' work a year on them. This was generally evaded and, as the roads got worse and worse, it was followed by all sorts of foolish Acts regulating the weight of loads, the width of tires, or the number of animals drawing each vehicle: almost everything was tried except the building of good roads.

In general as much as possible was sent by pack-animal rather than on wheels. For if a pack-horse became bogged in a mud-hole, it could generally be relieved of its load and dragged out; but a bogged wagon might have to wait there for the coming of summer. (Heavy trunks of trees needed for ship-building often took many months, or even several years, to travel to the coast.) And so long files of pack-animals, bearing bales of cloth from Gloucestershire, pottery from Staffordshire, and coal from the Black Country, were a familiar sight until little more than 200 years ago; and most of the few bridges built during medieval times were of the narrow, hump-backed kind now known as 'pack-horse bridges' (see BRIDGES).

In 1663 the first Turnpike Act made the experiment of collecting money for the upkeep of roads from those who used them. Toll-bars were built, each with its 'turnpike' or barrier, which stopped the traveller until he had paid his toll, and Trusts were appointed to see that the money was well spent. Under this system, in spite of its abuses, British roads gradually became good enough for the great coaching days of the 18th and early 19th centuries, when they were probably the best in Europe (see TURNPIKE).

The first good roads to be made in Britain after Roman times were built in Scotland by General Wade some years after the Jacobite Rebellion of 1715, and were military. Then, in 1737, Robert Philips read a paper on road construction to the Royal Society. In this he claimed, as McAdam did later, that the surface of a well-made road should be consolidated, not pulled up, by the action of the traffic passing over it. But Philips's paper brought no immediate

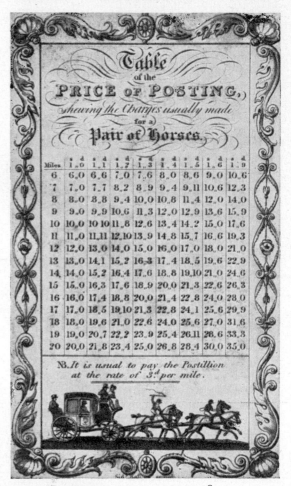

CHARGES FOR HIRING HORSES, 1824
This table of 'posting' prices is taken from Leigh's *New Pocket Road Book of England, Wales, and Scotland*

result. From 1765 onwards, however, a Yorkshireman, John Metcalfe, in spite of the fact that he was blind, built 180 miles of excellent turnpike roads. He was followed in the early 19th century by Telford, the famous engineer and bridge-builder, who built many hundreds of miles of roads in England, Scotland, and Wales. At about the same time John McAdam was working on the system of road construction that was to make his name famous. Unlike the roads of Trésaguet, Metcalfe, and Telford, MACADAM ROADS (q.v.) had no expensive foundation of heavy stone: they consisted simply of one layer of broken stone, laid direct on the subsoil. The idea was greatly ridiculed at first; but when it was found that such roads lasted well and were far less tiring to horses because of their slight 'give', McAdam's system triumphed.

For about 60 or 70 years after the coming of the railways in the middle of the 19th century, roads lost much of their importance until the development of motor transport in our own century. The invention of the pneumatic tire in 1888 raised quite new problems of road construction. Instead of rolling the stones of the surface into place, as iron tires do, the rubber tire tends to suck them loose; and the dust ground off these stones, which should help to cement them together, is blown away by the fast-moving car. Choking, blinding clouds of dust used to hang over the main roads of the late 19th century. Many experiments were tried, including the application of sea water and of various chemicals. But tar was found to be most effective in preventing dust and holding the broken stone firmly in place. At first the tar was applied either by brush or spray; but later it was found better to make a 'tarmacadam' surface in which the broken stones are completely coated with tar before being laid and rolled.

With the ever-increasing speed and weight of modern road vehicles, the foundations of main roads have to be immensely strong. The cost of such roads is far too heavy to be borne by anyone but the Government. The last of the Turnpike Trusts was abolished in 1895, when the roads were handed over to the Local Authorities.

See also ROADS, HISTORY OF; ROADS, MODERN; HORSE TRANSPORT; MOTOR TRANSPORT.
See also Vol. VIII: ROAD BUILDING.

ROADS, MODERN.
All industrial countries have been forced by modern motor transport to create road systems, or to improve those they had before. Britain, with 18,000 miles of road and 3 million licensed motor vehicles, carries more traffic for its length of roads than any other country. Main roads bearing long-distance traffic are so important to the nation's business, and their cost of building is so high (sometimes more than £100,000 a mile), that they cannot be paid for, as in the past, by the towns and counties through which they pass. The principal roads are therefore planned by the Ministry of Transport, a Government department set up in 1919. They are partly paid for with money raised by taxation. All other road costs are paid by local authorities, with money raised by rates.

British roads are classified in three groups under a system devised in 1919. The arterial roads, so called because they might be compared to the arteries in the human body, are known as

The Autocar

THE TRUNK ROADS OF BRITAIN AND THEIR ZONES

Fox Photos

PART OF CLOVER-LEAF ROAD CROSSING IN STOCKHOLM
The roads cross each other at three levels, allowing a continuous stream of traffic from seven directions

'A' or Class I roads; these include the principal roads radiating from London to far parts of the country, and many roads joining big cities. A certain number of 'A' roads, known as 'trunk roads', are of such special importance that the Government pays the whole cost. For all other 'A' roads the Government pays three-quarters of the cost of maintenance or improvement.

A second group of classified roads consists of 'B' or Class II roads, which are a little less important than 'A' roads. The Government pays a slightly smaller share of their cost. Last comes a third group, which has no official name, and for which the Government pays only half the cost. All other roads are described as 'unclassified', and are solely the responsibility of the county or borough in which they run.

Each road in the first two classes, 'A' and 'B', has a different number, which appears on all signposts, so that a motor driver can find his way across Britain if he has previously looked up the numbers on a map. For this purpose, England and Wales are divided into six zones marked by the six great trunk roads which radiate from London, and which are numbered A 1 to A 6. Scotland is divided in the same way by A 7, A 8, and A 9, which radiate from Edinburgh. All 'A' and 'B' roads starting in the sector between A 1 and A 2 begin with the figure '1'; all roads between A 2 and A 3 begin with '2', and so on. Thus a motorist might set off from London along the Bath Road, a trunk road which is called A 4, and on reaching Reading might turn off to an ordinary 'A' road called A 4009; then at the village of Nettlebed, he might turn into a Class 'B' road called B 481. A road keeps its number throughout its length: the A 6 road at Carlisle is still A 6 at London, 298 miles away. That means that some cross-country roads, if they are long enough, will continue to carry their zone number in a different zone. For instance, road A 428 runs from Coventry in Zone 4 across to Northampton in Zone 5, past Bedford into Zone 6, and after that it joins the A 1 road. The idea of road classification is not new. The Romans had three classes of roads, the most important being maintained by the State. The British system is roughly similar to those of France, U.S.A., and other countries.

The building of modern roads has developed slowly in Britain, partly because of their expense. Wherever possible, old roads are improved rather than new ones built. Trunk roads run in places over Roman or medieval roads, such as the Great North Road, BATH ROAD, and DOVER ROAD (qq.v.). Parts of Britain are so thickly populated that it has been difficult to plan the long-distance high-speed motorways which exist in some countries. The finest British road-building may be seen in by-passes, roads which allow heavy traffic to pass round a city, town, or village instead of through its narrow streets. Some by-passes are built in long, graceful curves, with two concrete carriageways for one-way traffic divided by a raised strip planted with shrubs; separate cycle tracks are sometimes laid. At the crossings of important roads, roundabouts are built (*see* ROAD TRAFFIC CONTROL). In London, the North Cir-

FLY-OVER JUNCTION, NEW YORK

Fox Photos

cular Road, although passing through populous suburbs, is an instance of a form of by-pass which enables fast traffic, free of speed limits, to avoid the centre of the city.

Germany, Italy, and the U.S.A. have been pioneers in building high-speed motorways. The German *autobahnen* and Italian *autostrade* are fenced in, and motorists are admitted to them only at special gates, where they pay a toll. Once inside, they can travel at 80 or 90 miles an hour if they like, for there are hardly any junctions, and

no slow-moving traffic is allowed. In Germany and U.S.A. modern devices such as 'fly-over' junctions and 'clover-leaf' crossings are used, so that traffic is carried over busy junctions by means of bridges, and drivers who wish to turn off the main road by moving to the 'pavement side' need not get in the way of faster traffic which is overtaking them.

See also ROADS, HISTORY OF; ROMAN ROADS; ROADS, BRITISH; ROAD TRAFFIC CONTROL.
See also Vol. VIII: ROAD BUILDING.

ROAD SERVICE STATION. The garage, or road service station, exists to provide the motorist with fuel and lubricating oil, and to clean or repair his car. Some garages perform only light, running repairs, but most are equipped for the skilled and intricate task of completely overhauling a car.

Re-fuelling is done by pumps, driven either by hand or by electricity, which draw the petrol from large tanks placed under the ground for safety. The amount used is registered on the dial on the pump. Lubricating oil for the engine, gear-box, and axle is usually supplied from a cabinet, from which it is poured into a measuring can. In most garages there is a high-pressure air outfit for pumping up the tires, sometimes consisting of a portable compressor and an air reservoir which supplies air at a pressure of about 250 lb. per sq. in., or a static compressor and a large reservoir, which can be used, not only for tires, but also in the workshops. Well-equipped garages also have apparatus for high-pressure chassis lubrication and gas and electric welding, lathes for machining small metal parts, and a sparking-plug cleaner and tester. In the larger service stations there are separate maintenance departments where engines can be taken out and overhauled. These are equipped with revolving engine stands, machines for reboring, and for testing the ignition and carburettor, as well as the necessary apparatus for repairing the bodies and electrical equipment of the cars. Service stations used to have special pits so that mechanics could work underneath a car, but now lifts, jacks, or trolleys are used to raise the vehicle to a convenient height.

See also MOTOR-CAR; MOTOR TRANSPORT.

ROAD TRAFFIC CONTROL. Since the speed and volume of road traffic has so greatly increased, it has become necessary to introduce more and more traffic regulations, especially in congested areas. These figures (to the nearest thousand) show how the numbers of licensed motor vehicles in Britain have grown in the 20th century:

	Private cars	Goods vehicles
1904	8,000	4,000
1924	474,000	203,000
1934	1,308,000	413,000
1948	1,961,000	769,000

Until it was repealed by the Road Traffic Act of 1930, there was legally a speed limit of 20 miles an hour for all vehicles—though it was in fact generally disregarded. By the Act of 1934 a new speed limit of 30 miles an hour was imposed in 'built-up areas' (that is, towns and most villages) for it had been shown that three-quarters of all accidents took place in these areas. Signs are put up to show the beginning and end of the restricted areas (*see* Fig. 1). The 1934 Act also introduced special pedestrian crossings marked by 'Belisha Beacons'—Mr. Hore Belisha being the Minister of Transport at the time. Driving tests were introduced for all new applicants for driving licences. Those who have not passed the test have to carry a learner's red 'L' on the front and back of the vehicle, and may not drive without a licenced companion beside them. Solo motor-cycle learners are allowed to ride alone.

As traffic continues to increase, further action is taken to control it, both for the sake of safety and speed. In most towns very narrow streets are made into 'one way streets'; official parking-places are marked, and parking in busy streets is forbidden. Busy cross-roads are controlled by automatic signals, thus releasing the police for general supervision. Automatic signals change from red to green either at fixed intervals or

GREASING A CAR

Fox Photos

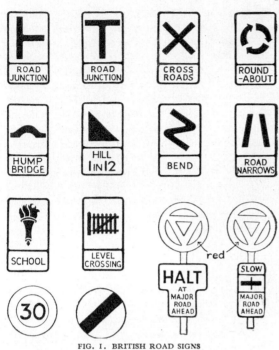

FIG. I. BRITISH ROAD SIGNS

up signs such as 'P' (for car park), 'Diversion' (to show that a road or street is closed for repairs), or a number which identifies a first-class road. All such signs appear in the Highway Code.

See RULE OF THE ROAD, Section I.

ROAD TRANSPORT ENGINES. Practically all vehicles on the roads, whether private cars, goods vehicles, or buses, are driven by some form of INTERNAL-COMBUSTION ENGINE (q.v. Vol. VIII), the type in widest use being the ordinary petrol-engine.

All the power of an engine could be produced in one cylinder; but most engines have four or six cylinders, as the power of a small engine can then be applied more evenly to a heavy load, and the moving parts need not be massive. MOTOR-CYCLES (q.v.) are an exception; their framework is so light compared with the power of even a very small engine that a well-designed single cylinder is efficient and cheap. The rated horse-power of private car engines ranges from 8 to 30 horse-power; the heavier commercial vehicles have engines of 30 to 50 horse-power, and some bus engines approach 100 horse-power. In buses and coaches, the cylinders are often designed to lie horizontally under the flooring to save space.

At times of acute petrol shortage, as in war, a petrol-engine can be adapted to burn gas instead of petrol; the gas can be either made from coal products in a miniature gasworks on a trailer drawn by the car, or it can be bought, ready-made, in a large balloon-like bag which is strapped to the roof of the car.

The second main type of internal-combustion engine, known as the compression-ignition engine or diesel engine, is being used more and more since the Second World War by the larger commercial vehicles, because it is cheaper and stronger in the long run for really heavy loads, and burns an oil which is easier to refine than petrol. This form of engine, invented by Rudolf Diesel in Germany in 1892, depends for its internal explosions (which drive the engine) on air compressed so tightly that it becomes hot, just as a bicycle pump warms up when pumped

according to the volume of traffic. The latter type work from a simple device underneath a rubber strip set in the road. This registers the passage of a vehicle on the principle of an electric bell-push, and is connected with a switch-box at the roadside which operates the lights.

Local highway authorities may erect in dangerous places traffic-signs as shown in Fig. 1, or paint signs such as 'Go Slow' or 'Look Left' in white or yellow letters at least 4 inches wide on the surface of the road itself. White lines or metal studs, with reflectors that catch the lights of cars at night, often called 'cat's eyes', show the middle of the road or the traffic lanes in an arterial road. These are particularly useful in dense fog when the motorist cannot easily see the side of the road. Associations such as the Royal Automobile Club and the Automobile Association, which are voluntarily supported by the subscriptions of their members, are also allowed, by arrangement with the police, to put

Cross-roads.   School.   No parking.   No cars.   No overtaking.   No entry.   Open crossing. Crossing gate.

FIG. 2. SOME INTERNATIONAL ROAD SIGNS. THESE ARE COLOURED RED AND BLACK.

SCAMMELL HEAVY-DUTY LORRY   *Topical Press*

40 miles to take on freshly charged batteries because all the electric power in the old ones would be used up. The used batteries would then have to be connected to the electric mains for several hours in order to be charged again. For that reason electric battery-powered cars have never been used to any great extent, except for the local collection and delivery of goods, such as milk and bread. A battery-powered motor is suitable for this purpose because it works at its best, as a petrol-engine does not, when it has frequent stops, which allow a battery to 'rest' (*see* Vol. VIII: ELECTRIC MOTOR and BATTERIES, ELECTRICAL).

Batteries are also used for other purposes where short journeys with frequent stops are involved. For instance, they drive porters' trucks which move luggage and mail-bags at big railway stations; and they propel invalid carriages, the occupant being thus spared the constant smell of petrol and exhaust fumes. There are also a few thousand battery-driven vans and lorries on the roads in Britain, carrying loads of 10 cwt. to 5 tons.

Until the 1920's, many motor-buses used a petrol-electric system of drive; an ordinary petrol-

hard; this heat causes the oil to explode. The pressure is so great that the engine must be made of thick metal, and is, therefore, too heavy for use in private cars.

A new and radically different type of engine, the GAS TURBINE (q.v. Vol. VIII) was first successfully applied to the motor car by British engineers. The first car of this kind in the world was demonstrated in Britain in March, 1950, by the Rover Company, and was later exhibited in America. The car, which was built to provide an experimental basis for future production models, had an engine of 100 horse-power, and in official trials it accelerated from a standstill to a speed of 60 miles an hour in 14 seconds.

Electric drive has many advantages. It is clean and silent, produces no exhaust gases, has fewer working parts to wear out, needs no gear-box, and has fewer hand-controls. It does not require petrol, which is inflammable, or a water-filled radiator, which may freeze in winter. Its great disadvantage is that, except for TROLLEY-BUSES (q.v.), an electric road vehicle is driven by batteries, and these, weight for weight, will drive a vehicle for a far shorter distance than a tankful of petrol. For instance, the driver of a battery-driven private car would have to stop every

Express Dairy Company

ELECTRIC MILK FLOAT

The power is stored in accumulators between the wheels

engine drove an electric GENERATOR (q.v. Vol. VIII), which created current to drive an electric motor connected to the road-wheels. This device was used because frequent stopping and starting at bus-stops was a strain on the engines and transmission of the early motor-buses (*see* MOTOR-CAR, Section 2).

See also MOTOR-CAR; MOTOR TRANSPORT.
See also Vol. VIII: INTERNAL COMBUSTION ENGINE; ELECTRIC MOTORS; GAS TURBINE.

ROCKET, *see* AIRCRAFT ENGINES, Section 6; AIRCRAFT TAKE-OFF; INTERPLANETARY TRAVEL. *See also* Vol. VIII: ROCKET PROPULSION.

ROMANCE LANGUAGES. This name is given to the group of languages, including FRENCH, ITALIAN, SPANISH AND PORTUGUESE (qq.v.), which are descended from LATIN (q.v.). After the collapse of the Roman Empire in the West in the 5th century, the Latin language began to change, changing in different ways in different parts of the Empire. From these changes there had grown up by the 9th century the beginnings of some of the main modern languages of Europe. The decaying Latin spoken from the 5th to the 9th centuries is known as Romance; therefore the great languages which sprang from it are called Romance Languages. French and Provençal (the tongue which was long spoken in southern France) developed from the form of Latin spoken in the territory which was once Roman Gaul; Spanish, Portuguese, and Catalan from the Latin of the Roman province of Iberia; Italian and its various dialects are descended from the Latin of Rome itself, and the different forms of Latin spoken in the various districts of the Italian peninsula. An interesting dialect still spoken on the Mediterranean island of Sardinia closely resembles Latin. Romanch, the language of eastern Switzerland, is a survival of the Latin once spoken in the Roman province of Rhaetia, and Roumanian is spoken in the area which was known to the Romans as Dacia.

The word Romance comes from the Latin *romanice* 'in the Roman way'. The modern French word *roman*, meaning a novel, and the English word 'romance', with its various meanings, are both derived from an early French word for anything written in Romance language.

See also LANGUAGE. HISTORY OF.

ROMAN ROADS. It is safe to say that, in Europe at least, the Romans were the first to create a well-planned system of well-built roads. The purpose of these was firstly military—to help their advancing armies by ensuring the quick movement of supplies and reinforcements, and then civil—to help their administration of the conquered countries and to provide a means of bringing their riches back to Rome. At the peak of its power the empire possessed more than 50,000 miles of excellent roads, radiating from Rome to the farthest corners of its dominions and connected by a network of minor cross-roads. In making them, great natural obstacles which could not be avoided were overcome: ravines and rivers were bridged with stone or timber, tunnels were driven through mountains, marshy ground was made firm with piles driven deep down and covered with cross-timbers or with successive layers of brushwood or 'wattles'—perhaps the origin of the Saxon name for Watling Street, the Roman road that runs from London to Shropshire.

B. C. Clayton
ROMAN ROAD NEAR PONTYPOOL, MONMOUTHSHIRE

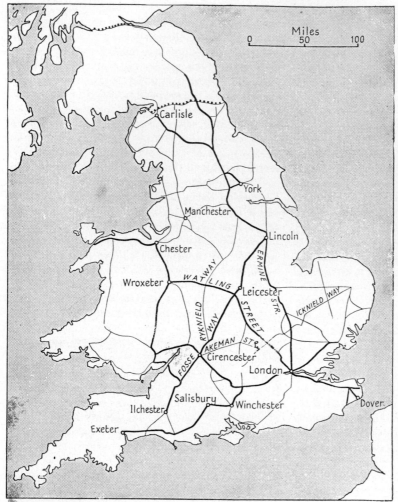

Miles
0   50   100

PRINCIPAL ROMAN ROADS IN BRITAIN (THE NAMES ARE POST-ROMAN)

the enforced labour of local inhabitants. Suitable materials were often fetched from considerable distances. The roads were usually from 14 to 16 feet wide, which allowed two legions, marching six abreast, to pass. In making them, the top soil was first removed and ditches were dug for drainage on either side. Then came the foundation of heavy stones carefully fitted together by hand, since there were no steam-rollers to consolidate them. Next followed a layer of smaller stones and another of broken tile, brick, or chalk, usually held together with mortar. Finally came the surface, well raised in the centre to throw off water. On the best roads this was made of flat stones, fitted together and cemented into place, with kerbs on either side. At other times it might be just small stones, well rammed down and cemented; or gravel alone might be used. The whole road surface was frequently raised well above the surrounding country—a fact that may be commemorated in our term 'the high road'.

From ruts which have been found in their surface we know that the roads were used by heavy wagons the width apart of whose wheels was 4 ft. 8 in. (see also CART AND WAGON). Officials and men of importance travelled more swiftly in light, two-wheeled carriages called cisia. In the stone pavements of Pompeii, near Naples, and other towns (from the streets of which heavy vehicles were frequently banned) grooves worn by the wheels of chariots have been found, and these are only 3 feet apart. Along the more important roads, at intervals of only a few miles, were built posting-houses where relays of fresh horses were kept. By this means a Roman official could easily cover 100 miles a day. On

Roman roads were by no means dead straight from end to end, as was once believed, though they often run exactly straight between the sky-line points, perhaps 20 miles apart, from which they were surveyed, and they are rarely far off the true lines. But they frequently make wide detours round deep valleys and other obstacles. In marking out their lines, the Roman surveyors probably lighted bonfires from sky-line to sky-line, and in some parts of England what are supposed to be the remains of these fires have been found by excavation. The lines of earlier roads are now found to have been followed more often than was once believed to be the case.

The work of road-making was carried out both by the Roman soldiers themselves, every Legion of the army having its own engineer, and by

one occasion the Emperor Tiberius actually did 200 miles in 24 hours. The regular time between Rome and London was 13 days—and it is interesting to note that nearly 2,000 years later, when Robert Peel was suddenly recalled from Italy to be Premier, the journey home took him exactly the same time, though he travelled post-haste all the way. To-day, little more than 100 years later, it could be flown in 2 hours.

The extent and length of the whole system of Roman roads is best known from two records compiled in Roman times, the *Itinerary of Antonius*, probably dating from the 3rd century A.D. and one made a century later which is now known as the Peutinger Table (*see* MAPS, HISTORY OF). They stretched from Scotland to Jerusalem and even beyond the Euphrates, from the heart of Egypt to the Spanish coast. The Roman-British roads are shown on the map. Many of these can still be traced to-day, sometimes as unusually straight stretches on our own roads, sometimes as deserted, grass-grown lanes running between hedges, sometimes as long mounds running across farm land, or even, with no difference in level to be seen, as straight strips in fields of pasture that turn brown in summer before the grass on either side.

See also ROADS; APPIAN WAY.
See also Vol. I: ROMAN CIVILIZATION.

ROPE RAILWAYS, *see* MOUNTAIN RAILWAYS, Section 3.

ROTORCRAFT. These are aircraft which are kept up in the air, not by fixed wings, like an ordinary aeroplane, but by several wings or blades spinning round on a spindle, rather like the wings of an old-fashioned windmill. The spindle is mounted upright on the top of the aircraft.

There are two main kinds of rotorcraft: the helicopter, in which the spindle and blades, made to spin round by an engine, move the aircraft; and the autogiro, in which an ordinary propeller or airscrew in front moves the aircraft.

1. HELICOPTER. The spindle and blades, which are spun round by the engine, provide the lifting action which raises the aircraft and keeps it in the sky. The blades act as a gigantic propeller: on a typical craft there are three blades, and each blade on the spindle is canted at an angle, again following the principle of the old-fashioned windmill. This angle can be varied by the pilot.

As the blades spin round, they begin to grip the air and slowly lift the aircraft off the ground. If the pilot of a rising helicopter wishes the aircraft to hover in the air, without motion, he reduces the speed of the spinning spindle and blades by reducing the speed of the engine, and he also alters the angle of the blades slightly. The series of blades (called a 'rotor') then ceases to grip the air enough to rise any farther, but just grips it enough to keep the aircraft at the height it has reached.

To move the aircraft forward, the entire rotor with its spindle and blades is canted slightly forward. The action is like that of a man holding an open umbrella in rain, who leans the umbrella slightly forward if the rain begins to blow from a forward direction. As soon as the spindle and blades lean away from the vertical towards any particular direction, the grip of the blades on the air not only continues to support the aircraft but also tends to pull it along in that direction.

That is the general principle of helicopters. There are many types. A helicopter can have two, three, four, or more blades on a rotor. It can have one, two, or three rotors, each with its spindle and blades. It can have two rotors close together above the cabin, the blades of one rotor interweaving with the blades of the other as they both spin round. It can have rotors mounted on outriggers on each side of the aircraft, in the way that oars are supported on each side of a racing boat on the river.

The method of steering a helicopter is unusual. A rudder would be useless, as there is not a fast enough stream of air being blown straight back (as from an airscrew) in which a rudder could work. Instead, a well-known principle of mechanics is made use of: when the helicopter's spindle and blades are being spun round, the effort applied to the spindle by the engine tends to cause the whole aircraft itself to spin round in the opposite direction to the spindle and blades. This turning tendency, which is common in engineering whenever anything is spinning, is known as 'torque'. The designer of a helicopter, when faced by this tendency of the aircraft to spin round on its own spindle, must provide some force as strong as the 'torque', which will keep the 'torque' in check. Therefore a small propeller, facing sideways, is mounted on one side of the tail of the aircraft. This little propeller, driven by an engine and continually

SIKORSKY S. 51 FOUR-SEAT HELICOPTER LIFTING A LOAD OF FREIGHT

spinning, thrusts a stream of air sideways, counteracting the 'torque' and preventing the tail of the aircraft from swinging round. Thus two forces are continually trying to push the tail of the aircraft sideways—'torque' on one side and the little propeller on the other. Those are the forces which the pilot uses for steering. If he wants to turn the nose of his aircraft to right or left, he simply causes the little propeller to increase or decrease the amount of its pressure for a few seconds, and at once the tail of the helicopter is pushed sideways until the whole helicopter is facing in the direction the pilot chooses. The pressure of the propeller is altered, not by making it go faster or slower, but by moving a lever which slightly changes the angle of its blades.

2. AUTOGIRO. The other distinctive kind of rotorcraft, the autogiro, works on quite different principles. The autogiro, for instance, has an airscrew or propeller at the front, like an ordinary aeroplane, which is driven by an engine in the usual way. The spindle and blades (the rotor) above the cabin of the autogiro are not con-nected with an engine, but are free to turn on their own account. They are caused to spin by the stream of air blown backward by the airscrew. Thus they spin round rather like the helicopter's blades, but, as we have seen, for a different reason. These spinning blades have the effect of lifting the aircraft into the air, much as the fixed wings of an ordinary aeroplane will lift it into the air. At the same time the airscrew of the autogiro moves the craft forward in the ordinary way. The autogiro is, therefore, much like the standard aeroplane, except that it has spinning wings instead of fixed ones. Its spinning wings act like a falling leaf spinning as it falls slowly to the ground. They will not allow the aircraft to fall, except very slowly. In the case of engine failure, therefore, an autogiro glides gently towards the ground and is easy to control.

The helicopter's spinning blades are not meant to act like a falling leaf; they are meant to have the active effect of a propeller, drawing the air-craft upward. In the event of engine failure, a helicopter is at a disadvantage compared with an autogiro until the pilot has had time to alter

Flight

CIERVA C.40 AUTOGIRO LANDING

the angle of the spinning blades to make them act on the autogiro's principle of a falling leaf. All forms of rotorcraft are noted for their power of slow flight and their ability to take off and land on a very small space without a runway. The helicopter can, if necessary, rise straight up in the air from the ground, although this is a strain on its structure. It can also hover, even when the air is absolutely still. The autogiro can rise from the ground at a very sharp angle. It can hover in a slight wind. Rotorcraft can also, if desired, take off and land just like a normal aeroplane.

The best speed of rotorcraft is from 75 to 100 miles an hour. The ordinary aeroplane is therefore five or six times faster, besides being able to fly a far longer distance non-stop.

The chief use of rotorcraft is for carrying mails or goods in districts where transport communications by land or water are bad. They are used also for the control of crowds by police (at events, for instance, such as the Oxford and Cambridge boat race); for spraying crops with chemicals to destroy insect pests; for the inspection of electric power lines; and for certain kinds of photographic surveying.

The rotorcraft is no new invention. LEONARDO DA VINCI, the Italian inventive genius of the 15th century, foresaw the idea. In France, experiments were made with helicopters in 1907. In 1923 the autogiro, invented by de la Cierva, a Spaniard, was first flown; his invention has been widely used. Several American helicopters, designed by Igor Sikorsky, a Russian emigrant, were much used by the American Army in the Second World War to rescue wounded from inaccessible places.

See also AEROPLANE; FLYING, HISTORY OF.

ROUMANIAN LANGUAGE, *see* ROMANCE LANGUAGES.

ROYAL TRAIN, *see* TRAIN, SPECIAL USES, Section 1.

RULE OF THE ROAD. 1. ROAD. The principle of the rule of the road is that all traffic—motor, horse-drawn, and bicycle—must move on one side only, except in special circumstances. In Great Britain, Eire, Malta, Sweden, and all British Dominions and Colonies except Canada, traffic keeps to the left: in all other countries it keeps to the right. As a result, in British cars the driver's seat is on the right-hand side, and in American and others on the left-hand side; for the driver is better able to control and steer his car when he is nearer the on-coming traffic. One exception to the left-hand rule is that a horseman leading a second horse usually moves on the right, because he must have his left or bridle-hand free, and the led horse should be as far away from the traffic as possible.

It is not known how the custom of keeping to the left began. Possibly it was because drivers of carriages wanted to keep their right or whip-hand free, which would not have been possible when driving on the right-hand side of the narrow wooded lanes of the country. But if this is so, we cannot tell why other countries adopted the opposite custom.

In Great Britain the *Highway Code* sets out many other rules and suggestions with which all users of the roads, pedestrians as well as bicyclists and motorists, should be familiar. Applicants for driving licences are questioned on the Code. Here are some of the main rules. When overtaking, a motorist must move out to the off-side of the road, that is, the right-hand side in Great Britain. But he should not overtake or turn to the right unless he can see that the road ahead is clear of on-coming traffic. He should not overtake, therefore, at a corner, at cross-roads, over a sharp rise, or at a pedestrian crossing (*see* ROAD TRAFFIC CONTROL). Motorists must give way to pedestrians who are getting on and off tramcars or buses, and they should go slowly when passing horses or herds of animals. Vehicles should be stopped as close to the side of the road as possible, and should not be left near bends or the brows of hills. The correct ways of giving signals for stopping, turning to the left and right, and so on are also shown in the *Highway Code*, a booklet published by His Majesty's Stationery Office.

2. SEA. The sea is an international highway, and any rule of the road at sea must be internationally recognized. The 'Regulations for the Prevention of Collision at Sea' were drawn up at an international conference in 1910, and a revised version—the one normally used—was agreed to at another conference in 1929, though it was never actually ratified by all the governments concerned.

The rules lay down which of two ships meeting is to give way. (The other vessel must, of course, maintain its course and speed to avoid confusion.) They describe the lights which must be shown at night by various types of vessels when under way or at anchor, ranging from the familiar red and green side lights carried by all ships when under way to less well-known ones such as those shown by a ship drifting out of control. They also give the signals which must be sounded in fog, which, like the lights to be carried, are different for ships under way and at anchor.

A ship 'under way' (that is, neither anchored nor aground, though not necessarily moving), in addition to side lights, must show steaming lights and a stern light. The two side lights (sometimes known as bow lights) each shine over 10 points of the compass ($112\frac{1}{2}$ degrees) from right ahead on their respective sides, green to starboard, red to port. The stern light, which is white, shines over the remainder of the circle (*see* Fig. 1). These three lights are carried by all ships under way, of whatever sort. The steaming lights, which are only carried by steamers, are two white lights, one mounted above and behind the other, which shine over the combined arcs of the two side lights. In a ship with two masts, one is mounted on each mast. The purpose of all these lights is so that the officer on watch on the bridge of a ship can understand the course being steered by another ship near him, and know which ship has the right of way, and what he must do.

There are many other combinations of lights. A ship that is anchored shows two white lights, one higher and more forward than the other, shining all round. A ship afloat but not under control shows two all round red lights, one above

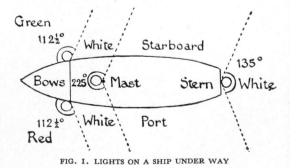

FIG. I. LIGHTS ON A SHIP UNDER WAY

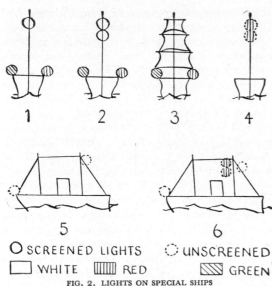

O SCREENED LIGHTS ⊙ UNSCREENED
☐ WHITE ▥ RED ▨ GREEN

FIG. 2. LIGHTS ON SPECIAL SHIPS

1. Steamer under way. 2. Steamer towing another vessel under way. 3. Sailing ship under way. 4. Ship out of control, not under way. 5. Vessel at anchor or fishing. 6. Vessel aground in a fairway

the other. She puts out her steaming lights, and, if she is not moving, her side lights also. A tug when towing shows two, or in some circumstances three, white lights, one above the other, in place of the normal steaming lights. Various lights are carried by different types of fishing-vessels to show in which direction their nets are lying. Lights are not shown by day, of course, but a ship at anchor hoists a black ball 2 feet in diameter up in the rigging, while a ship not under control hoists two, one above the other.

In fog, sound signals are made on the siren by steamers, on the fog-horn by sailing ships, and on the ship's bell by ships at anchor. Ships under way make their signal every 2 minutes, and ships at anchor every minute. As with lights, there are special signals for special ships.

The rule which lays down which of two ships approaching each other is to give way is as follows. If two steamers are meeting end on, each keeps to starboard. If one ship is overtaking another, it must keep out of the way of the ship being overtaken until it is 'finally past and clear'. If two ships are approaching each other on converging courses, the one which has the other on its starboard has to give way. A steamship always gives way to a sailing ship. The rules for sailing ships, which are more involved as they have to take into account the direction of the wind, are nowadays really only of interest to yachtsmen (*see* SAILING, Vol. IX).

The rules are the authority on which lawsuits arising out of collisions at sea are judged, and every officer who has to keep watch on the bridge must know their meaning—as every motorist must know the *Highway Code*. The well-known doggerel rhymes summarizing the various rules are good aids to the memory. In the case of two ships converging:

> If to your starboard red appear
> It is your duty to keep clear;
> To act as judgement says is proper
> To starboard—or port—back—or stop her.

> But when upon your port is seen
> A steamer's starboard light of green,
> There's not so much for you to do,
> For green to port keeps clear of you.

3. AIR. The advent of the fast, all-weather aircraft, and the demand for frequent and regular services, have made it essential to establish strict rules for air-traffic control. Air control is based on railway signal-box principles. Between stations, a train is always under the control of a signalman, who ensures its safe conduct through his own section and then passes it on to the next. Each signalman receives news in advance of a train's approach, and can refuse to accept it if the line is not clear (*see* SIGNALLING, RAILWAY).

So it is in the air; but instead of running on lines, aircraft fly within air 'corridors' called Flight Information Regions, and instead of seeing signal posts, they rely entirely on radio contact (*see* NAVIGATION, AIR). Language difficulties are largely overcome by the use of an international code of simple words.

Before taking off, a pilot must give details of his intended flight to the airfield authority. These intentions are signalled to control centres all along his route. Thus an aircraft on a long journey flies from one Flight Information Region to another, possibly along a defined 'corridor', or at any rate at a known height and speed. For a long way round each airport there exists an Approach Control Zone, which filters all traffic destined for the airport. Close to the airport itself is a much smaller zone, known as Airfield Control Zone, which handles aircraft only when they are landing or taking off. The pilot must ask permission from the zone controller to leave any zone. This is normally given at once, and

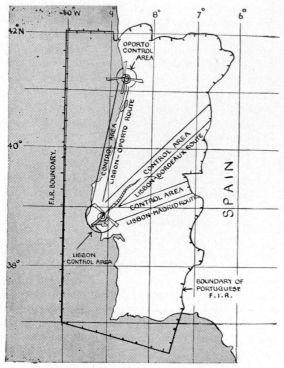

THE PORTUGUESE 'FLIGHT INFORMATION REGION'

country, and the Volga and Don, Dnieper, and Dniester rivers, are navigable to sea-going ships. The construction of three canals has made it possible to travel by water right across Russia from the Baltic to the Black Sea (*see* Fig. 1).

The linking of Russia's waterways was an important part of the second Five Year Plan of the Soviet Union. The first canal to be completed links the White Sea through Lakes Onega and Ladoga to the Baltic Sea, with an extension from Lake Onega to connect with the River VOLGA (q.v. Vol. III). The last canal in the scheme connects the River Don to the Volga near Stalingrad. But the greatest and perhaps most important achievement was the opening, in 1937, of an 80-mile canal to connect the Volga with Moscow, which lies on the unnavigable River Moskva, and so make possible the development of Moscow as an important inland port. This canal also brings a fresh supply of water to meet the increasing industrial and domestic needs of Moscow; a 13-mile stretch of the canal is made into a great reservoir for this purpose. More excavation and earth and concrete work were required to build this canal than any other, except the PANAMA CANAL (q.v.). Everything on its route had to be cleared away; even

the pilot must immediately report his position to the controller of the next zone. That routine is repeated at intervals on a long flight.

As a pilot nears his destination, he makes radio contact with Approach Control, and flies under their directions until they hand him over to Airfield Control (*see* AIRPORT).

In fair weather certain control instructions are relaxed. A pilot must be ready, however, to revert to full control from the ground at a minute's notice and to place himself completely in the hands of the controller. In bad weather, the work of Airfield Control becomes very complicated. Some aircraft have to 'queue up' by circling in the sky while awaiting permission to land; at the same time other craft on the ground are queuing to take off.

See also SAFETY AT SEA; NAVIGATION, AIR.

RUNIC WRITING, *see* ALPHABET.

RUNWAY (AERODROME), *see* AIRPORT.

RUSSIAN CANALS. Russia has more great inland waterways than any other European

FIG. 1. RUSSIAN WATERWAYS

whole villages were removed. Great barrages and dams were built, and many pumping-stations and hydro-electric power-stations set up. Seventeen road and railway bridges cross the canal.

The most serious engineering difficulty which faced the builders was the rise of land which lay between the Volga and Moscow. This was overcome by a series of ten great LOCKS (q.v.), which raised the canal in steps and then lowered it again. Fig. 2 shows how these locks were spaced; at one place the water is raised 105 feet by a series of four locks in quick succession. These great locks, each of them 951½ feet long and 98½ feet wide, empty and fill in 13 minutes, and are worked by a centralized automatic control with the minimum use of human labour and the least possible risk of mistake or accident. From one single control-point, one man can control the working of the canal and the movement of

FIG. 2. DIAGRAM OF THE LOCKS ON THE MOSKVA–VOLGA CANAL

all the ships along the whole 80-mile stretch, and know exactly what is happening at every point.

With the help of these three canals, the best use can be made of Russia's navigable rivers, and the development of Moscow as an industrial centre becomes much more practical. Russian rivers, however, are not navigable for many months of the year, because stretches of them are ice-bound.

See also CANALS; RIVER NAVIGATION.
See also Vol. III: U.S.S.R.

RUSSIAN LANGUAGE, *see* SLAVONIC LANGUAGES.

S

SAFETY AT SEA. Nowadays rules to safeguard the lives of sea-passengers and sailors are laid down for all ships. It had been a long-standing rule that every ship must carry lifeboats; but after the sinking of the *Titanic* in 1912, it was made compulsory for British ships to carry enough lifeboats to hold all their passengers and crew, and one out of every thirteen must be a motor lifeboat. As well they must carry light rafts, such as the Carley float, shaped like a large lifebuoy, on which people can sit. Many ships carry rafts on quick-release launching chutes on each side of the vessel.

Boat drill must be carried out on board ship once a week to ensure that crew and passengers know where to go and what to do in an emergency. Lifeboats carrying 100 or more people must be provided with a motor, and must carry wireless and searchlight installation. Each lifeboat must have a full equipment, including masts and orange-coloured sails, a gallon of oil for smoothing broken water, lines for use in case the lifeboat overturns, an electric signalling torch, hand flares, parachute signals with red lights, buoyant smoke signals giving off orange-coloured smoke, and a supply of food and water. With the aid of the equipment in modern ships' lifeboats many long voyages have been made from wrecks, and hundreds of lives saved. Life-jackets must be provided for every person on board. They are usually made of kapok or cork, and so designed that an unconscious man wearing one of them has his head held out of the water.

Ships are divided into watertight safety compartments, which are shut off by watertight bulkheads, with doors that can be mechanically closed from the ship's bridge. A ship 400 feet long will be divided into eight such compartments by seven bulkheads, one bulkhead being added for every extra 80 feet on the ship's length.

Ships are built with double bottoms, so that even if the outer skin is pierced, water will not come into the ship. The space between the two skins is used for carrying such commodities as oil fuel. The cry of 'All hands to the pumps' used to be heard in ships in danger; but now all ocean-going ships have pumps worked by machinery.

Appliances for detecting fire before it has got a hold have greatly lessened the danger from fire. Modern ships often have ducts which draw air from all parts of the vessel into the chart room, so that the officer of the watch there can immediately detect smoke and can tell where it comes from. Bulkheads and doors are made of fire-resisting materials as far as possible. The ceilings of cabins and public rooms are often fitted with sprinkler points which hold a store of water kept in by wax or some similar material; this melts and lets the water out when the heat in the room rises.

All ocean-going ships bear the Plimsoll mark or 'load line' (a line passing through a circle),

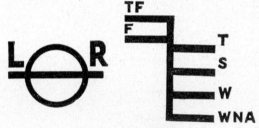

THE PLIMSOLL MARK

Line through circle is general line below which a ship may not be loaded. LR stands for 'Lloyd's Register'. The density of water differs according to temperature and saltiness, and a ship may be more heavily laden in some waters. Horizontal lines on the right show variations allowed. WNA. Winter North Atlantic; W. Winter elsewhere; S. Summer; T. Tropics; F. Freshwater; TF. Tropical Freshwater

painted on the hull (*see* diagram). A ship must not be loaded so heavily that the mark sinks below sea-level. This mark is named after Samuel Plimsoll, M.P., whose agitation in the 1870's put an end to the practice of sending to sea overloaded and heavily insured old ships (known to sailors as 'coffin ships'), from which the owners made a profit if they sank.

Safety at sea concerns all maritime nations, and international conferences are held to discuss life-saving devices and safety rules.

See also LIGHTHOUSES AND LIGHTSHIPS; LIFEBOAT; CLIMATE AND COMMUNICATIONS, Section 3; RULE OF THE ROAD, Section 2; WRECKS.

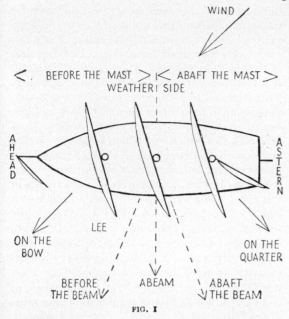

FIG. I

ing, she can sail on courses through 20 points of the COMPASS (q.v.), but cannot sail on courses less than 6 points either side of the direction from which the wind is blowing. In Fig. 2 the wind is blowing from the south-west. The ship, therefore, can sail WNW. (close-hauled on the port tack), NW. (wind abeam—the easiest course to sail the ship on), N. (wind on the quarter, and the ship sailing her fastest for the particular strength of wind blowing, every sail in full use), NE. (sailing dead before the wind—uncomfortable and wasteful as the after canvas stops the wind reaching the fore canvas, and the ship sails her slowest), and so on, round to SSE., when the ship will be sailing close-hauled again, but on the starboard tack. The ship cannot sail on courses between SSE. and SW. or between SW. and WNW.

Fig. 2 will help to explain the meaning of sailing 'close-hauled' and on the 'starboard' or 'port tack', for the three lines across the hulls show diagramatically how the yards are braced to suit the wind (a yard is the long piece of wood placed horizontally to support the top of the sail). It will be noticed that, when the ship is sailing as close to the wind as she can (that is, as nearly into the wind), the yards are braced sharp up, so as almost to lie fore and aft; she is then said to be sailing close-hauled. The other phrase is more difficult; the lower corners or 'clews' of the square mainsail or foresail of a full-rigged

SAILING. Some of the words in the special vocabulary of sailing must be explained first of all. In his own ship a sailor reckons position by the mast—he speaks of things as 'before' (in front of) or 'abaft' (behind) it. He says just 'the mast' in the singular, as if he were referring to the single great tree in the medieval ship before A.D. 1450 (*see* SAILING SHIPS); his own ship may have three or four masts. As he looks round the horizon from the deck of his ship, he describes objects as being ahead, astern, abeam, abaft, or before the beam, on his bow, or on his quarter (*see* Fig. 1). This gives the angle they make with the ship's course. The side on which they are may be shown by adding port (left) or starboard (right). Starboard was originally 'steerboard', and was the side on which the steering rudder was hung in Viking ships. The port side was earlier known as larboard. But in sailing ships the side is more often described in relation to the wind: it is called 'lee' on the side sheltered from the wind, and 'weather' on the side from which the wind is blowing.

Any floating body drives before the wind, but an efficient sailing ship can make her way, though not directly, in any direction, even to windward, without using paddle, oar, or motor. Let us consider a three-masted sailing ship of the last days of sail (*see* Fig. 3), and see on what courses she can sail in relation to the wind's direction, and how she is steered. Roughly speak-

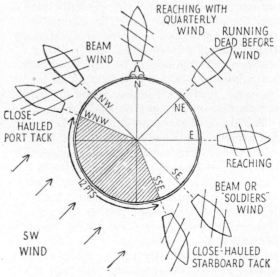

FIG. 2. DIRECTIONS IN WHICH A SHIP CAN SAIL WITH THE WIND SW.

The lines across the ship show the direction of the sails

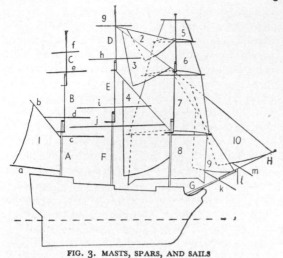

FIG. 3. MASTS, SPARS, AND SAILS

A. Mizzen mast; *B.* Mizzen topmast; *C.* Mizzen top-gallant mast; *D.* Main top-gallant mast; *E.* Main top-mast; *F.* Main mast; *G.* Bowsprit; *H.* Jib-boom; *a.* Spanker boom; *b.* Gaff; *c.* Crossjack yard; *d.* Mizzen topsail yard; *e.* Mizzen topgallant yard; *f.* Mizzen royal yard; *g.* Main royal yard; *h.* Main topgallant yard; *i.* Main topsail yard; *j.* Main yard; *k.* Spritsail yard; *l.* Dolphin striker; *m.* Sprit-sail topsail yard. 1. Mizzen or spanker; 2. Main topgallant staysail; 3. Middle staysail; 4. Main topmast staysail; 5. Fore royal sail; 6. Fore topgallant sail; 7. Fore top-sail; 8. Fore course or foresail; 9. Fore topmast staysail; 10. Jib.

ship are controlled by two ropes to each clew, of which one leads aft and is called the sheet, and the other leads forward and is called the tack. When a ship is sailing close-hauled and her yards are sharp braced to meet the wind, the fore-sail and the main-sail have their lee-sheets hauled taut (leading aft) and their weather tacks hauled taut (leading forward); in this position the weather tacks are said to be hauled on board; and according to which side the tacks are hauled on board, port or starboard, so the ship is said to be sailing on the 'port' or 'starboard tack'.

A full-rigged ship cannot, as has been said, sail nearer to the wind than 6 points. Even so, when sailing close-hauled, her hull is pushed by the wind to leeward as well as being driven forwards; this is called making leeway. The ship can thus only work right 'into the wind's eye' by taking a zigzag course; she must sail a certain distance on one tack, then alter her course, trim her sails again, and continue a certain distance on the other tack. By this method, which is called 'beating to windward', she will slowly work her way against the wind.

So far only the sails of the ship have been considered, but the hull also has its part to play. It

has already been seen how the ship may be pushed to leeward; a hull that is long and deep will resist this sideways movement, and will slip easily forward through the water. But the wind in the towering pile of canvas, 145 feet high, will also heel the ship over and strive to overset her. To withstand this force she must have stability, the power to return to an upright position when heeled over. Stability is obtained by breadth of hull and also by ballast, which is weight carried low down within the hull. A ship that stands up to her canvas well and keeps reasonably upright is said to be 'stiff'. The trim or adjustment in this respect of a ship can be altered. Ballast or a heavy cargo in the hold makes a ship stiff; the same ship, unballasted, and with a deck cargo, would be top-heavy and dangerous under sail. The proper trim of a sailing ship is very important and of great concern to her officers. Thus it will be seen that the design of a sailing ship, as of all ships, is a matter of compromise: she must slip easily through the water for the sake of speed, have stability for the sake of safety, and also be roomy within so that she may carry a big cargo.

The ship is steered by means of her rudder, which is hinged on the stern-post by a number of rings (or gudgeons) on the rudder, which fit over projections called pintles on the stern-post. It is free to move from side to side when operated by the tiller, a long bar which is slipped through or over the rudder-head. For several centuries, when the helm order 'Starboard' was called out, the tiller was pushed to starboard; this moved the rudder to port; the water driving past the ship's side caught against the rudder, and pushed the ship round, so that her stern turned to starboard and her bow to port (*see* Fig. 4). By an international agreement made in 1931 to avoid confusion, the practice was reversed; the helm order 'Starboard!' now means that the ship's head should turn to starboard. The tiller is now moved by a wheel, except on very small vessels.

Helm orders in sailing ships, however, are usually given in terms relating to the wind and the sails. Thus 'Up helm!' and 'Bear up!' mean move the tiller to windward; 'Down helm!', move it to leeward; 'Helm 's alee!', the tiller is to leeward. The order may also be given 'Bear down on' something; this means direct the ship's head to leeward towards some object.

When beating to windward, the change from sailing on one tack to sailing on another is made by using the rudder and trimming the sails so

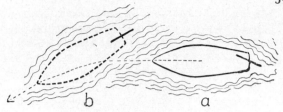

FIG. 4. THE ACTION OF THE RUDDER

a. Rudder to port, ship begins to alter course; *b.* Rudder straight, ship steady in new course

that the ship turns either into the wind through 12 points of the compass, or before the wind through 20 points of the compass. The first manœuvre is called tacking; the second wearing. To tack a square-rigged ship requires perfect weather conditions, for only in a calm sea can one be sure that she will 'come up' into the wind and that her sails will fill on the other tack. Her yards must be braced round at exactly the right moment or else she will fail to come round or 'miss stays'. In that case she will have to be sailed again in the original tack so as to gather steerage way for another attempt. In bad weather it may be dangerous for a ship to miss stays; she may hang up in the wind or even move stern-first. The surer way of changing tacks is to sail the ship the long way round before the wind, squaring off the yards and then bracing them up sharp on the other tack.

See also SAILING SHIPS.

See also Vol. IX: SAILING.

SAILING SHIPS. The sailing ship took many centuries to reach its final and most efficient forms. The story of sail from the earliest days has been traced, in historical order, in the articles PRIMITIVE SHIPS, CLASSICAL SHIPS, and VIKING SHIPS. The present article deals with the growth of ships from the Middle Ages, the period in which the full-rigged ship of the great days of sail had its origins.

The fleet built for the Norman invasion of England in 1066 is shown in the famous pictorial record of the Conquest, the BAYEUX TAPESTRY (q.v. Vol. XII). The Norman ships were very similar to the Viking and other Norse ships, to which the Normans were accustomed. In the next 400 years ships developed very slowly.

At the time of the Conquest, men-at-arms, knights, horses, and stores were carried over in clinker-built vessels which could be sailed only if the wind blew the way the fleet wanted to go;

otherwise they had to be rowed. The vessels were alike at either end and carried shields along the gunwales or sides. It is difficult to judge the size of these ships, but we know that the *White Ship*, which was lost on the Normandy coast in A.D. 1120, had 300 persons on board. Her crew included fifty experienced rowers as well as men-at-arms. She was moving under sail and oars, trying to overtake the rest of the Royal Fleet, when she was wrecked.

Ships grew in size and made longer voyages as trade increased. English ships went to Iceland for fish, to the Baltic for timber, to Gascony for wine, and they took wool to the Low Countries. The Genoese and Venetians sailed ships direct to England and Flanders from the Mediterranean. CRUSADES and PILGRIMAGES (qq.v. Vol. I) meant that large bodies of men travelled long distances by sea.

The ships of northern Europe and those used in the Mediterranean differed considerably. In the north, sail almost took the place of the oar, while in the south, the rowed galley was used as much as sail. The southern sailing ship hoisted the triangular fore-and-aft sail known as the lateen. Fig. 1, a ship of the 13th century from an illuminated manuscript, shows the single square sail used in the north and the steering oar slung from the starboard (steer-board) quarter. The top of the stem is ornamented with the carved figure of a bird. The mast is supported by fixed ropes or shrouds. Nail-heads are prominent along the ship's sides.

FIG. I. 13TH CENTURY SHIP

Voyage of St. John to Patmos. From an *Apocalypse* in the Bodleian Library

FIG. 2. A SEA-FIGHT

From a manuscript in the Fitzwilliam Museum of about
A.D. 1270

In those days merchant ships seized for the Royal service were quickly turned into fighting ships. Light stages were erected as 'castles' fore and aft, and at the mast-head. A captain, lieutenant, and men-at-arms were placed on board to 'fight the ship', and the civilian master and ship's company were retained to sail the ship. In action, ships were brought close together and fought castle to castle (Fig. 2). Later, cabins were made under these castles, which were soon built into the ships as permanent structures, useful both in peace and war. Fig. 3, copied from the seal of the town of Ipswich of 1200, shows permanent castles fore and aft. It also shows a ship with differently shaped ends, a long, high, over-hanging stem-post, and a shorter, straighter stern-post. Instead of the steering oar slung over the quarter, there is a rudder of the form we know to-day, hung in the centre line of the ship from the stern-post. Important ships, usually those in the Royal service, were gay with shields hung up and devices painted on the hull, with decorated sails, and flags and banners waving from mast and flagstaffs.

Figure 4, copied from an Admiralty seal, gives a good idea of a warship of the early 15th century. Banners fly from large staves on the castles, and a swallow-tail pennon flies from a staff in the top castle. In such a vessel as this, the *Grâce Dieu*, *Jesus*, or *Holigost*, Henry V and his men went forth to Normandy. This *Grâce Dieu* should not be confused with Henry VIII's GREAT HARRY (q.v.).

By the 15th century ships were getting much larger. The *Grâce Dieu*, whose remains have been discovered in the Hamble River near Bursledon, Southampton, measured 130 feet along the keel by 48 feet beam; this ship was 1,400 tons—a gigantic size for those days. The tonnage at this date referred to the capacity of a ship for carrying casks of Bordeaux wine, a ton of wine in two butts being estimated to occupy 60 cubic feet of space. No doubt the big main-sails of these monster ships made them very

FIG. 3. SHIP WITH PERMANENT CASTLES

From the First Common Seal of Ipswich, A.D. 1200

FIG. 4. EARLY 15TH CENTURY WARSHIP

From the Seal of the Sub-Admiralty of England

unhandy. Perhaps the flagstaffs gave the idea of the next big step forward; at any rate, the

FIG. 5. 3-MASTED SHIP OF ABOUT A.D. 1450

three-masted ship appears quite suddenly about 1450 (*see* Fig. 5). Two-masted ships were evidently tried out—Henry V's *Grâce Dieu* was a two-master. Probably the foremast was tried before the mizzen-mast, but both positions may have been tried. The lateen mizzen (or rear) sail is a Mediterranean sail, as we have already seen. The top-sail was set at first on a small top-mast erected in the 'fighting top' (a platform on top of the mast).

An important Mediterranean feature introduced into the north during the 15th century is carvel building, a method whereby the planks are placed edge to edge, giving a smooth surface, and not overlapping as in the earlier clinker-built northern ships. During this period the larger ships were all four-masted, and remained so, until the beginning of the 17th century.

Careful planning of the shapes and positions of the sails—the 'sail-plan'—enabled the sailor to suit his vessel to the varying wind and weather, and so make it more seaworthy and able to sail to windward—that is, against the direction of the wind, which was probably not possible with the single square-sail (*see* SAILING). This made possible the great voyages of discovery of the 15th and 16th centuries. Hulks, barges, balingers, and pinnaces were rigged much the same, differing only in size—indeed the same ship is often described by different names in old records.

Towards the end of the Middle Ages ships of 200 or 300 tons were in common use. These had three or four masts with a square head-sail, the sprit-sail set under the bowsprit, top-sails set over the fore- and main-sails, and lateens set on the mizzen-mast. The fore- and main-sails were known as the 'courses'. A small sail called a bonnet was laced to the body of a big sail, and could be removed in strong winds to reduce canvas. The shrouds (or fixed ropes) carried ratlines (forming rope ladders) so that men could easily climb aloft (*see* Colour Plate opposite p. 320).

The Mediterranean carrack, a combination of northern and southern forms, was recognizable by its overhanging forecastle and a big inverted V-shaped opening under it. Men went aloft by a simple rope ladder up the mainmast, and this mast was set up with tackles (movable ropes) instead of shrouds (fixed ropes). This carrack type was copied by the shipwrights of Bayonne on the west coast of France, who introduced it in northern waters, where it became popular, though in time it lost its distinctive features (*see* Fig. 6).

The caravel (sometimes spelt 'carvel') was a small ship of Spanish or Portuguese origin, rigged with two lateen sails.

During the 16th century the differences between a merchant ship and a warship became more obvious. The galley, the oar-driven ship of the Mediterranean, was never used successfully in the north. The galleass, a large galley also using sails, was much used by the seafaring

FIG. 6. CARRACK

FIG. 7. GALLEON OF 1588

people of the famous Italian republics of Venice and Genoa. The Portuguese attempted to build a sailing ship called a galleon on galley lines, though longer and lower, with the galley's pointed beak-head for boarding the enemy. Elizabethan seamen copied and modified the galleon. The successful men-of-war of Queen Elizabeth's Navy, the ARK ROYAL and REVENGE (qq.v.) were built like galleons. The rig and sail-plan was the same for all; the form of the hull distinguished the type of vessel (see Fig. 7).

The beginning of the 17th century saw a marked development in rigging. A little mast was erected on the round platform or 'top' at the end of the bowsprit, called the sprit-sail topmast, and on it was set the top-sail. This remained a characteristic feature of the rig of ships from about 1615 to the end of the century. After its introduction, the fourth mast, or bonaventure mizzen, began to disappear, and instead a square mizzen top-sail was set over the lateen sail. The yard which spread the foot of the mizzen top-sail was called in English 'the crossjack', and no sail was carried on it until late in the 19th century. During the 17th century reef points for reducing the size of a sail began to appear. Foot ropes were fitted under the yards for the men to stand on when reefing or furling the sails.

At this time the hulls of ships, especially English ships, were very beautifully and elaborately carved. The tops were round, and the crows' feet and other elaborate arrangements of rigging were unmistakable marks of the 17th-century ship. Large flags and streamers were flown on festive occasions.

The cutter, which became a famous English type of ship, probably came from Holland at the

Restoration. Schooners and brigs also appear after 1700. During the 18th century the sail-plan changed little. By the end of the century 'royals' (small sails above the top-gallant sails) were commonly carried on all three masts. The 18th-century hull had less ornamentation and none of the expensive gilding of the 17th century, decoration being almost entirely confined to the figurehead and stern ornaments. In larger ships about 1705 wheel steering replaced the cumbersome whipstaff (a long lever working the rudder).

About 1760 the practice of fastening sheets of copper to the outside of ships below the water-line made for greater speed. Copper did not become fouled by crusts of vegetation and shell-fish nor was it eaten by the Teredo worm, as had been the wooden hulls of earlier ships, and so the ships could move more easily through the water. Coppering, although expensive, soon became popular, for it did away with the necessity for periodic scraping.

By the end of the 18th century the maximum size in oak-built ships had been reached. Ships of the EAST INDIA COMPANY (q.v. Vol. VII), the finest English merchantmen, were about 1,000 tons, and the VICTORY (q.v.) herself no more than 2,162. Timber for shipbuilding was getting scarce, and experiments were made by replacing certain natural shapes of timber with iron fittings. This was the beginning of a great change. The mixture of wood and metal was soon followed by the all-iron hull, which made it possible to build much larger ships. Then came the first steam-engines, with paddle and screw, and these altered the whole build and character of ships.

But while these changes were coming in, sailing ships reached the height of their development in the famous CLIPPER SHIPS (q.v.). American rivalry in the middle of the 19th century caused British merchant shipbuilders to build for speed, and soon British clipper ships were competing with Americans in carrying tea or other kinds of cargo at record speeds. But as steamships improved, large sailing ships began to lose their place, though they continued for a time to run the long routes carrying wool, and then grain from Australia round the Cape, and nitrates from Chile round the Horn.

For a time great iron ships of 2,000 tons were built, which could be handled by small crews. The four-masted barque with its much divided sail-plan used small steam-engines to haul on the

National Maritime Museum

EAST INDIA COMPANY'S SHIP 'ATLAS', BUILT IN 1812 AND CARRYING 28 GUNS
Oil painting by W. J. Huggins

ropes, and had chain and wire in place of rope wherever possible. The steel topmasts and lower masts were made in one piece. But by the end of the 19th century sail was little used for commerce. To-day it survives only for pleasure in the form of yachts (*see* SAILING BOATS, Vol. IX), and in a few small coasting vessels.

See also SHIP; SAILING; SEA TRAVEL; STEAMSHIPS.
See also Vol. X: BATTLESHIP.

SAILOR, *see* SHIP'S COMPANY.

SALVAGE. The salvage of wrecked ships may mean the refloating of stranded ships, or the lifting of sunken ships, or the recovery of treasure or valuable cargo lost at sea.

A stranded vessel is usually pulled into deep water by TUGS (q.v.); and then salvage pumps keep her afloat while she is repaired enough to reach dry dock for more permanent repairs.

When a sunken ship is to be lifted, divers are sent down to place huge wires under her. These wires are secured at low tide to two specially constructed salvage vessels, one on each side of the wreck. When the rising tide lifts the vessels on the surface, they lift with them the sunken ship on the wire cradle. The three vessels, two on the surface and one submerged, are then taken to a suitable beach where the wreck can lie for temporary repairs. Sometimes, when conditions are suitable, floating structures known as 'camels' are filled with water and submerged on each side of the sunken vessel to which they are then attached. When the water is pumped out of them, they rise, lifting the wreck with them.

The raising of the German fleet, scuttled in Scapa Flow at the end of the First World War, was a spectacular work of salvage. Twenty-three destroyers were raised with wires and 'camels' as described and towed to shore to be broken up. The huge battleships and cruisers, most of which had capsized and were lying on the bottom upside down, were more difficult to raise. After several experiments, divers succeeded in bolting

Port of London Authority

WRECK LIGHTERS AT WORK IN THE THAMES TIDEWAY

air-locks on to the ships, and compressed air was pumped into them until one after another they rose, still upside down, to the surface. These also were towed away and broken up for their steel and fittings.

Probably the most difficult salvage work ever undertaken was the recovery of a large amount of gold and silver from the wreck of the P. and O. liner, the *Egypt*. The ship was sunk by collision in a fog off Ushant in 1922. The wreck's position was in some doubt, and the water was about 300 feet deep—too much for the diving gear normally used. An Italian salvage company, which had developed an observation chamber and special grabs, decided to try to salvage the treasure. After locating an obstruction on the bed of the ocean believed to be the wreck of the *Egypt*, the diver was lowered in the observation chamber. He confirmed by telephone that he was alongside a great sunken ship, and the work began. The diver gave directions by telephone for the lowering of explosive charges, and when these had been fired, he directed the lowering and working of the powerful grabs which tore away the shattered steel work. Fragment by fragment the charges and grabs ate into the ship until the diver could direct the grabs to the ship's safe.

The salvage company then began the slow and difficult work of blasting and tearing a way to the strong room where the treasure was kept. The work went on, in spite of severe set-backs, until on 22 June 1932, 10 years after the *Egypt* had foundered, the first ingots of gold were recovered from the strong room. The salvage company finally ceased work in July 1935, having recovered gold and silver valued at £1,183,000.

Another famous salvage undertaking was carried out by a handful of men with no special gear or equipment. In October 1940, the tanker *San Demetrio* sailed in convoy from Halifax with a cargo of petrol. The convoy was attacked, and the *San Demetrio* set on fire by a German warship. Knowing the dangerous nature of their cargo, the crew abandoned the ship. After some hours the crew of one of the lifeboats found the *San Demetrio* again, drifting and deserted, and still burning. They boarded her and set about putting out the fires; then, with a crew of only sixteen, several of whom were injured and burned, and one of whom was dying, and with practically no navigational aids, they sailed the ship over to Britain and berthed her under her own power. They saved not only a valuable ship but also a substantial part of her cargo. The owners of the vessel willingly paid out the sums awarded to the men for salvage, and guaranteed to them the costs of the necessary legal action. Salvage awards are always made by special legal courts, and the amounts awarded to the salvors are based on the value of the ship and cargo saved and the skill and risks taken in the work.

Flotsam and jetsam are goods lost at sea, as distinct from property lost ashore. Flotsam covers all goods that float, jetsam all that sink to the sea-bed. When flotsam reaches the shore and is washed up on the beaches, it becomes wreck. Flotsam and jetsam belong to their original owner, if he can be found; if not to the Crown. All wreck is Crown property.

See also DERELICTS; WRECKS AND WRECKERS; DIVERS AND DIVING APPARATUS.

SANSKRIT. This literally means 'refined, perfected', and is the name given to the ancient classical language of India, in which is written the Hindu literature of centuries. Strictly, the name applies only to the form of the language defined by the grammar of Pāṇini about 400 B.C.: he composed his grammar in order to teach the

Like Latin and Greek, Sanskrit is highly inflected, that is, it has many different word endings which are used to show the part the word plays in the sentence. The noun has eight cases, having, in addition to Nominative, Vocative, and the others found in Latin, separate forms for Locative or place-case, and Instrumental or agent-case. For example, *hastas* means 'the hand'; *haste* 'in the hand'; *hastena* 'by means of the hand'. The similarity in structure led western scholars to realize, towards the end of the 18th century, that Sanskrit was closely related to Latin and Greek; and they soon discovered that all INDO-EUROPEAN LANGUAGES (q.v.) formed one family of which Sanskrit is the oldest known member. Below are a few examples of words in Sanskrit which resemble words in English and Greek.

Sanskrit	Greek	English
duhitar	thugatēr	daughter
dvār	thūra	door
trayas	treis	three
madhu	methu	mead
ūdhar	outhar	udder

See also INDIAN LANGUAGES; LANGUAGE, HISTORY OF.
See also Vol. I: INDIAN CIVILIZATIONS; HINDUISM.

BUDDHIST MANUSCRIPT FROM BENGAL
Bodleian Library
Written in Sanskrit (Kutila script) A.D. 1095–1105 with illuminations showing Buddha and Indra

correct form of speech of the learned men of his day, and to protect the language from 'popular' corruptions. But Sanskrit is often used in a wider sense to include the older form of the same language in which is written the ancient religious literature of the Vedas. The oldest Vedic language is found in the collection of religious hymns known as the *Rig-Veda* (*see* SACRED BOOKS, Section 2, Vol. I) which was probably completed before 1000 B.C., and possibly much earlier. The language of the *Rig-Veda* differs from Classical Sanskrit both in vocabulary and grammar. Many words common in the older period have gone out of use, and new ones have become current. Vedic has also a much more complicated grammar.

SANTE FÉ TRAIL, *see* AMERICAN TRAILS.

SANTA MARIA, THE. This was the ship in which the Italian-born sea-captain Christopher COLUMBUS (q.v. Vol. V) sailed across the Atlantic and discovered the New World. Columbus did not set out to discover new land, but to find a new way to China and India. In the light of the belief that the world was a round shape, he very reasonably thought he could do so by sailing westward across the Atlantic, for he knew nothing of the whole continent of America nor of the Pacific Ocean which lay between. For some time he tried to persuade the King and Queen of Spain to provide him with ships and men to

A SHIP OF THE TIME OF COLUMBUS
Woodcut from *De Insulis Inventis* by Columbus, 1493

make this voyage of discovery. When, in 1492, Columbus had received the King's support, he was sent to a little port near Seville, where the inhabitants were in disfavour with the King and as a punishment were ordered to provide and equip two caravels, small, fast-sailing ships. Columbus chartered in addition a larger ship, the *Santa Maria*, direct from its owner.

We learn from the diary kept by Columbus that the *Santa Maria* was rigged as a typical ship of the period and carried a mainsail, foresail and mizzen, spritsail, and main-topsail. He had ninety men with him in all, and the *Santa Maria* probably carried forty of them. Her size has been variously estimated; she is unlikely to have measured more than 75 feet in over all length, and was probably of a carrack construction (*see* SAILING SHIPS), relatively short on the keel compared with her over-all length, and with great breadth. We know she carried her ship's boat

on her deck. There would have been a poop-deck aft, with cabins below, and a higher forecastle over the stem, raking forward.

Columbus sailed for the Canaries with his three vessels at dawn on 3 August. After delay amongst the Canary Islands he sailed away into the unknown on 6 September. On 10 October there was nearly a mutiny among the frightened sailors; but the next day one of the caravels, the *Nina*, picked up in the water a green branch bearing a little flower, which indicated the nearness of land. That night Columbus himself saw an unexplained light, and at 2 a.m. on the morning of 12 October 1492, the lookout on the forecastle of his other caravel, the *Pinta*, saw a white sand-cliff gleaming in the moonlight. This was the first sight of the New World; the land was part of one of the many islands off the coast of the American mainland; the island is unknown, though some geographers believe it was Watling Island in the Bahama group. The *Santa Maria* was later wrecked on Christmas Eve, and Columbus came home in the *Pinta*, believing that he had reached the Indies. Ever since then, the islands near America have been known as the West Indies.

See also EXPLORATION; SAILING SHIPS.

SCANDINAVIAN LANGUAGES. These, which include Danish, Swedish, and Norwegian, are all descended from Old Norse, the Northern branch of the parent language, Primitive Germanic (*see* GERMANIC LANGUAGES). Swedish is not confined to Sweden but is also spoken by a large number of people in Finland.

During the Middle Ages, Danish gradually replaced Norwegian as the language of the upper classes in Norway, the peasants continuing to speak Norwegian. This state of affairs has really survived until the present day, so that there are now two languages in Norway. *Riksmål* 'state language' is really a form of Danish, and is the language in which the Norwegian dramatist Ibsen wrote, and what we normally mean when we speak of Norwegian. It has been developed until it is entirely different from Danish in its spelling, which has been several times reformed, and also in pronunciation, grammar, and vocabulary, many native Norwegian words having been taken into it. The second language of Norway is *Landsmål* 'country language', which was created in the 19th century out of the various Norwegian peasant dialects, and has become more widely used since, because of a definite movement to encourage it.

Several other languages have developed out of Old Norse, which spread to the colonies invaded by the Vikings from the 8th to the 11th centuries. These include Icelandic, the language of Iceland, and Faeroese, spoken in the Faeroe Isles. Icelandic is specially interesting because it has one of the best medieval literatures; the SAGAS (q.v Vol. I) and the two famous mythological collections of ancient poems called *eddas* are well known.

See also Vol. I: DANES; NORWEGIANS; SWEDES.

SCHOONER, *see* SAILING SHIPS.

SEALS. A seal is the impression made on a substance, usually soft, such as melted sealing-wax, from a design engraved on metal or some other hard material. The word is sometimes used of the object on which the design is engraved, but the proper name for this is a die or matrix. Finger rings often have a device engraved on a gem, or, where there is no gem, directly on the metal: another type of small seal is the fob-seal, so called from the fob or pocket in which it could be carried. Both of these types are commonly called signets.

The seal is applied to a document to show that it is authentic; sometimes it is used in place of a signature, or sometimes with it, as further proof that the document is authorized by the owner of the seal. Seals may also be used to close up an envelope or packet; the wax hardens when it is allowed to cool after the die has been pressed upon it.

The art of seal-engraving was practised in very early times, and matrices have been found among ancient remains of Babylon, Egypt, and Crete. In the Old Testament (Gen. xli. 42) Pharaoh passes on his ring, a signet, to Joseph as a token of authority. In Roman times both seal and signature were used to give authenticity to documents, and the seal was used for closing or fastening documents. With the collapse of the Western Roman Empire in the 5th century A.D. there was a decline in the art of seal-engraving. Later, in the Dark Ages, when few

GREEK SEAL OF THE MID-
5TH CENTURY B.C.

SEAL OF CHICHESTER CATHEDRAL, EARLY 13TH CENTURY
Above is the matrix with which the seal (below) is impressed

could write, a sign, usually a cross, took the place of the signature, though some kings used a seal as well. In the 8th and 9th centuries the use of the classical intaglio (engraved gem) was revived and continued throughout the Middle Ages. In England, apart from one lead seal-impression (*bulla*) of Coenwulf, King of Mercia, the oldest surviving seals date from Edward the Confessor in the 11th century. After this there is a continuous series of royal seals, though before Henry I seals were not commonly used by persons other than kings.

In England the Great Seal of the King is the chief official seal, and is used for the authentication of the most important national documents, such as Acts of Parliament. The Privy Seal goes back as far as King John, and was originally used to authenticate documents connected with the King's chamber, and occasionally as a substitute for the Great Seal. The use of the Privy

OBVERSE AND REVERSE OF THE SEAL OF ROBERT FITZWALTER, EARLY 13TH CENTURY

Seal was abolished in 1884, although there is still a member of the British Government who holds the title of Lord Privy Seal—a post which carries no duties. The earliest municipal seals date from the end of the 12th century. There are also religious seals, belonging to churches or monasteries or their officers, as well as private seals of a religious character.

Matrices, other than engraved gems, were mostly of metal, especially silver or bronze, and the commonest shapes were circular or pointed ovals. They were either in two pieces to be used in a press, giving an impression on both sides of the wax, or single, usually with some form of handle. The design of a seal is made up of two parts—the device or picture, and the legend or words. The legend normally gives the person or institution concerned, or may be a verse or motto surrounding the device. From early medieval times the legends were generally in Latin, though French and English are also found, and English had become common by the end of the 17th century. The devices were very varied, including human figures, scenes from Scripture and the lives of saints, natural and fabulous beasts, ships, flowers and foliage, crosses and other symbols, and shields of arms either alone or combined with other subjects. Heraldic devices are first

seen on seals in the 12th century. The impressions were usually made on wax, though metal was sometimes used, especially in hot countries, and the seal was then impressed on wax spread on the document itself or attached to the strip of parchment or cord hanging from the lower end.

From being in medieval times a legal necessity on official documents, on which it is still used, the seal came to be a formality, and is now often replaced by a wafer or disk of red paper stuck on the document to represent the seal.

See also HERALDRY.

SEAPLANE. This term includes any type of aeroplane which can take off and alight on water. There are two distinct groups of such aircraft—flying boats and seaplanes proper, and many sub-divisions of each group.

With a flying boat the actual body of the aircraft (known as the hull, instead of the fuselage as in most other aircraft) floats on the water when at rest. A seaplane proper, which has an ordinary fuselage, like a land aeroplane, is supported on the water by floats, which are fitted to struts below the fuselage.

The hull of a flying boat has a planing bottom, like a speedboat (*see* MOTOR BOATS, Vol. IX). Although it is buoyant, the hull is not wide

Pan-American World Airways

FLYING BOAT WITH SPONSONS ATTACHED TO THE FUSELAGE

A TWIN FLOAT SEAPLANE

De Havilland Aircraft Co.

A Canadian de Havilland 'Beaver' used on Canadian lakes and rivers

enough to keep the aircraft balanced on water; so stabilizers, wing-tip floats and sponsons, must be provided to prevent its rolling over. The wing-tip floats are normally fitted to struts beneath the wing; to reduce drag in the air, they are generally made to retract into the wing or to fold up to form the wing-tip. Sponsons, or sea wings, are short stub wings mounted low on the sides of the hull. They are sturdier than wing-tip floats and will stand up to rougher seas; but they are heavier, cause more drag in water, and normally cannot be folded up in flight. They do, however, provide some lift after flying speed has been reached.

In the ordinary seaplane, buoyancy may be provided by two floats, mounted side by side on struts beneath the fuselage. Sometimes, instead, there is only one large float, in which case it must be fitted with wing-tip floats on each side, as with flying boats.

A combination of landplane and seaplane is known as an amphibian craft. The amphibian

is usually like a flying boat in design, but is fitted with retractable wheels which can be lowered for use on land aerodromes. One great advantage of aircraft which can alight on sheltered stretches of the sea or in harbours or river estuaries is that they do not need the vast and expensive land airports. Their navigation, however, requires seamanship as well as the qualities of an air pilot.

The large flying boat is mainly used for passenger transport and for long-range military reconnaissance. Some long-distance British air lines have used flying boats for many years. In Canada and Scandinavia flying boats and other seaplanes are in wide use; the ordinary seaplane with floats is the more popular, as the floats can be replaced by skis for use on frozen lakes in winter.

With all kinds of seaplane the shape of the hull and floats is of great importance. A shape suitable for fast movement through air is not always suitable for stability on water, nor for a clean take-off when rising from water to air. Flying boats with airscrew engines have to have these mounted fairly high to keep the airscrews clear of spray; the consequence is a deep hull, which reduces the speed of the craft in the air. The use of jet propulsion, by dispensing with airscrews, enables flying boats to be built with a shallower hull and consequently to give a better air performance.

See also AEROPLANE; AIRCRAFT ENGINES.

SEA TRAVEL. Until the invention of the steamship in the 19th century (see STEAMSHIP, HISTORY OF), travel by sea was always uncomfortable and often dangerous. People went to sea to trade, to make war, to emigrate, or to explore, but not for pleasure or for health, as they do to-day.

In the ancient world very little was known about navigation: there were no COMPASSES or SEXTANTS (qq.v.); so that ships kept as near to land as they could and, when possible, put to sea only in good weather, avoiding the spring and autumn storms. The ships of the ancient Egyptians, Greeks, and Romans (see CLASSICAL SHIPS) were not built for comfort. Egyptian ships about 1500 B.C. sometimes had canopies on deck for important people, but the rowers and other passengers sat at open benches exposed to the weather. Later Greek triremes, which were chiefly war vessels, had little room for passengers,

British Museum

THE WRECK OF THE WHITE SHIP
Drawing from a 14th century manuscript

National Maritime Museum

LORD GEORGE GRAHAM IN HIS CABIN

With Lord George Graham, the Captain, are the Chaplain and Purser; the Cook brings in a dish, a Blackamoor plays
the pipe and tabor, and a poodle performs to the music. Painting by William Hogarth, 1697–1764

and the few who did travel—traders, scholars going to places of learning such as Alexandria, or citizens going to exile—were expected to take their turn at the oars. When the ships were swamped in heavy storms, there were no life-saving means as we know to-day; drowning was a likely result; and it is small wonder that before putting to sea, sacrifices were offered to the sea-god Poseidon (the Romans called him Neptune) for a calm voyage. The Bible narrative (Acts xxvii) gives a vivid account of St. Paul's journey in A.D. 61 from Crete to Rome, in an Alexandrian cornship with 276 people on board—a journey which ended in wreck.

The achievements of the Saxons, Danes, and Normans were remarkable, for in their ships, some 80 feet long (*see* VIKING SHIPS), they sailed to the Mediterranean, down the west coast of Africa, and even across the North Atlantic Ocean. On long voyages shelters were put up on deck at night when the sail was lowered: otherwise the ships were open.

During the Middle Ages sea travel was still mainly a matter of war or trade; and the writings of those days are full of complaints about conditions on board ship. The historian Froissart tells how Sir Hervé de Lion took to the sea at Southampton for Harfleur; he met with a storm which lasted for a fortnight, during which his horse fell overboard, and Sir Hervé himself was 'so sore troubled that he had never health again'. A certain Simon Attefeld was provided with an estate by Edward I on condition that he should always accompany the King on his frequent crossings to France, to hold the King's head if need be.

Cabins first began to appear about the 13th century; the best cabins in the ships built at this time by the Venetians for the Kings of France were called 'Paradise'. But cabins were still only for privileged people. Merchants were probably allotted accommodation on deck according to the quantity of goods they were taking. The pilgrims who went to Rome, Palestine, and Spain had the minimum of comfort. A 15th-century poem describes the overcrowded travellers sitting or lying on the deck, feeling sea-sick, or trying to concentrate on their holy books in spite of headaches, while below the cook is making ready a meal, and the steward sets the board, putting bread and salt on it. Sea-sickness prevented most people from eating more than salted toast, though a solid meal of boiled or roast meat was provided. A 15th-century guide book advised pilgrims on reaching Venice to get a place in the 'overest stage' of the galley because the lower part was 'smoldering hote and stynkyng'.

During the 16th and 17th centuries ship building and navigation improved, and ships sailed long distances from Europe to the tropics, where food and water soon went bad. There are terrible descriptions of conditions on board. John Coad, who fought in the Monmouth rebellion in 1685 and was consequently transported to Jamaica, wrote in his journal how ninety-nine people were crammed into a small room under deck where they could not lie down properly: nor could they go on deck for air. The ship was soon infested with diseases such as smallpox. Smollett in *Roderick Random* gives a description of similar conditions in the 18th century: there was no proper sleeping room, no means of keeping food fresh, and even in the sick-bay the air was foul.

Until the end of the 18th century one of the chief dangers of a long sea-voyage, especially to the tropics, was the disease called scurvy, caused by lack of fresh food; and it was not until 1770 that Captain James Cook showed that this could be prevented by including in the sailors' diet lime, lemon, and orange juices, which would serve the same purpose as green vegetables. In the next year Cook returned from his voyage of nearly 3 years in the ENDEAVOUR (q.v.) without losing a man from scurvy.

In the 19th century there was a great increase in sea-travel, both for trading and diplomatic

ON THE DECK OF AN EMIGRANT SHIP IN 1840

The longboat amidships is roofed over and used as a chicken-house. Drawing by R. C. Leslie from his book *Old Sea Ways, Wings, and Words.* 1890

reasons, and because many people emigrated to America and Australia. In 1833 the *Royal William* crossed the Atlantic by steam. In this ship there was a cabin under deck with about fifty sleeping-berths and a well-furnished parlour; in the upper deck there was a dining-room with tables and benches. Emigrants to America or Australia, however, continued to travel in sailing ships, and as their ticket covered transport only, they had to bring their food with them or buy it on board. The emigrant ships were very overcrowded and unhealthy, and even water was scarce. When wealthy people travelled they took with them everything they could want. Honoria Lawrence, wife of Sir Henry Lawrence, when she sailed to India in 1837 to join her husband, furnished her own cabin and took with her large supplies of soap, tea, candles, matches, and other necessaries. Even much later it was not uncommon to take a milch cow on a long voyage as the only way of providing fresh milk for babies over so long a period.

By 1870 propeller-driven ships had become general, travel became more comfortable, even for people who travelled 'steerage'. Modern ships have refrigerator systems to keep food fresh; they are equipped with libraries, swimming-baths, and children's playrooms. Ships like the *Queen Mary* and QUEEN ELIZABETH (q.v.) have become, in fact, floating hotels, with every kind of comfort and entertainment provided for the passengers (*see* PLEASURE CRUISES, Vol. IX).

See also EXPLORATION; TRADE ROUTES; SAILING SHIPS.

SECRET WRITING, *see* CODES AND CIPHERS.

SEDAN CHAIR. This was a portable covered chair popular in England and on the Continent in the 17th, 18th, and 19th centuries. Two poles were placed through rings in its side to form shafts, by which two men, chairmen, carried the chair.

Soane Museum

A SEDAN CHAIR

'The Arrest', one of the paintings in the series 'The Rake's Progress', by W. Hogarth, 1697–1764

The name came from the French town of Sedan, where the chairs were first used. They made their way to England, and became fashionable in London during the reign of Charles I, when the King restricted the use of carriages because they blocked the streets. Some people had their own sedans, but generally they were hired like TAXIS (q.v.). The longest journey in a sedan was made by Princess Amelia who, in 1728, was carried by eight chairmen, working in reliefs, from London to Bath, a distance of 107 miles; but in general they were used, mainly by ladies, for short journeys in the towns. Sedans were most popular in Dr. Johnson's day, in the 18th century, and many of them were magnificently built. They went out of use as roads improved and travel in CARRIAGES (q.v.) became more comfortable.

SEMAPHORE. Before electric TELEGRAPHY (q.v.) was invented, various devices for visual signalling, known as 'telegraphs' or 'semaphores', were in use. They were large mechanical structures placed on hills or open sites where they could easily be seen, and often had movable arms whose position could be changed according to a code. One of the earliest was invented by a Frenchman, named Claude Chappe, in

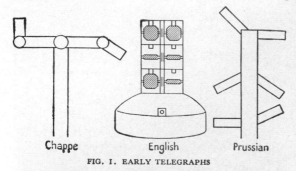

FIG. I. EARLY TELEGRAPHS

Chappe   English   Prussian

1792, and consisted of an upright post with movable wooden arms and hands which could be arranged in different ways, and were capable of sending as many as 192 signals (*see* Fig. 1).

A similar system was used in England to send messages between the coastal stations. During the Napoleonic wars, however, when invasion from France was feared, a rather different device was used, by which messages could be sent quickly between the Admiralty and the naval ports of Deal, Portsmouth, Plymouth, and Yarmouth. It consisted of two large, rectangular, vertical, wooden frames, each divided horizontally into three, in each of which an octagonal plate could be set either upright, to fill the frame, or flat to leave it empty. The six frames could thus be arranged in sixty-four different ways. This device gave its name to several Telegraph Hills in the south of England, such as those at New Cross and Swanscombe.

From 1832 a third type of telegraph, a Prussian device, was in use on the Continent. It resembled three double railway signals mounted on a vertical post, which, arranged at different angles, could send as many as 4,096 different signals.

These different forms of signalling were developed in chains of telegraph stations which ran across Europe, by which signals could be sent remarkably quickly; a message could be sent from Paris to Toulon, for instance, in 10 or 12 minutes.

The Semaphore code in use to-day was originally invented by a colonel of the Royal Engineers in 1822, but was not used until much later. The Royal Navy were using it for signalling with mechanical signal arms in the 1870's, but it was not transmitted by hand-flags for another 20 years. Flags are held in the hands to make the movements more conspicuous, the signaller always facing the person who is to receive the message. The arms move round in a circle divided into eight parts. For the first seven letters of the alphabet only one arm is used; but all the rest need both (*see* Fig. 2). A semaphore flag is white with a blue horizontal bar and 2 feet square, fixed on a stick 3 ft. 6 in. long. On a clear day it can be seen with binoculars about 4 miles away. Ships' mechanical arms can be seen 10 to 12 miles off.

Signallers usually work in pairs, one man reading out or writing down the messages, and the other making the signals or watching the distant station to spell out the answer. For all kinds of visual signalling, in which words have to be spelt out aloud, special 'phonetic alphabets'

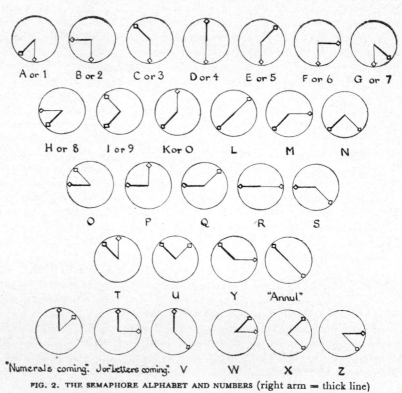

A or 1   B or 2   C or 3   D or 4   E or 5   F or 6   G or 7

H or 8   I or 9   K or 0   L   M   N

O   P   Q   R   S

T   U   Y   "Annul"

"Numerals coming".   "J or letters coming".   V   W   X   Z

FIG. 2. THE SEMAPHORE ALPHABET AND NUMBERS (right arm = thick line)

are used, each letter having a name by which it can be distinguished. The alphabet used by the British Army in the First World War has given us several familiar expressions; from the name 'Toc' for T we get 'Toc H' (the initials of Talbot House), and amongst other familiar terms are Pip Emma (P.M.), Ack Emma (A.M.), and Ack-Ack (anti-aircraft). During the Second Word War a phonetic alphabet was jointly used by the British and American Forces, beginning Able, Baker, Charlie, Dog.

See also SIGNALS; FLAG SIGNALLING; MORSE CODE; TELEGRAPHY.

SEMITIC LANGUAGES.

SEMITIC LANGUAGES. Semitic languages are so called because, according to a Hebrew tradition derived from the Book of Genesis, they were spoken by the descendants of Shem, the son of Noah (*see* SEMITES, Vol. I). These languages all sprang from a parent language, now lost beyond recovery. It was spoken by the Semites in the earliest times, when they lived in their original home, which is thought to have been Arabia. Semitic languages were spoken in Mesopotamia, Syria, and Palestine, and from these countries they spread later to Egypt, Abyssinia, north Africa, and other places. The most important of them are Hebrew and Aramaic (*see* HEBREW LANGUAGE), Phoenician, Assyrian, Babylonian, ARABIC (q.v.), and Ethiopic. Hebrew, Arabic, and Aramaic are still spoken to-day. Ethiopic, the ancient language of Abyssinia, gave way in the course of time to Amharic, a largely non-Semitic language spoken in Abyssinia to-day, but Ethiopic still lives on as the language of the Abyssinian Church. To the Arabic family belongs Maltese, the language of Malta, which has been much influenced by Italian. The Semitic languages are closely related to one another both in structure and vocabulary. They are very different from the INDO-EUROPEAN LANGUAGES (q.v.), such as English and French, for almost all Semitic words are derived from verbs consisting of three consonants. For example, from the Arabic *KaTaBa*, which means 'he wrote', are derived *KāTiB* 'scribe',

KiTāB 'book' and *maKTaB* 'school'. Semitic languages are usually written from right to left. It seems likely that in the very distant past some family relationship existed between these and the Hamitic languages (those supposedly spoken by the descendants of Ham, another son of Noah) which include ancient Egyptian, and certain African languages, such as those spoken by the Berbers and Somalis.

See also LANGUAGE, HISTORY OF.

SEVERN TUNNEL. This tunnel, which runs under the estuary of the River Severn, connecting the west of England with South Wales, is one of the longest under-water tunnels in the world. It measures 4 miles 624 yards, of which $2\frac{1}{4}$ miles run under the Severn. Before it was built, all railway lines connecting the west of England with South Wales had to make a long detour by way of Gloucester, crossing the Severn by bridge: now the main line between London and South Wales is shortened by 25 miles, and trains between Bristol and Cardiff take half as long as they did formerly. Plans on the tunnel began in 1873 and work actually started 4 years later; but because of the great difficulties involved, the tunnel was not opened for traffic until 1886. The deepest part of the tidal estuary on the north side, which is known as the 'Shoots', is about 400 yards wide and 80 feet deep, even at low water. So that 45 feet could be left between the bottom of this and the roof of the tunnel, the railway had to be dropped down a steep gradient for nearly $3\frac{1}{2}$ miles, to a depth of 115 feet below sea-level, and then, after a short level strip under the 'Shoots', lifted out again up another gradient to join the old South Wales main line.

The worst delays were caused by the breaking in of an underground spring which poured 6,000 gallons of water a minute into the workings, and so completely flooded them that nearly 14 months elapsed before it had been sealed off and the works had been cleared of water. In October 1883, there was a further disaster, for not only did the spring break through a second time, but also within a week the regular tidal

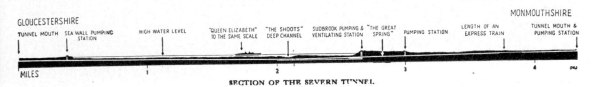

SECTION OF THE SEVERN TUNNEL.

wave known as the 'bore' (*see* TIDES, Vol. III) came up the estuary to such a height that the open cutting and the workings at the Monmouthshire end were completely flooded out. Pumping machinery sufficient to pump out as much as 30,000,000 gallons a day was installed. From one of the shafts at the Monmouthshire end a side heading was driven, parallel with the main tunnel, in the hopes of intercepting and controlling the great spring. For a time these measures were successful, and at the end of 1884, when the tunnel was nearly completed, it was thought that no further pumping would be needed. But by December 1885, pieces of the lining were breaking out with loud reports, and water was again spouting through. Permanent pumping machinery was, therefore, installed, and this now deals with from 13,370,000 to 36,550,000 gallons of water daily. There is also a ventilation plant.

See also TUNNELS.

SEXTANT. This instrument is used in a ship or aircraft for measuring the altitude, or angle above the horizon, of a star or other heavenly

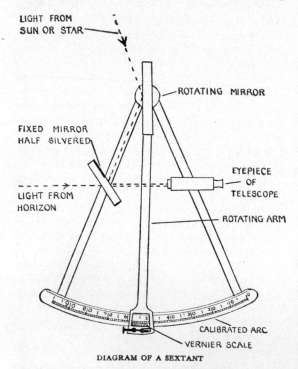

DIAGRAM OF A SEXTANT

body, and so to fix the craft's position (*see* NAVIGATION, MARINE). A navigator holds the

sextant in his hand and looks into its eyepiece; he then carefully adjusts a movable mirror in order to bring the reflected image of the star he has chosen to the level of the horizon; the exact angle of the mirror, which is marked on the instrument, shows the angle of the star. Since an aircraft is above earth level, an airman must look at a 'false horizon' in his instrument which is a 'bubble sextant'. He keeps this level by watching a bubble floating in liquid in a curved tube, on the principle of a spirit-level.

See also NAVIGATION, MARINE; NAVIGATION, HISTORY OF; COMPASS; CHRONOMETER.

SHIP. There are about 30,000 sea-going and ocean-going ships in the world to-day, totalling nearly 81 million tons. All except a very few are now driven through the water by the action of a screw propeller or propellers, or by a pair of paddle-wheels. The number of screws by which a ship is driven depends on such things as the depth of water in which she is normally used and the total power needed to drive her at her designed speed. The 'screw', as the name suggests, is somewhat like part of an ordinary screw used in carpentry. As the carpenter's screw advances into the wood with every turn of the screwdriver, so a ship's screw moves forward in the water with every turn, propelling the ship forward. But a ship's screw is operating in sea water, which is not solid as is the carpenter's wood, and so it tends to slip. Therefore with every turn of the screw there is a certain amount of wasted effort. The alternative to the screw is the paddle-wheel, generally used in pairs, the edge of the wheel bearing flat boards known as 'paddles'. As the wheel turns round, the boards thrust against the water in which the ship is moving.

Whether a ship is driven through the water by means of a screw or paddle-wheels, there must be an engine which turns them. Ships' engines are of two kinds, either reciprocating (to-and-fro) or rotary. In the first kind a piston moves to and fro, rather like the up-and-down motion of a cyclist's knees, causing circular motion on the principle of the cyclist's feet and pedals, and so turning the propeller. Reciprocating machines may work by steam or by oil. STEAM ENGINES (q.v. Vol. VIII) get their power from the pressure of steam in a boiler. In the INTERNAL COMBUSTION ENGINE (q.v. Vol. VIII), power comes from a series of explosions of fuel-oil, which has

Nautical Photo Agency

THE 'SCORTON', A TRAMP STEAMER
The derricks are for loading and unloading a general cargo

been previously forced into a very hot cylinder at high pressure.

Rotary engines, usually known as 'turbines', operate on steam. A turbine consists of a large drum which can spin round inside a circular casing. Steam is forced against a number of blades which are set round the edge of the drum; this moves round at high speed and turns the shaft to which it is attached (*see* STEAM TURBINE, Vol. VIII). Most turbines to-day are used with steam boilers heated by oil because this is the cheapest way of making steam. Apart from driving the ship, power is needed for many other purposes, such as lighting, cooking, heating, ventilation, and the working of deck gear needed for moving cargo in and out of the ship's hold.

In the whole world of ships there are probably nearly a hundred different types and kinds. Few can carry out the work of others because each type of cargo requires special characteristics in the way of winches, masts, derricks, and hatches, as well as speed. All ships can be classified as liners, tramps, or auxiliaries.

LINERS (q.v.) are ships which trade regularly between the same ports. Their size is set by the size of the harbours to which they regularly run; their speed is designed to suit the number of journeys they make in a year; the number of hatches they have is decided by the crane facilities on the quayside at each end of the voyage. A supreme example of a liner is one of the *Queens*, such as the *Queen Mary* or QUEEN ELIZABETH (q.v.), running between Southamp-

ton and New York. But a cross-channel ship running between Dover and Calais is also a liner. In each case the vessel carries passengers, a limited amount of freight, and mails, and runs to a schedule as rigid as that of an express train.

The tramp ship is required to trade mainly with bulk cargoes in almost any part of the world. A bulk cargo, in contrast to a cargo of goods packed in cases, is a heavy 'dead-weight' cargo, such as coal, grain, or iron ore. It is loaded in bulk and removed in bulk. The tramp must be available to run in any part of the world, perhaps carrying coal outwards from South Wales ports to ports on the River Plate in South America, and trading homewards with grain. Tramp ships must always be prepared to operate 'in ballast', that is to say, without any cargo in their holds. Therefore they must be specially built so that even when the holds are empty the ship does not rise so high in the water that the screws show above the surface. Sea water is pumped into ballast tanks to make the ship heavy, and so keep the screws under water. The tramp is usually smaller than the cargo liner, and rarely exceeds 10,000 tons gross. She carries more cargo-handling gear than liners, and generally more fuel, for her work takes her to out-of-the-way ports which have limited equipment and supplies.

Specialized vessels such as tankers and fruit ships can be either liners or tramps. The oil-tanker is probably the most important of all ship types to-day; a third of the ships built in

Port Line

THE 'PORT BRISBANE', A REFRIGERATED SHIP
This modern design has clean lines for fast travel

Britain in the years following the Second World War were tankers. These are vessels built to carry liquid cargoes in bulk; generally the liquid is some kind of oil, but ships have been built to carry acid and other liquid chemicals. Some tankers are owned by oil companies; others are chartered for a period of years. The largest tanker can carry some 30,000 tons of cargo. The basic design of all tankers is the same; they have a single deck, with the engines near the stern. The rest of the ship is filled with oil, stored in small tanks, sometimes as many as thirty. Pipes lead to each tank, so that the entire cargo, passing through the ship's pumps, can be loaded or unloaded through hoses in a few hours.

The life of a tanker is limited by corrosion, for the tanks are attacked by oil vapours and, when they are carrying sea-water ballast, by salt. Dry-cargo ships last about 25 years, but oil tankers only about 15. When the ship passes through tropical waters the oil becomes heated and so expands; therefore piping is fitted to the tanks to let out the oil vapour and prevent pressure in the tanks rising; the vapour is led to the tops of the masts to prevent inflammable gases being present at deck level.

Fruit, meat, and other perishable goods brought from places as far away as Canada and South Africa must travel in a refrigerated hold, where the low temperature prevents decay (*see* REFRIGERATION, Vol. VIII). Fruit grows and is picked at special seasons, so that a regular run throughout the year cannot be expected. Some ship-owners have built ships which can operate from California or from South Africa or the eastern Mediterranean, taking any fruit which is in season. Ships engaged in the Mediterranean fruit trade sometimes take cargo from ports of the United Kingdom or the Continent of Europe to ports on the Great Lakes of North America during the ice-free season, which is some 8 months of the year. They are small, fast, well-equipped ships, and may have accommodation for a dozen or so passengers.

Refrigerated ships vary from the 1,000-ton fish carrier to the large meat ships on ocean routes, which may run to 14,000 tons and a speed of 17 knots. Fruit ships, which are usually motor-vessels of 2,500 to 4,000 tons, have very high speeds for ships of this size. The holds and 'tween decks of fruit ships are insulated with cork or glass silk to prevent changes of temperature. The ship's refrigerating machinery can either keep the cargo spaces at a very low temperature so that the cargoes are frozen hard, or reduce the temperature only enough to chill the cargoes and prevent them going bad. This may affect the design of the ship. If a meat cargo is completely frozen, the carcases can be piled up in the hold, like any other solid cargo; if the meat is only chilled, however, each carcase has to hang by a separate hook, and several low

A Shell Photograph

A TURBO-ELECTRIC TANKER
The long low line is characteristic of tankers

'tween decks are needed. Chilled meat is therefore more expensive to carry.

Grain can be carried in any dry-cargo ship which has room for a cargo bulky in proportion to its weight, and in which the cargo can be prevented from shifting at sea and endangering the balance of the vessel. Every ship carrying grain has a bulkhead or partition running lengthways down its centre to keep the cargo in place. This can be dismantled when the ship has to carry other cargoes.

Besides vessels that ply in the main seaways of the world, there are many 'coasters' engaged in short-distance trading.

Auxiliary ships, such as DREDGERS, TUGS, CABLE SHIPS, and ICEBREAKERS (qq.v.) are mostly concerned with the important work of keeping open the sea lanes upon which the other kinds of ship work. Tugs move big ships into port or alongside quays. Dredgers maintain a sufficient depth of water in the sea lanes which lead to quaysides and ports. Lightships (*see* LIGHTHOUSES AND LIGHTSHIPS) are moored to mark some danger area, such as a sandbank or stretch of shallow water, and to give warning to other ships by their light signals.

See also MERCHANT SHIPPING; LINER; MOTOR-SHIP; ELECTRIC SHIP; PORTS AND HARBOURS.
See also Vol. VIII: SHIP BUILDING.

SHIP CANAL, *see* CANALS; MANCHESTER SHIP CANAL.

SHIPS, *see* PRIMITIVE SHIPS; CLASSICAL SHIPS; VIKING SHIPS; SAILING SHIPS; STEAMSHIPS.

SHIP'S COMPANY. Duties and discipline in a ship at sea are the result of traditions which have changed slowly with the centuries, although changes have been greater since the coming of steamships and motor-ships. The head of every merchant ship is the master, who has the courtesy title of captain. If he is master of a passenger ship, he wears upon his sleeves, while afloat, the distinguishing gold lace of his rank. Some shipping companies have their own cuff or shoulder design, but the usual mark of master's rank is four rows of gold lace with a lace diamond between the centre rows. On his uniform cap is the Merchant Navy standard badge or the company's badge, with a row of gold oak leaves on the peak. The master of a small cargo liner probably wears full uniform only when entering or leaving harbour, or on other special occasions. The master of a tramp steamer may wear no other outward sign of authority than a uniform cap, and even that may be discarded in favour of a more comfortable shore-going hat.

Masters of all types of ships, whether liner or tramp, lead the lonely life of leaders whom custom does not allow to mix freely with those under them. The master keeps no watches (fixed spells of duty), but he is always on call. He takes over the bridge when entering or leaving harbour, or during an emergency or some unusual

Cunard White Star

THE BRIDGE OF THE LINER 'CARONIA'

The magnetic compass can be seen in front of the helmsman, and the gyroscopic compass to his right. Behind the officer of the watch are the engine-room telegraphs

manœuvre. Before he can sit for his master's certificate, a sailor must usually serve 4 years at sea as an apprentice, a further 18 months after passing for his second mate's certificate, then 2 years after passing for his first mate's certificate. Then he must wait until the owners consider him experienced and responsible enough to be given command.

The next senior deck officer is the first mate, or chief officer, as he is now more popularly called. He is probably an officer in possession of his master's certificate, and waiting for a command. He is the senior deck (as opposed to engine-room) watch-keeping officer, and is in general charge of the deck department. The other deck watch-keeping officers are the second and third officers. (In the giant passenger liners, there may be as many as eight watch-keeping officers.) They are responsible to the master for the navigation and safety of the vessel. Most of the better-class companies also carry apprentices,

known (from the place where their quarters were in sailing vessels) as 'the half deck'. These boys may be cadets from one of the cadet training-schools or raw new-comers to the sea. The shipping company accepts a premium (a sum of money paid in advance) in return for teaching them the rudiments of their profession, until they are qualified for the second mate's certificate. The greater part of the premium is often returned to the boys in the form of pocket money.

The engineering department is administered by the chief engineer, known as 'the chief'. He is responsible only to the master and, like him, keeps no regular watch. Under the chief engineer there are three or more engineer watch-keeping officers, whose first responsiblity is the ship's main engines. But a constant watch must also be kept upon the temperature and lubrication of all other machinery—pumps, dynamos, fans, and so on. During a gale, when the ship is pitching badly, the watchkeeping engineer will stand by the throttle, and every time the up-flung stern brings the propeller out of the water, he will ease down to avoid racing the engines. If the ship has refrigerated holds, she will carry a separate staff of refrigerating engineers.

There are probably other officers in the ship, who are neither of the deck nor engineer branches. If the ship carries enough passengers, there is a purser on board, who is the ship's business-manager and deals with all money, stores, and documents. He also looks after passengers' valuables, and any small valuables that are being carried as cargo. The clerks, caterers, cooks, and stewards are his responsibility. If the ship is solely a cargo vessel, most of these duties are usually performed by the chief steward.

If there are more than 100 men in the crew, the ship carries a doctor. All ships of any size now carry one or more radio officers, who may be employed either by the shipping company or by the company which supplies and installs the ship's radio.

Chief of the 'lower deck', as the seamen are collectively called, is the boatswain, pronounced 'bos'n'. He is a sort of senior non-commissioned officer of the ship, and takes charge of all manœuvres under the supervision of the chief officer. 'Chips', the carpenter, is responsible for the maintenance of fresh-water tanks, sounding the bilges to see if water is leaking into the ship, letting go and heaving up the anchor, attending to the cargo hatches, and so on. The cook must hold a certificate, and usually has under him a butcher, baker, and other assistants. The donkey-man is to the chief engineer what the boatswain and carpenter are to the chief officer.

The seamen begin their career as ordinary seamen, and must serve 3 years before they can be 'rated up' and paid as able seamen. Quartermasters are higher-paid able seamen employed as helmsmen, and greasers are the assistants to the engineer of the watch. In the stokehold are the firemen who tend the fires and the trimmers who wheel supplies of coal from the bunkers. The use of oil-fired boilers or the internal combustion engine at sea is altering the duties of firemen, and doing away with the trimmers.

In passenger liners there are many other workers —stewards, lecturers, librarians, hostesses, hairdressers, shop assistants, telephonists, lift attendants, and others.

All the crew of a merchantman sign a contract known as the Articles of Agreement. The Government lays down rules about their feeding and accommodation.

See also SHIP.

SHORTHAND. This word applies to any system of shortened handwriting which can be put down as quickly as anyone can speak; an alternative word is 'stenography' (Greek: *stenos* 'narrow' or 'space-saving', *graphein* 'to write'). The use of such quick writing is not new: the ancient Greeks may have used shorthand; the Romans certainly did so: it seems to have been taught in their schools.

Modern shorthand in England can be traced back to 1588, when Dr. Timothy Bright published his *Characterie: An Arte of Shorte, Swifte and Secret Writing by Character*. This system was difficult to learn, for nearly every word had its own special sign. The system of John Willis, whose *Art of Stenographie* ran into fourteen editions between 1602 and 1647, was simpler to learn, but must have been clumsy for fast writing. The diarist Samuel PEPYS (q.v. Vol. V) kept all his diaries in shorthand, using the method of T. Shelton (1620), an imitator of Willis.

The systems of Willis and his successors were based on the alphabet, each letter being represented by a straight line or curve, some with hooks added. Vowel sounds were indicated rather vaguely, and confusion could easily arise. Gradually these systems were superseded by 'phonetic' systems (Greek: *phōnē* 'sound'), based on sounds, and not on the written alphabet. The basis of shorthand is the realization that

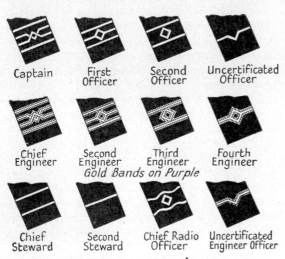

Captain · First Officer · Second Officer · Uncertificated Officer

Chief Engineer · Second Engineer · Third Engineer · Fourth Engineer

Gold Bands on Purple

Chief Steward · Second Steward · Chief Radio Officer · Uncertificated Engineer Officer

MERCHANT NAVY OFFICERS' RANKS

ordinary spelling uses far too many symbols (or letters) for short and simple sounds. Therefore shorthand, in writing a word, leaves out as many unnecessary symbols as possible; for those symbols which are left, it uses easy strokes in place of the complicated shapes of ordinary written letters. Where ordinary letters have more than one sound (as, for instance, the letter *g* has the sound in 'give' or that in 'ginger'), shorthand invents extra symbols to represent those sounds.

In the 18th century one improved system followed another, though none were quite satisfactory. The best was that of Samuel Taylor, 1786, the brevity and simplicity of which attracted the attention of the great stenographer, Sir Isaac Pitman (1813–97). Pitman's first effort was, in fact, a manual of Taylor's system; but presently he began anew on his own lines. Wishing to make shorthand generally available, he issued his *Stenographic Sound-Hand* in 1873, at the low price of 4*d.* a copy. The system achieved great popularity in Great Britain and America, and was adapted to several foreign languages. Continuously modernized and improved, it is still the most widely used shorthand, although many others, such as Bell's, Sloan's, and Gregg's, are also in common use

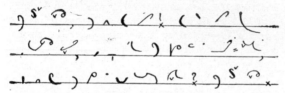

The above is the nursery rhyme, *Three Blind Mice*, written in Pitman's shorthand. It shows how use is made of thick and thin strokes and curves. The most common words are represented by grammalogues, very brief symbols, such as a dot on the line for 'the', and a dot above the line for 'a', and often-used phrases, such as 'in the circumstances', are shown by phraseograms in which the symbols for each of the words are joined together and abbreviated. Vowel sounds can be shown by dots and dashes placed beside the consonant symbols; but they can be mainly dispensed with by writing the symbols above, on, or through the ruled lines of the notebook. In this way the symbol for 'tn' written above the line means 'tan', on the line is 'ten', and through the line 'tin'.

In competitions, shorthand has been written at 250 words a minute, which is faster than any-one normally talks. Public speakers average not more than 150 words a minute, a speed which a good shorthand writer can follow.

SHORT-WAVE WIRELESS. A great part of wireless transmission takes place on short wavelengths. There are several reasons for this. Short-wave stations are cheaper to operate than long-wave stations, as they need smaller transmitters and less costly aerial equipment, requiring smaller maintenance staffs. Many more short-wave stations than medium or long ones can be tuned-in for an equal amount of knob-turning on an ordinary receiver; medium and long-wave transmission tends to 'spread', because the length of the wave makes a larger area of the tuning circuit become active. Short waves can be directed as a 'beam' in any direction, which greatly adds to the distance they travel and reduces the power needed to send them.

Speech is most easily conveyed across the world if the short-wave transmission is sent out as a 'beam'. In a motor-car headlight, the reason the light is so strong and goes so far is that the whole of the light from the small electric bulb is caught up in a reflector, which is merely a curved mirror behind the bulb, and is concentrated in one narrow beam. Beamed wireless works on the same principle. The energy from the short-wave transmitting aerial is caught up by wire screens behind the aerial, and is reflected forward in one narrow path. The inventor, Marconi (*see* WIRELESS), when experimenting in 1921, found that signals which he received were 200 times stronger if reflecting screens were fitted round the transmitting aerial. Long waves, like short waves, can be reflected in theory; but in practice they would require enormous assemblies of reflectors, perhaps miles in size, and even then transmissions might not be satisfactory.

The short-wave beam system is used as the 'radio link' in all telephone calls between Britain and the Commonwealth countries, the United States, and other distant places, as well as calls to ships at sea. It also plays a part in broadcasting. If the B.B.C. wish to include in their ordinary home programmes a talk by a commentator from America, they arrange for him to speak from New York to London by short-wave beam. His voice, on reaching London, can be linked with a B.B.C. transmitter, and so broadcast while he is actually speaking. Otherwise the voice can be recorded on a disk or other recording device to be broadcast later. The short-wave beam also makes it possible for people in different countries to take part in the same broadcast programme, talking to one another as if they were in the same room. The traditional 'round-the-world' broadcast from the B.B.C. on Christmas Day is organized in this way.

Even a carefully directed beam transmission can become very faint at a distance of some thousands of miles; but its range can be increased by using a relay station. Any short-wave wireless station can serve as a relay. Spoken commentaries on cricket Test Matches played in England have been transmitted on a short-wave beam from England, picked up on a high-quality receiver at Singapore, in the Malay Straits, magnified to their original strength in a local transmitting station, and then transmitted afresh by short-wave beam from Singapore to Australia and New Zealand. There the commentaries have been taken to local broadcasting stations and broadcast on medium waves in the local programmes. This kind of relaying is sometimes known as 'boosting'.

Aerials linked with transmitting and receiving stations for beam wireless are situated in various parts of Britain; generally a site is chosen in the country, away from disturbing influences such as high hills. The presence of mineral deposits underground might upset delicate electrical adjustments; so might the industrial plants and power station of a large city. One British beam station in the west of England operates with South America along a route almost the whole of which is over water, which offers less interference to wireless transmission than large areas of land.

Receiving aerials and transmitting aerials are sometimes erected miles apart, so that they will not interfere with one another electrically. A beam station, of course, is not concerned with the control of the spoken messages which pass through it. All the connexions are handled at a special telephone exchange, usually called the 'radio terminal'; the only task of the transmitting station is to convert the sounds which it receives on the telephone land-line into strong wireless signals, beamed in the right direction. In the same way, the receiving station has to pick up the incoming beam signals from a distant transmitter to strengthen them so that they make good audible speech, and to transfer them to the telephone land-line on their way to the telephone exchange. From there they are connected with the customer.

See also WAVELENGTHS; SPEECH, TRANSMISSION OF.

SHUNTING, *see* MARSHALLING YARDS.

SIAMESE LANGUAGE, *see* CHINESE AND ALLIED LANGUAGES.

SIGNALLING, RAILWAY. British signalling is based on the 'block' system, under which every length of line is divided into sections, guarded by signals, and no train or locomotive is allowed to enter any section if another is already there. The more trains running on a line, the shorter the sections; otherwise a train would often have to wait for another train a long way ahead to pass out of a long section.

Many gradual changes are taking place in signalling. The semaphore arm is being replaced on many lines by electric colour-light signals, which have no moving parts, and which throw a powerful beam by day or night. At busy places the many small signal-boxes (one for each section of line) are giving way to a central box with ELECTRIC SIGNALLING control (q.v.). Where traffic is very dense AUTOMATIC SIGNALLING (q.v.) takes the place of a human signalman. Sometimes the flow of traffic over main lines is kept moving by TRAIN CONTROL (q.v.) many miles away, although the signalmen on the spot still handle each train. The system of safety which underlies all these developments, however, is based on the traditional rules of the one-man signal-box and the old-fashioned semaphore signal, whose working will now be described.

A signal-box stands where one section of line ends and the next begins; each signal on a signal-

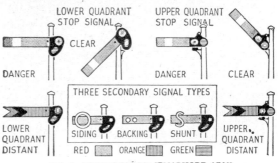

FIG. I. FIXED SIGNALS: SEMAPHORE ARMS

post is known as a 'fixed' signal, to distinguish it from signals made with the hand, or by flag or hand-lamp. The semaphore 'stop' arm, red in front and white at the back, stands horizontally for 'danger' and diagonally for 'clear'. On some lines the arm points upward for 'clear', and on others downward; the upward angle or 'upper quadrant' is now standard on British Railways. The arm is worked by wires, but is weighted so that it swings to 'danger' if a wire breaks. A red and a green glass in a 'spectacle' attached to the arm move in front of a lighted lamp at night (Fig. 1).

Signals which the driver is not allowed to pass if they stand at 'danger' are called 'stop' signals. But since no train could travel very fast if the driver had to be ready to stop dead at any 'stop' signal, a cautionary signal known as a 'distant' signal is placed from $\frac{1}{2}$ to $\frac{3}{4}$ mile from

to protect shunting movements. All those signals are mechanically interlocked in the signal-box, so that the lever which operates the 'distant' signal cannot be pulled to 'clear' unless all the 'stop' signals are also at 'clear' (Fig. 2).

Let us see how these signals are used in a typical box, that of Signalman B, which is half-way between signal-boxes A and C (Fig. 3). A 'block' section extends from the 'starter' of one box to a point about a quarter of a mile beyond the 'home' signal of the next box ahead. The boxes are connected by bells, and also by an electric circuit which moves a needle to one of three positions on a dial: 'Line clear', 'Train on line', or 'Line blocked'; this last is the normal setting when no traffic is being handled. Signalman B hears one stroke on the bell from A, 'Calling attention'. B answers with one stroke.

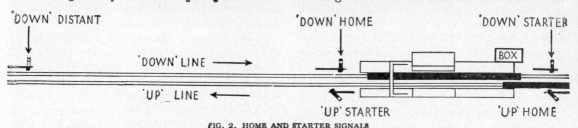

FIG. 2. HOME AND STARTER SIGNALS

Down 'Home' signal guards rear of train standing at platform. Down 'Starter' is cleared when box ahead accepts train. Up 'home' and 'starter' are shown cleared for express accepted by next box

the signal-box to warn the driver of a coming 'stop' signal. If the 'distant' signal is 'clear', the train can continue at full speed; if not, the driver has time to slow down. The arm of a 'distant' signal is fish-tailed, while a 'stop' signal has a square end. The standard colours for the 'distant' signal are a yellow arm and an orange light at night for 'caution'.

There are usually at least two 'stop' signals near a signal-box for each direction of running. As a train approaches the box, it comes to the 'home' signal. Rather more than a train's length farther on is the 'starting' signal or 'starter'. A train standing between 'home' and 'starter' is protected by that signal-box. There may also be an 'advanced starter' a little farther ahead,

If a passenger express is coming, A then rings four strokes in even succession, meaning, 'Is line clear for passenger express?' If B's section, from B to C, is clear, B rings back four strokes to A, and moves the needle of his dial from 'Line blocked' to 'Line clear'. The move is shown also on A's dial, and he then sets his signals to 'clear'. As the train passes A's box, he rings two strokes (meaning 'Train entering section') to B, who then readjusts the needle of his dial to 'Train on line'. Meanwhile B has been ringing C's bell, and offering the train, just as A had done, and on acceptance from C, has pulled off his signals also. When the train reaches B's box, he sets each signal at 'danger' as the train passes, then rings back to A, 'Train out of section' (two

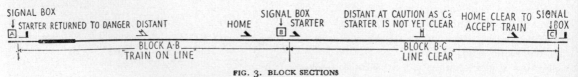

FIG. 3. BLOCK SECTIONS

Signals on Block A–B are in position for 'train on line'. Signals on Block B–C are in position for 'Line clear'

FIG. 4. BRITISH RAILWAYS HEADLAMP CODE

1. Passenger express train; 2. Passenger stopping train; 3. Express freight, not less than one-third of train with continuous brakes or empty passenger stock; 4. Express freight, without continuous brakes; 5. Through freight or ballast; 6. Light engine or engines, with one or two brakevans; 7. Express parcels, milk, &c., in coach-type stock; 8. Mineral or empty wagon train; 9. Goods stopping train; 10. Royal train. In addition a lamp at bottom centre and right indicates certain other express freight trains.

strokes, pause, one stroke), and sets his dial to the normal 'Line blocked'.

Any train can be described by this bell code; thus a stopping passenger train is three strokes, pause, one stroke. Signalmen identify trains by the locomotive headlamps (Fig. 4). A lamp over

each buffer marks a passenger express; one at the base of the chimney shows a passenger stopping train; goods and various other trains have other combinations. On busy lines, white disks indicate the routes which trains are to travel. On other lines, large figures in front of the engine are used to show the number of the train. The tail-lamp of the last coach shows a signalman that no part of a train is missing.

In some cases electrical contacts, worked by the trains themselves, lock the signal-box levers, and the 'Train on line' dial, to prevent a signalman making a mistake. The more usual protection against forgetfulness is the 'track circuit' (*see* ELECTRIC SIGNALLING, Section 2). In the signal-box the levers are interlocked to prevent signalmen from moving signals on points in such a way that trains might collide with one another. 'Locking-bars' are attached to points so that a signalman, having locked the points after moving them, cannot move them again until the train has passed.

The principal levers in a signal-box are usually

British Railways

NO. 2 SIGNAL BOX, EUSTON

at opposite ends, according to the track which they control. Between them are minor levers controlling cross-overs and sidings. Levers of 'stop' signals are red, 'distant' signals yellow, points black, and locking-bars blue. Spare levers are white. Each lever is numbered, corresponding with a diagram in front of the signalman.

See also ELECTRIC SIGNALLING; AUTOMATIC SIGNALLING; TRAIN CONTROL; RAILWAYMEN, Section 4.

SIGNALS. A signal is an action by which one person sends a message to another without speaking. Signalling usually consists of moving conspicuous objects, such as lights or flags, that can be seen at a distance, or of loud, echoing, or piercing noises, such as drums, whistles, or horns, that will rise above other sounds and carry a long way. Such means of communication enable messages to be sent over very long distances where direct speech would be impossible. Indeed, it was even thought that it might be possible to communicate with intelligent beings on Mars (if such existed) by a series of light flashes made from vast reflecting mirrors.

A very old method of signalling by night is with lighted beacons (like bonfires) set up on commanding sites. The news of the fall of Troy is supposed to have been sent 400 miles to Argos in Greece by a chain of beacons built on eight mountain-tops. The Romans, by a network of beacons along certain main routes, sent important State messages from one end of their Empire to the other. Signallers were always at hand along the fortified boundaries of the Roman Empire to report instantly the approach of hostile forces. Hadrian's Wall, the Roman boundary between England and Scotland, had watch-towers and signalling stations along it at intervals. A famous line of beacons ran across Asia Minor in the 8th century, when the Byzantine Empire was ruled from Constantinople, and there was constant fear of invasion by the Saracens. Watch was kept at a place called Lulon (about half-way along the southern side of what is now Turkey); from there, with only eight beacons in all, danger signals could be sent to Constantinople, some 500 miles away. Beacons have been used in England in times of national danger: a chain of them, reaching from the English Channel to the Scottish border, gave news of the approach of the Spanish Armada in 1588. Beacon stations were set up all along the hills of southern England during the Napoleonic wars,

when invasion from France was expected; the signal was to be fire by night and smoke by day. Smoke-signalling was a method practised especially by the North American Indians. They would make a fire of partly dried grass which they covered at intervals with a wet blanket; whenever the blanket was lifted a puff of smoke rose into the sky; various combinations of puffs had various meanings.

Audible signals usually take the form of high penetrating noises, or of deep reverberating ones which carry a long way, and which tend to be made stronger by echoing. The human voice can sometimes be used for the first kind: the North American Indians, for example, had special calls which could be heard at a distance; yodelling, now practised as an art among Alpine mountaineers, was originally simply a means of signalling. Whistling, too, is often used as a signal, as when we whistle to a dog. A code of whistle signals exists in parts of Africa. Since earliest times pipes and horns have been used for this kind of signalling. Pipes were used by shepherds in ancient Rome, Greece, and the East. The bos'n's pipe, a very high-pitched kind of whistle, is used in the British Navy as a signal to the crew. It has a wide range of calls to convey different orders, many of which have been put out of use with the passing of sail. Among those that survive is that used for 'piping the side', when a senior officer or other distinguished person is received on board. But now the pipe is mostly used merely as a call to attention before an order is passed by word of mouth.

The horn is a practical signalling instrument, for its note will carry a great distance. The earliest horns, the hollowed-out horns of bulls, were used by shepherds, foresters, huntsmen, and soldiers. Horns were widely used in the Middle Ages, and many of the heroes of medieval legend, such as Roland and Robin Hood, carried a horn on which they sounded a special blast to summon their followers. Roland, one of the captains of the great Frankish emperor Charlemagne in the early 9th century, is reputed to have had a magic horn called Olivant, on which, when fatally wounded in a battle in the Pyrenees Mountains against the Saracens, Roland sounded a call for help to Charlemagne. The blast was so loud that the horn cracked in two, but Charlemagne in France heard it and rushed to the rescue—though too late. It was the practice in the Middle Ages for the look-out who kept watch from a castle-tower to sound a horn as a danger signal. 'Waits' or watchmen, who used to patrol the fortified walls of the towns, sounded the hours upon a horn. The horn is still used by huntsmen, who make their signals by means of a simple code of rhythmic blasts. The trumpet and bugle were long used for military signals in battle, the trumpet by the cavalry, the bugle by the infantry. They are now mainly used on ceremonial occasions.

Among the echoing types of signal are bells. In Roman times bells were hung round the necks of cattle, sheep, and goats so that their herdsmen could find them; this is still done in lands of unfenced pastures, such as mountains. From the Middle Ages onwards the small handbells of hawkers and others were frequently to be heard in the streets. Lepers had to carry a bell or a rattle to warn people to keep away from them, as their

Pitt Rivers Museum

WEST AFRICAN DRUMMER
Modern woodcarving made in Ashanti

disease was contagious. Bells are now used for many purposes in ordinary life, especially in the Navy, where each half-hour in a spell of duty (watch) is marked off by a special number of bells.

Church bells, which will carry a long way, have always been used for other purposes than calling people to worship. They were tolled to call people to their duties in the fields, or to summon them to a municipal function. The 'Pancake bell' was tolled on Shrove Tuesday as a signal to begin preparation for the Lenten fast and the 'passing bell' was tolled when someone was dying, so that everyone might pray for the departing soul. The church bell, which was sometimes the property of the town, was the town alarm signal, or 'tocsin', to spread news of dangers such as plague or fire, and to muster the soldiers in time of war. During the Second World War, the church bells were silenced in Britain so that they might be used as a signal in case of invasion. The church bell sounded the 'CURFEW' (q.v. Vol. X) in the Middle Ages, the signal for people to cover their fires and retire to bed—a custom probably introduced to Eng-

land by William the Conqueror. Until the 12th century it was a punishable offence in England to be out after the curfew had tolled the sunset, and the bells were still often rung at this hour centuries after the rule had ceased to be observed. In Oxford, Great Tom, the bell over the gateway of Christ Church, still tolls at 9.5 p.m. every night, the normal time for closing the college gates, its hundred-and-one strokes representing the hundred-and-one original students of Christ Church. (*See also* BELL-RINGING, Vol. IX.)

The drum, a common instrument in ancient religious rituals, was probably also used very long ago as a signalling instrument. It has been so used in the British army for some centuries. Side-drums, cylindrical drums with parchment at either end, were used in the infantry, and kettledrums, drums with a rounded underpart, in the cavalry. From the special code of army drum signals are derived such expressions as 'to beat a retreat', or 'to beat a tattoo'. Drums were also used at sea; in the 16th and 17th centuries galley slaves rowed to the rhythm of drums. In British men-of-war of the 18th century certain drum signals were familiar, such as 'beating to quarters', and the 'ruffle' with which a senior officer was saluted when he came on board. The drum was also used to inform ships in company of each other's whereabouts during foggy weather. The 'tom-tom' of India and the 'talking drum' of Africa can be made to carry messages over long distances. The 'talking drum', sometimes made from a hollow log, gives out a high note at one end and a low note at the other; sometimes two skin-topped drums are used, one high in pitch and the other low. To cut a note short, the drummer places his hand over the opening in the log, or else flat on the skin cover, to stop the vibrations. Because water is a good carrier of sound, a drum is sometimes placed low down near a river's edge. If the drum is placed over an anthill in which a hole has been cut, its hollow shape, like the belly of a violin, vibrates and increases the sound. The biggest African drums can be heard at a distance of about 20 miles; messages can be passed on by other drummers stationed at intervals. These messages are generally of a simple nature—perhaps to inform a village that a lion is raiding a neighbouring village, or that a certain farmer is urgently wanted. In villages where a talking drum exists, a code of signals with certain meanings is handed down by word of mouth from one generation to the next. This method of communicating in bush or jungle is known as 'the bush telegraph'.

See also FLAG SIGNALLING; LIGHT SIGNALLING; MORSE CODE; SIGNALLING, RAILWAY; SIGNS AND SYMBOLS.

SIGNALS (AVIATION), *see* NAVIGATION, AIR.

SIGNALS AT SEA. Formerly many merchant ships could 'speak' to one another only by shouting through a hand-trumpet or megaphone, or by hanging in the rigging a blackboard bearing a chalked message. Even to-day, some fishing fleets still use these methods.

The Royal Navy from early days began to devise codes of signals for FLAG SIGNALLING by day, and LIGHT SIGNALLING by night. Both methods could use the MORSE CODE, while in daytime SEMAPHORE signals (qq.v.) could be seen many miles away.

All ships of any size now use WIRELESS (q.v.). Smaller ones, which do not carry a qualified wireless operator, are often fitted with radio-

telephony, by which the captain can speak to other ships or to shore (*see* SPEECH, TRANSMISSION OF). Wireless signals of distress are preceded by the emergency call S O S, chosen because of its simplicity in Morse, . . . - - - . . . Distress signals are transmitted on one wavelength, and ships which have not sufficient wireless operators to keep up a continuous watch have an automatic listening apparatus which rings alarm bells if a distress signal is picked up.

SIGNS AND SYMBOLS have been used in many countries to communicate ideas by other means than speaking and writing. Some gestures are symbolic; they may be simple ones like taking off one's hat or saluting an officer, or they may be elaborate like the gestures used in MIME (q.v. Vol. IX) or DEAF LANGUAGES (q.v.). These gestures often differ from country to country; the Greeks, for instance, jerk their heads backwards when they say 'No'. The handshake as a symbol of friendship and the seal of a bargain is very old; the ancient Jews, Greeks, and Romans used it.

Colours make convenient signs. Often the same colours have been used to express the same ideas among different nations. Red, for instance, in the knots and beads sent as messages in ancient Peru and among the Iroquois tribes meant war or danger, just as red lights in modern streets mean danger. Black among the same peoples meant death or other misfortune, as it did among the Egyptians and Romans, and still does to-day; and white meant peace and innocence. Green usually expresses spring, youth, joy, or victory. Purple is the colour of kings, and yellow that of traitors. In France, until modern times, the doors of traitors' houses used to be painted yellow.

Plants and flowers have their meanings. The ancient Greeks hung laurel outside a house to show that someone inside was ill. In the 18th century Turkish women used to send long messages, without touching pen or paper, by making up bouquets of flowers. In their language, flowers signified things with which their names rhymed. In the 19th century a conventional 'language of flowers' was popular in Britain, France, and the U.S.A. Dictionaries and other books were published to describe the meanings of flowers. The violet meant innocence, and the marigold despair. Different colours and varieties of rose had special meanings: the dog rose meant

'CARNATION—FASCINATION'
Illustration from *The Language of Flowers*, 1858

'pleasure mixed with pain', the white rose full of buds 'secrecy', and the yellow rose 'infidelity'. Thus messages could be sent to a sweetheart to show the sender's feelings. Red roses were a declaration of love.

Secret signs have often been used to convey to people information of a special kind. In Britain, until the early 20th century, begging tramps, who called from house to house to ask for food, money, or clothes, used to leave marks on the gate or wall of a house they had visited to indicate to other tramps whether the householder was likely to give charity or not, what excuse to offer for begging, whether there was an angry dog, and so on.

Sometimes signs have been used as symbols of violence, rioting, and war. The Highland clans of Scotland used to be called to arms by a fiery cross, symbolical of fire and sword. It was a cross whose ends had been burnt and then dipped in blood. In violence between races in parts of

U.S.A. in modern times the fiery cross has been revived by the Ku Klux Klan (*see* SECRET SOCIETIES, Vol. X).

See also SIGNALS.

SIMPLON TUNNEL. This tunnel, which crosses the Alps on the line between Lausanne in Switzerland and Milan in Italy, is the longest main-line railway tunnel in the world, running for 12⅓ miles beneath the Simplon Pass (*see* MOUNTAIN PASSES). It is the most important of the five tunnels which now pierce the Alps, making railway travel possible through this great mountain range, formerly a barrier between western Europe and Italy, which could be crossed only by roads through the passes.

The first proposal for a tunnel under the Simplon Pass was made as early as 1857; but it was not until 1895 that agreement was reached finally between the Swiss and Italian Governments, and work did not begin until 1898. Although the south end of the tunnel is in Italian territory, the agreement provided that the entire tunnel and its Italian approach from Domodossola should be a Swiss undertaking; and the Swiss Federal Railways still operate the Simplon line as far as Domodossola.

The Simplon consists of twin tunnels, 56 feet apart at the centres, one for each direction. The one on the eastern side is the original tunnel, which was opened in 1906. The one on the western side was originally a pilot tunnel, much smaller, driven to help in the work on the main tunnel. This pilot tunnel has been opened out to full size to take a second track, a task which was begun soon after the opening of the main tunnel, but was delayed by the First World War and was not completed until 1921.

Making the tunnel was an extremely difficult engineering feat. About five miles from the northern entrance, where the tunnel is at its deepest, the temperature in the workings rose so high that to enable the men to continue work at all the rock at the working face had to be sprayed with ice-cold water, specially pumped into the tunnel. Underground streams frequently broke into the workings, flowing in at times at a rate of as much as 3,000 gallons a minute, and sometimes hot springs would break in, adding greatly to the problems of heat. At other points the work was slowed down and made dangerous by the kind of material through which the tunnel had to be driven: at one point, for instance, there

THE NORTH ENTRANCE TO THE SIMPLON TUNNEL

Swiss Federal Railway.

was a pocket of micaceous lime schist, a kind of rock which, if disturbed, will thrust in all directions as if it were a liquid, and which exerted such enormous pressure on the structure of the tunnel that powerful steel reinforcements were liable to be bent by it. Because of this no less than 7 months were spent over only 138 feet of tunnel. At this point the masonry lining is now reinforced permanently by a series of extremely strong curved steel internal girders.

The original tunnel, with the pilot tunnel, cost a total of 86,720,000 Swiss francs. The pilot tunnel was connected with the main tunnel by small passages from the sides, at intervals of 220 yards, and was used for pumping cold air up to the working faces, and water for the drills, as well as carrying out of the tunnel the water that broke in at many points. Enlarging it to full size was, of course, a much simpler and less costly

task than that of building the original main tunnel.

See also TUNNELS.
See also Vol. VIII: TUNNELLING.

SKI, *see* SNOW AND ICE TRAVEL.

SLANG. This is the name given to words, word-usages, and phrases found only in loose, colloquial language, and not in standard speech or writing. The words used in slang may themselves be new; but they are very often substitutes for, or variants of expressions already in the standard language.

We use slang for all sorts of reasons, sometimes 'for fun'; sometimes because it seems picturesque or concise; sometimes to avoid the ordinary word, as when we say 'Adam's ale' for water; and sometimes because it seems to express our feelings better than more dignified language. We are more likely to use slang when speaking to friends and acquaintances than when addressing strangers or superiors; for it is essentially a casual and intimate form of speech. We might describe it as language in its shirtsleeves: it is informal, without necessarily being faulty.

There are numerous varieties of slang, and its sources are endless. Groups of people who have common interests tend to create their own slang; and since most people belong to more than one such group, some of the slang of each group comes into general use (though its precise, original meaning may weaken), while the rest remains known only to a few people. The main groups are:

1. Gipsies, and thieves, and tramps who do not wish the outsider to understand all they say. Some of the earliest European slang words we know are of this kind, and a few have come into general slang use: 'pal' which was originally a gipsy word for 'brother', 'quid' which was used as far back as the 17th century for 'guinea' or 'sovereign', 'bob' for a shilling, and 'tanner' for sixpence.

2. Trades and professions, especially theatrical and military. This slang must be distinguished from technical terms used in the trade. Military slang tends to come into general use in times of war. For example, in the Second World War the slang expressions 'browned off', 'pranged', and 'shooting a line', which were originally used by the R.A.F., were spoken by all kinds of people.

3. Schools and universities. Here slang perhaps develops partly in reaction to the more precise speech of teachers and lecturers. Some Public Schools have a slang of their own: it was from Rugby that the habit of abbreviating words and adding -*er* spread to Oxford, producing words like 'brekker', 'toggers', and 'rugger', the last of which is now generally used for Rugby Football.

4. Fashionable society or sections of it. This slang tends to consist of meaningless phrases that can be used to keep conversation going, for example: 'Oh I say', 'don't you know'.

5. Family slang. Most families evolve a small vocabulary of their own, which will include names and phrases mystifying to other people.

All these groups have their own peculiar ways of coining slang: Cockney costermongers, for example, used to be fond of 'back slang', which consists in pronouncing words backwards, as 'ecilop' for 'police'. Rhyming slang, such as 'trouble and strife' for wife, 'plates of meat' for feet, 'Oxford scholar' for dollar, is said to be Cockney in origin though it is also found in Australia and America.

The slang of almost all groups has certain common tendencies. It makes light of a serious or tragic situation, or refers to it by paraphrase. Thus a man who dies is said to 'go west', or 'kick the bucket' or to have 'gone for a Burton' (all of which phrases are now used by speakers unaware of their original meaning). In the same way the dangerous flying bomb of the Second World War became known as a 'doodle-bug'.

It identifies objects or institutions with well-known persons. Thus policemen were at first known as 'bobbies' or 'peelers', after Sir Robert Peel, who established the modern police force. The first name survives to-day. 'Belisha beacons' commemorate the Minister of Transport who introduced them.

It gives a new meaning to a common word. Thus 'bacon' comes to mean 'body', as in the phrase 'to save one's bacon' or 'skin'.

It uses a word of precise or powerful meaning in a context where it cannot carry such a meaning; so that the word becomes debased and weakened, for example 'nice' which formerly meant amongst other things, 'delicate', 'precise' —a 'nice' judgement meant a finely discriminating judgement. The adverb 'nicely' merely means 'well'; 'terribly' and 'awfully' have now become mere equivalents to 'very', as in 'awfully glad you came'. Slang delights in abbreviations: the hols (holidays), the High (Street), the Raf (R.A.F.), the Wrens (W.R.N.S.). It invents grotesque parodies of high-sounding words such as 'rumbustious'.

Languages borrow each other's slang, just as they borrow more respectable words. In the last 100 years America has been especially prolific in slang, partly native, partly adapted from the speech of emigrants from Europe; and some words that began as American slang are now in common use in English—'bunkum', 'stunt', 'movies', or 'talkies'. Several words of Australian slang, too, are by now familiar to us, such as 'to barrack'.

In view of the vividness and conciseness of much slang, it may seem pedantic to consider it as separate from and inferior to STANDARD ENGLISH (q.v.). To be sure Shakespeare used words that were doubtless slang in his day, though we do not always recognize them as such now; and other words that were once certainly slang are now used in serious writing, for example 'mob' (from *mobile vulgus*), which Swift thought a 'vulgar' word; 'hoax' (from hocus-pocus); 'prig' (originally a person overscrupulous about dress); and 'joke'. To take an example from another language, French *tête*, meaning head, is from Latin slang *testa*, meaning a pot. But comparatively few slang words change their status in this way, though there are many borderline cases This is partly because slang words are often intentionally grotesque in sound or appearance, and partly because slang that does become generally used is often applied so loosely or is so overworked that people become tired of it.

See also DIALECTS; ENGLISH LANGUAGE.

SLAVONIC LANGUAGES. The group of languages and dialects known as Slavonic belongs to the INDO-EUROPEAN (q.v.) family, of which, with the Baltic Languages, Lithuanian and Latvian (or Lettish) spoken by the inhabitants of Lithuania and Latvia, it forms one of the main divisions. Some 200 million people speak these languages, which include Russian, Polish, Czech, and others. They are all descended from the same language, Common Slavonic, which probably broke away from the main Indo-European family before Christian times. Slavonic languages have many characteristics in common: their nouns and adjectives are highly inflected (that is, they show very many different endings according to their functions in the sentence), Russian and Polish having as many as seven cases. They have few tenses, but their verbs preserve an ancient distinction called 'aspect' between actions thought of as finished or limited in time, and those which are regarded as continuous (see LANGUAGE STRUCTURE). They also use varied changes in the final syllables to produce subtle shades of meaning: Russian *Vasili* 'Basil', for instance, may also take the forms *Vaska*, *Vasya* and *Vasyenka*, to show changes in the attitude (affection and so on) of the speaker.

There are two principal Slavonic alphabets to-day, the Cyrillic and the Latin (see ALPHABET). Cyrillic (named after St. Cyril) was based on Greek letters as used by St. Cyril and St. Methodius when they converted some southern Slavs in the early Middle Ages. It has remained, with some modern changes, the method of writing for languages of all those Slavonic peoples whose Christianity and culture came from the Greek civilization of medieval Constantinople, directly or indirectly (see ORTHODOX EASTERN CHURCH, Vol. I). East Slavonic languages, such as Russian, all use it, and the Russians have applied it to many non-European languages in the U.S.S.R. The West Slavs, such as the Poles and Czechs, who came to accept Christianity and culture through Catholic Latin-using teachers, write their languages in adaptations of the Latin alphabet. In the Balkans, Serbians and Bulgarians use Cyrillic, while the Croats (whose language is practically the same as Serbian), and the Slovenes write in Latin characters. Russian, with its 32 letters of the alphabet, is able to express its sounds roughly according to a rule of one sound, one letter, with a fairly consistent phonetic spelling; whereas Polish finds it necessary to use many complex-looking groups of letters and marks to express some single sounds. Czech has the most practical Latin alphabet.

Apart from the differences in the alphabet, the following are some of the characteristics which distinguish one Slavonic sub-group from another: Polish has fixed the word-stress on the last syllable but one, and Czech largely on the first; Slovene has kept a good deal of the old dual number of nouns (that is, a special form for a pair of things); Bulgarian has considerably

ahs (a)	а	*khayr* (kh)	х
bookee (b)	б	guttural as in 'LOCH'	
vaydee (v)	в	*tsee* (ts)	ц
glahgol (g)	г	*tchervay* (ch)	ч
dobroh (d)	д	(as in 'CHURCH')	
yaist (e *or* ye)	е	*shah* (sh)	ш
zheevaytay (zh)	ж	*shtshah* (shch)	щ
zemlyah (z)	з	(as in 'ASHCHURCH')	
eeshay (ī)	и	*yayr* (*mute* sign)	ъ
*eeshay (ī)	і	*yayree* (oui)	ы
eeshay (ī)	й	(as in French 'oui')	
kahkoh (k)	к	*yayr* (*mouillé* sign)	ь
lyoodee (l)	л	(makes e.g. t = ty)	
meesslaytay (m)	м	*yaht (e *or* ye)	ѣ
nahsh (n)	н	*a* (e *initial*)	э
on (o)	о	(as in EXTEND, EPIC)	
pohkoee (p)	п	*you* (iou)	ю
rtsee (r)	р	(as English 'you')	
sslovoh (s)	с	*yah* (ya)	я
tverdoh (t)	т, ш	*feetah* (f)	ѳ
oo (u)	у	(not TH in Russian)	
fayrt (f)	ф	*eezheezah (ī)	ѵ

* i, ѣ, ѵ now obsolete.

MODERN RUSSIAN ALPHABET

simplified its various grammatical endings, but has developed a definite article (equivalent to English 'the') added after its noun.

Russian, the most important Slavonic language, belongs to the East Slavonic group. It is divided into Great Russian, or Russian proper, spoken by about 100 million people, and centred in Moscow; Ukrainian, or Little Russian, a language spoken in the Ukraine, of which the capital is Kiev; and White Russian, centred at Minsk, and now often called Byelo-Russian to avoid confusion with White Russian as a political term. About 40 million people speak either Ukrainian or White Russian; of the two, White Russian is less distinct from Russian proper. A kind of Little Russian, or Ruthenian, is spoken by about 10 million people in Ruthenia.

Russian differs from the other Slavonic languages in several ways. Its word-order is very free, and its sentence construction simple. It is very rich, and new compound words are readily formed by joining already existing words (such as *pravoslavny* 'orthodox', made from *pravo* and *slavny* which are direct translations of the Greek words *orthos* 'straight' and *doxa* 'opinion'). Russian also includes a few words of Turkic or Tatar origin, from early Asiatic invasions. That Russian is an Indo-European language, as is English, can be seen by comparing similar words in the two languages, such as *kot*, 'cat', *gus* 'goose', *sestra* 'sister', *syn* 'son'.

Russian has absorbed some words from German, French, and even English since the 16th century: it uses certain technical terms which are common in Europe, but it has otherwise remained strictly Slavonic.

Polish, Czech, and Slovak belong to the West Slavonic group. Polish is spoken by about 25 million people, Czech by 8 million, and Slovak, which is closely related to it, by about 3 million. Another language of the West Slavonic group is Wendish, spoken by about 100,000 people in districts on the Spree near Berlin.

Russian, Polish, and Czech have each a literature of European importance; and the influence of Russian classical literature and that of the new Soviet way of life, combined with the fact that Russian is the official language for the vast U.S.S.R., make Russian one of the great languages of the world.

Other Slavonic languages, Serbo-Croat, spoken by about 12 million, Bulgarian by about 7 million, and Slovene by about 1,500,000, with

Проказница-Мартышка,
Осел,
Козел
Да косолапый Мишка
Затеяли сыграть Квартет.

THE FIRST LINES OF A FABLE BY THE RUSSIAN AUTHOR KRYLOV
Published by the State Publishing House of Belles Lettres, Moscow

The tricksome little monkey
The donkey
The goat
And the clumsy-pawed bear
Ventured to play a quartet

mixed dialects of Slavonic parts of Macedonia in Yugoslavia, together make up South Slavonic, which is the meaning of Yugoslav.

See also LANGUAGE STRUCTURE.

See also Vol. I: RUSSIANS; POLES; CZECHOSLOVAKS; YUGOSLAVS; BULGARIANS.

SLEDGE. The earliest form of vehicle used by man before the WHEEL (q.v.) was invented was the sledge. Probably in very early days the hunter found that if he put his kill across a branch torn from a tree, he could drag it home more easily. Later he would begin to shape the branch, or to tie two branches together and bend up the front to make them slide easily over the rough ground. When he had fixed cross-pieces between his branches and attached leather thongs for pulling, he had formed a primitive sledge. Sledges, we know, were used in ancient Egypt for transporting the huge stone blocks for erecting pyramids, temples, and other buildings.

Even when the wheel was invented and generally used for vehicles, the sledge was still used over surfaces such as deep snow, where wheels would sink and stick. In Canada and Alaska dogs haul the sledges of trappers, prospectors, and traders. Timber, also, is often carried on heavy sledges in the winter. In northern Europe and Asia, particularly in Lapland, sledges are drawn by reindeer. In Russia a sledge called a 'troika' is drawn by three horses

Swiss Federal Railways

SWISS ARMY TRANSPORT BY SLEDGE AND SKIS

abreast. In Switzerland and other mountainous districts the sledge is used to carry food and fuel. It is used also, of course, on Polar expeditions for transporting equipment.

Sledges are also used in hot countries over soft ground where wheels might stick. In Siam a sledge like a wooden platform mounted on bamboo runners is drawn by water buffalo from the rice-fields to the village. Sledges on heavy wooden runners are drawn by oxen or by men over the cobbled streets of Madeira, for the runners of the sledge travel more smoothly on the cobbles than do the wheels of a cart.

See also SNOW AND ICE TRAVEL: BEASTS OF BURDEN.
See also Vol. IX: TOBOGGANING.

SLEEPING-CAR, *see* RAILWAY COACHES, Section 4.

SLIP-COACH, *see* RAILWAY COACHES, Section 7.

SMUGGLERS, *see* Vol. X: SMUGGLERS.

SNOW AND ICE TRAVEL. The traveller on snow and ice has not only to contend with extreme cold, for which he requires special windproof clothing, but also with the difficulties of the surface over which he is travelling, which is usually very soft, very slippery, or both; he may even be on floating ice. His problem is to avoid either sinking into snow or breaking through ice. He therefore has to use devices for spreading the weight of himself and his goods over a large area, so that the chances of sinking in or breaking through are reduced.

Travel over snow and ice has been carried on by Eskimoes, North American Indians, Lapps, and other tribes of northern Europe and Asia for centuries, and all have evolved their own methods of overcoming the difficulties. In open regions where the snow tends to be relatively hard, such as the lands of the ESKIMOES and some of the SIBERIAN PEOPLES (qq.v. Vol. I), the people wear soft sealskin boots to keep them warm. But in regions where the snow is very deep and soft, they have to wear special footgear to prevent their sinking into the snow. The AMERICAN INDIANS of the north (q.v. Vol. I), who live mostly in thickly wooded country, wear snowshoes, which consist of bent wood frames with a network of raw-hide thongs, the shoe being sufficiently wide to spread the weight well.

The LAPPS (q.v. Vol. I), also inhabitants of wooded country which is under snow for long periods of the year, have developed a long, narrow, wooden shoe or ski, which slides easily over the snow, in place of the broad snowshoe, which has to be lifted from the ground at each step. These skis give the Lapps considerable speed, which is important to a people who live by herding reindeer. Skis are used, not only for the sport of SKI-ING (q.v. Vol. IX), but also as the normal way of getting about in lands, such as Norway or Switzerland, where soft deep snow usually lasts for a long period of time. In such countries children often go to school on skis, instead of bicycles. Skis are also used on expeditions into POLAR REGIONS (q.v. Vol. III). Skates, on the other hand, have never been used as a means of travelling across ice by primitive people, largely because the ice is usually too rough. They were developed, however, by the Dutch, who used them in Holland on the large areas of inland water which become covered with smooth ice in the winter. Now they are used almost entirely for the sports of SKATING and ICE HOCKEY (qq.v. Vol. IX).

Wheeled transport is impracticable over snow and ice, and other methods have been developed. Probably the most primitive are the flat-bottomed toboggans of the Red Indians and the boat-shaped *pulkas* of the Lapps, both of which spread the weight of the load over the surface of soft snow. The Eskimoes lift the load off the ground on a SLEDGE (q.v.) with two separate narrow runners which are often shod with bone. Modern polar expeditions usually use sledges of the Eskimo type, with either broad wooden runners, or narrow steel-shod ones, according to the kind of surface expected. In some conditions the sledge runs better if the runners are kept scraped clean, while in other conditions friction can be reduced if a layer of ice is allowed to form on the runners; occasionally, at very low temperatures, the runners grip the ice better if they are covered with a layer of ice mixed with mud, or even something like porridge or blood.

Different draft animals and various methods of hauling vehicles over snow and ice are used in different regions (*see* BEASTS OF BURDEN, Sec-

E.N.A.

A LABRADOR TRAPPER WEARING SNOWSHOES

tion 5), dogs and reindeer being the most common. In recent years mechanical transport with caterpillar tracks has been increasingly used with considerable success.

Travel in polar and other snow and ice-bound regions has been revolutionized in modern times by the use of aeroplanes and by the invention of radio communication. Much more is now known about suitable clothing, tents, stoves, and the kind of food necessary to keep the traveller warm and healthy. The explorer no longer runs the same risk of disaster which befell expeditions of earlier times.

See also BEASTS OF BURDEN, Section 5; SLEDGE.
See also Vol. IX: SKATING; SKI-ING; TOBOGGANING.

SOVEREIGN OF THE SEAS, THE. This three-masted ship was launched at Woolwich in 1637. She was built by Phineas and Peter Pett, father and son, members of a distinguished family of shipwrights. She is said to be the first three-decker, or ship mounting three complete tiers of guns, 104 in all, on decks one above the other; but this is disputable. It is certain, however, that she was a ship notable for her very lavish

THE 'SOVEREIGN OF THE SEAS' AND HER BUILDER, PETER PETT
Probably painted in 1659–60 by W. van de Velde

ornamentation. A certain Peter Munday wrote in 1639: 'Her head, waist, quarter, and stern is so largely enriched with carved work overlaid with gold that it appears most glorious even from afar, especially her spacious lofty stern, whereon is expressed all that art and cost can do in carving and gilding.' She was steered by tackles on the tiller and the helmsman was directed from above through a voice-pipe. Her cook-room was in the hold, 'the work therein done by candlelight'. To pay for her, Charles I in 1634 had revived an obsolete power of the Crown to impress ships for naval service from the seaport towns; but instead of ships he asked for money, and he also approached the inland towns. This was the celebrated SHIP MONEY (q.v. Vol. X), and John Hampden's refusal to pay and subsequent trial played its part in bringing about the Civil Wars which lost King Charles both his crown and his head.

The *Sovereign of the Seas* saw service at the battle of the Kentish Knock in 1652, when the English fleet, commanded by Admiral Blake, defeated the Dutch off the mouth of the Thames. The ship was rebuilt in 1659 and again in 1684, and was accidentally burnt at Chatham in 1696.

See SHIPS, SAILING.

SPANISH AND PORTUGUESE LAN-GUAGES. These are two closely related lan-

guages which are descended from LATIN, and therefore belong to the group known as the ROMANCE LANGUAGES (qq.v.). Both include many Arabic words which have stayed in use since the time when the MOORS (q.v. Vol. I) dominated Spain, from about the 8th to the 15th century.

Spanish is spoken by about 115 million people: 27 million in Spain, and the rest in the former Spanish colonies of Central and South America. Mixed with local and Malay words, it is also spoken by many people in the Philippine Islands in the Pacific Ocean, which were once colonized by Spain. There are various dialects, ranging from those in north-west Spain which resemble Portuguese, to those in the east which are more like French and Provençal. The standard language of Spain is Castellano, or Castilian, the language of the province of Castile. In sound it is very like ITALIAN (q.v.). It has a strong 'r' sound, and a sound like the Scottish 'ch' (written 'j' or 'g'). One letter characteristic of Spanish is 'ñ' like the letters 'ni' in the English word 'onion' similar to French and Italian 'gn'. As in many European languages, nouns are either masculine or feminine in gender; and as in Italian, many masculine words end in 'o' and many feminine ones in 'a'. The spelling of Spanish is very simple, for almost every letter corresponds to one sound only, and vice versa. Spanish is studied in most British universities and in many schools, mainly for its value in trade relations with South America, but also for its literary importance. Among the best works written in Spanish is *Don Quixote* by CERVANTES (qq.v. Vol. V).

Portuguese is spoken by about 8 million people in Portugal, and 46 million in Brazil, which was for a long time a Portuguese colony. Forms of it are spoken in parts of Africa, such as Guinea, Angola, and Mozambique, and parts of Asia, such as Goa in India and Timor in the East Indies, which are or were once under Portuguese domination. It contains many sounds which are not in Spanish, including certain nasal vowels, ã, õ, and so on. About half a million people in the north of Spain speak the Basque language, which, as far as is known, is not related to any other language.

See also LANGUAGE STRUCTURE.
See also Vol. I: SPANIARDS; PORTUGUESE.

SPEECH. Speech is the most important, though not the only means by which men communicate their thoughts and feelings to each other. Whistling, gestures like shrugging the shoulders, SIGNALS (q.v.) like church bells or traffic-lights, are other ways. Indeed, we may think of speech as the act of making a signal by means of the breath, tongue, teeth, vocal cords, and the nose and mouth passages. So great a variety of distinct sounds can be produced by these organs, acting on messages from the brain, that any other system of sending complex 'signals' seems inadequate when compared with speech. WRITING (q.v.) is simply a way of representing speech in the absence of a speaker.

Speech would not exist if we did not feel the need to communicate to others our thoughts and feelings. Many kinds of animals communicate with each other: birds and monkeys, for example, give warning and courting cries, and some, such as the parrot, can imitate human sounds. But there is no evidence that any animals can, of their own accord, make special sounds to describe particular objects. Animal sounds are instinctive, and only very general meanings can be attached to them: they are not the same as words (*see* ANIMAL LANGUAGE, Vol. II).

Many early myths give explanations of how man learned to talk; and philosophers and scholars still differ among themselves on this subject. For no one can be certain how speech began, or how primitive speech was related to the sounds and gestures of animals. It has been suggested that speech as we now know it began only after the larynx in the throat had developed in tree-climbing animals, whose climbing gestures were accompanied by regular emissions of breath, or interjections. But interjections of this kind would be involuntary, whereas human speech has a definite purpose. Some scholars believe that gesture was the first means of communication, and that words, or sentences, were originally 'mouth-gestures', which at first accompanied and in some way imitated 'hand-gestures', and later replaced them. But there is no evidence that gestures developed before sounds. Chimpanzees, it is true, use gesture to express emotions, but never to indicate objects: unlike human beings they have no way of making statements; and though they may react to signs accompanying speech or to tones of voice, they do not understand human speech alone. Other scholars have held that primitive speech was an attempt to imitate directly the action, object, or sensation that the speaker was describing. But even in the most primitive languages, imitative words make up only a small part of the vocabulary. In fact, no known language gives us more than a faint clue as to what the very earliest speech was like; so that it is impossible to prove any of these theories.

Whatever its origin, we can be reasonably sure that speech did not develop until men began to live in communities and to act together. But it is not clear how certain sounds came to represent always particular objects or to have certain values. 'Giving things names' is one way of describing this stage of development. But if we use this phrase, we must remember that in the earliest languages there was probably no distinction between nouns and other words: just as in at least one language still spoken—Malayan— it is not always easy to say when a word is noun, verb, or adjective (*see* INDONESIAN LANGUAGES). At the very beginning all words possibly had some kind of inflexion or special ending to show their function in the sentence. Thus 'primitive' languages were probably not primitive in structure: Bantu, one of the most primitive languages now known, has some twenty classes of nouns. Indeed, it is in some ways misleading to describe these early languages as primitive: they were probably adequate and suitable for the kind of society in which they were first used.

At first the connexion between things and their 'names' was felt to be so close that the names were credited with a certain magical power, just as in some societies a child named after a famous ancestor is thought to be given some of that ancestor's qualities. Amongst primitive peoples, when so much in nature was unknown and mysterious, words, especially if used in incantations, probably had a great magical significance; for example, a god's name was thought of as part of him, and if, when praying to him, the right name was not used, the prayer would be thought ineffectual (*see* SPELLS AND INCANTATIONS, Vol. I).

The discovery that everything can be given a 'name' must have been as decisive in the history of mankind as it was in the life of Helen Keller, the blind, deaf-mute girl who, at the age of seven, suddenly began asking, by the use of the finger-alphabet, the name of everything she touched, and then ceased to use signs. (*See* DEAF LANGUAGES.) The next step must have been to learn that one can use various words to express the same object, that is, to learn that words are simply symbols. It was probably not till much later that men began to find names to describe whole classes of things or actions ('animal'; 'moving') or abstract qualities ('redness'; 'goodness').

See also LANGUAGE, HISTORY OF; NAMES.

SPEECH, TRANSMISSION OF. A spoken sentence—'Mr. Watson, come here; I want you' —was the first ever heard by electric means. The words were spoken over a length of a wire in 1876. This was the climax of 40 years of effort to find a way of electrically conveying SOUND (q.v. Vol. III).

During those years inventors in many countries claimed to have made 'electric speech', and in 1861 a German experimenter, Philip Reis, came near to producing the first telephone. A knitting-needle, an animal membrane, some sealing-wax, platinum, and a violin were some of the objects he used; but, though he could transmit sound of constant pitch, he could not send speech.

The man who succeeded in 1876 was Alexander Graham Bell, a Scot whose family had emigrated to Boston, Massachusetts; it was there that he invented the telephone.

His apparatus, though primitive, had all the elements of to-day's instrument. His 'microphone' was a horn-like speaking-tube, at the narrow end of which was a flat disk, or 'diaphragm'. This, as the sound waves from the

Crown Copyright

EARLY BELL TELEPHONE, 1876
From an exhibit in the Science Museum, London

D.D.C.

A PROGRAMME ENGINEER IN A LISTENING CUBICLE
The engineer controls the transmission from the studio

voice struck it, vibrated in sympathy with the waves, setting up variations of electric current (supplied by a battery) in an electro-magnetic coil. These variations were then carried over the connecting wire, at the other end of which was a receiving apparatus exactly like the transmitter. Vibrations in the diaphragm of this receiver caused sound-waves in the air which were very like those caused by the human voice.

Bell made his successful experiment in a noisy electrical workshop, he being in an attic-room, and Watson, his assistant, in the basement. This followed an experiment in the previous year when, in trying to work out an idea for transmitting many dot-and-dash telegraph messages over one wire at the same time, he heard on his instrument a twanging sound, accidentally caused by his assistant at the other end of their connecting wire. He realized then that not only dots and dashes but lifelike sounds might be passed over the wire.

From then on, experiments were made on both sides of the Atlantic. Among those who contributed most were the American inventor, Thomas Edison, and an English professor, D. E. Hughes, whose experiments with early microphones greatly improved the quality of speech. Hughes (the first to use the word 'microphone') had found that a loose contact in a telephone circuit made sounds corresponding to any vibrations affecting the contact; on this principle he invented the first carbon microphone—one of the principal types in use to-day.

While speech communication over wires was itself being developed, scientists were working on the idea of taking the human voice from one place to another without wires, and by 1888 a crude form of wireless speech communication up to 2 or 3 miles was demonstrated by Bell and Edison in America, Sir William Preece in Britain, and others. Something more was needed, and the answer came with the development of WIRELESS TELEGRAPHY (q.v.). But before telegraph methods could be used to carry speech, many questions had to be answered, such as how to produce from the transmitter continuous 'carrier' waves to 'carry' speech; how to 'modulate' them —that is, superimpose speech-waves on the carrier; and how to amplify the weak currents set up by the impact of the voice on a microphone.

There were notable developments even before those difficulties were overcome. Soon after 1900 an American professor, R. A. Fessenden, had used wireless waves to carry the human voice over a distance of a mile, and in 1906 he transmitted speech and music over a distance of 25 miles—thus staking a strong claim to be regarded as the first broadcaster. The following year he increased the range of communication to 100 miles. By 1910 the wireless telephone had spanned 500 miles. Technical shortcomings, however, were still so serious that the practical range of communication was not expected to be more than 100 miles or so.

The British professor, Sir Ambrose Fleming, made widespread speech possible when he invented the THERMIONIC VALVE (q.v. Vol. VIII) in 1904. This was like an ordinary electric-light bulb, but with a third wire sticking into it, and was intended to provide a more sensitive device for detecting wireless telegraph waves. Dr. Lee de Forest in America improved it, but it was still regarded merely as a device for receiving telegraph signals. Later the valve became the means of transmitting 'continuous waves', which greatly added to the distance telegraph signals could travel; it also amplified very weak signals which reached a receiver. Many years went by before its marvellous resources were fully known, and the valve was used to 'modulate' wireless waves, or to impress on them the characteristics of speech. Then, in 1915, a transmitter fitted with hundreds of valves was set up in Arlington, U.S.A., and succeeded in speaking to Paris, 3,500 miles away. For the next few years similar experimental transmissions were carried out on both sides of the Atlantic.

Long wave-lengths up to 6,000 metres were used because they were thought to be the best for long distances; but by this time the usefulness of the SHORT WAVE (q.v.) was being explored, and in 1921 they were used for two-way telephony between London and Amsterdam. In 1924 came the first transmission of speech from England to Australia. In 1926 a two-way telephone service was opened between London and New York, and the first stations set up in a vast network by which the member-nations of the British Commonwealth might speak to one another.

Already, in the early 1920's, the great step had been taken from wireless telephony to broadcasting (see BROADCASTING, HISTORY OF). The methods of that time became standardized, but before broadcasting had been in use for 20 years, one of its big limitations became clear. Since transmitters and receivers all over the world were based on the same technical principles, it was found to be hard to introduce any radical improvement. If broadcasting methods were changed, it would take some years to replace all the receivers. During that time, unless many listeners were to be cut off from radio, the B.B.C. and other corporations would have to double their transmission plant and broadcast all their programmes on both the old and new methods. Engineers had to face this problem with the development of frequency modulation (see WIRELESS, Vol. VIII). This is a method of broadcasting, or radio-telephony, which greatly improves the quality of voice or music, and reduces background noise and other blemishes. Hundreds of 'F.M.' stations are broadcasting in U.S.A., where there are many radio corporations for listeners to choose from. 'F.M.' is also much used for private wireless, as in police patrol cars (see TELEPHONE, MOBILE). But the equipment of most of the world's main broadcasting systems continues to be based on the older principle, that of 'amplitude modulation'.

See also BROADCASTING; TELEPHONE SERVICE.
See also Vol. VIII: RADIO ENGINEERING.

SPEED. Until man learnt to fly, little was known of the effect on the human body of movement at high speeds. When railways were first being built, it was feared by some people that to travel much faster than the speed of a horse would be injurious to health. All modern transport, and particularly flying, has taught man much about the effect of fast travel on the body.

The speed of many modern aircraft is over 500 miles an hour, yet no matter how great the speed of flight, even if faster than sound, it is not felt, provided that it is uniform, that there is full protection against the force of the wind, and that there are no passing objects to give visual clues. The earth rotates round its axis at over 600 miles per hour in Britain (1,034 m.p.h. at the Equator), and revolves round the sun at 65,000 m.p.h.: all that we experience is the force of gravity holding us down to the earth.

We do, however, feel acutely any changes in speed or direction if they are sudden; a passenger may stand safely in a moving bus for a long time, but he will be thrown off his feet by any sudden increase or decrease in the speed of the bus, or a sudden turn to left or right; in the same way, one may drink a cup of tea without spilling it while sitting in a fast-moving express train, but a slight nudge from someone's elbow will spill the tea. This illustrates Newton's First Law of Motion (q.v. Vol. III), by which any object, whether at rest or moving, will stay in that condition unless something forcibly changes its position, speed, or direction. Acceleration or deceleration, acting on a man or an aircraft, is expressed in terms of the force of gravity (g), which causes a body to have weight (*see* GRAVITATION, Vol. III). A force of 6 'g' will cause a body to have six times its normal weight, so that the blood becomes as heavy as molten iron, and the heart has considerable difficulty, or even inability, to maintain the circulation to the head. During a steep turn or dive, this force acts from the centre outwards, like swinging a chestnut on the end of a string. It tends to drain or spin the blood to the farthest parts of the body, so that the eyes and brain are momentarily starved of blood, causing dimming or blacking-out of vision, and even unconsciousness if the force is great and maintained for more than a few seconds. In the normal sitting position blacking-out occurs in the average healthy individual when a force of over $4\frac{1}{2}$ 'g' is applied and maintained for at least 4 seconds. Some people in the upright sitting position, can withstand 7 or more 'g' before blacking-out occurs. Legless pilots have a high resistance to blacking-out, as there is less area into which the blood can drain.

In ordinary commercial passenger flying, blacking-out does not occur, as forces greater than 2 'g' are not normally met with. In military aviation high forces of 'g' are attained; pneumatic anti-gravity trousers have been devised to stop the blood pooling in the legs and so prevent blacking-out happening to fighter pilots during aerobatics.

See also AEROBATICS; HIGH-ALTITUDE FLIGHT.

SPEED RECORDS, RAILWAY, *see* RAILWAY SPEED RECORDS.

SPELLING. The object of alphabetic writing is to represent the sounds of speech (*see* ALPHABET). Ideally a reader should be able to pronounce any word accurately at sight, and a writer should be able to spell any word correctly once he has heard it. This ideal would be possible only if the alphabet had one separate symbol for every distinct sound, but—except for the International Phonetic Alphabet which is too unwieldy and unfamiliar for ordinary use—there is no such alphabet in existence. The Roman Alphabet which is used throughout Europe has evolved during the course of centuries, being adapted to suit different languages. As it contains too few letters for all the sounds of speech, many sounds have to be represented in other ways; often one letter is given several different sounds, which are indicated in many languages, such as French and German, by accents and other symbols. In French, for example, the letter e may be written as e, é or è, each representing a different sound. In German an *umlaut* (··) over a, u, or o changes the sound of the letter. In French and English the pronunciation of a consonant can often be gathered from the letter following it. G or c, for instance, are 'soft' in sound when followed by e, as in words like 'race' or 'large'. Some sounds are represented by the combining together of different consonants such as ch, th, sh and so on, or by the joining of vowels to form diphthongs as with ou, ai, au. Nearly all languages have inconsistencies—several different letters which represent the same sound: in English, for example, we have x and ks, qu and kw, ph and f. Many languages, such as German and Italian, which use the Latin alphabet, have managed to remain roughly phonetic—that is, their spelling is a fairly accurate copy of pronunciation. In English, however, spelling has for various historical reasons ceased to be mainly a copy of pronunciation, and is very irregular. The main reason is that it has not kept pace with the many changes there have been in pronunciation.

Anglo-Saxon (Old English) spelling was based on Latin and was roughly phonetic—that is, it represented words as the scribe, or the writer of the manuscript he was copying, pronounced them. The system was not perfect because some Anglo-Saxon sounds could not be represented by the Latin alphabet. After the Norman Conquest English spelling came very much under French influence. Scribes, used to French spelling, began to try to spell English words; they found some English letters misleading, for instance, c in Anglo-Saxon *cild* had a different sound from c in the word *cyn*, and the scribes began to write one as 'child' and the other as 'kyn'. But they introduced other confusing spellings into the language themselves. For example, the Anglo-Saxon ў represented the sound expressed in French by u, and the French therefore often replaced it by the letter u when they were writing English. Since Anglo-Saxon u, representing the sound in the word 'full', remained in use, the result was that words of different sounds often had similar spellings.

Later there grew up the conventions by which some vowels were written double to show that they were long (as in 'see', 'sooth'), and consonants were usually written double to show that a preceding vowel was short (as in 'better', 'matter'). And a mute final e, which remained in some words as a relic of grammatical endings that were no longer pronounced, came to be used as a means of indicating the lengthened vowel in words such as 'life', 'bone' and 'came' (Anglo-Saxon *lif*, *bān*, *com*).

Though pronunciation changed a good deal between the 13th and the 16th centuries, spelling became increasingly conventional, so that it ceased to represent current pronunciation accurately. Confusion increased in the 16th century, when letters were inserted into words where they were not pronounced—either to make certain words look like each other: thus *delit(e)* became 'delight', to make it resemble 'light', with which it has nothing in common by origin; or else (following a French fashion) to show the connexion between an English and a Latin word: thus *doute* came to be spelt 'doubt', b being inserted, as sometimes in French spellings of the 15th and 16th centuries, to show the original connexion with Latin *dubitare*.

In the 16th century, too—whilst several changes in pronunciation were still in progress —the spread of printing and of printed books helped to fix and regularize spelling. In later centuries pronunciations, originally confined to a particular dialect-area, have sometimes replaced those represented by the traditional spelling ('bury', for example, is now pronounced like 'berry' in standard speech); and some distinctions of pronunciation have been lost, leaving meaningless variants in spelling: thus, 'name', 'day', 'they', each formerly had different vowel-sounds, and their spellings reflect these original differences, though they are now pronounced alike. Confusion has been still further increased by the modern tendency to retain the spelling and approximate pronunciation of words adopted from foreign languages—such as 'chauffeur', 'garage'. Finally, since the 18th century, spelling has tended to influence pronunciation, and especially the pronunciation of those people not accustomed to hearing STANDARD ENGLISH (q.v.) spoken: thus 'waistcoat', which had come to be pronounced 'wesket', is to-day often pronounced as it is spelt.

Since the 16th century there have been many proposals to simplify English spelling, or to add new letters to the alphabet. But only in America, where Noah Webster, author of the famous American *Dictionary of the English Language* (1828), was a strong advocate of spelling reform, have there been any considerable changes—for example, the dropping of 'silent' letters as in 'ax', for 'axe', 'catalog' for 'catalogue', and the development of uniform groups, as in 'humor', 'labor', 'honor', in line with 'humorous', 'honorable', and so on. The strongest arguments against more far-reaching reforms are that they would make existing books and documents unintelligible (in part, at least) to those familiar with the new system alone; and that it is useful to have the visual distinction between words like 'hole' and 'whole', 'wright' and 'write', 'taut' and 'taught', 'dying' and 'dyeing', which our present system preserves.

See also ENGLISH LANGUAGE; VOICE.

STAGE-COACH. Before the coming of the railways in the middle of the 19th century, the chief means of travel in the 18th and 19th centuries were the stage-coaches, which travelled regular 'stages' over the country, running to definite time-tables, like modern buses. During the 17th century wealthy people began to have their own coaches (*see* CARRIAGES); but everyone could not afford such a luxury. The first

Parker Gallery

ROYAL MAIL COACHES LEAVING 'THE SWAN WITH TWO NECKS' INN, LONDON, FOR THE WEST OF ENGLAND
Coloured engraving, 1831

stage-coach is believed to have appeared in 1657, running between London and Chester. Others soon began to run between London and Exeter (a 5 days' journey) and London and York (a week's journey) so long as the weather was reasonably good and no accident occurred. The coaches were heavily built vehicles, drawn by four horses, and carrying six passengers inside and others outside. They were badly sprung and uncomfortable, and the windows were either wooden shutters or leather curtains.

After the passing of the first Turnpike Act in 1663 (*see* TURNPIKE), the condition of a few of the main roads began to improve; so did the coaches. They became lighter, and were swung from thick leather straps attached to the axle-trees of the front and back wheels. Windows were provided with glass. More stage-coach services were run, and the speed increased. By about 1750 the regular service between London and Edinburgh took 8 days, all being well.

The introduction of Palmer's mail-coaches in 1784 marked a great improvement in comfortable and speedy travelling. These coaches carried only four passengers inside instead of six; armed guards travelled on the coaches to protect them from HIGHWAYMEN (q.v.); and fresh relays of horses waited every 7 or 8 miles. The length of travelling time was greatly reduced. For example, in 1784 the London to Newcastle coach took only 3 days, whereas in 1754 it had taken 6 days; and Birmingham to London took 19 hours in 1785 instead of 2 days in 1754. By 1800 regular stage-coach services were running between all the big towns in England, and those carrying mails ran to a fast fixed time-table. 'Fast', however, still meant an average of only about 5 miles an hour.

The great coaching days in England were in the beginning of the 19th century. The rivalry between coaches led to great activity at the posting INNS (q.v.), where fresh horses were led out of the yard as the guard's horn announced the arrival of the coach. Some of these coaches, drawn by six horses, covered about 50 miles a day. One of the most picturesque sights of London each evening in those days was the departure of twenty-seven mail-coaches from the G.P.O. in Lombard Street to various parts of the country (*see* POST OFFICE, HISTORY OF). The introduction of MACADAM ROADS (q.v.) in the early years of the 19th century also increased the efficiency of the stage-coach service, as well as increasing the working life of the coach horse (*see* HORSE TRANSPORT).

See also CARRIAGES; ROADS, BRITISH.

STAMPS, *see* POSTMARKS AND POSTAGE STAMPS.

STANDARD, *see* FLAGS, Section 1.

STANDARD ENGLISH. No two people speak or write their native language in exactly the same way. But in any country or community there is generally some agreement about the type of the common language which should be used in writing, and sometimes in speech also. Thus certain usages come to be regarded as 'standard'. Such a standard is not fixed and permanent, but changes, as the language changes, from generation to generation.

By the beginning of the 11th century the dialect of Wessex, which had grown in prestige with the growth of West Saxon political power, was probably recognized as the standard language for official and literary use (*see* ENGLISH LANGUAGE). But its prestige declined after the Norman Conquest, and for several hundred years writers who wrote in English wrote in their local DIALECT (q.v.), often using many local words, and spelling in their own way. By the 14th century, however, the law, government, culture, and much of the commerce of England was centralized in London; and the prestige of the dialect written and spoken there rose accordingly. It included, of course, a good many naturalized French words. It became the language of official documents and of the earliest printed books. By Elizabeth's reign (1558–1603) it was regarded as the type of spoken English that provided the best model for literary use, though most writers and courtiers probably continued to speak their native dialects, to a certain extent.

As more people learned to read, and grammars and dictionaries were printed, the type of written English based on that used in London became standard for the whole country. But it did not replace local variations of speech quickly, for travel was still slow and difficult, and the social classes did not mix very much. To-day, however, the spread of education and the wireless have influenced the pronunciation and idiom (the characteristic expression of a language) of people in all parts of the country in the direction of 'standard' spoken English—that is, the type of English generally spoken by well-educated people. This standard English is known as 'Received Standard'.

One result of this has been the growth of a 'Modified Standard', a form of English spoken by most people in England to-day. This differs from 'Received Standard' in being tinged with local words or expressions, with usages not yet recorded in dictionaries, or with words pronounced as they are spelt. There is no absolute division between this and 'Received Standard'. Each influences the other. Opinions about what is 'correct' in spoken English are always gradually changing, and what one generation considers as vulgar or absurd is often accepted by the next as proper and polite.

See also ENGLISH LANGUAGE; DIALECTS; SLANG.

STATIONMASTER, *see* RAILWAYMEN, Section 1.

STATIONS, RAILWAY. In British railway stations the platforms are always built fairly near the level of the railway coach. In other countries it is more usual to enter the coaches by climbing up from ground level, or from a very low platform. In Great Britain passengers wait on the platforms for their trains, whereas in the United States and Canada they wait inside the main station buildings, which are quite separate from the platforms.

The Grand Central Station in New York is a remarkable example of the palatial American railway stations; the vast central hall, surrounded by shops and station offices, is 275 feet by 120 feet, and can accommodate 30,000 people comfortably; 20 feet below it is the main-line station, with forty-two tracks, and 24 feet below that the suburban station, with another twenty-five tracks. From the central hall of an American station the passengers pass through gates to the platforms, which are little more than covered passage-ways alongside the trains. It is the general practice in large American cities to build

THE RED ROVER, LONDON TO SOUTHAMPTON STAGE COACH

Coloured aquatint, 1851

central or 'Union' terminals, used by most, if not all, the various railways serving the city.

In Great Britain the nearest approach to the American idea of a central hall, equipped with shops, from which the platforms open through gates, is probably the City station in Leeds. A somewhat similar principle has been adopted with certain modern London tube stations, such as Piccadilly Circus, which have a large circulating area immediately below the street, provided with shops, from which escalators carry passengers down to the platforms. A fine example of modern terminal station building in Britain is Waterloo, with twenty-one platforms, and an immense hall at their inner end running the full width of the station. Waterloo handles over 1,300 trains daily. In earlier days, terminal stations generally were built with all-over roofs, some with very large spans—St. Pancras station in London, with a single roof span of no less than 210 feet, being a fine example. But now the ridge-and-furrow type of glass roof is mostly used, for it is less costly both to build and to maintain.

The longest station platform in Great Britain is the single 2,194-foot platform connecting the Victoria and Exchange stations at Manchester; the stations at York, Edinburgh Waverley, and Crewe also have exceptionally long platforms. The busiest stations in Britain are London Bridge, of the Southern Region, with twenty-one platforms, partly terminal and partly 'through', handling 2,100 trains daily, and Clapham Junction, with seventeen platform lines, through which about 2,050 trains pass every day. In Paris, St. Lazare terminus has thirty-one tracks and handles 250,000 passengers a day, while the Gare de l'Est has thirty very long platforms, from which 23,000 suburban passengers make their way every evening within the space of a single hour.

See also UNDERGROUND RAILWAYS.

STEAM LOCOMOTIVE, *see* LOCOMOTIVE, STEAM.

STEAMSHIPS, HISTORY OF. An early suggestion for using steam to move ships was made in 1690 by the French scientist Denis Papin. In 1702 Thomas Savery, the engineer, constructed in Britain a water-pump worked by steam; he wrote that his pump 'may be made very useful to ships, but I dare not meddle with that matter'. The first use of steam power on land was by Thomas Newcomen about 1712. In 1736 Jonathan Hulls of Gloucestershire patented a steam tug-boat, in which a paddle-wheel at the stern was to have been driven by a Newcomen engine; but his proposal did not receive the support it deserved, and the scheme was never tried.

In 1775, however, J.-C. Périer actually drove a small boat by steam power for an experiment on the River Seine, near Paris. It had paddle-wheels, driven by a steam-cylinder and piston 8 inches in diameter. Three years later the Marquis Claude de Jouffroy d'Abbans made some further experiments with what he called 'palmipede' or web-footed paddles; but real success came in 1783, when his steamboat *Pyroscaphe* (Greek for 'fire-ship') of 182 tons, and 148 feet long, mounted the River Saône, near Lyons. The paddle-wheels were 13 feet across, driven by a steam-cylinder and piston.

Pioneer work on steam

PATRICK MILLER'S STEAMBOAT ON DALSWINTON LAKE, DUMFRIES, 1788
By courtesy of the Director of the Science Museum, London

Parker Gallery

THE 'BRITISH QUEEN' PADDLE STEAMER
Coloured aquatint, about 1839

power for ships was not confined to Europe; James Rumsey made important experiments in America with a steam-driven pump to draw in water at the bow of the vessel and force it out, like a jet, at the stern. In 1784 he constructed a model on this principle, and later made trials with a boat on the River Potomac. Another American pioneer, John Fitch, after experiments with a number of paddle-floats moving round in an endless chain, fitted a boat with twelve vertical oars or paddles, used like the hand paddle of an Indian canoe, and tried it under steam power on the River Delaware, near Philadelphia.

In 1788 a certain Patrick Miller in Britain, after experimenting with paddle ships driven by hand power, which soon exhausted the crew, began to consider the use of steam power. He tried a steam-engine, constructed by William Symington, in a double-hulled boat on Dalswinton Lake, Dumfries, with the poet Robert Burns on board. Three years later Symington made the engine for a steam tug-boat, the *Charlotte Dundas*, which was tried on the Forth and Clyde canal. She ran well; but the canal owners said

the wash from the paddles would harm the canal banks, and so nothing more was done.

Then in 1803 the American pioneer Robert Fulton had a steamboat built at Paris, and tried on the River Seine. It was 74 feet long, and had 12-foot paddle-wheels. The engine, made by J.-C. Périer, developed 8 horse-power, and the boat reached a speed of nearly 3 miles an hour. In 1807 Fulton had a second larger steamboat, the *Clermont*, built at New York. With her one-cylinder steam-engine of 20 horse-power, she reached a speed of nearly 5 miles an hour on the River Hudson.

In Europe the first steamer to run commercially was the *Comet* of 28 tons, length 51 feet, built at Glasgow in 1812 for Henry Bell to run on the River Clyde. Her single-cylinder, low-pressure steam-engine of 4 horse-power gave the vessel a speed of over $7\frac{1}{2}$ miles an hour. Steamboats began to appear on the Thames in 1815, and in 1816 there started a steam-packet service to Ireland (so called because packets of mails were carried for the Post Office).

The first steam-propelled vessel to cross the Atlantic, or indeed any ocean, was the packet-

Parker Gallery

THE 'GREAT BRITAIN' IRON STEAMSHIP
Coloured aquatint, 1845

steamer *Savannah* of 320 tons, length 98 feet, built of wood at New York in 1818. When she arrived off the coast of Ireland, with smoke rising from her, she was naturally mistaken for a ship on fire. Her paddle-wheels could be lifted up on deck when sails alone were used; in this way she returned to America. The first east-to-west journey across the Atlantic by steam power was by the *Rising Star* of 428 tons, a ship built at Rotherhithe in 1821 as a private warship. As protection from bombardment her paddle-wheels were placed inside the ship, and worked through large openings in the bottom of the hull. In 1825 steam communication with India was established by the *Enterprise* of 470 tons. Speeds gradually increased. In 1833 the Canadian packet-ship *Royal William*, built at Quebec, crossed from Nova Scotia to Cowes in 19 days, at a mean speed of about 6 knots (one knot equals 1·15 miles an hour).

Marine boilers up to this time were fed with sea-water, and had to be shut down every few days to clear out salt deposits. At length the surface CONDENSER (q.v. Vol. VIII), patented by Samuel Hall in 1834, enabled the boilers to be fed with fresh water, distilled from the used steam, which formerly had been wasted. Thus an engine could be kept in constant operation. The paddle-steamers *Sirius* and *Great Western*, which both crossed to New York in April 1838 under continuous steam power, were fitted with these new condensers.

Two years later, in 1840, Samuel Cunard, merchant-ship owner, started a steam mail service between Britain and America which was to become famous. His first vessel was the *Britannia* of 1,156 tons, length 207 feet, built of wood at Greenock on the Clyde, with engines of 740 horse-power; her speed was 10 knots. Charles Dickens crossed on her in 1842, when he visited America. The last of the Cunard paddle-steamers, built in 1861, was the *Scotia* of 3,871 tons, length 379 feet, with engines of 4,570 horse-power and paddle-wheels 40 feet across. She represented the final development in ocean paddle-steamers.

From about the mid-19th century the propeller or screw began to take the place of the paddle-wheel, although both ways of propelling a ship were in use together for many years. More than 2,000 years ago the Greek experimental thinker ARCHIMEDES (q.v. Vol. V) devised the principle

Cunard White Star

THE 'MAURETANIA', BUILT IN 1906 AND BROKEN UP IN 1935
From a photograph in the Science Museum, London

of the screw. The Greeks were not interested in the practical application of their thought, and nothing came of the idea. The practical use of the screw as a marine propeller dates from about 1837, when experiments were made by Francis Pettit Smith. A screw was spun round in the water, and forced the ship forward (*see* PRO-PELLER, Vol. VIII). In 1838 the *Archimedes* of 237 tons began the transition from paddle-wheel to screw propulsion. Another change was also in hand: timber suitable for shipbuilding had become so scarce and expensive that naval architects were forced to consider the use of wrought iron.

Both the changes from paddle-wheel to screw, and from wooden to iron shipbuilding, were embodied in an ocean steamer for the first time with the *Great Britain* of 3,270 tons, the first of her kind to cross the Atlantic. She was built at Bristol in 1843, to the plans of Isambard Brunel, a British engineer whose father had come to England as a refugee from the French Revolu-tion. Her engines developed about 1,500 horse-power, and propelled her at 11 knots. In 1846 she was stranded on the coast of Ireland; but as her iron hull did not break up as a wooden one would have done, iron-built ships won public confidence.

Next came the most ambitious failure in steamship history, the GREAT EASTERN (q.v.), an over-large ocean liner thought out by Brunel, and built 40 years in advance of practical ex-perience. This great ship, the only vessel in history to be propelled both by paddle-wheels and by screw propeller, was a commercial failure, and was sold in 1888 as old iron, and broken up.

In 1881 the Cunard ship *Servia* of 7,392 tons was constructed entirely of steel, instead of iron. Great advances were made later in steel manu-facture; and when the *Campania* of 12,950 tons was built in 1892, it was possible to use steel plates 25 feet long for her hull. The last Cunard liner to be fitted with piston steam-engines was the twin-screw *Caronia* of 19,524 tons, built in 1904. Her sister-ship, the triple-screw *Carmania*, launched in 1905, was the first large ship to be propelled by steam turbines.

In a STEAM TURBINE (q.v. Vol. VIII), rotary motion is produced by the direct action of the steam on the blades of the turbine wheel (somewhat like a water-mill). The development of this idea and its application to ships are due to Sir Charles Parsons, whose experimental *Turbinia*, a little ship of 44 tons, was built in 1894. This famous little vessel made its dramatic appearance at the naval review held at Spithead in 1897; the spectators were thrilled to see the *Turbinia* race down the lines of anchored ships at 34·5 knots, a speed never before attained on water.

After such a success, it was natural that turbines should come into use for ocean liners; and in 1904 the *Victorian* of 10,754 tons appeared. She had Parsons turbines of 12,000 total horse-power, and her three screws, each 8 feet across, turned at 280 revolutions a minute. On trial in 1905 a speed of 19·8 knots was reached.

The vessel with the proudest record in the whole of steamship history was the famous old Cunard *Mauretania* of 31,938 tons, length 762 feet, launched in 1906. She had Parsons turbines of 70,000 total horse-power. On her trials the vessel made 27·4 knots. She soon captured the Blue Riband of the Altantic as the fastest liner, and held the honour from 1907 until 1929, when the new German liner *Bremen*, with turbines of 130,000 horse-power, won it from her.

In 1932 there appeared the French turbine steamer *Normandie*, built at St. Nazaire in Brittany, with a tonnage of 86,496 tons, a length of 1,029 feet, and four independent sets of turbines, each set driving one of the four screws, and developing a total of 160,000 horse-power. The top speed of the vessel on trial was 32·1 knots.

In 1934 the *Queen Mary*, built for the Cunard White Star Line, reached nearly 33 knots on trial. The QUEEN ELIZABETH (q.v.), an even larger and more powerful ship built in 1938, on her first trip from Southampton to New York, in October 1946, crossed at an average speed over the whole journey of 28 knots.

See also SHIP.
See also Vol. VIII: STEAM-ENGINE.

STILUS, *see* WRITING INSTRUMENTS.

STRATOSPHERE FLIGHT, *see* HIGH ALTITUDE FLIGHT.

STREETS. The modern use of the word street to mean a roadway in a town or village rather than in open country is only about 400 years old. Before that, the word indicated a paved Roman

P. Hart

A STREET IN POMPEII
The stepping stones were to prevent pedestrians getting their feet muddy

National Gallery

A MEDIEVAL STREET IN FLANDERS
Detail from 'The Virgin and Child before a Firescreen',
painted by Roger Campin about 1430

Like the country roads, town **streets** everywhere were neglected after the fall of Rome in A.D. 410 (*see* ROADS). In England the Saxons did not use the old Roman cities, but built their villages nearby. As the villages grew into the towns of the Middle Ages, the unpaved streets remained, rough and muddy, with wooden houses crowded close on to them. The streets were built highest in the centre with 'kennels' or channels running along each side, or sometimes down the middle; these were all that the town had for drainage, and into them all refuse was thrown. Passers-by jostled each other off the comparatively dry street into the dirt of the kennel. The over-hanging upper-storeys of the 15th and 16th century houses held back both light and air from the streets which seldom got really dried out. There was no street-lighting, and little attempt at order. Theft was prevalent; beggars, tumblers, and pedlars filled the streets with their cries and antics. Apprentices advertised their masters' wares, calling 'What do ye lack?'. Cattle were driven through the streets, even in London where they were still to be seen as late as 1855. The streets were, in fact, in so bad a state that people always travelled, if they could, by river. In 1555 the Highways Statute, which applied to all parishes, decreed that each parish should mend its roads by means of 6 days' statute (or forced) labour levied on all males; but in fact this resulted in little improvement in the state of town streets in Tudor times.

Street names reveal much of the organization of trade; Goldsmiths, Butchers, Fishmongers, and Fullers each had their own street or row, as in the great fairs; Threadneedle Street in London echoes the tailor's trade.

During the 18th and early 19th centuries, architects occasionally planned a few streets in some towns, though this was confined mainly to the façade of the houses facing the streets. The great terraces of Bath grew up in the 18th century, and in the Regency period between 1810 and 1820 John Nash designed London's famous Regent Street. But proper sanitation and drainage were yet to come. In 1826 the streets near Westminster Abbey were still so insanitary that a cholera epidemic broke out. Many streets were unpaved, and as there was no system of REFUSE DISPOSAL (q.v. Vol. X), it was even known for a herd of swine to feed on rotting vegetables and other refuse in the heart of 19th-century London. The streets of the 18th and

road, such as Watling Street or Ermine Street (*see* ROMAN ROADS).

The streets of the city of Rome, narrow, haphazard, and winding, were paved, and some had raised footpaths; but they were quite inadequate for the traffic of the centre of a vast empire. Consequently wheeled traffic was forbidden in the day-time, and the rich were carried in LITTERS (q.v.) by slaves. Shopkeepers spread out their wares on the pavement, and wedding and funeral processions added to the confusion. In the newly built towns of the conquered provinces, a definite street plan was used. Roads crossed at right angles, and in the centre the market-place or forum commanded the main **streets** leading to the city gate, as is still to be seen in the ruins of Silchester in Berkshire and of Verulamium near St. Albans in Hertfordshire.

PARIS: THE CHAMPS ÉLYSÉES FROM THE TOP OF THE ARC DE TRIOMPHE

early 19th centuries which, during the daytime, echoed with the cries of milkmaids, fish-sellers, and the muffin-man, were practically unlit at night, and the night-watchmen, often old and incapable, could do little to patrol them. People were guided along the streets by 'link-boys' who carried torches of pitch and tow. The crossing-sweeper, who swept a clean passage for those who wished to cross the streets, was a well-known figure of 19th and even early 20th century London.

Gas street-lighting was first introduced in the streets of Westminster in 1814, and soon became widely used. The lamps were lit by the lamp-lighter with his ladder and pole, who was a familiar figure until 1920, and in some towns until much later. Electricity has now become the most usual form of street-lighting. Both gas and electric street-lamps can now be switched on and off automatically by a clock fixed to each lamp standard. In streets where the electric lights are supplied with current from a special main cable, not from the ordinary house mains, the lights can be switched on and off from a central station (see STREET SERVICES, Section 2, Vol. X).

The obligation for the upkeep of streets, except for a few main trunk roads, now falls upon the local authorities, who are assisted by government grants. They keep the surface in good repair, provide adequate drainage and lighting; they control the planning, width, and type of new streets in their area, the planting of trees, and siting of bus stops and shelters; they are responsible for naming roads and numbering houses.

Certain streets have achieved historic importance—the Rows of Chester, with their double lines of shops; Piccadilly, the site of famous London clubs and hotels; Oxford Street and Regent Street which house the great shopping centre of London; Downing Street and White-hall, the streets of government offices. The Royal Mile and Princes Street in EDINBURGH, Fifth Avenue, NEW YORK, the Champs Élysées in PARIS, and the Unter den Linden of BERLIN (qq.v. Vol. III) are all internationally famous.

TOWN PLANNING (q.v. Vol. X) to-day is greatly concerned with streets—their width and use, the houses fronting them, and the crossings involved, and an attempt is being made to distinguish between the road which takes long-distance 'through traffic' and the 'service' road solely for residents. By-pass roads reduce congestion in some of our old 'High Streets', which, though picturesque, were never intended for motor traffic, and easily become badly congested.

See also ROADS; ROAD TRAFFIC CONTROL.
See also Vol. X: STREET SERVICES; TOWN AND COUNTRY PLANNING.
See also Vol. XI: TOWNS, HISTORY OF.

SUEZ CANAL. This canal, 103 miles long, cuts through the narrow passage of land dividing the Mediterranean from the Red Sea. Before the construction of the canal, ships sailing from any part of Europe to India or the Far East had to journey all round the continent of Africa. The canal shortens the journey from Britain to India by 4,000 miles and that to Australia by 1,200 miles.

The idea of connecting the Mediterranean to the Red Sea by a canal is very old indeed. In the days of the Pharaohs, canals were planned and even dug to connect the Nile with the Red Sea. The idea of a canal through the Suez isthmus was conceived in the 8th century A.D., and again in the 16th century by the poet Christopher Marlowe. But it was not until the 19th century that any step was taken. Then a canal was proposed by a French priest, Père Enfantin, who wanted to improve communications with the East for missionary purposes. He succeeded in interesting Ferdinand de Lesseps, the French consul, in the scheme. By 1859 de Lesseps had made his plans, overcome opposition such as that of the Sultan of Turkey, and formed his company. Most of the money was subscribed in France and Turkey, for Britain, the most likely to benefit from the canal, viewed the scheme with misgivings. Some British statesmen feared that the canal would weaken Britain's supremacy at sea and give the French too much power in the East. They said the canal was a physical

SUEZ CANAL

E.N.A.

STEAMERS IN THE SUEZ CANAL

and Little Bitter Lake. The land is so flat that the whole canal was cut without a single lock. The main problem was one of excavation and dredging, for which bucket DREDGERS (q.v.) were used. The canal was opened in 1869. It had cost £20 million, and a further £20 million had to be spent in widening and deepening the canal in 1876 and 1885. In spite of the cost of construction the canal has brought much profit to its shareholders. In 1870, 451 ships passed through it; in 1948, 8,868. More than three-fifths of the ships and about half the tonnage were British. In 1875 the British Prime Minister, Disraeli, bought up £4,000,000 worth of shares, which are now calculated to be worth £22 million. The administration of the canal was vested in an international body called the Suez Canal Commission, and the dues for passage through the canal were the same for ships of all countries and were calculated by the ships' tonnage. It takes a ship about 15 hours to make the passage, and there is a strict speed limit.

See also CANALS.

impossibility. The workmen provided by Said Pasha, the Viceroy of Egypt, though on the whole well paid and cared for, worked under compulsion, an idea disliked by British people. In 1863 compulsory labour had to be given up, and de Lesseps, deprived of a large number of workmen, used modern engineering machinery to do the excavation.

The first step was to build two enormous embankments in the Mediterranean, forming a sort of triangular harbour with a narrow opening to the sea, to keep out silt brought down by the Nile. These were made of great blocks of concrete taken out on barges and dumped on the sea bottom until they rose above the sea level, and the spaces filled by loads of small stones. The canal was then cut along the edge of Lake Menzala for 28 miles, and then through Lake Balah and a sandy hollow called Lake Timsa, at the north end of which is now the town of Ismailia. Next a cut of 8 miles was made across desert, in the course of which the engineers had to blast through a mass of granite. The canal then came to a chain of sandy hollows which had once been pools of brackish water. When the sea was let into the canal, these filled up into lakes 25 miles long, called the Great Bitter Lake

SUPERSONIC FLIGHT. Sometimes an aeroplane flying fairly low is seen to approach without noise. As it passes overhead, a great burst of noise is suddenly heard, which grows fainter as the aircraft flies on. Then, after a brief moment, the sound of an approaching aircraft is heard. These are the signs that the craft was flying faster than the speed of sound. Thus the aeroplane approaches the spectator faster than its own noise. Once it is directly overhead, of course, it ceases to approach the spectator, and he can hear it flying away just like any slower aeroplane. Then the new sound, which reaches the spectator's ear a moment later, is the sound

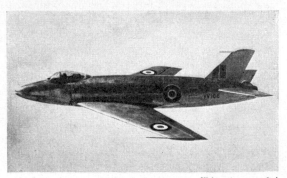

Vickers-Armstrong Ltd.

HIGH-SPEED AIRCRAFT WITH SWEPT-BACK WINGS
The aircraft shown can fly at supersonic speeds

which that aeroplane had been making while it was still coming towards him. SOUND (q.v. Vol. III) travels 760 miles an hour at sea-level at freezing-point; the speed of sound is less as altitudes or temperatures rise; aircraft often approach supersonic speed at a little over 600 miles an hour.

Special difficulties arise in building and manœuvring an aeroplane which will fly faster than sound. One difficulty arises from the nature of air. Air can be squeezed; scientists call it 'a compressible fluid'; if pressure is applied to it, its volume becomes smaller. Water, on the other hand, is regarded as not compressible; heavy pressure makes hardly any change in its volume. At most ordinary aeroplane speeds, the air maintains the volume unchanged; therefore designers can safely work out their calculations in the knowledge that the volume of air will remain the same. So great, however, is the speed of very fast modern aircraft that the air is compressed as they rush by. A body moving through the air causes a disturbance, which travels at the speed of sound, and which spreads out from it and causes particles of air in front of it to move out of its way; thus the air flows round the moving body. When an aeroplane itself is travelling as fast as sound, it hits the air in front of it before the particles of air can get out of the way. The result is a 'shock wave' in the air, which greatly increases the pressure of the air; as a result, the volume of the squeezed air becomes smaller. The air, when thus compressed, causes troublesome strains, as well as strong 'drag' effects in the aircraft (*see* HIGH ALTITUDE FLIGHT). But modern jet engines can produce sufficient thrust to overcome this drag. Besides the change of volume, an increase of pressure causes an increase of temperature, as those who have pumped up bicycle tires will know. An aeroplane travelling at very high speeds, therefore, gets quite hot. Already the cockpits of high-speed aeroplanes have to be kept cool by a refrigerator. The next limit to aeroplane speeds may prove to be the amount of heat which the craft can stand.

See also FLYING.

SWAHILI LANGUAGE, *see* AFRICAN LANGUAGES.

SWEDISH LANGUAGE, *see* SCANDINAVIAN LANGUAGES.

SYDNEY HARBOUR BRIDGE

SYDNEY HARBOUR BRIDGE. The city of Sydney in Australia grew up around a magnificent natural harbour, which made it an important trade centre; but until 1932 the north and south sides were connected only by ferry or by a roundabout 10-mile road. Now, one of the most famous arched bridges of modern times connects the north and south parts of the city. The width of water to be spanned would suggest that the bridge should have been of the suspension type, like the GOLDEN GATE BRIDGE (q.v.) at San Francisco; but the authorities decided to build an enormous arched bridge. The foundations were begun in January 1925, and to save the expense of transport, foundries and workshops were built on the site. As soon as the different parts were ready, they were carried on barges to the spot where they were needed, and then hauled into place by huge cranes. The construction went on from both sides of the harbour at once.

The bridge was completed early in 1932. The main span is 1,650 feet long, and the total length, including the approaches, is 2¾ miles. Across it run four railway lines side by side, as well as a wide roadway and pavements. It was expected to be the longest arched span in the world; but in fact the Bayonne Bridge over the Kill van Kull estuary in New York, which was begun 5 years later and finished 4 months earlier, with a span length of 1,652 feet 1 inch, is 25 inches longer. The Sydney Harbour Bridge, however, still holds two world records: it is the heaviest arched bridge and, with its width of 137 feet, the widest long bridge of any type.

See also BRIDGES.
See also Vol. III: SYDNEY.
See also Vol. VIII: BRIDGE BUILDING.

T

TABLET, *see* WRITING INSTRUMENTS.

TANK ENGINE, *see* LOCOMOTIVE, STEAM

TANKER AIRCRAFT, *see* FUELLING IN FLIGHT.

TANKER SHIP, *see* SHIP.

TANKER VEHICLE, *see* MOTOR TRANSPORT.

TAXI. Carriages for hire were first used in London early in the 17th century. They were often disused private carriages, licensed for public use, and were known as hackney-carriages, from the 'hackney' or slow-moving type of horse which drew them. In 1633 a Captain Bailey had the idea of setting four hackney-carriages in the Strand, and there people could hire them for journeys in the town. Others took up the idea, and within a short time there were so many hackney-carriages crowding the streets of London that special laws were necessary to restrict their numbers and organize them. In 1635 only fifty were allowed, but the number gradually increased, and by the early 18th century there were about 800 operating in London.

Early in the 19th century a new light two-wheeled carriage, called a 'cabriolet', was intro-

HANSOM CAB

duced into England from France, and from this came the name 'cab' for any type of hired carriage. In 1834 an architect named Hansom designed and patented a kind of cabriolet known as the 'hansom cab'. This held two passengers, and the driver's seat was raised over the back, the reins coming over the roof. The hansom was extremely popular, though it did not wholly replace the old hackney-carriage or four-wheeler —the 'growler' as it was sometimes called, possibly from the noise it made, or from its driver's tendency to grumble.

With the coming of the MOTOR-CAR (q.v.) early in the 20th century, motor-driven cabs began to replace both the hackney and the hansom cab. These were fitted with the taximeter, a clockwork device linked with the cab wheels, showing the distance covered and the fare, and so they were called 'taximeter cabs', or 'taxi-cabs', and finally 'taxis'.

In London taxi-cabs and their drivers are still largely governed by the laws made for the old horse-drawn hackney-carriages. Cabs are subject to inspection by the police before they are licensed, and afterwards should the occasion arise. The drivers have to pass a severe driving test, and prove that they have a good knowledge of London before they can be licensed. There is a large number of taxi ranks where the taxis may wait to be hired. A taxi may be hailed and hired while on its way to a rank, although the driver is not obliged to stop.

A licence to run a cab in a town or area outside London must be obtained from the local council, who can make regulations to govern the cabs on such matters as fares, the location and size of ranks, the fitting of taximeters, and the driver's responsibilities towards the hirer.

See also CARRIAGES; MOTOR-CAR.

TELECOMMUNICATIONS, *see* TELEGRAM; TELEPHONE SERVICE; CABLE; SHORT-WAVE WIRELESS.

TELECOMMUNICATIONS, INTERNATIONAL. These are the telephone and telegraph systems communicating with other countries and with ships at sea, either over submarine cables or by wireless. British international telegraph communications are handled by the Post Office, apart from a few private companies. The international telephone service from Britain is run solely by the Post Office; a telephone subscriber can speak with almost any other country and to passengers on the largest ocean-going liners, while a coastal service reaches small ships and trawlers. Apart from European calls, most of Britain's overseas telephone traffic passes over 'radio links' (*see* SHORT WAVE WIRELESS). Over 955,000 international calls were made from Britain in 1948.

The U.S.A. has the world's largest internal telecommunications system; it has about 35 million telephones, or one for every four persons, while in Britain (which has the next greatest number) there are 5 million telephones, or one for every ten persons. U.S. telegraphs and telephones are privately owned.

See also CABLE; TELEGRAM; TELEPHONE SERVICE.

TELEGRAM. The Post Office telegraph service operates through a number of large offices, called 'instrument rooms', which are connected by telegraph lines to teleprinter switchboards (rather like telephone exchange switchboards) in different parts of the country. Through these teleprinter switchboards an instrument room in one part of the country may be connected to other instrument rooms in other parts, just as one telephone subscriber is connected to another on a telephone trunk call.

TELEPRINTERS (q.v.) are used for sending and receiving telegrams in these instrument rooms, and the lines connecting the various instrument rooms with the teleprinter switchboards are called the 'teleprinter switching network'. There are, of course, many small telegraph offices not connected with the switching network; the larger of these have a teleprinter connected to the nearest instrument room, while the smaller ones (because they handle only a few telegrams) usually send their telegrams by telephone to the nearest instrument room from which they can be dispatched.

The name of every telegraph office in the country is abbreviated into a short two or three-letter code (for example, Birmingham is known as BM) and these letters appear on the teleprinter switchboards so that the operator may know which instrument is calling. When a telegram has been handed in to a Post Office it is passed to the nearest telegraph office or instrument room. Here a circulation clerk has a record of all the offices in the country, and he writes on the telegram the code of the telegraph instrument room nearest the destination of the telegram. He then passes the telegram to a teleprinter operator.

This operator starts typing on her teleprinter the code letters of the distant teleprinter she wishes to communicate with. A small lamp lights up on the distant teleprinter switchboard to tell the switchboard operator who is calling, and the code letters of the calling teleprinter are automatically typed on the teleprinter at the switchboard. When the switchboard operator reads from her teleprinter the letter code of the required instrument room, she connects the calling teleprinter to it, and the telegram can then be typed from one to the other on to long gummed-paper ribbon. When the whole of the telegram has been received, this ribbon is torn off in suitable lengths and stuck on to an ordinary telegram form. The telegram is then ready for delivery.

If the person to whom the telegram is to be sent is on the telephone, the message may be telephoned to him; but otherwise the telegram is sent out by messenger. The period which elapses between the handing in of a telegram at a Post Office until it is finally delivered depends on the number of times the telegram is handled; for example, a telegram handed into a very small Post Office will take longer to transmit and deliver than one handed in at a large Post Office with an instrument room of its own.

43,396,000 inland telegrams were handled by the POST OFFICE (q.v.) in 1948.

See also TELEPRINTER; TELECOMMUNICATIONS, INTERNATIONAL.

NEWSPAPER HANDBILL ANNOUNCING NAPOLEON III'S DEFEAT AND CAPTURE AT SEDAN IN 1870, DURING THE FRANCO-PRUSSIAN WAR

TELEGRAPHY, HISTORY OF. Electric telegraphy began just before the middle of the 19th century. The many inventors who helped to devise a working system were spurred on by the demands of the newly built railways for some means of conveying messages between signalmen about the safety of trains (*see* SIGNALLING, RAILWAY). Towards the end of the 18th century, the name 'telegraph' from the Greek words meaning 'writing at a distance', had come to be used for an Admiralty system of wooden signalboards (*see* SEMAPHORE). But although electricity was then little more than an amusing novelty, the years round 1800 were marked by many efforts to use it to convey messages. Men were just becoming aware of electrical or magnetic currents. They had been thrilled by the experiment in 1752 of Benjamin Franklin, the American statesman and thinker. When Franklin flew a kite during a storm, loose strands of the kite-string stuck out stiffly and his hand felt a slight shock; thus he had proved that lightning was an electrical discharge. Two Italians, Galvani and Volta (from whose names we get the two electrical terms 'galvanize' and 'volt') had devised early forms of battery which caused weak currents to flow (*see* ELECTRICAL ENGINEERING, HISTORY OF, Vol. VIII). Once it was found that an electric current would run along a piece of wire and cause objects to move, people tried to devise an electrical telegraph. Experiments were made using a separate wire for each letter of the alphabet; near each wire was a light-weight ball made of pith from a plant, which, when charged by the current, would attract a piece of paper bearing a letter of the alphabet. Other experimenters used the flash of a spark (caused by interrupting a circuit along which electricity flowed) to light up a letter.

It was known that a steel needle could be made magnetic by being rubbed against a magnet. In 1819 H. C. Oersted found that, if a current were passed through a wire near a needle which had been made magnetic, the needle would be turned away from its normal position, according to the direction of the current. This had important results. Galvani made a machine in which the twenty-six letters of the alphabet were pointed to by magnetic needles at the ends of twenty-six wires. William Sturgeon, a Lancashire shoemaker who was a keen amateur experimenter, produced the first electro-magnet, which consisted of a number of turns of wire around a horseshoe-shaped piece of 'soft' iron (not tempered hard like steel); this attracted smaller pieces of soft iron whenever current was passed along the wire coil (an invention which led later to the modern electric motor and dynamo). Within 6 years, in 1831, electro-magnetic signalling apparatus, in which the attracted piece of iron was made to strike a bell, had been demonstrated (*see* ELECTRIC SIGNALLING).

In America Samuel Morse, who later became Superintendent of Telegraphs to the United States Government, tried making signals by opening and closing an electrical circuit, so that the signals could be recorded. He fitted a pencil to a lever worked by an electro-magnet so that the pencil would mark a moving paper strip whenever the electrical circuit was completed or broken. For the use of this pencil recorder he invented the dot-and-dash alphabet which has made his name famous (*see* MORSE CODE). Later he invented a simple relaying instrument for automatically repeating signals from one section of the communication line into the next, so preserving the strength of the signals over any distance. Then he devised the Morse key or tapper, as a convenient way of making and breaking the flow of current.

A friend of Morse's, Alfred Vail, found that it was possible to 'read' the code by ear, from the sharp tapping sound made by the lever in the recording machine. So the original Morse recorder was no longer used (although, of course, telegraph systems to-day use elaborate systems for recording messages in Morse at high speed).

Morse was granted his first patent in 1848, nearly 9 years after he had demonstrated telegraphy over a line 40 miles long—the first line to be opened for public business. Within 3 years his telegraph system was being operated in America by fifty companies.

The first practical telegraph in Britain was set up in 1837 by two scientists, Cooke and Wheatstone, and linked Euston railway station in London with Camden Town station, only a mile away. A few years later, when this railway telegraph helped to bring about the arrest of a murderer, public interest in the invention was assured. Before long, telegraph lines were laid under the sea. The first cable between Europe and America was laid in 1858 (*see* CABLE, Section 2).

In 1861 Wheatstone brought in Britain's first

automatic sending and receiving apparatus. Sending by hand and receiving by ear were too slow to be practical on busy lines, their greatest speed being forty-five words a minute. If enough messages had to be sent from one city to another every day to keep ten dot-and-dash operators busy, it would be a great waste to have ten separate telegraph lines, one for each operator. Wheatstone's idea was that the ten operators should punch out their messages in a code consisting of holes on strips of paper; an automatic fast transmitting instrument, which would tap out dots and dashes ten times as fast as an operator, would then turn the punched strips of paper into dots and dashes for the telegraph wire, so that one line could take the messages of ten operators. The principle of high-speed transmission is still the same to-day, although later inventions have gone much farther; one line can now transmit high-speed messages for a number of automatic transmitters at the same time.

Shortly after 1850 Professor D. E. Hughes, the British professor of music who is chiefly famous for inventing a microphone, designed a typewriting telegraph—a startling novelty, for the ordinary TYPEWRITER (q.v.) itself had not then been invented. This device was the fore-runner of the modern TELEPRINTER (q.v.).

Another early novelty was the writing 'telegraph'. At the transmitting end of the telegraph line a pencil was moved by hand to shape a letter, as in handwriting; this movement, through a lever, varied the amount of electric current flowing to the receiving end. Here the varying current caused a recording pen to repeat the movements, thus providing a copy of the writing. This device, however, has never become much more than a toy.

See also TELEGRAM.

TELEPATHY. This word, which means 'feeling from afar', was invented about 1882 to cover all mysterious cases in which one mind was apparently able to communicate with another by unknown means, not using the SENSES (q.v. Vol. II) of sight, hearing, touch, taste, or smell. Since then the Society for Psychical Research has recorded many cases in which communication of this kind appears to have occurred.

A typical case is the following. A little girl of 10 years was walking along a country lane, reading a book on geometry. Suddenly her surroundings seemed to fade away, and she thought she saw her mother lying, apparently dead, on the floor of a little-used room at home, known as the 'white room', with a lace handkerchief beside her. The child was so impressed that instead of going home she hurried to a doctor's house and persuaded him to go home with her. He found the mother lying on the floor of the white room, suffering from a severe heart attack. Beside her was a lace handkerchief. The doctor was in time to save her life. Here it would seem that the mother's mind, in some mysterious way, reached out to the child's mind and generated a powerful picture or hallucination (see PSYCHOLOGY, Vol. XI).

It is important to distinguish between genuine and false telepathy. If two people think of a performing seal with a bottle balanced on its nose at about the same time, that may not be due to telepathy but, for example, to the fact that a few minutes earlier they were both looking

Crown Copyright

WHEATSTONE'S ABC TRANSMITTER AND RECEIVER
The hand on the transmitter (left) is moved to letters round the dial. The hand on the receiver (right) spells out the message as it is transmitted. From an exhibit in the Science Museum, London

at the famous 'Guinness' poster. Demonstrations of so-called 'thought transference' by professional entertainers are practically never genuine. Such people communicate with one another by cleverly concealed codes of signals, usually of a visual kind. A piece of chalk left lying on a table may indicate one of several objects, according to the direction in which it points. Two performers usually work together, one as 'transmitter' and the other as 'receiver', and their success depends largely on skilful planning beforehand. Music-hall 'telepathists' can be distinguished from genuine researchers who appear to possess a special gift by the fact that the latter readily submit their powers to scientific examination.

In recent years telepathy has been the subject of a large number of careful scientific experiments carried out in America and Britain. In the best of these experiments the sender (or 'agent', as he is called) sat in one room with a pack of twenty-five cards; the face of each card bore one of five different types of geometrical symbols such as a square, circle, or star, or a picture of one of five different animals. The pack was shuffled so that the symbols were in haphazard order. The receiver (or 'percipient') sat in another room, either adjoining the sender or even hundreds of miles away. The sender lifted off a card, one at a time, and looked at its face. The receiver had to guess which of the five symbols the sender was looking at. By pure chance alone he should guess correctly on the average one card in every five. If he made, for instance, 400 guesses, he would expect, by the mathematical laws of chance, to get about one-fifth right, or 80 out of the 400. But suppose he has guessed 112 right. The difference between 112 and 80 (= 32) is called the 'deviation'. This deviation is compared with tables of 'standard deviations' which have been worked out by mathematicians; the comparison shows that in this case a deviation of 32 could occur by pure luck alone only once in 10,000 such experiments. Therefore there is reason to suppose—though no certainty—that telepathy may have operated in this case. If the receiver repeatedly guesses a much larger proportion right, some explanation, such as telepathy, seems to be called for.

A telepathy experiment works as successfully when the sender is in London and the receiver in Belgium as when they are in adjoining rooms of the same house. But an important condition for success is that the sender and receiver should be friends or well acquainted with each other. So far as we can judge, therefore, telepathic communication is unaffected by distance. More remarkable still, it is to some extent independent of time. For instance, an experimenter has succeeded in guessing correctly—not the card the sender was looking at during the actual moment of guessing—but the card he would be looking at in two or three seconds' time. That is to say, the receiver was guessing correctly the card which would be in the sender's mind two or three seconds later. This receiver became known as 'the man who was three seconds ahead of time'.

It has been shown that when we do a sum in our head, electrical impulses occur within the brain (see NERVOUS SYSTEM, Vol. XI). This has led many people to suppose that thought-transference is a kind of wireless. But there are many difficulties in the way of accepting such a theory. In the first place a wireless signal is never received at one end before it has been transmitted at the other, as in the case just described. Again, all normal modes of communication between human beings depend on some kind of code or language, such as Morse or ordinary speech, by means of which wireless wave patterns can be interpreted and given a meaning. But it is difficult to understand how such codes or language could have originated in the case of 'brain waves'.

It might be thought that the harder the sender concentrates on sending the message, the easier it will be for the receiver to pick it up. Experiment shows that this is not the case. It is not even necessary that the sender should have the image in his conscious mind at the moment when the other person receives it. It is sufficient that he should have been thinking of it consciously, say a moment earlier. These facts suggest that the transfer takes place between the subconscious regions of the sender's and receiver's minds rather than between their conscious minds.

Persons acting as telepathic receivers who can produce some of the remarkable results described are apparently very uncommon, but experimenters think it probable that quite ordinary persons have at times short-lived spurts of telepathic reception. Telepathy, as a subject of serious scientific study, is sometimes described by the terms 'parapsychology' and 'extra-sensory perception'. Some people think it is an almost extinct faculty possessed by primitive man before he developed the power of speech. Others believe that it is the beginning of a new and more subtle means of communication between human beings, which may replace speech and writing in ages to come.

See also Vol. XI: PSYCHOLOGY.

TELEPHONE SERVICE. Shortly after Graham Bell had invented the telephone in America (*see* SPEECH, TRANSMISSION OF), a British company opened a telephone exchange in the City of London in 1879 to provide a service for seven or eight subscribers. The Post Office opened its first exchange at Swansea in 1881, and others later at Newcastle-on-Tyne, Bradford, and Middlesbrough. Private companies and some municipal authorities also set up telephones in other areas; but in 1889 the chief telephone companies merged in the 'National Telephone Company'. The Post Office took over all 'trunk' long-distance lines in 1896, and 6 years later opened the first of several large London exchanges, the 'Central', with 14,000 lines. Finally in 1912, the Post Office took over the National Telephone Company, and in the same year the first automatic exchange was opened at Epsom in Surrey. The Post Office now controlled all the telephones in the country, except those run by the municipal authorities of Portsmouth and Hull, and by the States of Jersey and Guernsey. The services of Hull and the Channel Islands are still locally owned and run, under Post Office licence. By 1918 the Post Office operated over 819,000 telephones. During the 1920's a few automatic exchanges were opened in the provinces, and in 1927 the first of the present large London automatic exchanges was opened at Holborn.

The 1930's saw the evolution of the present-day system; the 'trunk' service was completely re-organized; new standard automatic equipment was designed, and small automatic exchanges were specially made for rural areas. By 1939 there were 3,235,000 telephones, and about 2,236 million calls were made in a year.

During the Second World War, the Post Office was mainly concerned with providing telecommunications for war use; but by 1949 there were 5 million British telephones. In that year the Post Office had 5,848 local telephone exchanges, of which nearly 4,000 were automatic, while the total traffic reached 3,137 million calls a year— about 9 millions a day. The trunk service carried twice as many calls as it had done before the Second World War, and the number of trunk circuits rose from 6,770 in 1939 to 15,562 in 1949.

When two people speak on the telephone, their lines are joined through the local telephone exchange, to which all subscribers in a district are connected. Each subscriber pays a regular rent for the hire of his telephone instrument, as well as other charges based on the number of calls he makes, and extra charges for long-distance calls; no charge is made for the calls he receives. Most subscribers and exchanges are linked by underground cables; 24 million miles of wire are carried in these cables, and only 2 million miles on overhead poles. Some modern cables, although containing only two metal conductors, enable 600 different telephone conversations to take place at once (*see* CABLE).

Calls between telephone subscribers on the earlier systems were connected by operators at 'magneto' telephone exchanges—so called because the subscriber had to turn the handle of a small magneto generator to call the operator.

Crown Copyright

A TABLE TELEPHONE OF ABOUT 1895
From an exhibit in the Science Museum, London

G.P.O.

TELEPHONE OPERATORS AT WORK IN A MANUAL EXCHANGE

Each telephone also had its own small battery to supply electric current to allow the subscriber to speak. Later, large batteries in the exchanges gave all the current needed.

The standard method of connecting subscribers in Britain is the automatic exchange (*see* TELEPHONE ENGINEERING, Vol. VIII). A subscriber who wants to ring up a friend must know the number of the friend's telephone, which he will find in the local directory's list of names. He then 'spells out' this number on the figures of the dial on his instrument, and the connexion is made at the automatic exchange without the help of any operator. Special numbers or letters on the dial are reserved for special things: the figures '999' warn an exchange official that a caller urgently wants the fire-brigade, police, or ambulance service. The letters 'TIM' connect the caller to an automatically recorded voice controlled by a clock, which 'speaks' the exact time. There are still, however, many of the older 'manual' (hand-operated) exchanges in use; there, the connexion is made with a 'cord' of flexible wire, the ends of which the operator plugs into numbered holes in a board. Both methods can be used in public telephone boxes, from which both

local and trunk calls can be made. The money for the call is placed in slots in a box; or the call may be reversed—that is, the person receiving the call may direct that it be charged to his account.

The plan enabling any subscriber to dial any other number in Britain has had to be spread over a number of years. Although an automatic exchange can cover the area of a large town or country district, all distant calls to subscribers outside the town or district must pass through special 'trunk' exchanges; these are hand-operated, but modern switchboard design is replacing plugs and cords by small levers.

The 'trunk' service is now extended to an international service; the first telephone cable between Britain and France was opened in 1891. Now, by cable or 'radio link', Britain is linked by telephone with most of the world (*see* TELE-COMMUNICATIONS, INTERNATIONAL).

See also SPEECH, TRANSMISSION OF; POST OFFICE.
See also Vol. VIII: TELEPHONE ENGINEERING.

TELEPHONES, MOBILE. Small portable wireless transmitters are used for ordinary telephonic conversation; the smallest set can be

PORTABLE RADIO

B.B.C.

The transmitter and receiver, powered by batteries, are strapped to the man's back

luggage compartment. It is connected with a short vertical flexible aerial on the roof. On the dashboard, facing the driver, are control switches; under the dashboard is a small loud-speaker; close to the driver's hand is a hand-microphone; when he wants to speak to police headquarters he touches a switch and speaks into his microphone.

The police headquarters is connected with a number of fixed transmitting and receiving stations, each with its own aerial. These stations, which are automatic and unattended, are located in various parts of the county or city concerned, so that no car is ever out of range of a headquarters aerial, whether for sending or receiving. When an officer at headquarters wishes to give instructions to car patrols he speaks into a microphone and his words are transmitted from the aerials of all the fixed stations.

The device of a portable radio-telephone is occasionally used by the B.B.C. (*see* NEWS BROADCASTING). It is also sometimes used on foreign railways, for instance to link the guard's van with the engine-driver on mile-long American goods trains; but it has nowhere taken the place of signalling. On some American railways it connects passengers in a train with ordinary telephone exchanges.

The 'walkie-talkie', which weighs about 12 lb., may be used by the man on whose back it is strapped; but often the set is carried by an assistant. A small collapsible aerial attached to the set sticks up above the wearer's head. Earphones and a mouthpiece may be fixed to a head-band, so that the speaker's hands can be free. Batteries supply the power. Several 'walkie-talkie' sets may be used at once by firemen fighting a big fire, making it possible for the controlling officer to receive information and give instruction to crews hidden by smoke or intervening walls. The police also use this instrument to control large crowds.

See also SPEECH, TRANSMISSION OF.

strapped to a man's back ('walkie-talkie'), and the largest can be fitted in any kind of vehicle or craft. This form of radio-telephone is used in police cars, ambulances, fire-brigade tenders, newspaper reporters' cars, and sometimes in taxis. It has even been fitted to cranes and bulldozers engaged in large works of civil engineering, in which control from a central point is important. It is also used in ports by tugs, firefighting vessels, and official launches.

The method of communicating with a police car will explain the general principles. The entire transmitting and receiving apparatus of the car fits into a space of one cubic foot, because the set, unlike the broadcast receiver in the home, does not need the numerous coils and condensers necessary for tuning in to different stations. It is tuned permanently to wavelengths chosen by the local police force, and makes use of frequency modulation (*see* RADIO ENGINEERING, Vol. VIII); it is therefore difficult for outsiders to pick up. The set, which derives its power from the car's battery, is mounted on rubber shock-absorbers, generally in the rear

TELEPRINTER. This is a machine used by the POST OFFICE (q.v.) to send and receive telegraph messages over wires. It looks very like a large typewriter and works in much the same way: it has a keyboard with keys arranged to print both letters and figures, and can be operated by a typist. When the operator types out a message, the teleprinter not only transmits the same message to the distant teleprinter with which it is connected but can be arranged so that it will also type a copy itself. The distant receiving machine automatically types an exact copy, and it is this which is delivered (*see* Telegram).

Briefly, the teleprinter works in this way: each key of the keyboard sends out a different kind of electrical impulse when it is pressed. On the receiving teleprinter there is an electro-magnet which receives these electrical impulses, and these cause it automatically to operate the appropriate letters on the machine, and thus to produce a copy of the telegram. The receiving machine does not have to be attended all the time by an operator, for the sending machine can make it start up and receive a message.

Telex is a private teleprinter service by means of which business firms may send typewritten messages from their own offices over ordinary telephone lines. The Telex teleprinters are, in effect, 'telephone subscribers', for each has its own telephone line to the Post Office telephone exchange with its own number. When a Telex subscriber wishes to send a typed message, he merely calls the other Telex subscriber by telephone, switches on his teleprinter and types out his message. Unlike the machine used in the Post Office public service, however, the Telex teleprinter types on sheets of paper and not on a paper ribbon. Telex calls may be made not only within Great Britain but also to other European countries.

See also Telegram; Telephone Service.

TELEVISION. The power of seeing things a long way off by means of electricity—which we now call television—was a dream which attracted scientists for 60 years before they made it come true. When electric Telegraphy (q.v.) came into use in the middle of the 19th century, inventors began to think of sending pictures by electric wire. They were not yet thinking of using telegraphy to watch things actually moving; the most they hoped for was to transmit still pictures. But soon their thoughts turned to the transmitting of moving vision, an achievement which did not come until the wireless broadcasting of speech had been already established.

Between 1860 and 1880 many experimenters in Europe and America began to tackle the problem of turning the variations of light and shade of an image into electrical currents, transmitting and receiving them, and then turning them back into the original variations of light and shade, ready to reproduce them for the eye.

The discovery of a chemical element, selenium, the electrical qualities of which vary with changes in light and shade, is described in the article Picture Transmission, as well as the simplest way of 'scanning' a picture, or recording every part of its surface by means of a small beam of light. The same broad principle is used for television, but since in television everything that is seen is actually moving, the 'scanning' must be done with great speed. Just as the cinema is made possible by the natural slowness of the human eye, which fails to notice interruptions of vision which last less than about one-twentieth of a second, so the television transmitter can produce a satisfactory moving picture so long as it can send out at least thirty complete images every second of any scene which it is intended to transmit. Each image, during the one-thirtieth of a second which it lasts, must convey a record

G.P.O.

TELEPRINTER SWITCHBOARD AND KEYBOARD

of the precise amount of light and shade which exists all over its surface. The light and shade of more than 100,000 separate spots in the image must be recorded each time. Thus the transmitter and the receiver must be able in each second to send and receive about 4 million clues to what is happening in the television studio.

The early attempts at scanning were mechanical. In 1884 a German called Nipkow invented a revolving disk, in which he pierced holes in a spiral shape. Light was thrown through the holes, which lit up various parts of a picture in regular order. Later another inventor devised a revolving drum of mirrors for the same purpose. But no mechanical apparatus was quick enough; the scanning had to be electrical. High-frequency oscillations in an electronic circuit can number millions in a second, and if those oscillations could be influenced by the 100,000 details of light and shade thirty times a second, the problem would be solved.

The answer was found in scanning by electronic tube, a task now carried out by an instrument known as the iconoscope. When the television camera is pointed at the image, the light rays from the image fall on a sensitive plate at the back of the iconoscope. This plate is made up of hundreds of thousands of sensitive particles, each insulated from the other, and each electrically responsive to the light and shade of the minute part of the picture that fall upon it. The plate is somewhat like the layer of nerve-cells which form the retina at the back of the human eye. A stream of electrons from an electron 'gun' is then directed at the plate, and moves across the particles line by line, rather as the eye moves across the lines of a printed page when one is reading. This movement of the stream of electrons does not mean the movement of any mechanical parts, but arises out of electronic oscillations. Its effect is to charge the sensitive particles of the plate with energy sufficient to set up a series of differing currents in a connecting wire.

The number of lines into which a television picture is divided varies with different systems. The system of interlaced scanning used in Britain is technically described as '405 lines, 25 frames per second'. That means the camera scans, or 'reads', the picture in a series of lines—10,125 of them per second. To overcome 'flicker' in the picture, the camera's electrical 'eye' traverses the whole of the picture twice, reading alternate lines in one-fiftieth of a second, and the intermediate lines in the next fiftieth. This is the operation we call 'interlacing', and each reading of the lines is known as a 'field'. The effect obviously is to produce twenty-five complete pictures, or frames, every second.

The first real sign-post to modern television came in 1908, when the British experimenter, A. A. Campbell Swinton, suggested using electronic tubes for this purpose.

It was not until 1925 that John L. Baird in Britain and Charles Jenkins in the United States gave the first public demonstrations of television. They had been working on separate schemes, but both used mechanical scanning. They first transmitted outlines of figures, but within a few months Baird transmitted a living image in London, using an office-boy as his model. Baird's experimental work gives him a permanent and honoured place among the pioneers of radio communication. His first practical systems made use of the sensitivity to light of photo-electric cells; later, he employed the intermediate-film process in which the image is first photographed on moving film, which is then developed, washed, and fixed, so that it can be transmitted within 20 or 30 seconds of being 'shot'. Finally he used the electronic-tube method. At the time of his death in 1946 he was studying television in colour and in three dimensions (stereoscopic vision).

The next problem was to arrange to broadcast sound at the same time as vision, to receive both on the same aerial and in the same receiving set.

In 1929 began an experimental service from a B.B.C. transmitter. The service passed to full B.B.C. control in 1932. This early system sent out a new image only 12½ times a second; it also gave less detail in each image, which meant that a fairly small range of WAVELENGTHS (q.v.) was needed; so Baird's signals were radiated on 261 metres, one of the normal medium-wave B.B.C. figures.

In 1934 the Postmaster-General (who acts on behalf of the Government in giving the B.B.C. permission to carry on broadcasting) asked a committee to advise him on the various systems. As a result, an official B.B.C. service began at Alexandra Palace, north London, on 2 November 1936, and for the next 4 months used alternately the Baird system and an electronic-tube system known as the Marconi-E.M.I. In 1937, as advised by the committee, the B.B.C.

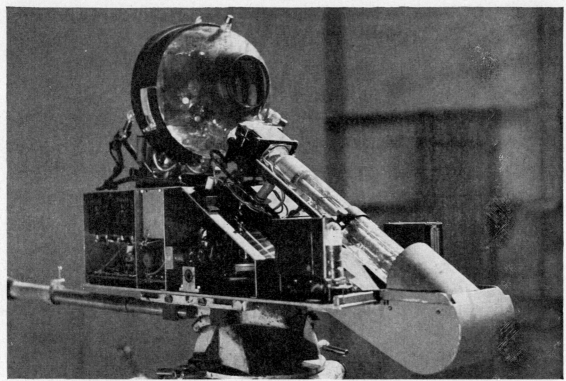

B.B.C.

EMITRON TELEVISION CAMERA WITH COVER REMOVED

adopted the Marconi-E.M.I. system exclusively. This brought into regular use an outstanding device, the 'Emitron' camera, which was based on the iconoscope invented by Dr. Vladimir Zworykin of the United States in 1933.

Competition in television methods was introduced in Britain following the setting up of the Independent Television Authority in 1954 (*see* BROADCASTING CORPORATIONS, Section 2).

Latest developments have led to experiments in coloured television, as well as stereoscopic television, in which images will appear to be solid, and not flat.

For the high-definition television of today, with its great variety of detail, a wide band of wavelengths is necessary. To crowd a great number of wavelengths together to achieve this detail meant using very short waves (*see* WAVE-LENGTHS), as these take up less room in a waveband. Very short waves do not reach very far from the transmitter. They do not make their way round the curve of the earth's surface, as most wireless waves do; in a general sense it is true to say that they cannot reach any receiver which is not within sight of the transmitting aerial.

The problem is even more difficult in countries of vast distances, such as the United States. An experimental aircraft has been used as a relaying station. The aircraft was fitted with apparatus for picking up the vision signals from the main sending station on the ground, and for re-transmitting them while in flight. The higher the aeroplane, the greater the stretch of country within its range, and so the wider the area of reception. Circling over Pittsburgh at a height of 25,000 feet, the aircraft picked up the signals from a transmitter at Washington, and, it was claimed, relayed them satisfactorily over an area 525 miles wide.

See also PICTURE TRANSMISSION; SHORT-WAVE WIRELESS.
See also Vol. VIII: TELEVISION ENGINEERING.
See also Vol. IX: TELEVISION.

TELEX, *see* TELEPRINTER.

TEST FLYING, *see* Vol. VII: AIRCRAFT IN-DUSTRY.

TIBETAN LANGUAGE, *see* CHINESE LANGUAGE.

TIME-TABLES. All forms of transport which run regularly work to a time-table of some sort. Railway time-tables are the most complicated; since all trains in any one direction have to use the same set of lines, delay and accidents would occur if exact timing to a minute were not planned out beforehand for every journey.

A graph is the basis of all railway time-tables. Large sheets of squared paper are used, with the 24 hours of the day marked along the top, and the stations and sidings of the section of line concerned marked down the side. Across these sheets the paths of the trains are plotted; a steep line indicates high speed, such as that of a streamlined express train, and every flattening of the inclination indicates a reduction of speed. Horizontal breaks in any train-line indicate stops. From such diagrams a comprehensive view of the train service may be obtained, and it is easy to see how train-paths might be improved, or paths for new trains found.

From the graphs the printed time-tables are compiled. In Great Britain the practice is now to issue these twice a year, the summer service about mid-May and the winter service about the beginning of October. The time-table books issued to the public are in the familiar form of *Bradshaw's Guide*. The *A.B.C. Guide* is an alphabetical guide to trains from London to all other British stations. The large sheets posted at the stations have to be compiled and printed, as well as the more complicated railway working time-tables, which give much information not accessible to the general public but necessary for all members of the staff concerned in operating the trains. This information includes the times at which non-stopping trains pass the principal stations and junctions, the working of empty carriages, freight trains, light engines, and so on, and many operating details. To avoid unnecessarily bulky books and excessive cost, the working books are sectionalized into a number of parts, and the various members of the staff are given only the section or sections with which they are concerned.

At monthly intervals supplements are printed for both the public and the working books, showing any interim changes in times or any train additions or cancellations. A bigger task still is the preparation of the staff weekly working notices, which list the special trains to be run during the week of their currency. A companion weekly issue is that for which the civil engineering departments are responsible, showing the various engineering works that may make speed restrictions necessary, the appearance and purpose of new and altered signals, and so on. In railway working, nothing is left to chance, and as little as possible to last-minute improvisation.

See also STATIONS, RAILWAY; RAILWAYMEN.

TITANIC, *see* CLIMATE AND COMMUNICATIONS, Section 3.

TOLLGATE, *see* TURNPIKE.

TONNAGE. Tonnage is a measurement of the size or capacity of a ship. The term originated in the early days of British merchant shipping, when the principal trade was the importation of wine from France. The casks in which the wine came were known as 'tuns', and were all about the same size. The size of the ships varied, and it became the practice to differentiate between them by saying how many tuns they carried. Even if ships were not carrying wine, their capacity was estimated by this method. Gradually the word changed its spelling and became 'ton'.

Tonnage is now calculated in four different ways. Displacement tonnage is the weight of water displaced by the ship, and is in fact the actual weight of the vessel. This term is used mostly in relation to warships. Deadweight tonnage is the weight of cargo, bunkers, water, and consumable stores necessary to load the ship down to the Plimsoll mark (*see* SAFETY AT SEA).

Gross tonnage is a measure of capacity, the ton in this case being 100 cubic feet of capacity. Certain spaces in the ship are excluded from measurement. They are: open-shelter deck space; any closed-in space fitted for machinery, other than the main engine room; wheel-houses; galleys, buildings on the upper deck for the shelter of passengers; and the ship's double bottom.

Net register tonnage is the measure of the cubic space available for the carriage of cargo and passengers, and is used as the basis for harbour charges. It is calculated by subtracting non-profit-earning spaces, that is, spaces for machinery, ballast tanks, and living-room for the crew, from the gross tonnage.

See also Vol. VII: SHIPPING.

TOWER BRIDGE. This is the last bridge across the Thames down the river. Just above the bridge lies a part of what is called the Pool of London, to which large ships can have access because the roadway of Tower Bridge can be lifted, on the principle of a drawbridge, to let them through. The bridge was built in 1894 from a design by Sir Horace Jones, and is the largest bridge of the 'bascule' type in the world.

A bascule bridge is one which can be lifted, either to allow passage under it or prevent passage across it, by a lever apparatus. A short bascule bridge, such as is often found on canals or in docks and harbours, is lifted in one piece from one end only; a long bridge is generally opened in two halves by lifting apparatus at each end. The bascule bridge built over the River Ouse in 1839 can be opened by two men in a minute and a half, making a passage 45 feet wide for ships.

The two heavy Gothic towers of the Tower bascule bridge are built of grey granite and hard red brick. Within them is the machinery for lifting the leaves of the iron drawbridge which runs between them across the centre of the river. These leaves, when open, stand upright against the towers, allowing a clearance of some 135 feet at high water. When closed, the bridge allows clearance for all ordinary river traffic. The opening and closing of the drawbridge takes about 4 or 5 minutes. Foot passengers can cross when the drawbridge is up by an upper footway suspended between the towers and reached by lifts or staircases inside the towers. Bridges from these towers to the embankment on each side are built on the suspension principle.

The bascule bridge is a rather slow and clumsy device for making crossways over rivers along which big ships must pass. Modern suspension bridges can be built high enough for the biggest ocean ships to pass under (*see* BRIDGES). Farther down the Thames the river is crossed by TUNNELS (q.v.) at Rotherhithe and Blackwall.

See also LONDON BRIDGE.
See also Vol. III: LONDON (picture); THAMES.

TRACK CIRCUIT, *see* ELECTRIC SIGNALLING, RAILWAY, Section 2.

TRACKED VEHICLES. A tracked vehicle is one whose wheels run on a road or track which it lays itself as it goes. The track is to provide the wheels with a firm surface on which to run,

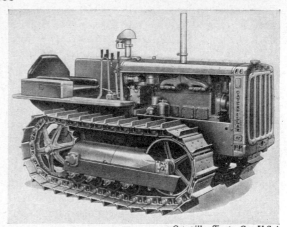

Caterpillar Tractor Co., U.S.A.
A 'CATERPILLAR' DIESEL TRACTOR

for wheels of a very large diameter, especially when under a heavy load, tend to sink into the ground, so that the softer the ground the greater the effort needed to move the wheels. The first 'caterpillar' or 'track-laying' vehicle had two endless chain tracks or metal belts, which gripped the ground by means of bars or indentations running transversely. The inside of the track took the weight of the vehicle on several roller or idler wheels (wheels not connected with the engine). Power from the engine was transmitted through a series of gears to two toothed (or 'sprocket') wheels on either side of the machine, which fitted into corresponding teeth or grooves on the track.

The principle was first used in 1900, and the track was also adapted for pneumatic-tired vehicles. The possibilities of the invention were most fully exploited by the army, who found these vehicles useful for crossing difficult country. Several machines were fitted with tracks from 1910 to 1914, before the First World War. The idea of the endless chain was then applied to tractors in the United States by a man named Holt; and his work led to further development in the tracked vehicle by the army, especially during the First World War, when armoured caterpillar tractors and later TANKS (q.v. Vol. X), were used.

Besides being useful in war, the tracked vehicle is valuable in the production of food and for building. On farms, 'caterpillar' or 'crawler' tractors, as they are often called, are used to plough and harvest fields where the ordinary wheeled vehicle would be unable to go. In any place where there are no roads the tracked vehicle is invaluable. A tractor fitted with endless tracks can be taken across ditches and over boggy fields, and can surmount the most difficult obstacles. It can also draw any type of agricultural machinery (*see* POWER FOR FARMING, Vol. VI).

Tracked machines such as the 'bulldozer' are used in civil engineering for clearing and levelling the ground, and for demolition, especially in roadmaking, where work has to be done over undulating surfaces, and where vast quantities of earth have to be moved. Tracked vehicles have also been used over snow or hard frozen ground (*see* SNOW AND ICE TRAVEL), the tracks being made of rubber, joined together by flexible steel bands, so that they can be used on the roads as well. Tracked vehicles are now much faster than they were when first invented: some can travel at a rate of 60 miles an hour on level ground.

See also Vol. VIII: TRACK MECHANISM.

TRADE ROUTES. Almost all communication, ancient and modern, is connected with trade. The attempt to discover details about ancient and medieval trade routes is exciting and baffling, for merchants are not generally writers. We have to piece together their story from the stray finds of explorers, or from chance facts mentioned for some different purpose by ancient writers. How did a piece of Irish gold, or indeed a piece of white nephrite, a stone found no nearer than China, reach Troy, in Asia Minor, about the year 2000 B.C.? How did an Egyptian glass bead come to be buried with a chieftain in his 'long barrow' in England, about that same time? We cannot answer. Earlier than 3000 B.C. there came to Ur in Mesopotamia, a great commercial city even by the standards of to-day (*see* SUMERIANS, Vol. I), lapis lazuli stones from the Pamirs in Central Asia, goods from the Indus valley (doubtless by sea and up the Persian Gulf), and silver from Syria. Objects from Ur have been found in Egypt But of the details of these contacts, next to nothing is known. There are written records of Egyptian expeditions by sea to the 'Land of Punt' (Somaliland) not much later, expeditions which brought back cargoes of ebony and myrrh, and some of King Solomon's treasure may have come from as far afield. But the expeditions of these distant times were not made along beaten

tracks of trade routes. Nevertheless, the track-ways along the ridges of the English Downs (*see* ROADS, BRITISH) may have been regularly used by traders in the Bronze Age, soon after 2000 B.C., and local trade was certainly considerable at a time when men were able to transport the 'blue' stones for the smaller circle of STONEHENGE (q.v. Vol. I) from Prescelly in Pembrokeshire to the heart of Wiltshire.

Both legend and the finds of archaeologists show that the travels of the Cretans 1500 B.C. extended to Sicily and the western Mediterranean as well as to Greece, Syria, and Egypt (*see* MINOANS, Vol. I). The PHOENICIANS (q.v. Vol. I) for many centuries from about the 12th century B.C. sailed from Syria to Egypt, westwards to Carthage and Spain, and through the Pillars of Hercules (Straits of Gibraltar) to Britain whence they fetched tin. The Greek traders of the Mediterranean from the 7th to the 4th centuries B.C. were less adventurous, carrying mainly olive-oil, wheat, wool, and herbs—the necessities of life—to and from southern Russia, the eastern Balkans, and north Africa. The sea route from Athens to Italy carried so many Greek painted vases of this period that archaeologists, finding these in Italian graves, thought that they must have been made in Italy; but they came, in fact, from the factories of Corinth or Athens. Many Greek cities lived by this foreign trade, and Athens, in particular, depended on food from abroad; in the 5th century B.C. cities were already scheming to control trade routes because of the political power that this would bring. When Athens lost control of the sea route through the Dardanelles, by which corn was brought from the lands on the north of the Black Sea, she was doomed to starvation or surrender (405 B.C.).

We begin now to trace more definitely the lines of routes stretching out far beyond the Mediterranean lands. Thus amber from the Baltic came across central Europe by way of the Rivers Rhine and Rhone, or the River Elbe and the Brenner Pass in the Alps, or the Rivers Vistula and Dniester. Little was known about the land from which it came, the land 'at the back of the north wind'.

The conquests made by ALEXANDER THE GREAT (q.v. Vol. V) opened up vast new regions, including India, to Mediterranean traders, and in course of time Alexandria in Egypt grew to be a city of more than a million people, through

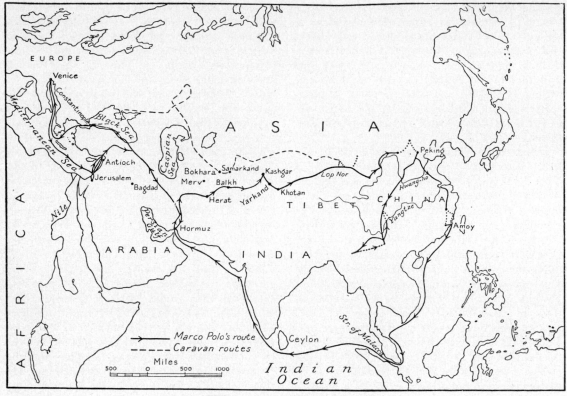

MEDIEVAL TRADE ROUTES TO THE EAST

which passed a rich traffic of jewels and spices from India, and frankincense from Arabia. In the 1st century A.D. the changes in the monsoon came to be understood; men learned to make an outward voyage to India with a following wind in July, and the return voyage with a following wind in January. Hundreds of ships every year made that voyage, and attempts were made to make a canal from the Red Sea to the Nile, so that ships might sail straight through to Rome.

Most of the overland trade—chiefly in silks —reaching Europe from central Asia and China, passed through Antioch in Syria. A geographer describes (about A.D. 140) how the caravans started from 'Sera Metropolis' (in China, on the Hwang Ho River) travelled across western China, thence to Merv (Turkestan) and by way of the Caspian gates either by the Caucasus route to the Black Sea or by Mesopotamia to Syria. This route crosses the terrible desert of Lop Nor (Sinkiang), so extensive, as Marco Polo afterwards said, that 'they report it would take a year to ride from one end of it to the other. If a traveller strays, he will hear spirits talking, and suppose

them to be his company.' Much of it has been crossed by European explorers in modern times. We know that parts of central Asia were then much more fertile, and that prosperous cities, now deserted and overwhelmed by sand, once flourished along the caravan route.

In western Europe the vast system of ROMAN ROADS (q.v.) opened up regular overland routes through north Italy and across the Alps, round into Spain, or to the Channel ports, and thanks to these a civilization of linked cities and townships was built up, of which trade was the lifeblood.

The safety of trade along these great trunk roads was imperilled by the barbarian invasions of the 4th century A.D. and later. Even more disastrous was the threat to the Mediterranean sea routes with the rise of the power of ISLAM (q.v. Vol. I), in the 7th and 8th centuries. This threat, more than anything else, brought the DARK AGES (q.v. Vol. I) to northern Europe, and for a long period there was little regular trade by sea or by road. It began again in the 12th and 13th centuries with the rise of the Italian trading republics, VENICE and GENOA (qq.v. Vol. III). Venice thrust her influence as far as the ports of the Black Sea to secure the western end of the caravan routes. She had a fleet of trading galleys, which came round every year into the Bay of Biscay, and up the Channel, calling at English and Flemish ports, bringing eastern products, such as silks, spices, and sugar, to exchange for raw wool and cloth (*see* TRADE, HISTORY OF, Vol. VII).

It was from Venice that MARCO POLO (q.v. Vol. V) set out to visit the fabulous East. For most of the journey he followed the way that the caravans had been taking for centuries; but he made a diversion south to Hormuz on the Persian Gulf, one terminus of the sea route from China. From Hormuz he went up through Persia to Herat and Balkh (Afghanistan), then along the ancient track through eastern Turkistan which led by way of Kashgar, Yarkand, and Khotan, across Lop Nor, and so at last to Peking. 'Out of this city', he wrote, 'go every day a thousand cartloads of silk.' When he came back years later to Venice (having made the journey by sea, by way of the Straits of Malacca and Ceylon, with jewels stuffing the lining of his clothes) he wrote down his gorgeous account of the rich East, which fired the imagination of western adventurers for centuries. For, not long after his return, disturbances in Asia closed the routes that he had followed, and other routes had to be found for reaching China.

Diaz and Vasco da Gama chose the route by the south of Africa (*see* EXPLORATION). On their way they found the Guinea coast, from which the Sahara caravans had brought, from time immemorial, gold dust to the north African ports. Da Gama, in reaching India by sea from western Europe, opened up a new route of incalculable importance. Columbus, a Genoese, set out to find a bolder way to China across the western ocean and round the world; though it was a generation before the route of which he was pioneer began to prosper. Then it was not the China trade but the gold of Peru that made its fortunes. Meanwhile in the Far East the Portuguese were pushing their way round into the China seas. They were followed, later, by the Dutch, who made the Cape of Good Hope one of their trading stations.

The English set out to find yet another new route of their own. Men were beginning to think of the world as a globe. Anyone who tries with a piece of thread on a globe to find the shortest way from London to Peking will discover that it passes through the Arctic Circle, north of Siberia, and is about the length of the shortest route from London to Panama. So English sailors attempted again and again to find the 'great-circle route' of the north-east and the north-west passages to China. All things seemed possible to that wonderful generation of Elizabethans. 'There is no land unhabitable, and no sea innavigable' wrote one of them. The explorations in the north-east opened up a route by the White Sea to Moscow, and English merchant explorers attempted to pass thence overland to China. They reached Persia, with which English merchants of the Levant Company had already made contact through the Mediterranean (*see* MERCHANT ADVENTURERS, Vol. VII).

By the mid-17th century the pattern of the great sea routes was already traced—with few exceptions. For a hundred years, till the abolition of the slave trade, there was a constant traffic of Liverpool ships from West Africa to the West Indies carrying slaves. And it was not till the opening of the SUEZ CANAL in 1869 and the PANAMA CANAL in 1914 (qq.v.) that the present tracks of the oceans were finally established. A map has been made showing the position of every British ship at sea on 1 January 1912. It shows three thick bands reaching from the Channel; west to Halifax and New York; south-west to Buenos Aires; and through the Mediterranean and Red Sea to the Far East. A thinner chain girdles almost all the coastlines of the world, except in the far north.

The last hundred years have seen the opening of vast new inland routes. The Mississippi–Missouri river system was opened up in the early days of the steamship (*see* RIVER NAVIGATION). Two generations later, transcontinental railways in the U.S.A. and Canada opened up the trade of the prairies (*see* RAILWAY SYSTEMS). The 'great-circle' routes of air transport have brought Africa within a few hours of London, and the journey to any part of the world is a matter not of months but of days (*see* CIVIL AVIATION).

See also EXPLORATION; NAVIGATION, HISTORY OF; PORTS, HISTORY OF; ROADS, HISTORY OF; SEA TRAVEL.

See also Vol. VII: COMMERCE; EXCHANGE AND TRADE; OVERSEAS TRADE.

TRAFFIC CONTROL, *see* ROAD TRAFFIC CONTROL; TRAIN CONTROL; RULE OF THE ROAD.

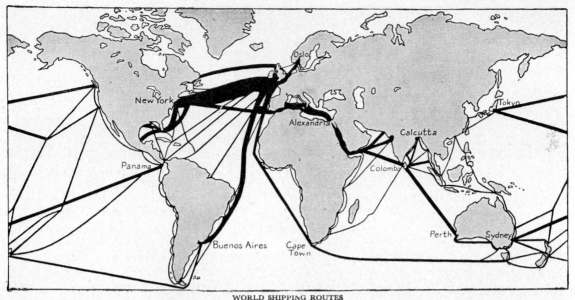

WORLD SHIPPING ROUTES

The thickness of each line indicates the volume of traffic

TRAFFIC-LIGHTS, *see* ROAD TRAFFIC CONTROL.

TRAILER, *see* MOTOR TRANSPORT.

TRAIN CONTROL. Many central traffic-control offices have been set up in the railways, so that the movement of the trains can be kept constantly under review, and the best use made of locomotives and train crews.

The principal main lines are divided into a series of controls, and there are further controls in busy areas, each with its control office. Large panels on the walls of the control office show the whole of the area, divided into sections, each in charge of a separate member of the control staff. The control office can receive information by telephone from every signalbox and yardmaster in the area; the position of every freight train in the area, moving or standing, is marked on the diagrams; the information includes the identity number of the engine, the number of wagons, the names of the driver, fireman, and guard, and the time at which they are due for relief. Although some freedom is allowed to individual signalmen in controlling the movements of the freight trains, especially in keeping them clear of passenger trains, the general direction of the traffic comes from the control offices, which keep accurate and detailed records of all that has happened in their areas throughout the day.

The most complete traffic-control systems in Britain are those of the western and midland divisions of the London Midland Region. The central 'brain' of the complex western division is the control office at Crewe. This applies the 'master' control over train movements throughout the 299 miles between Euston and Carlisle, and can also communicate at any moment with any part of the 2,400 route-miles of line in the division. Every morning the district operating superintendent at Crewe holds a conference by telephone with his district controllers, scattered over the entire division. His staff at Crewe numbers thirty, and, as at all control offices, works 24 hours a day in relays.

Centralized traffic control or 'C.T.C.' is much used in the U.S.A., especially on single lines. The large and very powerful American locomotives, and the long distances to be covered, have led the U.S. railways to concentrate the traffic in relatively few and very heavy trains, as against the British practice of a frequent service of lighter trains. Many important American main lines, particularly in the west, are therefore single-tracked, often for hundreds of miles continuously, and many of these lines, run by 'C.T.C.', can carry a daily tonnage both ways nearly equal to that of double-track lines. A central control

Union Pacific Railroad

A CENTRALIZED TRAIN TRAFFIC CONTROL BOARD
A diagram of the routes can be seen above the switchboard

office contains electrically illuminated diagrams which show the position of every train in the area controlled, and small thumb switches allow all the signals and points, even at stations 50 miles or more away, to be worked from the same central control room. At intervals on a single line there are passing loops, so that trains travelling in opposite directions can pass one another. These loops are very long, and the control from the 'C.T.C.' is so accurate that two trains often pass at a loop without stopping. Some of the fastest American streamlined passenger expresses run over single tracks for part of their route.

See also AUTOMATIC SIGNALLING; SIGNALLING, RAILWAY.

TRAINER AIRCRAFT, *see* AIRCRAFT, SPECIAL USES.

TRAIN FERRY, *see* FERRY, TRAIN.

TRAINING-SHIP. In a training-ship boys are educated as they would be at school or college, and they also become familiar with ships and the sea. In the early years of the present century most European countries had sea-going training-ships; these were sailing-vessels, since even after the advent of steam propulsion it was considered, and still is in the Scandinavian countries, that training in a sailing-ship made the best seamen. Before the First World War, the White Star Line (now absorbed in the Cunard White Star Line) maintained the sea-going training or cadet ship *Mersey* for those who wished to qualify as deck-officers in ships run by the associated companies of this line. Two other sea-going training ships were kept up by a private firm which supplied cadets to other shipping companies. These vessels were all sailing-ships.

There are now four merchant-service training-ships in Britain. They do not go to sea, but are moored permanently near their swimming-baths, sports grounds, lecture halls, and dormitories on shore. They still give a practical training in rope work, boat construction, sailing, and the use of sails in large ships; but their principal advantage over training-schools entirely on shore is that they give the ship atmosphere: watchkeeping is part of the routine, and nautical words are used all the time. The *Arethusa* provides training for boys of good character who are unable to pay fees, and the *Mercury* is a kind of secondary school for future ships' officers; H.M.S. *Conway* (founded in 1859) and H.M.S. *Worcester* (founded in 1862) are akin to public schools of the sea.

See also Vol. X: NAVAL TRAINING.

TRAINS, SPECIAL USES. Apart from the ordinary passenger and goods services, many trains are run for special purposes and are therefore specially equipped.

1. ROYAL TRAINS. Special coaches are used for journeys made by royalty. A train with separate sleeping-saloons for the King and Queen, and other sleeping-cars for their suite, is chosen for long journeys, as between London and Ballater (for Balmoral); another train makes the shorter journeys, as from King's Cross to Sandringham. If the King or Queen are travelling, special timetables are prepared, and precautions are taken to patrol the line to guard against mishap or delay.

2. HOSPITAL TRAINS. These are run in wartime to carry the wounded to hospital. They are made up of ambulance cars, with berths for all the lying-down cases and a space for seated patients, a restaurant car, and a car for the medical staff.

3. ARMOURED TRAINS. The armoured trains of the period of the South African War (1899–1902) were mostly formations of wagons, heavily covered with steel, which carried mobile guns. They were drawn by locomotives protected with armour-plate. Self-propelled guns make such trains unnecessary in modern war, but an armoured train is sometimes used as a mobile military headquarters.

4. PERISHABLE-GOODS TRAINS. Many special trains are run to carry foodstuffs. Fish trains travel at express-passenger speed; there are also meat trains composed of refrigerator wagons, and fruit trains in which the fruit, such as bananas, must be kept at an even temperature. The wagons for these trains are fitted with continuous brakes (*see* BRAKES, RAILWAY).

5. CATTLE TRAINS. Special wagons with adjustable partitions are built for live cattle, so that they may be carried standing, without being thrown over by sudden starts or stops or uncom-

THE QUEEN'S SALOON LOUNGE ON A ROYAL TRAIN

British Railways

fortably packed. Complete cattle trains are run, as far as possible, as this simplifies the work of watering and feeding the animals on the way.

6. BOAT TRAINS. Apart from the regular express trains between London and the ports from which the ships sail to Ireland and the continent, many special boat trains are run for Transatlantic and other ocean liners. To carry the passengers and luggage for the *Queen Mary* or QUEEN ELIZABETH (q.v.), for example, as many as seven or eight special trains may be needed between Waterloo and Southampton.

TRAMP SHIP, *see* SHIP.

TRAMWAY. The tramcar, a passenger-carrying vehicle running on lines through the streets, was invented in New York in 1830, by an Irish coachbuilder named John Stephenson. In 1832, work began on the first tramway, the New York and Harlem Railroad. About 20 years later tramways were opened in other parts of the U.S.A., and were later established in other countries, such as France and Great Britain. The first trams were horse-drawn, but as tramways developed, experiments were made in the use of other kinds of power. Steam, for example, was used to some extent in Great Britain in the 1880's and 1890's, and is still used in some Continental countries. In many places, such as San Francisco, which is built on steep hills, Edinburgh, and Melbourne, cable tramways were used for some time. These were worked by a cable running beneath the road, engaged by a grip rod from the tram through a continuous slot in the road.

The most important development in tramways was, of course, the introduction of electric power. The first commercial electric tramway was opened at Lichterfelde, near Berlin, on 12 May 1881. The first electric system in Great Britain was the Giant's Causeway line between Portrush and Bushmills in Ulster. In this, current was taken from a third rail. The use of overhead wires was developed first in Germany, and then in the United States, before it spread elsewhere. In later years conduit tramway systems were established in some places, notably in parts of London. In these the conductor rail was below ground and was contacted with a 'shoe'. The conduit system was, however, expensive to construct and maintain.

The use of double-deck tramcars is confined almost entirely to Great Britain, but many single-deck trams in other countries can carry as many passengers because there is room for them to

A HORSE-DRAWN TRAM AT MARBLE ARCH

stand. In Stockholm, for example, modern trams carry 104, of whom 70 are expected to stand. Often, one or more trailers are attached to a tram, and in some countries, such as Belgium, France, and the Netherlands, many of the trams are more like trains with several carriages, running on a kind of light railway.

Tramcars can move greater loads more smoothly than can buses, and, when electricity is cheap, they are more economical. Since the Second World War, however, the increased cost of electricity and of essential materials, such as copper and steel, has resulted in many tramways being taken up and buses used instead. Trams have been more developed in North America, but even there the statistics for 1948 showed that the number had dwindled by a quarter in 2 years. In Stockholm tramways have been converted into light railways, with an underground section in the centre of the city; and a similar plan has been put forward for Glasgow. Many towns have now replaced trams with trolley-bus routes.

See also TROLLEY-BUS.

TRANS-SIBERIAN RAILWAY, *see* RAILWAY SYSTEMS.

TRAVEL AGENCIES. These are firms whose business is to relieve a traveller of his major worries and anxieties. The story of travel agencies is largely the story of Thomas Cook (1808–92), a native of Melbourne, Derbyshire, who started work as a gardener's help at the age of 10 and founded the company of Thomas Cook and Son, which is still one of the foremost names associated with touring.

The germ of Cook's business lay in his connexion with the temperance movement, which he strongly supported. A mass temperance meeting had been arranged in Loughborough, in July 1841, soon after the opening of the first railways, and Cook suggested to a railway company that they run a special train to the meeting from Leicester. The company agreed, and carried 570 passengers there and back for a shilling each. This proved so successful that Cook was asked to plan and conduct outings of temperance societies and Sunday-school children during the following three summers. In 1845 he gave up his other occupations and settled in Leicester to concentrate on organizing excursions, being paid by the Midland Railway a percentage of the money received for all the tickets he sold.

One of the first pleasure trips he arranged was from Leicester to Liverpool, on 4 August 1845. To ensure its smooth running Cook went in advance round the places to be visited and prepared a 'handbook of the trip'; he also arranged accommodation for his party with hotel-keepers.

His next excursion was slightly more adventurous: he conducted 350 tourists from Leicester to Glasgow, at one guinea each. At Glasgow they were welcomed with bands and a salute of guns. When the Paris Exhibition opened in 1851 he planned an excursion from Leicester to Calais, his first excursion abroad. Next year began his 'grand circular tours' of Europe. In 1863 he took a party to Switzerland, and in 1864 to Italy.

The number of tourists had become too many for his personal guidance, and so he started the business of issuing tickets for British and European destinations, the purchasers travelling on their own account. In 1864 his son, John Mason Cook, joined him in partnership, and next year they moved to London to open up the head office of Thomas Cook and Son. From that time on their business expanded very quickly and the company's network of offices spread all round the world.

Many other agencies have since come into competition, in various countries, to serve the ever-growing needs of travel. Their tasks are now, principally, the issue of rail, steamer, and air tickets, hotel reservations, the provision of guides and interpreters, the dispatch of baggage, money exchange, and the supply of Travellers' Cheques (*see* BANKING, Vol. VII).

TRAVEL-BOOKS AND GUIDE-BOOKS. In every age men have been curious about the world beyond their own sea or their own mountain range, and from HERODOTUS (q.v. Vol. V) onwards there have been travellers and writers to satisfy their curiosity. The greatest of medieval traveller-writers was the Venetian MARCO POLO (q.v. Vol. V), who spent 24 years (1271–95) at the court of the Grand Khan of Tartary, or travelling there and back. His long account, dictated in French while a prisoner of war of the Genoese, was translated into many languages and became a classic all over Europe.

The 16th century brought the great outburst of EXPLORATION (q.v.) of which a noble part is recorded in Richard Hakluyt's *Principal Navigations Voiages and Discoveries of the English Nation*

A BRIDGE OVER THE BLACK RIVER, A BRANCH OF THE SENEGAL
Engraving after Mungo Park, from his *Travels in the Interior Districts of Africa*, 1799 (1816 edition)

(1589). By the 18th century, books of travel had become one of the most popular classes of polite literature, and alongside the stories of adventures and discovery there was growing up a new type of travel-book, the light, charming, unpretentious narrative of wanderings through countries that, though strange and picturesque, are perfectly well known. The *Turkish Letters* of Ogier de Busbecq, a Flemish nobleman who was ambassador at the Court of the Sultan Sulaiman the Magnificent in 1554–62, is an early and pleasant example of this new kind: it was published in English in 1694, and may have inspired Lady Mary Wortley Montagu to write home her own *Turkish Letters* from Constantinople in 1716 (first published in 1763). The older and newer types may be compared in a famous pair of travel books, Dr. Samuel Johnson's *Journey to the Western Islands of Scotland* (1775) and James Boswell's *Journal of a Tour to the Hebrides* (1786). They were fellow travellers; but while Dr. Johnson informed the educated public about

the peculiarities and customs of a remote and savage quarter of the kingdom, Mr. Boswell published a diary of an agreeable and amusing tour. During the 19th century the great narratives of exploration mostly dealt with Africa. Mungo Park's *Travels to the Source of the Niger* (1819) and Stanley's *Through the Dark Continent* (1878) are famous examples. Books were also written about the interior of South America and the Polar Regions. As late as 1932 Bertram Thomas could chronicle in *Arabia Felix* the story of the first European crossing of the 500-mile-wide 'Empty Quarter' of Arabia—which T. E. Lawrence called 'the last unwritten plot of earth'.

Travel-books may be written about any country into which some explorer is bold enough to venture. Guide-books are written to meet a specific business demand, and so they provide different and in some ways more valuable evidence of the state of communications and the habits of travellers. Until 1830–40, when the first of Murray's *Handbooks* and the first of

Baedeker's *Guides* made their appearance, all guide-books had dealt with things to see, and hardly at all with how to reach them. Tourists used to visit Greece in the 2nd century A.D.; but after the break-up of the Roman Empire, tourist travel became so difficult that it was almost unknown until the 17th century. The nearest thing to it in the Middle Ages was the pilgrim travel to the Holy Land, to Rome, and to shrines such as that of the Apostle St. James at Compostela in Spain; and little guide-books for the pilgrims were compiled. Even in the 17th and 18th centuries tourists were mostly well-to-do persons travelling along the great highways with a certain degree of state, or else poor scholars who expected to lie hard. Conditions of travel were unstable: you had to bargain for your lodging and your meal and your horse: it was more sensible to get hints from knowledgeable friends about local conditions than to rely on a guide-book which would probably be quite out of date. You turned to the guide-book as soon as you were safely installed.

The growth during the 19th century of an educated middle class, combined with the invention of railways and steamship services, produced a revolution in travel, and Murray and Baedeker showed the nature of the change. The traveller expected to be looked after all the way out and home again. Murray and Baedeker told him what clothes to take, what seasons to choose, how to be comfortable on the ship and in the train, and how, on arrival, to get safely from the railway station to one of a series of hotels whose prices and quality were indicated. Only when the traveller was safely established did Murray and Baedeker turn to sights and excursions, and here again hours, prices of admission, and similar practical questions have foremost place. These *Handbooks* and *Guides* symbolize the railway age: their main routes are all railway (or steamship) routes, and a glance at a Baedeker published in any year around 1900 will show how easy and smooth European travel had become for the tourist ready to face the minor discomforts of railway travel. Later, other series modelled on the pattern of Murray and Baedeker, such as the *Blue Guides*, obtained a foothold.

The development of motor-car and air travel have produced in the Michelin and similar guides a throw-back to the 18th and early 19th century road-books, of which *Cary's New Itinerary* (1798) was an outstanding example. Travelling in one's own car is somewhat like travelling in one's own coach—the 18th or 20th century traveller is free, as his rail-bound grandson (or grandfather) was not. He does not have so much use for a comprehensive account of the sights of any one place; and should he want one, he can be fairly sure of finding a local publication, in a language he understands, which will tell him most of what he needs to know.

TRAVELLING POST OFFICE, *see* POST OFFICE, MODERN.

TRINITY HOUSE. The ancient body known as the Corporation of Trinity House, London, is responsible for LIGHTHOUSES AND LIGHTSHIPS, BUOYS (qq.v.), and other navigation marks round certain of the coasts of Britain, and it is the chief authority for controlling ships' PILOTS (q.v.). It also has charge of some charities and almshouses for needy seamen and their dependants.

The origin of the Corporation is unknown; but it has been claimed that a body carrying out its early functions was established in the reign of Alfred the Great. The Corporation's first royal charter was granted by Henry VIII.

At the head of the Corporation to-day, as in ancient times, is a master, assisted by people known as elder brethren and younger brethren. The master and some of the elder brethren are generally eminent people who are offered the position as an honour. The other ten elder brethren, who run the Corporation, are elected from among experienced younger brethren, all of whom are officers in the Navy or the Merchant Service.

TRIREME, *see* CLASSICAL SHIPS.

TROLLEY-BUS. This is a public vehicle driven by electric power which it receives from overhead wires. Like the tram, it moves forward smoothly and rapidly, but it does not have the disadvantage of being confined to rails. The horsepower of a modern trolley-bus varies according to the type of chassis and the kind of service for which it is intended. An average modern two-axle trolley-bus has a 100/120 horsepower motor, and a three-axle trolley-bus one of 120/140 horsepower. The trolley-bus has a very quick rate of acceleration: from a standstill position it can reach a speed of 25 miles an hour in as little as 10 seconds.

Experiments were carried out with trolley-buses as early as 1899 and, as with tramcars, much of the pioneer work was done in Germany. Trolley-buses were first installed successfully in Britain at Leeds, Bradford, and Aberdare in 1911, to be followed by others at Rotherham, Keighley, and Dundee in the following year. They appeared on regular service in the London area on 16 May 1931, between Twickenham and Teddington, on the route of what was then the London United Tramways. By 1949 some 4,000 trolley-buses were at work in Great Britain, and 5,700 in the United States. This number now shows signs of declining. Trolley-buses have been used to replace tramcars in many places, but as costs and equipment have increased since the Second World War, oil-engined buses are being used increasingly for new conversion schemes.

See also BUS; TRAMWAY; LONDON TRANSPORT.

TUBE RAILWAY, *see* UNDERGROUND RAILWAY.

TUGS. These can be divided roughly into three classes—lighterage tugs used for towing lighters and barges, towage tugs used for towing ships, and big ocean-going rescue or salvage tugs.

Most of the 6,000 'dumb' barges (barges without means of propulsion) daily carrying cargo to and from ships in the Port of London are towed by little lighterage tugs, driven by steam or by internal combustion engines. Great skill and a profound knowledge of the tides are needed by the tugmaster who threads his way through the traffic of the world's busiest river with a tow of, say, six barges carrying together up to 1,000 tons of cargo—as much as could be carried by 100 ordinary-sized lorries.

Towage tugs are usually steam driven, and are used chiefly to assist large ocean-going vessels into and out of docks, or to and from riverside wharves. They do not so much tow the vessels as guide them and check their way, or hold them while they swing in the stream to anchor head-on to the tide. When the tug arrives alongside the incoming ship, a heaving line is thrown and is

Cunard White Star

TUGS MANŒUVRING THE LINER 'QUEEN MARY' INTO HER BERTH AT SOUTHAMPTON ON 29 SEPTEMBER 1946, AFTER HER LAST VOYAGE AS A TROOP CARRIER

then made fast to the great towing hawsers, which are in turn hauled across the intervening water. The hawsers are secured to the tug's slipping hook, an ingenious device which permits the tugmen to release the rope in an emergency with a blow from a large mallet. A towage tug's successful working depends upon the skill and co-operation of the tugmaster and engineer. A good tugboat engineer will sense when an order is about to come over the bridge telegraph, and be ready to act almost before the telegraph gong in the engine-room has clanged. Towage tugs from London saved thousands of tons of shipping at the evacuation in 1940 from Dunkirk by helping troopships amidst bombs and shell-fire, and towing to safety disabled ships which would otherwise have fallen into the hands of the enemy.

There are not many large tugs devoted to salvage work, for they have to lie in port waiting with steam up for a radio call to go to the rescue of some ship in trouble. The expenses of maintaining the tug in idleness are heavy, but a big job of SALVAGE (q.v.) successfully completed may bring the owners and crew a very large reward. The rescue tug must be prepared to go out in all weathers, and so has extremely powerful engines (usually diesel). Speed is important, for the first tug alongside the ship in trouble gets the job of salvage. The rescue tug sometimes tows dredgers or floating docks for long ocean voyages, sometimes half round the world. In 1944 the largest fleet of tugs ever gathered together towed the concrete units of the 'Mulberry harbour' across the Channel to France for the invasion of the Continent (see SUPPLY SERVICES (MILITARY), Vol. X).

See also BARGE; PORTS AND HARBOURS.

TUNNELS. 1. Tunnelling is a difficult, expensive, and dangerous engineering feat. Before the 19th century men had not acquired enough skill in engineering to carry out any extensive tunnelling. Tunnels, however, were known in ancient times: they were, for instance, driven into the rock under the Pyramids of Egypt to lead to the burial chambers of the kings; and the Romans built one in Rome for their chief drain, parts of which still remain.

In more recent times natural tunnels, hollowed out of the rock by the sea, were frequently used by SMUGGLERS (q.v. Vol. X) to bring their goods up from their boats unknown to the revenue men. The smugglers made many ingenious entrances

to these tunnels, hiding the door under the hearthstone of a cottage or behind a fireplace, so that it could not be reached while a fire was burning.

There is hardly an old castle or abbey in England without a legend about a tunnel, and sometimes a piece of the tunnel can still be seen. Many of them, however, were only drains. Tunnels have often been made as a way of escape from prison. In the last two World Wars, prisoners-of-war succeeded in making quite long escape tunnels in spite of the difficulty of having practically no tools and of having to hide their activities from their guards. They ventilated them by means of home-made bellows and air tubes made of biscuit tins; sometimes they even fitted them with electric light.

Modern tunnels made by engineers are constructed to carry canals, railways, and roads. There are forty-five canal tunnels in England and Wales, the largest being the Standedge Tunnel on the Huddersfield narrow canal. It is 5,415 yards long. The first canal tunnel in England was the Harecastle Old Tunnel of 2,897 yards on the summit level of the Trent and Mersey; it was begun by James Brindley in 1766, and not finished until 1777.

2. RAILWAY TUNNELS. The simplest form of railway tunnelling is known as 'cut-and-cover'. This consists in excavating a cutting, with vertical sides, and then roofing it over, a construction which is usually found only in towns. But the great majority of tunnels are bored from the two ends. If the depth of the bore below the surface is not too great, shafts, generally vertical, are driven down to the line of the tunnel, so that the driving of the tunnel may be begun at several points simultaneously, and the work thus hastened. These shafts are often used for the removal of the excavated material, and when the tunnel is complete, they are turned into ventilating shafts, acting like tall chimneys in drawing out smoke and fumes.

Exceedingly accurate survey work is needed in tunnelling—especially when a long tunnel is being driven from the two ends. There is no possibility of using any external checks to discover if any deviation is being made from the centre-line that has been planned. High temperatures, foul air, breaking in of water and noxious gases, or collapses of the rock all add to the difficulties. The accounts of the APENNINE, SIMPLON, and SEVERN TUNNELS (qq.v.) mention

THE THAMES TUNNEL AT ROTHERHITHE, WHICH WAS OPENED IN 1843
Above is a longitudinal section, and below a cross section and a diagram of men working in Brunel's 'shield'

some of these difficulties. Even tunnels through rock generally have to be lined throughout with masonry, the rock being seldom hard enough to be left with safety in its natural condition after the work of boring is complete. Automatic machinery has been invented for tunnelling through gravel or clay; it has not as yet been applied to any tunnels of normal double-line size, but only to the small circular tube-tunnels, with a maximum diameter of about 12 feet.

A double-line tunnel is about 26 feet in width, and 20 feet or so in height above the rails. The main arch is generally about three-quarters of a circle, with the centre some 7 feet above rail level. It stands on an inverted arch of much greater radius, called the 'invert', which provides plenty of space to accommodate the ballast and to allow for efficient drainage. Unless a tunnel is on a gradient throughout, it is customary to provide some fall in each direction from the centre, for drainage purposes.

After the Simplon and Apennine Tunnels— the longest double-line tunnels in the world— are two Swiss tunnels, the St. Gotthard, 9¼ miles, and the Lötschberg, 9 miles. The Mont Cenis, earliest of the Alpine tunnels to be bored, and open in 1871, is some 8 miles long. In the United States the record is held by the Cascade Tunnel on the Great Northern Railway, of nearly 8 miles, followed by the Moffat Tunnel of the Denver and Rio Grande Western, a tunnel of just over 6 miles which, with its railway approaches, cuts no less than 175 miles from the journey between Denver and Salt Lake City.

In Great Britain the longest main-line tunnel is the Severn Tunnel of the W.R., between Bristol and Newport, 4¼ miles. This is followed by three tunnels from east to west through the Pennines: Totley, L.M.R., 3½ miles; Standedge, L.M.R. (one double and two single-line tunnels), 3 miles; and Woodhead E.R. (two single-line tunnels), 3 miles. In view of maintenance difficulties and to accommodate the overhead conductors of the electrification scheme planned between Sheffield and Manchester, a new double-line Woodhead tunnel, costing £3,800,000, was begun in 1949. In the London Tube system, of course, it is possible to make continuous tunnel journeys of far greater length. The longest such tube journey, which is a world's record for continuous railway tunnelling, is the 16½ miles from Golder's Green to Morden, via the Bank (see UNDERGROUND RAILWAYS).

It has often been suggested that there should

be a Channel tunnel to connect England and France, and, indeed, digging actually began towards the end of the 19th century. By 1882 over a mile had been bored on either side, from Sangatte near Calais and from Shakespeare's Cliff near Dover. But the British Government advised the work to stop, because they were afraid of losing the safety from invasion then given by the Channel. Later schemes proposed a tunnel 33 miles long and at least 100 feet below the Channel bed. They suggested that it should be under the control of the British War Office, and made so that, in emergencies, it could be flooded to stop the passage of troops. In 1935 it was estimated that such a tunnel would take about 8 years to build, and cost over £30 million.

3. ROAD TUNNELS. There are several important road tunnels in England, usually under rivers and at points where the use of ferries has caused 'bottle-necks' in the flow of passengers and goods on important arterial routes. The first tunnel roadway was made under the River Thames near the London docks; it was built by the famous engineer Sir Marc Brunel, and opened in 1843. The driving of this tunnel, running from Wapping to Rotherhithe, was made possible by the invention of the 'shield' by Brunel. This early shield was a large rectangular framework containing thirty-six cells, erected below ground, facing the intended tunnel (*see* diagram). A man in each cell scooped out the clay in front of him to the depth of a few inches. Then the cells, in groups of three, were pushed that much further forward, and the men started to scoop again, while other men lined the newly-cut tunnel with bricks and iron rings. Years later men devised the circular 'Great-head' shield which cut tube railway tunnels under London. Brunel's tunnel, though built for road use, now carries an Underground railway to New Cross. Shortly before the First World War two road tunnels under the Thames were constructed, at Rotherhithe and Woolwich. A tunnel for foot-passengers only, between the Isle of Dogs and Greenwich, was opened soon after the original one of 1843.

The tunnels described are undoubtedly notable engineering feats, but they have since been com-

BUILDING THE MERSEY ROAD TUNNEL IN 1930

Stewart Balt

pletely overshadowed by the great Mersey Tunnel (q.v.), which links Liverpool with Birkenhead.

The Holland Tunnel and the Lincoln Tunnel take New York traffic under the Hudson river, and tunnels are used in Paris to by-pass the surface traffic.

See also Apennine; Mersey; Severn; Simplon Tunnels; Underground Railway.

See also Vol. VIII: Tunnelling.

TURBINE, STEAM, *see* Ship; *see also* Vol. VIII: Steam Turbine.

TURBINE, GAS, *see* Gas Turbine Locomotive; Road Transport Engines; Aircraft Engines, Section 2; *see also* Vol. VIII: Gas Turbine.

TURKISH AND ALLIED LANGUAGES.
Turkish (the language of Turkey), the language of the Turkic people of the U.S.S.R., the various Mongolian languages, and Tungus, which is spoken in part of Siberia, have all descended from one single language of long ago (*see* Language, History of). These languages, which are members of the Turkic-Mongol-Tungus family, differ in many ways from languages like English. The words are complicated and are often formed by means of chains of suffixes. The Mongol word *Gadzardagi*, for instance, means 'he who is on the earth' and is formed from *Gadzar* 'the earth', with *da* a suffix (or additional term) indicating 'where', and *gi* the relative pronoun ('he who'). The same word in Turkish is *yār-dā-ki*. The verb has many voices or moods: there are, for instance, not only passive, reflexive, and negative forms, but also forms for expressing the impossibility of an action.

The largest branch of this group is the Turkic family. There are about 30 million speakers of Turkic languages, all members of the many Turkish races which inhabit not only Turkey itself but also parts of Russia, Siberia, and Mongolia. The Mongolian languages are spoken by about 3 million people, in Mongolia and parts of Siberia and Tibet. The Tungus languages, which are spoken by probably fewer than a million people, mainly inhabitants of Siberia, include Manchu, which is spoken in Manchukuo (formerly Manchuria, then part of the old Chinese Empire). It has been a written language since the 13th century.

See also Language Structure.

See also Vol. I: Turks; Soviet Central Asian Peoples; Mongols; Siberian Peoples.

TURNPIKE.
During the 17th century, when wheeled traffic was rapidly increasing in England, something had to be done to improve the condition of the roads. It seemed reasonable that those who used them should pay for their upkeep; so from 1663 a number of Turnpike Acts were passed, which first made the local Justices of the Peace, and later boards of trustees known as 'Trusts', responsible for the highways, and gave them the right to collect fees or 'tolls' from those who took wheeled vehicles or animals along the roads. The Trusts collected their tolls by having barriers built at various places along the roads. The first barriers were wooden bars studded with pikes, which turned on a pivot, so the barriers, and the highways on which they occurred, were called 'turnpikes'. Often little toll-houses were built near the barriers for the use of the keeper. These cottages, many of which are still to be seen, were usually hexagonal in shape, so that the windows commanded a view in all directions.

When the fees collected were wisely spent, the condition of the highways rapidly improved; but unfortunately permission to levy tolls was granted to too many small Trusts, and these did not always work together. The number of toll-gates increased until they became a great nuisance. In some districts there was a gate every 6 or 8 miles, and on one road to the north of London there were ten gates in 3½ miles. This made travelling so slow and expensive that people began to protest. At the beginning of the 18th century the tolls were quite moderate—a shilling was charged for a wagon, and sixpence for a coach; but as time went on the fees increased enormously, so that before long a coach drawn by four horses was paying as much as 3½d. a mile. In 1837 it was estimated that each coach running between London and Manchester was paying £1,700 in turnpike fees every year. The Trusts, also, were sometimes corrupt, levying exorbitant tolls and not spending the money on the roads. In 1741, when extra tolls were levied on vehicles over 3 tons, gentlemen's coaches and wagons on government business were exempted from tolls. This privilege was much resented, and the turnpikes became very unpopular. In some places riots occurred and gates were broken down or burnt by the mob. Although the Government introduced severe penalties for rioters, even the death penalty, riots in Bristol in 1749 lasted for 3 days and had to be put down by soldiers.

A COACH ARRIVING AT A TURNPIKE

A coloured engraving from *Voyage en Angleterre* by L. E. Lami, 1830

As railway travel developed, the Trusts, many of whom had become bankrupt, were gradually reduced in number, until by 1859 almost all toll-gates had been removed from public roads in England, and the responsibility for highways was taken over by County Councils and later partly by the Ministry of Transport. Up to 1930, however, there were in Britain fifty-five private roads and eighty-eight bridges for which tolls were still levied; but these tolls also are being gradually done away with.

See also ROADS, BRITISH; ROADS, MODERN.

TWENTIETH CENTURY LIMITED TRAIN.

It is said that no trip to the United States is complete without 'riding the "Century" ' the famous luxury express of the New York Central System, which runs every night between New York and Chicago, covering the 958 miles in 16 hours, travelling west, and in $15\frac{1}{2}$ hours travelling east,

inclusive of all stops. The train has sixteen cars: single-room sleeping-cars of various types, dining, lounge, and buffet cars, and an observation car at the rear end, as on many American trains. Two of the sleepers take the Santa Fé route to Los Angeles on the Pacific Coast. The principal rival of the 'Century' is the 'Broadway Limited' of the Pennsylvania Railroad. Both use electric motors for running out of New York, but for most of their journeys powerful diesel-electric locomotives are used.

TYPEWRITER.

The first practical typewriter was manufactured in 1873; but as early as 1714 an Englishman, Henry Mill, was granted a patent for 'an artificial machine or method for the impressing or transcribing of letters singly or progressively one after another, as in writing'. No trace has been found of Mill's machine, if he ever made one.

HANSEN 'WRITING BALL' 1870–5

This typewriter is said to have been the first actually manufactured and sold to the public. From an exhibit in the Science Museum, London

For a long time inventors were most concerned with writing-machines for the use of blind people. By the middle of the 19th century there existed many different machines for making 'embossed' printing, the most successful being the BRAILLE writer (q.v.). During the 19th century various methods for typewriters were tried out, none of which proved satisfactory.

On 1 March 1873, however, the firm of Remington & Sons signed a contract with two Americans, Scholes and Gliddon, to manufacture the first really practical typewriter. It had forty-four keys, providing only capital letters, and so arranged that the letters which most often occur together—such as T and H, S and T, O and N—were placed as far apart as possible. The reason for this was that adjoining type-bars (the little levers with the letters on the end) tended to catch on each other when moving at any speed. This arrangement of the letters on the keyboard, which varies with every language, continues in most typewriters to-day; although a different arrangement, for which greater speed is claimed, is used in some American offices. The type-bars were arranged in 'basket' formation, so that each letter strikes inward towards the same spot on a roller which carries the paper.

Other designs have been used, including models with the letters set round the edge of a wheel, as in some 19th-century telegraphic instruments. The Scholes and Gliddon typewriter, however, has proved to be generally the most practical, and the history of the typewriter has consisted mainly of a series of improvements upon this design. In 1880 the introduction of the 'shift key' made possible a more compact, easily worked machine. Instead of there being a separate key for every capital and every small letter, these were combined in pairs, two on one type-bar. By the pressing of the shift key, the roller was slightly lifted and a capital letter resulted; in its normal position small letters were made. The next improvement was a machine which made it possible for the typist to see what he was writing—which had been impossible in the earlier machines. In the 'noiseless' typewriter, which appeared in 1910, the type-bar of each letter is made very light, and the rubber-covered roller replaced by a metal one, to reduce the smacking sound of the type-bar striking the paper. Light portable machines have been on the market since 1893. In 1935 an electric machine was brought out, which does very fast typing of excellent quality. The keys need to be struck only lightly, the electric power doing the rest. A very even impression results, and, with a specially hard roller, up to twenty-five carbon copies can be made at a time, compared with the normal six or seven.

The letters, numerals, and punctuation marks of all modern typewriters are arranged on the keyboard in a standard pattern. The typist has to memorize these, so that his fingers can find them automatically, while his eyes remain on his copy. This is called 'touch typing', and is essential for speed. A normal typing speed is about 40 words a minute, though an expert typist on an electric machine can work at some four times this speed. The paper is inserted round the roller fixed on a sliding carriage which moves from right to left as the keyboard is worked. When it reaches the end, a line space lever is pushed to move the paper up to a new line and return the carriage to the right. Ink is supplied from an inked ribbon which passes between the raised type-bar and the paper on the roller. The space-bar is pressed by the thumb between each word to make a white space. There is also a back-spacer so that the typist can go back to make a correction.

See also SHORTHAND.

U

UNDERGROUND RAILWAY. Many large cities have railway lines which, in places, lie slightly or wholly below street level. An entire 'underground' system is rare. In London, Paris, and Moscow, electric railways of an ordinary type run below the surface in shallow tunnels and cuttings. 'Subway' lines in New York, a city built on rock, are only a few feet below the streets; in other American cities elevated railways, carried on steel viaducts above the streets, were common, but many are now replaced by underground lines. London, however, with its clay subsoil which makes for easy tunnelling, is the one city with an extensive system of deep-level 'Tubes', which are literally circular pipes made of metal segments, into which a train will just fit.

The first underground railways were shallow tracks, dug down from street level, and built for steam trains. They formed London's 'Inner Circle', part of which was opened in 1863, and which was completed by 1884. Later, Tube railways burrowed 80 or 90 feet below ground level, to avoid interference with sewers, gas and electricity mains, and the basements of buildings, and also to lessen the vibration of buildings overhead when the trains were running. The first Tube, opened in 1890, ran under the River Thames from the City to the Elephant and Castle. In 1890 came the novelty of the 'Twopenny Tube', from the Bank of England to Shepherd's Bush, which followed for some years the French and American system of charging only one fare for any length of journey.

The Tubes are too deep to be reached by stairs, except in an emergency. The lifts which used to carry passengers between the street and the railway platform have almost all been replaced by moving stairways (*see* LIFTS AND ESCALATORS), which keep the passenger stream flowing more smoothly. Some of the biggest stations have four escalators, two going up and two down.

There are many other devices for saving time on a journey. Most tickets at busy stations are bought from batteries of electrical ticket machines, which can give change up to a shilling. Each ticket price covers a zone, so that the same ticket will serve destinations in various directions.

Train indicators on the platforms are automatically illuminated by each train as it approaches, the information having been electrically compiled at the start of the journey. When a train stops at a station, all its doors are slid open by compressed air under the guard's control. Wide double doors allow passengers to get in and out quickly, so that the train can start again in less than 25 seconds. Compressed air closes the doors, and the guard's starting signal cannot be worked until they are shut. Many stations have a 'headway' clock, on which the driver of an outgoing train can see how many seconds ahead the previous train has left. If two trains are very close, the second one can start slowly, to save current and avoid being needlessly halted by a signal later on. AUTOMATIC SIGNALLING (q.v.) is used in all Tubes, except at junctions. In addition, an automatic train-stop will pull up any train which has failed to stop at a signal.

In some earlier Tubes the tunnel dipped on leaving a station, to help the train to gain speed, and rose on entering a station, to help the

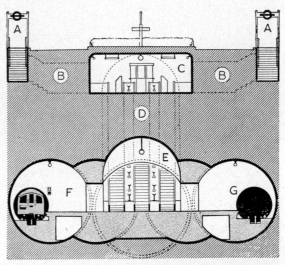

DIAGRAM OF AN UNDERGROUND STATION

A. Entrance steps from pavements; *B.* Subway under road; *C.* Booking-hall beneath roundabout; *D.* Escalator shaft; *E.* Circulating hall between platforms; *F.* Station tunnel section; *G.* Tunnel mouth

London Transport Executive

THE PLATFORM OF A LONDON TUBE STATION

braking. Modern trains do not need this assistance. The speed in the Tubes is seldom greater than 45 miles an hour, but on the ground-level sections of line in the outer suburbs, where stations are farther apart, trains may reach 60 miles an hour.

Many safety devices are fitted, including the 'dead man's handle'. The driver applies current to the electric motors by a controller which is in the driver's cab. This is fitted with a spring device on which the palm of the driver's hand presses lightly. If the driver is taken ill and his hand falls from the controller, the release of the spring stops the current and applies the brakes. Two bare wires may be seen running along the wall of each tunnel, where they can be most easily reached by the train staff. If an accident occurs, the pinching together of the bare wires by the fingers works a relay, which at once cuts off the current from the live rails in the section of line in which a train is standing. A telephone links the driver and guard of Tube trains; their voices can sometimes be heard from a small loud-speaker at the end of a compartment.

Parts of London's Tubes have been freed from noise by spraying the tunnel wall with asbestos fluff, to deaden sound, and by welding rails into continuous lengths to reduce the number of joints in the rails.

See also ELECTRIC RAILWAYS; LONDON TRANSPORT.

URDU LANGUAGE, *see* INDIAN LANGUAGES.

V

VACUUM BRAKES, *see* BRAKES, RAILWAY.

VATICAN LIBRARY. The Vatican, now a tiny independent State in the centre of ROME (q.v. Vol. III), has been for centuries the official residence of the Popes and their principal officials. The library is in the north wing of the palace of the Pope. A wide corridor leads through a series of halls, each containing hundreds of cases of books, to the impressive Great Hall built in 1588 by the Pope Sixtus V. The walls, ceiling, and even the six large pillars which support the roof are covered with paintings by the great artists of the time. Round the walls stand ornamented cabinets in which the most important books and manuscripts in the library are kept.

Alinari

A GALLERY IN THE VATICAN LIBRARY

The Vatican library originated in collections of manuscripts written in the early days of the Church by the different Popes, many of whom were men of learning. Boniface VIII in the late 13th century catalogued these writings, which became the inherited property of the Popes. In the 15th century Pope Nicholas V, generally considered the real founder of the library, added 5,000 volumes—a very large number for those days when all books had to be copied by hand—and ordered many translations to be made. Gradually the library grew, becoming one of the great treasures of Europe. Scholars flocked there —many of them poor men whom the Church helped with grants of money while they studied. Illuminated manuscripts were brought from the monasteries, and noblemen presented rare books; learning was fashionable, and powerful Italian families such as the Medicis were proud to be considered patrons of learning. Gifts came from other countries, and many books were left by devout Catholics in their wills.

Some of the famous original manuscripts in the Vatican are as much as 1,600 years old. Among them is the Codex Vaticanus, one of the earliest known copies of the New Testament, made before A.D. 400. There are also two manuscripts of the 4th century of the works of the Latin poet Virgil, and a 5th-century volume of the speeches of the Roman statesman and orator, Cicero.

See also LIBRARIES.

VELLUM, *see* PAPER.

VICTORY, H.M.S. Nelson's flagship, the fifth of her name in the Royal Navy, was launched at Chatham in 1765. A vessel of 2,162 tons, she cost £83,000 to build, and was designed by Sir Thomas Slade, then Surveyor of the Navy. Her original armament was 102 guns. Muzzle-loading guns of the period were named according to the weight of the solid iron shot they fired. Ninety guns, 32, 24, and 12 pounders, were mounted on three decks; thirty 32-pounders were mounted on the lowest deck, known as the gun deck; thirty 24-pounders on the middle deck; and thirty 12-pounders on the main deck. The remaining twelve 12-pounder guns were mounted on the quarter-deck and forecastle. The *Victory*, with a gun-deck length of 186 feet and a beam of 52 feet, was colloquially a 'three-decker'; in the Navy List she appeared as a 'first rate'.

National Maritime Museum

H.M.S. 'VICTORY'
Painted by Monamy Swaine before 1800

She was also sometimes called a ship-of-the-line, or 'liner', because she was of sufficient strength to lie in the 'line of battle'.

'First rates' were commonly used as flagships, the ships chosen by the admirals who commanded the fleet and who were distinguished by special flags. During her active career the *Victory* bore the flags of fourteen different admirals. Some of them, Kempenfelt, Howe, Hood, and St. Vincent, were among the most distinguished in our naval annals. Nelson, when a Commodore in H.M.S. *Captain*, was summoned on board H.M.S. *Victory* to be congratulated by the Commander-in-Chief, Admiral Jervis, after the victory over the Spaniards off Cape St. Vincent in 1797. Nelson flew his own flag in the *Victory* from the time of his blockading of Toulon in 1803 until he died in her cockpit at the Battle of Trafalgar on 21 October 1805. The *Victory* was paid off from active service at Portsmouth in 1812. She has escaped being broken up, and to-day can be seen by visitors to Portsmouth Dockyard,

carefully restored to her condition as at the Battle of Trafalgar when she checked Napoleon's scheme for the invasion of England.

See also Vol. X: BATTLESHIP.
See also Vol. V: NELSON.

VIKING SHIPS. In the 9th and 10th centuries A.D. Norse sailors, commonly known to-day as Vikings, set out in their longships from the creeks and fiords of Scandinavia and Denmark in a series of adventurous journeys. 'From the fury of the Northmen deliver us, O Lord!' chanted the monks of the Scottish Isles whose monasteries early felt the heavy hand of the plunderers. The Vikings were first reported off British shores in 787 when three longships appeared off the coast of Dorset, plundered, and went away, having killed the local magistrate. Soon they were arriving in fleets of several hundred ships, killing and burning, and in some cases settling in the country, until in 1016 King Canute the Dane ruled over a united kingdom of Denmark, Norway, England, and the Hebrides. The Vikings were merchants and colonizers as well as warriors and seamen, and their way of life depended to a great extent on their ships. They were splendid craftsmen. Their more distant voyages of discovery led to the colonizing of Iceland, Greenland, and un-identified localities in North America which they discovered nearly five centuries before Colum-bus. Perhaps these transatlantic voyages are the most exciting achievement of the Vikings in modern eyes, for great sailors such as Eric the Red, Lief the Lucky, Harald Haardraade, and others crossed the ocean in open boats, not only in northern seas but also southwards as far as Constantinople.

Actual examples of the Vikings' ships can be seen to-day because of their habit, shared with the Saxons, of placing a dead chief in his long-ship (with all the ship's gear on board) and covering the whole with soil to make a huge burial mound. When this soil was blue clay, the ship was sometimes preserved from decay; examples have been excavated almost intact. The few ships completely excavated date from different periods and follow a recognizable line of development. One ship, found at Gokstad in Norway, and preserved to-day in the Viking Ship Hall of Oslo University, dates from about A.D. 900. She is built of oak throughout, and her greatest length over all is 78 feet and breadth 16 ft. 9 in. The ship is built up of planks nailed together by iron rivets. There are sixteen planks a side, the edges overlapping 'clinker-built' fashion. The keel has a length of 66 feet, and from the ends of the keel the stem and stern posts rise in easy curves. The midship section shows the sides flaring outwards. The general form of the ship is of a long open boat, broad in the middle, with low freeboard and with sharp

and high ends. Bow and stern are alike, and the easy lines suggest a fast and good seaboat, able to make long voyages in capable hands (*see* Fig. 1). A modern replica of the Gokstad was built in 1892 and sailed across the Atlantic: she is credited with having reached a speed of 10 knots. There are sixteen oars a side, the oar-holes or rowlocks being placed in the third plank down from the gunwale, or upper plank. These oar-holes have cunning shutters fitted to them to keep the water out. The oars are about 18 feet long, and could be handled by one or two men as required. It is thought the rowers sat on benches, though these have not been found. The single mast was stepped amidships and arranged so as to be easily lowered; one square sail was probably set with a yard.

We learn from the Norse sagas that Viking ships were rated according to the number of spaces between the rowing benches or thwarts. This space was called a *rúm*: the word 'room' is used to-day by English fishermen in the same sense, meaning the space between the thwarts (or benches) in open boats. The Gokstad ship, with sixteen oars a side, was a ship of sixteen 'rooms'. The construction of the ship is perfectly adap-ted for a seagoing vessel which does not carry cargo and which must on occasions be hauled out of the water. Iron spikes secure the ends of the

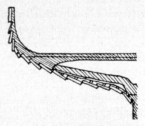

FIG. 2. MIDSHIP SECTION OF THE GOKSTAD SHIP

planks to the stem and stern posts. The ribs or timbers are fastened to the upper two planks by tree nails (wooden pins), and to the remain-ing planks by lashings made of flexible twigs (*see*

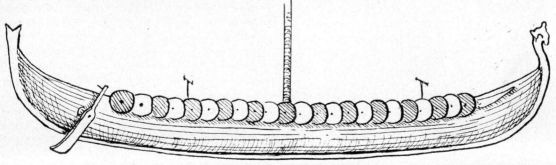

FIG. 1. RECONSTRUCTION OF THE GOKSTAD SHIP

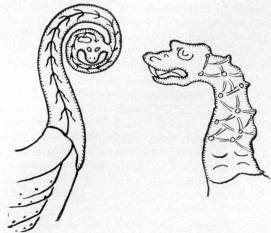

FIG. 3. FIGURE-HEAD OF OSEBERG SHIP, A.D. 850 (LEFT), AND CARVING OF THE SAME DATE

Fig. 2). Shields were found fixed along the gunwale and are painted alternately yellow and black.

The sagas tell us how the Vikings delighted in brave ships, with carved animal or serpent figure-heads surmounting the stemposts, and the carved tail-end of the animal at the sternposts, the ships gay with bright shields and decorated sails. The figureheads were passed on from favoured ship to favoured ship, and some of these carved heads survive (*see* Fig. 3). The ship was steered by means of a special oar or paddle slung over the starboard or 'steerboard' quarter (the right-hand side). The helmsman grasped a tiller which came inboard across the stern of the ship (*see* Fig. 4). The Gokstad ship was fitted with an awning, but had only a light deck, laid between the beams which passed across the ship between the ribs. At the bow and stern this deck was

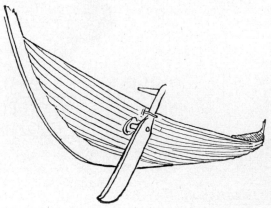

FIG. 4. RUDDER OR STEERING BAR OF THE GOKSTAD SHIP

higher and of a more permanent nature. Iron anchors are found in the ships excavated, and also the remains of small boats which were carried on board at sea. No doubt the ship's company lived roughly and hardily when compelled to keep to the sea; but when possible the Vikings seem to have cooked their meals and slept ashore.

The Gokstad ship is small, and may have had a crew of seventy men. Olaf Trygvason's ship, the *Long Serpent* of A.D. 1000, carried thirty-four pairs of oars, while King Canute, we are told, had a ship of sixty pairs of oars, which must have been some 300 feet in length. The Gokstad is probably typical of the rather smaller and commoner Viking ship, the sort of craft with gaily coloured sails in which America was first discovered by Norsemen and in which the Viking pirates sailed from the Baltic to the Mediterranean.

See also SAILING SHIPS.
See also Vol. I: DANES; NORWEGIANS.

VOICE. When man had achieved SPEECH, the sounds he uttered became very complicated. Various kinds of ALPHABET were devised to record the spoken word, and continuous changes in the fashions of SPELLING (qq.v.) show the difficulty of keeping pace with the delicate changes in the human voice.

1. PHONETICS is the science which studies spoken sounds, classifies them according to the part of the mouth used in making them, and observes what happens when sounds are strung together in spoken sentences. When we wish to speak, we draw in extra air through mouth and nose, and expel it again as breath, through the wind-pipe, throat, and mouth. The top of the wind-pipe, which is known as the larynx, contains two folds of muscular tissue (the 'vocal cords'), one on each side. These folds normally lie apart; when we want to speak, their free edges draw near to each other. The breath, passing through the chink between these edges, causes them to vibrate. This vibration, which is the beginning of a spoken sound, is carried forward by the stream of breath into the throat and mouth, which act as a megaphone and increase the volume of sound, helped by the resonance of the hollow bones over the eyes (sinuses).

Several parts of the mouth affect the spoken sound (*see* Diagram). First comes the soft palate, the soft muscular end of the roof of the mouth

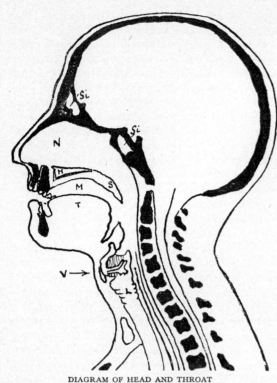

DIAGRAM OF HEAD AND THROAT

Si. Sinus; *N.* Nasal cavities; *H.* Hard Palate; *S.* Soft Palate;
M. Mouth; *T.* Tongue; *V.* Vocal Cords; *L.* Larynx

hanging over the throat. Normally this stands away from the back of the throat, allowing the breath to pass to the nose. When we are speaking, the soft palate reaches back to close the nose channel, so that our rising breath is forced out through the mouth where it can be shaped into speech sounds. The soft palate is lowered (allowing some breath to pass out through the nose) for only three sounds in the English language—'m', 'n', and 'ng'. That is why a cold in the head and a blocked nose makes it difficult to pronounce such sounds properly, and the word 'money' sounds like 'buddy'. In other languages, such as French, there are more of these nasal sounds than in English.

Several distinct parts of the tongue are used to shape sounds. We can raise and lower the tip or the middle (leaving the tip touching the lower teeth) or the back or sides, each movement producing a different sound. We can add to the number of sounds by dropping the lower jaw, which increases the size of the inside of the mouth. The lips give the final shape to sounds passing between them, particularly to vowel sounds. They can be stretched, as in a smile, or rounded as for whistling. Every change of position between those two extremes produces a slightly different sound.

In spoken English, as distinct from the written alphabet's five vowels, there are twelve vowel sounds, besides nine diphthongs (a tongue-glide from one vowel to another, as in 'boys'). One vowel sound, known as the 'neutral' vowel, is the sound uttered in English when any short unstressed vowel is spoken—as in the second syllable of 'written', 'madam', 'cannon', and in the first syllable of 'enough' or 'about', and in the two central syllables of 'Adam and Eve'. The neutral vowel sounds the same no matter how it is spelt. There are twenty-six consonant sounds in spoken English. Several written letters have more than one sound. 'G' may be 'hard' as in 'go', or 'soft' as in 'general'. 'Th' may be 'voiced' as in 'then', or 'voiceless' as in 'thin'. Thus there are forty-seven English speech sounds or 'phonemes': each sound into which a spoken language can be broken up is called a phoneme (*see* LANGUAGE STRUCTURE). A complete set of phonemes makes up a phonetic alphabet. Almost every dictionary contains a list of model words showing how the editor has tried, with printed letters or symbols, to represent every spoken sound. Some dictionaries use ordinary letters with various kinds of accent marks, such as á à â ȧ ā ă; others use more elaborate systems. The phonetic alphabet of the *Oxford English Dictionary* includes the following signs for some of the consonants: ʃ for the 'sh' sound in 'shop', ʒ for the 's' sound in 'vision', þ for the 'th' sound in 'thin' and ð for the 'th' sound in 'then', and the following for some of the vowels: ū° for the sound in 'poor', iū for that in 'pure', and æ for that in 'man'.

Phonetics also records the way that sounds are changed by other sounds which come before or after them. For instance, 'oo' is not always pronounced in exactly the same way. Between the 'oo' in 'moon' and in 'goose' there is a slight difference, the consonants before and after causing the tongue to be in a slightly different position. In practice, however, the ear does not detect the difference, and the 'oo' of 'moon' and of 'goose' are regarded as the same phoneme.

2. ACCENT. Spoken sounds are not uttered with dead regularity like the ticking of a clock. In most languages people tend to emphasize a word or a syllable, or even part of a sentence.

Sometimes one word is uttered more loudly than another; or an important word may be said very slowly. Sometimes a word or a syllable is spoken at a special musical pitch. All spoken emphasis of this kind is generally referred to as 'accent'. The word is also often used to describe the peculiarities of a person's speech, including not only peculiar alterations of stress or pitch, but also mispronunciations, or pronunciations and intonations peculiar to DIALECT (q.v.). Thus a Scotsman who 'rolls his r's', thus showing that he comes from north of the Tweed, is said to speak English with a 'Scottish accent'; a Londoner who talks like Eliza in Shaw's *Pygmalion* is said to have a 'Cockney accent'; and an Englishman speaking a foreign language may apply his native pronunciation and intonation to the foreign tongue, and so to speak it with 'an English accent'.

In classical GREEK (q.v.) and some other ancient languages, words had a well-marked musical accent or intonation. In modern CHINESE (q.v.) intonation is part of the word-form and affects its meaning: for example, the Cantonese word *fan* means either 'powder', 'sleep', 'burn', 'brave', or 'duty' according to the tone in which it is pronounced. In English, French, and many other languages, intonation is used to mark emphasis (in English, usually a high pitch), punctuation (for example, a falling tone at the end of a statement), and expression (a phrase like 'a fine fellow!' can express praise or sarcasm according to the intonation we give it). But in most modern European languages stress is more important than musical pitch. All INDO-EUROPEAN languages (q.v.) showed, at an early stage, a tendency to throw the stress back towards the beginning of a word; and in the Germanic languages, of which English is one, it now normally falls on the first syllable of a word. The chief exceptions in English to this rule are:

(*a*) Words of English origin with adverbial prefixes that have lost their adverbial or pre-positional force, such as understánd, indéed, to-dáy.

(*b*) Words borrowed from the Romance languages, such as FRENCH (q.v.). French loan-words at first kept the stress on the last syllable, but by the 15th century at the latest, the stress had usually shifted to the first syllable, except in words compounded with a prefix, such as com-mánd, replý. Later French borrowings have usually kept their French stress, such as coquétte, promenáde, though short words that have come into common use, and three-syllable words, often follow the English pattern: for example, chaúffeur, gárage, pétrol, ménu, réstaurant, and énvelope.

Words borrowed from Latin and Greek (as well as some borrowed through French) often show variation even in standard speech (for example, láboratory or labóratory). In long words the stress tends to be on the third syllable from the end (photógraphy), except in words ending in -ic, when it is on the last but one, as in geométric.

There is at present a tendency to shift the accent forward in many-syllabled words of classical origin—to say hospítable, capítalist, instead of as formerly, hóspitable, cápitalist. This avoids a series of weakly stressed syllables, which tend to become shortened and sometimes lost: láboratory tends to become labrotry, just as boatswain became bos'n. In American speech long words tend to have two main stresses as in nécessáry, ádvertísement. Accent sometimes varies if a word is used as a noun or a verb; for example, we say 'a safe cónduct', but 'I will condúct you there'.

Sentence-stress is usually governed by meaning, though also by contrast and rhythm. The main word is emphasized by being given a stronger stress than the rest, and often a distinct intonation. Thus, in a sentence like 'What shall I do with this boy?' almost any word can bear the chief stress, according to the point of the question.

See also ENGLISH LANGUAGE.

VOLAPÜK, *see* INTERNATIONAL LANGUAGES.

W

WAGON, *see* CART AND WAGON.

'WALKIE-TALKIE', *see* TELEPHONES, MOBILE.

WAVE-LENGTHS (WIRELESS). Every wireless transmission consists of a series of electrical oscillations or vibrations. If the rate of oscillation of a transmitting station is known, and if one adjusts or 'tunes' a receiving set to the same rate of oscillation, one can hear the transmission —provided, of course, that the receiver is strong enough to make the transmission audible.

Wave-lengths range from very short to very long (*see* WAVE MOTION, Vol. III). The real difference between short and long waves lies in the frequency of their oscillation, or electronic vibrations. It happens that a long-wave transmission oscillates comparatively slowly; for instance, by the time it has travelled 10 miles (17,600 yards), a 3,000-metre wave (3,280 yards) will have vibrated about five times, or once every 2 miles (actually 3,280 yards × 5 equals 16,400 yards). But a 30-metre wave is 100 times shorter than a 3,000-metre wave. It will therefore vibrate 100 times more often in travelling any given distance; in travelling 10 miles it will vibrate 500 times.

One may compare wireless waves with waves in water, as far as this simple arithmetic goes. If one starts tiny ripples in a hand-basin while washing one's hands, it will be seen that the length of a wave or ripple (that is the distance from crest to crest of two adjoining waves) may be only a quarter of an inch. Such a wave will rise and fall (vibrate) a couple of dozen times before reaching the side of the hand-basin 6 inches away. But a large wave at sea may be 20 feet from crest to crest, that is, nearly 1,000 times longer than the tiny quarter-inch wave in the hand-basin. The larger wave will rise and fall (vibrate) only once in that distance. The tiny wave, if it had travelled so far, would have vibrated nearly 1,000 times. So that talking about the 'length' of a wireless wave is only a way of describing the frequency of vibration of a transmission. It is a very old-fashioned way to describe it, dating from the early days of wireless when the nature of waves was less understood than now; the word is retained, out of habit, by the general public. The term used by modern radio engineers is 'frequency', that is, the number of vibrations a second that the transmitter sets up in the air. Frequency is expressed in 'kilocycles'. 'Kilo' is from the Greek word for 1,000, so 75 kilocycles means 75,000 vibrations or oscillations a second. This would be equal to a wave-length of 4,000 metres.

With the growth of wireless TELEGRAPHY, and later of BROADCASTING (qq.v.), the principal countries were obliged to discuss with one another the use of the various wave-lengths. European broadcasting organizations, warned by the example of America, where so many stations began to broadcast that most listening was jammed, met in London in 1925 and set up an International Broadcasting Union, with headquarters in Geneva. The Union made a plan providing each country with wavebands free from interference by others, and set up a checking post which warned stations when they strayed from their wave-lengths. Changes are periodically made as the result of international agreement—for instance in 1950 some B.B.C. station wave-lengths were altered.

Various groups of wave-lengths were classed together as wave-bands. It was agreed that the long waves (now reckoned to be those above 3,000 metres in length) should be used for medium and long distance communication from station to station; the medium waves (100–3,000 metres) for broadcasting, marine and aircraft communication, and direction-finding; the short waves (10–100 metres) for long-distance broadcasting, and communication from station to station; and the ultra-short waves (below 10 metres) for short-distance communication, TELEVISION (q.v.), and aircraft-guidance systems (*see* NAVIGATION, AIR). Mobile military units, 'walkie-talkie' systems, and the wireless cars of the police, for example, operate on these waves (*see* TELEPHONES, MOBILE).

The very first experiments in wireless had been made on wave-lengths of only a few metres. But the scientists found they could transmit farther with longer waves, and for many years they worked on medium and long wavelengths. It was Marconi (*see* WIRELESS, HISTORY OF), in making tests for army signalling during the First World War, who revived interest in short waves. The wave-bands now given to sound broadcasting on short waves—are the 11, 13, 16, 19, 25, 31, 41, and 49 metre bands.

Waves of under a metre offer a field for more experiment. Meanwhile there are still not enough wave-lengths for all the stations that want to broadcast.

See also WIRLESSS, HISTORY OF; SHORT-WAVE WIRELESS. See also Vol. III: WAVE MOTION.

WEIRS, *see* LOCKS AND WEIRS.

WELLAND CANAL. This canal is an important trade link between Canada and the U.S.A. It forms part of the great chain of waterways which stretches for 2,339 miles, from the Straits of Belle Isle at the entrance to the Gulf of St. Lawrence, along the St. Lawrence river, and through the Great Lakes to Duluth on Lake Superior. The Welland Canal is built across the high ground which separates Lake Ontario,

where the St. Lawrence rises, from Lake Erie. It is valuable not only to local traffic: it shortens the journey from Liverpool in England to Duluth or Chicago via Montreal by about 450 miles, and ships can convey cargo direct from Manchester to ports 1,000 miles inside the American continent.

The canal was built in 1829 by the Welland Canal Company. At first it stretched only from Port Dalhousie on Lake Ontario, as far as Port Robinson on Chippewa Creek, and then down to the Niagara river, above the Falls. Since then it has been rebuilt several times, and greatly enlarged and extended. In 1841 it was bought by the Government of Upper Canada, who rebuilt it three times. The final canal, completed in 1932, has a depth of 30 feet, and eight locks, each 829 by 84 feet, capable of accommodating all but a very few of the largest ships in the world. The lock gates are of steel and weigh as much as 425 tons each, 11,000 horse-power being needed for opening them and for lighting the canal. The canal is crossed by 22 bridges.

The Welland Canal is ice-bound for nearly 5 months of the year, and it is limited on the north by the shallowness of the canals on the St. Lawrence. The largest lake vessels, however,

National Film Board of Canada

A LOCK ON THE WELLAND CANAL
A railway bridge spanning the canal is lifted to allow a lake freighter to pass

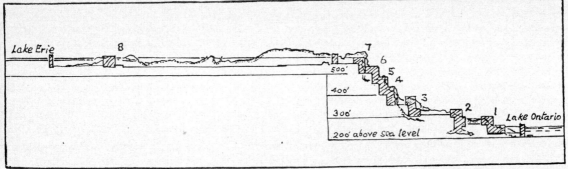

Lake Erie

8

7

6

5

4

500'

400'

3

300'

2

1

Lake Ontario

200' above sea level

Department of Transport, Ottawa

SECTION OF THE LOCKS ON THE WELLAND CANAL

some of them of 15,000 tons, can enter Lake Ontario from the south, and the canal now carries an annual tonnage of several millions.

See also CANALS.

See also Vol. III: GREAT LAKES; ST. LAWRENCE.

WELSH LANGUAGE. Welsh is a Celtic language, as are also IRISH or Erse and GAELIC (qq.v.). It belongs to the British or Brythonic group, and it has grown from the language spoken by the Ancient Britons at the time of the Roman invasion. This language borrowed a number of Latin words during the Roman occupation. When in the 5th and 6th centuries Britain was invaded from the east by Angles and Saxons speaking a GERMANIC language (q.v.), the language of the Britons died out in the greater part of the country, but survived in the mountainous and more remote west—Wales, Cumberland, parts of the Scottish Lowlands, and Cornwall, and was also carried by British emigrants across the Channel, where it now exists as the Breton language in Brittany. By the 6th century in Wales British had developed into Welsh, and by the end of the century there is evidence that poetry was being composed in the language. Manuscripts exist containing short pieces of prose and verse dating from the 9th to the 11th century, and when the laws of Wales were compiled in the 10th century, they were written down in Welsh. From the 12th century onwards the Welsh language has much literature, in the medieval period the best known being the prose tales called the *Mabinogion*, and the Arthurian romances of the ancient British legendary hero, King Arthur (*see* ARTHURIAN LITERATURE, Vol. XII).

When Wales was united with England in 1536,

it seemed likely that Welsh would disappear as a living language; but in 1588 a Bible in Welsh was published, and this played an important part in preserving the language. In 1931 Welsh was spoken by about 900,000 people in Wales, mostly in the country places, and also by communities of Welshmen in the large towns of England, in the United States of America, and in Canada, and in a Welsh settlement in South America. Welsh is now taught in the schools, colleges, and universities of Wales; it is compulsory in some counties, and some 'all-Welsh' schools have been established recently. To-day, Welsh is used more than ever before for a wide range of books on subjects such as philosophy and science and as the language of public administration.

Each of the twenty-eight signs in the Welsh alphabet, with the exception of *y*, has one standard sound only, and Welsh is therefore said to be written almost phonetically—that is, exactly as it is sounded. Welsh *c* is always like *c* in 'cat'; *g* is always like *g* in 'gun'; *ch* corresponds to the sound in Scottish *loch*; *dd* is sounded as *th* in 'this'; *f* is like English *v*, while *ff* is like English *f*; *ng* is as in 'singing', though occasionally it is like *ng* in 'anger'; *ll*, which usually gives so much trouble to strangers, is produced by putting the tongue in the position for sounding *l* and then releasing the breath sharply without bringing any sound from the throat; *ph* has the same sound as *ff*; *rh* is as *r* in 'carry' followed by a sudden release of breath; *th* is as in 'thin'; *y* has a sound like English *ee* in 'feet', except that it is produced towards the back of the mouth—Welsh *u* has the same sound; *y* also has sometimes a sound like *u* in 'dumb' in words of more than one syllable, but not in the last syllable.

In words of more than one syllable the accent normally comes on the last syllable but one: for example, *tref* 'town', *cártref* 'home', *cartréfi* 'homes'. In certain circumstances the first consonant undergoes a change known as 'initial mutation': for example, *pen* 'head', *fy mhen* 'my head', *ei ben* 'his head', *ei phen* 'her head'. As a rule the subject comes immediately after the verb, and if the subject is a noun, the verb is always in the singular even if the subject is plural: for example, *Gwêl y dyn y plant* 'The man sees the children', and *Gwêl y dynion y plant* 'The men see the children'; but when the subject is a pronoun, the verb agrees with it in number: *Gwêl ef y plant* 'He sees the children', and *Gwêlant hwy y plant* 'They see the children'.

See also Vol. I: WELSH.

WHEEL. The wheel has been described as the one thing man has invented entirely by himself, with no hint from anything found in nature. Certainly the idea of it had never occurred to any of the original inhabitants of the Americas until it was introduced from Europe in the 16th century, although high civilizations had flourished there for centuries, and great skill had been reached in building, road-making, metal-working, and other arts. In the western hemisphere wheeled chariots were used many thousands of years ago by the armies of Assyria and Egypt, and no doubt crude carts on wheels had been helping farmers to harvest their crops in even earlier times.

The idea of the wheel probably came from the use of rollers to help in moving heavy weights such as dug-out canoes or blocks of building stone. But the tree-trunk roller did not become a wheel until someone had thought of chopping away the middle part to leave only an axle with a disk wheel at each end. This could then be fixed beneath a SLEDGE (q.v.), making it into a wheeled vehicle.

Fixed axles, on which the separate wheels revolved, no doubt followed when some one-piece axle broke or wore through where it rubbed in its bearings. The next improvement would be to make a stronger, lighter wheel. Some of the very earliest pictures of chariots show the form of construction which is still followed in the wheels of farm carts and wheelbarrows. The central hub, stock, or nave is socketed to receive the spokes, the outer ends of which are held in a circular band built up of a number of curved pieces of wood called 'felloes' (pronounced 'fellies'). Round the whole a metal tire is put on while hot so that it may shrink and grip tight as it cools.

The steel tires of railway rolling-stock are shrunk on in exactly the same way, though here the rest of the wheel is also made of metal. The tires of these are not flat, but have a rib or 'flange' running round the outer face for the purpose of keeping them on the rails. The flanged wheel dates only from 1800, when it was invented by William Jessop. Some 40 years earlier the practice arose of casting a flange along the whole length of the rails (which were therefore like the letter L in section) to keep flat-tired wheels on the track (*see* RAILWAYS, HISTORY OF).

The invention which did most to lessen the work needed to move a wheeled vehicle not running on rails was that of the pneumatic tire, first used successfully by J. B. Dunlop of Belfast in 1888 (although an English patent for the idea had been taken out 40 years earlier). When a solid tire meets a small obstacle, such as a hard

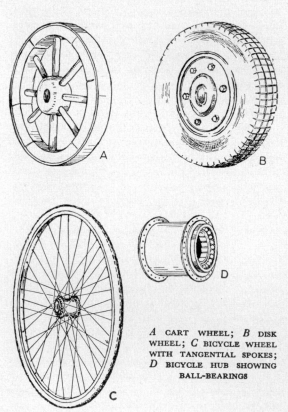

A CART WHEEL; *B* DISK WHEEL; *C* BICYCLE WHEEL WITH TANGENTIAL SPOKES; *D* BICYCLE HUB SHOWING BALL-BEARINGS

Metropolitan Museum of Art, New York

ETRUSCAN CHARIOT MADE 550–540 B.C., OF WOOD WITH BRONZE SHEATHING

stone on the road, it has to ride over it: that is to say both the wheel and its load have to be taken up a tiny hill. But a pneumatic tire, if the stone is not too big, is able to absorb it into its own circumference while it passes over, merely suffering a slight increase in the pressure of the air inside for a moment. The saving of work and the increase of speed were even more valuable to the early cyclist, for whom this kind of tire was originally made, than the increased comfort given by its cushioning effect.

The invention of ball-bearings had reduced enormously the friction between hubs and axles (*see* BEARINGS, Vol. VIII). The improvement can easily be seen if the wheels of a bicycle and of a wheelbarrow be set spinning at the same speed and notice be taken of how much sooner the latter stops. These bearings, too, were first perfected for the benefit of the cyclist.

We have seen how the first wheel or disk of solid wood was replaced by the spoked wheel, which was far stronger and lighter, but still fairly heavy. The spokes had always to be stout enough to bear the weight pressing down from the axle. So a still lighter wheel was invented to reduce the cyclist's work—the wire wheel in which the spokes are of steel wire and the weight of the axle hangs from the rim above instead of

pressing on it below. At first these spokes were fitted pointing straight at the centre of the wheel, but later, 'tangent spokes', as shown in the diagram, were invented. By this means the twisting forces between the axle and the rim, due either to pedalling or braking, were also converted into straight pulls, thus allowing the spokes to be made still lighter. This is the latest form of wheel, to be found on the majority of motor-cars to-day. Heavy-duty vehicles, however, usually have disk wheels made with solid steel pressings instead of spokes, often lightened by being cut away in places.

See also CART AND WAGON; BICYCLE; MOTOR-CAR.

WIRELESS EXCHANGE, *see* REDIFFUSION.

WIRELESS TELEGRAPHY, HISTORY OF.
Wireless was not invented. It was the result of many years of thought, discussion, and practical experiments by many people in several countries. Most of those early experimenters and thinkers were concerned only with their own problems of magnetism, astronomy, or mathematics, and did not know to what their thoughts would lead. The idea that messages might one day be sent without wires was not held until the last quarter of the 19th century (although it was known

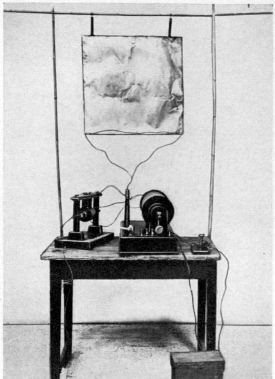

Marconi's Wireless Telegraph Co.

MODEL OF THE TYPE OF WIRELESS TRANSMITTER FIRST USED
BY MARCONI, WITH COPPER SHEET AERIAL

earlier that electrical activity could be detected at a distance). It was even later that men began to think of the idea of broadcasting actual sounds, such as music and spoken words.

All through the 19th century men had been experimenting with the recently discovered forces of ELECTRICITY and MAGNETISM (qq.v. Vol. III). In 1864 a British physicist named James Clerk Maxwell (1831-79), Professor of Experimental Physics at Cambridge University, proved by means of mathematics the existence of those electro-magnetic disturbances in the air that we call 'waves' (*see* WAVE MOTION, Vol. III). He did more: he showed that these waves obey the same natural laws as LIGHT (q.v. Vol. III), and that they travel at the same speed—186,000 miles a second. It was a masterly feat of pure mathematics, for he used no apparatus in reaching his conclusion.

Clerk Maxwell's theory received practical proof 24 years later from a German named Heinrich Hertz. He set up two rods, each with a knob at the end, and applied to the knobs an electrical current, doing so through an induction coil, which had the effect of increasing the strength of the current. The current became so strong that it jumped across the gap between the knobs, making a spark. Then, a short distance away from this apparatus, Hertz set up an exact copy of it. He found that, when he made a spark with the first machine, a current was caused in the second machine, also producing a spark. The German scientist described the result of his experiments as 'the outspreading of electric force'; it was the great British scientist, Lord Kelvin, translating Hertz's written report into English, who first used the term 'ether waves'. (Scientists thought for a long time that some substance must exist throughout the universe, to which they gave the name of 'ether'. It was thought that wireless waves and light waves were waves 'in the ether'. Later the belief in the existence of the ether was abandoned.) The waves set up by Hertz were extremely short in length—about 12 inches. Although the waves were projected only the length of a laboratory, we can say that at that moment 'wireless communication' came into being.

Hertz's great achievement led to much scientific study of wireless waves, and many practical things happened. One was the making of a kind of wave-detector known as a 'coherer'. Men already knew that if small loose particles of some material which was a conductor of electricity (such as powdered carbon, or iron filings) were placed in the path of an electric current, the passing of the current caused the particles to stick together, or 'cohere', and so form a solid conductor of electricity. Towards the end of the century Sir Oliver Lodge of Britain, and Professor E. Branly of France, made use of this fact in the invention of coherers. These were short, tube-like containers, carrying loose particles which would respond to the currents set up by Hertzian waves. By this time, ordinary telegraphy over an electric wire had made scientists and inventors familiar with the MORSE CODE (q.v.). They therefore sought ways of sending out groups of waves to represent the dots and dashes of the code, and also ways of making the tiny currents work a Morse ink-writer, printing the dots and dashes on a strip of paper (*see* TELEGRAPHY, HISTORY OF).

Sir Oliver Lodge, in 1894, first showed how the waves could be used as signals or messages, using Branly's coherer to do so—although, as he admitted later, he did not know the great meaning of his discovery. In Russia, in 1895, Professor A. Popoff, using a coherer, invented a method of recording lightning flashes, and showed how to use this method for signalling.

At the same time Guglielmo MARCONI (q.v. Vol. V) was at work in Italy, and early in 1895 he made a device like Popoff's, but which was expressly meant to send and receive electromagnetic signals. His work brought practical wireless communication into sight; from then on he was the leading experimenter in wireless telegraphy. In 1896, when he was only 22 years of age, he came to England; there he received help from the Chief Engineer of the Post Office, Sir William Preece, who had himself been studying the subject.

One early difficulty was that signals from several transmitters would interfere with one another. That meant that it was hard for a receiver to pick up only the wanted signal, and not others. In 1897 Sir Oliver Lodge supplied the answer by inventing the 'tuned circuit'—a means of controlling the wave-length of a receiver by adjustments to coils of wire. Just as a string of a violin will vibrate and hum if a particular note of music is played near it, so the receiver could be tuned to a particular wave-length. Lodge's tuning was an historic event. The wave-length became all-important. In the earliest experiments the length (the distance between the peak of one wave and that of the next) was very short; later, very long wave-lengths became customary, because scientists then thought that the longer the wave, the longer the distance the signal would travel. Years later they were to be proved wrong (see WAVE-LENGTHS).

The 'spark' method of transmission continued in use for many years; (because of this ships' operators, the chief users of wireless, were called 'Sparks'). But the spark was a crude method; it needed a good deal of power, and much of the electric current was wasted in making the spark. It became the aim of scientists to transmit not a mere series of sparks in a wave, but a continuous wave. That would mean, among other advantages, wireless telephony —the transmission of speech. Improvements gradually increased the distance spanned by wireless telegraphy, and at last the continuous wave was to be generated; but it did not lead to the immediate discovery of a way of transmitting speech.

Marconi's Wireless Telegraph Co.

DIAGRAM OF WIRELESS EXPERIMENTS WITH KITE AERIALS ACROSS THE BRISTOL CHANNEL in 1897

Soon after Marconi's arrival in England in 1896 he had demonstrated his apparatus over the 400 yards between the General Post Office at St. Martin's-le-Grand, in London, and Queen Victoria Street. Next he sent a signal across 8 miles of Salisbury Plain, and then over the 9 miles of the Bristol Channel between points near Penarth and Weston-super-Mare. In the following year, during naval manœuvres, a distance of 60 miles was covered.

Wireless stations were set up at Alum Bay in the Isle of Wight and at Bournemouth in 1898; from Alum Bay the first paid wireless message was sent. Two months later, wireless telegraphy enabled Queen Victoria to keep in touch from the Isle of Wight with her son, the Prince of Wales, who was at sea aboard the Royal yacht *Osborne*: in 16 days about 150 messages were exchanged. In March 1899 the English Channel was bridged by wireless, between Chelmsford and a spot near Boulogne—a distance of 85 miles. In the same year wireless telegraphy began to be used in a small way in the British Navy. Soon apparatus was installed aboard the *Lake Cham-*

Marconi's Wireless Telegraph Co.

SOME OF THE APPARATUS AT POLDHU WIRELESS STATION USED BY MARCONI FOR THE FIRST TRANSATLANTIC TRANSMISSION IN 1901
On the left are the transformers. The banks of condensers are in metal containers on the wooden rack. On the right is the spark-gap, consisting of two steel spheres mounted on insulating rods

plain, the first British merchant vessel to be equipped.

The year 1901 was a milestone. On 12 December, using an aerial hung from a kite, Marconi and two assistants listened at St. John's, Newfoundland, to the 'dot-dot-dot' of the letter 's' in the Morse code sent across the Atlantic from a station in Poldhu, Cornwall, nearly 2,000 miles away. It was 6 years, however, before the first public transatlantic service was opened between Glace Bay in Canada and Clifden in Ireland.

Marconi's feat raised a question of vital interest to the scientists. Clerk Maxwell had shown, and Hertz had confirmed, that wireless waves must travel in a straight line. But the earth is round. How, then, did the waves, in their journey from Britain to America, get over the bulge of the earth's surface? If one drew a straight line through the earth from the British Isles to America, the line would be nearly 2,000 miles long and the bulge 200 miles high.

A British physicist, Oliver Heaviside, and an American, Dr. A. E. Kennelly, answered the question in 1902. Each, independently but almost at the same time, put forward the idea of some kind of layer in the upper atmosphere, miles above the earth, that had the property of stopping the waves in their upward path and turning them back towards the earth, just as a hand mirror would reflect a beam of light. Thus, they said, the waves travelled on in a series of bounces between earth and sky. In spite of early doubts this theory had to be accepted; 23 years passed before the existence and height not only of the Kennealy-Heaviside layer, but of others above and below it, were proved by another British physicist, Sir Edward Appleton. He proved that each of these layers in the 'ionosphere' (as the region in which they exist has been named) had an effect on the movement of wireless waves. Recent knowledge of their behaviour and properties has explained not only how the waves travel around the world, but the reasons for other phenomena, such as the fading of signals.

Between 1907 and the end of the First World War, wireless telegraphy spread a network of communication over the world. In 1919 a message from England was received by wireless telegraphy in Australia. The war itself had proved the value of wireless to the armed forces, and stimulated developments which were to lead to wireless telephony and then to broadcasting —though that was not then suspected (*see* SPEECH, TRANSMISSION OF).

The ways in which the electro-magnetic waves may be used are beyond count, for even yet their value is only partly known. Their value to navigation reached a spectacular climax in the development of radar (radio-location) before and during the Second World War. By 1945, a vessel at sea in fog could 'see' its way past obstacles such as icebergs; an aircraft in flight above thick cloud could 'see' when it crossed a coastline. Both could obtain an accurate 'fix' of their position at any instant, and could be guided to port or airfield by a radio beam (*see* NAVIGATION, MARINE, and NAVIGATION, AIR). The 'beam', which is a concentration of waves on a selected object or area, is the basis of international communication by two-way telephony (*see* SHORT-WAVE WIRELESS). Wireless waves are used to carry still pictures from one side of the globe to the other (*see* PICTURE TRANSMISSION); to control mechanical apparatus many miles away (remote control); to give information to mobile police units so swiftly that criminals have been caught as they were leaving the scene of their crime (*see* TELEPHONE, MOBILE); to ascertain differences in longitude and latitude; to track the path of electric storms; and to be one of the principal means of entertainment for people all over the world (*see* BROADCASTING PROGRAMMES, Vol. IX). Recently the further service of TELEVISION (q.v.) has been developed.

See also SPEECH, TRANSMISSION OF; BROADCASTING, HISTORY OF.

See also Vol. VIII: RADIO ENGINEERING.

WRECKS AND WRECKERS. 1. WRECKS.
The causes of shipwreck are many and, in spite of all the safety devices and scientific aids to navigation of to-day, ceaseless vigilance is needed to preserve ships from disaster. Shipwrecks are most often caused by striking a rock, perhaps through an error of judgement on the part of the master, an incorrect chart, or a breakdown of the engines. Collision between two ships, often in fog, has accounted for almost as many wrecks. Collision with icebergs has cost thousands of lives, and was responsible for the loss of the *Titanic* (*see* CLIMATE AND COMMUNICATIONS, Section 3); and fire at sea, especially common in the days when ships used oil lanterns, has proved even more deadly. Ships may also be overwhelmed in typhoons and hurricanes, capsize because their cargo is carelessly loaded, or founder as a result of bad leaks.

In the late 18th century repairs to the bottom of a ship were carried out by heeling the ship over. This was usually done by shifting ballast and running out all the guns on one side and running them in on the other. In August 1782 the *Royal George*, a wooden man-of-war then lying at Spithead, was heeled over too far, and with little warning water entered the gun ports, and the *Royal George* turned over and sank, with the loss of about 900 lives.

In 1874 the famous sailing-vessel the *Cospatrick*, carrying outward-bound emigrants for Australia, was destroyed by fire. The whole of the ship's company, passengers and crew, were lost, except for five men who escaped in a boat and were later picked up. It is not known how the fire started. In the emigrant ships fire was so much feared that lanterns were usually padlocked after being lit.

Sometimes vessels have just disappeared without trace, and the cause of the disaster can only be guessed. This happened to the steamship *Waratah*, a big twin-screw ship with a displacement of 16,800 tons, and well equipped, except that she carried no wireless installation. When homeward bound from her second voyage to Australia in 1909 she was signalled by another vessel between Durban and Capetown. The other vessel watched the *Waratah* disappear over the horizon, and since then no trace of her or of her 200 passengers and crew has ever been found. It is surmised that she capsized in a bad storm, but it has never been explained why no wreckage or bodies were found.

Those who have escaped from a wreck have sometimes perished on the savage lands upon which they have been cast. The *Grosvenor*, an East Indiaman homeward bound from India in 1782, with ship's company and passengers totalling 135 and a very valuable cargo, was wrecked, owing to an error in navigation, on the coast of

Parker Gallery

THE CREW OF THE 'LADY HOBART' ABANDONING HER AFTER SHE HAD STRUCK AN ICEBERG IN 1803
Coloured lithograph

Africa. A few survivors, with the help of a rope, managed to struggle to the land, and a good many more, huddled on the after part of the ship, were miraculously saved when the vessel broke up and the part on which they were gathered floated to the land. They found, however, that they were some 600 miles from Cape Town, surrounded by unfriendly Africans in a country infested by wild beasts, and only nineteen succeeded in reaching safety.

There are records of panic among passengers and of crews who have deserted their duty during shipwreck; but there are many more records of heroism than of cowardice. When the *Titanic* was lost in 1912, the ship's orchestra remained at their posts and played the hymn 'Nearer, my God, to Thee' as the vessel went down. When the *Birkenhead*, an iron paddle-wheel troopship, was lost off the African coast in 1852, more than 500 troops, knowing that there was little chance of survival, remained drawn up in their ranks in perfect order while the women and children were

put into the few remaining boats. They went down with the ship, their ranks unbroken. Similar discipline was shown in 1893 when the collision between H.M.S. *Victoria* and H.M.S. *Camperdown* resulted in the foundering of the *Victoria* with the loss of 336 seamen and 22 officers.

During the First and Second World Wars there were many disasters at sea, not from natural sea hazards, but caused by submarine attacks, mines, and other enemy action. Such was the disaster of the steamship *Lusitania* which was torpedoed without warning off the south coast of Ireland in 1915 and sank within 20 minutes, carrying 1,198 people to their death.

In modern times there are so many scientific aids to SAFETY AT SEA (q.v.) that disasters are fewer and rescue more effective. But shipwrecks still occur even to-day, as was shown in 1949 when the 17,500-ton liner *Magdalena* was wrecked off the coast of Brazil on her maiden voyage. The vessel was a fine twin-screw passenger and cargo vessel, more than 550 feet in length, com-

The Times

THE ITALIAN STEAMER 'SILVIA ONORATO' AGROUND ON THE GOODWIN SANDS, OFF DEAL, KENT

plete with all modern aids to navigation and staffed by an experienced ship's master and six certificated officers. She struck a reef while travelling at 13 knots (13 sea miles per hour), and became stuck hard and fast. The passengers were all rescued, and the crew tried to save the vessel. The weather grew worse, and the *Magdalena* was swept off the reef by wind and tide and anchored by her crew in deep water. She was eventually taken in tow, but the quantity of water in her holds made her so unhandy that she finally broke her back and split into two. No lives were lost, but the disaster shows that science cannot wholly do away with the perils of the sea.

2. WRECKERS. Wreck of the sea from the earliest times was regarded as royal property. But until the Tudor monarchs began to enforce the royal writ in the outlying parts of England and Ireland, that fact meant little. The coast-dwellers of medieval days, often miserably poor, regarded wrecks as a blessing from God, going so far as to pray 'Lord, send her to us', when they saw a ship coming dangerously near the shore.

Plunder of wreck was not, however, confined to the poor and ignorant. In 1305 the Prior of St. Nicholas in the Scilly Isles and the leader of the garrison were ringleaders in an attack on a coroner who inquired too closely into a wreck and its cargo. Thirty years later several monks were cited among sixty-one persons who broke an Irish ship to pieces and carried away the cargo.

In the 16th century the law of wreck was revised. The coast was divided into districts under the authority of Vice-Admirals. A vessel was to be counted as a wreck only if neither man, woman, child, dog, nor cat remained on board. Unfortunately this Act led to brutal abuses, for local plunderers and even the Vice-Admirals themselves found it paid them to see that no one survived from a wrecked ship. Every borough corporation tried to obtain the right of wreck for itself, but in lonely districts, especially on the west coast, neither the corporation nor the district Vice-Admirals had any real authority.

In 1526 the cargo saved from a Portuguese wreck on the coast of Cornwall was carried off; the justices called the Captain of Mount St

Michael to account, but he replied that it was 'the custom of the country', and no court in the country could convict him. Many cases came before the courts during the 16th century, showing that men of property, as well as the peasants, were concerned in plundering wrecks, and that certain towns such as St. Ives were regular markets for stolen goods.

During the 17th century private lighthouses were built; but these were often so unreliable that they were a menace to shipping. Indeed, lights were reputed often to be used to bring about wrecks rather than prevent them. The St. Agnes light was a public scandal, and its first keeper stole unashamedly from wrecks. In fact, lighthouses were looked upon as an unjustifiable way of robbing the people of their hereditary right to plunder wrecks.

By the middle of the 18th century the Cornish tinners were the most active plunderers. When a ship was reported near the coast they would leave their work, and armed with axes would follow the ship till she struck. Two thousand of them would then strip the vessel within a single tide, preventing the crew from refloating the ship, and often barbarously ill-using them. The townsfolk condoned and profited from such crimes. The law could do little, and pressure was brought even in Parliament to save condemned wreckers from execution.

The work of the National Institute for the Preservation of Life from Shipwreck, instituted in 1824, and the slow amendment of the law of wreckage in the second half of the 19th century led to a more humane attitude towards shipwrecked seamen. Wrecking continued through the 19th century on a smaller scale, the Cornish coast still being the chief scene of wreckers' activities, which not even the coastguards or troops could stop.

To-day harbour authorities generally have the right to remove wrecks and recover the money they spend from what they salvage. If they intend to raise or remove wrecks they must give notice of their intention, and allow owners to take their property on paying the fair market value.

See also DERELICTS; LIFEBOAT; SALVAGE.

WRITING, HISTORY OF. The chief way by which we record our thoughts and speech and pass them on to other people is by writing them down. But before he learned to write man invented other ingenious means of doing this, by using everyday objects as tokens or symbols of what he wanted to say. For example, the Scythians, the ancient inhabitants of southern Russia, once sent a 'letter' to the Persians consisting of a bird, a mouse, a frog, and five arrows. It meant, 'Persians, can you fly like a bird, hide yourselves in the ground like a mouse, leap through swamps like a frog? If you cannot, then do not try to go to war with us: we shall overwhelm you with arrows.' Similar kinds of methods are found among various primitive peoples. The 'calumet', a decorated reed tobacco-pipe, was used by some North American Indian tribes as the symbol of peace or war. When the leaders of hostile tribes met to discuss peace they sat around a camp fire and the peace-pipe was passed round the circle: to accept it meant to accept friendship; to reject it meant to choose war. Another device was the 'wampum' of the North American Iroquois, which consisted of little flat beads strung on to a cord; sometimes they made whole belts of these strings of beads, which were arranged in patterns (see picture), and worn as an ornament or girdle. White beads stood for peace, red for war or danger, black for death or misfortune, and yellow for gold or tribute. The Lu-tze, on the Tibeto-Chinese frontier, used similar means of communication: a piece of chicken liver, three pieces of chicken fat, and a chili, wrapped in red paper, meant 'prepare to fight at once'. The *aroko* (meaning 'to convey news') of the Yebu and other negro tribes of Nigeria, may also be mentioned: two cowrie shells, strung back to back, indicated a reproof for non-payment of debt; four cowries, in pairs, face to face, denoted a message of good will and request for a personal interview; and so on (*see* SIGNS AND SYMBOLS).

To-day, when we want to remember to do something, we often make a note of it on paper. Ancient people used memory devices for the same purpose. The most widely known are the knotted cord and the message stick. The ancient Chinese, Tibetans, Persians, and Mexicans 'wrote' in this way, and so did some primitive tribes from Melanesia to Formosa, in central and western Africa, in California or southern Peru; even to-day we sometimes tie a knot in a handkerchief to remind us of something. The knot device is the basis of the ancient Peruvian *quipus*, consisting of a number of threads or cords of different length, thickness, and colour, hang

Pitt Rivers Museum

NORTH AMERICAN WAMPUM BELTS OF THE 17TH AND EARLY 18TH CENTURIES

Top: 'The Double Calumet Treaty Belt' represents a Council Hearth flanked by double calumets. Next: 'The Peace-Path Belt' belongs to the same treaty. Third: 'The Jesuit Missionary Belt' has a Council Hearth in the centre, flanked by a lamb and dove and three crosses. Bottom: 'The Four Nations Alliance Belt' records a treaty respecting lands. Four towns or tribes (squares) are flanked by protecting white men's houses

ing from a top band. The nearer a knot was to the stick the more important was the matter to which it referred. A black knot meant death; a white one, silver or peace; a yellow one, gold; a red one, war; and a green one, grain (*see* PERU, ANCIENT, Vol. I). Notched sticks were used in ancient Scandinavia and until recently among some primitive Australian tribes for carrying messages about war, assemblies, and so forth. Notched sticks, or 'tallies', were also used by the Exchequer of England; as late as 1812 the English Government issued 'tallies' to those who lent it money.

The first primitive picture-writings were rough drawings made on the walls of caves, on animals' bones, or on stone. It is not certain, however, to what extent these drawings were the beginning of art, or attempts to record events. In this kind of picture-writing the written symbol represents an object or the idea behind an object, and has no connexion with the spoken words as in later phonetic writing, where the written symbol represents a sound of the VOICE (q.v.). Picture-writing is still found to-day among primitive peoples of Polynesia and Australia, of western Africa, of North and Central America, among the Yukaghirs of north-eastern Siberia, and others. In a primitive picture-writing the pictures represent the actual object drawn, such as a man or animal: and a circle might represent the sun. But in a developed picture-writing, known as 'ideography', the pictures represent

not so much the objects themselves as the ideas associated with them, in the same way that the frog sent to the Persians represented the idea of hopping. Thus, a moon might represent a month; a circle might represent not only the sun, but also the day or heat, or light, or a god associated with the sun; a man's legs or feet indicated walking; a man's mouth, speaking; the eye, seeing; and the ear, hearing. In North American Indian ideography 'wind' was represented by an inflated sail; 'life' by a snake (there was a belief that snakes live for ever); 'bravery' by an eagle; 'happiness' by a turtle (the turtle was believed to bring good luck, like the horseshoe among superstitious people to-day); and so on.

Only a few ancient ideographic scripts were complete systems of writing, with definite conventional pictures always used for the same objects. Among these were the systems of the MESOPOTAMIAN peoples (*see* CUNEIFORM WRITING), the EGYPTIANS (*see* HIEROGLYPHICS), the people of the Indus Valley in India (*see* INDIAN LANGUAGES), the Chinese, the inhabitants of Easter Island in the South Pacific (*see* POLYNESIAN LANGUAGES) and the AZTECS and MAYAS of Mexico and Central America (qq.v. Vol. I). But these scripts were complicated, for they were a mixture of pure picture-writing and phonetic writing. Some of the symbols represented objects or ideas and others represented spoken sounds, the two kinds being combined together in various ways. The confusion was increased by

PETITION OF CHIPPEWA CHIEFS PRESENTED AT WASHINGTON IN 1849

The chief, represented by his Crane Totem (1) is followed by warriors of the 'Marten' (2, 3, 4), 'Bear' (5), 'Man-Fish' (6), and 'Cat-Fish' (7) clans. Lines joining the eyes of the animals to the leader's signify unity of views, those joining the hearts, unity of purpose. The line drawn forward from the Crane's eye denotes the course of the journey, another joins the four lakes (8), the grant of which was the object of the journey. The long lines (10) are Lake Superior with a path (9) leading to it

the fact that some of the phonetic symbols were 'polyphones'—signs representing several possible sounds; and others were 'homophones'—signs which had the same phonetic value as each other, but represented different objects. The result was that many words, though written identically, were pronounced differently or had different meanings. To avoid this confusion two methods were introduced into Egyptian hieroglyphics, Chinese, and the cuneiform scripts.

Firstly, symbols called 'determinatives' were placed before or after the ideogram to show the general class to which it belonged—deities, countries, mountains, men, rivers, birds, or fishes. Secondly, symbols called 'phonetic complements' were put after a polyphone to show its phonetic or spoken value. In cuneiform writing the 'phonetic complement' consisted of a consonant (having the same value as the last consonant of the word indicated by the polyphone) and a vowel, usually 'a'.

The Mesopotamian peoples, and particularly the ASSYRIANS (q.v. Vol. I), not only succeeded in developing signs for syllables, they also discovered that there are sounds of a special kind,

which we call vowels, and set aside symbols to express them; at a later stage the Assyrian cuneiform script became practically a syllabic writing (see below). The EGYPTIANS (q.v. Vol. I) succeeded in isolating the consonants in the same way as the Assyrians had isolated the vowels, but used these consonantal signs mainly for writing grammatical inflexions, foreign words, and proper names. On the whole, none of the great systems known as 'ideographic' (Egyptian, cuneiform, Cretan, Hittite, Chinese, and so on), succeeded in moving completely across from the pure ideographic writing to the pure phonetic writing.

In pure phonetic writing each written symbol is a phonogram, that is, it corresponds to a sound or a group of sounds, and language and writing become closely connected. Generally, there is no connexion between the form of the written symbols and the sounds or words they represent. There are two main forms of phonetic writing, syllabic and alphabetic. In syllabic writing each sign or symbol represents a syllable of a word, which is generally 'open', that is to say, it is a consonant+a vowel (*ba, ta, la, mo,* and so on)

The main ancient syllabic writings—apart from the aforementioned Assyrian cuneiform writing—are the so-called pseudo-hieroglyphic script of Byblos in northern Syria, which was used by the Semitic population of Byblos in about 1500 B.C., and the script used by the ancient population of the island of Cyprus from the 6th to the 3rd century B.C. Of the modern syllabic writing the most interesting are the two Japanese scripts which derived from Chinese in the 8th and 9th centuries A.D.: the *katakana*, or *yamato* (Japanese) *gana*, used mainly in learned works, official documents, and for writing personal names, especially of Europeans; and the *hira* (= plain, simple) *gana*, used mainly in newspapers and light literature. These two systems are seldom used independently; they are generally written alongside Sino-Japanese ideograms, also of Chinese origin, and are used as phonetic complements or indications of the grammatical variations which are not needed in Chinese and cannot be expressed by Chinese ideograms.

Alphabetic writing is the most highly developed and widely used method. It is described under ALPHABET (q.v.). Some scripts may be described as nearly alphabetic: they are partly syllabic and partly alphabetic; the early Persian cuneiform script, which was the official script of the ancient Persian monarchy, and was used from the 6th to 4th centuries B.C., was nearly alphabetic.

See also ALPHABETS; HANDWRITING; WRITING INSTRUMENTS; HIEROGLYPHICS; CUNEIFORM WRITING.

WRITING INSTRUMENTS.

1. The earliest writing instruments were finely pointed flints, with which primitive peoples drew pictures on the walls of caves. Specimens about 100,000 years old have been found in the Altamira caves in Spain, in which early men have left wall-paintings of animals (*see* CAVE MAN, Vol. I). Mineral pigments were also used—yellow, blue-grey, and black—mixed with animal fat. In early civilizations numbers of different writing materials were used, such as sheets of metal, bark of trees, and the leaves of plants and trees: palm leaves, for example, were used in India; and the Latin word for a book, *liber*, originally meant the bark of a tree. About 3500 B.C. the Babylonians and Assyrians began to scratch (and later to stamp) their writings on moist tablets of clay, which were then dried in the sun or baked in ovens (*see* CUNEIFORM WRITING). Tablets of wax were widely used by the Greeks and

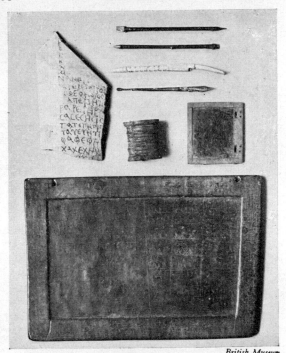

British Museum

ROMAN WAX TABLETS, POTSHERD USED FOR WRITING, AND PENS

Romans. These consisted of small pieces of wood coated on one or both sides with wax. The writing was scratched by a pointed instrument of metal or bone, known as a 'stilus'. These tablets were used for school exercises, legal documents, and private notes; their name of *codex* from the Latin word for 'tree trunk' is now used for any writing in book form as opposed to roll form.

2. PEN. When papyrus became the chief writing material of the ancient world (*see* PAPER, Section 2), the letters were traced with a kind of pen made from the hollow stem of a reed, known as a *calamus*. The Egyptians used it with a soft point, rather like a paint brush; and the Greeks and Romans sharpened it to a sharp point and slit it like a quill pen. The word 'pen' is derived from the Latin *penna*, 'a feather', and was originally applied to the quill pen. This is first mentioned in the 7th century, though it was probably used much earlier. Goose feathers were generally used, the quill being cut with a knife (the pen-knife) and the nib split to make it hold INK (q.v.), and then shaped to a point. Bronze pens dating from old Roman times, however, have also been found—one example was found

FOUNTAIN PEN
(short-barrelled type)

HEAD OF A
BALL-POINT
PEN

in the ruins of Pompeii, the city buried under volcanic dust for many centuries. Quill pens remained the standard pen until the beginning of the 19th century, when steel nibs began to be made in Birmingham. The first nibs cost 5s. each and were very hard and stiff, but gradually the present nib with holes and slits in it was developed. In 1926 stainless steel was used for pen-nibs.

Fountain pens were first made about 1886. Modern pens work by means of a suction lever, which draws the ink into a barrel, from where it flows towards the nib. Although a fountain-pen works on a simple principle, its manufacture can be elaborate; 200 separate operations go to the making of some pens. The nib is generally made of gold, and is sometimes tipped with a hard and expensive metal called iridium. A later invention was the ball-point pen. This holds enough special ink to last for some time; it writes like a pencil, and the ink dries immediately. The pen consists of an inner plastic tube containing the ink, which is forced in under pressure, and the little cylinder holding the ball. The ball, a standard 1-millimetre diameter ball-bearing, is forced into the metal end of the tube, which is slightly turned in to prevent the ball coming out.

3. PENCIL. The word 'pencil' comes from the Latin *penicillum*, meaning 'a little tail'; this name was applied by the Romans to fine brushes used for drawing and painting. In about 1600 the discovery of a graphite mine in Borrowdale, in Cumberland, led to the use of wooden pencils filled with graphite, or blacklead, a mineral which consists largely of carbon.

To-day pencil leads are made of powdered graphite and clay moistened into paste, then forced out of holes in a cylinder. They are then baked hard. For the cases narrow grooves are cut in thin boards of wood; the leads are laid in them, and other grooved boards are glued over them. A cutting machine divides the boards into individual pencils, ready for smoothing and finishing. Juniper wood is used for the better pencils, and pine wood for the cheaper ones.

The hardness or softness of the lead depends on the proportion of graphite to clay and the temperature to which it has been heated. Indelible and coloured pencils are made in the same way as ordinary lead pencils, but other substances are added to the composition, such as gum, tallow, wax, and various dyes.

4. INDIA-RUBBER. Before india-rubber was discovered ink was erased by scratching with a knife; pencil-marks were removed with soft breadcrumbs. India-rubber was first discovered in South America by Columbus, but was not introduced into England until the 18th century. Now it is chiefly grown in the East Indies.

5. BLOTTING-PAPER. We know that this was used in the 15th century, but it was a rarity for a long time after that. The usual way of drying what had been written was to sprinkle it with fine sand.

See also HANDWRITING; WRITING, HISTORY OF; PAPER; INK.

Y

YIDDISH LANGUAGE, *see* GERMANIC LANGUAGES.

Z

ZEPPELIN, *see* AIRSHIP.